AF181261

Wilhelm Neuefeind · Raymond G. Riezman (Eds.)

Economic Theory and International Trade

Essays in Memoriam
J. Trout Rader

With 30 Figures

Springer-Verlag
Berlin Heidelberg New York
London Paris Tokyo
Hong Kong Barcelona
Budapest

Prof. Dr. Wilhelm Neuefeind
Department of Economics
Washington University
One Brookings Drive
Box 1208
St. Louis, MO 63130
USA

Prof. Dr. Raymond G. Riezman
Department of Economics
University of Iowa
Iowa City, IA 52242
USA

ISBN-13: 978-3-642-77673-1 e-ISBN-13: 978-3-642-77671-7
DOI: 10.1007/978-3-642-77671-7

This work is subject to copyright. All rights are reserved, whether the whole or part of the material is concerned, specifically the rights of translation, reprinting, reuse of illustrations, recitation, broadcasting, reproduction on microfilms or in other ways, and storage in data banks. Duplication of this publication or parts thereof is only permitted under the provisions of the German Copyright Law of September 9, 1965, in its version of June 24, 1985, and a copyright fee must always be paid. Violations fall under the prosecution act of the German Copyright Law.

© Springer-Verlag Berlin · Heidelberg 1992
Softcover reprint of the hardcover 1st edition 1992

The use of registered names, trademarks, etc. in this publication does not imply, even in the absence of a specific statement, that such names are exempt from the relevant protective laws and regulations and therefore free for general use.

2142/7130-543210 - Printed on acid-free paper

Preface

John Trout Rader III died on May 23, 1991 after a long bout with multiple sclerosis. At the time of his death he was Professor of Economics at Washington University in Saint Louis. He was born on August 23, 1938 and received his B.A. from the University of Texas in 1959 and his Ph.D. from Yale University in 1963. In 1965, after brief stints as assistant professor at the Universities of Missouri and Illinois, he joined Washington University where he was promoted to Professor in 1970. In Saint Louis, he divided his energies between his two lifelong loves: his family (his wife Deanna and children Kathy, Wendy, David, and Sarah) and ECONOMICS. Already in the seventies, his long and painful illness started to interfere with his work.

During his brief but productive career he succeeded in assembling an impressive record as a scholar: He wrote three books and more than thirty articles covering a remarkably broad range of topics. His two books on microeconomics and general equilibrium (1972a, 1972b)[1] are research monographs rather than textbooks; they contain many ideas which anticipated lines of research his fellow economists took up only later. The topics in his articles range from consumer analysis (1963, 1973a, 1976c, 1976d, 1978a, 1979b), production theory (1968c, 1970a, 1974), equilibrium and welfare theory (1964, 1968a, 1970a, 1972c, 1972d, 1976b, 1976c, 1980), growth theory and dynamics (1965, 1975, 1985), international trade (1968b, 1971b, 1973b, 1978c, 1979a), and public choice (1973d, 1978b). He also wrote on development (1971a) and macro topics (1977a, 1977b) and contributed technical results (1973c). The breadth of Trout's work becomes evident when one examines the publication dates and discovers that he was always working on a variety of topics.

He was equally successful as a teacher: his undergraduate students found the ECONOMICS he taught exciting and his enthusiasm infectious. Many of them decided that it must be worthwhile to pursue an academic career in such an intriguing field. They and most of his graduate students went on to be productive economists of their own. Seven of them have contributed to this volume, attesting to the influence of his teaching.

The editors had planned this volume to be in honor of rather than *in memoriam* J. Trout Rader. Some time ago, we started soliciting contributions. We had told Trout that we were putting together a volume with papers from his students, colleagues, and friends. He knew the contributors and was aware that a number of distinguished scholars were among them. He was very pleased and greatly appreciated the efforts of so many friends. He had a chance to read some of the papers and most of the abstracts. Trout did not live long enough to see the finished product which honors his considerable achievements. We trust that he would approve of it.

Many of the articles in this volume have been influenced by Trout's research or teaching and will serve as evidence of his scholarly achievements and the considerable impact he had on the profession.

It seems appropriate to conclude with a more personal note. Trout was a productive scholar who continued to do his work until the very end. He also was a very

[1] These publication dates refer to the bibliography given below.

warm and deeply religious man. He suffered a great deal during his long illness. His courage and faith in dealing with this illness were quite remarkable to those of us who were fortunate enough to meet Trout during that period. A nurse, who had cared for many terminally ill people and who cared for him in the last year of his life, remarked that he never complained about his fate and never felt sorry for himself. In exasperation, she one day asked him why he never complained or felt resentment because his life was to end prematurely; he stared at her with a penetrating gaze and calmly said:

> "I have been very lucky in life and have a great deal to be thankful for. Don't forget that you are going to die too. I'm just going a little sooner."

We would like to thank everybody who helped Trout through the difficult last years, the authors for their contributions to this volume, and Karen Rensing for her help in turning many differing manuscripts into a book.

March 1992

Wilhelm Neuefeind
Saint Louis, Missouri

Raymond Riezman
Iowa City, Iowa

Economic Theory and International Trade
Essays in memoriam J. Trout Rader

Edited by
WILHELM NEUEFEIND
Washington University in Saint Louis
and
RAYMOND RIEZMAN
University of Iowa

Table of Contents

Bibliography of John Trout Rader III

1963 "The Existence of a Utility Function to Represent Preferences," *Review of Economic Studies, 30,* 229-232.

1964 "Edgeworth Exchange and General Economic Equilibrium," *Yale Economic Essays, 4,* 133-180; and, *Two Corrections,* Yale Economic Essays, 5 Spring 1965.

1965 "On Intertemporal Efficiency," *Metroeconomica, 17,* 152-170.

1968a "Pairwise Optimality and Non-Competitive Behaviour," in *Papers in Quantitative Economics, Vol. I,* ed. J.P. Quirk and A.M. Zarley. Lawrence, Kansas: University of Kansas Press, 101-128.

1968b "International Trade and Development in a Small Country," in *Papers in Quantitative Economics, Vol. I,* ed. J.P. Quirk and A.M. Zarley. Lawrence, Kansas: University of Kansas Press, 399-431.

1968c "Normally, Factor Inputs are Never Gross Substitutes," *Journal of Political Economy, 76,* 38-43.

1970a "Resource Allocation with Increasing Returns to Scale," *American Economic Review, 60,* 814-825.

1970b "New Ideas in Pure Theory: Discussion," *American Economic Review, May Supplement,* 463-464.

1971a *Economics of Feudalism.* New York: Gordon and Breach.

1971b "International Trade and Development in a Small Country, II," in *Papers in Quantitative Economics, Vol. II,* ed. A.M. Zarley. Lawrence, Kansas: University of Kansas Press, 177-207.

1972a *Theory of Microeconomics.* New York: Academic Press.

1972b *Theory of General Economic Equilibrium.* New York: Academic Press.

1972c "General Equilibrium Theory with Complementary Factors," *Journal of Economic Theory, 4,* 372-380.

1972d "Impossibility of Qualitative Economics: Excessively Strong Correspondence Principles in Production-Exchange Economies," *Zeitschrift für Nationalökonomie, 32,* 397-416.

1973a "Nice Demand Functions," *Econometrica, 41,* 913-936.

1973b "Heckscher-Ohlin Hypothesis and Scarce-Factor Theorems" (with P. Van Moeseke), *Tijdschrift Voor Economie, 18,* 445-50.

1973c "Absolutely Continuous Maximizers," *Journal of Optmization Theory and Applications, 12,* 107-128.

1973d "An Economic Approach to Social Choice," *Public Choice, 15,* 47-75.

1974 "Aggregate Laws of Production," *Zeitschrift für Nationalökonomie, 34,* 249-282.

1975 "Turnpike Theory with (Under)Consumption," *Review of Economic Studies, 42,* 155-165; and, "Turnpike Theory: A Revised Proof," *Review of Economic Studies, 43,* 1976, 369-370.

1976a "Pairwise Optimality, Multilateral Optimality and Efficiency, With and Without Externalities," in *Theory and Measurement of Economic Externalities,* ed. S. Y. Lin. New York: Academic Press, 135-152.

1976b "The Welfare Loss of Price Distortion," *Econometrica, 44,* 1253-1258.

1976c "Equivalence of Consumer Surplus, the Divisia Index of Output, and Eisenberg's Addilog Social Utility," *Journal of Economic Theory, 13,* 58-66.

1976d "Preferences Which Have Open Graphs" (with T. Bergstrom and R. Parks), *Journal of Mathematical Economics, 3,* 265-268.

1977a "Many Good Multiplier Analysis: Classical, Neoclassical and Keynesian," in *Equilibrium and Disequilibrium in Economic Theory,* ed. G. Schwödiauer. Dordrecht, Holland: Reidel, 611-649.

1977b "A Note on What's Wrong with IS-LM," *Journal of Economics, 3,* 242.

1978a "Induced Preferences on Trades When Preferences May be Intransitive and Incomplete," *Econometrica, 46,* 137-146.

1978b "An Economic Approach to Social Choice II" (with T. Bergstrom), *Public Choice, 53,* 17-31.

1978c "On Factor Price Equalization," *Journal of Mathematical Economics, 5,* 71-82.

1979a "Factor Price Equalization With More Industries than Factors," in *General Equilibrium Growth and Trade,* ed. J. Green and J. Scheinkman. Academic Press: New York, 347-354.

1979b "Nice Demand Functions II," *Journal of Mathematical Economics, 6,* 253-262.

1980 "The Second Theorem of Welfare Economics When Utilities are Independent," *Journal of Economic Theory, 23,* 420-424.

1981 "Utility Over Time: The Homothetic Case," *Journal of Economic Theory, 25,* 219-236.

1985 "Market Dynamics and the Law of Demand" (with D. Keenan), *Econometrica, 53,* 465-472.

1987 "Production as Indirect Exchange," in *The New Palgrave,* ed. J. Eatwell, M. Milgate and P. Newman. MacMillan: London, 1000-1002.

Cooperative Capital Accumulation Games and the Core

ROBERT A. BECKER*
Indiana University

This study is dedicated to Professor Trout Rader whose influence on my choice of career and research program was profound. I wish to express my deep appreciation for his contributions as a researcher and teacher as well as my gratitude for his guidance and friendship over the past twenty-three years.

1 Introduction

The purpose of this study is to examine the core of a cooperative capital accumulation game.[1] The basic approach recognizes both the recursive structure of consumption and capital accumulation decisions as well as the open-endedness of the future. The ultimate objective of undertaking an examination of the core concept is to obtain qualitative statements about the long-run evolution of the model economy.

In this paper agents are permitted to trade in a model with all possible forward markets in place. Each agent is given a utility function evaluated once, for all time, at time zero. In the spirit of cooperative game theory, agents are permitted to make binding futures contracts of any kind they can mutually agree upon. The allocation of resources in the present and future results in a solution to the model. A *core solution* is singled out for study in this paper. Specifically, an allocation (for all time) is a *core allocation* if no coalition of agents can propose an alternative allocation for itself resulting in a larger utility payoff for each member at time zero given the endowments of productive factors available to that coalition. The existence of core allocations is addressed in this paper. Some examples of core allocations are given to clarify the interest in the core solution concept. A *recursive core* solution concept is introduced as well to permit recontracting to take place on any date. A recursive core allocation results when no coalition can form and improve upon the given allocation from some time on by use of its own resources. The requirement that an allocation be in the recursive core is obviously more restrictive than requiring

*This research was supported by NSF Grant SES 85-20180.

[1]The core solution for exchange and production economies played a prominent role in Professor Rader's lectures on distributive justice. See Rader (1972, pp. 108-109) for a summary of his views on the importance of the core in equilibrium theory and welfare economics.

it to belong to the core. Several examples of core allocations are constructed to illustrate the dynamic possibilities under this solution concept.

Recursive Pareto optimal allocations are also defined which permit recontracting by the grand coalition at any date. A recursive Pareto optimal allocation results when the grand coalition cannot improve upon the given allocation at any time. If agents preferences admit a recursive utility function representation, then the set of Recursive Pareto optimal allocations are shown to be equal to the set of weak Pareto optimal allocations for contracts entered into at time zero. This implies that weak Pareto optimal allocations have a time consistency property in the sense that the grand coalition will never recontract at any future time.

The model proposed here consists of a finite number of households endowed with an initial vector of capital goods and having access to a constant returns to scale technology. Aggregate resource limitations may bound the production possibilities of the economy in some cases (for example, if labor is the only primary factor of production). There is a single all purpose consumption good that is produced from the technology using a vector of inputs. The model is a generalization of the one found in Becker (1982, 1983).

Dynamic cooperative games have been proposed in the resource economics literature by Munro (1979). He formulated a two-country Nash bargaining problem over the optimal management of a shared fishery. The model developed below can, in principle, be applied to a discrete time version of Munro's model. The Nash bargaining solution is just one possible core allocation. A core concept for exchange economies with a complete set of forward markets extending into the indefinite future was first proposed by Peleg and Yaari (1970). They proved the existence of a core allocation by arguing that the characteristic form of the game fit the schema proposed by Scarf (1967). Their focus on payoff space was also used in Becker (1982, 1983); the results derived below utilize that idea again. The Scarf based existence proof was also used by Aliprantis, Brown and Burkinshaw (1987) to give a general core existence result for production and exchange economies modeled on a symmetric Riesz dual system. The order structure of the commodity space defined in Section 2 is not used to generate the core existence theorem below in contrast to the core existence proof given in Aliprantis, *et al.* Most recently, the Peleg and Yaari methodology has been pursued by Boyd and McKenzie (1990) in the context of a capital theoretic model. The consumption sets in their model were not restricted to the positive cone of the commodity space as commonly found in the literature on infinite dimensional space models.[2] They demonstrated the existence of core allocations and the equal treatment property for replica economies along with the existence of an *Edgeworth equilibrium* allocation which lies in the equal treatment core of every replica economy. Their approach also yielded the existence of a competitive equilibrium price system in ℓ_1.

The study of core allocations in a capital theoretic setting also links the study of intertemporal distribution, the core and efficiency concerns that were prominent themes in Professor Trout Rader's writings and lectures. The problem of characterizing the long-run distribution of wealth in economies with heterogeneous infinitely

[2]See Becker (1991) for a discussion of capital theory models in infinite dimensional general equilibrium theory.

lived agents served as the motivation for some of his most important research. Indeed, I recall as an undergraduate student of his an assignment of finding the long-run distribution of consumption resulting from a weak Pareto optimal allocation in a two person exchange economy. Each agent's utility function was of the time additive separable form with constant discount factor; agents were assumed to have different discount factors.[3] The long-run pattern of consumption turned out to yield the most impatient agent's consumption converging to zero while the more patient consumer enjoyed all the available consumption good. Understanding the intertemporal inequality arising from different discount factors subsequently became a major theme in my research program. Indeed, the portion of my doctoral dissertation at the University of Rochester devoted to heterogeneous household models of capital accumulation was stimulated by my early encounter with long-run distributional issues met in that class.[4]

The paper is organized as follows: the commodity space is defined in Section 2 and the representation of intertemporal preferences is discussed in Section 3. The cooperative game is developed in Section 4 while the existence of core allocations is discussed in Section 5. Examples are presented in Section 6 and the recursive core is introduced in Section 7. Concluding comments are given in Section 8.

2 The Commodity Space

The basic commodity space is the vector space, s, of sequences of real numbers. An element $X \in s$ is written as a sequence $X = \{x_t\}, t = 1, 2, \ldots$, with $x_t \in \mathbf{R}$. We use the notational convention that upper case letters represent sequences and lower case letters their terms unless otherwise noted. The nonnegative cone, s_+, of s is defined by $X \in s_+$ if and only if $x_t \geq 0$ for all t. Define the space $s_0 = \{X' \in s :$ There exists a T (depending on X') with $x'_t = 0$ for all $t > T\}$. This is the vector space of sequences with finitely many non-zero terms. Given $X \in s, X' \in s_0$, define a bilinear map $< X, X' >$ by the formula

$$< X, X' >= \Sigma_{t=1}^{\infty} x_t x'_t.$$

Under this bilinear map the spaces (s, s_0) form a dual pair. Give s the weak topology, $\sigma(s, s_0)$, determined by s_0. A sequence $\{X^n\}_{n=1}^{\infty} \subset s, X^n = \{x_t^n\}$, converges to $X = \{x_t\} \in s$ in the $\sigma(s, s_0)$-topology if and only if $x_t^n \to x_t$ for each t as $n \to \infty$. The $\sigma(s, s_0)$-topology is equivalent to the product topology on s when viewed as the cartesian product of a countable number of copies of $\mathbf{R}$. The space s endowed with the $\sigma(s, s_0)$-topology is a Fréchet space, i.e., it is a complete and metrizable locally convex linear space. Robertson and Robertson (1973) contains additional information on Fréchet spaces.

The topological interior of s_+ is empty in the $\sigma(s, s_0)$-topology. The boundary of s_+ is s_+. Consequently, this model is another example of a resource allocation

[3] See Rader (1971, pp. 32-34) for the underlying model and his solution.

[4] See Becker (1980), Becker and Foias (1987), and Becker, Boyd and Foias (1991) for samples of my research on heterogeneous agent models.

problem in an infinite dimensional commodity space where the nonnegative cone of the commodity space has an empty interior.[5]

The set s^m is the set of sequences of real m-vectors with nonnegative cone s^m_+. The basic topological description of s carries over to s^m with straightforward changes. The space s^m_0 is defined similarly. The $\sigma(s^m, s^m_0)$*-topology* is defined for this dual pair in an analogous manner. The term σ*-topology* is used when the meaning is clear.

Capital stocks and net investment vectors, denoted k and z respectively, are elements of $\mathbf{R}^n$, Euclidean n-dimensional space. If x and y are elements of $\mathbf{R}^n$, then the inequality $x \geq y$ means $x_i \geq y_i$ for each component $i=1,\ldots,n$. The symbol $x > y$ is used to designate that $x \geq y$ and $x \neq y$ both hold. The notation $x >> y$ means that $x_i > y_i$ in every component.

3 Intertemporal Utility

A household's preference order over alternative consumption profiles is described by a utility function defined on the commodity space. A consumption program is a point $C \in s_+, C = \{c_t\}$, where c_t is the consumption flow of the single commodity during period t. The basic properties of intertemporal utility are stated as axioms. The simplest expression of these postulates occurs when utility is a continuous function on the commodity space. Both recursive and non-recursive utility functions satisfying the basic postulates are given as examples.

3.1 The Basic Postulates

A *utility function*, U, is a real-valued function defined on the commodity space that has the property $U(C) \geq U(C')$ whenever C and C' are commodity profiles and C is at least as preferred as C' by the player. Assume that intertemporal preferences are *weakly monotonic* in the sense that U is non-decreasing in each argument. The *strong monotonicity* axiom states that utility is an increasing function of consumption at any fixed date. The weak monotonicity property is to be understood as a maintained characteristic of the utility function without further comment. In an infinite dimensional commodity space context, hypotheses concerning continuity and concavity of U must be framed with some care. The axioms for this situation are stated as

($U1$) *U is continuous in the $\sigma(s, s_0)$-topology.*

($U2$) *U is a concave function.*

Lemma 3.1 characterizes the class of functions satisfying ($U1$). Note that a set is compact in the $\sigma(s, s_0)$-topology if and only if it is closed and bounded.

LEMMA 3.1 : *A utility function U satisfies* ($U1$) *iff* $U(c_1, c_2, \ldots, c_N, 0, 0, \ldots)$ *is a continuous function in the variables* $(c_1, c_2, \ldots, c_N)$ *for each N and*

[5] Aliprantis, Brown and Burkinshaw (1989) may be consulted for other examples of infinite dimensional commodity spaces arising in general equilibrium analysis whose positive cones have an empty interior.

$$\sup |U(c_1, c_2, ..., c_N, 0, 0, ...) - U(C)| \to 0 \text{ as } N \to \infty$$

uniformly on each $\sigma(s, s_0)$*-compact subset* $\mathbf{D}$ *of* s_+.

When $(U1)$ holds, we can express U as the limit of finite dimensional utility functions, $U(C) = \lim_{N\to\infty} U(P_N C)$. The projections P_N are defined by $P_N(C) = (c_1, c_2, \ldots, c_N, 0, 0, \ldots)$.

3.2 Examples of Utility Functions

In many applications, a household's preference order is described by a *recursive utility function.* These utility functions treat the future in the same way at each point in time. Current utility is expressed as a fixed function (aggregator) of current consumption and the utility of future consumption. Postulates governing intertemporal preference are most easily expressed in terms of the aggregator. The original work on this approach was carried out in a series of papers by Koopmans and his collaborators (Koopmans, 1960, 1972; Koopmans, Diamond and Williamson, 1964; Diamond, 1965; Beals and Koopmans, 1969). The aggregator first appeared as a primitive concept in the work of Lucas and Stokey (1984). Further development of this idea may be found in Boyd (1990) and Streufert (1990).[6]

More formally, a utility function is *recursive* if there is a function W, the *aggregator*, such that

$$U(C) = W(c_1, U(SC)) \tag{3.1}$$

where $SC = (c_2, c_3, \ldots)$ is the future consumption stream. For example, when $W(0,0) = 0$, Boyd (1990) has shown the utility function can be computed from the aggregator as the limit of "partial sums" by

$$U(C) = \lim_{N\to\infty} W(c_1, W(c_2, \ldots, W(c_N, 0)) \ldots) = \lim_{N\to\infty} U(P_N C). \tag{3.2}$$

The *Inada condition at zero* is met if $W_1 = \partial W/\partial z \to \infty$ as $z \to 0^+$.

The time additive separable (TAS) utility function $U(C) = \sum_{t=1}^{\infty} \delta^{t-1} u(c_t)$ is recursive; take $W(z, y) + \delta y$ and call u the *felicity function.* Recall, $\sigma(z) = -zu''(z)/u'(z)$ is the *elasticity of marginal felicity.* The constant marginal elasticity of marginal felicity functions, $u(z) = z^{1-\sigma}/(1-\sigma), \sigma > 0, \sigma \neq 1$, and $u(z) = \log z, \sigma = 1$, obey the Inada condition at zero and are not bounded. The corresponding TAS utility functions fail to satisfy $(U1)$. Two felicity functions that enjoy the Inada property and obey $U(0) = 0$ as well as $(U1)$ and $(U2)$ are given by $u(z) = \text{arcsec}\,(1+z)$, and $u(z) = \arctan z^\mu, 0 < \mu < 1$.

Many other types of utility functions are recursive. Koopmans, Diamond and Williamson (1964) used the KDW aggregator $W(z, y) = (1/\theta)\log(1 + \beta z^\delta + \gamma y)$ where $(z, y) \in [0,1] \times [0,1], \theta = \log(1 + \beta + \gamma), \beta > 0, 1 > \delta > 0$, and $\theta > \gamma > 0$. The associated utility function does not have a closed form representation. The UEH

[6]See Becker and Boyd (1990) for a survey of recursive utility theory with applications to equilibrium analysis and growth theory.

aggregator $W(z,y) = (-1+y)\exp[-u(z)]$ as used by Uzawa (1968), Epstein (1983), and Epstein and Hynes (1983) yields a recursive utility function which satisfies ($U1$) and ($U2$):

$$U(C) = -\Sigma_{t=1}^{\infty} \exp[-\Sigma_{s=1}^{t} u(c_s)], \tag{3.3}$$

where $y \leq 0$ and u is an increasing, strictly concave function with $u(z) \geq \epsilon$ for some $\epsilon > 0$. The Rawls maximin utility function is also recursive; the aggregator is $W(z,y) = \inf\{z,y\}$. The Rawls utility function is then given by $U(C) = \inf_t c_t$. This utility function is weakly monotonic in consumption at any date, but it is not strongly monotonic.

The recursive utility functions represent stationary preferences. Streufert (1985) gives a generalization of this class. One family of non-recursive utility functions was proposed by Majumdar (1975, pg. 149). Epstein (1986, Theorem 3) develops another class of utility functions, called implicitly additive functions. The core existence theorems are applicable to the Majumdar, Streufert and the implicitly additive functions with suitable parameterization.

The recursive utility functions are open to a different interpretation than the standard one of an infinitely lived household. The second interpretation is that each household is a sequence of altruistic generations (or at least non-malevolent generations). Let each generation live for one period and derive utility from its consumption as well as from the consumption stream enjoyed by **all** of its descendants. Suppose that the preference of a member of generation t is described by an aggregator function W over it's own consumption c_t and that of its heirs as registered by the utility $U(c_{t+1}, c_{t+2}, \ldots)$. Let C be a consumption sequence. Then $U(c_t, S^tC)$ is the utility achieved by generation t provided that each generation follows the path C. The altruism of each generation is limited by the impatience properties of the aggregator (or utility function). The usual interpretation of the Rawlsian aggregator (utility) in models of intergenerational justice fits this intergenerational framework. The aggregator is also a forward looking evaluation of the consumption stream since generation t does not care about the consumption enjoyed by members of preceding generations. Indeed, this freedom from the past is a consequence of the weak separability property of the present from the future that is built into the recursive utility concept. The main application of the intergenerational interpretation of recursive utility is in the section on the recursive core.

4 The Cooperative Game

The purpose of this section is to develop the economic structure underlying the core solution concept for dynamic capital accumulation games. The first task is to describe the model economy and the second is to describe the cooperative game. The formal study of the core solution concept is deferred to the next section.

4.1 The Economy

The economy is described by the production technology, the households characteristics (preferences and endowments), and their productive opportunities. Time is taken to be discrete or given by periods indexed by $t = 0, 1, 2, \ldots$. The economy under study contains H households (players or agents) denoted by the indices $h = 1, 2, \ldots H$. For simplicity, there is a single consumption good which is either consumed or freely disposed of in the period in which it is produced. Let c_t^h denote the consumption of household h in period t. A consumption sequence is denoted by $C^h = \{c_t^h\}_{t=1}^{\infty}$. Consumption at any date is always nonnegative so $C^h \in s_+$. The agents payoff functions are specified to be a utility function in the class satisfying axioms $(U1)$ and $(U2)$. There is a single primary factor, labor, and each household's labor is identical. The model is said to be *open.* A *closed* model occurs whenever labor constraints are absent.

The technology is given by a set of possible inputs and outputs. Labor is treated in one of two ways. The open version of the model will be subject to diminishing returns at the individual and economy-wide level whereas the closed model will not be subject to that limitation. The main implication of whether or not labor is a primary factor has to do with compactness of the feasible or attainable set. It turns out that compactness of the feasible sets for the economy as well as any coalition will be met in either case given the technology axioms described below. There are n types of capital-investment goods. In the open model, labor is combined with capital stocks to produce the consumption and investment goods. In the closed model, the consumption and investment goods are produced from capital stocks only. The open model is presented in this section. An example of the closed model is briefly discussed in Section 5.

The derivation of each coalition's characteristic function is based upon the assumption that contracts entered into at the starting period are enforceable over the entire horizon. Therefore, the payoff function to household h is given by the utility value of the realized consumption sequence. In the open economy model, a player's characteristics are defined by the triple $\{U_h, k^h, \ell^h\}$ where U_h is the utility function, k^h is the vector assigning the initial endowment of capital goods to h, and ℓ^h is the player's labor endowment (available at each date). Notice that the agent does not derive utility from leisure. In a core allocation, each player will act as if his labor supply is perfectly inelastic. The restriction of the model in this way is not essential, but rather is made for simplicity. In the open economy model each household is assumed to have one unit of labor available during each period.

The technology set specifying the input-output possibilities between adjacent periods is described by a convex cone denoted by T in both the case of an open or closed model. In either case, this set is available at each date and every agent is assumed to have access to the common technology set. Therefore, each coalition will also have access to this common technology set. The use of a convex cone technology simplifies the analysis (see Boehm [1974] for a core concept in the static production economy case). This specification of the technology set is also consistent with the standard examples found in the capital theory literature.

Let $y = [c, z, k, \ell] \in T \subseteq \mathbf{R}_+ \times \mathbf{R}^n \times \mathbf{R}_+^n \times \mathbf{R}_+$ denote an input-output vector. The **gross investment** vector is defined by $g = z + \Lambda k$, where Λ is an $n \times n$ diagonal matrix whose diagonal entries, λ_j satisfy $0 < \lambda_j \leq 1$ where λ_j is the depreciation rate of capital good j for $j = 1, \ldots n$. The scaler c denotes the **consumption** good output, z is the vector of **net investments** or increments to the capital stock,

k is the vector of **capital stocks**, and ℓ is the **labor** input. The intertemporal technology set is the cartesian product of the sets T given by $\mathcal{T} = \Pi_{t=1}^{\infty} T$. Of course $\mathcal{T}$ is a subset of the corresponding product of the spaces $s_+ \times s^n \times s_+^n \times s_+$.

The axioms for the open technology set model are listed next; interpretations are given after each assumption. The axioms are virtually identical to the technology axioms in Cass and Shell (1976, pp. 34-37). This specification of the technology is sufficiently general to admit several interesting examples (see Section 6 and Rader [1974, Appendix]).

($T1$) *Feasibility of nonnegative inputs.*
If $(k, \ell) \geq 0$, then there exists (c, z) such that $[c, z, k, \ell] \in T$.

($T2$) *Feasibility of boundary production.*
T is a closed set.

($T3$) *Diminishing returns in production.*
T is a convex set.

($T4$) *Productivity of the technology.*
A point $[c, z, k, \ell] \in T$ exists such that $(c, z) >> 0$.

($T5$) *Constant returns to scale and inaction is possible.*
T is a convex cone and $0 \in T$.

($T6$) *Necessity of primary factors.*
If $[c, z, k, \ell] \in T$ and $\ell = 0$, then $c = 0$ and $z_j \leq 0$ according as $k_j \geq 0$ for $j = 1, 2, \ldots, n$.

($T7$) *Nonnegative Gross Investment.*
For the $n \times n$ diagonal matrix Λ with $1 \geq \lambda_j > 0$ for $j = 1, 2, \ldots n$, if $[c, z, k, \ell] \in T$, then $z + \Lambda k \geq 0$.

($T8$) *Free disposal in allocation.*
If $[c, z, k, \ell] \in T$, $[c', z', k', \ell']$ satisfies (i) $(c', z') \leq (c, z)$ with $c' \geq 0$ and $z' \geq -\Lambda k'$, and (ii) $(k', \ell') \geq (k, \ell)$, then $[c', z', k', \ell'] \in T$.

The production axioms are self-explanatory. The existence of a bound on depreciation rates (Axiom ($T7$)) implies there is an upper bound on feasible capital stocks given fixed labor inputs. A production point $[c, z, k, \ell] \in T$ with $\ell = \ell^*$ for some fixed ℓ^*(say $\ell^* = H$) and $z \geq 0$ is *replicable*. Axioms ($T2$), ($T5$) and ($T6$) imply $\{[c, z, k] : [c, z, k, \ell] \in T, z \geq 0 \text{ and } \ell = \ell^*\}$ is bounded. *Feasible programs* are sequences $[C, Z, K, L] \in \mathcal{T}$ having the properties that $z_t = k_t - k_{t-1}$ and $k_0 \leq x$ with $\ell_t = \ell^*$ for all t where x is the vector of initial capital. The following BOUNDEDNESS LEMMA drawn from Cass and Shell (1976, pg. 36) applies and is quoted below. The notation $||y||$ signifies the usual norm of a vector y in an appropriate finite dimensional real vector space.

LEMMA 4.1: *There is a bound $B < \infty$ such that every production point $[c, z, k, \ell] \in T$ which is replicable or feasible satisfies the boundedness restriction*

$$||(c, z, k)|| < B. \tag{B}$$

One application of Lemma 4.1 is to show that the set of attainable consumption and capital accumulation programs is σ-compact. Sequences $Y = (C, Z, K, L)$ define a *possible program* provided $[c_t, z_t, k_{t-1}, \ell_t] \in T$ and $z_t = k_t - k_{t-1}$ for $t = 1, 2, \ldots$. The sequence (C, Z, K, L) is an *attainable program* if it is possible and $k_0 \leq \Sigma_{h=1}^{H} k^h$ and $\Sigma_{h=1}^{H} \ell^h \leq H$.[7] Recall, each household is endowed with one unit of identical labor so the aggregate endowment is H units of labor. Let $\mathcal{A}$ denote the attainable set for given aggregate endowments of capital goods and labor. The corresponding attainable consumption set, $\mathcal{C}$, is defined by $\mathcal{C} = \{C : [C, Z, K, L] \text{ is attainable}\}$, where L denotes the labor input sequence. The compactness of attainable sets for the open model result follows easily and is recorded without proof.

LEMMA 4.2: *The set of attainable programs $\mathcal{A}$ for an open model satisfying axioms $(T1) - (T8)$ is a σ-compact subset of s_{+}^{2n+2}. Moreover, the attainable consumption set $\mathcal{C}$ is a σ-compact subset of s_{+}.*

Lemmas 4.1 - 4.2 provide the basis for several crucial properties of the capital accumulation model necessary to cast it into a cooperative game without side payments in characteristic function form.

An *economy*, $\mathcal{E}$, is defined by the objects $\{(U_h, k^h, \ell^h), T\}$ where $h = 1, \ldots, H$ is the list of agents, U_h is the utility function of agent h, k^h is the initial capital of agent h, ℓ^h is the labor endowment of h, and T is the technology set. The economy $\mathcal{E}$ is said to satisfy the **basic assumptions** if $(U1)$-$(U2)$ and $(T1)$-$(T8)$ are met with $\ell^h = 1$ the normalized labor endowment for each agent h in every period.

4.2 The Game Model

The game model is derived in this subsection from the economy $\mathcal{E}$. Let $A = \{1, 2, \ldots, H\}$, with $h \in A$, denote the set of players. A *coalition* S is a non-empty subset of A; the set of coalitions is given by the set of all non-empty subsets of A and denoted by $\mathcal{P}(A)$. The number of agents in a coalition S is written as $|S|$; evidently $|A| = H$. If S is a coalition, then $A \backslash S = \{h \in A : h \notin S\}$ is called the *adverse coalition.*

The derivation of each coalition's characteristic function is based on the assumption that contracts entered into at the starting time period are enforceable over the entire infinite horizon. Therefore the payoff to household h is the (present) utility value of its consumption profile. The characteristic function form of the capital accumulation game is based on modelling the players as forming *path strategies* consisting of their time sequences of desired capital "supplies," investment "demands," and consumption "demands." Path strategies are also called *open loop* decisions. The use of an open loop decision concept corresponds to the requirement that all decisions be taken at time zero and that those decisions are optimal for a player when viewed at that time. This conception of the decision process is possible because binding agreements have been made by the players.

Consumption, net investment, capital, and labor sequences which are possible plans for a coalition are denoted by $[C(S), Z(S), K(S), L(S)]$ and are elements of $\mathcal{T}$ with $z_t(S) = k_t(S) - k_{t-1}(S)$ for all t. A possible program $[C(S), Z(S), K(S), L(S)]$ for S is termed an *S-possible program.* The consumption sequence $C(S)$ represents the aggregate consumption enjoyed by the members of S; the consumption of $h \in S$

[7] An attainable program is a feasible program for the values of $x = \Sigma_h k^h$ and $\ell^* = H$.

at time t is denoted by $c_t^h(S)$. The other sequences have similar interpretations. If a coalition S forms, then that coalition acts as a subeconomy in the model. This means that the coalition may access the technology set and distribute output at each time to the members. The characteristic form of the game will then specify the utility payoffs that the coalition can provide for its members. The initial resources of the coalition are its capital, $k(S) = \Sigma_{h \in S} k^h$, and labor resources consisting of $|S|$ workers. An *S-attainable program* is an S-possible program that also meets the coalition's resource constraint. An $|S|$-tuple $(Y^h(S) : h \in S) \equiv (Y^h)$ is an *S-allocation* if $\Sigma_{h \in S} Y^h(S)$ is an S-attainable allocation. The term *allocation* is used in place of *A-allocation* when the meaning is clear.

The use of the convex cone technology implies that the coalition S must only calculate the possible distribution of consumption goods to its members based on the total resources available to S. In particular, the distribution of capital across members of S along an S-attainable program is irrelevant for the determination of what S can guarantee for itself in the way of payoff vectors. However, it is useful to keep track of the individual ownership rights in capital and investment goods since the core concept is defined relative to an initial disbursement of resources. Notice that if $[C^h(S), Z^h(S), K^h(S), 1] \in \mathcal{T}$, then $\Sigma_{h \in S}[C^h(S), Z^h(S), K^h(S), 1] \in \mathcal{T}$ with $L(S)$ equal to the constant sequence whose t-th element is $|S|$.

Define a correspondence $V : \mathcal{P}(\mathcal{A}) \to \mathbf{R}^H$ according to

$$V(S) = \{v \in \mathbf{R}^H : \exists [C^h(S), Z^h(S), K^h(S), 1] \text{ such that for all } h \in S, (4.1)\text{-}(4.5) \text{ hold}\}.$$

$$\Sigma_{h \in S}[C^h(S), Z^h(S), K^h(S), 1] \in \mathcal{T}, \tag{4.1}$$

$$z_t^h(S) = k_t^h(S) - k_{t-1}^h(S), \tag{4.2}$$

$$z_t^h(S) + \Lambda k_{t-1}^h(S) \geq 0, \tag{4.3}$$

$$\Sigma_{h \in S} k_0^h \leq k(S), \tag{4.4}$$

$$v_v \leq U_h(C^h). \tag{4.5}$$

The correspondence V is called the *characteristic function* of the economy $\mathcal{E}$. Let $\pi_s : \mathbf{R}^H \to \mathbf{R}^S$ be the projection map from $\mathbf{R}^H$ into $\mathbf{R}^S$ where $\mathbf{R}^S$ has coordinates corresponding to $h \in$ S. Let $\mathcal{V}(S) = \pi_S V(S)$ denote the projection of $V(S)$ into $\mathbf{R}^S$; write $v \in V(S), v_S = \pi_S v$, and note $\mathcal{V}(A) = V(A)$.

The pair (A, V) is a *cooperative game without side payments in characteristic function form* if the conditions (C.1)-(C.5) listed below hold.

(C.1) For all $S \in \mathcal{P}(A), V(S)$ is a non-empty, non-full and closed subset of $\mathbf{R}^H$;

(C.2) For all $S \in \mathcal{P}(A), V(S)$ is comprehensive in the sense that $V(S) = V(S) - (\mathbf{R}_+^H)$;

(C.3) For all $S \in \mathcal{P}(A), V(S)$ is cylindrical in the sense that if $w \in V(S)$ and $y \in \mathbf{R}^H$ such that $w_S = y_S$, then $y \in V(S)$;

(C.4) There exists $v^0 \in \mathbf{R}^H$ such that $v^0 >> 0$ and for each $h, V(\{h\}) = \{v \in \mathbf{R}^H : v_h \leq v_h^0\}$;

(C.5) $V(S)$ is bounded from above for each $S \in \mathcal{P}(\mathcal{A})$ in the sense that there exists a real number $q_S > 0$ such that if $v \in V(S)$ and $v_S \geq 0$, then $v_h < q_S$ for all $h \in$ S.

LEMMA 4.3: *If* $(U1)$,$(U2)$, *and* $(T1) - (T8)$ *are satisfied, then* (A, V) *defined by* (4.1)-(4.5) *is a cooperative game without side payments in characteristic function form.*

The proof of this is standard given Lemmas (4.1) and (4.2), so it is omitted to save space. The core is translation invariant, so the standard assumption that $U_h(0) = 0$ (given $(U1)$) with $0 \in V(S)$ is replaced by the normalization condition (C.4). The advantage of this new normalization is that v^0 may be regarded as the vector of payoffs that each agent can obtain acting alone by solving his individual Ramsey optimal growth problem given his preferences, access to the common technology, endowment of capital, and unit level of labor resources. The basic hypotheses on preferences, the technology, and the endowment are sufficient to yield the existence of a vector v^0 with v^0_h interpreted as player h's individual Ramsey optimal payoff.[8] The following Lemma summarizes the properties enjoyed by the projection correspondence $\mathcal{V}$.

LEMMA 4.4: *If* $(U1)$,$(U2)$, *and* $(T1) - (T8)$ *are satisfied, then for* (A, V) *defined by* (4.1)-(4.5), $\mathcal{V}(S)$ *is a convex set and* $\mathcal{V}(S) \cap \mathbf{R}^S_+$ *is a non-empty compact convex set.*

5 The Core of (A, V)

The existence of core solutions for the game (A, V) and corresponding core allocations for $\mathcal{E}$ is established in this section. The interest in the core is defended on the usual grounds of reasonableness of this solution concept.[9] The first result covers games meeting the basic assumptions on preferences and technology. Extensions to games where U may not be continuous on the entire commodity space are discussed next. Existence for growing economies with convex technologies including closed one-sector models is taken up as another direction for a generalized core existence result.

5.1 The Basic Existence Theorem

The formal definition of the core of (A, V) is given with the main existence theorem.

DEFINITION: $v \in \mathbf{R}^H$ is *improved upon (or rejected)* by a coalition S if there exists a $v' \in \mathcal{V}(S)$ having $v'_h > v_h$ for each $h \in$ S. The *core* of the cooperative game (A, V) without sidepayments in characteristic function form is the set of $v \in \mathbf{R}^H$ that cannot be improved upon by any coalition S.

The set of core allocations for the game (A, V) is denoted by $C(A, V)$.

[8] If player h has a zero capital endowment, then by translating the value of $U_h(0)$ condition (C.4) may be met.

[9] Becker and Chakrabarti (1991) have shown that von Neumann-Morgenstern solutions exist for the game (A,V) meeting the basic assumptions. Chakrabarti (1989) has also shown the existence of a Shapley value for this non-transferable utility game.

DEFINITION: A coalition S *improves upon an allocation* (Y^h) if there is an S-allocation $(Y^h(S))$ such that $U^h(C^h(S)) > U^h(C^h)$ holds for each $h \in S$. A *core allocation* for $\mathcal{E}$ is an allocation that cannot be improved on by any coalition. The *core* of $\mathcal{E}$ is set of all core allocations for the economy $\mathcal{E}$.

DEFINITION: A collection $\mathcal{B} = \{S\}, S \in \mathcal{P}(A)$, is called a *balanced collection* if there exists weights $w_S \geq 0$ satisfying the equations

$$\Sigma_{\{S \in \mathcal{B}: S \supseteq \{h\}\}} w_S = 1 \qquad (h = 1, 2, \ldots, H). \tag{5.1}$$

DEFINITION: (A, V) is a *balanced game* if for every balanced collection $\mathcal{B} = \{S\}$ of subsets of A we have

$$\cap_{S \in \mathcal{B}} V(S) \subseteq V(A). \tag{5.2}$$

The main existence result for games (A, V) is Scarf's (1967) Theorem:[10]

THEOREM 5.1: A *balanced game* (A, V) *has a non-empty core.*

THEOREM 5.2: *If an economy* $\mathcal{E}$ *satisfies the basic assumptions, then* $C(A, V)$ *is non-empty for the game* (A, V) *defined by* (4.1). *The core of* $\mathcal{E}$ *is also non-empty.*

PROOF: The proof of this theorem is a modification of Becker's (1982,1983) arguments. The key step is to verify that the game is balanced. Let $\mathcal{B} = \{S\}$ be a balanced collection with weights w_S satisfying (5.1) and let $v \in \cap_{S \in \mathcal{B}} V(S)$. Then there exists for each $S \in \mathcal{B}$ sequences $\{Y^h(S)\}$ for $h \in S$ such that (4.1)-(4.5) hold with $v_h \equiv v_h(S)$. Define

$$Y^h = \Sigma_{\{S \in \mathcal{B}\}: S \supseteq \{h\}\}} w_S Y^h(S).$$

The vector Y^h is a convex combination of the vectors $Y^h(S)$ as S varies over coalitions in $\mathcal{B}$ having h as a member. By $(U2)$,

$$U_h(C^h) \geq \Sigma_{\{S \in \mathcal{B}: S \supseteq \{h\}\}} w_S U_h(C^h(S)) \geq$$

$$\Sigma_{\{S \in \mathcal{B}: S \supseteq \{h\}\}} w_S v_h = v_h.$$

Therefore $v \in V(A)$ if and only if

$$\Sigma_{h \in A} Y^h \in \mathcal{T} \text{ and} \tag{5.3}$$

$$\Sigma_{h \in A} z_t^h = \Sigma_{h \in A}(k_t^h - k_{t-1}^h), \ \Sigma_{h \in A} \ell^h = H. \tag{5.4}$$

The assumption that $\mathcal{T}$ is a convex cone implies for each $h \in S$ and t that $w_S y_t^h(S) \in T$ and $\Sigma_{h \in S} y_t^h(S) \in T$. Therefore $w_S Y^h(S) \in \mathcal{T}$ and $\Sigma_{h \in S} Y^h(S) \in \mathcal{T}$. Thus

$$\Sigma_{h \in A} Y^h = \Sigma_{h \in A} \Sigma_{\{S \in \mathcal{B}: S \supseteq \{h\}\}} w_S Y^h(S)$$

$$= \Sigma_{\{S \in \mathcal{B}: S \supseteq \{h\}\}} w_S (\Sigma_{h \in A} Y^h(S)) \in \mathcal{T}.$$

Thus (Y^h) is in the intertemporal production set $\mathcal{T}$ for the entire economy. A similar calculation shows that the relations in (5.4) hold. Therefore, (Y^h) is

[10] Also see Shapley and Vohra [1991] for the form of Scarf's Theorem fitting the game defined with properties (C.1) – (C.5).

an attainable allocation for this economy implying $v \in V(A)$. Applying Scarf's Theorem yields the conclusion $C(A,V) \neq \emptyset$.

Suppose $v \in C(A,V)$. Let (Y^h) be any attainable allocation for the grand coalition with $U^h(C^h) \geq v_h$. Evidently (Y^h) is an element of the core of $\mathcal{E}$. Q.E.D.

The Scarf theorem applies because the characteristic function form of the game places the existence analysis in the finite dimensional space of utility payoffs. The dimension of the payoff space is independent of the dimension of the commodity space. The structure of the infinite dimensional commodity space enters through the verification of the key compactness property (Lemma 4.2) needed for (A,V) to qualify as a game. This in turn implies the compactness in payoff space reported in Lemma 4.4. Incidentally, the full power of Scarf's theorem is not needed because the attainable utility sets $V(S)$ are convex (see Ekeland [1974, pp. 79-80]).

5.2 The Extended Existence Theorem

The central examples of unbounded utility functions are found in the TAS forms with constant elasticity of marginal felicity. The purpose of this section is to extend Theorem 5.2 to some cases of unbounded utility functions which fail to satisfy $(U1)$. The hypotheses of the extended existence result restrict agents utility functions to be bounded from below. The one-sector model is used to in order to give a concrete illustration to the extension of the basic existence theorem.

The one-sector production model can be described for a fixed labor force ℓ^*. Output in any period depends on the level of variable input x. Given input x, output net of depreciation is denoted $g(x) - \lambda x$, where λx allows for proportional depreciation of capital in a single period and $0 \leq \lambda \leq 1$ is a given parameter. The total output available in the period is denoted by $f(x) = g(x) + (1-\lambda)x$. Assume that g is derived from a neoclassical constant returns to scale production function G with labor input fixed at ℓ^*: Write $g(x) = G(x, \ell^*)$. Recall that a production function G is *neoclassical* provided it is concave, positively homogeneous of degree one, increasing in both arguments, and twice continuously differentiable for positive values of its arguments. In many applications $G(0,0) = G(x,0) = G(0,\ell) = 0$ and Inada conditions at the origin may also hold (see $(F1)$). The notation f_S and g_S refers to the cases where $\ell^* = |S|$ for a coalition S. The S subscripts are suppressed when the meaning is clear. The basic properties of f may be summarized in the statement:

$(F1)$ The function $f : \mathbf{R}_+ \to \mathbf{R}_+$ with $f(0) = 0$. On $\mathbf{R}_{++}$,f is C^2 with $f'' < 0$ and $f' > 0$. Moreover, $1 < f'(0+) \leq \infty$ and $f'(\infty) < 1$.[11]

Assumption $(F1)$ implies there is a maximum sustainable stock, $b = f_A(b) > 0$, available to the grand coalition. An example motivates the assumptions of the extended existence theorem. The aggregator $W(z,y) = z^\mu + \delta y$, $0 < \mu, \delta < 1$, defines a utility function U, on s_+ which is not continuous at 0.[12] Even though U is

[11] The notation $f'(0+)$ stands for the limit of the expression $f'(x)$ as $x \to 0$ from the right. Similarly, $f'(\infty)$ denotes the corresponding limit as $x \to \infty$.

[12] See Beals and Koopmans (1969, pg. 1014). This utility function is lower semicontinuous but it is not upper semicontinous at the origin.

not continuous on all of s_+, there are relevant subsets of s_+ where U is continuous. These sets are proper subsets of $\mathcal{X}(\beta) = \{X \in s : \sup_t |\frac{x_t}{\beta^t}| < \infty\}$ where $\beta > 1$ is a fixed weighting factor.[13]

Define f^t inductively by setting $f^1 = f$ and $f^t = f(f^{t-1})$. The *path of pure accumulation starting from seed k* is $\{f_A^t(k)\}$. The set $D = \{C \in s_+ : 0 \leq c_t \leq f_A^t(k), t = 1, 2, \ldots\}$ contains all feasible consumption profiles for the grand coalition. For $\alpha \geq 1$, D is said to be an *α-bounded* set if $\sup_t |\frac{x_t}{\alpha^t}| < \infty$ whenever $X \in D$. The concavity of f_A and $k \in (0, b)$ imply D is an α-bounded subset of $\mathcal{X}(\beta)$ for any $\alpha > f'_A(\infty)$. [14] Boyd (1990) has shown that U is continuous on $\mathcal{X}(\beta)$ provided $\delta\beta^\mu < 1$. If $\beta > \alpha$, then $D \subseteq \mathcal{X}(\beta)$ is a relatively σ-compact subset of s. Continuity of U on D is enough to define this single players characteristic function. For an economy $\mathcal{E}$ populated by agents with this utility function, continuity of U on D is more than enough to define the game (A, V) given the concavity of f. The set D contains all consumption profiles that could ever occur in any core allocation. The condition $\delta\beta^\mu < 1$ is a joint condition on preferences and technology insuring the continuity of U on an economically important subset of the program space.

The definition of the domain D actually opens the possibility for accommodating models permitting unbounded growth in the capital stocks.[15] These models can arise in the one sector context in either a linear or nonlinear production framework. The nonlinear case can arise when there is no depreciation. The linear case, $f(x) = \gamma x, \gamma > 1$, corresponds to the closed economy model where labor is not a scarce factor of production. In both cases, the path of pure accumulation starting with the social endowment of capital is an element of D. For example, if $f(x) = 2x + \sqrt{x}$, then the concavity of f once again implies D is α-bounded for any $\alpha > 2$. If $\beta > \alpha$ and $\delta\beta^\mu < 1$, then U is continuous on the relatively σ-compact set D.

For the open economy one-sector model, Axiom (T) describes the technology whereas Axiom (TC) governs the one-sector closed model case. Analogs of Lemmas (4.2)–(4.4) may be derived for models meeting either Axioms (T) or (TC).

(T) $T = \{(c, z, k, \ell) \in \mathbf{R}^4 : c + z + \lambda k \leq G(k, \ell),\ c, k, \ell \geq 0,\ z + \lambda k \geq 0\}$, *where* G *is a neoclassical production function and* $0 \leq \lambda \leq 1$.

(TC) $T = \{(c, z, k) \in \mathbf{R}^3 : c + z \leq \gamma k,\ c, k \geq 0,\ z + \lambda k \geq 0\}$, *where* $\gamma > 1$.[16]

The following axioms are stated for arbitrary utility functions.[17] The social endowment of capital is k. The set D is to be defined using the path of pure accumulation starting from k.

AXIOM OF FINITUDE: *The utility function* U_h *is defined on a convex subset of* s_+ *containing* D *and may take the value* $+\infty$. *Moreover,* U_h *is concave and increasing with*

$$0 \leq U_h(C^h) \leq U_h(f(k), f^2(k), \ldots) < \infty.$$

[13] Boyd (1990) contains detailed information about this construction.

[14] Boyd (1990, pg. 337).

[15] See Jones and Manuelli (1990) for a detailed motivation for interest in convex growth models allowing for unbounded growth of capital stocks.

[16] Let $\gamma = \xi - \lambda$ be the net marginal product of capital.

[17] These axioms are adapted from Becker, Boyd and Foias (1991).

AXIOM OF CONTINUITY: *The utility function U_h is σ-continuous on D .*

The same proof as Theorem (5.2) carries over to economies with technologies satisfying either (T) or (TC) and the Axioms of Finitude and Continuity. The **extended basic assumptions** are said to be met by an economy $\mathcal{E}$ provided the Axioms of Finitude and Continuity hold, and either property (T) or (TC) governs the technology set. In the open economy case it is understood that $\ell^h = 1$ is the normalized labor input of each player. The extended existence theorem for one sector models (open or closed versions) is

THEOREM 5.3: *If an economy $\mathcal{E}$ satisfies the extended basic assumptions, then $C(A, V)$ is non-empty and the core of $\mathcal{E}$ is non-empty.*

Open multisector economies may provide suitable structure for creation of analogs of Theorem (5.3). For example, two-sector models may be employed with the path of pure accumulation found by producing only the capital good with all the economy's labor. In this case, the bounds derived from the one-sector case have counterparts in the two-sector framework and the existence result remains valid.

The adaptation of the extended basic assumptions to cases where the aggregator is not bounded from below, such as $W(z,y) = \log z + \delta y$, remains open. One way to attack the extension to these functions may be found in Becker, Boyd and Foias (1991). There, an agent is always able to construct a consumption profile which is strictly bounded away from the origin and no consumption program actually chosen in that model economy would yield less consumption to an agent at any time than given by that special path. In the present core model, the Becker, Boyd and Foias domain construction could be utilized in one-sector models where $f_{\{h\}}(0) > 0$, that is, capital is not an essential input in the production process. Further exploration of core existence theorem for utility unbounded from below is a project for future study.

6 Examples of the Core Solution Concept

The examples in this section illustrate some of the possible properties of core allocations. Aggregate capital and consumption models are studied for illustrative purposes. The first set of examples explore the case of time additive separable utility functions. All of the examples focus on the distributional aspects of core allocations. It should be noted that since core allocations are Pareto optimal, the extensive literature devoted to optimal allocations may be used to state results concerning the time paths of aggregate consumption and capital holdings.

6.1 Additive Separable Utility Examples

Example 1:

There is one consumption good and one investment good; each is produced according to a neoclassical production function and there is no joint production. Labor and capital are the inputs. The two-sector technology set may be described in the usual way.[18] It is enough to assume that both labor and capital are required for the production of a positive output from any sector.

Assume there are H agents. Each player's utility is given by a TAS utility function specified by a concave, increasing felicity u_h satisfying $u_h(0) = 0$. The discount factor satisfies the relation $0 < \delta_h < 1$. Suppose that player one is the only player endowed with capital (in amount k) and each player may supply one unit of labor. Then the only coalitions that can produce any positive utility payoffs for some player must contain player 1; all coalitions S with $1 \notin S$ cannot produce anything from their labor alone. Therefore, one core allocation is the payoff assigning $v_h = 0$ to $h \geq 2$ and v_1 equal to the maximum discounted utility found by solving the optimal growth problem for player one from starting stocks k, using all the economy's available labor (H units at each time), and satisfying the technology constraints at each time. Players $h \geq 2$ contribute their labor to the grand coalition but do not receive any benefit.

This solution is extreme, since the players $h \geq 2$ might threaten to withdraw their labor services in the event that they do not get any consumption in this "solution." In fact, other core allocations do exist in this example. Any Pareto optimal distribution of utility giving player one a payoff $v_1 > v_1(\{1\})$ will be a core allocation.

If this example is modified to permit another agent (say player 2) to have a positive endowment of capital, then other "winning coalitions" may form. A core allocation must give players 1 and 2 at least as much utility as either could achieve in isolation as well as in the case where they form the coalition $S = \{1, 2\}$. If $\delta_1 > \delta_2$, then it is known that any Pareto optimal allocation (in particular core allocation) must have player 2's consumption converging to zero.

Example 2:

The technology is described by a two-sector model summarized by the transformation function available to coalition S, $F_S(x, x')$, expressing the maximum production of the consumption good given capital inputs x and net outputs x' with labor input $|S|$. Gross investment is $g = x' - (1 - \lambda)x$ for $0 \leq \lambda \leq 1$ and $F_S(0,0) = F_S(0, x') = 0$. The production functions underlying the consumption and capital investment goods sectors are taken to yield a technology consistent with the basic axioms.[19] The transformation function F_S for each coalition is a concave function which is increasing in the first argument and decreasing in the second. Let $D(S)$ denote the domain of F_S in $\mathbf{R}^2_+$. The sets $D(S)$ are non-empty convex sets having a non-empty interior relative to $\mathbf{R}^2_+$. Use the notation $D(A) = D$ and $F_A(x, x') = F(x, x')$ for the grand coalition A.

In this example U_h is a TAS utility function with linear felicity function $u_h(c_t^h) = c_t^h$ for $h = 1, \ldots, H$. Let $\gamma(S) \in \mathbf{R}^S_+$ be a row vector of weights for $h \in S$, with $\Sigma_{h \in S}\gamma(S) = 1$; γ is the vector of weights for the grand coalition A. The basic assumptions on utility are not met by this specification, however the extended existence theorem may be easily seen to accommodate this model.

The following discussion is presented for the case of the grand coalition A and carries over to an arbitrary coalition with the appropriate notational changes. Fix γ

[18] Some additional details may also be found in Example 2 below.

[19] Consult Boldrin (1989) for a detailed development of the two-sector model appropriate for the analysis in this example.

and define $1 \times H$ vectors $\Gamma_\gamma(t) = (\gamma_1\delta_1^{t-1}, \ldots, \gamma_H\delta_H^{t-1})$ and let $e = (1, 1, \ldots, 1)$. Let $c_t = [c_t^1, \ldots, c_t^H]$ denote an $H \times 1$ column vector. Define for each $(x, x') \in D$,

$$V_\gamma(x, x', t) = \sup \Gamma_\gamma(t) c_t \tag{6.1}$$

by choice of c_t subject to the constraints

$$ec_t \leq F(x, x'),\ c_t \geq 0.$$

Problem (6.1) is a linear programming problem with optimal basic solution

$$\bar{c}_t = (\bar{c}_t^1, \ldots, \bar{c}_t^H)$$

with

$$\bar{c}_t^{h(t)} = F(x, x'),\ \bar{c}_t^h = 0$$

for $h \neq h(t)$, where $h(t)$ satisfies $\gamma_{h(t)}\delta_{h(t)}^{t-1} \geq \gamma_h \delta_h^{t-1}$ for all h. The lexicographic rule may be used to break ties as needed, so $h(t)$ is the first h occurring in ties. Thus

$$V_\gamma(x, x', t) = \gamma_{h(t)}\delta_{h(t)}^{t-1} F(x, x'). \tag{6.2}$$

Define a value function

$$J_\gamma(k) = \sup \Sigma_{t=1}^\infty V_\gamma(x_{t-1}, x_t, t) \tag{6.3}$$

by choice of a capital sequence $\{x_t\}_{t=1}^\infty$ satisfying $(x_{t-1}, x_t) \in D$ for $t = 1, 2, \ldots$ and $x_0 \leq k$. The problem defined by (6.3) is a reduced form model of the variety studied by McKenzie (1986). Thus, the general theory developed for those models applies to (6.3).

In general, the reduced form objective is not time stationary. However, if $\delta_h = \delta$ for all $h, 0 < \delta < 1$, then the value function J_γ is proportional to

$$J(k) = \sup\{\Sigma_{t=1}^\infty \delta^{t-1} F(x_{t-1}, x_t) : (x_{t-1}, x_t) \in D, x_0 \leq k\}. \tag{6.4}$$

In this case, (6.4) and (6.5) generate equivalent optimal paths of capital accumulation. The weights serve to redistribute consumption. Thus the core capital accumulation program separates from the distribution of consumption problem. The specific choices of the weights for a core allocation depend on the distribution of initial capital: agents having no capital need not receive a positive weight as observed in the first example.

If $1 > \delta_1 > \delta_2 > \cdots > \delta_H > 0$ and $\gamma_1 > 0$, then (6.3) has the form: There exists $T(\gamma)$ such that

$$V_\gamma(x, x', t) = \gamma_1\delta_1^{t-1} F(x, x') \text{ for } t \geq T(\gamma);$$
$$V_\gamma(x, x', t) = \gamma_h\delta_h^{t-1} F(x, x') \text{ for } t < T(\gamma),$$

where $h = h(t)$ from (6.2) and $T(\gamma) = 0$ may occur in which case only the first one period return function is active. Thus, (6.3) becomes for $T(\gamma) \geq 1$:

$$J_\gamma(k) = \sup\{\Sigma_{t=1}^{T(\gamma)} \gamma_{h(t)}\delta_{h(t)}^{t-1} F(x_{t-1}, x_t) + \Sigma_{t=T(\gamma)+1}^\infty \gamma_1\delta_1^{t-1} F(x_{t-1}x_t)\} \tag{6.5}$$

subject to the usual constraints. Therefore household 1 eventually dominates the objective function if $\gamma_1 > 0$.

Let $J_{\gamma(S)}(k(S)), S \in \mathcal{P}(\mathcal{A})$, be the analog of the optimal return function in (6.3). Then a payoff vector $v \in C(A, V)$ if and only if there exist weights $\gamma(S) \in \mathbf{R}^S_+, S \in \mathcal{P}(\mathcal{A})$, such that $\gamma(S)v_S \geq J_{\gamma(S)}(k(S))$ holds for all S.

Suppose v is a core payoff vector and $k(\{1\}) > 0$. Let $J_1(k(\{1\})$ denote player 1's optimal value function for his individual Ramsey problem. Then $v_{\{1\}} \equiv v_1 \geq J_1(k(\{1\}) > 0$ implying that γ_1 must hold. Indeed, if $\gamma_1 = 0$, then $h(t) \neq 1$ for all t and $c_t^1 = 0$ holds for all t by (6.1) with $\{x_t\}_{t=1}^{\infty}$ the corresponding solution to (6.3). But this implies $v_{\{1\}} = 0$, a contradiction. Thus $k(\{1\}) > 0$ implies $v_1 > 0$ and player 1's core consumption is eventually positive. This result only depends on $1 > \delta_1 \geq \delta_h > 0$ for $h \neq 1$. Consideration of additional subcases leads to sharper conclusions.

Case 1. $\delta = \delta_h$ for all h.

Let $I = \{h : k(\{h\}) > 0\}$. Then $h \in I$ implies $\gamma_1 = \gamma_h > 0$ must also hold. If $h \notin I$, then $\gamma_1 = \gamma_h$ may also hold if $h \in S$ for some S having $k(S) > 0$. The actual distribution of consumption in a core allocation is otherwise indeterminate. Note the reason that $\gamma_1 = \gamma_h$ must hold by virtue of the linear programming structure of (6.1) and the condition that all agents have a common discount factor in Case 1. Indeed, agent h has positive consumption at time t if and only if $\gamma_1 = \gamma_h$ as each optimal basic solution gives all the consumption to one agent and every optimal solution is a convex combination of optimal basic solutions.

Case 2. $1 > \delta_1 > \delta_2 > \cdots > \delta_H$.

In this case, $\gamma_1 > 0$ implies only player one eventually has positive consumption by the same reasoning used to support (6.5). In this case, if some player has the role of $h(t)$ in an optimal basic solution and $h(t) \neq 1$, then that player trades present consumption against future consumption. Notice that this means

$$v_{h(t)} \geq J_{h(t)}(k(\{h(t)\}) > 0, \text{ if } k(\{h(t)\}) > 0.$$

Thus for t large enough, a core allocation may give zero consumption to agents with a positive capital endowment. Even though player $h(t)$ has positive stocks for all t when calculating the optimal value of his single agent Ramsey problem, he (presumably) gives up claims to his capital stock to player 1 for a larger initial consumption in the core allocation. This partly answers a conjecture in Becker (1982) concerning the possibility that higher impatience players will eventually or asymptotically receive a zero payoff per period even though a positive payoff at each time t would be realized in isolation. The core allocation provides a preferred discounted stream of rewards than the optimal value achieved in isolation.

The general pattern of capital accumulation for the program (6.3) may be ascertained by piecing together results for stationary two-sector problems. The preceding analysis shows that there will always exist a finite time T such that J_γ may be decomposed into the form:

$$J_\gamma(k) = \sup \Sigma_{t=1}^{T} \gamma_{h(t)} \delta_{h(t)}^{t-1} F(x_{t-1}, x_t) + \Sigma_{t=T+1}^{\infty} \gamma_1 \delta_1^{t-1} F(x_{t-1}, x_t).$$

It is clear from backward induction dynamic programming considerations that the optimal path of capital stocks can be characterized as the solution to

$$\sup\{\Sigma_{t=1}^{T}\gamma_{h(t)}\delta_{h(t)}^{t-1}F(x_{t-1},x_t)+M_\gamma(x_T)\}$$

by choice of $(x_0, x_1, \ldots, x_T)$ subject to $(x_{t-1}, x_t) \in D$ for $t = 1, 2, \ldots, T$ and $x_0 \leq k$ where

$$M_\gamma(x'_T) = \sup \Sigma_{t=T+1}^{\infty}\gamma_1\delta_1^{t-1}F(x_{t-1},x_t)$$

by choice of $\{x_t\}_{t=T+1}^{\infty}, (x_{t-1}, x_t) \in D, t = T+1, \ldots,$ and $x_T \leq x'_T$. This later program is just a standard quasi-stationary realization of the two-sector model.[20]

The dynamics of the optimal program starting from time T depends on the sign of the second order partial derivative of $F, \partial^2 F(x,y)/\partial x \partial y \equiv F_{12}$, evaluated along an optimal program. In particular, if $F_{12} > 0$, then the optimal capital program is monotonic, if $F_{12} < 0$, then it oscillates.[21] Indeed, for δ_1 sufficiently small, factor intensity reversals may induce a chaotic optimal program.[22] It follows, for example, in the case $F_{12} > 0$, that the optimal program starting from $t = 1$ is **eventually** monotonic in a core allocation: the first T periods capital stocks may oscillate but eventually the optimal capital path settles into a monotonic regime. A similar statement applies to the cases where $F_{12} < 0$ always holds. If player 1 is sufficiently impatient and there is a factor intensity reversal, the optimal capital path may follow a chaotic trajectory as noted in Boldrin (1989).

Example 3:

Let there be two households with utility functions as in example one. Assume here that $\delta_1 > \delta_2$. Suppose for simplicity that the model is an exchange economy. At each date t, agent h has 1 unit of a single consumption good; the economy's aggregate endowment of the good is 2 units at each time. Agents exchange consumption goods over an infinite time horizon to achieve a profile of consumption preferred to the no-trade state. The cooperative exchange game (A, V) may be defined by letting $V(A)$ equal the set of Pareto optimal utility payoffs (plus those payoffs $v_h \leq u_h(1)/(1-\delta_h)$). Clearly $C(A, V)$ is non-empty and any core allocation results in a Pareto optimal distribution of the consumption goods over time. By using the methods in Lucas and Stokey (1984) and Rader (1981) it is easy to show that any core allocation has the property that player 1's consumption asymptotically approaches 2 while player 2's consumption converges to 0. The most patient player receives all the consumption in the limit.

Notice that player 2 is bound to follow the sequence of trades implicit in any core allocation because contracts made at time zero are binding on all the players. This is important because agent 2 would renege on his agreement if this was possible. At some time T (which depends on the particular core allocation), agent 2 gets consumption permanently smaller that one unit (his endowment). If that agent could cheat by abrogating the contract with player 1 from time T on into the indefinite future, then player 2 would be able to consume his endowment at each date $t \geq$ T. This strategy would yield a higher payoff to the player from time T on than the strategy of following with the agreed trades made at the start of the game.

[20]See Boldrin (1989) and McKenzie (1986) for a discussion of this model.

[21]See Benhabib and Nishimura (1985) for details.

[22]See Boldrin (1989).

This example suggests that the core solution concept is not time consistent. Put differently, if agents may revise their trades as time proceeds, then agreements made at time zero may not necessarily be followed forever. Can the core concept be strengthened to one which is time consistent? This problem is addressed in Section 7.

6.2 Recursive Utility Examples

Example 4:

This example is based on a two player model where each player has Rawlsian utility given by the aggregator $W(x, y) = \min\{x, y\}$. The technology is a one sector linear model. This corresponds to a closed model specification in the general theory. The constraints are that $x_0 \leq k$, the usual nonnegativities, and for $t \geq 1$:

$$c_t^1 + c_t^2 + x_t \leq \gamma x_{t-1}. \tag{6.6}$$

The social endowment of capital is k. The Pareto optimal payoffs are given by a linear utility possibility frontier. This frontier has the equation $v_1 + v_2 = \gamma k - k$, where v_h is player h's payoff. The shape of the utility possibility frontier is a reflection of the conservative nature of the maximum criterion: players do not have any incentive to either save or dissave. Now fix the initial capital at k^h with $k^1 + k^2 =$ k. It is easy to show that the "disagreement point" given by payoffs $v_h = \gamma k^h - k^h$ are on the utility possibility frontier. Therefore, the core allocation is uniquely determined by the initial distribution of capital. The consumption of each player is stationary. In this case, neither player would have any reason to cheat on an agreement made at the beginning of time. The results for the closed economy used here may be extended to the open case with a one-sector neoclassical production function provided the total capital is below the golden-rule stock for that technology. In the case total capital exceeds the golden-rule stock, one player enjoys a consumption binge at time one with the golden-rule state reached in one step. This path will be in the core as well.

Example 5:

This example uses the same technological setup as the previous one but specifies UEH utility functions of the class (3.3) for the players. The example is motivated by a analogous continuous time example in Epstein and Hynes (1983). Assume that $u_1 \leq u_2$ and let k denote the aggregate endowment of capital. Assume that $u_h(0) < \log \gamma < u_h(\infty)$. A *stationary Pareto optimal* allocation can be shown to satisfy the relations

$$\gamma \exp(-u_h(c^h)) = 1 \tag{6.7}$$

for all h. This consumption allocation is a *stationary perfect foresight equilibrium* if the player's have initial capital

$$k^h = c^h / r, \tag{6.8}$$

where $\gamma^{-1} = 1 + r$ for $r > 0$. For the initial distribution of capital given by (6.8) and total capital $k = k^1 + k^2$, the payoff $v_h = -1/(1 - \rho_h)$ corresponds to a core allocation where $\rho_h = \exp(-u_h(c^h))$. It follows that for this distribution of capital stocks, that the stationary perfect foresight equilibrium is a core allocation which is time stationary. In this case, neither agent will have an incentive to deviate from the given allocation even if such a deviation were permitted by the rules. Also notice that $u_1 \leq u_2$ implies that $c^1 \geq c^2$ and $k^1 \geq k^2$. If the initial distribution of capital differed from the stationary distribution, then other Pareto optima and core allocations would, of course, be possible.

7 The Recursive Core

The core solution does not use the recursive structure of production or utility in those cases where players preferences are recursive. If all agents utility functions are members of the recursive class, a refinement of the core solution concept may be defined which takes advantage of the weak separability of the future form the present. This new solution concept is called the *recursive core* and it is developed in this section. The main difference between the recursive core and the core is that a recursive core allocation must remain a core allocation in each subgame that starts at an arbitrary time t given the evolution of assets to time t implied by that allocation started at time zero. The idea is to impose a time consistency condition on core allocations made at time zero. No coalition should be able to take the assets available to it at any time t and improve upon the continuation of the allocation that began at time zero. Recursive core allocations are self-enforcing even though binding agreements across period may not be possible. The recursive core has built-in dynamic features that the more static looking core concept is incapable of exhibiting along solution paths.

7.1 Motivation for the Recursive Core

Example 3 of the previous section is the motivating game for the recursive core concept. There are two interpretations of that exchange game (A, V) and the core allocations in $C(A, V)$. In the first case, there is a single representative agent of each type h that selects a path strategy C^h once and for all in a giant forward market with settlement made at time zero. A second interpretation is that of a sequence of altruistic generations composed at each t of a type 1 or type 2 trader that come together in a giant intertemporal market and arrive at path strategies C^h by face-to-face bargaining. Agreements between generations are binding, so all trades may be executed at time zero. Altruism and the bargaining power of future generations are linked in this process (see Page [1977]).

In the two player core-exchange game, the core solution has generation one of the impatient player ($h = 2$) receiving a consumption larger than one unit and infinitely many future generations consuming less than one unit. Why would so many future generations follow the plan initiated by the earlier generations? If the generations cannot directly meet or cannot come to binding agreements, the later generations would try to escape from the early generations agreements as already noted. Indeed, each generation receiving less than one unit of the good would reject the initial core allocation if it could do so. The latter generations are clearly better off in a no-trade position. This time inconsistency of the core allocation would obtain for any core allocation that did not give everything to one player for all time; this is possible only in the case where the player who receives all the consumption is also the only one endowed with that good. An analogous situation arises in Example 1 when $\delta_1 > \delta_2$ and agent two's endowment of capital is positive. On the other hand, Examples 4 and 5 display a time consistency property. The recursive core is introduced in order to frame a solution concept that will provide each generation with an incentive to voluntarily maintain inherited agreements.

7.2 Formulation of the Recursive Core

The normal form of the game (A, V) is used to spell out the recursive core concept for open models. Player h selects a *strategy*, Y^h, which is a sequence of consumption, investment goods, capital stocks, and labor supply profiles. The case of a closed one-sector model is similar. The time zero endowment is fixed. Player h's payoff function is defined by the aggregator W^h with associated utility function U^h. An *allocation* is a list of sequences $(Y^h, h \in A) \equiv (Y^h)$ such that $\Sigma_{h=1}^H Y^h \in \mathcal{T}$, with $\Sigma_{h=1}^H z_t^h = \Sigma_{h=1}^H (k_t^h - k_{t-1}^h)$, and $k_0^h \leq k^h$ is h's endowment of capital goods.

DEFINITION: An allocation (Y^h) is *rejected by a coalition S at time T* if there exist sequences $Y^h(S)$ such that for $t \geq T$ and $h \in S$,

$$W^h(c_T^h(S), U^h(S^T C^h(S)) > W^h(c_T^h, U^h(S^T C^h)), \tag{7.1}$$

$$\Sigma_{h\in S} Y^h(S) \in \mathcal{T} \text{ and } \Sigma_{h\in S} \ell^h(S) = |S| \text{ for } t \geq T, \tag{7.2}$$

$$\Sigma_{h\in S} z_t^h(S) = \Sigma_{h\in S}(k_t^h(S) - k_{t-1}^h(S)) \text{ for } t \geq T, \tag{7.3}$$

$$\text{and } \Sigma_{h\in S} k_{T-1}^h(S) \leq \Sigma_{h\in S} x_{T-1}^h, \tag{7.4}$$

where x_{T-1}^h is the capital stock achieved by h at the end of period $T-1$ when following the path (Y^h).

An allocation is rejected by S at time T if, when that allocation is followed up to time T, with the resources accumulated to that date by the members of coalition S, it is possible for the members of S to initiate a new profile which is technologically possible and improves the welfare of each coalition member.

DEFINITIONS: The *recursive core* is the set of all allocations which are not rejected by any coalition at any date. The set of recursive core allocations is denoted by $R(A, V)$. An allocation is a *recursive Pareto optimum* if it is not rejected by the grand coalition A at any date. The set of recursive Pareto optima is denoted by $P(A, V)$. An allocation is a *weak Pareto optimum* if it is not rejected by the grand coalition A at time 1. The set of weak Pareto optima is denoted $WP(A, V)$.[23]

An allocation in the recursive core has a *time consistency property:* no coalition would voluntarily depart from the allocation at any date T given the resources available to it at T either through past accumulation decisions or by way of primary factor endowments. If agreements between generations at time zero are not legally

[23] Haurie and Delfour (1976) discuss the related notion of a closed-loop Pareto optimal path.

binding, then the recursive core allocations are self-enforcing. For intertemporal-intergenerational bargaining games where binding agreements between generations are impossible to enforce, the recursive core solution yields a path that no generation would deviate from in the manner seen in the exchange Example 3.

It is also interesting to note that allocations in $WP(A,V)$ are time-consistent when utility is recursive. This is a consequence of the stationarity property enjoyed by recursive utility.

PROPOSITION 7.1: *Suppose the basic assumptions on preferences and technology hold. If each agent's utility function is recursive, then* $WP(A,V) = P(A,V)$.

PROOF: Evidently $P(A,V) \subseteq WP(A,V)$ — apply the recursive Pareto optimum definition at time 1. To prove the reverse inclusion, $P(A,V) \supseteq WP(A,V)$, holds, suppose (Y^h) is a weak Pareto optimum allocation but it is not a recursive Pareto optimal allocation. Then (Y^h) is rejected by the grand coalition A at some time T. Therefore there is an A-attainable allocation $(Y^h(A))$ starting from time T with $\Sigma_{h=1}^{H} k_{T-1}^h(A) \leq \Sigma_{h=1}^{H} k_{T-1}^h$, and such that

$$W^h(c_T^h(A), U^h(S^T C^h(A)) > W^h(c_T^h, U^h(S^T C^h)), \tag{7.5}$$

where $\Sigma_{h=1}^{H} k_{T-1}^h$ is the total capital stock achieved by the grand coalition at the end of period $T-1$ when following the path (Y^h). Equation (7.5) is equivalent to

$$U^h(c_T^h(A), c_{T+1}^h(A), \ldots) > U^h(c_T^h, c_{T+1}^h, \ldots) \tag{7.6}$$

Now define a program $(\overline{Y}_h)$ coordinatewise by $\overline{y}_t^h = [\overline{c}_t^h, \overline{z}_t^h, \overline{k}_t^h, \overline{\ell}_t^h]$ with $\overline{\ell}_t^h = 1$ for all h by the formulas:

$$\overline{Y}_t^h = Y_t^h \ (t \leq T-1)$$
$$\overline{Y}_t^h = Y_t^h(A) \ (t \geq T).$$

The program $(\overline{Y}^h)$ is feasible for the grand coalition given the initial stocks k and is preferred by every player to the path (Y^h) since utility is recursive and (7.6) holds if and only if

$$U^h(\overline{c}_1, \ldots, \overline{c}_{T-1}, c_T^h(A), c_{T+1}^h(A), \ldots) > U^h(\overline{c}_1, \ldots, \overline{c}_{T-1}, c_T^h, c_{T+1}^h, \ldots).$$

But this inequality and the feasibility of $(\overline{Y}^h)$ contradicts the weak Pareto optimality of the program (Y^h). Q.E.D.

7.3 Properties of the Recursive Core

One elementary property of the recursive core is stated as

PROPOSITION 7.2: *Given the basic assumptions on preferences and technology, if each agent's utility function is recursive, then* $R(A,V) \subseteq P(A,V)$.

The proof of Proposition 7.2 is immediate. It is important to stress here that both $R(A,V)$ and $P(A,V)$ may be empty.[24] This Proposition merely asserts that

[24]However, the existence of individually rational weak Pareto optima is guaranteed in the case of models meeting the basic assumptions: just apply results in Aliprantis, Brown and Burkinshaw (1989, pp. 222-223) noting that the utility space in this case is compact.

if an allocation is in the recursive core, than it is necessarily a recursive Pareto optimum. By an appropriate distribution of the initial stocks (possibly different from the given stocks), the particular recursive Pareto optimum need not be a recursive core allocation. Indeed, the criterion for an allocation to belong to the recursive Pareto optimal set is independent of the initial distribution of capital stocks. The recursive core test requires a specification of that initial distribution of stocks.

The Pareto optimal allocation in Example 3 is a recursive Pareto optimum, but clearly it does not belong to the recursive core. To see this, fix any time T and let c_t^1 and c_t^2 for $t \geq T$ denote the consumption assigned to each player in the Pareto optimum starting at T. Clearly, there is no way to redistribute the two units of the good available at each future date to improve one player's welfare without lowering the other player's welfare. Thus, imposing the condition that an allocation belong to the set of recursive Pareto optima may not be strong enough by itself to remove the incentive for some generation to break it's obligation made at time zero. The distribution of endowments does matter in the determination of which (if any) recursive Pareto optima are also recursive core allocations. Notice that the allocations giving everything to one player (when the other's endowment is zero) are recursive core allocations.

The inclusion $C(A,V) \supseteq R(A,V)$ holds but the $C(A,V) \subseteq R(A,V)$ inclusion is generally false as noted in the examples. Moreover, an attempt to argue for the later inclusion along the lines of the proof of Proposition 7.2 fails since the calculation showing the existence of an allocation improving on the given weak Pareto optimal assignment uses the grand coalition in a non-trivial fashion. For the argument to carry over, it must be possible for the improving coalition to construct the analogous improving program within its own resources starting from the beginning of the game. However, this may not be feasible for a coalition S without calling on the resources of the adverse coalition. This is a serious issue since S is not, in general, the grand coalition.

The core allocation found in Example 4 is a recursive core allocation for that game. Indeed, it is not surprising that the payoff functions motivated by a "theory of justice" are consistent with both core allocation ideas. The existence of recursive core allocations in Examples 4 and 5 imply the recursive core is non-empty for at least some games. One problem remaining for future work is to determine what class of games have non-empty recursive cores. The examples constructed above of recursive core allocations are all stationary. This suggests another question: does a non-stationary recursive core allocation exist? A partial solution to this problem has been obtained by Becker and Chakrabarti (1991) in the form of an "Implementation Theorem." Their result states that for an economy meeting the basic assumptions, any core allocation yields a recursive core allocation when the capital stocks held by agents are suitably redistributed at each time. The complete analysis of recursive core allocations awaits further research.

8 Conclusion

This paper has introduced two solution concepts for dynamic cooperative games of capital accumulation. The first, the core, corresponds to an open-loop solution idea while the second, the recursive core, corresponds to a closed-loop solution. In general, these two solutions will not agree in the sense that the core contains the recursive core. The interest in core allocations lies in the additional structure imposed and the implications for distribution theory. The problem of completely characterizing both core concepts remains a problem for future work.

References

ALIPRANTIS, C.D., D.J. BROWN, AND O. BURKINSHAW (1989): *Existence and Optimality of Competitive Equilibria.* Berlin: Springer-Verlag.

ALIPRANTIS, C.D., D.J. BROWN, AND O. BURKINSHAW (1987): "Edgeworth Equilibria in Production Economies," *Journal of Economic Theory,* 43, 252-292.

BEALS, R., AND T.C. KOOPMANS (1969): "Maximizing Stationary Utility in a Constant Technology," *SIAM Journal of Applied Mathematics,* 17, 1001-1015.

BECKER, R.A. (1980): "On the Long-Run Steady State in a Simple Dynamic Model of Equilibrium with Heterogeneous Households," *Quarterly Journal of Economics,* 95, 375-382.

BECKER, R.A. (1982): "The Existence of Core Allocations in a One Sector Model of Capital Accumulation," *Economics Letters,* 9, 201-207.

BECKER, R.A. (1983): "The Existence of Core Allocations in a Multi-Sector Model of Capital Accumulations," Working Paper, Indiana University, Bloomington.

BECKER, R.A. (1991): "The Fundamental Theorems of Welfare Economics in Infinite Dimensional Commodity Spaces," in *Equilibrium Theory with Infinitely Many Commodities.* Ed. M.A. Khan and N. Yannelis, Berlin: Springer-Verlag.

BECKER, R.A., AND J.H. BOYD III (1990): "Recursive Utility: Discrete Time Theory," *Cuadernos Economicos de ICE,* 46, forthcoming.

BECKER, R.A., J.H. BOYD III, AND C. FOIAS (1991): "The Existence of Ramsey Equilibrium," *Econometrica,* 59, forthcoming.

BECKER, R.A., AND S.K. CHAKRABARTI (1989, revised 1991): "The Recursive Core," Working Paper, Indiana University, Bloomington.

BECKER, R.A., AND C. FOIAS (1987): "A Characterization of Ramsey Equilibrium," *Journal of Economic Theory,* 41, 173-184.

BENHABIB, J., AND K. NISHIMURA (1985): "Competitive Equilibrium Cycles," *Journal of Economic Theory,* 35, 284-306.

BOEHM, V. (1974): "The Core of an Economy with Production," *Review of Economic Studies,* 41, 429-436.

BOLDRIN, M. (1989): "Paths of Optimal Accumulation in Two-Sector Models," in *Economic Complexity: Chaos, Sunspots, Bubbles, and Nonlinearity.* Ed. W.A. Barnett, J. Geweke, and K. Shell, Cambridge, England: Cambridge University Press.

BOYD, J.H., III (1990): "Recursive Utility and the Ramsey Problem," *Journal of Economic Theory,* 50, 326-345.

Boyd, J.H., III, and L.W. McKenzie — The Existence of Competitive Equilibrium over an Infinite Horizon with Production and General Consumption Sets, — University of Rochester Discussion Paper No 224, Rochester — 1990.

CASS, D., AND K. SHELL (1976): "The Structure and Stability of Competitive Dynamical Systems," *Journal of Economic Theory,* 12, 31-70.

CHAKRABARTI, S.K. (1989): "On Value Allocations in a Multi-Sector Model of Capital Accumulation," Indiana University-Purdue University at Indianapolis Working Paper, Indianapolis.

DIAMOND, P.A. (1965): "The Evaluation of Infinite Utility Streams," *Econometrica,* 33, 170-177.

EKELAND, I. (1974): *La Theorie Des Jeux.* Paris: Presses Universitaires de France.

EPSTEIN, L.G. (1983): "Stationary Cardinal Utility and Optimal Growth Under Uncertainty," *Journal of Economic Theory,* 31, 133-152.

EPSTEIN, L.G. (1986): "Implicitly Additive Utility and the Nature of Optimal Growth," *Journal of Mathematical Economics,* 15, 111-128.

EPSTEIN, L.G., AND J.A. HYNES (1983): "The Rate of Time Preference and Dynamic Economic Analysis," *Journal of Political Economy,* 91, 611-635.

HAURIE, A., AND M.C. DELFOUR (1976): "Individual and Collective Rationality in a Dynamic Pareto Equilibrium, forthcoming" in *Multicriteria Decision Making and Differential Games.* Ed. G. Leitman, New York: Plenum Press.

JONES, L.E., AND R. MANUELLI (1990): "A Convex Model of Equilibrium Growth: Theory and Policy Implications," *Journal of Political Economy,* 98, 1008-1038.

KOOPMANS, T.C. (1960): "Stationary Ordinal Utility and Impatience," *Econometrica,* 28, 287-309.

KOOPMANS, T.C., P.A. DIAMOND, AND R.E. WILLIAMSON (1964): "Stationary Utility and Time Perspective," *Econometrica,* 32, 82-100.

KOOPMANS, T.C. (1972): "Representation of Preference Orderings Over Time," in *Decision and Organization.* Ed. C.B. McGuire and R. Radner, Amsterdam: North-Holland.

LUCAS, R.E., JR., AND N.L. STOKEY (1984): "Optimal Growth with Many Consumers," *Journal of Economic Theory,* 32, 139-171.

MAJUMDAR, M. (1975): "Some Remarks on Optimal Growth with Intertemporally Dependent Preferences in the Neoclassical Model," *Review of Economic Studies,* 42, 147-153.

MAS-COLELL, A. (1986): "The Price Equilibrium Existence Problem in Topological Vector Lattices," *Econometrica,* 54, 1039-1053.

MCKENZIE, L.W. (1986): "Optimal Economic Growth, Turnpike Theorems and Comparative Dynamics," in *Handbook of Mathematical Economics, Vol. III.* Ed. K.J. Arrow and M.D. Intriligator, Amsterdam: North-Holland.

MUNRO, G. (1979): "The Optimal Management of Transboundary Renewable Resources," *Canadian Journal of Economics,* 12, 355-376.

PAGE, T. (New York University Press — 1977): "Intertemporal and International Aspects of Virgin Materials Taxes, in" in *Resources Conservation.* Ed. Social and Economic Dimensions of Recycling, D.W. Pearce and I. Walter: New York.

PELEG, B., AND M. YAARI (1970): "Markets with Countably Many Commodities," *International Economic Review,* 11, 369-377.

RADER, T. (1971): *The Economics of Feudalism.* New York: Gordon and Breach.

RADER, T. (1972): *Theory of General Economic Equilibrium.* New York: Academic Press.
RADER, T. (1974): "Aggregative Laws of Production," *Zeitscrift für Nationalökonomie,* 34, 249-282.
RADER, T. (1981): "Utility over Time: The Homothetic Case," *Journal of Economic Theory,* 25, 219-236.
ROBERTSON, A.P., AND W. ROBERTSON (1973): *Topological Vector Spaces.* Cambridge, U.K.: Cambridge University Press.
SCARF, H. (1967): "The Core of an N-Person Game," *Econometrica,* 35, 50-69.
SHAPLEY, L., AND R. VOHRA (1991): "On Kakutani's Fixed Point Theorem, the $K-K-M-S$ Theorem and the Core of a Balanced Game," *Economic Theory,* 1, 107-116.
STREUFERT, P. (1985): "Dynamic Allocation with Consistent Intergenerational Benevolence," IMSSS Technical Report #471, Stanford.
STREUFERT, P. (1990): "Stationary Recursive Utility and Dynamic Programming Under the Assumption of Biconvergence," *Review of Economic Studies,* 57, 79-97.
UZAWA, H. (1968): "Time Preference, the Consumption Function, and Optimum Asset Holdings," in *Value, Capital and Growth: Papers in Honour of Sir John Hicks.* Ed. J.N. Wolfe, Edinburgh: Edinburgh University Press.

When Non-transitive Relations Take Maxima and Competitive Equilibrium Can't be Beat

TED BERGSTROM
University of Michigan

I had the great good fortune of being a new assistant professor at Washington University when Trout Rader was a young associate professor with no other theorists around him to talk to. For me these were exciting times. Here was a person with powerful technical skills, full of imaginative ideas and eager to share them—someone to learn from, to admire, and to emulate. Trout was working on a two-volume treatise on economic theory, and I would read the chapters as he produced them. Trout's first drafts were not paragons of clarity, but they were full of clever stuff and I could get him to try to explain this stuff to me. At least at first, the main coin I could offer in return for his tutelage was typographical errors from his manuscript. Luckily, this currency was readily available and could always be redeemed for good value.

Trout wrote his Ph. D. dissertation on competitive equilibrium theory, a subject that I had almost entirely evaded in graduate school. Trout convinced me that this was a rich subject whose applications were only beginning to be tapped. With his encouragement, I wrote papers on general equilibrium in a slave economy, general equilibrium with benevolent consumers, and general equilibrium with public goods. In the process, I found that competitive equilibrium as described in Debreu's *Theory of Value* was not as general as it could be or as one would like it to be in "realistic" applications.

I accumulated a stock of ideas and tricks to use in existence proofs, many of which were inspired by Debreu's 1962 paper, McKenzie's 1959 and 1961 papers, the drafts of Rader's 1972 book on general equilibrium, and Sonnenschein's 1971 paper on non-transitive consumers. In 1973, I put these tricks into a paper called "Competitive Equilibrium Without Transitivity, Local Nonsatiation or Monotonicity". Not only were the consumers in that paper locally sated and nonmonotonic, they were afflicted with Sonnenscheinian nontransitivity.[1] Not long after the 1973 paper was written, Trout and I came across Gale and Mas-Colell's brilliant reformulation of equilibrium existence theory (1975), which handled equilibrium with nontransitive consumers much more elegantly and powerfully. We collaborated with Robert Parks on an exploration of Gale and Mas-Colell's open graph assumption (1976). Trout wrote a paper extending his own earlier work on induced

---

[1] Trout suggested that the paper should be called "On the Existence of Equilibrium in a Lunatic Asylum".

preferences and household production to the Gale-Mas-Colell environment (1975). I wrote a paper, "The Existence of Maximal Elements and Equilibria in the Absence of Transitivity", (1975) which I believed to be an elegant and useful extension of the Gale Mas-Colell theory. The referees of the journal I sent it to did not share my enthusiasm for this paper, and I put it in my desk to ripen.

In the meantime, several good papers extended the Gale-Mas-Colell theorem. Papers dealing with finite-dimensional spaces include Shafer and Sonnenschein (1975), (1976), Shafer (1976), Borglin and Keiding (1976), Gale and Mas-Colell (1979), McKenzie (1981), Geistdoerfer-Florenzano (1982), Schofield (1984), and Blume (1986).[2] Other writers, including Aliprantis and Brown (1983), Florenzano (1983), Yannelis and Prabhakar (1983), Khan (1984), Toussaint (1984) and Mehta (1987), extended many of these results to infinite-dimensional commodity spaces and to infinite numbers of consumers.

Most of the theorems found here are taken from my unpublished 1975 paper and can now be found somewhere in economics literature. But an expository paper laying the story out all at once in a consistent format seems called for. The results on existence of competitive equilibrium fall into the category that McKenzie (1981) calls the "modern form of the classical theorem on existence of competitive equilibrium".[3] I have added some new results stimulated by the work of Geistdoerfer-Florenzano (1982), Moore (1975), McKenzie (1981) and Mehta (1987) as well as several examples, motivating discussions and references to more recent literature.

This paper shows that Nash equilibrium and competitive equilibrium exist as maximal elements of judiciously chosen non-transitive binary relations that are continuous enough and convex enough to have maximal elements. That this should be possible is strongly suggested by the structure of Gale and Mas Colell's proof. To accomplish this result, the convexity and continuity assumptions made in existence theorems of Fan, Sonnenschein, and Gale-Mas-Colell are relaxed in such a way as to unify and extend their results.

1 A Generalization of Theorems by Fan and Sonnenschein

In 1961, Ky Fan discovered the remarkable fact that even a nontransitive binary relation must take maximal elements on compact, convex sets so long as there is sufficient continuity and convexity. This idea was introduced to economists by Hugo Sonnenschein (1971) who independently proved a similar result and showed that an interesting demand theory can be constructed without transitivity.

Let S be a set and $P \subset S \times S$ a binary relation. If $(y, x) \in P$, we write yPx. Where $x \in S$, let the "better than" sets be denoted by $P(x) = \{y|yPx\}$ and the

---

[2] Authoritative discussions of early and more recent developments in equilibrium existence theory are found in Debreu (1982) and Sonnenschein (1977).

[3] McKenzie defines the "classical theory" as dealing with finite numbers of consumers and a finite dimensional commodity space. Although many of our results on existence of maximal elements apply in infinite-dimensional spaces, the competitive equilibrium theory here is all finite-dimensional.

"worse than" sets by $P^{-1}(x) = \{y|xPy\}$. Where $X \subset S$, $x^* \in X$ is a *maximal element* for P on X if $P(x^*) \cap X = \emptyset$.

Fan (1961) and Sonnenschein (1971) have proved the following results on the existence of maximal elements.

Ky Fan's Theorem. *Let $P \subset S \times S$ be a binary relation where S is a linear topological space and where*

(i) P is irreflexive,

(ii) For all $x \in S$, $P(x)$ is convex or empty,

(iii) (Open graph.) P is an open set in $S \times S$.

Then if $X \subset S$ is non-empty, convex, and compact, there exists a maximal element for P on S.

Hugo Sonnenschein's Theorem. *Let $P \subset \Re^n \times \Re^n$ be a binary relation such that:*

(i) P is asymmetric,

(ii) For all $x \in \Re^n$, $P(x)$ is convex or empty,

(iii) (Open "worse than" sets.) For all $x \in \Re^n$, $P^{-1}(x)$ is open.[4]

Then if $X \subset \Re^n$ is non-empty, convex and compact, there exists a maximal element x^* for P on X.

Neither of these two theorems implies the other. Fan's open-graph assumption is stronger than Sonnenschein's assumption of open "worse than" sets. On the other hand, Fan's theorem applies to arbitrary linear topological spaces, while Sonnenschein's theorem is proved only for finite-dimensional Euclidean space.

Theorem 1 generalizes both Fan's theorem and Sonnenschein's theorem.

Theorem 1. *Let $P \subset S \times S$ be a binary relation where S is a linear topological space and where:*

1.A For all $x \in S$, $x \notin \text{con}\,\text{P}(\text{x})$.[5]

1.B For all $x \in S$, $P^{-1}(x)$ is open.

Then if $X \subset S$ is non-empty, convex, and compact, there exists a maximal element for P on X.

To prove Theorem 1, we use a lemma due to Ky Fan, which extends the well-known theorem of Knaster, Kuratowski, and Mazurkiewicz to topological linear spaces of arbitrary dimension.

Lemma 1. *(Ky Fan) Let S be a linear topological space and $X \subset S$. For each $x \in X$, let $F(x)$ be a closed set in S such that:*

(i) The convex hull of any finite subset $\{x_1, ..., x_n\}$ of X is contained in $\bigcup_{i=1}^{m} F(x_i)$.

[4] Bergstrom, Parks and Rader (1976) call this property "open lower sections", Schofield (1983) calls it "lower demi-continuity".

[5] For any set, S, con S denotes the smallest convex set containing S. Schofield defines a relation with property 1.A to be "semi-convex".

(ii) $F(x)$ is compact for at least one $x \in X$.

Then $\bigcap_{x \in X} F(x) \neq \emptyset$.

Proof of Theorem 1:

Let $\{x_1, ..., x_n\}$ be a finite subset of X. If $z \in \bigcap_{i=1}^{n} P^{-1}(x_i)$, then by Assumption (i) of Theorem 1, $z \notin \text{con}\{\text{x}_1, ..., \text{x}_\text{n}\}$. Therefore $\bigcap_{i=1}^{n} P^{-1}(x_i) \subset (\text{con}\{\text{x}_1, ..., \text{x}_\text{n}\})^c$ and hence $\text{con}\{\text{x}_1, ..., \text{x}_\text{n}\} \subset \left(\bigcap_{i=1}^{n} \text{P}^{-1}(\text{x}_\text{i})\right)^c = \bigcup_{i=1}^{n} (\text{P}^{-1}(\text{x}_\text{i}))^c$. For all $x \in X$, let $F(x) = (P^{-1}(x))^c \cap X$. Then the sets $F(x)$ satisfy condition (i) of Lemma 1. Also, since $P^{-1}(x)$ is open (by Assumption 1.B and X is compact, $F(x)$ is compact for all $x \in X$. Therefore according to Lemma 1, $\bigcap_{x \in X} F(x) \neq \emptyset$. Therefore $x^* \in \bigcap_{x \in X} F(x)$ for some x^*. From the definitions, it follows that x^* is a maximal element for P on X. ∎

1.1 *Remarks on the convexity assumption*

Fan assumes that $x \notin P(x)$ (P is irreflexive). Sonnenschein assumes that P is asymmetric, which implies that P is irreflexive. Both Fan and Sonnenschein assume that $P(x)$ is either convex or empty, and hence that $\text{con}\,\text{P}(\text{x}) = \text{P}(\text{x})$. Therefore both authors' assumptions imply Theorem 1's assumption that $x \notin \text{con}\,\text{P}(\text{x})$.

There are economically interesting examples of preferences that satisfy $x \notin \text{con}\,\text{P}(\text{x})$, but do not have $P(x)$ convex. Consider a consumer who consumes two desirable goods, but finds that fractional units of both goods are useless. For this consumer, $(2,1) \in P(1,1)$ and $(1,2) \in P(1,1)$, but $.5(2,1) + .5(1,2) = (1.5, 1.5) \notin P(1,1)$. Although this example violates convexity of $P(x_1, x_2)$, it does not violate $x \notin P(x)$.

For another example, consider a consumer who takes the trouble to recognize that commodity bundle x differs from y only if the Euclidean distance $d(x,y)$ between these two bundles exceeds some threshold amount ϵ. Let the consumer also have a continuous strictly quasi-concave utility function, u_i and suppose that she prefers x to y if and only if $u_i(x) > u_i(y)$ and $d(x,y) > \epsilon$. This consumer would not have convex preferred sets, but her preferences do have the property that $x \notin \text{con}\,\text{P}(\text{x})$.

1.2 *Remarks on the continuity assumption*

Continuous preferences, as defined by Debreu (1959) have open "better than" sets, $P(x)$, and open "worse than" sets, $P^{-1}(x)$. The open-graph assumption made by Ky Fan and also by Gale and Mas-Colell is stronger than Debreu's continuity.

Bergstrom, Rader and Parks show examples of preferences that do not have open graph but are continuous in the sense of Debreu. They show that Debreu's continuity assumption implies open graph if P is transitive and "order dense". They also adapt a theorem of Shafer (1974) to show that if X is the entire non-negative orthant in $\Re^n$ and if $P(x)$ is a convex set for all $x \in X$, then Debreu's continuity assumption implies the open-graph property.

Theorem 1, like Sonnenschein's theorem, requires only that the "worse than" sets be open. If some commodities are useful only in discrete units, it is reasonable to assume that all "worse than" sets are open, but it is not reasonable to assume that all "better than" sets are open. For example, consider the relation P on $\Re^2$ such that $(x,y)P(x',y')$ if and only if $x + \lfloor y \rfloor > x' + \lfloor y' \rfloor$, where $\lfloor y \rfloor$ is the greatest integer smaller than y. The set $P(1,1)$, is not open. To see this, notice that $(1,2)P(1,1)$, but every open neighborhood of $(1,2)$ contains points (x,y) such that $(1,1)P(x,y)$. On the other hand, it is easy to verify that for every point (x,y) in the nonnegative orthant, the set $P^{-1}(x,y)$ is open.

2 Lower Semi-continuous Preferences and Existence of Maximal Elements

Some familiar and useful asymmetric binary relations have neither open "better than" sets nor open "worse than" sets, but are "continuous enough" to take maximal elements on closed, bounded convex sets. Consider the following examples:

- (the lexicographic ordering, P_{lex}) Define P_{lex} on $\Re^2$ so that $(x_1, x_2)P_{lex}(y_1, y_2)$ if $x_1 > y_1$ or if $x_1 = y_1$ and $x_2 > y_2$.
- (the "Nash improvement relation", $\hat{P}$) Consider a game where players have strategy sets X_i and continuous individual preferences P_i defined on the outcome space, $X = \prod_i X_i$. Define $\hat{P}_i$ on X so that $x\hat{P}_iy$ if player i prefers x to y and if x differs from y only by i's choice of strategy. Define $\hat{P}$ on X so that $x\hat{P}y$ if and only if $x\hat{P}_iy$ for *some* player i.

Each of these relations has the property that if xPy then for all points y' "close to y", there are points x', "arbitrarily close to x", such that $x'Py'$. This property is known as *lower semi-continuity* of the correspondence that maps each point x to the set $P(x)$. We will define a relation with this continuity property to be *lower semi-continuous.* In finite-dimensional spaces, we can replace Theorem 1's assumption of open "worse than" sets by the weaker assumption that P is lower semi-continuous.[6] Lower semi-continuity is a nice property to work with because complicated lower semi-continuous binary relations can be built from simple ones. For example, unions, intersections, Cartesian products, projections, and convex hulls of lower semi-continuous correspondences are lower semi-continuous. Several propositions that are useful for identifying and constructing lower semi-continuous correspondences are presented in the Appendix.

6 This possibility was also noted by Gale and Mas-Colell (1979).

DEFINITION 1: *(Lower semi-continuous correspondence.)*[7] *Let X and Y be topological spaces and 2^Y the set of all subsets of Y (including the empty set). The correspondence $\phi : X \to 2^Y$ is lower semi-continuous (l.s.c.) if for every set V which is open in Y, the set $\{x \in X \mid \phi(x) \cap V \neq \emptyset\}$ is open in X.*

DEFINITION 2: *(Lower semi-continuous binary relation.) Let S be a topological space, $P \subset S \times S$, and $X \subset S$. The relation P is lower semi-continuous on X if the correspondence $\phi : X \to 2^Y$ where $\phi(x) = P(x) \cap X$ is l.s.c. (where X is endowed with the relative topology).*

Theorem 2. *Let $P \subset \Re^n \times \Re^n$ be a binary relation and let $X \subset \Re^n$ be non-empty, convex and compact where:*

2.A For all $x \in X$, $x \notin \mathrm{con}\, \mathrm{P(x)}$.

2.B P is lower semi-continuous on X.

Then there exists a maximal element for P on X.

To prove theorem 2, we use a lemma which is a special case of Michael's selection theorem (Michael (1956), Theorem 3.1‴).

LEMMA 2: *Let $X \subset \Re^n$ and $\phi : X \to 2^X$ a l.s.c. correspondence such that for all $x \in X$, $\phi(x)$ is a non-empty convex set. Then there exists a continuous function $f : X \to X$ such that for all $x \in X$, $f(x) \in \phi(x)$.*

Proof of Theorem 2:

Suppose that for all $x \in X$, $P(x) \cap X \neq \emptyset$. By Assumption 2.B, the correspondence $\phi : X \to 2^X$ where $\phi(x) = P(x) \cap X$ is l.s.c. Then the correspondence $\Psi : X \to 2^X$ where $\Psi(x) = \mathrm{con}\, \phi(\mathrm{x})$ for all $x \in X$ is also l.s.c. (Proposition 9, the Appendix) and $\Psi(x)$ is non-empty and convex for all $x \in X$. By Lemma 2, there exists a continuous function $f : X \to X$ such that for all $x \in X$, $f(x) \in \Psi(x)$. Since X is non-empty, convex, and compact, by Brouwer's fixed point theorem there exists $\bar{x} \in X$ such that $\bar{x} = f(\bar{x}) \in \Psi(\bar{x})$. But then $\bar{x} \in \mathrm{con}\, \mathrm{P}(\bar{\mathrm{x}})$ which is contrary to Assumption 2.B. Therefore it must be that $P(x^*) \cap X = \emptyset$ for some $x^* \in X$. ∎

As we show in Proposition 2 of the Appendix, P will be l.s.c. if $P^{-1}(x)$ is open for all x. Thus for finite dimensional spaces, Theorem 2 generalizes Theorem 1.

For proving the existence of competitive equilibrium where the set of feasible trades is not necessarily convex, it will be useful to have the following corollary to Theorem 2.

COROLLARY: *Let P be a binary relation defined on $X \times X$ where $X \subset \Re^n$ and let S be a convex, compact subset of X such that if $x \in S$ and $y \in X \sim S$, then $(x,y) \notin P$. Then if P satisfies conditions 2.A and 2.B of Theorem 2, there exists $x^* \in S$ such that x^* is a maximal element for P on X.*

---

[7] The term *lower hemi-continuous* is sometimes used instead, with *semi-continuous* being reserved for functions. We will follow Michael (1956) in using *semi.*

To prove the Corollary, notice that Theorem 2 implies that P has a maximal element on S and under the assumptions of the corollary, a maximal element of P on S is also a maximal element of P on X.

2.1 *Extensions to infinite-dimensional spaces*

Our Theorem 1 applies in spaces of infinite as well as finite dimension, but requires that "worse than sets" all be open. As Aliprantis and Brown (1983) show, this theorem can be used to establish the existence of competitive equilibrium in an economy with an infinite-dimensional commodity space. Theorem 2 allows us to weaken the assumption of open "worse than" sets to the assumption that preferences are lower semi-continuous, but at the cost of requiring the consumption space is finite-dimensional.

Mehta (1987) proves an alternative weakening of the continuity assumption that allows the existence of maximal elements on infinite-dimensional spaces.[8]

THEOREM $1'$: *(Mehta) Theorem 1 remains true if Assumption 1.A is replaced by the (weaker) assumption:*

$1'.A$ *if $P(x) \neq \emptyset$, then there exists at least one point in the interior of $P^{-1}(x)$.*[9]

Theorem $1'$ is stronger than Theorem 1, but not strictly comparable with Theorem 2 since the assumption of weak lower demi-continuity is neither weaker nor stronger than the assumption of lower semi-continuity.

Another infinite-dimensional alternative to Theorem 2 is the following result:

THEOREM $2'$: *Let $P \subset S \times S$ where S is a separable Banach space and let $X \subset \Re^n$ be non-empty, convex and compact where:*

$2'.A$ *For all $x \in X$, $x \notin \operatorname{con} \mathrm{P}(\mathrm{x})$.*

$2'.B$ *P is lower semi-continuous on X.*

$2'.C$ *If $P(x) \neq \emptyset$, then either $P(x)$ has an interior point or $P(x)$ is closed.*

Proof of Theorem $2'$:

We appeal again to Michael's Theorem $3.1'''$, which informs us that a lower semi-continuous correspondence has a continuous selection if the image sets are nonempty and convex and either finite-dimensional, closed, or have interior points. If $\operatorname{con} \mathrm{P}(\mathrm{x}) \neq \emptyset$ for all x in then there exists a continuous function f mapping X into itself. By Schauder's fixed point theorem, f must have a fixed point $\bar{x}$. But this can not be since then we would have $\bar{x} \in \operatorname{con} \mathrm{P}(\bar{\mathrm{x}})$, contrary to $2'$.A. ∎

---

[8] In a separate theorem, Mehta shows that Theorem 2 can be extended to any Banach space if Assumption 2.A is strengthened to the assumption that $P(x)$ is closed and convex for all x and $x \notin P(x)$. Of course the assumption that P would not be sustainable in the usual model of strict preference.

[9] Mehta calls this property "weak lower demi-continuity".

2.2 *Other Extensions*

It is known that an acyclic binary relation with open "worse than" sets takes maximal elements on compact sets. (Bergstrom (1975), Walker(1977), Birchenhall (1977)). Schofield (1984) was the first to relate these results to the Fan-Sonnenschein theorems. Schofield shows that assuming that preferences satisfy a local convexity property is equivalent to assuming the nonexistence of "local cycles". He also shows that if the set X is either a convex set or a smooth manifold of a certain topological type, then the global condition $x \notin \text{con}\,\mathrm{P(x)}$ can be replaced by a local version of the same assumption in theorems guaranteeing that P has a maximal element on X.

In a very useful compendium of results on the existence of maximal elements, Mehta (1987) shows that the assumption that the set X be compact can under certain conditions be weakened to paracompactness or alternatively to the assumption that $P^{-1}(x_0)^c$ is compact for some $x_0 \in X$.

3 The Existence of Nash Equilibrium

Nash (1950) showed how to prove the existence of "Nash" equilibrium in a game where the strategy sets are compact and convex and where each individual's preferences are represented by a continuous function that is quasi-concave in his own strategy. Nash observed that with his assumptions, the reaction correspondence (he called it the countering correspondence) has a closed graph and convex image sets and he applied Kakutani's fixed point theorem to show the existence of a fixed point, which in turn must be an equilibrium.

Nash's convexity and continuity assumptions can be relaxed and the transitivity assumption (made implicitly when preferences on outcomes are represented by real-valued payoff functions) can be eliminated. This is done by finding a binary relation for which a maximal element must be a Nash equilibrium and which satisfies the conditions of Theorem 2.

DEFINITION 3: *(Game.) A game* $(P_i, X_i)_{i\in I}$ *consists of a set of players* $I = \{1, ..., m\}$, *a strategy set* X_i *for each* $i \in I$, *a set of possible outcomes* $X = \prod_{i\in I} X_i$, *and for each* $i \in I$, *a preference relation* $P_i \subset X \times X$.

A Nash equilibrium is an outcome $\bar{x} \in X$ such that no player can gain by choosing an alternative strategy if all other players persist in their choice of the strategies named in $\bar{x}$. To establish Nash equilibrium as a maximal element of a binary relation, it is useful to define $\hat{P}_i \subset P_i$ so that $x\hat{P}_iy$ if player i prefers x to y and if player i can single-handedly change the outcome from y to x. Also, define $\hat{P}$ so that $x\hat{P}y$ if *someone* who prefers x to y can single-handedly change the outcome from y to x. An outcome is a Nash equilibrium if and only if it is a maximal element of $\hat{P}$ on the set of possible outcomes.

DEFINITION 4: *(Nash improvement relations.) The Nash improvement* $\hat{P}_i \subset X \times X$ *for player* i *is defined so that* $x\hat{P}_iy$ *if and only if* xP_iy *and for all* $j \neq i$,

$x_j = y_j$. The (overall) Nash improvement relation is defined to be $\hat{P} = \bigcup_I \hat{P}_i$. For all $x \in X$, define $P_i^*(x) \subset X_i$ to be the projection of $\hat{P}_i(x)$ on X_i.

DEFINITION 5: *(Nash equilibrium.) A Nash equilibrium for the game $(P_i, X_i)_{i \in I}$ is a point $\bar{x} \in X$ such that $\hat{P}(\bar{x}) = \emptyset$.*

Theorem 3. *Let $(P_i, X_i)_{i \in I}$ be a game such that $X_i \subset \Re^n$ is non-empty, convex, and compact for all $i \in I$ and:*

3.A For all $x \in X$ and all $i \in I$, $x \notin \operatorname{con} \hat{P}_i(x)$.

3.B For all $i \in I$, $\hat{P}_i$ is lower semi-continuous.

Then there exists a Nash equilibrium.

The continuity assumption in Theorem 3 is that $\hat{P}_i$ is l.s.c. for all $i \in I$. This assumption is weaker than the assumption that P_i is lower semi-continuous and is equivalent to lower semi-continuity of the mapping $P_i^* : X \to X_i$. [10]

Proof of Theorem 3:

We will show that $\hat{P}$ satisfies the conditions of Theorem 2. First we show that for all $x \in X$, $x \notin \operatorname{con} \mathrm{P}(x)$. If $y \in \operatorname{con} \hat{P}(x)$, then $y = \sum_{j \in J} \lambda_j y^j$ where $J \subset I$, where $\sum_{j \in J} \lambda_j = 1$ and for all $j \in J$, $\lambda_j \geq 0$ and $y^j \in \hat{P}_j(x)$. Then $y - x = \sum_{j \in J} \lambda_j z^j$ where $z^j = y^j - x$. Assumption 3.A requires that $z^j \neq 0$ for $j \in J$. The correspondences $\hat{P}_j$ are constructed so that the z^j's are linearly independent and therefore $y - x \neq 0$. It follows that $x \notin \operatorname{con} \hat{P}(x)$.

Since $\hat{P}_i$ is assumed to be l.s.c. and since unions of l.s.c. correspondences are also l.s.c., (Appendix, Proposition 3), it must be that $\hat{P}$ is l.s.c. It follows from Theorem 2, that $\hat{P}(\bar{x}) = \emptyset$ for some $\bar{x} \in X$. By definition, $\bar{x}$ must be a Nash equilibrium. ∎

4 Existence of Free-Disposal Competitive Equilibrium

In a "Robinson Crusoe" economy,[11] where Robinson has convex preferences and a convex production possibility set, a competitive equilibrium allocation can be found simply by maximizing Robinson's utility on the production possibility set. In general for an exchange economy, even where individual preferences are continuous, transitive, and convex, there is no continuous "aggregate utility function" that can

---

[10] Treat P_i^* and $\hat{P}_i$ as correspondences which map x to $P_i^*(x)$ and $\hat{P}_i(x)$, respectively. Since P_i^* is the ith projection of $\hat{P}_i$, while $\hat{P}_i$ is the Cartesian product of P_i^* with "identity" correspondences for each $j \neq i$, propositions 5 and 6 of the Appendix imply that if $\hat{P}_i$ is l.s.c., then so is P_i^* and conversely.

[11] or for that matter in any economy where aggregate demand behaves as if it is the demand of a single utility-maximizing consumer.

be maximized to find a competitive equilibrium. Nevertheless, under very general conditions there exists a non-transitive binary relation satisfying the conditions of Theorem 2, which is maximized at a competitive equilibrium.

This section proves existence of equilibrium for an exchange economy with free disposal and where consumer preferences are locally nonsatiated. As will be seen later, these assumptions are not essential for existence of equilibrium. Free-disposal and local nonsatiation assumptions can be eliminated, but in order to see the structure of the existence proofs more clearly, it is helpful to work through this special case first.

DEFINITION 6: *(Exchange economy.) An exchange economy consists of* m *consumers, indexed by the set* $I = \{1, ..., m\}$. *For each* $i \in I$, *there is a consumption set* $X_i \subset \Re^n$ *and an initial endowment* $w_i \in \Re^n$.

DEFINITION 7: *(Allocations and preferences.) An allocation is a point* $x = (x_1, ..., x_m) \in \prod_I X_i = X$. *Each consumer has a preference relation* $P_i \subset X \times X$. *For each consumer, define i's Nash improvement preference relation,* $\hat{P}_i$ *as in Definition 4.*

Preference relations P_i are defined over the allocation space X rather than simply over i's own consumption space X_i. This allows for the possibility of "consumption externalities". This allows for the possibility of benevolence, envy, emulation and other direct effects of others' consumption on consumer preferences. Although consumers may care about the consumption of others, the equilibrium model allows them to choose only their own consumption bundles subject to their own budgets. McKenzie (1955) was the first to extend existence theory to this model. Others who study existence with externalities include Arrow and Hahn (1971) and Shafer and Sonnenschein (1975).

DEFINITION 8: *(Free-disposal competitive equilibrium.) A price vector* $\bar{p} > 0$ *and an allocation* $\bar{x}$ *constitute a free-disposal competitive equilibrium if :*

(i) For all $i \in I$, $\bar{p}\bar{x}_i = \bar{p}w_i$.

(ii) For all $i \in I$, $\hat{P}_i(\bar{x}) \cap \{x \in X \mid \bar{p}x_i \leq \bar{p}w_i\} = \emptyset$.

(iii) $\sum_I \bar{x}_i \leq \sum_I w_i$.

A free-disposal competitive equilibrium for an exchange economy is equivalent to competitive equilibrium in a production economy where the only "production" possibilities are disposal activities for every good. In equilibrium supply for some goods can exceed consumers' demand, but any excess supply is removed by the disposal activity. Profit maximization in the "free-disposal industry" requires that equilibrium prices of all goods be nonnegative and prices of goods that are in excess supply must be zero. Since equilibrium prices must be non-negative, conditions (i) and (iii) of equilibrium imply that any good in excess supply must have zero price.[12]

[12] If the budget constraint in (i) were relaxed to require only that $\bar{p}x_i \leq \bar{p}w_i$, then the weakened definition of equilibrium would not imply that prices of goods in excess supply be zero. On the

We follow a path first marked out by Debreu (1962), who proved the existence of "quasi-equilibrium" under relatively weak assumptions and then showed that additional assumptions imply that a quasi-equilibrium is a competitive equilibrium.

DEFINITION 9: *(Free-disposal quasi-equilibrium). A price vector $\bar{p} > 0$ and an allocation $\bar{x}$ constitute a free-disposal quasi-equilibrium if conditions (i) and (iii) of Definition 8 are satisfied as well as:*

(ii′) *For all $i \in I$, $\hat{P}_i(\bar{x}) \cap \{x \in X_i \mid \bar{p}x_i < \bar{p}w_i\} = \emptyset$.*

THEOREM 4: *There exists a free-disposal quasi-equilibrium for an exchange economy if:*

4.A *For all $i \in I$, the consumption set X_i is a convex, compact*[13] *set in $\Re^n$ and $w_i \in X_i$.*

4.B *For all $i \in I$, preference relations P_i are l.s.c.*

4.C *For all $i \in I$ and for all $x \in X$, $x_i \notin \text{con}\,\hat{P}_i(x)$.*

4.D *(Local nonsatiation.) For all $i \in I$, if $x \in X$, then every open neighborhood of x_i in X_i contains a point $x'_i \in \hat{P}_i(x)$.*

Let S^n be the unit simplex $\{p \in \Re^n_+ | \sum_{i=1}^n p_i = 1\}$ and let $\hat{X} = S^n \times X$. The following correspondences will with domain $\hat{X}$ will be useful:

DEFINITION 10: *(Price-adjustment correspondence ϕ_p.) Define $\phi_p : \hat{X} \to S^n$ so that*

$$\phi_p(p,x) = \{p' \in S^n | p' \sum_I^n (x_i - w_i) > p \sum_I^n (x_i - w_i)\}.$$

DEFINITION 11: *(Allocation-adjustment correspondence ϕ_i.) For each $i \in I$, define $\phi_i : \hat{X} \to X$*

(i) If $(p,x) \in \hat{X}$ and $px_i \leq pw_i$, then $\phi_i(p,x) = \hat{P}_i(x) \cap \{x' | px'_i < pw_i\}$.

(ii) If $(p,x) \in \hat{X}$ and $px_i > pw_i$, then $\phi_i(p,x) = \{x' | px'_i < px_i$ and $x'_j = x_j$ for all $j \neq i\}$.

DEFINITION 12: *(Disequilibrium correspondence ϕ.) Define $\phi : \hat{X} \to \hat{X}$ so that*

$$\phi(p,x) = (\phi_p(p,x) \times x) \bigcup \left(p \times \bigcup_I \phi_i(p,x) \right).$$

Consider a binary relation Q such that $(p',x')Q(p,x)$ if and only if $(p',x') \in \phi(p,x)$. Lemma 3, which is proved in the Appendix, shows that if preferences

other hand, if $\bar{p}x_i \leq \bar{p}w_i$ for all i and if all prices are non-negative and goods in excess supply have zero prices, then it must be that in equilibrium, $\bar{p}\bar{x}_i = \bar{p}w_i$ for all i.

[13] The assumption that consumption sets are compact can be replaced by the weaker assumption that these sets are closed and bounded from below. To do so, one can use the truncation technique devised by Debreu (1962).

satisfy the assumptions of Theorem 4, then Q will satisfy the assumptions of Theorem 1 and will have a maximal element. Theorem 4 will then be proved by showing that a maximal element of Q is a free-disposal quasi-equilibrium.

LEMMA 3: *Under the assumptions of Theorem 4, the correspondence ϕ is l.s.c. and for all $(p,x) \in \hat{X}$, $(p,x) \notin \text{con}\,\phi(p,x)$. If $\hat{\phi}(p,x) = \emptyset$, then $\hat{\phi}_p(p,x) = \emptyset$ and for all $i \in I$, $\hat{\phi}_i(p,x) = \emptyset$.*

Proof of Theorem 4:

Let Q be the relation on $\hat{X}$ such that $Q(p,x) = \phi(p,x)$. According to Lemma 3, Q satisfies the hypothesis of Theorem 2. Therefore there exists $(\bar{p},\bar{x}) \in \hat{X}$ such that $\phi(\bar{p},\bar{x}) = \emptyset$. This implies that $\phi_p(\bar{p},\bar{x}) = \emptyset$ and for all i, $\phi_i(\bar{p},\bar{x}) = \emptyset$. If $px_i > pw_i$ for some i, then since $w_i \in X_i$, it must be that $\phi_i(p,x) \neq \emptyset$. Since for all $i \in I$, $\phi_i(\bar{p},\bar{x}) = \emptyset$, it follows from the definition of ϕ_i that $\bar{p}\bar{x}_i \leq \bar{p}w_i$ and if $x'\hat{P}_i\bar{x}$, then $\bar{p}x'_i \geq pw_i$. Since preferences are assumed to be locally nonsatiated, this can be the case only if $\bar{p}\bar{x}_i = \bar{p}w_i$ for all $i \in I$.

Therefore $\bar{p}\sum_I(\bar{x}_i - w_i) = 0$. Since $\phi_p(\bar{p},\bar{x}) = \emptyset$, it must be that $\bar{p}\sum_I(\bar{x}_i - w_i) \geq p\sum_I(\bar{x}_i - w_i)$ for all $p \in S^n$. Unless $\sum_I(\bar{x}_i - w_i) \leq 0$, it would be possible to find $p \in S^n$ such that $p\sum_I(\bar{x}_i - w_i) > 0$. Therefore $\sum_I \bar{x}_i \leq \sum_I w_i$ and $(\bar{p},\bar{x})$ must be a quasi-equilibrium. ∎

The existence of a free-disposal competitive equilibrium can be established by adding sufficient assumptions to guarantee that a quasi-equilibrium is a competitive equilibrium. Here we choose assumptions that lead to a very simple proof. As will be shown in the next section, the assumption that initial endowments can be greatly weakened. Assumption 5.B is weaker than the assumption that "better than" sets are open.

THEOREM 5: *There exists a free-disposal competitive equilibrium if preferences satisfy the assumptions 4.1, 4.2 and 4.3 of Theorem 4 as well as*

5.A *For all i, w_i is in the interior of X_i.*

5.B *For all i, if $x\hat{P}_iy$ and if $x' \in X$ and $x'_j = x_j$ for $j \neq i$, then there exists a scalar, $\lambda \in (0,1)$, such that $\lambda x + (1-\lambda)x'\hat{P}_iy$.*

Proof of Theorem 5:

Suppose that $(\bar{p},\bar{x})$ is a quasi-equilibrium and $x\hat{P}_i\bar{x}$ for some i. Then it must be that $\bar{p}x_i = \bar{p}w_i$. Since w_i is in the interior of X_i, there exists some $z_i \in X_i$ such that $\bar{p}z_i < \bar{p}w_i$. For $\lambda \in (0,1)$, let $x(\lambda) \in X$ be the allocation such that $x(\lambda)_i = \lambda x_i + (1-\lambda)z$ and for $j \neq i$, $x(\lambda)_j = x_j$. According to Assumption 5.1, there is some λ for which $x(\lambda)\hat{P}_ix$. Since $\bar{p}z_i < \bar{p}w_i$, if $\bar{p}x_i \leq \bar{p}w_i$, it must be that $\bar{p}x(\lambda)_i < pw_i$. But this cannot be since $(\bar{p},\bar{x})$ is a quasi-equilibrium. Therefore it must be that if $x\hat{P}_i\bar{x}$, then $\bar{p}x \geq \bar{p}w_i$, so $(\bar{p},\bar{x})$ must be a competitive equilibrium. ∎

4.1 *Remarks on Quasi-equilibrium and Compensated Equilibrium.*

Debreu (1962) defined quasi-equilibrium to be a price vector and an allocation that satisfies all of the conditions of competitive equilibrium except that condition (ii) is weakened to

(ii*) If $\bar{p}\bar{x}_i > \min_{x \in X_i} \bar{p}x$, then $\hat{P}_i(\bar{x}) \cap \{x \in X \mid \bar{p}x_i \leq \bar{p}w_i\} = \emptyset$.

This condition implies that in a quasi-equilibrium, no consumer can find a bundle that is both cheaper and preferred to his competitive bundle. Debreu (1959) showed that quasi-equilibrium exists under weaker assumptions than are needed for competitive equilibrium.

Arrow and Hahn (1971) and Moore (1975) defined a slightly different notion of quasi-equilibrium from Debreu's which they call "compensated equilibrium." They define a compensated equilibrium that has properties (i) and (iii) of competitive equilibrium, while (ii) is replaced by the assumption that for any consumer, anything "at least as good" as his bundle in quasi-equilibrium must cost at least as much.

When preferences are not locally non-satiated, compensated equilibrium is not quite the appropriate tool for equilibrium analysis. If there are thick indifference curves, then for some price vectors and for some consumers there may be no commodity bundles such that the consumer spends his entire wealth (Condition (i)) and such that the consumer is also minimizing his expenditure on the set of bundles at least as good as the chosen bundle. This difficulty is remedied by weakening the Arrow-Hahn-Moore definition to replace condition (ii) of the definition of competitive equilibrium by the condition that "no consumer can find a preference bundle is both cheaper and strictly preferred to his equilibrium bundle." This is the definition of "quasi-equilibrium" that will be used here. This definition first appeared in Bergstrom (1975) and was adopted by Geistdoerfer-Florenzano (1982), who found it to be advantageous for the same reasons.

5 Equilibrium without Free Disposal, Monotonicity or Local Nonsatiation

If at some allocations, consumers prefer less of some commodities to more, and if there is no free disposal, then we must insist that in competitive equilibrium supply *equals* demand in every market. If this is the case, we must allow the possibility that some commodities have negative prices in competitive equilibrium.

DEFINITION 13: *(Competitive equilibrium.) A price vector $\bar{p} \neq 0$ and an allocation $\bar{x}$ constitute a competitive equilibrium if:*

(i) For all $i \in I$, $\bar{p}\bar{x}_i = \bar{p}w_i$.

(ii) For all $i \in I$, $\hat{P}_i(\bar{x}) \cap \{x \in X \mid \bar{p}x_i \leq \bar{p}w_i\} = \emptyset$.

(iii) $\sum_I \bar{x}_i = \sum_I w_i$.

DEFINITION 14: *(Quasi-equilibrium.) A price vector $\bar{p} \neq 0$ and an allocation $\bar{x}$ constitute a quasi-equilibrium if conditions (i) and (iii) of Definition 13 are satisfied as well as:*

(ii′) *For all* $i \in I$, $\hat{P}_i(\bar{x}) \cap \{x \in X_i \mid \bar{p}x_i < \bar{p}w_i\} = \emptyset$.

Existence of quasi-equilibrium can be proved using similar techniques to those used for proving free-disposal quasi-equilibrium, but without free disposal we will need two extra tricks.

The trick used to find equilibrium when prices may be negative was first used by Bergstrom (1973) and later applied by Bergstrom (1976) and Shafer (1976). Equilibrium prices will be found somewhere on the unit sphere $\{p \in \Re^n \mid \|p\| = 1\}$. Since the unit sphere is not a convex set, it is mathematically convenient to define correspondences over the unit ball, $B^n = \{p \in \Re^n \mid \|p\| \leq 1\}$ and to show that the equilibrium that is ultimately found lies on the unit sphere. To do this, we alter the "budget correspondences" for price vectors p such that $\|p\| < 1$ to give each consumer an "income" of $pw_i + \frac{1-\|p\|}{m}$ (where m is the number of consumers in I). As it turns out, our binary relation will have a maximal element only where $\|p\| = 1$, so that in the equilibrium that we establish, incomes are simply pw_i.

In order to do without the assumption of local nonsatiation, we borrow a trick from Gale and Mas-Colell. We define an augmented preference relation $\tilde{P}_i$ that includes $\hat{P}_i$ and shares the convexity and continuity properties of $\hat{P}_i$, but is locally non-satiated.

DEFINITION 15: *(Gale-Mas-Colell augmented preference relation $\tilde{P}_i$.) Define $\tilde{P}_i \subset X \times X$ so that $\tilde{P}_i(x)$ consists of all points in* $\operatorname{con}\{\hat{P}_i(x) \cup \{x\}\}$ *except for x itself.*

The following result, which is proved in the Appendix shows that $\tilde{P}_i$ inherits from $\hat{P}_i$ the nice properties needed for existence of maximal elements.

LEMMA 4:

(i) If $\hat{P}_i(x) \neq \emptyset$, then every neighborhood of x contains a point $x' \in \tilde{P}_i(x)$.

(ii) If $\hat{P}_i$ is l.s.c., so is $\tilde{P}_i$.

(iii) If $x \notin \operatorname{con}\hat{P}_i(x)$, then $x \notin \tilde{P}_i(x)$.

We define a series of correspondences that parallel the constructions for the free-disposal case except that the domain of prices is the unit ball rather than the unit simplex,

DEFINITION 16: *(Price-adjustment correspondence $\tilde{\phi}_p$.) Let $\tilde{X} = B^n \times X$. Define $\tilde{\phi}_p : \tilde{X} \to B^n$ so that* $\tilde{\phi}_p(p,x) = \{p' \mid p' \sum_I^n (x_i - w_i) > p \sum_I^n (x_i - w_i)\}$.

DEFINITION 17: *(Allocation-adjustment correspondence $\tilde{\phi}_i$.)* For each $i \in I$, *define $\tilde{\phi}_i : \tilde{X} \to X$ so that*

(i) If $(p,x) \in \tilde{X}$ and $px_i \leq pw_i + \frac{(1-\|p\|)}{m}$, then $\phi_i(p,x) = \{x' \mid x' \tilde{P}_i x \text{ and } px'_i < pw_i\}$.

(ii) If $(p,x) \in \tilde{X}$ and $px_i > pw_i$, then $\phi_i(p,x) = \{x' \mid px'_i < px_i \text{ and } x'_j = x_j \text{ for all } j \neq i\}$.

DEFINITION 18: *(Disequilibrium correspondence $\tilde{\phi}$) Define $\tilde{\phi} : \tilde{X} \to \tilde{X}$ so that*

$$\tilde{\phi}(p,x) = \left(\tilde{\phi}_p(p,x) \times X\right) \bigcup \left(B^n \times \bigcup_I \tilde{\phi}_i(p,x)\right)$$

If we define a relation Q such that xQy if $x \in \phi(y)$, then Lemma 5 ensures that Q takes a maximal element on $\tilde{X}$. A proof of Lemma 5 is found in the Appendix. In the proof of Theorem 6, we show that a maximal element of Q is a quasi-equilibrium.

LEMMA 5: *The correspondence $\tilde{\phi}$ is l.s.c., for all $x \in \tilde{X}$, $x \notin \text{con}\,\tilde{\phi}(x)$. If $\tilde{\phi}(p,x) = \emptyset$, then $\tilde{\phi}_p(p,x) = \emptyset$ and for all $i \in I$, $\tilde{\phi}_i(p,x) = \emptyset$.*

THEOREM 6: *There exists a quasi-equilibrium for an exchange economy if:*

6.A For all $i \in I$, the consumption set X_i is a convex, compact set, and $w_i \in X_i$.

6.B For all $i \in I$, preference relations P_i are l.s.c.

6.C For all $i \in I$ and for all $x \in X$, $x_i \notin \text{con}\,\hat{P}_i(x)$.

6.D (No feasible bliss points.) If $\sum_I (x_i - w_i) = 0$, then for all $i \in I$, $\hat{P}_i(x) \neq \emptyset$.

Proof of Theorem 6:

According to Lemma 5, the correspondence $\tilde{\phi}$ satisfies the hypothesis of Theorem 2. Therefore there exists $(\bar{p}, \bar{x}) \in \tilde{X}$ such that $\tilde{\phi}(\bar{p}, \bar{x}) = \emptyset$.

Since $\phi(\bar{p}, \bar{x}) = \emptyset$, it must be that $\bar{p} \sum_I (\bar{x}_i - w_i) \geq p \sum_I (\bar{x}_i - w_i)$ for all $p \in B^n$. This implies that either $\sum_I (\bar{x}_i - w_i) = 0$, or $\bar{p} = \frac{\sum_I (\bar{x}_i - w_i)}{\|\sum_I (\bar{x}_i - w_i)\|}$, in which case $\|\bar{p}\| = 1$. Therefore if $\|\bar{p}\| < 1$, $\sum_I (\bar{x}_i - w_i) = 0$. But if $\sum_I (\bar{x}_i - w_i) = 0$, then by Assumption 6.D, for all i, $\tilde{P}_i(\bar{x}) \neq \emptyset$. Suppose That $\bar{p}\bar{x}_i < \bar{p}w_i + \frac{1-\|p\|}{m}$ for some i. Then from Lemma 4(i), it follows that there must be $x' \in \tilde{P}_i(\bar{x})$ such that $\bar{p}x'_i < \bar{p}w_i$. but this cannot be since $\tilde{\phi}_i(\bar{p}, \bar{x}) = \emptyset$. Therefore $\bar{p}\bar{x}_i \geq \bar{p}w_i + \frac{1-\|p\|}{m}$ for all $i \in I$ and hence $\bar{p} \cdot \sum \bar{x}_i - \bar{p}w_i \geq 1 - \|p\| > 0$. But this is impossible since $\sum \bar{x}_i - w_i = 0$. We must conclude that $\|\bar{p}\| = 1$.

Given that $\|p\| = 1$ and that $\tilde{\phi}_i(\bar{p}, \bar{x}) = \emptyset$, it must be that $\bar{p}\bar{x}_i \leq \bar{p}w_i$ for all $i \in I$ and $\bar{p} \sum_I (\bar{x}_i - w_i) \leq 0$. Since $\phi_0(\bar{p}, \bar{x}) = \emptyset$, and $\bar{p} \sum_I (\bar{x}_i - w_i) \leq 0$, it must be that $\sum_I (\bar{x}_i - w_i) = 0$. Since $\phi_i(\bar{p}, \bar{x}) = \emptyset$, it must also be that $\tilde{P}_i(\bar{x}) \cap \{x | \bar{p}x_i < \bar{p}w_i\} = \emptyset$ and hence $\hat{P}_i(\bar{p}, \bar{x}) = \emptyset$ for all $i \in I$. But this implies that $(\bar{p}, \bar{x})$ is a quasi-equilibrium. ∎

A quasi-equilibrium can be shown to be competitive equilibrium under much weaker assumptions than Debreu's (1959) assumption that every consumer has a positive initial endowment of every good. Debreu's assumption is used to show that at any possible equilibrium prices, each consumer can always afford some bundle that costs strictly less than his budget constraint. A quasi-equilibrium will have this property if each consumer could survive after having surrendered some vector of commodities that could be used to make all other consumers better off. This idea is embodied in the "irreducibility" assumptions of McKenzie (1959), (1961) and Debreu (1962) and the "resource-relatedness" assumptions of Arrow and Hahn

(1971). The conflict of interest assumption used here is taken from Bergstrom (1976). Geistdoerfer-Florenzano (1982) discusses these alternative assumptions in detail and shows that our conflict of interest assumptions (1976) are weaker than either "McKenzie-Debreu irreducibility" or "Arrow-Hahn irreducibility".[14]

DEFINITION 19: *(Conflict of interest.) Let $P_i^*(x)$ be the projection of $\hat{P}_i(x)$ as in Definition 4. There is conflict of interest if for any allocation $x \in X$ such that $\sum_I (x_i - w_i) = 0$ and if for consumer $j \in I$, $w_j \notin P_j^*(x)$ then there exists $x' \in X$ and numbers $\theta_i > 0$ such that for all $i \neq j$, $x'_i \in P_i^*(x)$ and such that* $\sum_{i \in I} \theta_i (x'_i - w_i) = 0.$

If the conflict of interest condition holds with the θ_i's all equal, then for any j and any feasible allocation x that leaves consumer j no worse off than he would be without trading, there exists another feasible allocation that is better for all consumers other than j. Allowing the possibility that θ_i's may differ means that there is also conflict of interest if for some arbitrarily chosen numbers of persons of each type in the economy, it would be possible for the persons of all types other than j to be made better off (typically at the expense of the type j's.)

THEOREM 7: *A quasi-equilibrium $(\bar{p}, \bar{x})$ is a competitive equilibrium if :*

7.A *For all i, if $x\hat{P}_i y$ and if $x' \in X$ and $x'_j = x_j$ for $j \neq i$, then there exists a scalar $\lambda \in (0,1)$, such that $\lambda x + (1-\lambda)x'\hat{P}_i y$.*

7.B *There is conflict of interest.*

7.C $\sum_I w_i \in$ *Interior* $\sum_I X_i$.

Proof of Theorem 7:

Let $K = \{i \in I | \bar{p}x_i < pw_i$ for some $i \in I\}$. From Assumption 7.C and the fact that $\sum_I (\bar{x}_i - w_i) = 0$, it follows that K is not empty. Using Assumption 7.A, it is easy to show that for $i \in K$, $\hat{P}_i(\bar{x}) \cap \{x \in X \mid \bar{p}x_i \leq \bar{p}w_i\} = \emptyset$. Suppose that for some $i \in I$, $i \notin K$. By assumption 7.B, for all $j \neq i$, there exists $x'_j \in P_j^*(x)$ and $\sum_I (x'_i - w_i) = 0$. Since $(\bar{p}, \bar{x})$ is a quasi-equilibrium, it must be that for all $j \neq i$, $\bar{p}x'_j \geq \bar{p}w_j$ and since K is not empty, it must be that for some $k \neq i$, $\bar{p}x'_k > \bar{p}w_k$. Therefore $\bar{p}\sum_{j \neq i}(x'_j - w_j) > 0$. But $\bar{p}\sum_I (x'_j - w_j) = 0$, since $\sum_I (x'_j - w_j) = 0$. Therefore $\bar{p}x'_i < \bar{p}w_i$. But this contradicts the assumption that $i \notin K$. It follows that $K = I$ and hence $\hat{P}_i(\bar{x}) \cap \{x \in X \mid \bar{p}x_i \leq \bar{p}w_i\} = \emptyset$ for all $i \in I$. ∎

5.1 *Nonconvex consumption sets and consumers who can't survive without trade.*

We have assumed that consumption sets are closed, convex and that each consumer's initial endowment lies in his consumption set. Moore (1975) argued that for a modern economy it is unrealistic to assume that consumers can survive

[14] Moore's (1982) assumption that "Each consumer is productive" is very similar to, but slightly stronger than, our "conflict of interest" assumption.

without trade. Moore proves the existence of quasi-equilibrium without assuming $w_i \in X_i$ for a model with transitive, locally nonsatiated preferences. Moore uses an assumption that each consumer is "productive in the economy", which is very similar to our "conflict of interest" assumption. McKenzie (1981) extended Moore's results to the case of preferences which need not be transitive or locally nonsatiated.[15]

While it is probably true that in a modern economies, many consumers would not live long without trade, it is not obvious that the "consumption sets" of equilibrium theory should be identified with sets of commodity bundles that allow a person to "survive". In fact in an economy with dated commodities, there is some question of what is meant by survival. Few consumers would die immediately if they were unable to make any trades. Regardless of what trades they make, real-world consumers do not live forever.

In an exchange economy where tradables consist only of an existing stock of n "goods", it seems reasonable to let each consumer's consumption set be the entire non-negative orthant in $\Re^n$. Bundles of goods can be delivered or collected from each consumer's "warehouse", subject only to the constraint that warehouses always contain nonnegative stocks of each commodity.[16] This is true even if, after all deliveries and collections are made, some consumers are left with such meager bundles that they can not "survive". If each consumer has a nonnegative initial endowment, then $w_i \in X_i$ for all i, since this is just the outcome if no deliveries or collections occur. With this interpretation, it might not be reasonable to assume local nonsatiation or convex preferences over consumption bundles that lead to early starvation.[17] But the assumptions of the model considered here, which assumes neither local nonsatiation nor convexity of preferences, presents no difficulties for this interpretation.

In an economy where people exchange labor services for goods, and where commodities are distinguished by time of delivery as well as by type, it may not be appropriate to identify the consumption set with the nonnegative orthant. Feasible combinations of food input, years of survival and labor supply must be related in a fairly complicated way. Matters are clarified if we specify the set of "feasible trades" quite independently of the notion of survival. The set of feasible trades for a consumer with consumption set X_i and endowment w_i is the set $X_i - w_i$. Even if a consumer can not "survive" without trade, zero trade is a possible outcome and hence we can reasonably assume that $w_i \in X_i$. If zero trade leads to early demise, the problem that arises for equilibrium theorists is that it is not reasonable to assume that the set of feasible trades is convex.

For example, consider an economy with two commodities, bread and labor,

---

[15] McKenzie regards Moore's weakening of the survival assumption as "perhaps the most dramatic innovation since 1959" in the theory of existence of competitive equilibrium.

[16] The existence theorem in this paper permits the possibility that warehouses are of bounded capacity.

[17] With convex preferences, if $x\,P\,y$ then $\lambda x + (1-\lambda)y\,P\,y$. If consumptions below a certain threshold all lead to starvation and are equally bad, then this assumption would not be reasonable.

which can be made available in two different time periods. A consumer has no bread in his initial endowment and must have at least one unit of bread in the first period in order to survive to the second period. If he doesn't survive, then he can offer no labor in the second period. One feasible outcome has the consumer making no trade in either period and starving to death before the second period. Another possibility is that he offers one unit of labor in each time period and receives one unit of bread in each period. For the set if feasible trades to be convex, it must be feasible to supply half a unit of labor in each time period and consume half a unit of bread in each period. But we have assumed that if he gets less than one unit of bread in the first period, then he will be unavailable to supply any labor in the second period. Therefore the set of feasible trades is not convex.

Survival sets and feasible consumptions sets are distinguished as follows. For each consumer i, let there be a "survival set" S_i and a set of "feasible consumptions" $X_i \supset S_i$. The survival set can be interpreted as the set of commodity bundles that allow the consumer to reach some threshold of general health. As a formal matter, the set S_i is assumed to be convex and closed, while the set X_i is compact but need not be convex. We will also assume that consumer i never prefers consumption bundles not in $X_i \sim S_i$ to bundles in S_i.

We can now modify Theorem 6 on the existence of quasi-equilibrium to allow the possibility that the set of feasible trades is not convex.

THEOREM 6′: *There exists a quasi-equilibrium for an exchange economy if Assumptions 6.B, 6.C, and 6.D are satisfied and as well as assumption (6′.A). Every consumer i has a compact consumption set X_i and a closed, convex survival set $S_i \subset X_i$ such that if $y \in S_i$ and $x \in X_i \sim S_i$, then not xP_iy.*

With this weakened assumption, the proof of Theorem 6 goes through almost exactly as before. The correspondence $\phi(p, x)$ still satisfies conditions 2.A and 2.B of Theorem 2. Since X is not convex, we can not apply Theorem 2 directly, but the corollary that appears directly after Theorem 2 implies that $\phi(\bar{p}, \bar{x}) = \emptyset$ for some $(\bar{p}, \bar{x})$. The rest of the proof works as before.

Under the assumptions of Theorem 7, the proposition that a quasi-equilibrium must be a competitive equilibrium remains true with the weakened assumptions of Theorem 6′.

5.2 *Adding Production to the Model*

One might think that adding production to this model would be a tedious, notation-intensive chore, but Trout Rader has shown how to make this task easy. In his Ph. D. thesis, published in *Yale Economic Essays* in 1963, Rader showed that a pure exchange economy can be interpreted as an economy with household production. This is done by defining "induced preferences" on net trades in the natural way, given the consumer's initial endowment and his household production possibility set. Rader further shows that the standard Arrow-Debreu model of a "private ownership economy" with convex production possibility sets can be incorporated into this framework. Where consumer i owns fraction θ_{ij} of firm j which has production possibility set Y_j, the Arrow-Debreu model is equivalent to an exchange model in which each consumer i has a household production possibility set, $\sum_j \theta_{ij} Y_j$. In an unpublished paper, Rader (1975) shows that these ideas carry over nicely to the case of preferences that need not be transitive or complete.

Appendix

Properties of Lower Semi-Continuous Correspondences:

Here we report several useful properties of l.s.c. correspondences. Those propositions that are stated without proofs all have simple proofs which are reported elsewhere. See Berge (1963) and Michael (1956).

Proposition 1 simply restates the definition of lower semi-continuity in a useful way.

PROPOSITION 1: *The correspondence $\phi : X \to 2^Y$ in l.s.c. iff for all $x \in X$, $y \in \phi(x)$ implies that for every open neighborhood V of y in Y there exists an open neighborhood U of x in X such that for all $x' \in U$, $\phi(x') \cap V \neq \emptyset$.*

An immediate consequence of Proposition 1 is the fact that a sufficient (but not necessary) condition for a correspondence to be l.s.c. is that the "inverse images of points" are open sets.

PROPOSITION 2: *Let S be a topological space, $P \subset S \times S$ and $X \subset S$. If for all $x \in S$, $P^{-1}(x)$ is open in X, then P is l.s.c. on X.*

Proof: Let V be an open subset of S. Then $\{x \in X \mid P(x) \cap V \neq \emptyset\} = \bigcup_{y \in V} (P^{-1}(y) \cap X)$ which is a union of sets which are open in X and hence is open in X. Therefore P is l.s.c. on X. ∎

Unions and finite intersections of l.s.c. correspondence must also be l.s.c.

PROPOSITION 3: *For any index set I, let $\phi_i : X \to Y$ be l.s.c. for all $i \in I$. Then $\Psi : X \to Y$ is l.s.c. where $\Psi(x) = \bigcup_{i \in I} \phi_i(x)$.*

PROPOSITION 4: *For any finite index set I, let $\phi_i : X \to Y$ be l.s.c. for all $i \in I$. Then $\Psi : X \to Y$ is l.s.c. where $\Psi(x) = \bigcap_{i \in I} \phi_i(x)$.*

Projections and Cartesian products of l.s.c. correspondences must also be l.s.c.

PROPOSITION 5: *Let I be a finite index set and $X = \prod_{i \in I} X_i$. Let $\phi : X \to X$ be l.s.c. and let $\phi_i : X \to 2^{X_i}$ to be the projection of ϕ on X_i. Then ϕ_i is l.s.c.*

PROPOSITION 6: *Let I be a finite index set and $X = \prod_{i \in I} X_i$ where such X_i is a topological space. Let $\phi_i : X \to 2^{X_i}$ be l.s.c. for all $i \in I$. Let $\phi : X \to X$ be defined so that $\phi(x) = \prod_{i \in I} \phi_i(x)$. Then ϕ is l.s.c.*

PROPOSITION 7: *Let* $X = \prod_{i \in I} X_i$. *Let* $\phi_i : X \to X_i$ *be l.s.c. Let* $\hat{\phi}_i : X \to X$ *be defined so that* $\hat{\phi}_i(p, x) = \{x' \in X | x'_i \in \phi_i(x) \text{ and } x'_j = x_j \text{ for all } j \neq i\}$. *Then* $\hat{\phi}_i$ *is l.s.c.*

Proof: The correspondence $\hat{\phi}_i$ is just the Cartesian product of ϕ_i with the "identity correspondences" that maps $x_j \in X_j$ into the set $\{x_j\}$ for each $j \neq i$. These correspondences are all l.s.c. According to Proposition 6, the Cartesian product of l.s.c. correspondences is l.s.c. ∎

PROPOSITION 8: *Let* $X = \prod_{i \in I} X_i$. *Let* $\phi : X \to X$ *be l.s.c. For* $i \in I$, *define* $\hat{\phi}_i : X \to X$ *so that* $\hat{\phi}_i(x) = \{x' | x' \in \phi(x) \text{ and } x'_j = x_j \text{ for all } j \neq i\}$. *Then* $\hat{\phi}_i$ *is l.s.c.*

Proof: For $j \in I$, let $T_j(x) = \{x' \in X | x'_j = x_j\}$. The correspondences T_j are easily seen to be l.s.c. Now $\hat{\phi}_i(x) = \phi(x)_{j \neq i} T_j$. Since finite intersections of l.s.c. correspondences are l.s.c., $\hat{\phi}_i$ is l.s.c. ∎

If a correspondence is lower semi-continuous, then the correspondence whose image sets are the convex hulls of the image sets in the original correspondence will also be l.s.c.

PROPOSITION 9: *If* Y *is a linear topological space and* $\phi : X \to 2^Y$ *is l.s.c., then the correspondence,* Ψ, $X \to 2^Y$ *where* $\Psi(x) = \text{con}\, \phi(\text{x})$ *is l.s.c.*

The next result is useful for establishing existence of equilibrium when preferences are not monotonic and there is no free disposal.

PROPOSITION 10: *Let* $\phi_i : \prod X_i \to X_i$ *be l.s.c. and define* $\phi_i^* : \prod X_i \to X_i$ *so that* $\phi_i^*(x) = \{z \in X_i \mid z = \lambda y_i + (1 - \lambda) x_i \text{ where } y_i \in \phi_i(x) \text{ and } 0 < \lambda \leq 1\}$. *Then* ϕ_i^* *is l.s.c.*

Proof: Consider the correspondence $\Psi_i(x) = \phi_i(x) \cup I_i(x)$, where $I_i(x)$ is the ith projection of the identity correspondence. Then Ψ_i must be l.s.c., since it is the union of two l.s.c. correspondences. Where ϕ_i^* is the correspondence defined in Proposition 7, $\phi_i^*(x) = \text{con}\,\text{Psi}(\text{x})$ for all x and hence ϕ_i^* must be l.s.c., according to Proposition 6.

An alternative characterization of lower semi-continuous correspondences is in terms of sequences.

PROPOSITION 11: *Where* X *and* Y *satisfy the first axiom of countability,*[18] *the following property is necessary and sufficient that* $\phi : X \to 2^Y$ *be l.s.c. If*

[18] A topological space satisfies the first axiom of countability if the neighborhood system if every point has a countable base. This is true of all metric spaces. If X and Y lack this property, then lower semi-continuity may be characterized by the convergence of nets rather than sequences. This situation is in close analogy to the characterization of continuous functions by sequences or nets. See Kelley (1963).

$y \in \phi(x)$ and $x(n) \to x$, there exists a subsequence $x(n_k) \to x$ such that for some sequence, $y(k)$ in Y, $y(k) \to y$ and $y(k) \in \phi(x(n_k))$ for every integer k.[19]

Proof: Suppose that ϕ is l.s.c. Let $y \in \phi(x)$ and let $\{V_k \mid k = 1, 2, ...\}$ be a countable base at y. For each k, let $\hat{V}_k = \bigcap_{i \leq K} V_i$. Since ϕ is l.s.c., for each k there exists a neighborhood U_k of x such that for all $x' \in U_k$, $\hat{V}_k \cap \phi(x') \neq \emptyset$. Let $\hat{U}_k = \bigcap_{i \leq k} U_i$. Since $x(n) \to x$, there exists a subsequence $(x(n_k))$ such that for every k, $x(n_k) \in \hat{U}_k$. Then there exists $y(k) \in \hat{V}_k \cap \phi(x(n_k))$. Since $\{\hat{V}_k \mid k = 1, 2, ...\}$ is a base at y, $y(k) \to y$. Thus $(x(n_k))$ is a subsequence of $x(n)$ such that there exists a sequence $(y(k))$ in Y where $y(k) \to y$ and $y(k) \in \phi(x(n_k))$ for all k. This proves necessity.

Suppose that ϕ is not l.s.c. Then there exist $x \in X$, $y \in Y$ and a neighborhood V of Y such that for every neighborhood U of x, there exists $x' \in U$ such that $\phi(x') \cap V = \emptyset$. Let $\{U_n \mid n = 1, 2, ...\}$ be a countable base at x and for each k, let $\hat{U}_n = \bigcap_{i \leq n} U_i$. Then there exists a sequence $(x(n))$ such that for all n, $x(n) \in \hat{U}_n$ and $\phi(x(n)) \cap V = \emptyset$. Clearly $x(n) \to x$. But there is no subsequence $(x(n_k)$ of $(x(n))$ for which there exists a sequence $(y(k))$ where $y(k) \to y$ and $y(k) \in \phi(x(n_k))$ for every k. This proves sufficiency. ∎

Proofs of Lemmas in Text:

Proof of Lemma 3:

For all $p \in S^n$ and $z \in \Re^n$, the set $\{p' \in S^n | p'z > pz\}$ is open in S^n. It follows that for all $(p, x) \in \hat{X}$, $\phi_p^{-1}(p, x)$ is open in S^n. From Proposition 2, it follows that ϕ_p is l.s.c.

Let $B_i(p, x) = \{x' \in X | px'_i < pw_i\}$. Let $C_i(p, x) = \{x' \in X | px'_i < px_i$ and $x'_j = x_j$ for all $j \neq i\}$. From Proposition 2 it follows that $B_i(p, x)$ is l.s.c. From Propositions 2 and 8, it follows that $C_i(p, x)$ is l.s.c.

Let $\phi_i^a(p, x) = \hat{P}_i(x) \cap B_i(p)$ if $px_i \leq pw_i$ and $\phi_i^a(p, x) = \emptyset$ if $px_i > pw_i$. Let $\phi_i^b(p, x) = C_i(p, x)$ if $px_i > pw_i$ and $\phi_i^b(p, x) = \emptyset$ if $px_i \leq pw_i$. From Proposition 2 it follows that ϕ_i^a and ϕ_i^b are l.s.c. Since for all $(p, x) \in \hat{X}$, $\phi_i(p, x) = \phi_i^a \cup \phi_i^b(p, x)$, it follows from Proposition 3 that ϕ_i is l.s.c. From Proposition 3 it then follows that $\phi = \cup_I \phi_i$ is l.s.c.

From the definition of ϕ, it is immediate that if $\hat{\phi}(p, x) = \emptyset$, then $\hat{\phi}_p(p, x) = \emptyset$ and for all $i \in I$, $\hat{\phi}_i(p, x) = \emptyset$. ∎

---

19 The reader may be familiar with the following characterization of lower semi-continuity. Where $y \in \phi(x)$ and $x(n) \to x$, there exists a sequence $y(n) \to y$ such that $y(n) \in \phi(x(n))$ for all n. If the image sets are always non-empty and X and Y satisfy the first axiom of countability, then this property is necessary and sufficient that ϕ be l.s.c. as defined here. If $\phi(x)$ can be empty this property is not necessary. (In particular it may be that $\phi(x(n)) = \emptyset$ for some n.)

Proof of Lemma 4:

Result (i) is trivial. Result (ii) follows from Proposition 9 of the Appendix. To prove Result (iii), notice that if $x \in \tilde{P}_i(x)$, then $x = \lambda x + (1-\lambda)y$ for some $y \in \operatorname{con} \hat{P}_i(x)$ and some $\lambda \in [0,1)$. For $\lambda \neq 1$, $x = \lambda x + (1-\lambda)y$ if and only if $x = y$. So if $x \in \tilde{P}_i(x)$, then $x \in \hat{P}_i(x)$. Result (iii) follows. ∎

Proof of Lemma 5:

The proof of Lemma 5 closely parallels the proof of Lemma 3. The arguments for lower semi-continuity are unchanged when p comes from the unit sphere rather than the unit ball. The only other differences between the proof of Lemma 3 and this proof is that the Gale-Mas-Colell augmented preference relations $\tilde{P}_i$ replace $\hat{P}_i$ and the "budgets inequalities" $px_i < pw_i$ are replaced by $px_i < pw_i + \frac{(1-\|p\|)}{m}$. Lemma 4 ensures that $\tilde{P}_i$ inherits the properties of $\hat{P}_i$ that are needed for this proof. The change in the budget inequality does not affect the rest of the argument. ∎

References

ALIPRANTIS, C., AND D. BROWN (1983): "Equilibria in Markets with a Riesz space of commodities," *Journal of Mathematical Economics,* 11, 189-207.

ARROW, K., AND F. HAHN (1971): *General Competitive Analysis.* San Francisco: Holden-Day.

BERGE, C. (1963): *Topological Spaces.* New York: Macmillan.

BERGSTROM, T. (1973): "Competitive Equilibrium Without Transitivity, Local Nonsatiation or Monotonicity," Washington University, St. Louis, MO.

BERGSTROM, T. (1975): "The Existence of Maximal Elements and Equilibria in the Absence of Transitivity," Washington University, St. Louis, MO.

BERGSTROM, T. (1975): "Maximal Elements of Acyclic Relations on Compact Sets," *Journal of Economic Theory,* 10, 403-404.

BERGSTROM, T. (1976): "How to Discard Free Disposability—At No Cost," *Journal of Mathematical Economics,* 3, 131-134.

BERGSTROM, T., R. PARKS, AND T. RADER, (1976): "Preferences Which Have Open Graph," *Journal of Mathematical Economics,* 3, 265-268.

BIRCHENHALL, C. (1977): "Conditions for the Existence of Maximal Elements in Compact Sets," *Journal of Economic Theory,* 16, 111-115.

BORGLIN, A. AND H. KEIDING (1976): "Existence of Equilibrium Actions and of Equilibrium," *Journal of Mathematical Economics,* 3, 313-316.

BLUME, L. (1986): "Equilibrium and Optimality in a Sequence of Markets with Transaction Costs," in *Contributions to Mathematical Economics in Honor of Gerard Debreu,* ed. by Hildenbrand, W. and A. Mas-Colell. New York: Elsevier.

DEBREU, G. (1959): *Theory of Value.* New York: Wiley.

DEBREU, G. (1962): "New Concepts and Techniques in General Equilibrium Analysis," *International Economic Review,* 3, 257-273.

DEBREU, G. (1982): "Existence of Competitive Equilibrium," in *Handbook of Mathematical Economics, Volume II*, ed. by Arrow, K. and M. Intriligator. New York: Elsevier., 697-743.

FAN, K. (1961): "A Generalization of Tychonoff's Fixed Point Theorem,," *Math Annalen,* 142, 305-310.

GALE, D. AND A. MAS-COLELL (1975): "A Short Proof of Existence of Equilibrium Without Ordered Preferences," *Journal of Mathematical Economics,* 2, 9-15.

GALE, D. AND A. MAS-COLELL (1979): "Corrections to an Equilibrium Existence Theorem for a General Equilibrium Model Without Ordered Preferences," *Journal of Mathematical Economics,* 6, 297-299.

GEISTDOERFER-FLORENZANO, M. (1982): "The Gale-Nikaido-Debreu Lemma and the Existence of Transitive Equilibrium with or without the Free-Disposal Assumption," *Journal of Mathematical Economics,* 9, 113-134.

KELLEY, J. (1963): *General Topology.* Princeton, N.J.: Van Nostrand.

MCKENZIE, L. (1955): "Competitive Equilibrium with Dependent Consumer Preferences," in *Second Symposium on Linear Programming,* ed. by National Bureau of Standards and Department of the Air Force. Washington: D. C.

MCKENZIE, L. (1959): "On the Existence of General Equilibrium for a Competitive Market," *Econometrica,* 27, 54-71.

MCKENZIE, L. (1961): "On the Existence of General Equilibrium–Some Corrections," *Econometrica,* 29, 247-248.

MCKENZIE, L. (1981): "The Classical Theorem on Existence of Competitive Equilibrium," *Econometrica,* 49, 819-842.

MEHTA, G. (1987): "Maximal Elements of Preference Maps," Working Paper, University of Queensland, Department of Economics, Brisbane, Australia.

MEHTA, G. (1987): "Weakly Lower Demicontinuous Preference Maps," *Economics Letters,* 23, 15-18.

MOORE, J. (1975): "The Existence of "Compensated Equilibrium" and the Structure of the Pareto Efficiency Frontier," *International Economic Review,* 16, 267-300.

MICHAEL, E. (1956): "Continuous Selections, I," *Annals of Mathematics,* 63, 361-382.

NASH, J. (1950): "Equilibrium States in N-person Games," *Proceedings of the National Academy of Sciences of the U.S.A.,* 36, 48-49.

RADER, T. (1964): "Edgeworth Exchange and General Economic Equilibrium," *Yale Economic Essays,* 4, 133-181.

RADER, T. (1972): *Theory of General Economic Equilibrium.* New York: Academic Press.

RADER, T. (1975): "Induced Preferences on Trades When Preferences May be Intransitive and Incomplete," Washington University, St. Louis, MO.

SCHOFIELD, N. (1983): "Social Equilibrium and Cycles on Compact Sets," *Journal of Economic Theory,* 33, 59-71.

SCHOFIELD, N. (1984): "Existence of Equilibrium on a Manifold," *Mathematics of Operations Research,* 9, 545-557.

SHAFER, W. (1974): "The Nontransitive Consumer," *Econometrica,* 42, 913-919.

SHAFER, W. AND H. SONNENSCHEIN (1975): "Equilibrium in Abstract Economies without Ordered Preferences," *Journal of Mathematical Economics,* 2, 345-348.

SHAFER, W. AND H. SONNENSCHEIN (1976): "Equilibrium with Externalities, Commodity Taxation, and Lump Sum Transfers," *International Economic Review,* 17, 601-611.

SHAFER, W. (1976): "Equilibrium in Economies without Ordered Preferences or Free Disposal," *Journal of Mathematical Economics,* 3, 135-137.

SONNENSCHEIN, H. (1971): "Demand Theory Without Transitive Preference with Applications to the Theory of Competitive Equilibrium," in *Preferences, Utility and Demand,* ed. by Chipman, J., L. Hurwicz, M. Richter, and H. Sonnenschein. New York: Harcourt, Brace, Jovanovich., 215-223.

SONNENSCHEIN, H. (1977): "Some Recent Results on the Existence of Equilibrium in Finite Purely Competitive Economies," in *Frontiers of Quantitative Economics, Vol. IIIA,* ed. by Intriligator, M. New York: Elsevier., 103-109.

WALKER, M. (1977): "On the Existence of Maximal Elements," *Journal of Economic Theory,* 16, 470-474.

YANNELIS, N. AND N. PRABHAKAR (1983): "Existence of Maximal Elements and Equilibria in Linear Topological Spaces," *Journal of Mathematical Economics,* 12, 233-245.

The Algebraic Geometry of Competitive Equilibrium

LAWRENCE E. BLUME
Cornell University
AND
WILLIAM R. ZAME
The Johns Hopkins University and UCLA

1 Introduction

The classical tools of general equilibrium theory are convexity and general topology. One of Debreu's lasting contributions has been to show how the tools of differential topology may serve to yield more refined information about equilibrium. In particular, Debreu (1970) showed that differential topology could provide a rigorous formalization of "counting equations and unknowns" to provide a satisfactory result on the determinacy of equilibrium.

Debreu required that preferences be representable by C^2 utility functions with non-vanishing gradients and that indifference surfaces have non-vanishing curvature. Following Debreu, a natural question to ask is: Are there other interesting classes of preferences (or demands) exhibiting regularity of behavior sufficient to guarantee the generic local determinacy of equilibrium prices? The first results in this direction were obtained by Rader (1972, 1973), who showed that generic finiteness of the equilibrium price set was a consequence of demand being differentiable almost everywhere and satisfying condition N: that the image of a null set is null. Rader also gave conditions on preferences sufficient to generate demand meeting these hypotheses; a further set of sufficient conditions was developed in a later paper (1979). The concave-utility requirement of Rader (1973) has only recently been relaxed to local concavifiability of the preference relation, by Pascoa and Werlang (1989).

The work reported here extends the work of Debreu in a different direction. Its motivation comes from two sources. The first is a remark made by Rader at an NBER Conference in the 1970's about the nature of demand when preferences are analytic. The second is the work of Blume and Zame (1989) and Schanuel, Simon and Zame (forthcoming) on the applications of algebraic geometry in non-cooperative game theory. When asked about the potential applications of the methods of those papers to general equilibrium theory, our response was to be skeptical because the required hypotheses seemed to be so strong. However, we later realized that these algebraic-geometric methods could in fact be extended to a much wider class of preferences than we had previously thought (roughly, the piecewise analytic preferences), and that the strength of these assumptions bought many compensations. Our central result is that, for preferences in this class, generically in endowments, the equilibrium set is finite and depends nicely on endowments. We allow for flats and kinks of indifference surfaces, we make no curvature requirements, and we allow for equilibria on the boundary of the price simplex. Moreover, our conclusions are somewhat stronger than those in the smooth case in that they yield more structure on the exceptional set of endowments.

The classes of preferences we consider are those with utility representations that are semi-algebraic (roughly, piecewise algebraic) and finitely sub-analytic (roughly, piecewise analytic); precise definitions are given in Section 2. Most of the familiar preferences used in applications have representations that are finitely sub-analytic on the relevant portions of their domain: Cobb-Douglas, logarithmic, exponential, CES, HARA, piecewise-linear. However our methods, which are those of real algebraic geometry and mathematical logic, apply potentially to other classes of preferences. For our purposes, the crucial property of preferences is that their graphs belong to an O-minimal Tarski system containing the graphs of addition and multiplication (again, Section 2 provides a precise definition); the semi-algebraic sets and the finitely sub-analytic sets comprise the known examples. Once we know that preferences belong to such a system, the key properties of demand and the local finiteness of equilibrium follow from a few basic properties shared by all such systems. It seems preferable, therefore, to present the arguments in the somewhat more abstract setting of O-minimal Tarski systems rather than to carry around the excess baggage that comes from assuming that preferences are specifically semi-algebraic or finitely sub-analytic.

Section 2 contains the relevant mathematical background, including definitions and a summary of results about O-minimal Tarski systems, including the family of semi-algebraic sets and the family of finitely sub-analytic sets. Section 3 discusses preferences and demands. The local finiteness result and its proof are found in Section 4.

2 Mathematical Background

In this Section we set out, following van den Dries (1986), the basic properties of O-minimal Tarski systems. Our goal is to delimit a class of functions; we proceed, however, by delimiting a class of sets. This may seem less strange if we keep in mind that every property of a function $f : \mathbf{R} \to \mathbf{R}$ can be expressed in terms of its graph: f is measurable if and only if its graph is a measurable set, f is smooth if and only if its graph is a smooth manifold, etc.

A *Tarski system* is a family $\mathcal{S} = \{\mathcal{S}_n\}$ such that:

1. For each n, $\mathcal{S}_n$ is a Boolean algebra[1] of subsets of $\mathbf{R}^\mathbf{n}$.

2. If $X \in \mathcal{S}_n$, then $\mathbf{R} \times X \in \mathcal{S}_{n+1}$ and $X \times \mathbf{R} \in \mathcal{S}_{n+1}$.

[1]That is, $\mathcal{S}_n$ contains $\emptyset$ and $\mathbf{R}^\mathbf{n}$ and is closed under formation of complements, finite unions, and finite intersections.

3. For each n, $D_n = \{(x_1, \ldots, x_n) \ : \ x_1 = x_n\} \in \mathcal{S}_n$.

4. If $X \in \mathcal{S}_n$ and $\pi : \mathbf{R^n} \to \mathbf{R^{n-1}}$ is the projection onto the first $n-1$ coordinates, then $\pi(X) \in \mathcal{S}_{n-1}$.

A Tarski system $\mathcal{S}$ is *O-minimal* if, in addition:

5. It contains the graph of the less than relation: $L = \{(x, y) \ : \ x < y\} \in \mathcal{S}_2$.

6. For each $r \in \mathbf{R}$ the singleton $\{r\}$ belongs to $\mathcal{S}_1$.

7. Every set in $\mathcal{S}_1$ is a finite union of intervals and points.

It should be emphasized that a Tarski system is a *system*—that its properties achieve much of their bite in conjunction with each other. A simple example may make this point. Let $B \in \mathcal{S}_2$ and let B^s be the symmetrically reversed set: $B^s = \{(x, y) \ : \ (y, x) \in B\}$. Property 2 guarantees that $\mathbf{R} \times B \in \mathcal{S}_3$. Since properties 3 and 1 guarantee that $D_3 \in \mathcal{S}_3$ and $\mathcal{S}_3$ is a Boolean algebra, it follows that $(R \times B) \cap D_3 \in \mathcal{S}_3$. Since B^s is the projection of $(R \times B) \cap D_3$ into the first two coordinates, we conclude from property 4 that $B^s \in \mathcal{S}_2$.

To see the additional bite of O-minimality, observe that we may build a Tarski system by beginning with an arbitrary family $\{T_n\}$, adjoining the diagonal subsets, and closing under Boolean operations, products, and projections. However, such a process may already lead to a family which violates property 7. For instance, if we begin with the singletons in $\mathbf{R}$ and the single additional set $A = \{(x, y) \ : \ y = \sin x\} \subset \mathbf{R^2}$ (the graph of the sine function), we must include $\mathbf{R} \times \{0\} \subset \mathbf{R^2}$, and $A \cap (\mathbf{R} \times \{0\})$, and the image of $A \cap (R \times \{0\})$ under the first coordinate projection. But this last set is precisely the set of zeroes of the sine function, which is not a finite union of points and intervals.

If $\mathcal{S}$ is an O-minimal Tarski system, it is convenient to say that a set X *belongs* to $\mathcal{S}$ or X is an *$\mathcal{S}$-set* if $X \in \mathcal{S}_n$ for some n. We say that a function (or correspondence) $f : A \to B$ *belongs* to $\mathcal{S}$ or f is an *$\mathcal{S}$-function* if the graph of f belongs to $\mathcal{S}$.[2] It is useful to note that the inverse correspondence of every function belonging to $\mathcal{S}$ again belongs to $\mathcal{S}$. The simple proof follows along the same lines as the coordinate-reversal example above.

For our purposes, we shall mainly be interested in O-minimal Tarski systems which contain (the graphs of) addition and multiplication; i.e.,

8. $A = \{(x, y, z) \ : \ z = x + y\} \in \mathcal{S}_3$.

9. $M = \{(x, y, z) \ : \ z = xy\} \in \mathcal{S}_3$.

Two O-minimal Tarski systems are well known: The polyhedral (or piecewise linear) sets satisfy all the above properties but property 9, while the semi-algebraic sets satisfy all nine properties.

[2]Note that the domain of f is the projection of the graph of f, and so belongs automatically to $\mathcal{S}$ whenever f does.

A subset of $\mathbf{R^n}$ is *polyhedral* if it is a finite union of sets defined by linear equalities and inequalities; i.e., if it is a finite union of sets of the form $\{x : \lambda_i(x) = \alpha_i,\ \mu_j(x) < \beta_j,\ 1 \le i \le N,\ 1 \le j \le M\}$, where the α_i and β_j are real numbers, and the λ_i and μ_j are linear functionals.

A subset of $\mathbf{R^n}$ is *semi-algebraic* if it is a finite union of sets defined by polynomial equalities and inequalities; i.e., if it is a finite union of sets of the form $\{x : p_i(x) = \alpha_i, \quad q_j(x) < \beta_j, \quad 1 \le i \le M,\ 1 \le j \le N\}$, where p_i and q_j are polynomials.

It is easy to see that the polyhedral sets form an O-minimal Tarski system, and that they are contained in every O-minimal Tarski system satisfying property 8. (Of course they themselves do not satisfy property 9.) The polyhedral functions are precisely the familiar piecewise linear functions.

The semi-algebraic sets form the smallest O-minimal Tarski system satisfying properties 8 and 9. All of the defining properties of O-minimal Tarski systems except for property 4 are easily verified for the family of semi-algebraic sets. The fourth property is a consequence of a deep theorem of logic, the Tarski-Seidenberg Theorem. The semi-algebraic functions include the piecewise linear functions, all the familiar algebraic functions (polynomials, rational functions, roots, etc.), and their compositions, algebraic combinations, and their derivatives; but not the transcendental functions such as the exponential function, the logarithm and the trigonometric functions, and indefinite integrals of semi-algebraic functions.

A larger O-minimal Tarski system was discovered by van den Dries (1986), relying on the work of Lojasiewicz (1965) and Gabrielov (1968): the finitely sub-analytic sets. To define this family, we must first define semi-analytic sets and sub-analytic sets.

A subset $X \subset \mathbf{R^n}$ is *semi-analytic* if for each $y \in \mathbf{R^n}$ (not just $y \in X$) there is an open neighborhood U of y such that $U \cap X$ is the finite union of sets defined by real analytic inequalities and inequalities; i.e., $U \cap X$ is a finite union of sets of the form $\{x : f_i(x) = \alpha_i, \quad g_j(x) < \beta_j, \quad 1 \le i \le M,\ 1 \le j \le N\}$, where f_i and g_j are real analytic functions.

A subset $X \subset \mathbf{R^n}$ is *sub-analytic* if for each $y \in \mathbf{R^n}$ (not just $y \in X$) there is an open neighborhood V of y and a bounded semi-analytic set $Y \subset \mathbf{R^{n+m}}$ such that $V \cap X$ is the image of Y under the projection onto the first n coordinates.

A subset $X \subset \mathbf{R^n}$ is *finitely sub-analytic* if it is the image under the map

$$(x_1, \dots, x_n) \mapsto \left(\frac{x_1}{\sqrt{1+x_1^2}}, \dots, \frac{x_n}{\sqrt{1+x_n^2}} \right)$$

of a sub-analytic subset of $\mathbf{R^n}$.

Of course, semi-algebraic sets and functions are finitely sub-analytic, but many transcendental functions are finitely sub-analytic but not semi-algebraic, including the restrictions of the exponential function, the logarithm and the trigonometric functions to compact subsets of their domains. Compositions, algebraic combinations, and derivatives of finitely sub-analytic functions are finitely sub-analytic, but indefinite integrals are not. Neither are the exponential function, the logarithm and the trigonometric functions on their entire domains.

For our purposes, the crucial properties of O-minimal Tarski systems are the various finiteness properties (discussed below), and the fact that O-minimal Tarski systems are *closed under definability.* To see what this means, consider an O-minimal Tarski system $\mathcal{S}$ and a set $X \in \mathcal{S}_n$. The set

$$Y = \{(x_1,\dots,x_{n-1}) \ : \ \exists x_n \ (x_1,\dots,x_{n-1},x_n) \in X\}$$

is the projection of X onto its first $n-1$ components, and thus belongs to $\mathcal{S}_{n-1}$. Similarly, the set

$$Z = \{(x_1,\dots,x_{n-1}) \ : \ \forall x_n \ (x_1,\dots,x_{n-1},x_n) \in X\}$$

is the complement of the projection of the complement of X, and thus also belongs to $\mathcal{S}_{n-1}$. In like manner, if F is a first order formula involving the free variables x_1 through x_{n-1}, any finite number of quantified variables, and sets in $\mathcal{S}$, then it is a finite string of conjunctions and disjunctions of expressions such as those in the definitions of Y and Z and their negations. Negation corresponds to set complementation, conjunction corresponds to intersection and disjunction corresponds to union, so the fact that $\mathcal{S}$ is a Boolean Algebra (property 1) implies that the set

$$\{(x_1,\dots,x_{n-1}) \ : \ F(x_1,\dots,x_{n-1},x_n) \quad \text{is true}\}$$

is an element of $\mathcal{S}$.

At this point, closure under definability might seem to be an obscure property, but the fact that the O-minimal Tarski systems we are interested in contain (the graphs of) familiar relations and functions, including $=$, $<$, $+$ and $-$, make it quite powerful.

To give a simple example of the implications of closure under definability, let $\mathcal{S}$ be any O-minimal Tarski system that contains addition and scalar multiplication, and let X be any set belonging to $\mathcal{S}$; we show that the closure $\mathrm{cl}\, X$ of X also belongs to $\mathcal{S}$. To see this, let us write $\|w\| = \sum_n |w_n|$. Then the closure of X is:

$$\mathrm{cl}\, X = \{y \in \mathbf{R}^n \ : \ \forall \epsilon > 0, \ \exists x \in X, \ \|x - y\| < \epsilon\}$$

On the face of it, the expression that defines $\mathrm{cl}\, X$ is not a formula in the sense discussed above; however, it may easily be expanded into such a formula. Let π denote the projection from $\mathbf{R}^2$ onto the first coordinate. For any $X \in \mathcal{S}_2$, let X^s denote the symmetric reversal of X, and recall that L is the graph of the less-than relation. Note first that the sets of non-negative real numbers, non-positive real numbers, and positive real numbers are all $\mathcal{S}$-sets. This is trivially true for the systems of semi-algebraic and finitely sub-analytic sets. However, it can be shown to be true for all O-minimal Tarski systems satisfying properties 1 through 6. For instance:

$$\mathbf{R}_+ = \{x \ : \ 0 \le x\} = \pi\Big((L \cap (\{0\} \times \mathbf{R}))^s\Big) \cup \{0\}$$

Let $\mathbf{R_0}$ denote the set $\{0\} \times \mathbf{R}$. Property 6 implies that the set $\{0\}$ is an $\mathcal{S}$-set. Property 2 then implies that $\mathbf{R_0}$ is an $\mathcal{S}$-set. It follows from properties 5 and 2 that $L \cap \mathbf{R_0}$ is an $\mathcal{S}$-set, from properties 1 through 4 that $(L \cap \mathbf{R_0})^s$ is an $\mathcal{S}$-set, from property 5 that $\pi((L \cap \mathbf{R_0})^s)$ is an $\mathcal{S}$- set, and finally from property 1 that $\pi((L \cap \mathbf{R_0})^s) \cup \{0\}$ is an $\mathcal{S}$-set.

Next, observe that the graph of the absolute value function on $\mathbf{R}$ is:

$$\begin{aligned}\text{Graph}(|\cdot|) &= \{(r,s) \ : \ r \in \mathbf{R}_+ \quad \text{and} \quad s = r\} \\ &\quad \cup\{(r,s) \ : \ r \in \mathbf{R}_- \quad \text{and} \quad s = -r\} \cup \{(0,0)\}\end{aligned}$$

The first set is $(\mathbf{R} \times \mathbf{R}_+) \cap D_2$, which is clearly an $\mathcal{S}$-set. The third set is $(\{0\} \times \mathbf{R}) \cap D_2$, which is clearly an $\mathcal{S}$ set. The second set is $\{(r,s) \ : \ r \in \mathbf{R}_-\} \cap \{(r,s) \ : \ r+s=0\}$. The set on the left is clearly an $\mathcal{S}$-set. The set on the right is $A \cap (\mathbf{R} \times \mathbf{R} \times \{0\})$ (where A is the graph of addition). It follows from properties 8, 6 and 2 that this set is an $\mathcal{S}$ set. Thus the second set is an $\mathcal{S}$ set, and so Graph($|\cdot|$) is an $\mathcal{S}$-set. In other words, $|\cdot|$ is an $\mathcal{S}$-function for any O-minimal Tarski system satisfying properties 1 through 6 and 8.

Similarly we can use property 8 to conclude that $(x,y) \mapsto \|x-y\|$ is also an $\mathcal{S}$-function, and so $N = \{(x,y,\epsilon) \in \mathbf{R^n} \times \mathbf{R^n} \times \mathbf{R} \ : \ \|x-y\| < \epsilon\}$ is an $\mathcal{S}$-set. Now the closure of X may be expressed as:

$$\text{cl}\, X = \Big\{ y \in \mathbf{R^n} \ : \ \forall \epsilon \ \Big((\epsilon \in \mathbf{R}_-) \text{ or } (\epsilon \in \mathbf{R}_{++} \text{ and } (\exists \mathbf{x} \in \mathbf{X}, \ (\mathbf{x}, \mathbf{y}, \epsilon) \in \mathbf{N})) \Big) \Big\}$$

which is an $\mathcal{S}$-set, as asserted.

Closure under definability has been exploited by Blume and Zame (1989) and Schanuel, Simon and Zame (forthcoming) to show that, for finite games, the graph of the Nash equilibrium correspondence, and the graphs of many refinements of the Nash equilibrium correspondence, are semi-algebraic correspondences. We refer to these papers for more examples of the sort of $\epsilon - \delta$ manipulations used above.

We now turn to the basic finiteness properties. In what follows, we fix an O-minimal Tarski system $\mathcal{S}$ that contains addition and multiplication, and list some important consequences of properties 1 through 9. For further discussion, see van den Dries (1986) and Bochnak, Coste and Roy (1987).

GLOBAL FINITENESS: Every set X belonging to $\mathcal{S}$ has a finite number of connected components, and each of them belongs to $\mathcal{S}$. If $f : X \to Y$ belongs to $\mathcal{S}$, then each point inverse $f^{-1}(y)$ belongs to $\mathcal{S}$, and there is a positive integer $N(f)$ such that each point inverse $f^{-1}(y)$ has at most $N(f)$ connected components.

TRIANGULABILITY: If $X \in \mathcal{S}_n$, then there is a finite simplicial complex $K \subset \mathbf{R^n}$ and a homeomorphism h belonging to $\mathcal{S}$, mapping X onto K.

In view of this property, we may unambiguously define the dimension of X, $\dim X$, to be the largest dimension of any subsimplex of K.

DIMENSION: If $X \in \mathcal{S}_n$ then $\text{cl}\, X, \partial X \in \mathcal{S}_n$, $\dim \text{cl}\, X = \dim X$ and $\dim \partial X < \dim X$. If $f : X \to \mathbf{R^n}$ belongs to $\mathcal{S}$, then $\dim f(X) \leq \dim X$.

CONTINUITY: If $F : X \to Y$ is a closed-valued correspondence belonging to $\mathcal{S}$, then there is a subset $X' \subset X$ belonging to $\mathcal{S}$ such that $X \backslash X'$ is closed,

$\dim X \backslash X' < \dim X$, and the restriction of F to X' is continuous. In particular, if $f : X \to Y$ is an $\mathcal{S}$-function, then it is continuous on the complement of a closed, lower dimensional $\mathcal{S}$-set $X' \subset X$.

GENERIC TRIVIALITY: Let $f : X \to Y$ be a continuous function belonging to $\mathcal{S}$. Then there is a subset $Y' \subset Y$ belonging to Y such that $Y \backslash Y'$ is closed, Y' has a finite number of connected components, and for each such connected component Y_i of Y', there is a set Z_i belonging to $\mathcal{S}$ and a homeomorphism h_i belonging to $\mathcal{S}$ which maps $Y_i \times Z_i$ onto $f^{-1}(Y_i)$ and has the property that $f(h_i(y,z)) = y$ for all y, z.

As we shall see, Generic Triviality serves both as a version of Sard's Theorem and as a version of the Implicit Function Theorem, and we shall make extensive use of it. It is useful to understand the differences, however. Given smooth manifolds X, Y, and a smooth function $f : X \to Y$, Sard's Theorem guarantees that most points $y \in Y$ are regular values of f (i.e., that the differential df has rank equal to the dimension of Y at every point of $f^{-1}(y)$). The set Y' of exceptional (irregular) values is a set of measure zero.[3] If X is compact, the set of regular values is open and for every regular value $y \in Y \backslash Y'$ there is a neighborhood W of Y, a manifold Z, and a smooth homeomorphism $h : W \times Z \to f^{-1}(W)$ such that $f(h(w,z)) = w$. Generic triviality allows us to obtain the same product structure, in the complement of an exceptional set Y', when X and Y are $\mathcal{S}$-sets and $f : X \to Y$ is an $\mathcal{S}$-function, but there are some important differences. The first of these is that we do not need to insist that X be compact. (In the smooth case, compactness of X is required to guarantee that the set of regular values be open. If X is not compact the exceptional set Y' could be dense, in which case no open subset of Y will admit a product structure.) A bit more subtly, note that in the case of $\mathcal{S}$-sets and $\mathcal{S}$-functions, there is a *finite* covering of the complement of the exceptional set by neighborhoods whose inverse images are products; this need not be possible in the smooth case. Most importantly, in the case of $\mathcal{S}$-sets and $\mathcal{S}$-functions it will be possible to say a great deal about the structure of the exceptional set Y' and its inverse image $f^{-1}(Y')$. Indeed, Y' is an $\mathcal{S}$-set and of lower dimension than Y, $f^{-1}(Y')$ is also an $\mathcal{S}$-set, the restriction of f to $f^{-1}(Y')$ is an $\mathcal{S}$-function, and the entire apparatus can then be applied to the mapping $f : f^{-1}(Y') \to Y'$. In the smooth case, by contrast, Y' will be a closed set of measure zero, but otherwise may be entirely arbitrary. In particular, both Y' and $f^{-1}(Y')$ may fail to be manifolds.

3 Preferences and Demand

For the rest of the paper, we fix an O-minimal Tarski system $\mathcal{S}$ that contains addition and multiplication. (Recall that the two known examples of such systems are the semi-algebraic sets and the finitely sub-analytic sets.) We consider a consumer, characterized by a consumption set $X \subset \mathbf{R}^{\mathbf{L}}$ and a preference order $\succeq$. We assume that X is closed and convex, and that the preference order is complete, transitive and continuous. We show first that, if the consumption set and (the graph of) the preference order belongs to $\mathcal{S}$, then the preference order is representable by a utility

[3] The precise degree of smoothness required depends upon the dimensions of X and Y.

function belonging to $\mathcal{S}$.

Theorem 1 *If the consumption set X and (the graph of) the preference order $\succeq$ belong to $\mathcal{S}$, then $\succeq$ is representable by a continuous utility function belonging to $\mathcal{S}$.*

Proof: Fix an arbitrary reference point $x \in X$, and write $X' = \{y : y \succeq x\}$ and $X'' = X \backslash X'$. Both of these sets belong to $\mathcal{S}$. Now define a utility function $u(\cdot)$ by

$$u(y) = \begin{cases} +\inf\{\|z - x\| : z \succeq y\} & \text{for } y \in X', \\ -\inf\{\|z - x\| : y \succeq z\} & \text{for } y \in X''. \end{cases}$$

A standard and completely straightforward argument shows that u is lower semicontinuous and represents the preference ordering $\succeq$. The graph of u is:

$$\begin{aligned} \operatorname{Graph} u = \{(y,r) : y \in X' \text{ and } r > 0 \text{ and not}(\exists z(z,y) \in \operatorname{Graph} \succeq \text{ and } \|z - x\| < r) \\ \text{and } (\forall \epsilon > 0\, \exists z'\, (z',y) \in \operatorname{Graph} \succeq \text{ and } \|z - x\| < r + \epsilon)\} \\ \cup \{(y,r) : y \in X'' \text{ and } r < 0 \text{ and not } (\exists z\, (z,y) \in \operatorname{Graph} \succeq \text{ and } \|z - x\| < -r) \\ \text{and } (\forall \epsilon > 0\, \exists z'\, (z',y) \in \operatorname{Graph} \succeq \text{ and } \|z' - x\| < -r + \epsilon)\} \end{aligned}$$

Since O-minimal Tarski systems are closed under definability, we conclude that Graph u belongs to $\mathcal{S}$.

We now have an $\mathcal{S}$-function u which represents $\succeq$, but it may not be continuous. Next we modify it to make it continuous. Since u is an $\mathcal{S}$-function, its range must be a finite union of intervals and single points (Property 7). Using standard arguments it is easily seen that the range contains no isolated points, and is the union of a finite number of intervals such that each bounded interval is open from below and closed from above, and is such that the points of discontinuity are precisely those in the inverse image of the upper bound for each bounded interval. In other words, the range is

$$(a_1, b_1] \cup (a_2, b_2] \cdots \cup (a_{n-1}, b_{n-1}] \cup (a_n, \infty)$$

where each $b_i < a_{i+1}$ and $a_n < \infty$ if and only if $\succeq$ is globally non-satiated. Define

$$v(x) = \begin{cases} u(x) & \text{if } x \in u^{-1}(a_1, b_1], \\ u(x) - a_i & \text{if } x \in u^{-1}(a_i, b_i] \text{ for } i = 2, \ldots, n. \end{cases}$$

Each of the sets $u^{-1}(a_i, b_i]$ is an $\mathcal{S}$-set, and each of the functions $u(x) - a_i$ is an $\mathcal{S}$-function, so the set

$$\begin{aligned} \operatorname{Graph} v = \{\operatorname{Graph} u \cap (u^{-1}(a_1, b_1] \times \mathbf{R})\} \bigcup \\ \cup_{i=2}^{n} \Big(\{(x,r) : \exists s(r = s - a_i) \text{ and}((x,s) \in \operatorname{Graph} u)\} \cap \{u^{-1}(a_i, b_i] \times \mathbf{R}\}\Big) \end{aligned}$$

is in $\mathcal{S}$. The function v is a continuous utility representation for the preference order $\succeq$. □

It is convenient to collect here the following result, which assures us that the demand correspondence also belongs to $\mathcal{S}$ and has the "correct" dimension. The reader will recognize this result as the analog in our setting of a well-known result of Debreu for smooth preferences. Its proof employs a duality idea that seems novel. View demand as depending on price and income. For each price/income pair, we identify the utility level the consumer achieves, and then make use of some facts about the relationship between prices and those consumption bundles which minimize expenditure at the given price among all bundles achieving that level of utility. We make no assumptions about curvature or smoothness. In particular, we allow for the possibility that indifference surfaces have flats and kinks. (To prove the corresponding result for the case of smooth preferences, one would check for regularity of the value 0 for the mapping which describes the first order conditions characterizing demand. Of course, there would be no way to verify the regularity condition unless the mapping is smooth, ruling out flats and kinks.)

Write Δ for the simplex of non-negative prices in $\mathbf{R^L}$ which sum to 1. Demand depends on income y and prices p. We allow for some prices to equal 0, even though demand may be undefined at such prices. Let $d : \Delta \times \mathbf{R}_+ \to X$ denote the demand correspondence with arguments price and income, and define the demand correspondence $D : \Delta \times \mathbf{R}^\mathbf{L}_+ \to X$, with arguments price and endowment, by the equation $D(p,e) = d(p, p \cdot e)$. The conclusion of the Theorem states that the dimension of the graph of d is less than or equal to L, and that of the graph of D is less than or equal to $2L - 1$. The smooth-preference version of this Theorem says that the dimensions are *equal* to L and $2L-1$, respectively. We only have inequalities because our hypotheses are insufficient to guarantee the existence of demand for all price-income pairs.

Theorem 2 *If the consumption set X and preference order $\succeq$ belong to $\mathcal{S}$, then the graph of the demand correspondences $d : \mathbf{R}_+ \times \Delta \to X$ and $D : \Delta \times \mathbf{R}^\mathbf{L}_+ \to X$ generated by $\succeq$ belongs to $\mathcal{S}$,* $\dim \operatorname{Graph} d \leq L$ *and* $\dim \operatorname{Graph} D \leq (L-1) + L$.

The duality argument is facilitated by the following result on convex sets and their supports. Let $C \subset \mathbf{R^n}$ be a closed, convex set, and let $\rho : \partial C \to \mathbf{R^n}$ denote correspondence that assigns to each $x \in \partial C$ its supporting hyperplanes:

$$\rho(x) = \{p \ : \ p \cdot x \leq p \cdot z \quad \text{for all} \quad z \in C\}.$$

Lemma 1 *The map $(x,p) \mapsto x - p$ is one-to-one on the domain* $\operatorname{Graph} \rho$.

Proof of Lemma 1: Suppose that (x,p) and (y,q) are two points in $\operatorname{Graph} \rho$, and that $x - p = y - q$. Then

$$\begin{aligned} p \cdot x - p \cdot p &= p \cdot y - p \cdot q, \\ q \cdot y - q \cdot q &= q \cdot x - q \cdot p. \end{aligned}$$

Rearranging,

$$\begin{aligned} -p \cdot p + p \cdot q &= p \cdot (y - x) \geq 0, \\ -q \cdot q + q \cdot p &= q \cdot (x - y) \geq 0. \end{aligned}$$

Adding these two inequalities gives $(p-q) \cdot (p-q) \leq 0$, so $p = q$ and therefore $x = y$. □

Proof of Theorem 2: The first assertion, that Graph d is an $\mathcal{S}$-set, is again a simple exercise. The graph of the demand correspondence d is:

$$\begin{aligned}\text{Graph}\, d = \{(p, y, x) \ : \ & y \in \mathbf{R}_+ \text{ and } x \in X \text{ and } p \cdot x \le y \\ & \text{and not } (\exists z \ z \in Z \text{ and } p \cdot z \le y \text{ and } z \succ x)\}\end{aligned}$$

Since Graph d is definable from $\mathcal{S}$, it is an $\mathcal{S}$-set.[4]

The calculation of the dimension of the graph of demand relies upon a duality argument. We will apply Lemma 1 to "at least as good as" sets. Let $\succeq x = \{y : (y, x) \in \succeq\}$.

First take prices to be in all of $\mathbf{R}^{\mathbf{L}}_+ \backslash \{0\}$, and call the demand correspondence $\hat{d}$. The demand correspondence d is the restriction of $\hat{d}$ to the domain $\Delta \times \mathbf{R}_+$. Let $u : \mathbf{R}^{\mathbf{L}} \to \mathbf{R}$ be an $\mathcal{S}$-utility representation of the consumer's preferences $\succeq$.

It is a consequence of Lemma 1 that the $\mathcal{S}$-function

$$\phi : (p, y, d) \mapsto (d - p, u(d))$$

is one-to-one from Graph $\hat{d}$ to $\mathbf{R}^{\mathbf{L+1}}$. To see this, suppose that $\phi(p, y, d) = \phi(p', y', d')$. Then $u(d) = u(d')$. Since preferences are continuous and locally non-satiated, it follows that if z is demanded at any price q, then z is on the boundary of the closed set $\succeq x$ and q supports $\succeq x$ at z. Since $\succeq$ is locally non-satiated, d and d' are both on the boundary of $\succeq d$. Since p and p' support $\succeq d$ at d and d', respectively, it follows from the equality of $d - p$ and $d' - p'$ and Lemma 1 that $p = p'$ and $d = d'$.

Local non-satiation of $\succeq$ implies that $y = p \cdot d$. Since Graph $\hat{d}$ is the image of the $\mathcal{S}$-function ϕ^{-1}, and since $\mathcal{S}$-functions do not increase dimension, dim Graph $\hat{d} = \dim \phi(\text{Graph}\, \hat{d}) \le L + 1$.

Let $\|p\|$ denote the sum $\sum_l p_l$, and observe that the map $\pi : \mathbf{R}^{\mathbf{L}}_+ \times \mathbf{R} \times X \to \Delta \times \mathbf{R} \times X$ defined by $\pi(p, y, x) = ((1/\|p\|)p, (1/\|p\|)y, x, \|p\|)$ is an $\mathcal{S}$-isomorphism from Graph $\hat{d}$ to Graph $d \times \mathbf{R}_{++}$. Thus dim Graph $d + 1 \le L + 1$, so Graph d has dimension at most L.

Finally, let π_L denote the projection of vectors in $\mathbf{R}^{\mathbf{L}}$ onto their first $L - 1$ coordinates. The map $\phi : \Delta \times \mathbf{R}^{\mathbf{L}}_+ \times X \to \Delta \times \mathbf{R}_+ \times X$ given by $\psi(p, e, x) = (p, p \cdot e, x, \pi_L(e_1))$ defines an $\mathcal{S}$-isomorphism between Graph D and Graph $d \times \mathbf{R}^{\mathbf{L-1}}_+$. Thus Graph D has dimension no greater than $L + L - 1$. □

Having identified new classes of preferences, we ask which of the common specifications of preferences are included and which are not. Of course, preferences represented by piecewise linear utility functions are semi-algebraic. More generally, preferences represented by piecewise polynomial (spline) utility functions are semi-algebraic, as are preferences represented by Cobb-Douglas and CES utility functions with rational exponents (eg., $x^{1/4}y^{3/4}$, $x^{1/4} + y^{3/4}$). For irrational exponents, logarithmic, or exponential utilities the situation is slightly more complicated, because the logarithm and exponential function are not finitely sub-analytic on the domain

[4]Note that, even if preferences are piecewise linear, the definition of demand involves quadratic terms. Hence demand may fail to be piecewise linear even when preferences are.

$(0, \infty)$. However, a slight twist will frequently land us back in the finitely sub-analytic class. Consider for example an economy in which consumption sets are the positive orthant and utility functions are Cobb-Douglas. Let $K \subset \mathbf{R}_{++}^{\mathbf{NL}}$ be a compact set, and restrict attention to endowments lying in K. There is a compact set $K^* \subset \mathbf{R}_{++}^{\mathbf{NL}}$ that is a product of intervals (and hence polyhedral), and contains all feasible, individually rational allocations. The economy we obtain by restricting consumption sets to K^* is then finitely sub-analytic, and its competitive equilibria coincide with the competitive equilibria of our original economy.

We are also compelled to ask whether the requirement that preferences belong to some O-minimal Tarski system containing additional and multiplication (eg. the finitely sub-analytic sets or the semi-algebraic sets) places any restrictions on observable data; the answer is that it does not. Indeed, the now classic constructions of Afriat (1967) and Diewert (1973) construct piecewise linear utility functions that rationalize any finite number of demand observations satisfying the Strong Axiom of Revealed Preferences. Matzkin and Richter (1991) construct piecewise polynomial (hence semi-algebraic) utility functions that rationalize (in a stronger sense) any finite number of demand observations satisfying SARP.

4 Local Determinacy of Equilibrium

In this Section we present our main result, the local finiteness and determinacy of equilibrium prices when consumption sets and preferences belong to a given O-minimal Tarski system $\mathcal{S}$ containing the graphs of addition and multiplication. We shall state and prove our result first for strictly convex preferences (which generate demand functions), in order to compare our technical apparatus to that used for smooth economies, and then for general prefrences (which generate demand correspondences).

We consider exchange economies with L commodities and N consumers, having consumption sets X_n and preferences $\succeq_n$. Throughout, we assume that consumption sets are closed and convex, that preferences are complete, transitive, continuous, monotone and locally non-satiated, and that consumption sets and preferences belong to a fixed O-minimal Tarski system $\mathcal{S}$ containing the semi-algebraic sets. We view consumption sets and preferences as fixed an endowments as variable. Write e_n for the endowment of consumer n, and e_{-1} for the vector of endowments of consumers other than consumer 1. Write $\mathcal{E} = \prod X_n$ for the space of endowments, and $\mathcal{E}_n$ for the space of endowment vectors for all consumers other than consumer 1. The space of prices is the non-negative unit simplex $\Delta \subset \mathbf{R}_{+}^{\mathbf{L}}$.[5]

Theorem 3 *If preferences are strictly convex, then there is a closed, lower-dimensional $\mathcal{S}$-set $E_0 \subset \mathcal{E}$ such that, if $e \in \mathcal{E} \backslash E_0$, then the set of equilibrium prices is finite. Moreover, the restriction to $e \in \mathcal{E} \backslash E_0$ of the equilibrium price correspondence is continuous.*

[5]Since preferences are not required to be strictly monotone, we allow for the possibility that some equilibrium prices are 0. As in Section 3, we allow for the possibility that demand is undefined at some prices. Of course, such prices cannot be equilibrium prices, so this causes no difficulty.

Proof: The proof follows Debreu (1970). Define the map $F : \Delta \times \mathbf{R}_+ \times \mathcal{E}_n \to \mathbf{R}^{\mathbf{LN}}$ by:

$$F(p, y, e_{-1}) = \begin{pmatrix} d_1(p, y) + \sum_{n=2}^{N} d_n(p, p \cdot e_n) - e_n \\ e_2 \\ \vdots \\ e_N \end{pmatrix}.$$

Given our assumptions, for all $e \in \mathcal{E}$, the set $F^{-1}(e)$ is non-empty, and its projection onto Δ is the set of equilibrium prices when endowments are e. According to generic triviality, there is a closed, lower-dimensional $\mathcal{S}$-set $E_0 \subset E$ such that, for each of the finite number of connected components E_i of $\mathcal{E} \backslash E_0$, there is an $\mathcal{S}$-set A_i and an $\mathcal{S}$-homeomorphism $h : E_i \times A_i \to F^{-1}(A_i)$ such that $F(h(e, a)) = e$. Thus, for all $e \in E_i$, $\dim F^{-1}(e) = \dim A_i$. Now we count dimensions. Each E_i has dimension LN, and $E_i \times A_i$ is homeomorphic to a set of dimension LN, so $\dim A_i = 0$. Hence $F^{-1}(e)$ is 0-dimensional. Since it is an $\mathcal{S}$-set, it is finite. Since $F^{-1}(A_i)$ is a product, the restriction of the equilibrium price correspondence to each A_i (and hence to $\mathcal{E} \backslash E_0$) is continuous. □

Note how Generic Triviality simultaneously plays the roles of Sard's Theorem and of the Implicit Function Theorem: it tells us that almost all values are "regular" and gives us a device for counting dimensions. Notice, though, that unlike the Implicit Function Theorem, we have no criterion for identifying regular values.

Rader's (1972, 1973) result on the generic determinateness of equilibrium for absolutely continuous demand applies to semi-algebraic and finitely sub-analytic exchange economies. Semi-algebraic and finitely sub-analytic functions are continuously differentiable almost everywhere and satisfy his Condition N, that the image of a null set is null. According to Rader, equilibrium is therefore locally determined for almost all endowment allocations. Our result differs in two respects from that obtained through the application of Rader's Theorem. Our additional hypotheses allow us to say more about the exceptional set of endowments (closed and lower dimensional) and more about the equilibrium correspondence (generic continuity).

In the absence of strict convexity of preferences, demand is a correspondence, rather than a function. In this case, F will also be a correspondence, rather than a function, and we work with inverse images of appropriate projections of its graphs. The proof uses the same map and counts dimensions in much the same way the proof of the preceding Theorem does, but the argument requires that the graph of the map be cut up in such a way that the dimension of the demand sets and their supporting price sets can be controlled.

Theorem 4 *If preferences are convex, then there is a closed, lower-dimensional $\mathcal{S}$-set $E_0 \subset \mathcal{E}$ such that, if $e \in \mathcal{E} \backslash E_0$, then the set of equilibrium prices is finite. Moreover, the restriction to $\mathcal{E} \backslash E_0$ of the equilibrium price correspondence is continuous.*

Proof: Define the $\mathcal{S}$-set $H \subset \Delta \times \mathbf{R}_{++} \times \mathbf{R}^{\mathbf{L(N-1)}} \times \mathbf{R}^{\mathbf{LN}}$ such that:

$$H = \{(p, y, e_{-1}, d_1, \ldots, d_N) \ : \ d_1 \in D_1(p, y), d_n \in D_n(p, p \cdot e_n) \quad \text{for} \quad n = 2, \ldots, N\}$$

where D_n is consumer n's demand (correspondence) with arguments price and income. Let ϕ denote the map from H to $\mathbf{R^L}$ such that $\phi(h) = (d_1 + \sum_{n=2}^N d_n - e_n, e_{-1})$. The function ϕ on H is the analog to F in the previous Theorem: $(p, y, e_{-1}, d_1, \ldots, d_N)$ is in the inverse image of (z, e_{-1}) if and only if p is an equilibrium price for the economy with endowment allocation (z, e_{-1}). For a given (p, y, e_{-1}), let $y_1 = y$ and $y_n = p \cdot e_n$ for $n = 2, \ldots, N$. Let $k = (k_1, \ldots, k_N)$ be a vector of integers, and define $H_k \subset H$ to be the subset of H where consumer 1's demand has dimension k_1, and so forth:

$$H_k = \{h \in H \ : \ \dim D_1(p, y) = k_1, \ldots, \dim D_N(p, y_n) = k_N\}.$$

This set will be empty unless all $k_i \le L - 1$. Each H_k can be defined by linear inequalities, and so each H_k is an $\mathcal{S}$-set. The sets H_k partition H.

Next, let $\succeq d_n$ denote the consumption bundles consumer n finds at least as good as d_n. Define

$$H_{k,m} = \{h \in H_k \ : \ \dim\{p \ : \ p \text{ supports each } \succeq d_n\} = m\},$$

where $m \le L - 1$. All the $H_{k,m}$ partition H.

If the projection of the set of endowments of a particular $H_{k,m}$ has dimension less than L, the set of economies having some equilibria described by H_k is lower dimensional, and H_k can be ignored. Assume, then, that for each consumer $n = 2, \ldots, N$ the projection of H_k onto his endowments has full dimension L. Then

$$\dim H_{k,m} = m + a + L(N-1) + \sum_{n=1}^{N} k_n,$$

where a, the dimension of the projection of $H_{k,m}$ onto consumer 1's income, is either 0 or 1.

Define ϕ on $H_{k,m}$ such that

$$\phi(h) = (\sum_{n=1}^{N} d_n - \sum_{n=2}^{N} e_n, e_{-1}).$$

The price vector p is an equilibrium price for $e = (e_1, \ldots, e_N)$ if and only if there is a y and $d = (d_1, \ldots, d_N)$ such that (p, y, e_{-1}, d) is in the inverse image of e. We can suppose that the range of ϕ has dimension NL. Applying generic triviality to ϕ, there is a closed, lower dimensional set E_0 of endowment allocations such that, on each of the finite number of connected components E_i of $\mathcal{E} \backslash E_0$, $\phi^{-1}(e)$ is an $\mathcal{S}$-set of dimension $m + a - L + \sum_{n=1}^N k_n$.

Now h is in $\phi^{-1}(e)$ if and only if endowments of consumers 2 through N are correct and there are $d_n \in D_n(p, y_n)$ such that $\sum_{n=1}^N d_n = \sum_{n=1}^N e_n$. The set $\sum_{n=1}^N D_n(p, y_n)$ has dimension no more than $L - m$, since if $d \in \sum_{n=1}^N D_n(p, y_n)$, then $p \cdot d - \sum_{n=1}^N y_n = 0$ for an m-dimensional set of prices p. Thus the set of demands summing to d has codimension $L - m$, in other words, dimension $m + a - L + \sum_{n=1}^N k_n$. It follows from a routine generic triviality argument that, since the dimension of $H_{k,m}$ is the same as the dimension of each "fiber" over a price p in the projection of $H_{k,m}$ onto Δ, the dimension of this projection must be 0. Continuity follows as in the proof of the previous Theorem. □

The foregoing results extend the local finiteness results of Debreu to an important class of preferences which allows for kinks and flats. We have chosen to parameterize economies by endowments, rather than by endowment distributions, and for good reason: the corresponding results are not generally true in that setting. Consider, for example, an Edgeworth box economy. If consumers have identical Leontief utility functions $u_i(x_i, y_i) = \min(x_i, y_i)$, and the box is square (i.e., the aggregate endowments of the two goods are equal) then any individually rational diagonal allocation, which is to say any individually rational Pareto optimal allocation, can be supported as an equilibrium (and different allocations will be supported by different prices). Hence equilibrium prices will be indeterminate for every endowment distribution. Of course, for most endowments the box will not be square, and determinacy will be restored.

References

AFRIAT, S.N. (1967): "The Construction of Utility Functions from Expenditure Data," *International Economic Review,* 8, 67–77.

BLUME, L. AND W.R. ZAME (1989): "The Algebraic Geometry of Perfect and Sequential Equilibrium," CAE Working Paper #89-19, Cornell University.

BOCHNAK, J., M. COSTE AND M-F. ROY (1987): *Géométrie Algébrique Réelle.* Berlin: Springer-Verlag.

CHANG AND KEISLER, J. (1973): *Model Theory.* Amsterdam: North Holland.

DIEWERT, ERWIN (1973): "Afriat and Revealed Preference Theory," *Review of Economic Studies,* 40, 419–425.

VAN DEN DRIES, LOU (1986): "A Generalization of the Tarski-Seidenberg Theorem, and some Nondefinability Results," *Bulletin of the American Mathematical Society,* 15, 189–193.

GABRIELOV, A. (1968): "Projections of Semi-Analytic Sets," *Functional Anal. App.,* 2, 282–291.

LOJASIEWICZ, S. (1965): "Ensembles Semi-Analytiques," mimeographed notes, Inst. Hautes Études Sci.

MATZKIN, ROSA L. AND MARCEL K. RICHTER (1991): "Testing Strictly Concave Rationality," *Journal of Economic Theory,* 53, 287–303.

PASCOA, MARIO AND SERGIO WERLANG (1989): "Local Concavifiability of Preferences and Determinacy of Equilibrium," CARESS Working Paper #89-19, University of Pennsylvania.

RADER, J. TROUT (1972): *Theory of General Economic Equilibrium.* New York: Academic Press.

——————— (1973): "Nice Demand Functions," *Econometrica,* 41, 913–936.

——————— (1979): "Nice Demand Functions II," *Journal of Mathematical Economics,* 6, 253–262.

SCHANUEL, S., L. SIMON AND W. ZAME (forthcoming): "The algebraic geometry of games and the tracing procedure," in *Methods, Morals and Markets.* Ed. R. Selten, Berlin: Springer-Verlag.

Intra-Industry Trade, Factor Proportions, and Aggregation*

JOHN S. CHIPMAN
University of Minnesota

Introduction

In the literature on the empirical explanation of trade flows, it appears to have become a universally accepted dictum that the existence of so-called "intra-industry trade," i.e., trade between countries of products within the same industrial category, is *prima facie* evidence of the existence of economies of scale or monopolistic competition, or both, and in particular is incompatible with the "factor-proportions theory," by which is meant the theory developed by Heckscher and Ohlin according to which trade flows among countries are explained by differences in their relative factor endowments, it being assumed that production functions among countries are the same.

In this paper I shall argue, both on empirical and theoretical grounds, that there is nothing in the empirical observations of international trade statistics that cannot be explained perfectly easily by the "Heckscher-Ohlin theory" as formulated by Lerner (1952) and Samuelson (1953). (I shall refer to this as the HOLS model.) I do not wish to contend that alternatives to this theory are not worth exploring and developing; but if so, the reason for doing so should not be that the more conventional theory is unable to explain the observed facts. In the last analysis, that theory should be accepted which is able to explain them best; but before this can be done, a clearer understanding is needed of the extent to which the conventional theory is or is not able to do so. The belief that it is not able to do so is, in my opinion, based on a misunderstanding of the nature of that theory and a lack of appreciation of its rich potentialities.

In Section 1, I examine some empirical evidence which points to the conclusion that if commodity classification systems were to carry the disaggregation process sufficiently far, two-way trade could be expected to disappear from international trade statistics. In Section 2, I consider the pure theory of international trade in

*Presented at the Midwest International Economic Conference, East Lansing, 26 October 1985. An abridged version appeared in German (Chipman, 1986). Research was supported by the Riksbankens Jubileumsfond and National Science Foundation grant SES-8607652. Especial thanks are due to Joan R. Rodgers for criticisms, suggestions, and assistance, as well as to Elizabeth Dolan for help in producing the final manuscript including tables and charts.

the textbook case of two countries, two commodities, and two factors, and come to the conclusion that if (as is alleged to be the case in the literature on intra-industry trade) production processes are very similar as between the two commodities and factor endowments are very similar as between the two countries, it is possible for each country to export up to 50 percent of the output of its export good, the percentage *increasing* as the production processes become more similar. Finally, in Section 3, I consider the frequently repeated assertion that, when there are three or more countries, one would under the "factor-proportions theory" expect to find less trade between countries with similar than with dissimilar endowments; I find instead that, assuming identical and homothetic preferences within and across countries, if the two countries with similar endowments export goods with similar production processes, they may be expected to trade more with each other than with the third country, this effect being further accentuated when (1) there is a strong world preference for the goods which they export, or (2) when their absolute endowment levels are greater than those of the third country, or both.

1 Some empirical evidence

Grubel and Lloyd (1975, pp. 86–9) distinguish between two types of intra-industry trade: trade in goods which are close substitutes in use but produced by different production processes (e.g., wood and metal furniture); and trade in goods which are not close substitutes in use but are produced by very similar or identical production processes (e.g., steel bars and sheets). They also consider a third type of goods, such as automobiles, which are close substitutes and are also produced by similar processes. They allow that the first type of intra-industry trade is compatible with the HOLS model, and then introduce a second issue, (p. 87): "For this group of goods the intra-industry trade phenomenon is simply the result of statistical aggregation." It is implied but not stated explicitly that intra-industry trade in the other two cases is not a result of statistical aggregation.

Let me now take up this second issue. If it is granted in all the above cases that the goods being traded are physically distinct (and indeed, Grubel and Lloyd themselves emphasize that this is so, pp. 125–6), then a fine enough classification system will recognize the distinction. The fact that trade statistics using existing, cruder classification systems exhibit two-way trade within categories is as much a result of statistical aggregation in the case of one kind of good as in the other; for why should our description (as opposed to explanation) of an empirical phenomenon depend on our theories about it? The only question, then, is how much disaggregation would be necessary in order for two-way trade to disappear from international trade statistics. In this section I try to form a rough estimate, based on data presented by Grubel & Lloyd (1975) and Gray (1978); and on a new set of data for Sweden.

1.1 The Grubel-Lloyd data

Grubel and Lloyd (1975, p. 50) have presented a table showing the percentage of Australian intra-industry trade in its total trade with various countries and country groups, at various SITC digit levels, using a 7-digit refinement of the 5-digit Stan-

Table 1a

Australian Intra-Industry Trade, 1968–69
as a Proportion of Total Trade, with Major Trading Partners

Country or Country Group	SITC level of disaggregation				
	1	2	3	5	7
United States	0.397	0.250	0.146	0.100	0.032
United Kingdom	0.315	0.125	0.077	0.042	0.013
Japan	0.180	0.106	0.048	0.022	0.002
European Community	0.153	0.063	0.049	0.032	0.010
Canada	0.386	0.275	0.176	0.072	0.008
New Zealand	0.798	0.475	0.305	0.195	0.044
Hong Kong	0.505	0.173	0.133	0.065	0.014
India	0.495	0.095	0.055	0.018	0.002
South Africa	0.654	0.303	0.163	0.073	0.007
Southeast Asia	0.174	0.098	0.087	0.044	0.015
Rest of the world	0.520	0.270	0.189	0.106	0.031
All countries	0.429	0.259	0.202	0.149	0.062

dard International Trade classification. For Australia's leading trading partners in 1968–69 (the European Community consisted then of West Germany, France, Italy, Belgium and the Netherlands) their figures for the proportion of intra-industry trade in total trade (adjusted for global bilateral trade imbalances) are reproduced in Table 1a, ranked in order of decreasing value of exports to Australia in 1968–69 (except for the last two groups).

These figures show a very clear downward trend. It is tempting, therefore, to extrapolate. We do not, of course, possess a theory of how compilers of commodity classification systems decide to associate the number of digits in the classification code with the degree of fineness of the disaggregation. The best we can do at this stage is to fit a reasonably-shaped curve. Accordingly, I have chosen to fit the reciprocal power function[1]

$$P = 1 - aS^b \tag{1.1}$$

where S is the SITC level of disaggregation and P is the proportion of intra-industry trade in total trade. This function has the desirable property that at the null (0-digit) level of disaggregation, when the index has been adjusted for trade imbalances, 100% of trade is intra-industry trade. The curve (1.1) has been fitted to the data of Table 1a by the Fletcher-Powell (1963) method.[2] With two parameters and five data points, there are only three degrees of freedom; but given the limitations of data, presumably this is the best one can do. Table 1b gives the parameter estimates and

[1]I had originally chosen the form $P = a + bS^c$ for both intra- and inter-industry trade, but in the latter case this resulted in highly correlated estimates of a and b. The forms (1.1) and (1.2) were suggested by Joan Rodgers.

[2]Calculations were performed on the HP-71B handheld computer, equipped with mathematics and curve-fitting modules and additional 100K RAM.

the coefficient of determination (R^2), where $1 - R^2$ is defined as in Theil (1971, p. 164) as the ratio of the sum of squares of the residuals $P - 1 + aS^b$ to the sum of squares of the observations on the dependent variable P. The three panels of Figure 1 show the curves and the corresponding data points.

Table 1b
Australian Intra-Industry Trade, 1968–69

Parameters (a, b) of the reciprocal power function, coefficient of determination (R^2), and zero cutoff point (S^*), for the data of Table 1a.

Country or Country Group	a	b	R^2	S^*
United States	0.632151	0.226733	0.987579	7.56
United Kingdom	0.738451	0.164275	0.938998	6.33
Japan	0.832555	0.099745	0.981524	6.28
European Community	0.867818	0.072194	0.958070	7.13
Canada	0.617048	0.248759	0.998534	6.96
New Zealand	0.318901	0.581939	0.974533	7.13
Hong Kong	0.601277	0.277028	0.916313	6.27
India	0.651323	0.254798	0.806576	5.38
South Africa	0.472589	0.411547	0.939699	6.18
Southeast Asia	0.834666	0.085760	0.992714	8.23
Rest of the world	0.547025	0.308483	0.974598	7.07
All countries	0.603694	0.228339	0.990105	9.12

The last column of Table 1b provides the solution S^* of equation (1.1) for $P = 0$. Thus, for all of the individual countries and groups, the curves predict that intra-industry trade will cease to be observed if the SITC is refined to the ninth level of disaggregation; and for all countries together, to the tenth level.

Taken as a whole, these results support the hypothesis that intra-industry trade is a statistical phenomenon in the sense that it would cease to be observed if sufficiently disaggregated data were obtained, and that this would be achieved with a not unreasonable degree of refinement of existing classification systems.

1.2 Gray's data

The second data set I consider is taken from a study by Gray (1978) of West German and French trade with specified partners, in 1-digit SITC categories at each of the five SITC levels of aggregation.

In the case of West German trade, only for trade with Belgium and France—in SITC categories 6 (manufactured goods classified chiefly by material) and 7 (machinery and transport equipment)—are data furnished by Gray for all five levels of aggregation (cf. Gray, 1978, p. 105). These are therefore the only series from his table that I have attempted to analyze. The measure of intra-industry trade used

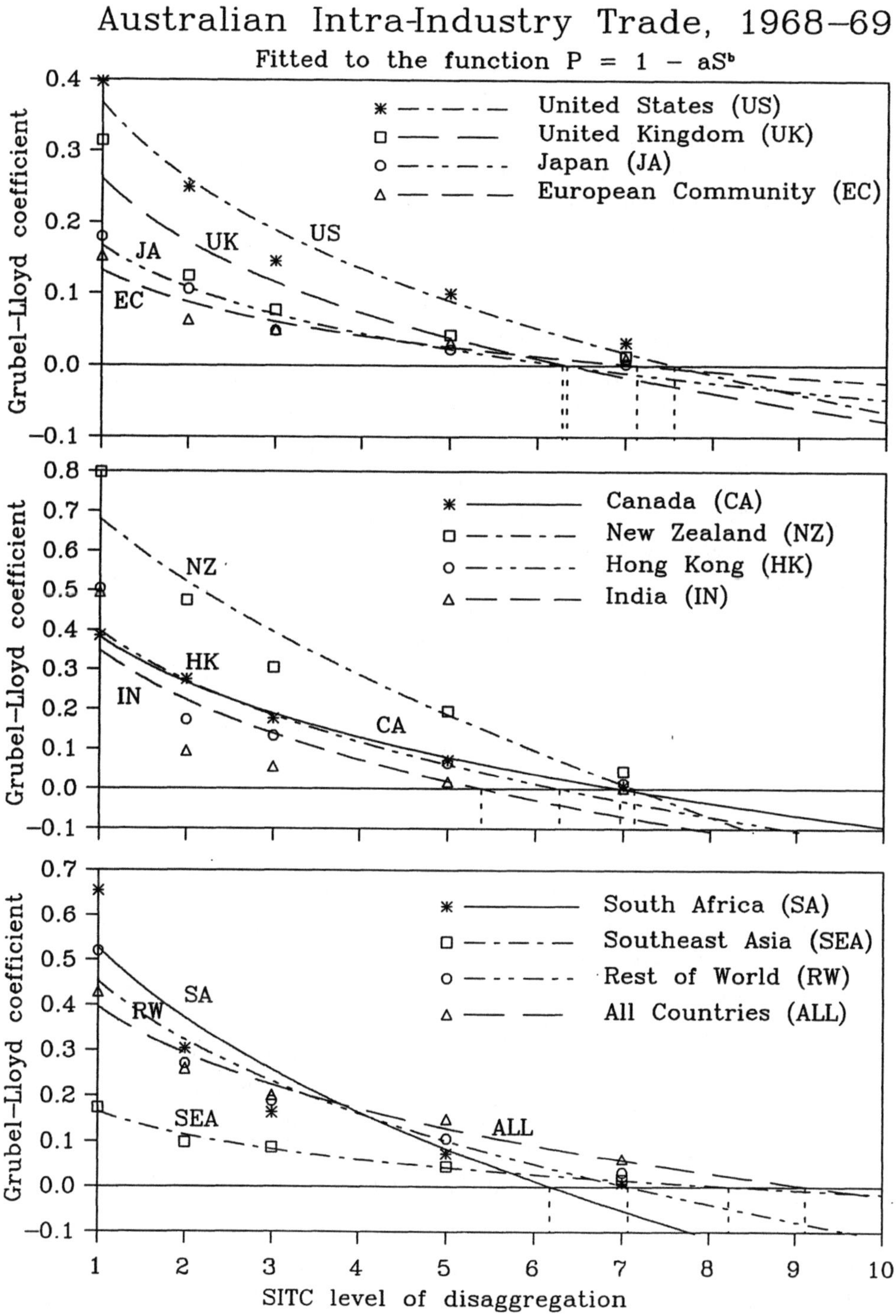
Australian Intra-Industry Trade, 1968–69
Fitted to the function P = 1 – aS^b
United States (US)
United Kingdom (UK)
Japan (JA)
European Community (EC)
US
UK
JA
EC
Canada (CA)
New Zealand (NZ)
Hong Kong (HK)
India (IN)
NZ
HK
IN
CA
South Africa (SA)
Southeast Asia (SEA)
Rest of World (RW)
All Countries (ALL)
SA
RW
SEA
ALL
Grubel–Lloyd coefficient
SITC level of disaggregation

Figure 1

by Gray is the Balassa index (cf. Balassa, 1966), defined as

$$B = \frac{1}{n}\sum_{i=1}^{n}\frac{|X_i - M_i|}{X_i + M_i}, \tag{1.2}$$

where X_i andM_i are the values of exports and imports in category i, and n is the number of categories at the given level of aggregation. The index actually measures *inter-* rather than *intra-*industry trade; it has the value zero when all trade is intra-industry trade, and unity when none of it is.

Table 2a

West German Inter-Industry Trade, 1973

Balassa coefficient for trade with Belgium & France in two SITC categories, with number of categories at each SITC level

Country	SITC level of disaggregation				
	1	2	3	4	5
1. SITC 6—manufactured goods classified chiefly by material					
Number of categories	*1*	*8*	*50*	*53*	*26*
Belgium	0.31	0.33	0.40	0.49	0.58
France	0.09	0.17	0.32	0.42	0.48
2. SITC 7—machinery and transport equipment					
Number of categories	*1*	*3*	*18*	*46*	*52*
Belgium	0.38	0.41	0.53	0.57	0.61
France	0.18	0.27	0.36	0.50	0.52

Table 2b

West German Inter-Industry Trade, 1973

Parameters (a,b) of the power function, coefficient of determination (R^2), and unit cutoff point (S^*), for the data of Table 2a.

Country	a	b	R^2	S^*
1. SITC 6—manufactured goods classified chiefly by material				
Belgium	0.265177	0.450626	0.994306	19.02
France	0.096109	1.025047	0.996071	9.83
2. SITC 7—machinery and transport equipment				
Belgium	0.358752	0.328844	0.998182	22.59
France	0.172730	0.707112	0.996856	11.98

As explained by Grubel & Lloyd (1975, p. 26), the Balassa measure has the disadvantage of being an unweighted average of the ratios $|X_i - M_i|/(X_i + M_i)$; if instead we weight industry i by its importance,$(X_i+M_i)/\sum_{j=1}^{n}(X_j+M_j)$, we obtain

$$C = \frac{\sum_{i=1}^{n}|X_i - M_i|}{\sum_{i=1}^{n}(X_i + M_i)}. \tag{1.3}$$

The Grubel-Lloyd measure P corresponds to $1-C$. The latter has the advantageous property of being necessarily nonincreasing as the degree of disaggregation becomes finer (cf. Grubel & Lloyd, 1975, p. 23). This monotonicity property is lost with the unweighted Balassa measure. Balassa himself has since (1986) adopted the Grubel-Lloyd measure.

The Balassa coefficient (1.2) has been fitted to the SITC data on inter-industry trade by the power function

$$B = aS^b. \tag{1.4}$$

This has the property that inter-industry trade, corrected for trade imbalance, has the value 0 at the null ($S = 0$) level of disaggregation.

Table 2a reproduces the relevant figures from Gray's table for West German inter-industry trade for the Balassa coefficient (1.2) and for the number of aggregated subcategories at each SITC level (the parameter n of (1.2)). Table 2b provides the estimates of the parameters a and b of (1.4), the coefficient of determination (R^2), and the unit cutoff point (S^*), i.e., the value of S that solves $B = 1$ in (1.4). The fitted curves are shown in Figure 2.

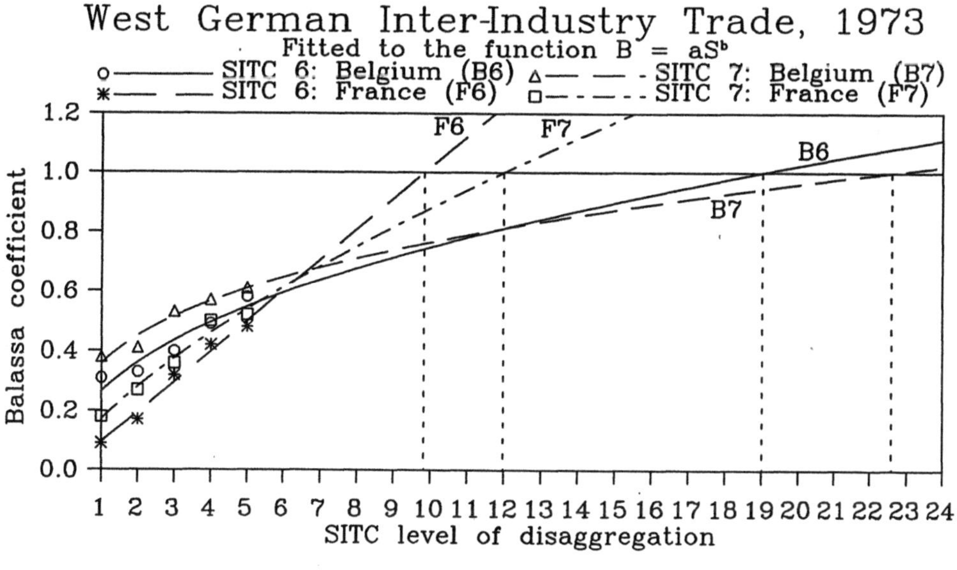

Figure 2

The curves for West German inter-industry trade with Belgium and France lend some support to the hypothesis that intra-industry trade in basic materials is more of a "statistical phenomenon" than is intra-industry trade in finished products, since they predict that intra-industry trade in the former will cease to be observed at the twentieth and tenth levels of disaggregation respectively, whereas it will continue to be observed in the latter up to the twenty-third and twelfth levels respectively. But this conclusion depends upon a willingness to extrapolate curves far from the observations used to fit them.

In the case of French inter-industry trade, Gray (1978, p. 106) provides calculations of the Balassa coefficients for French trade with Belgium, West Germany,

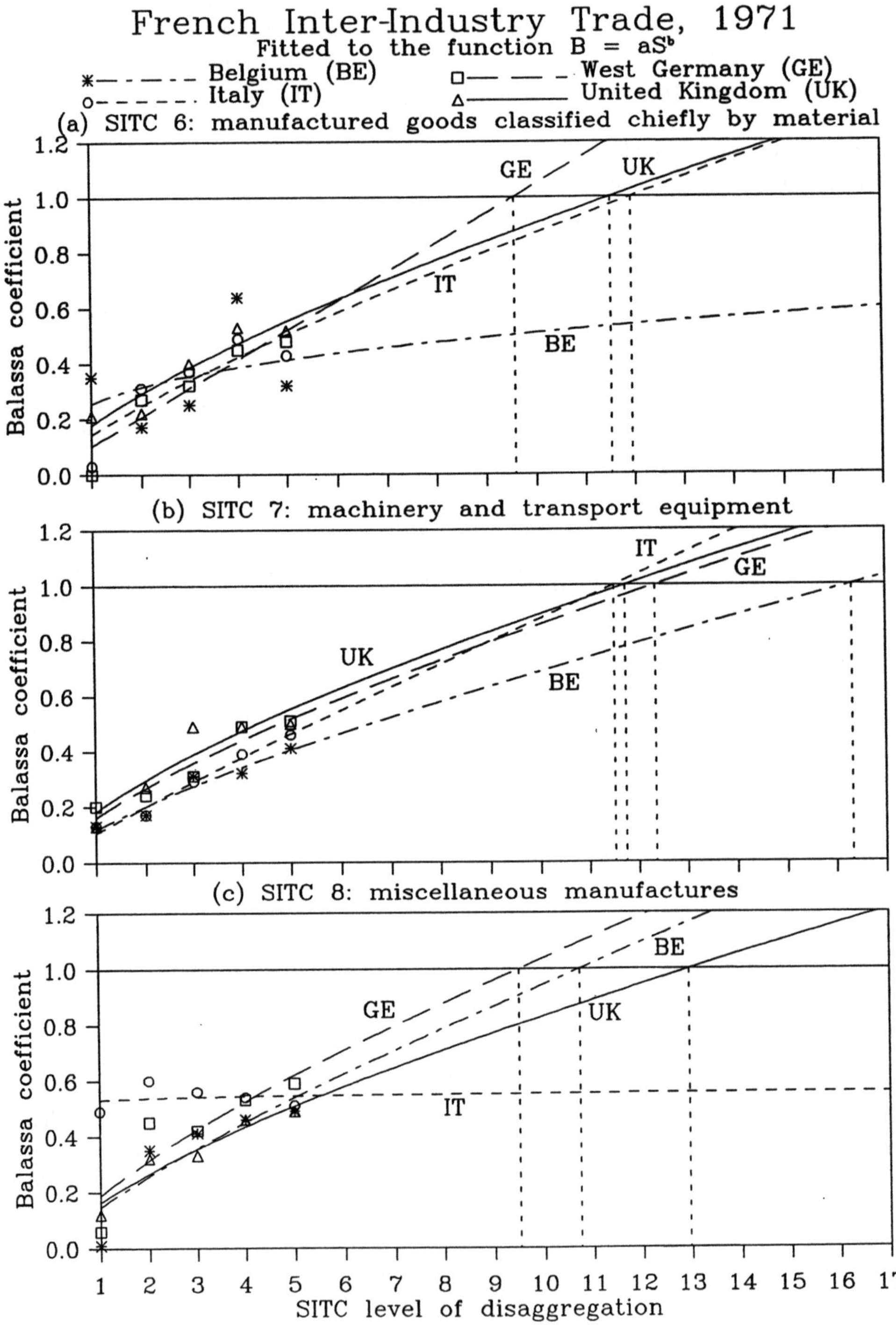
French Inter-Industry Trade, 1971
Fitted to the function B = aS^b
Belgium (BE)
West Germany (GE)
Italy (IT)
United Kingdom (UK)
(a) SITC 6: manufactured goods classified chiefly by material
(b) SITC 7: machinery and transport equipment
(c) SITC 8: miscellaneous manufactures
Balassa coefficient
GE
UK
IT
BE
0.0
0.2
0.4
0.6
0.8
1.0
1.2
1 2 3 4 5 6 7 8 9 10 11 12 13 14 15 16 17
SITC level of disaggregation

Figure 3

Italy, and the United Kingdom in SITC categories 6, 7, and 8. These figures are reproduced in Table 3a. Table 3b furnishes the estimates of the parameters *a* and *b* of (1.4), the coefficient of determination (R^2), and the unit cutoff point (S^*). The fitted curves are displayed in Figure 3.

Table 3a

French Inter-Industry Trade, 1971

Balassa coefficient for trade with selected partners and SITC categories, with number of categories at each SITC level

Country	SITC level of disaggregation				
	1	2	3	4	5
1. SITC 6—manufactured goods classified chiefly by material					
Number of categories	*2*	*7*	*32*	*129*	*21*
Belgium	0.35	0.17	0.25	0.64	0.32
West Germany	0.00	0.27	0.32	0.45	0.48
Italy	0.03	0.31	0.37	0.49	0.43
United Kingdom	0.21	0.22	0.40	0.53	0.52
2. SITC 7—machinery and transport equipment					
Number of categories	*1*	*3*	*18*	*73*	*75*
Belgium	0.13	0.17	0.31	0.32	0.41
West Germany	0.20	0.24	0.31	0.49	0.51
Italy	0.13	0.17	0.29	0.39	0.46
United Kingdom	0.13	0.27	0.49	0.49	0.50
3. SITC 8—miscellaneous manufactures					
Number of categories	*1*	*7*	*18*	*57*	*21*
Belgium	0.01	0.35	0.41	0.46	0.49
West Germany	0.06	0.45	0.42	0.53	0.59
Italy	0.49	0.60	0.56	0.54	0.51
United Kingdom	0.12	0.32	0.33	0.46	0.49

It is apparent from Table 3b and the graphs of Figure 3 that, except for two anomalous cases, the fitted curves predict the disappearance of intra-industry trade at reasonable levels of disaggregation. The two exceptional cases are those of trade with Belgium in SITC 6 (for which the curve fit is very poor—0.84 being a very low coefficient of determination given that there are only three degrees of freedom) and trade with Italy in SITC 8 (for which the Balassa coefficient is, beyond SITC level 2, monotone decreasing in the SITC level of disaggregation). In the cases of SITC 6 and 8 it is apparent from Table 3a that there are far fewer subcategories in the Balassa coefficient at the 5-digit than at the 4-digit level, indicating that numerous probably redundant 5-digit categories (categories for which the fifth digit is zero and no subdivision actually takes place) have been excluded from the calculations. This adds to the non-monotonicity of the Balassa coefficient itself. Taking account of these considerations, it seems a fair inference that one could expect intra-industry trade to disappear at or slightly above the sixteenth level of disaggregation.

Table 3b

French Inter-Industry Trade, 1971

Parameters (a, b) of the power function, coefficient of determination (R^2), and unit cutoff point (S^*), for the data of Table 3a

Country	a	b	R^2	S^*
1. SITC 6—manufactured goods classifed chiefly by material				
Belgium	0.255230	0.301232	0.843465	93.07
West Germany	0.102449	1.008442	0.971280	9.58
Italy	0.143065	0.784057	0.957771	11.94
United Kingdom	0.176951	0.708637	0.986922	11.52
2. SITC 7—machinery and transport equipment				
Belgium	0.118237	0.764512	0.993027	16.33
West Germany	0.160754	0.727198	0.989941	12.35
Italy	0.105163	0.921781	0.996672	11.51
United Kingdom	0.181954	0.691905	0.979750	11.74
3. SITC 8—miscellaneous manufactures				
Belgium	0.147025	0.807923	0.955960	10.73
West Germany	0.187742	0.742835	0.964668	9.50
Italy	0.531450	0.016625	0.995044	3.2+E16
United Kingdom	0.162729	0.708720	0.990619	12.96

1.3 The Swedish data

Unpublished monthly data on Swedish imports and exports have been supplied to the author by the Statistiska centralbyrån, Stockholm, covering the period 1977–1984.[3] These data are classified according to the Svensk standard för näringsgrensindelning (SNI), which is a 6-digit refinement of the 4-digit International Standard Industrial Classification of All Economic Activities (ISIC) constructed by the United Nations. The Grubel-Lloyd coefficients have been computed by Joan R. Rodgers, adjusted for trade imbalances by Aquino's (1978) method (cf. Chipman, 1987, p. 940), and are presented in Tables 4a and 4b for two different modes of calculation. In the first, when a k-digit category is trivially refined to a $(k+1)$-digit category by adding a zero to the code but not subdividing the category, this $(k+1)$-digit category is included in the calculations; in the second mode it is excluded.

Tables 4c and 4d furnish the coefficients of the fitted curves, the coefficient of determination, and the unit cutoff point, corresponding to Tables 4a and 4b respectively. The fitted curves for the pooled data in these two cases are displayed in Figure 4. As the tables and figure indicate, the two modes of calculation provide

[3]I wish to thank Professor Sten Johansson, General Director of the Statistiska centralbyrån (SCB), Mr. Gunnar Stolpe, Head of the Foreign Trade and Prices Division of the SCB, Dr. Edward Palmer and Mr. Randall Bowie of the Konjunkturinstitutet (National Institute of Economic Research), and Ms. Anna Odhner, of the Sveriges Riksbank, for all their efforts and cooperation in helping me acquire this data set at an affordable cost. These data have been further analyzed by Rodgers (1987, 1988).

Table 4a

Swedish Intra-Industry Trade 1977–1984

Grubel-Lloyd coefficients for SNI categories (with repetition of trivial subcategories)

Year	SNI level of disaggregation					
	1	2	3	4	5	6
1977	0.9108	0.6459	0.6300	0.5970	0.5911	0.5865
1978	0.8570	0.6344	0.6198	0.5895	0.5837	0.5761
1979	0.9037	0.6406	0.6238	0.5901	0.5825	0.5707
1980	0.8717	0.6511	0.6337	0.6020	0.5946	0.5821
1981	0.8401	0.6338	0.6222	0.5873	0.5840	0.5752
1982	0.8658	0.6558	0.6405	0.5967	0.5924	0.5855
1983	0.8297	0.6699	0.6598	0.6184	0.6154	0.6085
1984	0.8185	0.6819	0.6723	0.6307	0.6273	0.6199

Table 4b

Swedish Intra-Industry Trade 1977–1984

Grubel-Lloyd coefficients for SNI categories (without repetition of trivial subcategories)

Year	SNI level of disaggregation					
	1	2	3	4	5	6
1977	0.9108	0.6459	0.6604	0.6488	0.6174	0.4615
1978	0.8570	0.6344	0.6491	0.6261	0.5929	0.4425
1979	0.9037	0.6406	0.6536	0.6405	0.6052	0.4420
1980	0.8717	0.6511	0.6826	0.6600	0.6205	0.4606
1981	0.8401	0.6338	0.6728	0.6405	0.6047	0.4633
1982	0.8658	0.6558	0.6862	0.6437	0.6066	0.4727
1983	0.8297	0.6699	0.7059	0.6480	0.6159	0.4746
1984	0.8185	0.6819	0.7150	0.6543	0.6136	0.4759

Table 4c

Swedish Intra-Industry Trade 1977–1984

Parameters (a,b) of the power function, coefficient of determination (R^2), and zero cutoff point (S^*) for data of Table 4a.

Year	a	b	R^2	S^*
1977	0.195211	0.475726	0.991660	31.00
1978	0.224189	0.400879	0.994390	41.68
1979	0.199229	0.478432	0.991958	29.14
1980	0.208818	0.429991	0.994833	38.19
1981	0.231913	0.379543	0.995366	47.01
1982	0.209289	0.427409	0.995397	38.84
1983	0.221710	0.353183	0.997731	71.18
1984	0.221639	0.332268	0.998537	93.19
Pooled	0.213379	0.411247	0.994496	42.78

Table 4d

Swedish Intra-Industry Trade 1977–1984

Parameters (a,b) of the power function, coefficient of determination (R^2), and zero cutoff point (S^*) for data of Table 4b.

Year	a	b	R^2	S^*
1977	0.163248	0.619753	0.991455	18.59
1978	0.191203	0.547961	0.993529	20.48
1979	0.166576	0.626580	0.991254	17.47
1980	0.171347	0.579884	0.993090	20.95
1981	0.197004	0.504332	0.993971	25.06
1982	0.175331	0.568340	0.994906	21.40
1983	0.182338	0.530882	0.995756	24.68
1984	0.180543	0.532134	0.996123	24.95
Pooled	0.178127	0.564111	0.993473	21.29

a striking difference. The very high cutoff points in the first calculation can be interpreted by saying that if disaggregation merely consists in adding zeros to the code and not actually subdividing the categories, it may take a long time or even forever to eliminate statistical observations of two-way trade from international trade statistics.

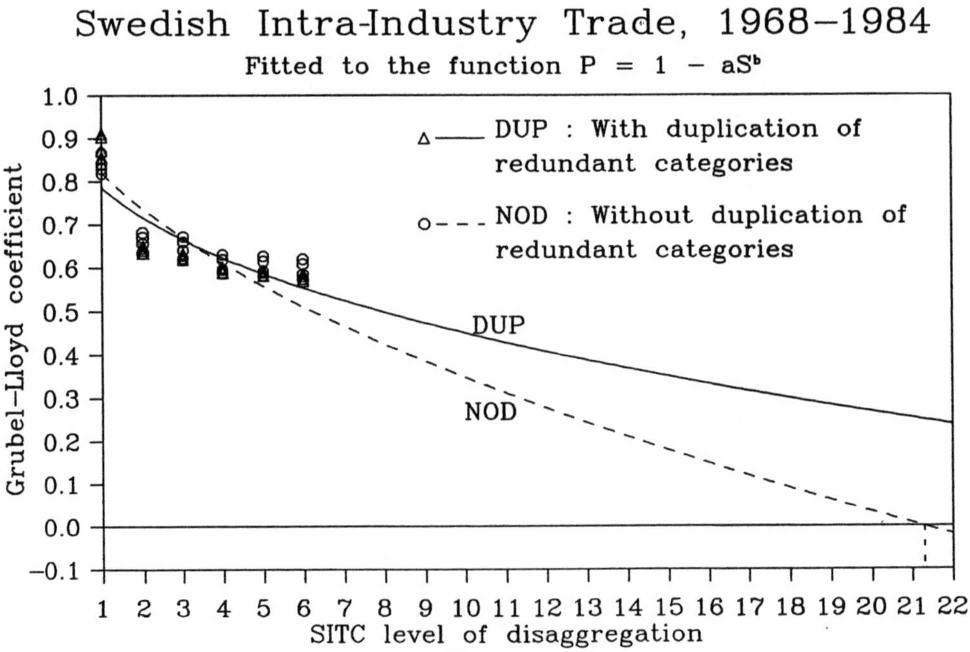

Figure 4

2 The two-commodity, two-factor, two-country case

The thesis was presented by Grubel and Lloyd (1975, pp. 88–91) that (1) a preponderant amount of intra-industry trade takes place in industries within which production functions are very similar to one another, between countries with very similar factor endowments, and (2) this fact is inconsistent with the Heckscher-Ohlin theory with its assumptions of perfect competition and constant returns to scale. In this section I take issue with the second of these propositions, and show that this type of intra-industry trade is readily explained in terms of the HOLS model.

In their words (Grubel & Lloyd, 1975, pp. 88–9):

> ...in certain industries, developed countries tend to produce large numbers of substitute products with input requirements ...so similar that they may be considered identical. The Heckscher-Ohlin model also assumes the identity of production functions across countries. ...therefore [*sic*] the constant rates of transformation between these products and their relative prices must be the same across countries. As a result the exchange of these commodities with identical input requirements for each other is not profitable, because profits arise from exploitation of differences in relative prices among countries. Yet we observe the exchange of such products. The inconsistency between the theory and reality can be explained by relaxing either the assumption that the production functions are identical across countries or the assumption that there are no economies of scale.

The assumption that the rates of transformation will be the same across countries requires the additional assumption of identical factor endowment ratios; however, this seems to be implicitly assumed, since the authors subsequently state (p. 92) that "countries trading in these products have similar endowments with human, knowledge, and real capital relative to labour and land."

In terms of the standard two-commodity, two-factor, two-country model, the case discussed by Grubel and Lloyd may easily be analyzed in terms of the well-known "Lerner diagram" (cf. Lerner, 1952; Chipman, 1966). In Figure 5 a case is shown in which the production isoquants (which are the same for the two countries) are extremely close and the diversification cone very narrow. It is assumed that commodity i uses factor i relatively intensively ($i = 1,2$). Then country 1 will specialize in the production of commodity 1, and country 2 will specialize in the production of commodity 2; both countries will be on the verge of diversifying. Now suppose the two production functions are completely symmetric to each other in their arguments, and suppose further that consumers in both countries have identical and homothetic, and also symmetric, preferences. Then it is clear that in world equilibrium the prices of the two commodities will be the same. To specialize the assumptions still further (for simplicity), suppose consumers have Mill-Cobb-Douglas preferences generated by a utility function

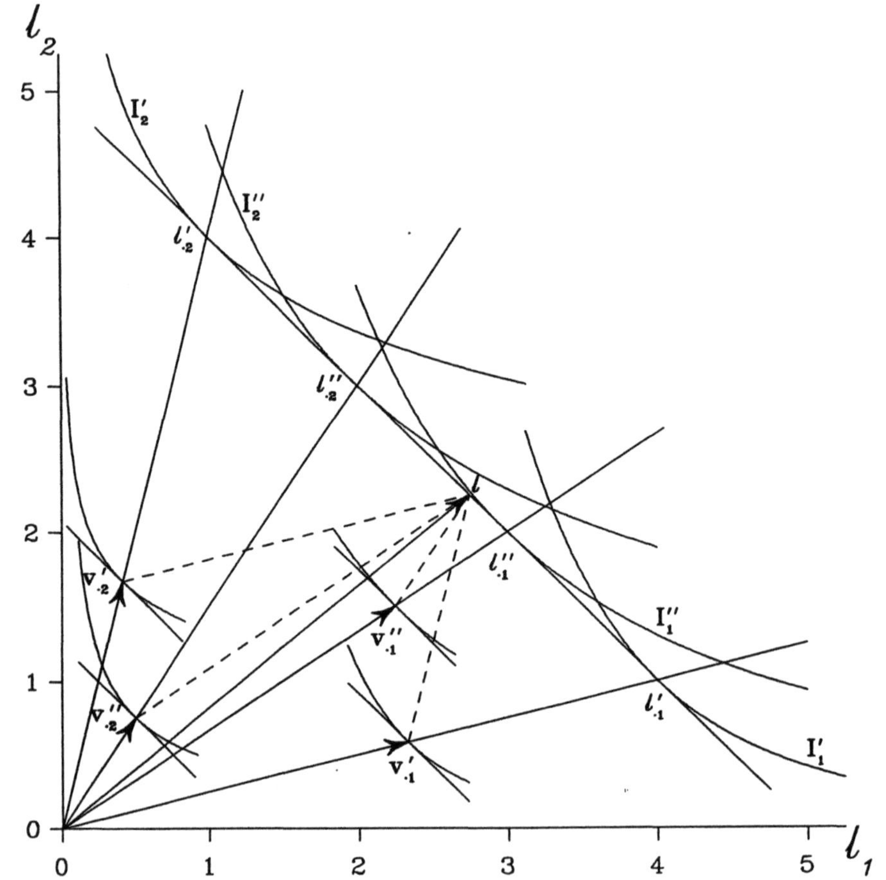

A country with resource endowments $l = (l_1, l_2)$ has technology characterized by isoquants I'_1, I'_2 in situation 1 and I''_1, I''_2 in situation 2. In situation 1, the endowment vector l is allocated between industries according to $v'_{.1} + v'_{.2} = l$, where $v'_{.j} = (v'_{1j}, v'_{2j})$; the diversification cone is $l'_{.1}0l'_{.2}$. In situation 2, this cone shrinks to $l''_{.1}0l''_{.2}$ in such a way that l is close to the lower edge of the cone; the endowment vector l is now allocated between the two industries according to $v''_{.1} + v''_{.2} = l$. A much larger fraction of resources is devoted to industry 1 (the export industry) in the second situation than in the first. In the limit, as $l''_{.1}$ approaches l, all the country's resources are allocated to industry 1, and since (with unit prices) half of the export good is consumed, the other half is exported.

Figure 5

$$U(x_1, x_2) = x_1^{\theta_1} x_2^{\theta_2} \quad (\theta_j > 0, \theta_1 + \theta_2 = 1) \tag{2.1}$$

where (by symmetry) $\theta_1 = \theta_2 = \frac{1}{2}$, x_j being the consumption of commodity j. Then in each country, with prices of the two commodities being equal to each other, one-half of the output of the good it specializes in is consumed; hence one-half is exported. This is true no matter how wide or narrow the diversification cone.

Now suppose we make the following construction. Let production functions be quite disparate (but still symmetric to each other), as indicated by the outside isoquants in Figure 5, but let the factor endowments remain close as before. Then the respective countries' resource allocations will be very close, and there will be very little trade. Now let the isoquants become closer and closer, until they reach the narrow diversification cone, that is, until the diversification cone is bounded by the given endowment vectors. Then each country will export a larger and larger proportion of the good in which it has a comparative advantage, up to the limit of one-half of its export good.

Let us now make this argument more precise. Using the model of Chipman (1985), suppose that there are two Cobb-Douglas production functions (identical between countries)

$$f_j(v_{1j}, v_{2j}) = \mu_j v_{1j}^{\beta_{1j}} v_{2j}^{\beta_{2j}} \quad (j = 1, 2), \tag{2.2}$$

where $\beta_{ij} > 0$ and $\beta_{1j} + \beta_{2j} = 1$ and v_{ij} denotes the allocation of factor i to industry j (a country superscript is omitted for notational convenience), and let the resource-allocation constraints (in each country)

$$v_{11} + v_{12} = l_1^k, \quad v_{21} + v_{22} = l_2^k \tag{2.3}$$

be satisfied, where l_i^k denotes the endowment of country k in factor i $(i, k = 1, 2)$. Let preferences be given by (2.1) for both countries. World equilibrium may then be computed as follows. First, denoting the rental of factor i by w_i, and assuming diversification of production in both countries, factor rentals are solved for by setting prices equal to minimum unit costs. The cost functions dual to (2.2) are

$$g_j(w_1, w_2) = \nu_j w_1^{\beta_{1j}} w_2^{\beta_{2j}} \text{ where } \nu_j = \frac{1}{f_j(\beta_{1j}, \beta_{2j})} \quad (j = 1, 2) \tag{2.4}$$

(cf. Chipman, 1985, p. 293); equating each of these to p_j we obtain

$$\begin{bmatrix} \log w_1 \\ \log w_2 \end{bmatrix} = \begin{bmatrix} \beta_{11} & \beta_{21} \\ \beta_{12} & \beta_{22} \end{bmatrix}^{-1} \begin{bmatrix} \log(\frac{p_1}{\nu_1}) \\ \log(\frac{p_2}{\nu_2}) \end{bmatrix}. \tag{2.5}$$

The cost-minimizing factor-output matrix is

$$B = \begin{bmatrix} b_{11} & b_{12} \\ b_{21} & b_{22} \end{bmatrix} = \begin{bmatrix} w_1 & 0 \\ 0 & w_2 \end{bmatrix}^{-1} \begin{bmatrix} \beta_{11} & \beta_{12} \\ \beta_{21} & \beta_{22} \end{bmatrix} \begin{bmatrix} p_1 & 0 \\ 0 & p_2 \end{bmatrix}. \tag{2.6}$$

Denoting its inverse and that of $[\beta_{ij}]$ by

$$B^{-1} = \begin{bmatrix} b^{11} & b^{12} \\ b^{21} & b^{22} \end{bmatrix} = \begin{bmatrix} b_{11} & b_{12} \\ b_{21} & b_{22} \end{bmatrix}^{-1}, \quad \begin{bmatrix} \beta^{11} & \beta^{12} \\ \beta^{21} & \beta^{22} \end{bmatrix} = \begin{bmatrix} \beta_{11} & \beta_{12} \\ \beta_{21} & \beta_{22} \end{bmatrix}^{-1} \tag{2.7}$$

respectively, we find from (2.4), (2.5), and (2.7) that

$$w_i = \prod_{h=1}^{2} (\mu_h \beta_{1h}^{\beta_{1h}} \beta_{2h}^{\beta_{2h}} p_h)^{\beta^{hi}}, \tag{2.8}$$

hence the elements of the inverse factor-output matrix are

$$b^{ji} = \frac{w_i \beta^{ji}}{p_j} = \frac{[\prod_{h=1}^{2}(\mu_h \beta_{1h}^{\beta_{1h}} \beta_{2h}^{\beta_{2h}} p_h)^{\beta^{hi}}]\beta^{ji}}{p_j}. \tag{2.9}$$

Now, country k's Rybczynski function for commodity j is, in the region of diversification, given by

$$y_j^k = \hat{y}_j(p_1, p_2, l_1^k, l_2^k) = b^{j1}(p_1, p_2)l_1^k + b^{j2}(p_1, p_2)l_2^k \tag{2.10}$$

(as is seen by substituting $v_{ij} = b_{ij}y_j$ in (2.3) and inverting), where the functions $b^{ji}(p_1, p_2)$ are given by (2.9). (The dependence of the b^{ji} on the parameters μ_j, β_{ij} is not explicitly indicated but should be kept in mind). Let world outputs, world consumption, and world factor endowments be denoted

$$y_j = \sum_{k=1}^{2} y_j^k, \; x_j = \sum_{k=1}^{2} x_j^k, \; l_i = \sum_{k=1}^{2} l_i^k. \tag{2.11}$$

Given that both countries are assumed to be diversifying, and that the production functions (2.2) satisfy the hypothesis of absence of factor-intensity reversal, we obtain from (2.10) and (2.11) the world Rybczynski functions

$$\hat{y}_j(p_1, p_2, l_1, l_2) = b^{j1}(p_1, p_2)l_1 + b^{j2}(p_1, p_2)l_2. \tag{2.12}$$

Since preferences in both countries are assumed to be generated by the utility function (2.1), which can be aggregated, equilibrium world consumption must satisfy

$$\frac{x_2}{x_1} = \frac{\theta_2}{\theta_1}\frac{p_1}{p_2}. \tag{2.13}$$

Setting $x_j = y_j$ for world equilibrium, and taking account of the homogeneity of degree 0 of the funtions b^{ji}, we obtain from (2.12) and (2.14) the equation

$$\frac{b^{21}(p_1/p_2, 1)l_1 + b^{22}(p_1/p_2, 1)l_2}{b^{11}(p_1/p_2, 1)l_1 + b^{12}(p_1/p_2, 1)l_2} - \frac{\theta_2}{\theta_1}\frac{p_1}{p_2} = 0. \tag{2.14}$$

Standard methods, such as Newton's method or the secant method, may be used to solve this equation for the world price ratio p_1/p_2.

Once the equilibrium world price ratio has been obtained, each country's export-output ratio is readily computed. Assuming that commodity j uses factor j relatively intensively (i.e., that $\beta_{11} > \beta_{12}$), the output of each country's export good is computed from the Rybczynski function (2.10), for $j = k$ (say, setting $p_2 = 1$). The value of the national-product function

$$\Pi(p_1, p_2, l_1^k, l_2^k) = \sum_{j=1}^{2} p_j \hat{y}_j(p_1, p_2, l_1^k, l_2^k) \tag{2.15}$$

is then computed, and the consumption of commodity j in country k is

$$x_j^k = \frac{\theta_j \Pi(p_1, p_2, l_1^k, l_2^k)}{p_j}. \tag{2.16}$$

For each country, the export-output ratio is then

$$\frac{y_k^k - x_k^k}{y_k^k} = 1 - \theta_k\left(1 + \frac{p_j y_j^k}{p_k y_k^k}\right) \quad (j \neq k). \tag{2.17}$$

Our object is now to show that, at least under certain additional hypotheses, these export-output ratios will increase as production functions become more similar. The additional hypotheses will impose complete symmetry as between the two commodities, factors, and countries. Specifically, I shall assume that $\mu_1 = \mu_2 = 1$ and $\beta_{12} = \beta_{21}$; the latter of course implies $\beta_{11} = \beta_{22}$, providing complete symmetry as between production functions. To obtain symmetry in consumption we set $\theta_1 = \theta_2 = \frac{1}{2}$, and to have symmetry as between the countries' factor endowments we set $l_1^1 = l_2^2$ and $l_2^1 = l_1^2$, where $l_1^1 > l_2^1$ (country k is relatively well endowed in factor k). With these symmetry assumptions, the solution of (2.14) may be bypassed, since clearly $p_1 = p_2$. Without loss of generality it will be assumed that $p_1 = p_2 = 1$, and for convenience we shall denote $\beta = \beta_{12} = \beta_{21}$ and $1 - \beta = \beta_{11} = \beta_{22}$. Since we assume $\beta_{11} > \beta_{21}$, this is equivalent to $\beta < \frac{1}{2}$.

With these symmetry assumptions, (2.8) reduces to

$$w_1 = w_2 = (1-\beta)^{1-\beta}\beta^\beta. \tag{2.18}$$

Thus, it is interesting to note that for $\beta < \frac{1}{2}$ both factor rentals are decreasing functions of β; that is, factor rentals decrease as production functions become more similar. The inverse factor-output matrix now becomes

$$B^{-1} = \frac{(1-\beta)^{1-\beta}\beta^\beta}{1-2\beta}\begin{bmatrix} 1-\beta & -\beta \\ -\beta & 1-\beta \end{bmatrix}, \tag{2.19}$$

and we find that

$$\frac{dB^{-1}}{d\beta} = \frac{(1-\beta)^{1-\beta}\beta^\beta}{1-2\beta}\begin{bmatrix} (1-\beta)\psi(\beta) - 1 & -\beta\psi(\beta) + 1 \\ -\beta\psi(\beta) + 1 & (1-\beta)\psi(\beta) - 1 \end{bmatrix}, \tag{2.20}$$

where

$$\psi(\beta) = \log\beta - \log(1-\beta) + 2(1-2\beta)^{-1}. \tag{2.21}$$

The Rybczynski functions (2.10) reduce to

$$y_j^k = \frac{(1-\beta)^{1-\beta}\beta^\beta}{1-2\beta}\left[l_j^k - \beta(l_1^k + l_2^k)\right] \quad (j = 1, 2). \tag{2.22}$$

From (2.22) and (2.17) (with $\theta = \frac{1}{2}$ and $p_1 = p_2 = 1$), it follows that country k's export-output ratio is equal to

$$\frac{y_k^k - x_k^k}{y_k^k} = \frac{l_k^k - l_j^k}{2\left[l_k^k - \beta(l_k^k + l_j^k)\right]} = \frac{L-1}{2[L - \beta(L+1)]} \quad (j \neq k), \tag{2.23}$$

(where $L = l_k^k / l_j^k$, $j \neq k$) which is an increasing function of β since $l_k^k > l_j^k$ for $j \neq k$. This proves the

Theorem. *If the symmetry conditions $\mu_1 = \mu_2 = 1$, $\beta_{12} = \beta_{21} = \beta$, $\theta_1 = \theta_2 = \frac{1}{2}$, $l_1^1 = l_2^2$, $l_2^1 = l_1^2$ hold in the model (2.1), (2.2), (2.3), if commodity j uses factor j relatively intensively ($\beta < \frac{1}{2}$) and country k is relatively will endowed in factor k ($l_k^k > l_k^j$ for $j \neq k$), and if both commodities continue to be produced in both countries, then as the production functions become more similar (i.e., β increases), each country's exports increase as a proportion of the output of the export good.*

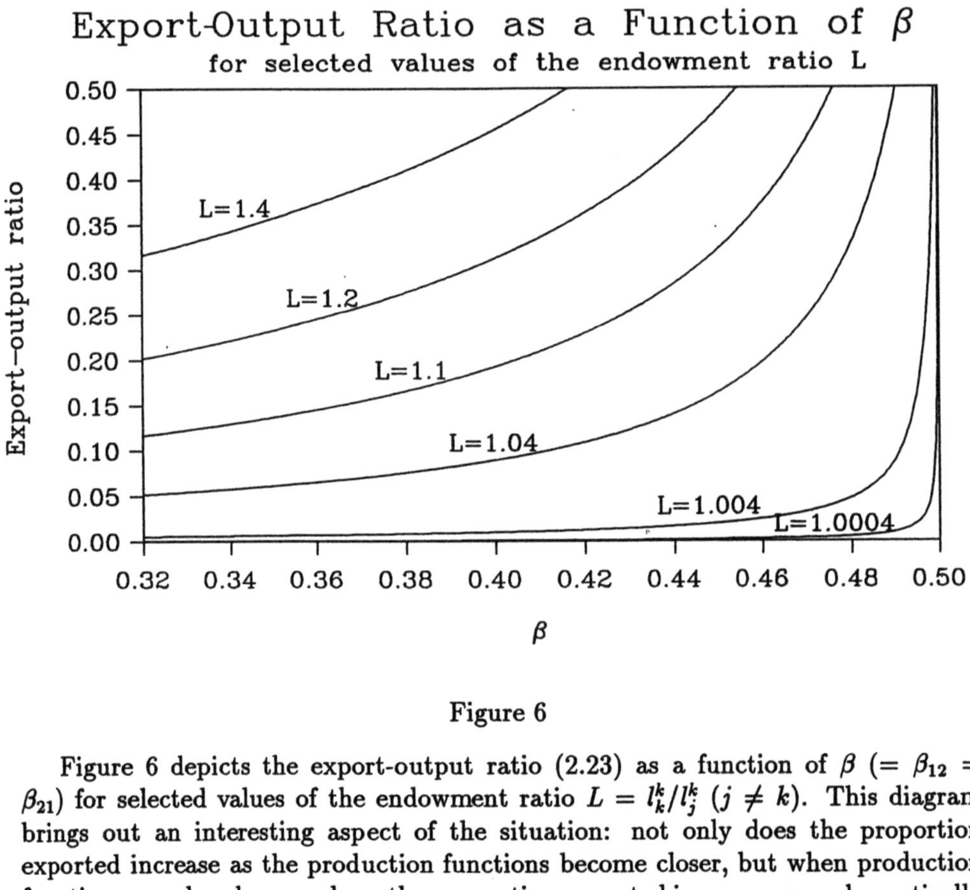

Figure 6

Figure 6 depicts the export-output ratio (2.23) as a function of β ($= \beta_{12} = \beta_{21}$) for selected values of the endowment ratio $L = l_k^k / l_j^k$ ($j \neq k$). This diagram brings out an interesting aspect of the situation: not only does the proportion exported increase as the production functions become closer, but when production functions are already very close, the proportion exported increases very dramatically when the distance between the production functions decreases only slightly. It is stated by Grubel and Lloyd (1975, p. 91) that "it is highly unlikely that the minor differences in input requirements between goods within ... industries could lead to the large observed trade if production were subject to constant returns to scale." But, as the above theorem and the figure show, *the more minor* the difference in input requirements, *the greater* is the percentage of output exported, and *the more sensitive* is the percentage exported to narrowing of the differences between production functions.

What happens in the limit as both the production functions for the two commodities and the factor endowments of the two countries become identical? In particular, what happens when $\beta_{12} = \beta_{21} = .5$ and $l_1^1 = l_2^1 = 1$? It is clear that the curves of Figure 6 approach a discontinuous correspondence in the shape of a backward *L*. The diversification cone shrinks to a ray on which lie both countries' endowment vectors; the countries' production-possibility frontiers become parallel straight lines. World trade becomes indeterminate.

The issue of indeterminacy was raised by Corden (1978, p. 4):

> Suppose that all goods in an "industry" used factors in identical proportions—that is, had identical factor intensities. In this case factor proportions theory could not explain intra-industry trade. For this purpose an industry must be defined in terms of the statistical classification used the intra-industry calculations. Usually the SITC three-digit classification is used though, with even narrower definitions, substantial intra-industry trade apparently remains. It follows that, in such a case, other theories must explain intra-industry trade.

One could argue by analogy with the indeterminacy in the size distibution of firms in an industry under constant returns and competitive equilibrium, that either the constant-returns or the competitive assumption (or both) must be relaxed in order to yield a determinate theory.

But the indeterminateness involved in the present case results from the totally improbable assumption that production functions are exactly the same; let them differ in only the slightest degree, as in the above example, and the determinacy is restored.

The indeterminacy of this limiting case points to what is a fallacy in Grubel and Lloyd's argument when they state (p. 89) that "exchange of these commodities for each other is not profitable, because profits arise from the exploitation of differences in relative prices among countries." It is a confusion between conditions for existence and conditions for uniqueness of equilibrium. Zero profits, and equal prices in the same market, are part of the defining conditions of competitive equilibrium in general and the HOLS model in particular. A competitive equilibrium certainly exists in this limiting case, but it is a neutral equilibrium, with each country's exports indeterminate—anywhere between zero and fifty percent of either good may be exported. Far from being inconsistent with the observation that there is a large haphazard amount of trade between similar countries, the model is entirely in conformity with it.

3 The three-commodity, three-factor, three-country case

The following statement by Hufbauer and Chilas (1974, p. 3) appears to express a widely-held and unchallenged point of view:

> Neoclassical trade theory once predicted that trade would wither between similar nations. After all, trade supposedly compensates for factor endowment disparities or differences in tastes, and if these disparities or taste differences are modest, the need for trade is small.

No references to "neoclassical trade theory" were cited to support this contention, and I doubt whether they could be easily found. Ricardo discussed the question of the *direction* of trade between two countries, but as far as I know he never concerned himself with explaining the *amount* of trade. The same appears to be true of neoclassical and, in particular, the Heckscher-Ohlin theory. But whether or not sources could be found in support of such a proposition, the result of the previous section shows it to be incorrect.

Somewhat similar contentions are frequently made in contexts that are relevant only if trade among more than two countries is involved. Fairly typical is the following argument put forward by Gray (1980, p. 447):

> ...a preponderant amount of international trade takes place among industrial nations with relatively similar resource endowments. ...this pattern of international trade cannot be readily accounted for by the orthodox, factor-proportions theory of international trade even in its multiple-factor version. The standard theory would suggest that the larger trade flows would take place among nations with markedly different factor endowments.

The only proposition known to me that relates trade patterns to relative factor endowments is the "Heckscher-Ohlin theorem," which states that if there are two countries, two factors, and two commodities produced competitively under constant returns to scale and freely traded with zero transport costs, and if (1) preferences are identical and homothetic within and between countries, (2) production functions are identical as between countries, (3) there are no factor-intensity reversals, and (4) trade is balanced, then each country will export the commodity in which its relatively abundant factor is used relatively intensively. If any of the above four conditions is removed, it is easy to construct a counterexample to the proposition; in fact, much of the literature on the "Leontief paradox" was devoted precisely to such exercises. Thus, very special assumptions are required even in the simple $2 \times 2 \times 2$ case to obtain unequivocal results; and even then, the results concern only the *direction* of trade, not the *amount* of trade.

Let us consider now a model of three countries, each producing three commodities with three factors. Countries 1 and 2 will be "similar" in their factor endowments, and they will have a comparative advantage in producing commodities 1 and 2, which have "similar" production functions. The object is to show that countries 1 and 2 may trade more, even much more, with each other than with the third country.

To produce some definite examples. I shall as in the previous section assume that production functions in each country have the Cobb-Douglas form

$$(3.1) \quad y_j^k = f_j(v_{1j}^k, v_{2j}^k, v_{3j}^k) = \mu_j v_{1j}^{\beta_{1j}} v_{2j}^{\beta_{2j}} v_{3j}^{\beta_{3j}} \quad (\beta_{ij} > 0, \sum_{i=1}^{3} \beta_{ij} = 1) \; (j = 1, 2, 3)$$

and that the resource-allocation constraints

$$(3.2) \qquad v_{i1}^k + v_{i2}^k + v_{i3}^k = l_i^k \quad (i = 1, 2, 3)$$

are satisfied. Here, $v_{ij} = v^k_{ij}$ denotes the input of factor i into the production of commodity j in country k (the superscript is omitted in (3.1) for notational simplicity); y^k_j is the output of commodity j in country k, and l^k_i is the endowment of factor i in country k. I shall finally assume that preferences in each country are identical and homothetic, generated by the Mill-Cobb-Douglas utility function

$$U(x_1, x_2, x_3) = x_1^{\theta_1} x_2^{\theta_2} x_3^{\theta_3} \quad (\theta_j > 0, \sum_{j=1}^{3} \theta_j = 1). \tag{3.3}$$

Now we must define "similarity". Since in the examples to follow I shall assume $\mu_1 = \mu_2 = \mu_3 = 1$, the dissimilarity between two production functions f^j and $f^{j'}$ may be defined simply as the Euclidean distance betweeen the vectors of exponents β_j and $\beta_{j'}$, where $\beta_j = (\beta_{1j}, \beta_{2j}, \beta_{3j})$, i.e.,

$$\sqrt{\sum_{i=1}^{3} (\beta_{ij} - \beta_{ij'})^2}. \tag{3.4}$$

In the case of factor-endowment vectors $l^k = (l^k_1, l^k_2, l^k_3)$ and $l^{k'} = (l^{k'}_1, l^{k'}_2, l^{k'}_3)$, I shall define the *relative dissimilarity* between them as the normalized distance

$$\sqrt{\sum_{i=1}^{3} \left(\frac{l^k_i}{\|l^k\|} - \frac{l^{k'}_i}{\|l^{k'}\|} \right)}, \text{ where } \|l^k\| = \sqrt{\sum_{i=1}^{3} (l^k_i)^2}, \tag{3.5}$$

i.e., the distance between them after they have both been normalized to unit length.

World equilibrium is solved for in the following manner. It is assumed that the equilibrium is one in which each country produces all three commodities, hence in view of the assumption that the countries have identical production functions, and of the form (3.1) (ruling out factor-intensity reversal), factor rentals are equalized; therefore, each country produces according to the same technical coefficients. World national product is then determined by the world national-product function

$$Y = \Pi(p_1, p_2, p_3, l_1, l_2, l_3) = \sum_{k=1}^{3} \Pi(p_1, p_2, p_3, l^k_1, l^k_2, l^k_3), \tag{3.6}$$

where $l_i = \sum_{k=1}^{3} l^k_i$, and world output of commodity j is determined according to the world Rybczynski function

$$y_j = \hat{y}_j(p_1, p_2, p_3, l_1, l_2, l_3) = \sum_{k=1}^{3} \hat{y}^k_j(p_1, p_2, p_3, l^k_1, l^k_2, l^k_3), \tag{3.7}$$

where $\hat{y} = \partial\Pi/\partial p_j$. To compute (3.6) and (3.7), we first obtain the factor rentals; this is done by solving from the system of minimum-unit-cost functions

$$p_j = g_j(w_1, w_2, w_3) = \nu_j w_1^{\beta_{1j}} w_2^{\beta_{2j}} w_3^{\beta_{3j}} \; (j = 1, 2, 3) \tag{3.8}$$

where $\nu_j = 1/f_j(\beta_{1j}, \beta_{2j}, \beta_{3j})$, given that this system is linear in the logarithms of the p_j/ν_j and w_i.

From these factor rentals, the matrix of factor-output coefficients $b_{ij} = \beta_{ij}p_j/w_i$ is obtained, and the world outputs (3.7) are obtained by solving the system of equations

$$\sum_{j=1}^{3} b_{ij}y_j = l_i \quad (i = 1, 2, 3). \tag{3.9}$$

World national product, (3.6), is then obtained from

$$Y = \sum_{j=1}^{3} p_j y_j. \tag{3.10}$$

From (3.10) and the assumption that world preferences are identical and homothetic and are generated by (3.3), world consumption is given by

$$x_j = \frac{\theta_j Y}{p_j}. \tag{3.11}$$

The system of equations to be solved to obtain world equilibrium prices is obtained by setting demand equal to supply for two out of the three commodities (since the third equality will follow by Walras' law); we may write this in the form

$$p_j y_j = \theta_j Y \quad (j = 1, 2) \tag{3.12}$$

where y_j and Y are obtained from (3.9) and(3.10), and x_j from (3.11).

To solve the equations (3.12), Wolfe's (1959) algorithm has been used. Setting $p_3 = 1$, three trial solutions p^1, p^2, p^3 are chosen, to form the matrix

$$P = \begin{bmatrix} p_1^1 & p_1^2 & p_1^3 \\ p_2^1 & p_2^2 & p_2^3 \end{bmatrix}. \tag{3.13}$$

The matrix

$$A = \begin{bmatrix} p_1^1y_1^1 - \theta_1Y^1 & p_1^2y_1^2 - \theta_1Y^2 & p_3^3y_1^3 - \theta_1Y^3 \\ p_2^1y_2^1 - \theta_2Y^1 & p_2^2y_2^2 - \theta_2Y^2 & p_2^3y_2^3 - \theta_2Y^3 \\ 1 & 1 & 1 \end{bmatrix} \tag{3.14}$$

is formed, where y_j^k and Y^k are obtained from (3.9) and (3.10) using the factor-output coefficients $b_{ij} = \beta_{ij}p_j^k/w_i^k$, the w_i^k being obtained from the p_k^k via (3.8). The norm of $p^k = (p_1^k, p_2^k)$ is defined as

$$\|p^k\| = \sum_{j=1}^{2} \left(p_j^k y_j^k - \theta_j Y^k\right)^2. \tag{3.15}$$

The Wolfe algorithm then proceeds as follows. A new average price vector $\bar{p}$ is obtained from the formula

$$\begin{bmatrix} \bar{p}_1 \\ \bar{p}_2 \end{bmatrix} = \tag{3.16}$$

$$\begin{bmatrix} p_1^1 & p_1^2 & p_1^3 \\ p_2^1 & p_2^2 & p_2^3 \end{bmatrix} \begin{bmatrix} p_1^1y_1^1 - \theta_1Y^1 & p_1^2y_1^2 - \theta_1Y^2 & p_3^3y_1^3 - \theta_1Y^3 \\ p_2^1y_2^1 - \theta_2Y^1 & p_2^2y_2^2 - \theta_2Y^2 & p_2^3y_2^3 - \theta_2Y^3 \\ 1 & 1 & 1 \end{bmatrix}^{-1} \begin{bmatrix} 0 \\ 0 \\ 1 \end{bmatrix}.$$

One of the columns, p^k of (3.13) of maximal norm (3.15) is then dropped and replaced by $\bar{p}$; from the new price vector, the factor rentals w_i, then factor-output coefficients b_{ij}, the outputs y_j, and the national product Y are recomputed and the new column of coefficients of A is substituted for the dropped one. When the maximal norm (3.15) has reached a prescribed small number, the process converges.

This algorithm assumes diversification by all three countries, but this assumption may be incorrect. That is, for a particular choice of matrices of exponents β_{ij} in (3.1) and factor endowments l_i^k $(i,j,k = 1,2,3)$, it could happen that the algorithm yields negative outputs for some commodities. This solution would have to be rejected, of course. In the examples to be give below, positive production has been verified for all cases.

I shall choose initially the matrix of exponents

$$\begin{bmatrix} \beta_{11} & \beta_{12} & \beta_{13} \\ \beta_{21} & \beta_{22} & \beta_{23} \\ \beta_{31} & \beta_{32} & \beta_{33} \end{bmatrix} = \begin{bmatrix} .49 & .46 & .1 \\ .46 & .49 & .1 \\ .05 & .05 & .8 \end{bmatrix}, \tag{3.17}$$

the matrix of factor endowments

$$\begin{bmatrix} l_1^1 & l_1^2 & l_1^3 \\ l_2^1 & l_2^2 & l_2^3 \\ l_3^1 & l_3^2 & l_3^3 \end{bmatrix} = \begin{bmatrix} 1180 & 1120 & 725/t \\ 1120 & 1180 & 725/t \\ 300 & 300 & 1300/t \end{bmatrix} \tag{3.18}$$

(where t is a positive parameter), and the vector of constant expenditure shares

$$(\theta_1, \theta_2, \theta_3) = \left(\frac{r}{2r+1}, \frac{r}{2r+1}, \frac{1}{2r+1}\right) \tag{3.19}$$

where $0 < r \leq 1$. The countries 1 and 2, as well as commodities 1 and 2, are completely symmetric in their differences, and the prices of commodities 1 and 2 in world equilibrium will necessarily be equal to one another. If $t = 1$ in (3.8), the length of country 3's endowment vector (1655.7) is just slightly larger than that of countries 1 and 2 (1654.3)—giving this country the benefit of the doubt. For $t = 1$ and $r = 1$ we find that the prices are[4]

$$p_1 = p_2 = .98441846365, \quad p_3 = 1. \tag{3.20}$$

The pattern of world outputs is given by

$$\begin{bmatrix} y_1^1 & y_1^2 & y_1^3 \\ y_2^1 & y_2^2 & y_2^3 \\ y_3^1 & y_3^2 & y_3^3 \end{bmatrix} = \begin{bmatrix} 908.11 & 71.94 & 224.42 \\ 71.24 & 908.11 & 224.42 \\ 150.32 & 150.32 & 885.09 \end{bmatrix}; \tag{3.21}$$

and the pattern of world consumption is

$$\begin{bmatrix} x_1^1 & x_1^2 & x_1^3 \\ x_2^1 & x_2^2 & x_2^3 \\ x_3^1 & x_3^2 & x_3^3 \end{bmatrix} = \begin{bmatrix} 377.58 & 377.58 & 449.31 \\ 377.58 & 377.58 & 449.31 \\ 371.71 & 371.71 & 442.32 \end{bmatrix}. \tag{3.22}$$

[4]Computations were carried out on the HP-71B handheld computer. A listing of the BASIC program is available from the author on request.

The row sums of the output and consumption matrices are equal to one another (except for rounding error). The matrix of world trade values is

$$(3.23)\qquad \begin{bmatrix} p_1 z_1^1 & p_1 z_1^2 & p_1 z_1^3 \\ p_2 z_2^1 & p_2 z_2^2 & p_2 z_2^3 \\ p_3 z_3^1 & p_3 z_3^2 & p_3 z_3^3 \end{bmatrix} = \begin{bmatrix} -522.27 & 300.89 & 221.39 \\ 300.89 & -522.27 & 221.39 \\ 221.39 & 221.39 & -442.77 \end{bmatrix},$$

where $z_j^k = x_j^k - y_j^k$. Thus we see that countries 1 and 2 trade more with each other than with country 3. Nevertheless, their factor endowments are closer to one another than to those of country 3 as measured by the indices of relative dissimilarity (3.5), yielding the matrix

$$(3.24)\qquad \begin{bmatrix} 0 & .0513 & .7054 \\ .0513 & 0 & .7054 \\ .7054 & .7054 & 0 \end{bmatrix}.$$

Likewise, the production coefficients of commodities 1 and 2 are much closer to each other than to that of commodity 3, as measured by the dissimilarity criterion (3.4), yielding the matrix

$$(3.25)\qquad \begin{bmatrix} 0 & .0424 & .9188 \\ .0424 & 0 & .9188 \\ .9188 & .9188 & 0 \end{bmatrix}.$$

As r increases, i.e., as the relative share of world expenditure devoted to commodities 1 and 2 increases, the ratio of trade between countries 1 and 2 to trade between countries 1 and 3 increases. The same is true as t increases, i.e., as countries 1 and 2's absolute endowments increase relatively to country 3's. Table 5 gives the ratio of trade between dissimilar countries as a function of t and r; note that the relationship between this ratio and the scale factor t is linear, for each r.

Table 5

Ratios of trade between similar and dissimilar countries (for the model (3.17)–(3.19)—countries 1 & 2 versus countries 1 & 3 and countries 2 & 3) for various values of the endowment ratio t and expenditure ratio r

Endow-ment Ratio	Expenditure Ratio									
	1	2	3	4	5	6	7	8	9	10
1	1.359	2.289	3.049	3.683	4.219	4.679	5.077	5.426	5.733	6.007
2	1.946	3.169	4.170	5.004	5.710	6.314	6.839	7.297	7.702	8.062
3	2.533	4.050	5.291	6.325	7.200	7.950	8.600	9.169	9.670	10.116
4	3.120	4.931	6.412	7.646	8.690	9.585	10.361	11.040	11.639	12.171
5	3.707	5.811	7.532	8.967	10.180	11.221	12.122	12.911	13.607	14.226
6	4.295	6.692	8.653	10.288	11.671	12.856	13.884	14.783	15.576	16.281
7	4.882	7.572	9.774	11.609	13.161	14.492	15.645	16.654	17.544	18.338
8	5.469	8.453	10.895	12.930	14.651	16.127	17.406	18.525	19.513	20.390
9	6.056	9.334	12.016	14.250	16.142	17.763	19.167	20.397	21.481	22.445
10	6.643	10.214	13.136	15.571	17.632	19.398	20.929	22.268	23.450	24.500

It seems quite reasonable to assume that there is a preponderance of world expenditure on the products of industrial countries which are similar to each other in both their endowments and in the production processes on which they concentrate; and that these countries have higher absolute productivity (whether measured by t in (3.18) or by the μ_j in (3.1)—which we have assumed = 1). Thus, there are three forces all of which lead to greater trade between similar countries: (1) similarity in the production functions for the goods which they export—a circumstance which (as we saw in the previous section) makes for *more* intra-industry trade; (2) greater world demand for their products; and (3) greater absolute productivity of the similar industrial countries compared to the dissimilar one.

References

AQUINO, ANTONIO (1978): "Intra-Industry Trade and Inter-Industry Specialization as Concurrent Sources of International Trade in Manufactures," *Weltwirtschaftliches Archiv*, 114, 275–296.

BALASSA, BELA (1966): "Tariff Reductions and Trade in Manufactures among Industrial Countries," *American Economic Review*, 56, 466–473.

— (1986): "Intra-Industry Specialization: A Cross-Country Analysis," *European Economic Review*, 30, 27–42.

CHIPMAN, JOHN S. (1966): "A Survey of the Theory of International Trade, Part 3, The Modern Theory," *Econometrica*, 34, 18–76.

— (1985): "Product Diversification, Equalization of Factor Rentals, and Consumer Preferences" in *Rationale Wirtschaftspolitik in komplexen Gesellschaften*, ed. Hellmuth Milde and Hans G. Monissen. Stuttgart: Verlag W. Kohlhammer, 284–295.

— (1986): "Intra-industrieller Handel, Faktorproportionen und Aggregation" in *Aspekte internationaler Wirtschaftsbeziehungen*, ed. Rainer Ertel and Hans-Joachim Heinemann. Hannover: Niedersächsisches Institut für Wirtschaftsforschung e.V., 81–108.

— (1987): "International Trade" in *The New Palgrave: A Dictionary of Economics*, ed. John Eatwell, Murray Milgate, and Peter Newman. London: The Macmillan Press, Vol. 2, 922–955.

CORDEN, W. M. (1978): "Intra-Industry Trade and Factor Proportions Theory" in *On the Economics of Intra-Industry Trade*, ed. Herbert Giersch. Tübingen: J.C.B. Mohr (Paul Siebeck), 3–12.

FLETCHER, R., AND M. J. D. POWELL (1963): "A Rapidly Convergent Descent Method for Minimization," *Computer Journal*, 6, 164–168.

GRAY, H. PETER (1978): "Intra-Industry Trade: The Effects of Different Levels of Data Aggregation" in *On the Economics of Intra-Industry Trade*, ed. Herbert Giersch. Tübingen: J.C.B. Mohr (Paul Siebeck), 87–110.

— (1980): "The Theory of International Trade among Industrial Nations," *Weltwirtschaftliches Archiv*, 116, 447–470.

GRUBEL, HERBERT G., AND PETER J. LLOYD (1975): *Intra-Industry Trade*. London: The Macmillan Press Ltd.

HUFBAUER, GARY C., AND JOHN G. CHILAS (1974): "Specialization by Industrial Countries: Extent and Consequences," in *The International Division of Labour, Problems and Perspectives*, ed. Herbert Giersch. Tübingen: J.C.B. Mohr

(Paul Siebeck), 3–38.
LERNER, ABBA P. (1952): "Factor Prices and International Trade," (1933), *Economica, N.S.,* 19, 1–15.
RODGERS, JOAN R. (1987): "An Analysis of Intra-Industry Trade Flows: The Case of Sweden," Ph. D. dissertation, University of Minnesota.
—— (1988): "Intra-Industry Trade, Aggregation and the HOS Model," *Journal of Economic Studies,* 15, No. 5, 5–23.
SAMUELSON, PAUL A. (1953): "Prices of Factors and Goods in General Equilibrium," *Review of Economic Studies,* 21, 1–20.
THEIL, HENRI (1971): *Principles of Econometrics.* New York: John Wiley & Sons, Inc.
WOLFE, PHILIP (1959): "The Secant Method for Simultaneous Nonlinear Equations," *Communications of the Association for Computing Machinery,* 2, No. 12, 12–13.

Compensating Variation as a Measure of Welfare Change*

JOHN S. CHIPMAN
University of Minnesota
AND
JAMES C. MOORE
Purdue University

1 Introduction

The concept of "compensating variation" introduced by Hicks (1939), and developed by Henderson (1941) and Hicks (1942, 1956), remains along with its sister concept of "consumer's surplus" the principal tool of analysis underlying present-day "cost-benefit analysis" and "applied welfare economics" (cf. Mishan, 1971; Harberger, 1964, 1971). In two previous papers (Chipman & Moore, 1976, 1980) we have respectively analyzed the consumer's surplus and the compensating and equivalent variations in the context of single-valued, differentiable demand functions. In the present paper we extend the analysis of the latter two concepts to the context of demand correspondences. Since the alternative specifications of homothetic and parallel[1] prefences turn out to be of particular importance in providing a rigorous justification for certain uses of the compensating variation as a welfare measure, we include a detailed development of the principal properties of demand correspondences and indirect preferences under these two specifications—particularly that of "parallel" preferences in Appendix B. Our main results (Theorems 1 and 3) establishing necessary conditions for the extended applicability of the compensating variation both make use of a basic duality theorem concerning the relationship between

*Research for this paper on the part of both authors was supported by National Science Foundation grant SOC77-27257.

[1]The concept of parallel preferences was first formulated by Auspitz & Lieben (1889, p. 471) and Edgeworth (1891, p. 237n), and may be regarded as implicit in Barone's (1894) concept of an "instrumental good"; the specification was subsequently taken up by Wilson (1939), Boulding (1945), and Samuelson (1942, 1964); see also Katzner (1970, pp. 23–4), where such preferences are described as "quasi-linear." In recent years (but largely independently of the preceding) it has played an important role in the concept of "willingness to pay" in the theory of public goods (cf. Hurwicz, 1975, 1981; Green & Laffont, 1979, p. 31; Laffont & Maskin, 1982, pp. 48, 56; Starrett, 1988, p. 269) as well as in allowing for the possibility of "transferable utility" in the theory of games (cf. Owen, 1982, p. 122). The use of the specification of parallel preferences in the theory of public goods may be regarded as implicit in Lindahl's (1919) original formulation.

indirect preferences and demand correspondences proved in Appendix A (Theorem 6).

The compensating variation was defined by Hicks (1942) as that loss of income that would make a consumer just as well off after a change in prices (and income) as he had been in the initial situation. If the compensating variation is positive, the consumer is better off in the new situation. This suggests that the compensating variation can be taken as a numerical measure of the welfare improvement. However, a question immediately presents itself: why should one wish to employ a particular cardinal index of welfare improvement when a mere ordinal comparison of the two situations would suffice?

One possible answer to this question is that one is interested only in the actual pecuniary amounts of compensation that would (or at least should) accompany the adoption of the contemplated alternative situation. Even if this is all that is admitted to by a practitioner of cost-benefit analysis, in practice such analysis frequently forms the basis for policy recommendations which are not contingent upon the actual payment or extraction of compensation. The specious nature of arguments based upon hypothetical but unrealized payment of compensation was brought out by Samuelson (1947, pp. 250–1), and has been further scrutinized by Chipman & Moore (1978, pp. 578–9). If actual payment or extraction of compensation is not contemplated, one is back to the question of how to interpret the cardinal magnitude of the compensating variation as an indicator of welfare itself.

There remains, then, a second possible answer to the above question, which is that one is interested in gauging the size of welfare improvement so as to be able to provide a ranking not only of one alternative situation relative to the existing one, but of two alternative situations relative to each other. That this is the fundamental object of the pursuit of welfare measurement seems clear from the original formulation put forward by Hicks (1941). Hicks distinguised two tasks of welfare economics: the first was the study of the conditions of [Pareto] optimality and productive efficiency; and the second was the study of deviations from this optimum. In his words (1941, p. 112):

> I define an *optimum* organization of production as one in which there is no further opportunity for *improvements*; no reorganization is possible which will leave any individuals so much better off that they can compensate the losers and still be left with a net gain. The first task of welfare economics is the formal study of the conditions of optimum organization in this sense ... The second task of welfare economics is the study of deviations from this optimum, and it is here that consumer's surplus has its part to play. The idea of consumer's surplus enables us to study in detail the effects of deviations from the optimum in a particular market. It is not merely a convenient way of showing when there will be a deviation (consumer's surplus is not necessary for that purpose, since the basic optimum conditions ... show us at once when there will be a deviation); it also offers us a way of measuring the size of deviation. This, if we are right in our general viewpoint, is a most important service. It will clearly not be worth while to take measures, which may have awkward repercussions on distribution, if they offer no more than

> a small improvement in productive efficiency. If the improvement is a large one, the case may well be altered.

The implication of the last two sentences in this passage is clear: there is a significance to be attached to the *magnitude* of the measured welfare loss, since it enables one to rank two alternative situations relatively to each other, not just relatively to the initial situation. In fact, in the article referred to, Hicks went on to provide a specific illustration of such a comparison.[2]

Stimulated by a contribution by Henderson (1941), Hicks proceeded to develop the concept of compensating variation, which he had first introduced in *Value and Capital* (1939). In his words (1942, p. 127): "There seems very little doubt that it is the Compensating Variation which is the magnitude that is economically interesting, and not the (perhaps pedantically defined) consumer's surplus." It is somewhat ironic that Hicks' subsequent and sustained concern with the numerous different definitions and varieties of variation and surplus (cf. Hicks, 1943, 1945–46, 1956) appear to have led him to lose sight of the question of precisely how these measures should be used in carrying out what he had previously defined as the "second task" of welfare economics; for he never came back to any illustrations of specific applications. Nevertheless there is little doubt that prominent practitioners of welfare measurement have continued to adopt and implement the point of view of Hicks' "second task"; one can do no better than quote from a widely cited and influential paper by Harberger (1971, p. 795):[3]

> The practitioner of applied welfare economics knows full well that his clients do not come to him in search of full optima or elegant suboptima. He is more likely to be asked which of two alternative agricultural programs is better .... Most applied welfare economics thus answers questions like ... "Which of two or three alternative actions helps most or hurts least, and by approximately how much?"

The question posed in the present paper is one that emerges directly from the question just quoted: under what conditions will the compensating variation correctly rank two or more alternative situations for an individual relatively to each other as well as relatively to the initial situation?

We provide the following answers to this question: (1) If no restictions are placed on the class of alternatives under comparison, then there are no conditions on pref-

[2]This was an illustration of the effect on welfare of a restriction of output on the part of the producers in a particular industry (Hicks, 1941, pp. 112–4). The main point of the illustration was to show that after an initial reduction in output from the optimal level, a further equal reduction would have an even more damaging effect: "When output has already been contracted below the optimum, a further contraction is very damaging" (p. 114). Such a conclusion could not be drawn unless one could compare the welfare loss after the further reduction in output with the welfare loss after the initial reduction in output. What is involved is a quaternary ordering of the form "the loss in going from a to b is greater than the loss in going from c to d," and it has been known since the time of Pareto (1909, pp. 264–5), Frisch (1926), and Alt (1936) that such rankings lead to a cardinal indicator. In fact, if the welfare indicator (be it the consumer's surplus or the compensating variation) has only ordinal significance, one is not even entitled to say that the further reduction in output is damaging—let alone "very damaging".

[3]A similar characterization of the purposes of applied welfare economics is found in Harberger (1964, p. 58); the relevant passage is cited in Chipman & Moore (1980, footnote 1).

erences under which the compensating variation will always correctly rank two or more alternatives to the existing situation. This is shown in Section 2. (2) If we confine attention to certain restricted pairwise comparisons, in particular (a) situations with differing prices but the same income, or (b) situations in which the price of one commodity is the same, then a necessary and sufficient condition for the compensating variation to rank such alternative situations correctly is that preferences be homothetic in case (a) (this is shown in Section 3) and parallel (with respect to the commodity whose price is unchanged) in case (b) (this is shown in Section 4). These happen to be precisely the same necessary and sufficient conditions on preferences that are required for constancy of the marginal utility of income—and thus for the validity of the Marshallian consumer's surplus as a measure of welfare change—in the same respective circumstances, as we have shown in Chipman & Moore (1976) (see also Samuelson, 1942). Thus, some of the perceived advantages of the compensating variation over the Marshallian consumer's surplus are more apparent than real.[4] On the other hand, the broader use of the *equivalent* variation to make comparisons among several alternative situations is valid under very general conditions, as we show in the next section.[5]

2 Compensating and equivalent variations

Let $p = (p_1, p_2, \ldots, p_n)$ denote the vector of (strictly positive) prices faced by a consumer, and m his money income, also strictly positive. Pairs $b = (p, m)$ will be called *budgets* or *situations*, and the space E^{n+1}_{++} of all such pairs will be called the *budget space*. The set

$$B(p,m) = \{x \in E^n_+ \mid p \cdot x \leqq m\} \tag{2.1}$$

will be called the *budget set*. The consumer will be assumed to have a total, transitive preference relation R (a weak order) on the set of commodity bundles x in the nonnegative orthant E^n_+, which is such as to generate a *demand correspondence*

$$h(p,m) = \{x \in B(p,m) \mid x' \in B(p,m) \Rightarrow xRx'\} \tag{2.2}$$

[4]See, for example, Mohring (1971), who takes the position that use of the compensating variation obviates the need to assume that the marginal utility of income is constant. This is true if use of the compensating variation is limited to making ordinal comparisons of alternative situations with an initial situation; but in many cases, the Marshallian consumer's surplus itself is also perfectly satisfactory in this regard (see, for instance, Chipman & Moore, 1980, footnote 18). But if one extends the use of the compensating variation to comparisons of the type of Hicks' "second task", then keeping in mind that the property of constancy of the marginal (indirect) utility of income is not invariant with respect to monotone transformations of the indirect utility function, what can be said is this: the compensating variation is a valid indicator of welfare change for "second-task" comparisons if and only if there exists some numerical indicator of indirect preferences (i.e., an indirect utility function) for which the marginal utility of income is constant over the set of prices and income to which comparisons are restricted. This is shown in Chipman & Moore (1980) for the cases in which the comparison sets are those with constant income and constant price of one commodity respectively. In a recent paper we have extended this proposition to a much wider class of comparison sets (Chipman & Moore, 1990).

[5]The same conclusion can be drawn from Hause's (1975) analysis.

satisfying the *budget-balance condition*

$$(2.3) \qquad (\forall (p,m) \in E^{n+1}_{++})(\forall x \in h(p,m)): \quad p \cdot x = m.$$

The *indirect preference relation* R^* induced by R is defined on E^{n+1}_{++} by[6]

$$(2.4) \qquad (p^1,m^1)R^*(p^2,m^2) \Leftrightarrow [(\exists x^1 \in h(p^1,m^1), x^2 \in h(p^2,m^2)) : x^1 R x^2].$$

It is easy to show that under the above assumptions, R^* is

(a) *homogeneous of degree zero* in (p,m), i.e.,

$$(\forall (p,m) \in E^{n+1}_{++})(\forall \lambda \in E^1_{++}): \ (p,m)I^*(\lambda p, \lambda m),$$

where I^* is the indirect indifference relation defined by

$$b^1 I^* b^2 \Leftrightarrow [b^1 R^* b^2 \ \& \ b^2 R^* b^1],$$

and

(b) *strictly increasing* in m, i.e.,

$$(\forall p \in E^n_{++})(\forall m^1, m^2 \in E^1_{++}): \ m^1 > m^2 \Rightarrow (p,m^1)P^*(p,m^2),$$

where P^* is the indirect strict preference relation defined by

$$b^1 P^* b^2 \Leftrightarrow [b^1 R^* b^2 \ \& \ \neg b^2 R^* b^1].$$

Moreover, if R is continuous, so is R^*.

If $\Omega \subseteq E^{n+1}_{++}$, we shall say that a a real-valued function $V : \Omega \to E^1$ *represents* R^* *on* Ω if and only if

$$\begin{aligned}&(\forall (p^1,m^1),(p^2,m^2) \in \Omega): \\ &\qquad V(p^1,m^1) \geqq V(p^2,m^2) \Leftrightarrow (p^1,m^1)R^*(p^2,m^2);\end{aligned}$$

and if V represents R on E^{n+1}_{++}, we shall say that V is an *indirect utility function* (representing R^*). Note that it follows immediately from (a) and (b) above that if V represents R^* on $\Omega \subseteq E^{n+1}_{++}$, we must have (cf. Chipman & Moore, 1976, Lemmas 1 & 2):

V1. $(\forall (p,m) \in \Omega)(\forall \lambda \in E^1_{++}): \ \lambda(p,m) \in \Omega \Rightarrow V(\lambda p, \lambda m) = V(p,m)$;

V2. $V(p,m)$ is a strictly increasing function of m on Ω.

In fact, we have the following necessary and sufficient characterization which we state for future use, the proof of which is left to the interested reader:

Lemma 1. *If R is a weak order on a non-empty subset of E^n_+, and R^* is represented by a function $V(p,m)$ on some non-empty open subset Ω of E^{n+1}_{++}, then h satisfies the budget-balance condition (2.3) if and only if V is strictly increasing in m.*

---

[6]Note that, since all elements of $h(p,m)$ are indifferent, this ordering is well-defined.

In dealing with a subset, Ω, of E^{n+1}_{++}, we shall often be interested in the image of Ω under h, defined by

$$h(\Omega) = \{x \in E^n_+ \mid (\exists (p,m) \in \Omega): \ x \in h(p,m)\}. \tag{2.5}$$

Let $(p^0, m^0) \in E^{n+1}_{++}$ be given. Following Hurwicz & Uzawa (1971) (see also McKenzie, 1957), we define the *income-compensation function* $\mu : E^{2n+1}_{++} \to E^1_{++}$ by[7]

$$\mu(p; p^0, m^0) = \inf\{m \in E^1_{++} \mid (p,m)R^*(p^0, m^0)\}. \tag{2.6}$$

The following properties of μ may be noted:

M1. $\mu(p; \lambda p^0, \lambda m^0) = \mu(p; p^0, m^0)$ for $\lambda > 0$;

M2. $\mu(\lambda p; p^0, m^0) = \lambda\mu(p; p^0, m^0)$ for $\lambda > 0$;

M3. $\mu(p^0; p^0, m^0) = m^0$.

If R is continuous, the following additional properties hold:[8]

M4. $(p,m)I^*(p^0, \mu(p^0; p, m))$ for all $(p,m) \in E^{n+1}_{++}$;

M5. $(p^1, m^1)I^*(p^0, m^0) \Leftrightarrow \mu(p^0; p^1, m^1) = m^0$;

M6. the function $V_{p^0} : E^{n+1}_{++} \to E^1_+$ defined by

$$V_{p^0}(p,m) = \mu(p^0; p, m) = \inf\{m' \in E^1_+ \mid (p^0, m')R^*(p,m)\} \tag{2.7}$$

is an indirect utility function[9] representing R^*.

Condition M5 is actually an immediate consequence of conditions M6 and M3. It has the following simple geometric interpretation in the budget space: the graph of $\mu(p; p^t, m^t)$ (for fixed (p^t, m^t) and variable p) is the indirect indifference surface through the point (p^t, m^t) (see Figure 1).

We shall assume for the remainder of this paper that R (and hence R^*) is continuous.[10]

Now, suppose one contemplates a change from an initial situation (p^0, m^0) to a new one (p^1, m^1). Hicks (1942, pp. 127–8; 1956, pp. 80–1) defined the compensating and equivalent variations only for the cases $m^0 = m^1$. The *compensating variation* in going from (p^0, m^0) to (p^1, m^0) is defined by

---

[7]We use this rather than the more popular "expenditure function" $e(p,u)$ since it deals directly with the space of entitities we are concerned with and does not require us to adopt a particular cardinal indirect utility function $V(p,m)$ satisfying $\mu(p; p^0, m^0) = e(p, V(p^0, m^0))$ (let alone prejudge the question of the existence of such a function).

[8]The statement of M5 as given also uses the assumption that h satisfies the budget-balance condition.

[9]In effect, this is what is established in Lemma 8 of Hurwicz & Uzawa (1971, pp. 129–30).

[10]It may be remarked, however, that certain of our results remain valid if this assumption is weakened. Specifically, continuity may be replaced by upper semi-continuity in the hypotheses of Theorems 1 and 3.

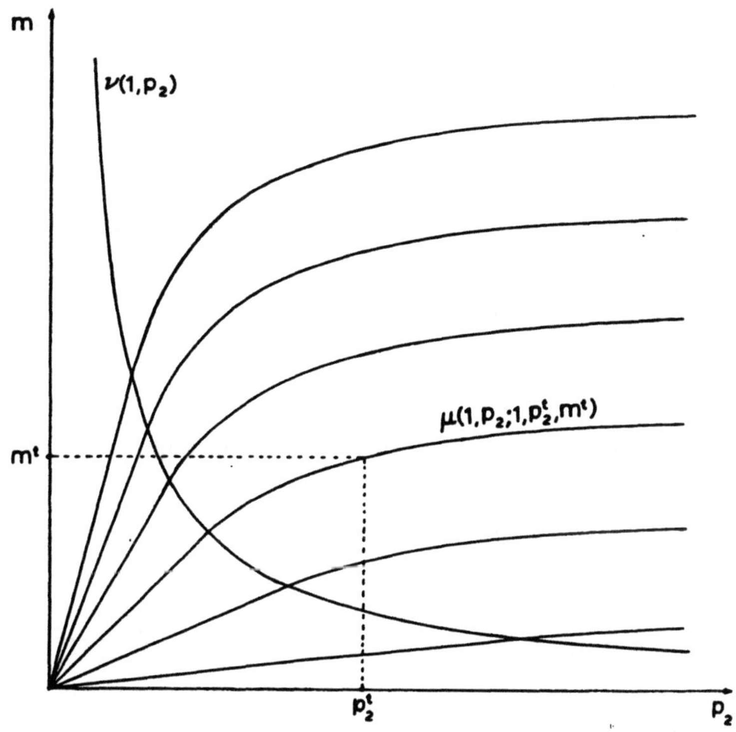

Figure 1

(2.8) $$C(p^1;p^0,m^0) = m^0 - \mu(p^1;p^0,m^0).$$

The *equivalent variation* in going from (p^0,m^0) to (p^1,m^0) is defined by

(2.9) $$E(p^0;p^1,m^0) = \mu(p^0;p^1,m^0) - m^0.$$

More symmetrically, we may rewrite (2.9) as

(2.10) $$E(p^0;p^1,m^1) = \mu(p^0;p^1,m^1) - m^1$$

(where $m^1 = m^0$); this shows that the equivalent variation in going from (p^0,m^1) to (p^1,m^1) is equal, with opposite sign, to the compensating variation in going from (p^1,m^1) back to (p^0,m^1) (cf. Hicks, 1942, p. 128; 1956, p. 81).[11]

[11]From properties M3 and M5 of μ it is clear that the compensating variation satisfies

$$V_{p^1}(p^1, m^0 - C(p^1;p^0,m^0)) = V_{p^1}(p^0,m^0)$$

(cf. Hicks, 1942, p. 131). Likewise, the equivalent variation satisfies

$$V_{p^0}(p^0, m^1 + E(p^0;p^1,m^1)) = V_{p^0}(p^1,m^1).$$

In order to consider the validity of these concepts when extended to comparison of two or more alternatives to the initial situation (p^0, m^0), we begin by defining a criterion for an acceptable indicator of welfare change. Given an indirect preference relation, R^*, on E_{++}^{n+1}, and a set $\Gamma \subseteq E_{++}^{2(n+1)}$, we shall say that a function $W : \Gamma \to E^1$ is an *acceptable indicator of welfare change (for R^*) on* Γ if and only if we have, for each $((p^1, m^1), (p^2, m^2)) \in \Gamma$:

$$(2.11) \qquad W((p^1, m^1), (p^2, m^2)) \geqq 0 \Leftrightarrow (p^2, m^2) R^* (p^1, m^1).$$

Since the natural extensions of (2.8) and (2.9) to the case of a comparison between (p^0, m^0) and a second budget (p^1, m^1) are given by

$$(2.12) \qquad \bar{C}(p^1, m^1; p^0, m^0) = m^1 - \mu(p^1; p^0, m^0),$$

and

$$(2.13) \qquad \bar{E}(p^1, m^1; p^0, m^0) = \mu(p^0; p^1, m^1) - m^0,$$

respectively, it is clear that the validity of the extended usage of the two concepts requires that the respective functions

$$(2.14) \qquad W^C((p^1, m^1), (p^2, m^2)) \equiv \bar{C}(p^2, m^2; p^0, m^0) - \bar{C}(p^1, m^1; p^0, m^0)$$

and

$$(2.15) \qquad W^E((p^1, m^1), (p^2, m^2)) \equiv \bar{E}(p^2, m^2; p^0, m^0) - \bar{E}(p^1, m^1; p^0, m^0)$$

be acceptable indicators of welfare change on some set $\Gamma \subseteq E_{++}^{2(n+1)}$. Suppose we consider these criteria in turn.

Considering first the function W^C defined in (2.14), we note that it follows from (2.12) that the requirement that $W^C((p^1, m^1), (p^2, m^2))$ be nonnegative is equivalent to the stipulation that

$$(2.16) \qquad m^2 - \mu(p^2; p^0, m^0) \geqq m^1 - \mu(p^1; p^0, m^0)$$

for $((p^1, m^1), (p^2, m^2)) \in \Gamma$. Because of the separability of the function W in this case, it is apparent that if the set Γ under consideration is of the form:

$$(2.17) \qquad \Gamma = \Omega \times \Omega$$

for some non-empty set $\Omega \subseteq E_{++}^{n+1}$, the question of whether W^C is an acceptable indicator of welfare change in this situation reduces to the question of whether the function Ψ defined on Ω by

$$(2.18) \qquad \Psi(p, m) = m - \mu(p; p^0, m^0)$$

represents R^* on Ω. Suppose, however, that Ω is a non-empty open subset of E_{++}^{n+1}, and let us take Γ to be of the form (2.17). If Ψ represents R^* on Ω, then by V1, Ψ is positively homogeneous of degree zero on Ω. On the other hand, by M2, $\mu(p; p^0, m^0)$ is positively homogeneous of degree one in p, so that for all $(p, m) \in \Omega$ and all $\lambda > 0$ such that $(\lambda p, \lambda m) \in \Omega$,

$$\Psi(\lambda p, \lambda m) = \lambda[m - \mu(p; p^0, m^0)] = \lambda \Psi(p, m).$$

However, since Ω is an open set, it follows that for each $(p, m) \in \Omega$, there exists $\varepsilon > 0$ such that if $|\lambda - 1| < \varepsilon$, then $\lambda(p, m) = (\lambda p, \lambda m) \in \Omega$. Obviously we can have

$$\Psi(p, m) = \Psi(\lambda p, \lambda m) = \lambda\Psi(p, m)$$

for all λ such that $|\lambda - 1| < \varepsilon$ only if $\Psi(p, m) = 0$. Since (p, m) was an arbitrary element of Ω, this implies that Ψ vanishes identically on Ω, which contradicts V2.

It follows from the above argument that the function W^C defined in (2.14) can never provide an acceptable indicator of welfare change on a set Γ of the form (2.17) with Ω a non-empty open subset of E^{n+1}_{++}. On the other hand, if Γ is of the form

$$(2.19)\quad \Gamma = \Gamma(p^0, m^0) = \{((p^1, m^1), (p^2, m^2)) \in E^{2(n+1)}_{++} \mid (p^1, m^1) = (p^0, m^0)\},$$

where (p^0, m^0) is the base-period budget, then W^C always (that is, under the assumptions being employed in this paper) provides an acceptable indicator of welfare change on $\Gamma(p^0, m^0)$; for if $(p^1, m^1) = (p^0, m^0)$, then by (2.12), (2.14), and M3, W^C takes the form:

$$\begin{aligned} W^C((p^1, m^1), (p^2, m^2)) &= m^2 - \mu(p^2; p^0, m^0) - [m^0 - \mu(p^0; p^0, m^0)] \\ &= \mu(p^2; p^2, m^2) - \mu(p^2; p^0, m^0). \end{aligned}$$

Since V_{p^2} is known to be an indirect utility function representing R^* on E^{n+1}_{++}, it follows that W^C provides an acceptable indicator of welfare change on $\Gamma(p^0, m^0)$.

The question then becomes: are there cases intermediate between these two in which W^C provides an acceptable indicator of welfare change, at least under some conditions? In Section 3, we show (simplifying slightly) that if Γ takes the form

$$\Gamma = \Gamma(\bar{m}) = \{((p^1, m^1), (p^2, m^2)) \in E^{2(n+1)}_{++} \mid m^1 = m^2 = \bar{m}\},$$

then W^C provides an acceptable indicator of welfare change on Γ if and only if preferences are homothetic; and in Section 4 we show that if Γ takes the form

$$\Gamma = \Gamma(\bar{p}_1) = \{((p^1, m^1), (p^2, m^2)) \in E^{2(n+1)}_{++} \mid p^1_1 = p^2_1 = \bar{p}_1\},$$

then W^C provides an acceptable indicator of welfare change on Γ if and only if preference are "parallel" in the first commodity, as defined in Section 4. It is evident that these are two special cases of a more general principle (cf. Chipman & Moore, 1990), but these are the only two cases with which we shall attempt to deal in this paper.

Turning now to the equivalent variation, we note that the function W^E defined in (2.15) is nonnegative if and only if

$$\mu(p^0; p^2, m^2) \geqq \mu(p^0; p^1, m^1).$$

Since $V_{p^0}(p, m) \equiv \mu(p^0; p, m)$ is known to be a valid indirect utility function under the assumptions of this paper, it follows at once that the function W^E defined in (2.15) provides an acceptable indicator of welfare change on $\Gamma = E^{2(n+1)}_{++}$.[12] This would

[12] In terms of the representation of the direct preference relation R, use of this measure amounts to choosing a particular numerical utility function, namely the Hurwicz-Uzawa (1971) function $U_{p^0}(x)$, where $U_{p^0}(h(p, m)) = V_{p^0}(p, m)$. Samuelson (1974) has called this the "money metric." We owe to E. Foster the remark that this is equivalent to using the equivalent variation as a welfare indicator.

appear to constitute a very strong reason for preferring the use of the equivalent variation to that of the compensating variation in applied welfare analysis; however, sometimes circumstances dictate the use of the latter [for more complete discussions of these points, see Hause (1975) and Chipman & Moore (1980)].

3 Budgets with unchanged income

In this section we shall investigate the conditions under which the function W^C defined in (2.14), above, provides an acceptable indicator of welfare change on a set $\Gamma \subseteq E^{2(n+1)}_{++}$ of the form

$$\Gamma = \Omega \times \Omega \tag{3.1}$$

where Ω is of the form

$$\Omega = \Pi \times \{\bar{m}\} \tag{3.2}$$

with $\Pi \subseteq E^{n+1}_{++}$ and $\bar{m} > 0$. As we have seen in the previous section, a necessary and sufficient condition for this is that the function Ψ defined in (2.18) represents R^* on Ω, i.e.,

$$(p^2,\bar{m})R^*(p^1,\bar{m}) \Leftrightarrow \bar{m} - \mu(p^2;p^0,m^0) \geqq \bar{m} - \mu(p^1;p^0,m^0). \tag{3.3}$$

Given Ω of the form (3.2), define the set $\Omega_{\bar{m}} \subseteq E^{n+1}_{++}$ by

$$\Omega_{\bar{m}} = \{(p,m) \in E^{n+1}_{++} \mid p/m \in \bar{m}^{-1}\Pi\}, \tag{3.4}$$

and suppose that $(p^1,m^1),(p^2,m^2) \in \Omega_{\bar{m}}$. Applying the criterion (3.3) to the price vectors $\bar{m}p^1/m^1, \bar{m}p^2/m^2 \in \Pi$, we have:

$$(\bar{m}p^2/m^2,\bar{m})R^*(\bar{m}p^1/m^1,\bar{m}) \Leftrightarrow$$
$$\bar{m} - \mu(\bar{m}p^2/m^2;p^0,m^0) \geqq \bar{m} - \mu(\bar{m}p^1/m^1;p^0,m^0).$$

Making use of the homogeneity of degree zero of R^*, as well as of property M2 of μ, this is easily seen to be equivalent to

$$(p^2,m^2)R^*(p^1,m^1) \Leftrightarrow 1 - \frac{\mu(p^2;p^0,m^0)}{m^2} \geqq 1 - \frac{\mu(p^1;p^0,m^0)}{m^1},$$

which in turn is obviously equivalent to

$$(p^2,m^2)R^*(p^1,m^1) \Leftrightarrow \frac{m^2}{\mu(p^2;p^0,m^0)} \geqq \frac{m^1}{\mu(p^1;p^0,m^0)}.$$

Thus we have established the following:

Lemma 2. *Given $(p^0,m^0) \in E^{n+1}_{++}$, the function Ψ defined by (2.18) represents R^* on a non-empty set $\Pi \times \{\bar{m}\} \subseteq E^{n+1}_{++}$ if and only if the function $V : E^{n+1}_{++} \to E^1_+$ defined by*

$$V(p,m) = \frac{m}{\mu(p;p^0,m^0)} \tag{3.5}$$

represents R^* on $\Omega_{\bar{m}} \subseteq E^{n+1}_{++}$, where $\Omega_{\bar{m}}$ is defined by (3.4).

Note that the homogeneity of degree zero of R^* enables one to extend an assumed property of R^* on $\Pi \times \{\bar{m}\}$ to a larger set $\Omega_{\bar{m}} \supseteq \Pi \times \{\bar{m}\}$; but this larger set still depends on the particular choice of $\bar{m}$. If, for example, we consider two different individuals with constant but unequal incomes $\bar{m}_1$ and $\bar{m}_2$, and facing the same set of prices varying in the set Π, we require their indirect preferences to be representable by functions of the form $m_i/\mu^i(p;p^0,m^0)$ on (in general) different sets $\Omega_{\bar{m}_i}, i = 1,2$. However, if Π happens to be cone,[13] so that $\bar{m}^{-1}\Pi = \Pi$, then $\Omega_{\bar{m}}$ is independent of $\bar{m}$ and takes the form $\Omega_{\bar{m}} = \Pi \times E^1_{++}$.

The function (3.5) has the important property of being positively homogeneous of degree one in m. Theorem 1 below states that if a function with this property represents R^* on a set Ω of the form $\Omega = \Pi \times E^1_{++}$, where Π is a non-empty open subset of E^{n+1}_{++}, then R must be homothetic on $h(\Omega)$, where, as usual, R will be said to be *homothetic* on a set $Z \subseteq E^{n+1}_{++}$ if and only if

(3.6) $$(\forall x^1, x^2 \in Z)(\forall \lambda \in E^1_{++}) : x^2 R x^1 \Leftrightarrow \lambda x^2 R \lambda x^1.$$

If, therefore, we choose Π to be an open cone in E^{n+1}_{++}, we have $\Omega_{\bar{m}} = \Omega$ for any $\bar{m} > 0$, and it then follows from Lemma 2 and Theorem 1 that when Π is an open cone, W^C provides an acceptable indicator of welfare change on the set Γ defined by (3.1) and (3.2) only if R is homothetic on $h(\Omega)$, where $\Omega = \Omega_{\bar{m}}$. This establishes proposition (b) stated at the close of the introduction.

Theorem 1. *If there exists an open non-empty set* $\Pi \subseteq E^{n+1}_{++}$ *and a function* V *satisfying*

(a) $V : \Omega \to E^1_{+}$, where $\Omega = \Pi \times E^1_{++}$;

(b) V *represents* R^* *on* Ω;

(c) V *is positively homogeneous of degree one in* m;

and if

(d) the demand correspondence, h, *is convex-valued;*

then:

(i) h *is positively homogeneous of degree one in* m, *i.e.,*

$$(\forall (p,m) \in \Omega)(\forall \lambda \in E^1_{++}) : \quad h(p,\lambda m) = \lambda h(p,m);$$

and

(ii) R *is homothetic on* $h(\Omega)$ *(and* $h(\Omega)$ *is a cone).*

Proof. (i) First we show that

(3.7) $$\lambda h(p,m) \subseteq h(p,\lambda m).$$

Let $(p^1,m^1) \in \Omega, x^1 \in h(p^1,m^1)$ and $\lambda \in E^1_{++}$. We are to show that $\lambda x^1 \in h(p^1,\lambda m^1)$.

[13] We follow Rockafellar (1970, p. 13) in defining a cone K by the property $\lambda K = K$ for $\lambda > 0$.

Let $(p, m) \in \Pi \times E^1_{++}$ be such that

$$p \cdot \lambda x^1 \leqq m.$$

For any such $(p, m) \in \Omega$ we have $h(p, m/\lambda) R x^1$; hence, since $(p, m/\lambda) \in \Omega$ and V represents R^* on Ω, it follows that

$$V(p, m/\lambda) \geqq V(p^1, m^1).$$

Using now the fact that V is positively homogeneous of degree one in m, we have

$$V(p, m) = \lambda V(p, m/\lambda) \geqq \lambda V(p^1, m^1) = V(p^1, \lambda m^1).$$

We conclude, therefore (since V represents R^* on Ω), that

$$(\forall (p, m) \in \Omega) : \; p \cdot \lambda x^1 \leqq m \Rightarrow (p, m) R^* (p^1, \lambda m^1);$$

and, since $\lambda x^1 \in B(p^1, \lambda m^1)$, and Ω is an open set, it follows from Theorem 6 of Appendix A [replacing x^1 by λx^1 and (p^1, m^1) by $(p^1, \lambda m^1)$] that $\lambda x^1 \in h(p^1, \lambda m^1)$. This establishes (3.7).

To establish

$$h(p, \lambda m) \subseteq \lambda h(p, m) \tag{3.8}$$

we begin by noting that (3.5) is equivalent to

$$\lambda^{-1} h(p, \lambda m) R \subseteq h(p, m).$$

Thus we see that an argument identical with that yielding (3.7), with a mere change of notation (λ^{-1} for λ and λm^1 for m^1), yields (3.8).

(ii) It follows at once from part (i) that $h(\Omega)$ is a cone. To prove that R is homothetic on $h(\Omega)$, let $x^1, x^2 \in h(\Omega)$ be such that $x^1 R x^2$, and let $\lambda \in E^1_{++}$. Since $x^t \in h(\Omega)$ for $t = 1, 2$, there exist $(p^t, m^t) \in \Omega$ such that

$$x^t \in h(p^t, m^t) \quad \text{for} \quad t = 1, 2;$$

and since V represents R^* on Ω it follows from (3.6) that

$$V(p^1, m^1) \geqq V(p^2, m^2).$$

However, by reason of the fact that V is positively homogeneous of degree one in m, we then have $V(p^1, \lambda m^1) \geqq V(p^2, \lambda m^2)$; and since V represents R^* on Ω, it follows that $(p^1, \lambda m^1) R^* (p^2, \lambda m^2)$. Since, by part (i), $\lambda x^t \in h(p^t, \lambda m^t)$ for $t = 1, 2$ it then follows that $\lambda x^1 \, R \, \lambda x^2$. ∎

Interestingly enough, the conclusions of the preceding result do not necessarily obtain if h is not convex-valued; as is shown by our next example. On the other hand, if we are willing to assume that $h(\Omega)$ is a cone (in place of the assumption that h is convex-valued) then the conclusions of Theorem 1 do hold. This is established by the Corollary which follows Example 1.

Example 1. Consider the utility function $U(\cdot)$, defined on E^2_+ by:

$$U(x) = \begin{cases} 3x_1 & \text{for } x_2 > 2x_1 \geqq 0 \ \& \ x_1 < 1, \\ 4x_1 & \text{for } x_2 > 2x_1 \geqq 0 \ \& \ x_1 \geqq 1, \\ x_1 + x_2 & \text{for } 2x_1 \geqq x_2 \geqq x_1/2 \ \& \ 0 < x_1 + x_2 < 3, \\ 2\max\{x_1, x_2\} & \text{for } 2x_1 \geqq x_2 \geqq x_1/2 \ \& \ x_1 + x_2 \geqq 3, \\ 3x_2 & \text{for } 0 \leqq x_2 < x_1/2 \ \& \ x_2 < 1, \text{ and} \\ 4x_2 & \text{for } 0 \leqq x_2 < x_1/2 \ \& \ x_2 \geqq 1. \end{cases}$$

This is illustrated in Figure 2. For $U(x) = u < 3$, the level sets $U^{-1}(u) = \{x|U(x) = u\}$ are broken lines as shown in the case $u = 1.5$: vertical above the cone, horizontal to the right of the cone, and with slope -1 inside the cone. For $u = 3$ the level set $U^{-1}(u)$ consists of the singleton $\{(1.5, 1.5)\}$. For $3 < u < 4$ the level sets consist of inverted L-shaped segments in the cone as shown for the case $u = 3.5$. For $u \geqq 4$, the level sets $U^{-1}(u)$ are staircase-shaped broken lines.

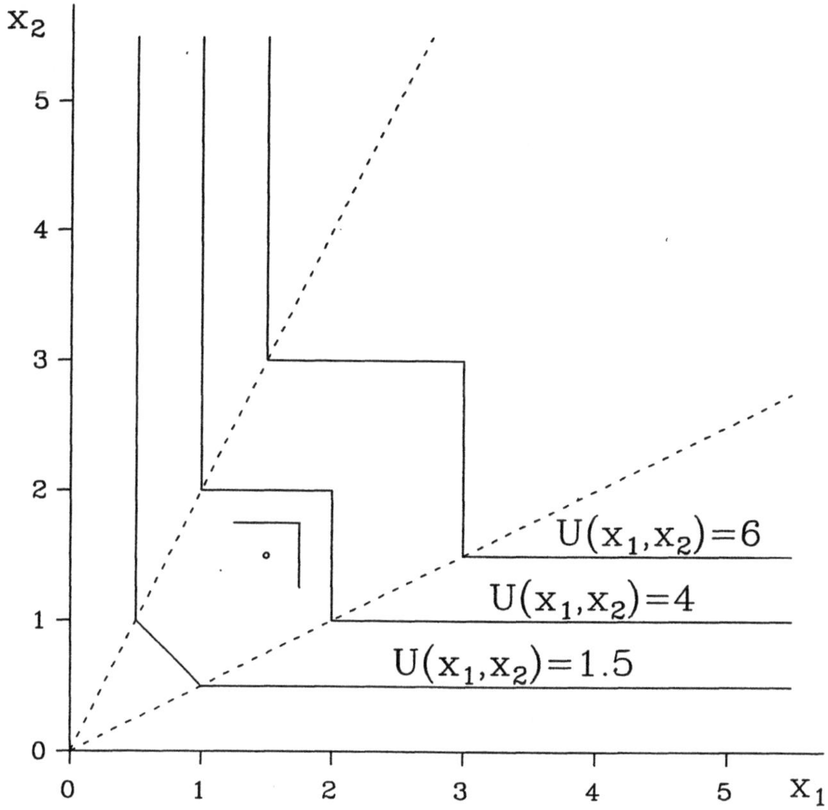

Figure 2

It is easily shown that the demand correspondence generated by $U(\cdot)$ is given by:

$$h(p,m) = \begin{cases} \left\{\dfrac{m}{p_1+2p_2}, \dfrac{2m}{p_1+2p_2}\right\} & \text{for } p_1 > p_2 > 0, \\ \{x \in E^2_+ | p \cdot x = m \ \& \ 2x_1 \geqq x_2 \geqq x_1/2\} & \text{for } \begin{cases} p_1 = p_2 > 0 \ \& \\ 0 \leqq m/p_1 < 3, \end{cases} \\ \left\{\left(\dfrac{m}{3p_1}, \dfrac{2m}{3p_1}\right), \left(\dfrac{2m}{3p_1}, \dfrac{m}{3p_1}\right)\right\} & \text{for } \begin{cases} p_1 = p_2 > 0 \ \& \\ m/p_1 \geqq 3, \end{cases} \\ \left\{\left(\dfrac{2m}{2p_1+p_2}, \dfrac{m}{2p_1+p_2}\right)\right\} & \text{for } 0 < p_1 < p_2; \end{cases}$$

and that an indirect utility function representing R^* is here given by:

$$V(p,m) = \begin{cases} \dfrac{3m}{p_1+2p_2} & \text{for } p_1 \geqq p_2 > 0, \\ \dfrac{3m}{2p_1+p_2} & \text{for } 0 < p_1 < p_2. \end{cases}$$

One can then easily check to verify the fact that h and V satisfy all of the assumptions of Theorem 1 *except* that h is not convex-valued. Nonetheless, neither part (i) nor part (ii) of the conclusion of Theorem 1 holds in this case.

Corollary. If in Theorem 1, we substitute the assumption:

(d') $h(\Omega)$ is a cone

for assumption (d), retaining all of the other assumptions of the result, then h and V satisfy (i) and (ii) of Theorem 1.

Proof.

(i) We proceed as in the proof of Theorem 1 to show that if $\lambda > 0$, then

$$(\forall (p,m) \in \Omega) : p \cdot \lambda x^1 \leqq m \Rightarrow (p,m) R^* (p^1, \lambda m^1) \tag{3.9}$$

[the interested reader can easily check to verify the fact that we did not invoke the convexity of $h(p^1, m^1)$ in deriving this extension in the proof of Theorem 1]. We then note that since $h(\Omega)$ is a cone, there exists $(p^*, m^*) \in \Omega$ such that:

$$\lambda x^1 \in h(p^*, m^*); \tag{3.10}$$

and from (3.9),

$$(p^*, m^*) R^* (p^1, \lambda m^1). \tag{3.11}$$

It then follows at once from (3.10), (3.11), and the definition of R^*, that

$$\lambda x^1 \in h(p^1, \lambda m^1);$$

and thus that:

$$\lambda h(p^1, m^1) \in h(p^1, \lambda m^1).$$

As was the case in the proof of Theorem 1, we can now establish that

$$h(p^1, \lambda m^1) \subseteq \lambda h(p^1, m^1),$$

by noting that this statement is equivalent to:

$$\lambda^{-1}h(p^1, \lambda m^1) \subseteq h(p^1, m^1).$$

(ii) Since we are here assuming that $h(\Omega)$ is a cone, our proof of part (ii) of the conclusion can proceed exactly as in the proof of Theorem 1. ∎

The converse of Theorem 1 is also true; that is, if R is homothetic on E^n_+, then given any base budget $(p^0, m^0) \in E^{n+1}_{++}$, any set $\Pi \subseteq E^{n+1}_{++}$, and any $\bar{m} > 0$, the compensating variation provides an acceptable welfare criterion on $\Pi \times \{\bar{m}\}$. Given Lemma 2, this is an immediate consequence of Theorem 2 below, which is proved in Chipman & Moore (1980, H4–H7); here we provide a simpler proof. First we state the following lemma, the proof of which is left to the interested reader.

Lemma 3. *If R is homothetic, R^* satisfies*

$$(\forall \lambda \in E^1_{++}): \quad (p^1, m^1)R^*(p^2, m^2) \Leftrightarrow (p^1, \lambda m^1)R^*(p^2, \lambda m^2).$$

Theorem 2. *If R is homothetic on E^n_+, then given any $(p^0, m^0) \in E^{n+1}_{++}$, the function (3.5) is an indirect utility function representing R^*.*

Proof. For any $(p, m) \in E^{n+1}_{++}$, we have by property M4 of μ and the definition (3.5) of V,

$$(p^0, m^0)\, I^*\, (p, \mu(p; p^0, m^0)) = \left(p, \frac{m}{V(p,m)}\right),$$

whence by Lemma 3 (and again using M4),

$$(p^0, m^0 V(p, m))\, I^*\, (p, m).$$

Using property V2 of indirect utility functions, it then follows that

$$V_{p^0}(p, m) \equiv \mu(p^0; p, m) = m^0 V(p, m). \tag{3.12}$$

The function V_{p^0} is, by M6, an indirect utility function representing R^*; and since it follows from (3.12) that the function V (defined by (3.5)) is an increasing transformation (in fact, a positive multiple) of V_{p^0}, the result follows. ∎

Given the definition (3.5) of V, (3.12) may be written in the form

$$\frac{m}{\mu(p; p^0, m^0)} = \frac{\mu(p^0; p, m)}{m^0}. \tag{3.13}$$

This may be interpreted as stating that, when R is homothetic, $\mu(p, p^0, m^0)$ may be considered as a "true cost-of-living index". However, Theorem 2 shows that it is only when R is homothetic that this interpretation is appropriate. This "if and only if" characterization was established, although under more restrictive conditions, by Samuelson & Swamy (1974).

4 Budgets with unchanged price of one commodity

We now consider pairs of budgets $(p^1, m^1), (p^2, m^2) \in E^{n+1}_{++}$ for which the price of one of the commodities, say the first, is the same as between all budgets under comparison. In dealing with this case it will be convenient to introduce the notation

$$(4.1) \qquad q = (p_2, p_3, \ldots, p_n), \quad y = (x_2, x_3, \ldots, x_n),$$

so that we may denote budgets and commodity bundles respectively by

$$(4.2) \qquad (p, m) = (p_1, q, m), \quad x = (x_1, y).$$

Thus we can write, for example, $p \cdot x = p_1 x_1 + q \cdot y$. Using this notation, we can state the problem to be investigated in this section as follows. We seek the conditions under which the function W^C defined in (2.14) provides an acceptable indicator of welfare change on a set $\Gamma \subseteq E_{++}^{2(n+1)}$ of the form

$$(4.3) \qquad \Gamma = \Omega \times \Omega,$$

where Ω is of the form

$$(4.4) \qquad \Omega = \{\bar{p}_1\} \times \Theta$$

with $\bar{p}_1 \in E_{++}^1$ and $\Theta \subseteq E_{++}^n$. As we saw in Section 2, a necessary and sufficient condition for this is that the function Ψ defined in (2.18) represent R^* on Ω, i.e., that

$$(4.5) \qquad (\bar{p}_1, q^2, m^2) R^* (\bar{p}_1, q^1, m^1) \Leftrightarrow \\ m^2 - \mu(\bar{p}_1, q^2; p^0, m^0) \geqq m^1 - \mu(\bar{p}_1, q^1; p^0, m^0).$$

Given a set Ω of the form (4.4), define the set $\Omega_{\bar{p}_1} \subseteq E_{++}^{n+1}$ by

$$(4.6) \qquad \Omega_{\bar{p}_1} = \{(p, m) = (p_1, q, m) \in E_{++}^{n+1} \mid p_1^{-1}(q, m) \in \bar{p}_1^{-1}\Theta\},$$

and suppose that $(p^1, m^1), (p^2, m^2) \in \Omega_{\bar{p}_1}$. Applying the criterion (4.5) to the vectors

$$\frac{\bar{p}_1}{p_1^1}(q^1, m^1), \quad \frac{\bar{p}_1}{p_1^2}(q^2, m^2) \in \Theta,$$

we obtain:

$$\left(\bar{p}_1, \frac{\bar{p}_1}{p_1^2} q^2, \frac{\bar{p}_1}{p_1^2} m^2\right) R^* \left(\bar{p}_1, \frac{\bar{p}_1}{p_1^1} q^1, \frac{\bar{p}_1}{p_1^1} m^1\right) \Leftrightarrow \\ \frac{\bar{p}_1}{p_1^2} m^2 - \mu\left(\bar{p}_1, \frac{\bar{p}_1}{p_1^2} q^2; p^0, m^0\right) \geqq \frac{\bar{p}_1}{p_1^1} m^1 - \mu\left(\bar{p}_1, \frac{\bar{p}_1}{p_1^1} q^1; p^0, m^0\right).$$

Using the homogeneity of degree zero of R^* as well as property M2 of μ, we obtain:

$$(4.7) \qquad (p^2, m^2) R^* (p^1, m^1) \Leftrightarrow \frac{m^2}{p_1^2} - \frac{\mu(p^2; p^0, m^0)}{p_1^2} \geqq \frac{m^1}{p_1^1} - \frac{\mu(p^1; p^0, m^0)}{p_1^1}$$

(cf. Chipman & Moore, 1980).

Thus we have established the following:

Lemma 4. *Given $(p^0, m^0) \in E_{++}^{n+1}$, the function Ψ defined by (2.18) represents R^* on a non-empty set $\{\bar{p}_1\} \times \Theta \subseteq E_{++}^{n+1}$ if and only if the function $V : E_{++}^{n+1} \to E^1$ defined by*

$$(4.8) \qquad V(p, m) = \frac{m}{p_1} - \frac{\mu(p; p^0, m^0)}{p_1}$$

represents R^* *on* $\Omega_{\bar{p}_1} \subseteq E^{n+1}_{++}$, *where* $\Omega_{\bar{p}_1}$ *is defined by (4.6).*

Note that the function (4.8) has the property

$$V(p,m^2) - V(p,m^1) = \frac{m^2 - m^1}{p_1}. \tag{4.9}$$

It will be shown in Theorem 3 below that if a function V with this property represents R^* on set $\Omega \subseteq E^{n+1}_{++}$ of the form

$$\Omega = \{(p,m) \in E^{n+1}_{++} \mid p \in \Pi \ \&\ m > \nu(p)\}, \tag{4.10}$$

where Π is a non-empty open subset of E^n_{++} and $\nu : \Pi \to E^1_+$ is a continuous function, then R must be parallel with respect to commodity 1 on $h(\Omega)$, where we define this condition as follows: a preference relation R is *parallel with respect to commodity 1* on a subset $Z \subseteq E^n_+$ if and only if, denoting $y = (x_2, x_3, \ldots, x_n)$, the conditions

$$(\forall (x_1^1, y^1), (x_1^2, y^2) \in Z) : [y^2 = y^1 \ \&\ x_1^2 > x_1^1] \Rightarrow (x_1^2, y^2)\, P\, (x_1^1, y^1) \tag{4.11a}$$

(where "P" denotes the relation of strict preference) and

$$(\forall x^1, x^2 \in Z)(\forall \lambda \in E^1 \text{ such that } x^1 + \lambda e^1, x^2 + \lambda e^1 \in Z) : \tag{4.11b}$$

$$x^2 R x^1 \Rightarrow x^2 + \lambda e^1 \, R \, x^1 + \lambda e^1$$

hold, where we define

$$e^1 = (1, 0, 0, \ldots, 0). \tag{4.12}$$

We may observe now that for an appropriate choice of Θ (given by (4.13) below) the form (4.10) coincides with the form (4.6) above, so that we shall be able to conclude from Lemma 4 and Theorem 3 that, for such sets Θ, the compensating variation provides an acceptable welfare criterion on $\{\bar{p}_1\} \times \Theta$ only if R is parallel with respect to commodity 1 on $h(\Omega)$. This establishes proposition (c) stated at the close of the introduction.

Let the set $\Theta \subseteq E^n_{++}$ have the form

$$\Theta = \{(q,m) \in E^n_{++} \mid q \in \Pi_1 \ \ \&\ \ m > \nu^*(q)\}, \tag{4.13}$$

where Π_1 is a non-empty open subset of E^{n-1}_{++} and $\nu^* : \Pi_1 \to E^1_+$ is a continuous function. Now define $\Pi \subseteq E^n_{++}$ and $\nu : \Pi \to E^1_+$ by

$$\Pi = \left\{ p = (p_1, q) \in E^n_{++} \;\middle|\; \frac{\bar{p}_1}{p_1} q \in \Pi_1 \right\} \tag{4.14}$$

(note that Π, so defined, is a cone) and

$$\nu(p) = \frac{p_1}{\bar{p}_1} \nu^*\!\left(\frac{\bar{p}_1}{p_1} q\right). \tag{4.15}$$

Then Π and ν satisfy the required properties and we verify from the definitions (4.6), (4.10), (4.14), and (4.15) that $\Omega = \Omega_{\bar{p}_1}$.

Conversely, if R is parallel with respect to commodity 1 on E^n_+, it will follow from Theorem 5 below that, for an appropriate $(p^0, m^0) \in E^{n+1}_{++}$, there exists a non-empty set Ω of the form (4.6) such that the function V of (4.8) represents R^* on Ω, and thus that the compensating variation provides an acceptable welfare criterion on $\{\bar{p}_1\} \times \Theta$, where Θ is a set of the form (4.13).

Theorem 3. *Suppose the demand correspondence h satisfies*

$$(\forall (p,m) \in E^{n+1}_{++}) : h(p,m) \text{ is a convex set,}$$

and suppose there exists a non-empty open set $\Pi \subseteq E^n_{++}$, and functions

$$\nu : \Pi \to E^1_+, \quad V : \Omega \to E^1$$

(where Ω is defined by (4.10)), satisfying:

(a) ν is continuous;

(b) V represents R^* on Ω;

(c) V satisfies (4.9) for all $(p, m^1), (p, m^2) \in \Omega$.

Then the following conditions hold:

(i) h satisfies the budget-balance condition on Ω;

(ii) if $(p^1, m^1), (p^1, m^2) \in \Omega$ and $x^1 = (x^1_1, y^1) \in h(p^1, m^1)$ satisfy

$$m^2 \geqq q^1 \cdot y^1 \quad (\text{where} \quad q^1 = (p^1_2, \ldots, p^1_n)), \tag{4.16}$$

then

$$(x^1_1 + \lambda, y^1) \in h(p^1, m^2), \quad \text{where} \quad \lambda = \frac{m^2 - m^1}{p^1_1};$$

(iii) R is parallel with respect to commodity 1 on $h(\Omega)$.

Proof. (i) Since V is strictly increasing in m on Ω, it follows at once from Lemma 1 that h satisfies the budget-balance condiion (2.3) on Ω.

(ii) Let $(p^1, m^1), (p^1, m^2) \in \Omega$ and $(x^1_1, y^1) \in h(p^1, m^1)$ satisfy (4.16), and define $x^2 \in E^n$ by

$$x^2 = (x^1_1 + \lambda, y^1), \quad \text{where} \quad \lambda = \frac{m^2 - m^1}{p^1_1}. \tag{4.17}$$

Then we have, from (4.16) and condition (i),

$$x^2_1 = x^1_1 + \lambda = x^1_1 + \frac{m^2 - m^1}{p^1_1} \geqq x^1_1 + \frac{q^1 \cdot y^1 - m^1}{p^1_1} = x^1_1 - \frac{p^1_1 x^1_1}{p^1_1} = 0,$$

and

$$p^1 \cdot x^2 = p^1 \cdot x^1 + p^1_1 \lambda = m^2.$$

Hence

$$x^2 \in B(p^1, m^2) = \{x \in E^n_+ \mid p^1 \cdot x \leqq m^2\}.$$

Suppose, by way of contradiction, that

(4.18) $$x^2 \notin h(p^1, m^2).$$

By the continuity of the function ν, the fact that Π is an open set, and the fact that $m^t > \nu(p^1)$ for $t = 1, 2$, there exists $\varepsilon > 0$ such that[14]

(4.19) $$(\forall p \in N(p^1, \varepsilon)) : \quad p \in \Pi \ \& \ |\nu(p) - \nu(p^1)| < \min\{m^1 - \nu(p^1), m^2 - \nu(p^1)\};$$

and, by Theorem 6 in Appendix A, there exists $(p^0, m^0) \in E^{n+1}_{++}$ satisfying[15]

(4.20) $$p^0 \in N(p^1, \varepsilon), \ p^0 \geq p^1, \ p^0 \cdot x^2 < m^0$$

and

(4.21) $$(p^1, m^2)\, P^*\, (p^0, m^0).$$

We then have, by (4.19) and (4.20),

$$\nu(p^0) - \nu(p^1) < m^2 - \nu(p^1),$$

so that

$$p^1 \cdot x^2 = m^2 > \nu(p^0).$$

Thus, using (4.20),

$$m^0 > p^0 \cdot x^2 \geqq p^1 \cdot x^2 > \nu(p^0),$$

so that $(p^0, m^0) \in \Omega$; and it then follows from (4.21) and hypothesis (b) that

(4.22) $$V(p^1, m^2) > V(p^0, m^0).$$

On the other hand, by (4.20) and the definition (4.17) of x^2, we have

$$m^0 > p^0 \cdot x^2 = p^0 \cdot x^1 + p_1^0 \lambda,$$

so that, again using (4.20),

(4.23) $$m^0 - p_1^0 \lambda > p^0 \cdot x^1 \geqq p^1 \cdot x^1 = m^1,$$

and thus

(4.24) $$(p^0, m^0 - p_1^0 \lambda)\ P^*\ (p^0, m^1).$$

However, it follows at once from (4.19) and (4.20) that

$$m^1 > \nu(p^0);$$

and thus, using (4.23), it follows that $(p^0, m^0 - p_1^0\lambda) \in \Omega$. Therefore, we have from (4.24) and hypothesis (b):

(4.25) $$V(p^0, m^0 - p_1^0 \lambda) > V(p^0, m^1) \ \text{ and } \ V(p^0, m^1) \geqq V(p^1, m^1),$$

---

[14] "$N(p, \varepsilon)$" denotes the neighborhood of p with radius $\varepsilon > 0$ in the Euclidean topology.

[15] We define the relation "$p^0 \geq p^1$" between vectors p^0 and p^1 to mean "$p^0 \geqq p^1$ and $p^0 \neq p^1$."

where the second inequality follows from the condition $p^0 \geq p^1$ of (4.20). However, it follows from hypothesis (c) that

$$V(p^0, m^0 - p_1^0\lambda) = V(p^0, m^0) - \lambda,$$

and thus from (4.25):

$$V(p^0, m^0) > V(p^1, m^1) + \lambda. \tag{4.26}$$

But then using hypothesis (c) once more we have

$$V(p^1, m^2) = V(p^1, m^1) + \frac{m^2 - m^1}{p_1^1} = V(p^1, m^1) + \lambda;$$

hence, from (4.26) we obtain

$$V(p^0, m^0) > V(p^1, m^2),$$

which contradicts (4.22). We conclude, therefore, that (4.18) cannot hold, i.e., that

$$x^2 \in h(p^1, m^2),$$

which establishes (ii) of our conclusion.

(iii) Suppose $x^1, x^2 \in h(\Omega)$ are such that

$$x_1^2 > x_1^1 \quad \& \quad y^2 = y^1. \tag{4.27}$$

Since $x^2 \in h(\Omega)$, there exists $(p^2, m^2) \in \Omega$ such that

$$x^2 \in h(p^2, m^2),$$

and we have from (4.27) that

$$p^2 \cdot x^1 < p^2 \cdot x^2 = m^2.$$

Therefore, it follows from the budget-balance condition that $x^2 P x^1$.

Next, let $x^1, x^2 \in h(\Omega)$ and $\lambda \in E^1$ be such that

$$x^1 R x^2 \text{ and } x^1 + \lambda e^1,\ x^2 + \lambda e^1 \in h(\Omega), \tag{4.28}$$

where e^1 is defined by (4.12). We wish to prove that

$$x^1 + \lambda e^1\, R\, x^2 + \lambda e^1. \tag{4.29}$$

This is obviously true for $\lambda = 0$. We shall provide a proof for the case $\lambda < 0$ only; the proof for $\lambda > 0$ is symmetric and is left to the interested reader.

Since $x^t + \lambda e^1 \in h(\Omega)$, there exists $(p^t, m^t) \in \Omega$ such that

$$x^t + \lambda e^1 \in h(p^t, m^t) \text{ for } t = 1, 2. \tag{4.30}$$

Furthermore, defining

$$\Delta^t m = -p_1^t \lambda \text{ for } t = 1, 2,$$

we have $\Delta^t m > 0$ hence

$$(4.31) \qquad (p^t, m^t + \Delta^t m) \in \Omega \text{ for } t = 1, 2;$$

consequently, by part (ii),

$$x^t \in h(p^t, m^t + \Delta^t m) \text{ for } t = 1, 2.$$

Hence by (4.28) and hypothesis (b),

$$(4.32) \qquad V(p^1, m^1 + \Delta^1 m) \geqq V(p^2, m^2 + \Delta^2 m).$$

Using the definition of $\Delta^t m$ and hypothesis (c) we have

$$V(p^t, m^t + \Delta^t m) = V(p^t, m^t) + \Delta^t m / p_1^t = V(p^t, m^t) - \lambda \text{ for } t = 1, 2;$$

hence, from (4.32),

$$V(p^1, m^1) \geqq V(p^2, m^2).$$

It then follows from (4.30) and hypothesis (b) that (4.29) holds. ∎

We now proceed to the converse proposition: that if R is parallel with respect to commodity 1 on E_+^n, then for an appropriate choice of (p^0, m^0) the function (4.8) represents R^* on a certain set $\hat{\Omega}(p^0, m^0)$ defined in the statement of Theorem 5 below. In order to establish this it will first be necessary to establish the precise dual property of R^* (and to determine the subset of E_{++}^{n+1} on which it holds) corresponding to the property enjoyed by R of being parallel with respect to commodity 1. This is given by the Corollary to Theorem 4. Theorem 4 in turn provides the characteristic property of demand correspondences generated by parallel preferences. The proof, which is rather elaborate, is contained in Appendix B.

Theorem 4. *Let R be convex and parallel with respect to commodity 1 on E_+^n. Define the set $\Pi \subseteq E_{++}^n$ by*

$$\Pi = \left\{ p \in E_{++}^n \;\middle|\; \left(\exists m \in E_+^1, \exists (x_1, y) \in h(p, m)\right) : x_1 > 0 \right\}$$

and the function $\nu : \Pi \to E_+^n$ by

$$\nu(p) = \inf\left\{ m \in E_+^1 \;\middle|\; \left(\exists (x_1, y) \in h(p, m)\right) : x_1 > 0 \right\}.$$

Then:

i. *ν is lower semi-continuous;*

ii. *for every $p^1 \in \Pi$ and every $m^1, m^2 \in E_+^1$ for which*

$$m^1 \geqq \nu(p^1) \quad \text{and} \quad m^2 \geqq \nu(p^1)$$

we have:

$$(\exists (x_1^1, y^1) \in h(p^1, m^1)) : \; (x_1^1, y^1) + \frac{m^2 - m^1}{p_1^1} e^1 \in h(p^1, m^2).$$

Remark. Writing $\lambda = (m^2 - m^1)/p_1^1$ we see immediately that part (ii) of Theorem 4 can be stated in the following equivalent form: If $m^1 \geqq \nu(p^1)$ and $\lambda \geqq -[m^1 - \nu(p^1)]/p_1^1$ then

$$(\exists(x_1^1, y^1) \in h(p^1, m^1)) : \ (x^1 + \lambda, y^1) \in h(p^1, m^1 + \lambda p_1^1). \tag{4.33}$$

An illustration for the case $\lambda < 0$ is given in Figure 3.

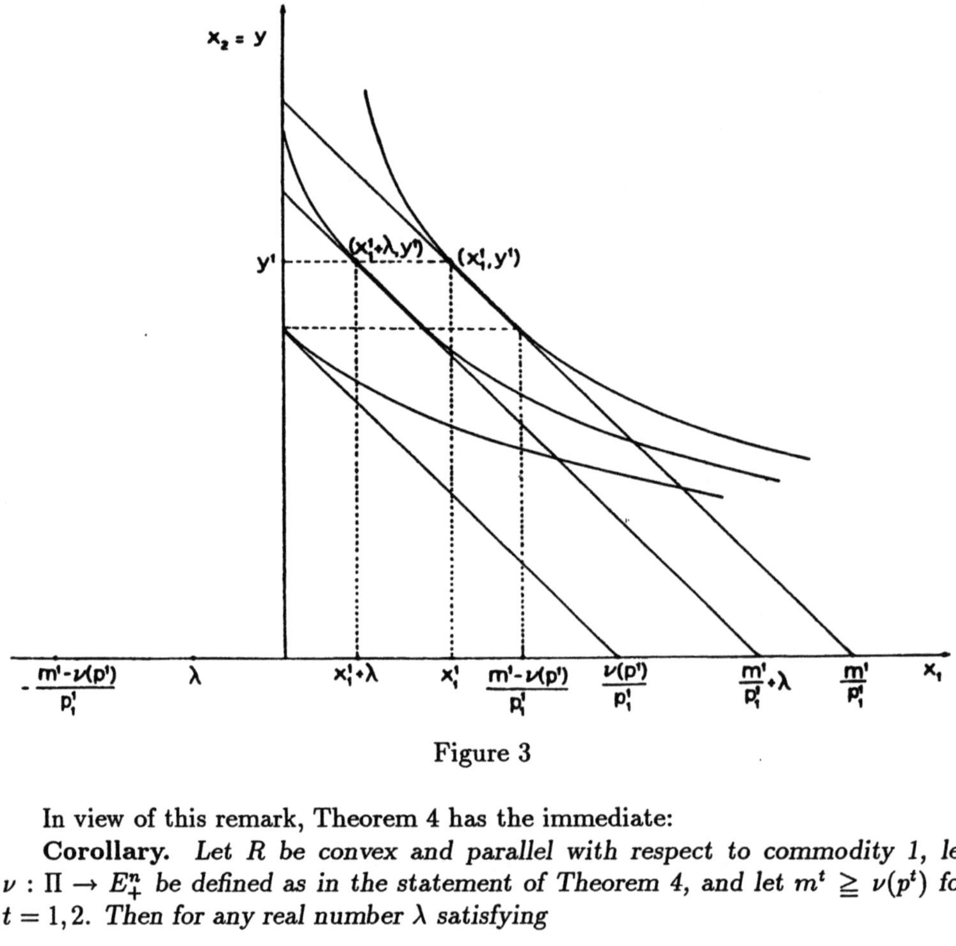

Figure 3

In view of this remark, Theorem 4 has the immediate:

Corollary. *Let R be convex and parallel with respect to commodity 1, let* $\nu : \Pi \to E_+^n$ *be defined as in the statement of Theorem 4, and let* $m^t \geqq \nu(p^t)$ *for* $t = 1, 2$. *Then for any real number* λ *satisfying*

$$\lambda \geqq \max\left\{-\frac{m^1 - \nu(p^1)}{p_1^1}, -\frac{m^2 - \nu(p^2)}{p_1^2}\right\}$$

we have

$$(p^1, m^1)R^*(p^2, m^2) \Leftrightarrow (p^1, m^1 + \lambda p_1^1)R^*(p^2, m^2 + \lambda p_1^2).$$

Note that this property corresponds to the property defined by Lemma 3 in the case of homothetic preferences. The following result, which is established by Theorem 4 and by propositions P4–P7 of Chipman & Moore (1980), completes the argument that if R is parallel with respect to commodity 1, then there exists a non-empty set Γ of the form defined in (4.5) and (4.6) such that W^C provides an acceptable indicator of welfare change on Γ.

Theorem 5. *Let R be convex and parallel with respect to commodity 1 on E^n_+, and let $\Pi \subseteq E^n_{++}$ and $\nu : \Pi \to E^n_+$ be defined as in Theorem 4. Let $p^0 \in \Pi$ and $m^0 \geqq \nu(p^0)$, and define the sets $\hat{\Pi}(p^0, m^0) \subseteq \Pi$ and $\hat{\Omega}(p^0, m^0) \subseteq E^{n+1}_{++}$ by*[16]

$$\hat{\Pi}(p^0,m^0) = \{p \in \Pi \mid \mu(p^0;p,\nu(p)) \leqq m^0\} = \{p \in \Pi \mid (p^0,m^0)R^*(p,\nu(p))\}$$

and

$$\hat{\Omega}(p^0,m^0) = \{(p,m) \in E^{n+1}_{++} \mid p \in \hat{\Pi}(p^0,m^0) \ \& \ m \geqq \nu(p)\}$$

respectively. Then the function V of (4.8) represents R^* on $\hat{\Omega}(p^0,m^0)$.

An important contrast between Theorem 5 and Theorem 2 should be noted. The situation in the case of parallel preferences differs from that in the case of homothetic preferences in that the base budget (p^0, m^0) cannot be chosen arbitrarily. Moreover one cannot, in general, choose a base budget (p^0, m^0) such that $\hat{\Omega}(p^0, m^0) = E^{n+1}_{++}$; while this possibility is not ruled out,[17]such a stipulation would carry much stronger implications over and above the requirement that R be parallel. The following example provides an illustration of the need for qualifications in the statement of Theorem 5.

Example 2.[18] Let R be the weak order on E^2_+ generated by the utility function

$$U(x_1, x_2) = x_1 + 2\sqrt{x_2}.$$

Then h is a single-valued function given by

$$h(p,m) = \begin{cases} (0, m/p_2) & \text{for } m < (p_1)^2/p_2 \\ (m/p_1 - p_1/p_2, (p_1/p_2)^2) & \text{for } m \geqq (p_1)^2/p_2, \end{cases} \tag{4.34}$$

so that an indirect utility function representing R^* is given by $F(p,m) = U(h(p,m))$, or

$$F(p,m) = \begin{cases} 2\sqrt{m/p_2} & \text{for } m < (p_1)^2/p_2 \\ m/p_1 + p_1/p_2 & \text{for } m \geqq (p_1)^2/p_2. \end{cases} \tag{4.35}$$

In terms of the notation used in Theorem 4, Π and ν are given in this case by

$$\Pi = E^2_{++} \quad \text{and} \quad \nu(p) = (p_1)^2/p_2$$

respectively. (The function $\nu(1,p_2) = 1/p_2$ is shown in Figure 1.) We note further that for $p \in E^2_{++}$,

$$F(p,\nu(p)) = 2p_1/p_2. \tag{4.36}$$

[16]Note that, as is easy to prove, given any $p \in \Pi$, there exists $m^0 \geqq \nu(p^0)$ such that $p \in \hat{\Pi}(p^0,m^0)$. The sets $\hat{\Pi}(p^0,m^0)$ and $\hat{\Omega}(p^0,m^0)$ are therefore non-empty.

[17]An example in which $\Pi = E^n_{++} = \hat{\Pi}(p^0,m^0)$ for any base budget (p^0,m^0), and where preferences are both homothetic and parallel on E^n_+, is that in which R is the lexicographic ordering of E^n_+. See the further remarks on this case in Chipman & Moore (1976, pp. 74–5).

[18]This example was used in Chipman & Moore (1990, p. 88) to illustrate similar points.

Let $(p^0, m^0) \in E^3_{++}$ be a base budget with $m^0 \geqq \nu(p^0)$. Using (4.35) and (4.36) we see that for $p \in E^2_{++}$,

$$p \in \hat{\Pi}(p^0, m^0) \Leftrightarrow \frac{m^0}{p_1^0} + \frac{p_1^0}{p_2^0} \geqq \frac{2p_1}{p_2}, \tag{4.37}$$

where $\hat{\Pi}(p^0, m^0)$ is defined as in the statement of Theorem 5. We note next that

$$\frac{m^0}{p_1^0} + \frac{p_1^0}{p_2^0} \geqq \frac{2p_1}{p_2} \Leftrightarrow p_1\left[\frac{m^0}{p_1^0} + \frac{p_1^0}{p_2^0} - \frac{p_1}{p_2}\right] \geqq \frac{(p_1)^2}{p_2} = \nu(p). \tag{4.38}$$

If the consumer has the budget $(p, m) \in E^3_{++}$ where

$$m = p_1\left[\frac{m^0}{p_1^0} + \frac{p_1^0}{p_2^0} - \frac{p_1}{p_2}\right]$$

we see from (4.35) and (4.38) that

$$F(p,m) = \left[\frac{m^0}{p_1^0} + \frac{p_1^0}{p_2^0} - \frac{p_1}{p_2}\right] + \frac{p_1}{p_2} = \frac{m^0}{p_1^0} + \frac{p_1^0}{p_2^0} = F(p^0, m^0).$$

Hence from (4.37) and (4.38) we see that

$$\mu(p; p^0, m^0) = p_1\left[\frac{m^0}{p_1^0} + \frac{p_1^0}{p_2^0} - \frac{p_1}{p_2}\right] \Leftrightarrow p \in \hat{\Pi}(p^0, m^0). \tag{4.39}$$

On the other hand, as can easily be shown,

$$p \notin \hat{\Pi}(p^0, m^0) \Rightarrow \mu(p; p^0, m^0) = \frac{p_2}{4}\left[\frac{m^0}{p_1^0} + \frac{p_1^0}{p_2^0}\right]^2. \tag{4.40}$$

(See Figure 1, where a number of graphs of the family of curves $m = \mu(1, p_2; p^t, m^t)$ are plotted for different $(1, p_2^t, m^t)$ such that $m^t \geqq \nu(1, p_2^t) = 1/p_2^t$; by M5, these are indirect indifference curves. Note that they are parallel—in the sense of having a constant vertical distance between them—in the region $m \geqq \nu(p)$.)

From (4.35) we see that for $(p, m) \in \hat{\Omega}(p^0, m^0)$, we have

$$F(p,m) = \frac{m}{p_1} + \frac{p_1}{p_2},$$

while from (4.39) and (4.8) we have

$$\begin{aligned} V(p,m) &= \frac{m}{p_1} - \frac{\mu(p; p^0, m^0)}{p_1} = \frac{m}{p_1} - \frac{m^0}{p_1^0} - \frac{p_1^0}{p_2^0} + \frac{p_1}{p_2} \\ &= F(p,m) - F(p^0, m^0). \end{aligned}$$

This verifies the fact that V represents R^* on $\hat{\Omega}(p^0, m^0)$. It is easy to show, however, using (4.40) and (4.35), that V does not represent R^* on $E^3_{++} \backslash \hat{\Omega}(p^0, m^0)$.

Appendix A

A duality theorem underlying the necessity results used in the proofs of Theorems 1 and 3.

Theorem 6. *Let R be an upper semi-continuous weak order on E^n_+, let h satisfy the budget-balance condition (2.3), and let R^* be the indirect preference relation induced by R. Let $(p^1, m^1) \in E^{n+1}_{++}$; then, given any*[19]

$$x^1 \in B(p^1, m^1)\backslash \text{conv } h(p^1, m^1)$$

and any $\varepsilon > 0$, there exists $(p^0, m^0) \in E^{n+1}_{++}$ such that

$$\|p^0 - p^1\| < \varepsilon,\ |m^0 - m^1| < \varepsilon,\ p^0 \geq p^1,\ p^0 \cdot x^1 < m^0, \tag{A.1}$$

and

$$(p^1, m^1) P^* (p^0, m^0). \tag{A.2}$$

Proof. Let (p^1, m^1) and x^1 be as in the hypotheses, let $\varepsilon > 0$ be given, and define the sets $A, B, C, D \in E^n_+$ by

$$\begin{aligned} A &= \{x \in E^n_+ \mid (\forall x' \in h(p^1, m^1)) : xRx'\}, \\ B &= A \cap B(p^1, m^1 + \varepsilon), \\ C &= \text{conv} B, \\ D &= C + E^n_+, \end{aligned}$$

respectively. Since R is upper semi-continuous, A is closed. Consequently B is compact, and therefore (cf. Nikaido, 1968, p. 25) so too is C. Therefore, D is closed and convex.

1. First we show that $x^1 \notin D$. Suppose the contrary; then there exist $x' \in C$ and $z \in E^n_+$ such that $x^1 = x' + z$. However, since it is clear from the budget-balance condition that $p^1 \cdot x \geqq m^1$ for all $x \in C$, it then follows from the fact that $x^1 \in B(p^1, m^1)$ that

$$p^1 \cdot x^1 = m^1; \tag{A.3}$$

and thus, since $p^1 > 0$, that $z = 0$. Therefore, $x^1 = x' \in C$; and consequently, there exist[20]

$$a \in S^n_+,\ \{z^1, z^2, \ldots, z^{n+1}\} \subseteq A$$

such that

$$x^1 = x' = \sum_{i=1}^{n+1} a_i z^i. \tag{A.4}$$

However, it follows from the budget-balance condition and the definition of A that

$$p^1 \cdot z^1 \geqq m^1 \text{ for } i = 1, 2, \ldots, n+1,$$

and thus from (A.3) and (A.4) we have

$$p^1 \cdot z^i = m^1 \text{ for } i = 1, 2, \ldots, n+1.$$

[19] Following Rockafellar (1970) we denote by "conv A" the convex hull of a set A.

[20] "S^n_+" denotes the unit simplex $S^n_+ = \{a \in E^{n+1}_+ \mid \sum_{i=1}^{n+1} a_i = 1\}$.

Therefore, by definition of A,

$$z^i \in h(p^1, m^1) \text{ for } i = 1, 2, \ldots, n+1. \tag{A.5}$$

But (A.4) and (A.5) imply that $x^1 \in \text{conv}\, h(p^1, m^1)$, contrary to our hypothesis. Therefore, $x^1 \notin D$.

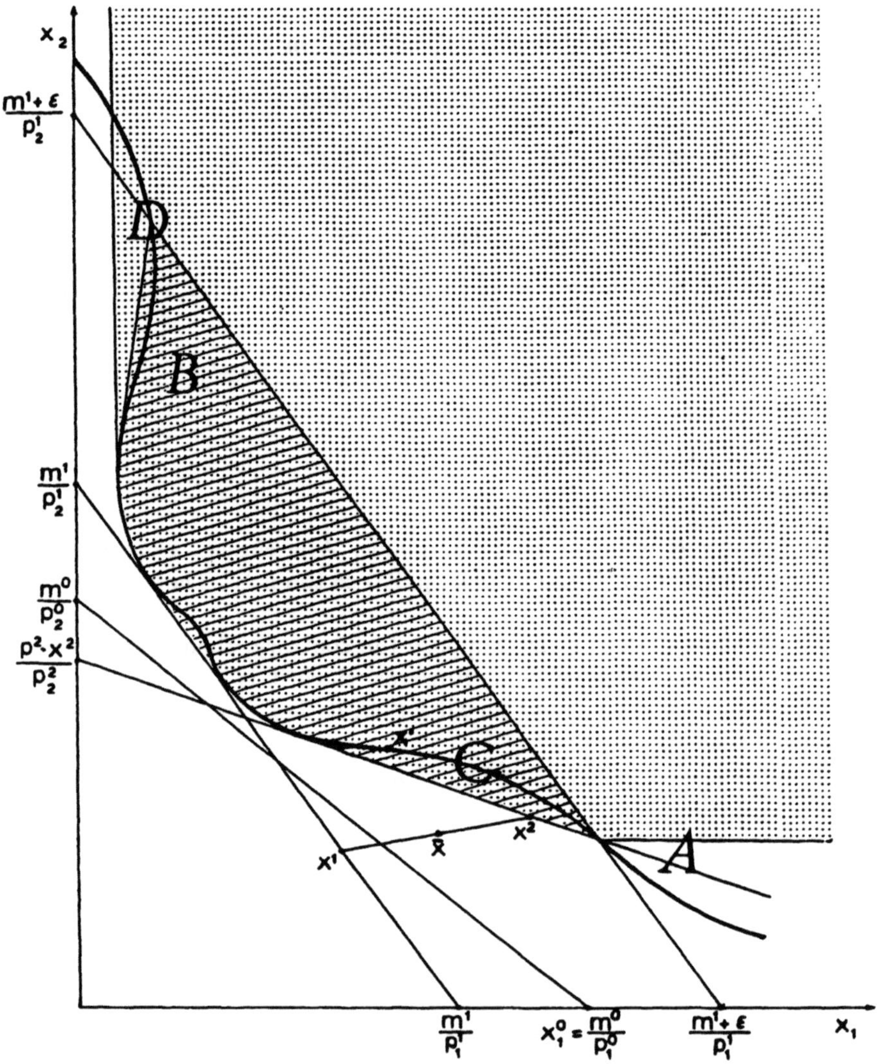

Figure 4

2. Next we establish (A.1). Since $x^1 \notin D$, and D is closed and convex, it follows by standard separating hyperplane results that there exist $p^2 \geq 0$ and $x^2 \in D$ satisfying (see Figure 4)

$$(\forall x \in D): \; p^2 \cdot x \geqq p^2 \cdot x^2 > p^2 \cdot x^1. \tag{A.6}$$

Defining $\bar{x} = \frac{1}{2}x^1 + \frac{1}{2}x^2$, we note that it follows from (A.6) that

(A.7) $$p^2 \cdot x^2 > p^2 \cdot \bar{x} > p^2 \cdot x^1;$$

and, since $p^2 \geq 0$ and $x^1 \geqq 0$ it follows that

(A.8) $$p^2 \cdot \bar{x} > 0.$$

Using (A.8), define

$$\delta = \min\left\{\frac{\varepsilon}{2p^2 \cdot x'}, \frac{\varepsilon}{2\|p^2\|}\right\}, \ p^0 = p^1 + \delta p^2, \ \text{and } m^0 = m^1 + \delta p^2 \cdot \bar{x}.$$

Then we note that $\|p^0 - p^1\| = \delta\|p^2\| \leqq \varepsilon/2 < \varepsilon, p^0 \geq p^1, |m^0 - m^1| = \delta p^2 \cdot \bar{x} \leqq \varepsilon/2 < \varepsilon$, and (using (A.7))

$$p^0 \cdot x^1 = (p^1 + \delta p^2) \cdot x^1 < m^1 + \delta p^2 \cdot \bar{x} = m^0.$$

3. Finally we establish (A.2). Now, consider the budget set $B(p^0, m^0)$. It is easy to prove that the maximum of $p^1 \cdot x$ subject to $x \geqq 0$ and $p^0 \cdot x \leqq m^0$ is achieved at $x = x^0$, where $x_i^0 = 0$ for $i \neq k$ and $x_i^0 = m^0/p_k^0$ for $i = k$, and where $k \in \{1, 2, \ldots, n\}$ is such that

$$p_k^1/p_k^0 \geqq p_i^1/p_i^0 \ \text{for } i = 1, 2, \ldots, n.$$

However, we have

(A.9) $$p^1 \cdot x^0 = m^0 p_k^1/p_k^0;$$

and, since $p^0 = p^1 + \delta p^2$, it follows that

(A.10) $$p_k^1/p_k^0 \leqq 1.$$

Furthermore, from (A.1) we have $m^0 \leqq m^1 + |m^0 - m^1| < m^1 + \varepsilon$, so that from (A.9) and (A.10) it follows that

$$\max\{p^1 \cdot x \mid x \in B(p^0, m^0)\} < m^1 + \varepsilon,$$

and thus

(A.11) $$B(p^0, m^0) \subseteq B(p^1, m^1 + \varepsilon).$$

However, if $x' \in B(p^1, m^1 + \varepsilon)$ is such that $x'Rx$ for some $x \in h(p^1, m^1)$, so that $x' \in A$, then by (A.6), (A.7), and the definition of D it follows that $p^2 \cdot x' \geq p^2 \cdot x^2 > p^2 \cdot \bar{x}$. Therefore, using the definition of m^0 and the budget-balance condition, it follows that for any such x',

$$p^0 \cdot x' = (p^1 + \delta p^2) \cdot x' = p^1 \cdot x' + \delta p^2 \cdot x' \geqq m^1 + \delta p^2 \cdot x^2 > m^1 + \delta p^2 \cdot \bar{x} = m^0.$$

Consequently, it follows that for $x^0 \in h(p^0, m^0)$, we must have xPx^0 for all $x \in h(p^1, m^1)$, and (A.2) follows. ∎

Appendix B

Properties of demand correspondences generated by parallel preferences: Proof of Theorem 4.

The proof of Theorem 4 will be preceded by a series of four Lemmas, and illustrated by Figures 5–7.

Lemma 5. *Let R be parallel with respect to commodity 1, and let $p^2 \in E^n_{++}$ and $m^1, m^2 \in E^1_+$. If $m^2 \geqq m^1$, and if $(x^2_1, y^2) \in h(p^2, m^2)$ is such that $x^2_1 \geqq (m^2 - m^1)/p^2_1$, then*

$$(x^2_1, y^2) - \frac{m^2 - m^1}{p^2_1} e^1 \in h(p^2, m^1).$$

Proof. Suppose p^2, m^1, m^2 and $(x^2_1, y^2) \in h(p^2, m^2)$ satisfy the hypothesis. Then, defining

$$x^1_1 = x^2_1 - \frac{m^2 - m^1}{p^2_1},$$

we see that (recalling the definition (2.1) of B)

$$(x^2_1, y^2) - \frac{m^2 - m^1}{p^2_1} e^1 = (x^1_1, y^2) \in B(p^2, m^1).$$

If for some $(x'_1, y') \in B(p^2, m^1)$ we were to have

$$(x'_1, y') P (x^1_1, y^2)$$

it would follow at once from the definition of parallel preferences and the definition of (x^1_1, y^2) that (see Figure 5)

$$(x''_1, y') \equiv (x'_1, y') + \frac{m^2 - m^1}{p^2_1} e^1 \; P \; (x^2_1, y^2);$$

and since $(x''_1, y') \in B(p^2, m^2)$, this would contradict our assumption that $(x^2_1, y^2) \in h(p^2, m^2)$. Therefore we have

$$(\forall (x'_1, y') \in B(p^2, m^1)) : \quad (x^1, y^2) R (x'_1, y'),$$

and we conclude that $(x^1_1, y^2) \in h(p^2, m^1)$, as desired. ∎

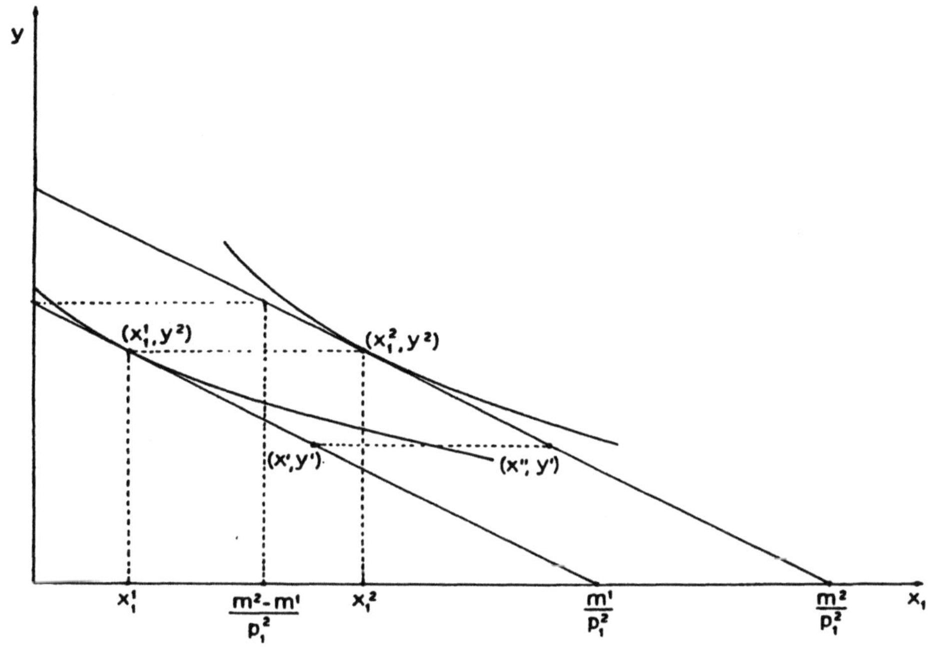

Figure 5

Lemma 6. *Let R be convex and parallel with respect to commodity 1 on E^n_+, and define the set $\Pi \subseteq E^n_{++}$ and the function $\nu : \Pi \to E^n_+$ as in the statement of Theorem 4. Then for any $p \in \Pi$ and any $m \geqq \nu(p)$, we have*

$$(\forall (x_1, y) \in h(p, m)) : x_1 \leqq \frac{m - \nu(p)}{p_1}.$$

Proof. Suppose by way of contradiction that there exist $(p^2, m^2) \in \Pi \times E^1_+$ and $(x_1^2, y^2) \in h(p^2, m^2)$ such that

$$x_1^2 > \frac{m^2 - \nu(p^2)}{p_1^2}.$$

Further, define $m^1 \in E^1_+$ by

$$m^1 = \nu(p^2) - \tfrac{1}{2}[p_1^2 x_1^2 - m^2 + \nu(p^2)] = \frac{\nu(p^2) + m^2 - p_1^2 x_1^2}{2}.$$

Then we have (see Figure 6)

$$\text{(B.1)} \qquad \begin{aligned} x_1^1 \equiv x_1^2 - \frac{m^2 - m^1}{p_1^2} &= x_1^2 - \frac{m^2}{p_1^2} + \frac{\nu(p^2) + m^2 - p_1^2 x_1^2}{2p_1^2} \\ &= \tfrac{1}{2}\left[x_1^2 - \frac{m^2 - \nu(p^2)}{p_1^2}\right] > 0, \end{aligned}$$

so that by Lemma 5,

$$(x_1^1, y^2) = (x_1^2, y^2) - \frac{m^2 - m^1}{p_1^2} e^1 \in h(p^2, m^1). \tag{B.2}$$

However, since $m^1 < \nu(p^2)$, (B.1) and (B.2) contradict the definition of $\nu(p^2)$. ∎

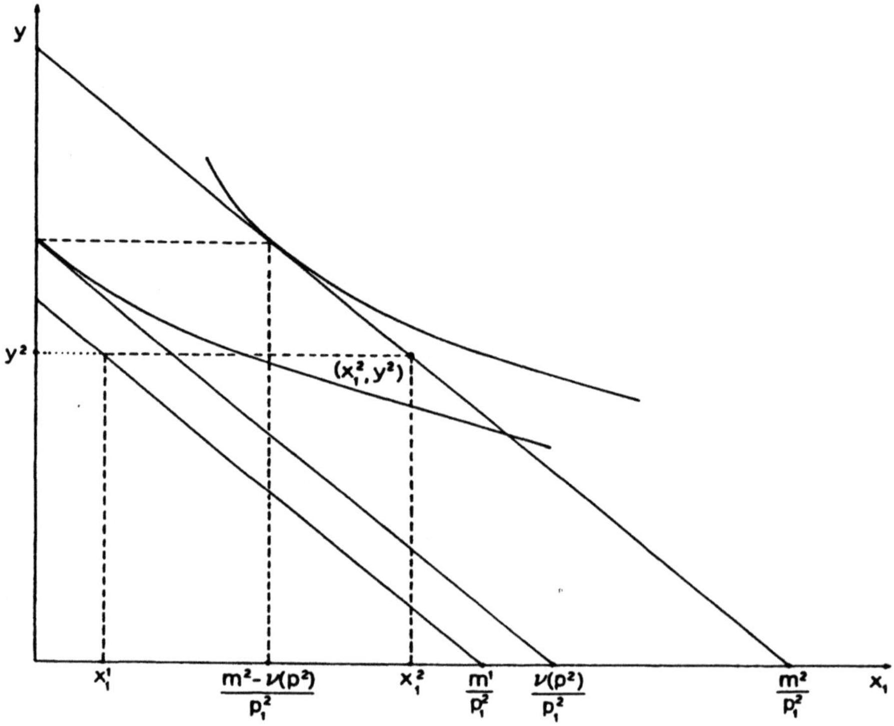

Figure 6

Lemma 7. *Let R, Π, and ν be as in the statement of Theorem 4, and let $p^1 \in \Pi$ and $m^1, m^2 \in E_+^1$ be such that*

$$m^2 \geqq m^1 \geqq \nu(p^1).$$

Then if $(x_1^1, y^1) \in h(p^1, m^1)$ is such that $x_1^1 > 0$, we have

$$(x_1^1, y^1) + \frac{m^2 - m^1}{p_1^1} e^1 \in h(p^1, m^2).$$

Proof. Let $(x_1^1, y^1) \in h(p^1, m^1)$ be such that $x_1^1 > 0$, and, defining

$$x_1^2 = x_1^1 + \frac{m^2 - m^1}{p_1^1}, \tag{B.3}$$

suppose by way of contradiction that

$$(x_1^2, y^1) \notin h(p^1, m^2). \tag{B.4}$$

Letting $(x_1'', y'') \in h(p^1, m^2)$ be such that

$$x_1'' = \max\{x_1 \mid (x_1, y) \in h(p^1, m^2)\},$$

we have by (B.4) and the fact that $(x_1^2, y^1) \in B(p^1, m^2)$ that

$$(x_1'', y'') P (x_1^2, y^1). \tag{B.5}$$

We now distinguish two cases:

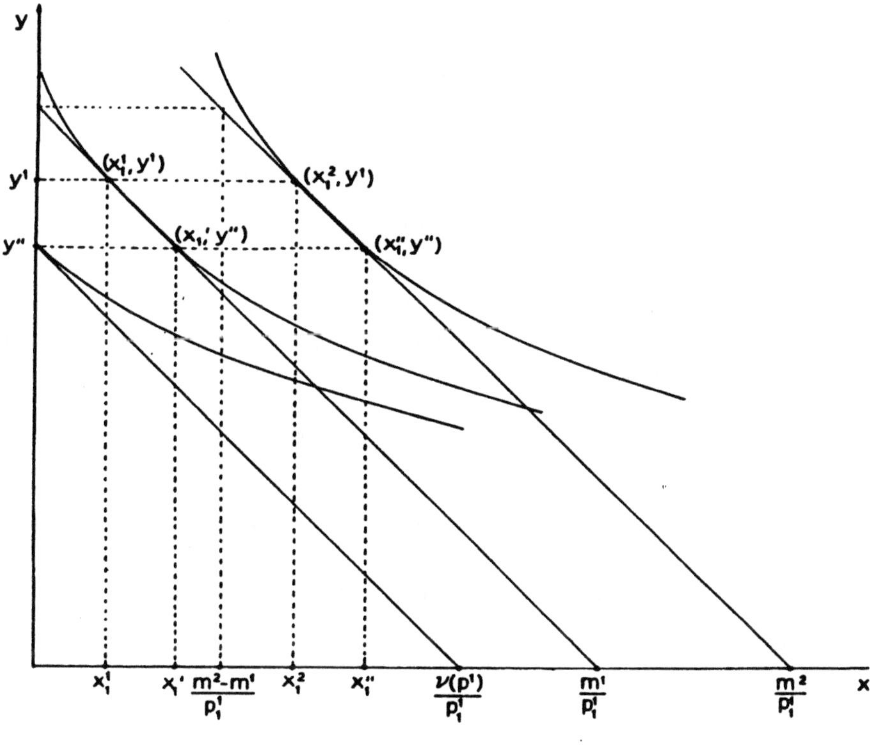

Figure 7

(a) $x_1'' \geqq (m^2 - m^1)/p_1^1$. Defining (see Figure 7)

$$x_1' = x_1'' - \frac{m^2 - m^1}{p_1^1} \geqq 0,$$

we have $(x_1', y'') \in B(p^1, m^1)$, hence it follows at once from (B.5), the definition (1.2) of parallel preferences, and the definition (B.3) of (x^2, y^1), that

$$(x_1', y'') = (x_1'', y'') - \frac{m^2 - m^1}{p_1^1} P (x_1^2, y^1) - \frac{m^2 - m^1}{p_1^1} = (x_1^1, y^1).$$

This contradicts the assumption that $(x_1^1, y^1) \in h(p^1, m^1)$.

(b) $x_1'' < (m^2 - m^1)/p_1^1$. Here it follows from (B.5) and the convexity of R that

(B.6) $$(\forall\lambda \in]0,1[) : \lambda(x_1'', y'') + (1-\lambda)(x_1^2, y^1) P (x_1^2, y^1).$$

However, since $x_1^1 > 0$, it can be seen that there exists $\lambda_0 \in]0,1[$ such that, defining

$$(\bar{x}_1, \bar{y}_1) = \lambda_0(x_1'', y'') + (1-\lambda_0)(x_1^2, y^1),$$

we will have

$$\bar{x}_1 - \frac{m^2 - m^1}{p_1^1} \geqq 0$$

(e.g., let $\lambda_1 = p_1^1 x_1^1/[m^2 - m^1 + p_1^1(x_1^1 - x_1'')]$). Thus we have

$$(\bar{x}_1, \bar{y}) - \frac{m^2 - m^1}{p_1^1} e^1 \in B(p^1, m^1);$$

and by (B.6), the definition of parallel preferences, and the definition of (x_1^2, y^1), we have

$$(\bar{x}_1, \bar{y}) - \frac{m^2 - m^1}{p_1^1} e^1 P (x_1^1, y^1),$$

contradicting the assumption that $(x_1^1, y^1) \in h(p^1, m^1)$. ∎

Lemma 8. *Let R, Π, and ν be as in the statement of Theorem 4. Then for any $p \in \Pi$ and for any $m \geqq \nu(p)$,*

$$(\exists (x_1, y) \in h(p, m)) : \quad x_1 = \frac{m - \nu(p)}{p_1}.$$

Proof. Let $(p^2, m^2) \in \Pi \times E_+^1$ be such that $m^2 \geqq \nu(p^2)$, let $(x_1^2, y^2) \in h(p^2, m^2)$ be such that

$$x_1^2 = \max\{x_1 \in E_+^1 \mid (x_1, y) \in h(p^2, m^2)\},$$

and suppose, by way of contradiction, that

$$x_1^2 < \frac{m^2 - \nu(p^2)}{p_1^2}.$$

Then $\nu(p^2) < m^2 - p_1^2 x_1^2$ so that, by the definition of ν, there exists $m^2 \in E_+^1$ satisfying

$$\nu(p^2) < m^1 < m^2 - p_1^2 x_1^2 \quad \text{and} \quad (\exists (x_1^1, y^1) \in h(p^2, m^1)) : x_1^1 > 0.$$

However, by Lemma 7 it follows that

$$(x_1'', y^1) \equiv (x_1^1, y^1) + \frac{m^2 - m^1}{p_1^2} e^1 \in h(p^2, m^2);$$

but since

$$x_1'' \equiv x_1^1 + \frac{m^2 - m^1}{p_1^2} > x_1^1 + \frac{m^2 - \nu(p^2)}{p_1^2} > x_1^1 + x_1^2 > x_1^2,$$

this contradicts our definition of (x_1^2, y^2).

We conclude, therefore, that

$$x_1^2 \geqq \frac{m^2 - \nu(p^2)}{p_1^2},$$

and our result follows at once from Lemma 6.

Proof of Theorem 4. (i) Define the function $\varphi : E_{++}^{n+1} \times E_+^n \to E_+^1$ by

$$\varphi(p, m, x) = x_1.$$

It is clearly continuous, and since h is upper hemi-continuous and compact-valued, it follows (cf. Berge, 1963, Theorem 2, p. 116) that the function $M : E_{++}^{n+1} \to E_+^1$ defined by

$$M(p,m) = \max\{\varphi(p,m,x) \mid x \in h(p,m)\}$$

is upper semi-continuous. Therefore, the function $N : E_{++}^{n+1} \to E^1$ defined by

$$N(p,m) = p_1 M(p,m) - m \tag{B.7}$$

is upper semi-continuous. However, for $p \in \Pi$ we have by Lemmas 6 and 8 that

$$M(p,m) = \begin{cases} 0 & \text{for } m < \nu(p) \\ \dfrac{m - \nu(p)}{p_1} & \text{for } m \geqq \nu(p). \end{cases} \tag{B.8}$$

It follows from (B.8) and (B.7) that for all $p \in \Pi$ and all $m > \nu(p)$, the function

$$N(p,m) = p_1 M(p,m) - m = -\nu(p)$$

is upper semi-continuous, and thus that ν is lower semi-continuous.

(ii) We have by Lemma 8,

$$(\exists (x_1^t, y^t) \in h(p^1, m^t)) : \quad x_1^t = \frac{m^t - \nu(p^1)}{p_1^1} \text{ for } t = 1, 2. \tag{B.9}$$

We now distinguish two cases.

(a) $m^2 \leqq m^1$. In this case, letting (x^1, y^1) be as in (B.9), we have, since $m^2 \geqq \nu(p^1)$,

$$x_1^1 + \frac{m^2 - m^1}{p_1^1} \geqq x_1^1 + \frac{\nu(p^1) - m^1}{p_1^1} = 0;$$

and then it follows at once from Lemma 5 that

$$(x_1^1, y^1) + \frac{m^2 - m^1}{p_1^1} e^1 \in h(p^1, m^2).$$

(b) $m^2 > m^1$. In this case it follows by the same basic reasoning as used in part (a) that

$$(x_1^2, y^2) + \frac{m^1 - m^2}{p_1^1} e^1 \in h(p^1, m^1). \tag{B.10}$$

Defining (x_1^0, y^2) by

$$(x_1^0, y^2) = (x_1^2, y^2) + \frac{m^1 - m^2}{p_1^1} e^1 \tag{B.11}$$

it follows from (B.10) that

$$(\forall (x_1, y) \in h(p^1, m^1)) : \ (x_1, y)\, I\, (x_1^0, y^2).$$

Consequently, it follows at once from the definition of parallel preferences and (B.11) that

$$(\forall (x_1, y) \in h(p^1, m^1)) : \quad (x_1, y) + \frac{m^2 - m^1}{p_1^1} e^1 I (x_1^2, y^2).$$

Thus we see that

$$h(p^1, m^1) + \left\{ \frac{m^2 - m^1}{p_1^1} e^1 \right\} \subseteq h(p^1, m^2). \quad \blacksquare$$

References

ALT, FRANZ (1936): "Über die Meßbarkeit des Nutzens," *Zeitschrift für Nationalökonomie,* 7, 2. Heft, 161–169. English translation: "On the Measurability of Utility," in *Preferences, Utility, and Demand,* ed. John S. Chipman, Leonid Hurwicz, Marcel K. Richter, and Hugo F. Sonnenschein. New York: Harcourt Brace Jovanovich Inc., 1971, 424–431.

AUSPITZ, RUDOLF, AND RICHARD LIEBEN (1889): *Untersuchungen über die Theorie des Preises.* Leipzig: Duncker & Humblot.

BARONE, ENRICO (1894): "Sulla 'consumers' rent'," *Giornale degli Economisti [2],* 9, 211–224.

BERGE, CLAUDE (1963): *Topological Spaces.* New York: The Macmillan Company.

BOULDING, KENNETH E. (1945): "The Concept of Economic Surplus," *American Economic Review,* 35, 851–869.

CHIPMAN, JOHN S., AND JAMES C. MOORE (1976): "The Scope of Consumer's Surplus Arguments," in *Evolution, Welfare and Time in Economics: Essays in Honor of Nicholas Georgescu-Roegen,* ed. Anthony M. Tang, Fred M. Westfield, and James S. Worley. Lexington, Mass.: D. C. Heath and Company, 69–123.

—— (1978): "The New Welfare Economics, 1939–1974," *International Economic Review,* 19, 547–584.

—— (1980): "Compensating Variation, Consumer's Surplus, and Welfare," *American Economic Review,* 70, 933–949.

—— (1990): "Acceptable Indicators of Welfare Change, Consumer's Surplus Analysis, and the Gorman Polar Form," in *Preferences, Uncertainty, and Optimality: Essays in Honor of Leonid Hurwicz,* ed. John S. Chipman, Daniel McFadden, and Marcel K. Richter. Boulder, Colo.: Westview Press, 68–120.

EDGEWORTH, F.Y. (1891): "Osservazioni sulla teoria matematica dell'economia politica con riguardo speciale ai principi di economia di Alfredo Marshall," *Giornale degli Economisti [2],* 2, 233–245.

FRISCH, RAGNAR (1926): "Sur un problème d'économie pure," *Norsk Matematisk Forenings Skrifter,* Serie I, Nr. 16, 1–40. English translation: "On a Problem in Pure Economics," in *Preferences, Utility and Demand*, ed. John S. Chipman, Leonid Hurwicz, Marcel K. Richter, and Hugo F. Sonnenschein. New York: Harcourt Brace Jovanovich, Inc. 1971, 386–423.

GREEN, JERRY, AND JEAN-JACQUES LAFFONT (1979): *Incentives in Public Decision-Making.* Amsterdam: North-Holland Publishing Company.

HARBERGER, ARNOLD C. (1964): "The Measurement of Waste," *American Economic Review, Papers and Proceedings,* 54, 58–76.

—— (1971): "Three Basic Postulates for Applied Welfare Economics, An Interpretive Essay," *Journal of Economic Literature,* 9, 785–797.

HAUSE, JOHN C. (1975): "The Theory of Welfare Cost Measurement," *Journal of Political Economy,* 83, 1145–1182.

HENDERSON, A. (1941): "Consumer's Surplus and the Compensating Variation," *Review of Economic Studies,* 8, 117–121.

HICKS, J. R. (1939): *Value and Capital.* Oxford: Clarendon Press. 2nd ed., 1946.

—— (1941): "The Rehabilitation of Consumer's Surplus," *Review of Economic Studies,* 8, 108–116.

—— (1942): "Consumer's Surplus and Index-Numbers," *Review of Economic Studies,* 9, 126–137.

—— (1956): *A Revision of Demand Theory.* Oxford: Clarendon Press.

HURWICZ, LEONID (1975): "On the Pareto-Optimality of Manipulative Nash Equilibria," presented at the Third World Congress of the Econometric Society, Toronto.

—— (1981): "On Incentive Problems in the Design of Non-Wasteful Resource Allocation Systems," in *Studies in Economic Theory and Practice: Essays in Honor of Edward Lipiński,* ed. N. Assorodobraj-Kula, C. Bobrowski, H. Hagemejer, W. Kula, and J. Łoś. Amsterdam: North-Holland Publishing Company, 93–106.

HURWICZ, LEONID, AND HIROFUMI UZAWA (1971): "On the Integrability of Demand Functions," in *Preferences, Utility and Demand,* ed. John S. Chipman, Leonid Hurwicz, Marcel K. Richter, and Hugo F. Sonnenschein. New York: Harcourt Brace Jovanovich, Inc., 114–148.

KATZNER, DONALD W. (1970): *Static Demand Theory.* New York: The Macmillan Company.

MCKENZIE, LIONEL W. (1957): "Demand Theory Without a Utility Index," *Review of Economic Studies,* 24, 185–189.

LAFFONT, JEAN-JACQUES, AND ERIC MASKIN (1982): "The Theory of Incentives: An Overview," in *Advances in Economic Theory,* ed. Werner Hildenbrand. Cambridge: Cambridge University Press, 31–94.

LINDAHL, ERIK (1919): *Die Gerechtigkeit der Besteuerung.* Lund: Gleerup. English translation of Part I, Chapter 4, pp. 85–98: "Just Taxation—A Positive Solution," in *Classics in the Theory of Public Finance,* ed. Richard A. Musgrave and Alan T. Peacock. London: Macmillan & Co. Ltd., 1958, 168–176.

MISHAN, E. J. (1971): *Cost-Benefit Analysis.* New York and Washington: Praeger Publishers.

MOHRING, HERBERT (1971): "Alternative Welfare Gain and Loss Measures," *Western Economic Journal,* 9, 349–368.

NIKAIDO, HUKUKANE (1968): *Convex Structures and Economic Theory.* New York: Academic Press.

OWEN, GUILLERMO (1982): *Game Theory.* 2nd edition. Orlando, Florida: Academic Press.

PARETO, VILFREDO (1909): *Manuel d'économie politique.* Paris: V. Giard et E. Brière.

ROCKAFELLAR, R. TYRRELL (1970): *Convex Analysis.* Princeton, N.J.: Princeton University Press.

SAMUELSON, PAUL A. (1942): "Constancy of the Marginal Utility of Income," in *Studies in Mathematical Economics and Econometrics, In Memory of Henry Schultz,* ed. Oscar Lange, Francis McIntyre, and Theodore O. Yntema. Chicago: University of Chicago Press, 75–91.

—— (1947): *Foundations of Economic Analysis.* Cambridge, Mass.: Harvard University Press.

—— (1964): "Principles of Efficiency—Discussion," *American Economic Review, Papers and Proceedings,* 54, 93–96.

—— (1974): "Complementarity: An Essay on the 40th Anniversary of the Hicks–Allen Revolution in Demand Theory," *Journal of Economic Literature,* 12, 1255–1289.

SAMUELSON, PAUL A., AND S. SWAMY (1974): "Invariant Economic Index Numbers and Canonical Duality: Survey and Synthesis," *American Economic Review,* 64, 566–593.

STARRETT, DAVID A. (1988): *Foundations of Public Economics.* Cambridge: Cambridge University Press.

Technical Progress, Terms of Trade and Welfare in a Mobile Capital Harris-Todaro Model

JAI-YOUNG CHOI
Lamar University, Beaumont
AND
EDEN S. H. YU
Louisiana State University
Chinese University of Hong Kong

1 Introduction

Recently, several trade theorists have investigated the implications of economic growth for a small economy in the mobile capital version of Harris-Todaro (1970) model of unemployment.[1] Corden and Findlay (1975) have analyzed the effects of factor accumulation and technical progress. They show that assuming a relatively capital-intensive manufacturing sector, the Rybczynski theorem and "ultra-biased" effect of technical progress on sectoral outputs derivable from the standard Heckscher-Ohlin-Samuelson model carries over to the Harris-Todaro (H-T henceforth) model with intersectoral capital mobility. Extending the analysis of Corden and Findlay, Neary (1981) has derived the necessary and sufficient condition for the stability of the model that an unspecialized long-run equilibrium is dynamically stable, if and only if the urban sector (i.e., manufacturing plus urban unemployed) is *capital-abundant* relative to the agricultural sector.[2] Recently, Beladi and Naqvi (1988) have shown that for a small country, economic growth resulting from either technical progress or factor growth cannot be immiserizing in the H-T model.

[1]In the original H-T model, there are three factors of production, labor, land, and capital. H-T assumed that land is specific to agriculture and capital is perfectly immobile between sectors. The capital-specific, H-T model was analyzed by Das (1982) when growth in the form of capital accumulation is introduced in a dynamic environment. Corden and Findlay (1975) brought the H-T model closer to the neoclassical two-sector model by incorporating intersectoral capital mobility. The capital- mobile H-T model has been used by Batra and Naqvi (1987) to study gains-from-trade issues, by Parai and Batra (1987) to examine welfare consequences of customs unions, and by Chao and Yu (1990) to consider the welfare effects of terms-of-trade changes.

[2]H-T showed that with sector-specific capital the model is always stable. Corden and Findlay (1975) assume that manufacturing is capital-intensive relative to agriculture without discussion of stability. Neary (1981) demonstrated that the Corden-Findlay assumption is only a necessary, though not sufficient, condition for stability.

The purpose of this paper is twofold. First, we will reconsider the implications of economic growth, specifically with reference to Hicks neutral technical progress, for a small country in conjunction with Neary's dynamic stability condition. In particular, the role of the stability condition for determining the Corden-Findlay and the Beladi- Naqvi results will be clearly identified.[3] We will show that the assumption of a capital-intensive manufacturing made by these writers is necessary, but not sufficient to establish their results. Second, we will extend the analysis to the case of a large country which is capable of influencing world prices by manipulating its volume of trade.[4] The effects of technical progress on capital-labor ratios, urban unemployment rate, labor allocation, sectoral outputs, import demand, terms of trade and social welfare will be systematically analyzed. It will be shown that for a large developing country, Hicks neutral technical progress occurring in manufacturing (importable) sector necessarily results in a higher social welfare, whereas technical progress in agricultural (exportable) sector may reduce welfare.

This paper is structured as follows. Section 2 briefly presents the capital-mobile Harris-Todaro model and its assumptions. Section 3 considers the implications of Hicks-neutral technical progress in manufacturing sector for sectoral employment, output and welfare for both a small as well as a large country. Section 4 examines the various effects of Hicks-neutral technical progress occurring agricultural sector. Section 5 offers the concluding remarks.

2 Assumptions and the Model

Consider a developing economy with two sectors: rural (sector 1) producing an agricultural output in the amount of X_1, and urban (sector 2) producing a manufactured product in the amount of X_2. Each sector utilizes two factors of production, labor (L) and capital (K), and a linearly homogeneous technology. Both factors are perfectly mobile between sectors. Flexible rental (r) ensures full-employment of capital. But the labor is fully employed in the rural sector only where the real wage (w_1) is flexible. In the urban sector where the real wage (w_2) is rigid (due to an institutional minimum wage), unemployment exists.

The production functions for the two sectors are expressed as

$$X_i = t_i F_i(L_i, K_i) = t_i L_i f_i(k_i) \qquad i = 1,2 \tag{1}$$

where X_i is the output of the ith sector, K_i and L_i are its employment of capital and labor, and k_i ($= K_i/L_i$) is its capital-labor ratio. The parameter t_i denotes the sectoral state of technology with t_i equals to unity initially, and f_i is F_i/L_i for $i = 1,2$.

Perfect capital mobility results in identical rental rates, equal to the value of

[3]The Corden-Findlay and the Beladi-Naqvi results are mostly derived from diagrammatic analysis, and hence the role of dynamic stability condition for their results cannot be clearly identified.

[4]Corden-Findlay and Beladi-Naqvi confined their analysis to the case of a small developing economy. It is instructive to extend their analysis to the case of a large developing country such as Brazil.

marginal product of capital, in both sectors.

$$r = t_1 F_{K1} = pt_2 F_{K2}$$

or

$$r = t_1 f_1'(k_1) = pt_2 f_2'(k_2) \tag{2}$$

where F_{Ki} is the partial derivative of F_i with respect to capital in the ith sector, f_i' is the derivative of f_i with respect to k_i (i = 1,2), and p is the relative price of the manufactured good in terms of the agricultural good.

The wage rates in the two sectors are usually unequal, and labor allocations are determined also through marginal productivity pricing by

$$w_1 = t_1 F_{L1} = t_1(f_1 - k_1 f_1') \tag{3}$$

$$\overline{w}_2 = pt_2 F_{L2} = pt_2(f_2 - k_2 f_2') \tag{4}$$

where F_{Li} is the partial derivative of F_i with respect to labor in the ith sector ($i = 1, 2$).

The unique feature of the H-T model is that labor migration from rural to urban sector occurs until the actual rural wage equals to the expected wage in the urban sector, which is the institutionally-set minimum wage ($\overline{w}_2$) times the probability of finding a job in the urban sector. Let λ be the urban unemployment ratio, i.e., the ratio of unemployed (L_u) to the employed (L_2) in the urban sector. Then labor force in the urban sector equals $L_2 + L_u = L_2(1 + \lambda)$. The labor market equilibrium implies

$$(1 + \lambda)w_1 = \overline{w}_2. \tag{5}$$

The employment condition in factor markets can be written as

$$K_1 + K_2 = L_1 k_1 + L_2 k_2 = \overline{K} \tag{6}$$

and

$$L_1 + L_2 + L_u = L_1 + (1 + \lambda)L_2 = \overline{L} \tag{7}$$

where $\overline{K}$ and $\overline{L}$ denote fixed supplies of capital and labor, respectively.

The demand side of the model is given by a strictly quasi-concave social utility function (U), which is dependent on the consumption for the two commodities (D_1 and D_2):

$$U = U(D_1, D_2) \tag{8}$$

where $U_1 > 0$ and $U_{ii} < 0$ for $i = 1, 2$. The economy's budget constraint stipulates that the value of production is matched by the value of consumption

$$X_1 + pX_2 = D_1 + p_2 D_2. \tag{9}$$

Following H-T, we will assume that the developing economy exports the agricultural product and imports the manufactured product.

$$E_1 = X_1 - D_1 \tag{10}$$

$$E_2 = D_2 - X_2 \tag{11}$$

where E_1 and E_2, respectively, stand for the export and import of the country.

This completes the specification of the mobile capital version of H-T model which allows for the presence of urban unemployment in a growing economy. The model can be used for studying the implications of Hicks-neutral technical progress in either the manufacturing or the agricultural sector, a task to be dealt with in the next two sections.

3 Hicks-Neutral Technical Progress in Manufacturing Sector

In this section, consider Hicks-neutral technical progress taking place in the manufacturing sector only, i.e., $dt_1 = 0$, $dt_2 > 0$. For notational simplicity, let $t_2 = t$ and $dt_2 = dt$, hereafter. For a moment, assume a small country which is a price-taker in the international market.

For analytical purposes, equations (2) - (5) are reduced to a system of three equations:

$$f_1' = ptf_2' \tag{12}$$

$$pt(f_2 - k_2 f_2') = \overline{w} \tag{13}$$

$$(1+\lambda)(f_1 - k_1 f_1') = \overline{w} \tag{14}$$

Note that the above three equations contain 3 endogenous variables, k_1, k_2 and λ, and 2 parameters p and t.[5] Thus we can solve for the unknowns: $k_i = k_i(p,t)$ $(i = 1,2)$ and $\lambda = \lambda(p,t)$. Totally differentiating (12) - (14) and expressing them in matrix form.

$$\begin{bmatrix} f_1'' & -ptf_2'' & 0 \\ 0 & -ptk_2 f_2'' & 0 \\ -(1+\lambda)k_1 f_1'' & 0 & f_1 - k_1 f_1' \end{bmatrix} \begin{bmatrix} dk_1 \\ dk_2 \\ d\lambda \end{bmatrix} = \begin{bmatrix} tf_2' dp + pf_2' dt \\ -tF_{L2} dp - pF_{L2} dt \\ 0 \end{bmatrix} \tag{15}$$

The determinant of the coefficient matrix of (15) is

$$D = -w_1 ptk_2 f_1'' f_2'' < 0 \tag{16}$$

because $f_i'' < 0 (i = 1,2)$ due to diminishing marginal productivity.

3.1 Sectoral Employment and Output

The effects of an exogenous change in the relative good price at constant technology and of Hicks-neutral technological progress at constant good price ratio can be easily ascertained. By virtue of Cramer's rule, (15) can be solved for dk_1, dk_2 and $d\lambda$. With constant technology ($dt = 0$), we obtain

[5] w_2 may be treated as a parameter, but this is not necessary for the present analysis.

$$\partial k_1/\partial p = -pt^2 f_2 F_{L1} f_2''/D < 0 \tag{17}$$

$$\partial k_2/\partial p = -tF_{L1}F_{L2}f_1''/D < 0 \tag{18}$$

$$\partial \lambda/\partial p = -(1+\lambda)pt^2 k_1 f_2 f_1'' f_2''/D > 0 \tag{19}$$

Holding the relative price of the manufacturing good constant ($dp = 0$), we derive

$$\partial k_1/\partial t = -p^2 t f_2 F_{L1} f_2''/D < 0 \tag{20}$$

$$\partial k_2/\partial t = -pF_{L1}F_{L2}f_1''/D < 0 \tag{21}$$

$$\partial \lambda/\partial t = -(1+\lambda)p^2 t k_1 f_2 f_1'' f_2''/D > 0 \tag{22}$$

It is clear that an increase in the relative price of the manufacturing good has effect on sectoral factor-intensities and urban unemployment similar to that of technical improvement in the manufacturing sector. That is, an increase in p or t reduces the capital-labor ratios in both sectors and raises the urban unemployment ratio (λ). Our result supports the finding obtained graphically by Corden and Findlay (1975) and Beladi and Naqvi (1988). It is notable that the dynamic stability condition has no bearing on this result.

The labor allocational effect of a change n the good price ratio or the state of technology in manufacturing can be deduced. Differentiating (6) and (7) with respect to p while holding technology constant, $dt = 0$, we obtain

$$\partial L_1/\partial p = [k_2 - (1+\lambda)k_1]^{-1}[(1+\lambda)(L_1\partial k_1/\partial p + L_2\partial k_2/\partial p) - k_2 L_2 \partial\lambda/\partial p] \tag{23}$$

$$\partial L_2/\partial p = -[k_2 - (1+\lambda)k_1]^{-1}(L_1\partial k_1/\partial p + L_2\partial k_2/\partial p - k_1 L_2 \partial\lambda/\partial p) \tag{24}$$

Differentiating (6) and (7) with respect to t holding p constant yields

$$\partial L_1/\partial t = [k_2 - (1+\lambda)k_1]^{-1}[(1+\lambda)(L_1\partial k_1/\partial t + L_2\partial k_2/\partial t) - k_2 L_2 \partial\lambda/\partial t] \tag{25}$$

$$\partial L_2/\partial t = -[k_2 - (1+\lambda)k_1]^{-1}(L_1\partial k_1/\partial t + L_2\partial k_2/\partial t - k_1 L_2 \partial\lambda/\partial t) \tag{26}$$

Note that the signs of the expressions (23) - (26) crucially depend on the sign of the denominator, $k_2 - (1+\lambda)k_1$. If $[k_2 - (1+\lambda)k_1]$ is positive (negative), then $\partial L_1/\partial p$ and $\partial L_1/\partial t$ are both negative (positive) *and* $\partial L_2/\partial p$ and $\partial L_2/\partial t$ are both positive (negative). What then is the meaning of $[k_2 - (1+\lambda)k_1]$? Neary (1981) demonstrated that the neoclassical H-T model is stable if and only if manufacturing sector is *capital abundant* relative to agriculture. Capital abundant in manufacturing is a stronger condition than capital intensive, because the former requires not only $k_2 > k_1$, but also $k_2 > (1+\lambda)k_1$.[6] So $k_2 > k_1$ is a necessary, but not sufficient condition for stability.

Assuming manufacturing is capital intensive, i.e., $k_2 > k_1$, Corden and Findlay argue that Hicks-neutral technical progress in manufacturing raises (reduces) employment of labor in manufacturing (agriculture). Our result clearly shows that Corden-Findlay argument holds, if and only if $k_2 > (1+\lambda)k_1$, and their argument

[6]McCool (1982) points out that Neary's dynamic stability condition, $k_2 > (1+\lambda)k_1$, implies that manufacturing is capital-intensive relative to agriculture in the value sense (see also Batra and Naqvi, 1987).

breaks down if $k_2 < (1+\lambda)k_1$ even if $k_2 > k_1$. To sustain Corden-Findlay argument, the assumption that manufacturing is capital-intensive should be replaced by a stronger condition that manufacturing is capital-abundant, a condition consistent with the stability of the model. Similarly, the effect of a change in p on sectoral employment depends upon whether or not manufacturing is capital abundant. For notational simplicity let $\alpha = [k_2 - (1+\lambda)k_1]$ hereafter.

We can now determine the effect of a change in p or t on sectoral outputs. Differentiating (1) holding t constant and utilizing (17), (18), (23) and (24), we obtain

$$\begin{aligned}\partial X_1/\partial p &= f_1\partial L_1/\partial p + L_1 f_1'\partial k_1/\partial p = \alpha^{-1}\{\partial k_1/\partial p[L_1 f_1'\alpha + f_1(1+\lambda)L_1] \\ &\quad -f_1[L_2 f_2 \partial\lambda/\partial p - (1+\lambda)L_2\partial k_2/\partial p]\} \qquad (27)\end{aligned}$$

$$\begin{aligned}\partial X_2/\partial p &= tf_2\partial L_2/\partial p + tL_2 f_2'\partial k_2/\partial p = -t\alpha^{-1}\{f_2[L_1\partial k_1/\partial p - k_1 L_2 \partial\lambda/\partial p] \\ &\quad +L_2[F_{L2} + f_2'(1+\lambda)k_1](\partial k_2/\partial p)\} \qquad (28)\end{aligned}$$

Similarly, differentiating (1), holding p constant, and using (20), (21), (25) and (26) yields

$$\begin{aligned}\partial X_1/\partial t &= f_1\partial L_1/\partial t + L_1 f_1'\partial k_1/\partial t = \alpha^{-1}\{(\partial k_1/\partial t)[L_1 f_1'\alpha + f_1(1+\lambda)L_1] \\ &\quad -f_1[L_2 k_2(\partial\lambda/\partial t) - (1+\lambda)L_2(\partial k_2/\partial t)]\} \qquad (29)\end{aligned}$$

$$\begin{aligned}\partial X_2/\partial t &= L_2 f_2 + tf_2\partial L_2/\partial t + tL_2 f_2' = L_2 f_2 - \alpha^{-1}t\{f_2[L_1\partial k_1/\partial t - k_1 L_2\partial\lambda/\partial t \\ &\quad +L_2[F_{L2} + f_2'(1+\lambda)k_1](\partial k_2/\partial t)\}. \qquad (30)\end{aligned}$$

Equations (27)-(28) reveal that the sectoral output will respond positively to a change in its relative price, if and only if manufacturing is relatively capital abundant, i.e., $\alpha > 0$. The price-output response would be perverse if $\alpha < 0$. Thus, assuming $k_2 > k_1$ cannot guarantee positive price-output response. Similarly, (29) and (30) shows that Hicks-neutral technical progress in manufacturing will raise the manufacturing output and lower the agricultural output at constant terms of trade, i.e., growth is ultra-biased, if and only if $\alpha > 0$.[7] It follows that assuming a dynamically stable system, the output effect of growth will be ultra-biased.

3.2 Welfare Effect

It is now relatively straightforward to analyze the welfare effect of technical improvement occurring in manufacturing sector. Differentiating the social utility function (8), utilizing consumer equilibrium condition ($U_2/U_1 = p$), and differentiating the budget constraint (9) with respect to t, we obtain

$$(1/U_1)dU/dt = dY/dt = dX_1/dt + pdX_2/dt - E_2 dp/dt \qquad (31)$$

[7] Corden and Findlay argued that growth is ultra- biased if $k_2 > k_1$. Again this assumption is insufficient; it should be replaced by $\alpha > 0$.

where dY is the change in the real income.

Note that Hicks-neutral technical progress in manufacturing will affect the output of either industry in two possible ways: (1) a direct effect on outputs due to technological improvements in manufacturing and the resulting reallocation of resources between manufacturing and agriculture; (2) an indirect effect results from the adjustment in the terms of trade consequent upon technical progress. Thus we may write

$$X_i = X_i(t, p(t)) \qquad i = 1, 2 \tag{32}$$

so that

$$dX_i/dt = \partial X_i/\partial t + (\partial X_i/\partial p)(dp/dt) \tag{33}$$

The first term of the RHS of (33) captures the direct output effect of technical progress at constant terms of trade, and the second term indicates the indirect output effect resulting from technical progress via changes in the terms of trade.

Substituting (33) into (31), we obtain the key expression for assessing the welfare effect of technical progress for the growing economy, as follows:

$$(1/U_1)dU/dt = (\partial X_1/\partial t + p\partial X_2/\partial t) + (\partial X_1/\partial p + \partial X_2/\partial p - E_2)dp/dt \tag{34}$$

The first term of the RHS of (34) captures the welfare consequence of technical change at constant terms of trade, while the second term shows the welfare effect of change in technology via induced changes in the terms of trade.

3.2.1 Small country

Consider first a small country which is incapable of influencing the world price, i.e., $dp/dt = 0$. Utilizing (29) and (30), (34) can be rewritten as

$$(1/U_1)dU/dt = \partial X_i/\partial t + p\partial X_i/\partial t = \alpha p L_2 f_2/k_2 \tag{35}$$

which is positive, if and only if $\alpha > 0$, i.e., $k_2 > (1 + \lambda)k_1$. Thus, the following proposition is immediate:

Proposition 1 *Technical progress in manufacturing improves the welfare of a small economy provided that the manufacturing sector is relatively capital abundant.*

This proposition restates a result of Beladi and Naqvi (1988). It is an interesting result in view of the now well-known general principle of immiserizing growth announced by Bhagwati (1975). The principle states that economic expansion in the presence of a distortion can entail a loss in welfare even for a small country. Note that the present model is characterized by two distortions regarding unequal wage rates between the urban and rural sector and rigidity in the urban wage rate. Surprisingly, growth cannot be immiserizing in thus unemployment plagued economy. Our analysis confirms the result of non-immiserizing growth of Beladi-Naqvi. It should, however, be noted that Beladi-Naqvi developed their argument by using the unit cost diagram without much discussion of stability about the model. Our analysis indicates that their result requires an important qualification; that is, manufacturing must be relatively capital abundant, $k_2 > (1 + \lambda)k_1$. Note that technical progress can reduce welfare, if $k_2 < (1+\lambda)k_1$ (even with $k_2 > k_1$ as was assumed by Beladi-Naqvi).

While Beladi-Naqvi provided some useful exploration as to why technical progress should result in a higher real income, we would furnish an alternative, but somewhat more rigorous, illustration of our non-immiserizing result by bringing out the significance of the stability condition. Using (29) and (30), we can rewrite (35) as

$$\begin{aligned}(1/U_1)dU/dt &= \partial X_1/\partial t + p\partial X_2/\partial t \\ &= pL_2f_2 + A\partial k_1/\partial t + B\partial k_2/\partial t + C\partial\lambda/\partial t \qquad (36)\end{aligned}$$

where the coefficients A and B are both zeroes and $C = -w_1L_2$. In view of (36), the welfare effect of technical progress can be decomposed into four components: the first term captures the primary gain of technical progress in manufacturing, the second and the third terms (here both vanishing) indicate the welfare impact of technical progress via changes in the capital-labor ratios, and the fourth term represents the welfare loss due to the increase in the urban unemployment ration. In the traditional Heckscher-Ohlin-Samuelson trade model of full employment, the fourth term is zero so that $dU/dt > 0$, indicating that technical progress in the absence of any distortions enhances the welfare of a small economy.

In the present model, it appear at first glance that growth may reduce welfare as technical progress raises the urban unemployment ratio, thus yielding a result consistent with the general principle of immiserizing growth. But it turns out that the stability condition rules out this immiserizing outcome. Using (22), the welfare loss associated urban unemployment is given by $-w_1L_2(\partial\lambda/\partial t) = -pL_2f_2(1+\lambda)(k_1/k_2)$. Comparing this loss to the primary gain of technical progress, pL_2f_2, it is clear that the latter dominates the former, if and only if $k_2 > (1+\lambda)k_1$. Thus growth cannot be immiserizing in a stable system. Conversely, growth will reduce welfare, if $k_2 < (1+\lambda)k_1$ (even if $k_2 > k_1$). Our result may be related in terms of market stability to the well-known problem of unilateral transfers.[8]

3.2.2 Large country

We now shift our analysis to a large country which has monopoly power to influence the world prices. Following H- T, let the home country export (import) agricultural (manufactured) products. In view of (34), it is necessary to obtain an expression for the effect of technical progress (t) on the terms of trade (p). Suppose for simplicity that only the home country experiences technical progress while the foreign country remains stationary.[9]

Following the two-stage procedure as delineated in Choi and Yu (1985), we can easily derive (from the balance of payments equilibrium condition):

$$dp/dt = (\partial E_2/\partial t)[(p/(a_h + a_f - 1))E_2] \qquad (37)$$

[8]Assuming stable markets, Samuelson (1952) has shown that the welfare of the receiving country always improves regardless of the direction of the shift in the terms of trade induced by the transfer; the primary gain from receiving the transfer dominates the negative induced terms of trade effect (in the event that terms of trade deteriorate).

[9]This assumption may be relaxed, and the effect of technical progress in both countries can be easily analyzed (see Choi and Yu, 1985).

where $a_h = -(p/E_2)(\partial E_2/\partial p)$ is the price elasticity of home import demand and $a_f = (p/E_1)(\partial E_1/\partial p)$ is the price elasticity of foreign import demand. Assuming that the Marshall-Lerner condition is satisfied, $a_h + a_f - 1 > 0$.

Using the import demand function, $E_2 = D_2(p, Y) - X_2(p, t)$, where Y $(= X_1 + pX_2)$ is the real national income, we obtain[10]

$$\partial E_2/\partial t = (m_h/p)(\partial X_1/\partial t) - (1 - m_h)\partial X_2/\partial t \tag{38}$$

where $m_h = -(\partial D_2/\partial Y)$ is the home marginal propensity to consume the importables. In the absence of inferior goods, $0 < m_h < 1$.

We have shown earlier that technical progress in manufacturing is ultra-biased, i.e., $\partial X_1/\partial t < 0$ and $\partial X_2/\partial t > 0$, if the system is stable. It follows immediately that assuming stability $\partial E_2/\partial t$ is negative. Thus, given normal consumer taste, technical progress in manufacturing necessarily results in a reduction in import demand, which implies, in view of the balance of payments condition, an anti-trade pattern of growth.

Given $\partial E_2/\partial t < 0$, it is immediate from (37) that dp/dt is unambiguously negative, provided that $(a_h + a_f - 1) > 0$. Thus, technical progress in manufacturing in the H-T economy necessarily improves the home country's terms of trade in the stable system. This result is consistent with that obtainable from the standard full employment, undistorted economy.

To deduce the full welfare effect of technical progress, we need to obtain an express for the term, $\partial X_1/\partial p + p(\partial X_2/\partial p)$, in (34). Using (27) and (28), we have

$$\partial X_1/\partial p + \partial X_2/\partial p = -w_1 L_2 \partial\lambda/\partial p \tag{39}$$

which is negative, if $k_2 \neq (1+\lambda)k_1$. Thus, an exogenous deterioration in the terms of trade ($\partial p > 0$) necessarily reduces real income and welfare of a *small* country because of an increased urban unemployment rate. It is notable that this result does not hinge upon Neary's stability condition.

Our aim here is to evaluate the impact of technical progress on a large country's welfare. So we substitute (19), (35) and (39) in (34) to obtain

$$(1/U_1)dU/dt = pL_2 f_2[k_2 - (1+\lambda)k_1]k_1^{-1} - dp/dt[(1+\lambda)tL_2 f_2 k_2^{-1} + E_2] \tag{40}$$

which is positive, if $k_2 > (1+\lambda)k_1$ (and also $a_h + a_f > 1$ to assure $dp/dt < 0$). Thus, the following proposition is immediate:

Proposition 2 *Technical progress in the manufacturing sector of the capital-mobile Harris-Todaro economy always enhances the welfare of a large country.*

This result is noteworthy because it differs drastically from the results obtainable from framework integrating many other forms of distortions. For example, Hazari (1978) has shown that technical progress may be immiserizing for a large economy in the fixed wage differential model. Choi and Yu (1985) have obtained similar

[10] For analytical purpose, prices are held constant to separate the effect of technical progress on the import demand from that of a change in the terms of trade. See, for example, Hazari (1978, chap. 5) for details.

immiserizing consequences for a large economy characterized by variable returns to scale.[11]

The economic intuition behind our result is simple. Since technical progress in the manufacturing (importable) industry improves the terms of trade, and the improvement in the terms of trade enhances welfare (due to a resulting reduction in urban unemployment rate), the (secondary) induced terms of trade effect is beneficial. Given the positive primary effect of technical progress, the overall welfare must be improved, despite the presence of dual distortions in the system.

4 Hicks-Neutral Technical Progress in Agriculture

Suppose now technical progress occurs in the agricultural instead of in the manufacturing sector, so that $dt_1 > 0$ and $dt_2 = 0$. Thus, the basic system of equations (2) - (5) reduces to

$$t_1 f_1' = p f_2' \tag{41}$$

$$p(f_2 - k_2 f_2') = w_2 \tag{42}$$

$$(1+\lambda)t_1(f_1 - k_1 f_1') = w_2 \tag{43}$$

Totally differentiating (41) - (43) and expressing them in matrix form

$$\begin{bmatrix} t_1 f_1'' & -pf_2'' & 0 \\ -t_1(1+\lambda)k_1 f_1'' & 0 & t_1(f_1 - k_1 f_1') \\ 0 & -pk_2 t_2'' & 0 \end{bmatrix} \begin{bmatrix} dk_1 \\ dk_2 \\ d\lambda \end{bmatrix} = \begin{bmatrix} f_2' dp - f_1' dt_1 \\ -F_{L1}(1+\lambda)dt_1 \\ -F_{L2} dp \end{bmatrix} \tag{44}$$

The determinant of the coefficient matrix of (44) is

$$D* = t_1 p k_2 f_1'' f_2'' w_1 > 0$$

terms of trade, and welfare of a small as well as a large country. The Appendix presents major equations obtained from the analysis.

To conserve space it suffices here to summarize our major findings:

1. The Corden-Findlay (1975) result that
   (a) Hicks-neutral technical progress in agriculture raises (does not affect) the capital-labor ratio in agriculture (manufacturing and
   (b) it reduces the urban unemployment ration (λ) is valid regardless of the dynamic stability condition.
2. The Corden-Findlay result that technical progress in agriculture increases (decreases) agricultural (manufacturing) employment and output is valid if and only if $k_2 > (1+\lambda)k_1$. The result breaks down if $k_2 < (1+\lambda)k_1$ even if $k_2 > k_1$.

[11] In the standard Heckscher-Ohlin-Samuelson model, growth can reduce a large country's welfare. A necessary condition for immiserizing growth to occur is that the terms of trade must deteriorate. In the trade model with distortions, e.g., factor market imperfection, growth can result in lower welfare even at constant or improved terms of trade. See Batra and Scully (1971) and Bhagwati (1975), among others.

3. Similar to technical progress in manufacturing, the outputs respond positively to changes in the relative good price, and growth is ultra-biased in the sense that technical progress is agricultural sector raises the output of agricultural products at the expenses of the output of manufacturing.

4. Unlike technical progress in manufacturing, the result that technical progress in agriculture improves welfare for a small country does not hinge on Neary's stability condition, i.e., the (normal growth) result holds as long as $k_2 \neq (1 + \lambda)k_1$, because technical progress now generates both the primary production gain as well as the gain associated with a reduction in the urban unemployment ratio.

5. Technical progress in agriculture (the exportable) sector leads to an increased import demand and hence a pro- trade pattern of growth. It also worsens the terms of trade in a stable system. These outcomes are just the opposite of those obtained under technical improvement in manufacturing.

6. The welfare effect of technical progress in agriculture (the exportable) sector at constant terms of trade is always positive, while the welfare effect via deterioration in the terms of trade is negative. Thus we may state the following proposition:

Proposition 3 *Technical progress in agriculture of a large country with mobile capital, Harris-Todaro economy, unlike technical progress in manufacturing, can be immiserizing.*

5 Conclusions

We have reexamined the effects of Hicks-neutral technical progress on sectoral employment and output, and the welfare of a small country in a mobile capital version of H-T model. It is shown that most of the results obtained for a small country by Corden-Findlay and Beladi-Naqvi crucially hinges on Neary's dynamic stability condition, i.e., manufacturing is relatively capital abundant, $k_2 > (1 + \lambda)k_1$. The results break down if $k_2 < (1 + \lambda)k_1$, even if $k_2 > k_1$. There is one exception in that for a small country, neutral technical progress in agriculture always leads to normal growth as long as $k_2 \neq (1 + \lambda)k_1$. Furthermore, for a large country, neutral technical progress in the importable (manufacturing) sector always enhances welfare, while technical progress in the exportable (agricultural) sector may be immiserizing in the stable system. Our findings are closer to the standard results derivable from the Heckscher-Ohlin-Samuelson model than to the results obtainable from the traditional distortionary model with fixed wage differentials.[12] It should be noted that most of our results in the present paper heavily depend on the dynamic stability condition requiring that manufacturing is capital-intensive relative to agriculture in value sense.

[12] See, for example, Johnson (1965), Batra and Scully (1971), Bhagwati (1975) and Hazari (1978).

TABLE 1
Effects of Technical Progress in the Capital Harris-Todaro Economy*

	Technical progress in manufacturing	Technical progress in agriculture
$\partial k_1/\partial p$	$-$	$-$
$\partial k_2/\partial p$	$-$	$-$
$\partial \lambda/\partial p$	$+$	$+$
$\partial k_1/\partial t_i$	$-$	$+$
$\partial k_2/\partial t_i$	$-$	0
$\partial \lambda/\partial t_i$	$+$	$-$
$\partial L_1/\partial p$	$-$	$-$
$\partial L_2/\partial p$	$+$	$+$
$\partial L_1/\partial t_i$	$-$	$+$
$\partial L_2/\partial t_i$	$+$	$-$
$\partial X_1/\partial p$	$-$	$-$
$\partial X_2/\partial p$	$+$	$+$
$\partial X_1/\partial t_i$	$-$	$+$
$\partial X_2/\partial t_i$	$+$	$-$
$\partial U/\partial t_i$ (small country)	$+$	$+$
$\partial E_2/\partial t_i$	$-$	$+$
$\partial p/\partial t_i$	$-$[a]	$+$[b]
$\partial X_1/\partial p + p\partial X_2/\partial p$	$-$	$-$
$\partial U/\partial t_i$ (large country)	$+$	$\pm$

* Assume that the system is stable, i.e., $k_2 > (1+\lambda)k_1$ and $a_h + a_f - 1 > 0$. Note that t_i indicates technical progress in either the manufacturing or agricultural sector, $i = 1, 2$.

[a] improvement
[b] deterioration

Appendix

This appendix presents the results obtained from comparative static analysis on Hicks-neutral technical progress occurring in agricultural sector only.

$\partial k_1/\partial p = pt_1 f_2 F_{L1} f_2''/D* < 0$
$\partial k_2/\partial p = t_1^2 F_{L1} F_{L2} f_1''/D* < 0$
$\partial \lambda/\partial p = t_1 p k_1 f_2 (1+\lambda) f_1'' f_2''/D* > 0$
$\partial k_1/\partial t_1 = -pt_1 k_2 F_{L1} f_1' f_2''/D* > 0$
$\partial k_2/\partial t_1 = 0$
$\partial \lambda/\partial t_1 = -pt_1 k_2 f_1 (1+\lambda) f_1'' f_2''/D* < 0$
$\partial L_1/\partial p = [(1+\lambda)(L_1 \partial k_1/\partial p + L_2 \partial k_2/\partial p) - k_2 L_2 \partial\lambda/\partial p]/\alpha < 0$
$\partial L_2/\partial p = -[L_1 \partial k_1/\partial p + L_2 \partial k_2/\partial p - k_1 L_2 \partial \lambda/\partial p]/\alpha > 0$
$\partial L_1/\partial t_1 = [(1+\lambda) L_2 \partial k_1/\partial t_1 - k_2 L_2 \partial \lambda/\partial t_1]/\alpha > 0$
$\partial L_2/\partial t_1 = -[L_1 \partial k_1/\partial t_1 - k_1 L_2 \partial \lambda/\partial t_1]/\alpha < 0$

$$\partial X_1/\partial p = t_1 f_1 \partial L_1/\partial p + t_1 L_1 f_1' \partial k_1/\partial p < 0$$
$$\partial X_2/\partial p = f_2 \partial L_2/\partial p + L_2 f_2' \partial k_2/\partial p$$
$$= -\{f_2(L_1 \partial k_1/\partial p - k_1 L_2 \partial \lambda/\partial p) + L_2[F_{L2} + f_2'(1+\lambda)k_1]\partial k_2/\partial p\}/\alpha > 0$$
$$\partial X_1/\partial t_1 = L_1 f_1 - (t_1 f_1 k_2 L_2/\alpha)\partial \lambda/\partial t_1 + [t_1 f_1 L_1(1+\lambda) + t_1 L_1 f_1' \alpha](\partial k_1/\partial t_1)/\alpha > 0$$
$$\partial X_2/\partial t_1 = f_2 \partial L_2/\partial t_1 < 0$$

5.1 *Small country*

(a) Welfare effect:

$$(1/U_1)(dU/dt_1) = \partial X_1/\partial t_1 + p\partial X_2/\partial t_2$$
$$= L_1 f_1 - w_1 L_2 \partial \lambda/\partial t_1 = f_1 \overline{L} > 0, \text{ if } k_2 \neq (1+\lambda)k_1$$

Thus, normal growth results independent of dynamic stability, if $k_2 \neq (1+\lambda)k_1$

5.2 *Large country*

(a) Import demand:

$$\partial E_2/\partial t_1 = m_h \partial X_1/\partial t_1 - (1-m_h)\partial X_2/\partial t_1 > 0$$

In view of $E_1 = pE_2$, this indicates protrade patter of growth.

(b) Terms of trade:

$$\partial p/\partial t_1 = [(p/(a_f + a_h - 1))E_2](\partial E_2/\partial t_1) > 0$$

Terms of trade deteriorate.

(c) Terms of trade effect on national income:

$$\partial X_1/\partial p + p\partial X_2/\partial p = -w_1 L_2 \partial \lambda/\partial p < 0$$

(d) Total welfare effect:

$$(1/U_1)(dU/dt_1) = \partial X_1/\partial t_1 + p\partial X_2/\partial t_2 + (\partial X_1/\partial p + \partial X_2/\partial p - E_2)\partial \lambda/\partial t \gtreqless 0$$

Hicks-neutral technical progress in agriculture sector may be immiserizing.

References

BATRA, R.N. AND SCULLY, G.W. (1971): "The Theory of Wage Differentials: Welfare and Immiserizing Growth," *Journal of International Economics,* 1, 241-7.

BATRA, R.N. AND NAQVI, N. (1987): "Urban Unemployment and the Gains from Trade," *Economica,* 54, 381-395.

BELADI, H. AND NAQVI, N. (May 1988): "Urban Unemployment and Non-Immiserizing Growth," *Journal of Development Economics,* 28, 365-376.

BHAGWATI, J.N. (1975): "The Generalized Theory of Distortion and Welfare," in *Trade, Balance of Payments and Growth.* Ed. J. Bhagwati, R. Jones, R. Mundell, and T. Vanek, Amsterdam: North-Holland.

CHAO, C.C. AND YU, E.S.H. (1990): "Urban Unemployment Terms of Trade and Welfare," *Southern Economic Journal,* 56, 743-751.

CHOI, J.Y. AND YU, E.S.H. (1985): "Technical Progress, Terms of Trade, and Welfare Under Variable Returns to Scale," *Economica,* 52, 365-377.

CORDEN, W.M. AND R. FINDLAY (1975): "Urban Unemployment, Intersectoral Capital Mobility and Development Policy," *Economica,* 2, 59-78.

DAS, S.P. (February 1982): "Sector Specific Minimum Wages, Economic Growth and Some Policy Implications," *Journal of Development Economics,* 10, 127-31.

HARRIS, J.R. AND TODARO, M. (1970): "Migration, Unemployment and Development: A Two Sector Analysis," *American Economic Review,* 126-42.

HAZARI, B.R. (1978): *The Pure Theory of International Trade and Distortions.* New York: John Wiley and Sons.

JOHNSON, H.G. (1965): "Optimal Trade Intervention in the Presence of Domestic Distortions," in *Trade Growth and Balance of Payments.* Ed. R. E. Baldwin et al, Chicago: Rand McNally and Co.

MCCOOL, T. (1982): "Wage Subsidies, Distortionary Taxes in a Mobile Capital Harris-Todaro Model," *Economica,* 49, 69-80.

NEARY, J.P. (1981): "On the Harris-Todaro Model with Intersectoral Capital Mobility," *Economica,* 48, 219-234.

PARAI, A.K. AND BATRA, R.N. (1987): "Customs Unions and Unemployment in LDCs," *Journal of Development Economics,* 26, 311-319.

SAMUELSON, P.A. (June 1952): "The Transfer Problem and Transportation Costs: The Terms of Trade When Impediments Are Absent," *Economic Journal,* 279-302.

Equilibrium of an Economy with Infinitely Many Indivisible Commodities and Consumers*

Karl Dunz
State University of New York at Albany

1 Introduction

This paper examines an economy that is a special case of what Ostroy (1984) has termed "large-square" economies. The economy can also be thought of as the "large-square" version of a "small-square" economy with indivisible goods presented by Shapley and Scarf (1974). In their economy, each consumer is endowed with a single indivisible good, which they call a house, and has preferences over houses such that they want exactly one house. Shapley and Scarf show that an equilibrium exists for this economy. The "large-square" version of this that is examined below has a continuum of indivisible goods and a continuum of agents each being endowed with exactly one indivisible good. Each agent has a utility function defined over these indivisible goods and wants to consume exactly one such good. It will be assumed that there are finitely many such utility functions. A quasi-equilibrium is shown to exist for this special kind of "large-square" economy.

The two papers that are most closely related to this model are Mas-Colell (1975) and Jones (1983). Both of these papers deal with the case of differentiated commodities and start with a compact metric space of characteristics. A point in this space of characteristics represents a commodity. Mas-Colell assumes that these commodities are available only in integral amounts. He assumes the existence of at least one homogeneous commodity that everyone desires. On the other hand, Jones assumes the commodities are perfectly divisible. So in Mas-Colell agents consume a non-negative integer-valued measure and a non-negative real number (of the homogeneous good). While in Jones they consume a non-negative (Borel) measure. Both papers prove the existence of an equilibrium and Mas-Colell also proves a core equivalence result.

The model presented below is slightly different from both of these other papers. As in Mas-Colell, there are nonconvexities in the consumption set since it is assumed that there is only one unit of each commodity. However, Mas-Colell's assumption of the existence of a homogeneous good is eliminated and it is assumed that agents

*This work is based on the author's dissertation. The support and encouragement of my thesis advisor, Gerard Debreu, is gratefully acknowledged. Michael Sheard deserves credit for teaching me nonstandard analysis. Of course, any errors are solely my own.

desire exactly one commodity. Therefore consumers do not consume sets of commodities as in both Mas-Colell and Jones. In Jones' framework the following model can be viewed as having each agent endowed with a Dirac measure[1] and having preferences such that every agent desires to consume a Dirac measure.

Another relevant paper is Weber (1981), which gives sufficient conditions for the existence of core allocations in games with infinitely many agents. The main condition is a translation (and strengthening) of balancedness to the continuum of players case. An example is presented below that shows that the model of this paper does not satisfy Weber's balancedness condition, yet an equilibrium and thus a core allocation exist. So this paper provides another example of a class of economies where Weber's balancedness condition is not necessary for the existence of core allocations.

2 The Model

In this section the model is described. Since it can be viewed as an extension of a house trading game of Shapley and Scarf (1974), the commodities will be called houses. However, all that is really being assumed is that agents are consuming an indivisible bundle of commodities.

The economy will be denoted by $\mathcal{E} \equiv \langle (H, \mathcal{H}, \mu), (E_1, \ldots, E_K), (u_1, \ldots, u_K) \rangle$.

The commodity space and space of agents is described by the measure space $(H, \mathcal{H}, \mu)$, where $H = [0,1]$, $\mathcal{H}$ is the Borel σ-algebra, and μ is Lebesgue measure.[2] The set H represents both the set of houses and the set of agents in the economy. This can be done since each agent is endowed with exactly one house; so, an agent can be identified with his endowment. So a point h in H will sometimes refer to house h and sometimes to the agent whose endowment is h.

Formally, since all the agents have different endowments and an agent's type is usually described by both endowment and preferences, there are infinitely many types of agents. However, it will be assumed that there are only finitely many different utility functions and an agent's type will refer to his utility function. There will be K such types with utility functions, $u_1, \ldots, u_K$. Each u_t is a continuous, bounded real-valued function on H, with $\forall h \in H, u_t(h) \leq B_t$. Each agent is assumed to desire exactly one house. So each type t agent's problem is to pick the h that maximizes $u_t(h)$ in the set of affordable houses.

The endowments of agents of type t are given by E_t. So $(E_1, \ldots, E_K)$ will be assumed to be a measurable partition of H. Each E_t can be interpreted as either the set of houses initially owned by agents of type t or the set of agents of type t.

Shapley and Scarf show that a competitive equilibrium exists for the case where H being a finite set. This paper extends their result to the continuum of agents case.

---

[1]That is, $\delta_x(A) = 1$ if $x \in A$ and 0 otherwise.

[2]The main result of this paper can be extended to the case where H is a compact metric space. The restriction to the unit interval simplifies the nonstandard analysis used in the proof.

3 Equilibria

In this section how to define an equilibrium is discussed. An example is given that shows why the concept of an equilibrium distribution is used. This concept is also used in Mas-Colell (1975) and is due to Hart, Hildenbrand, and Kohlberg (1974).

The following is a natural definition of an equilibrium for an economy with a continuum of agents and houses.

DEFINITION 1 *An* equilibrium *for an economy, $\mathcal{E}$, is a pair of maps, (p, m), such that:*

1) $p : H \to \Re_+$ is a measurable function, which is interpreted as a price function;

2) $m : H \to H$ is a measurable function implies $\forall S \in \mathcal{H}, \mu(S) = \mu(m^{-1}(S))$, where $m^{-1}(S)$ is interpreted as the set of agents moving to the set S; and

3) $m(a) \in argmax\{u_t(h)|p(h) \leq p(a)\}$ for almost every $a \in H \cap E_k, k = 1, \ldots, K$. This condition says that each agent moves to the "best" house he can afford.

When H is a finite set this definition of an equilibrium is the same as the one used in Shapley and Scarf (1974). Unfortunately, such an equilibrium might not exist in an economy with a continuum of agents. The reason for this is that it might not be possible to find a map, m, that satisfies conditions 2 and 3 simultaneously. An example of an economy without an equilibrium will now be given.

Suppose there are 2 types of agents and $H = [0, 1]$. Type 1 agents own houses to the right of 1/2 and type 2 agents live to the left of 1/2. So $E_1 = [1/2, 1]$ and $E_2 = [0, 1/2]$. The utility functions of each type are $u_1(h) = 1- \mid h - 1/4 \mid$ and $u_2(h) = (1 + h)/2$. Type 1 agents want to live as close to $h = 1/4$ as possible. The houses around this point are all owned by type 2 agents. All type 2 agents want to move as close to $h = 1$ as possible and all of these houses are owned by type 1 agents. So you would expect agents living around 1/4 to trade houses with those living around 1. Also, note that, for every $v \geq 3/4$, $\mu\{h \in H|u_1(h) \geq v\} = \mu\{h \in H|u_2(h) \geq v\}$.

This suggests that an equilibrium price function could be defined by

$$p(h) = \begin{cases} u_1(h) & \text{if } h \in E_2 \\ u_2(h) & \text{if } h \in E_1 \end{cases}$$

This price function would allow equal measures of agents around 1/4 and 1 to "switch place", i.e. buy each other's houses.

However, there is no function, $m : H \to H$, that satisfies conditions 2 and 3 for this price function. If there was such a function it would have to determine to which side of 1/4 each agent in E_1 moved. This has to be done in such a way that for every measurable subset of E_1 half of the set has to move to a house less than 1/4 and the other half moves to a house between 1/4 and 1/2. This is equivalent to finding a measurable subset, S, of E_1 such that, for every $v \geq 3/4$, $\mu\{h \in S|u_2(h) \geq v\} = 1/2$. It is well-known that such a set does not exist. Therefore, no equilibrium exists in this example.

The properties of the price function defined above does make it a reasonable "equilibrium" price function. This suggests using the notion of an equilibrium distribution, whose definition is now given.

DEFINITION 2 *An* equilibrium distribution *for $\mathcal{E}$ is $\langle(\nu_t), t = 1, \ldots, K; p\rangle$, where $p : H \to \Re_+$ is a measurable function and each ν_t is a measure defined on $\mathcal{H}$, such that:*

1) $\forall t = 1, \ldots, K, \nu_t(H) = \mu(E_t)$;

2) $\forall S \in \mathcal{H}, \sum_{t=1}^{K} \nu_t(S) = \mu(S)$; and

3) $\forall$ measurable $S \subseteq E_t$, $\forall t = 1, \ldots, K$,

$$\nu_t\{h \in H | h \in argmax\{u_t(x)|p(x) \leq p(a)\}, a \in S\} \geq \mu(S).$$

The interpretation of $\nu_t(S)$ is the fraction of the total population that lives in S and is of type t. So condition 1 says that almost every type t agent owns a house in H. Condition 2 requires that the fraction of the population living in any (measurable) subset of H be equal to the fraction of all houses in that subset. Recall that every agent owns exactly one house. The third condition implies that almost every agent moves to the most preferred house he can afford given the price function.

For technical reasons, the existence of an equilibrium distribution will not be shown. Instead, a quasi-equilibrium distribution will be shown to exist. In the usual definition, a quasi-equilibrium is the same as an equilibrium except that each agent moves to a house such that there is no preferred house that costs strictly less. If defined in this way, there is always a trivial quasi-equilibrium distribution in an economy $\mathcal{E}$. Let p be a constant function. Then any ν_t satisfying conditions 1 and 2 of an equilibrium will yield a quasi-equilibrium distribution since all houses in an agent's budget set cost the same. To exclude this trivial equilibrium, a quasi-equilibrium distribution will be required to have a price function that orders the houses that type t agents move to in the same way as u_t. One could interpret this as requiring quasi-equilibrium prices to reflect the "bids" of the agents buying the houses. The following is the definition of a quasi-equilibrium distribution.

DEFINITION 3 *$\langle(\nu_t), t = 1, \ldots, K; p\rangle$ is a* quasi-equilibrium distribution *for an economy, $\mathcal{E}$, if $p : H \to \Re_+$ is a measurable function and each ν_t is a measure defined on $\mathcal{H}$, such that:*

1) $\forall t = 1, \ldots, K$, $\nu_t(H) = \mu(E_t)$;

2) $\forall S \in \mathcal{H}$, $\sum_{t=1}^{K} \nu_t(S) = \mu(S)$;

3) $\forall$ measurable $S \subseteq E_t$,

$$\nu_t\{x \in H \,|\, a \in S, p(x) \leq p(a) \text{ and } \forall y,\ p(y) < p(a) \Rightarrow u_t(x) \geq u_t(y)\} \geq \mu(S);$$

and

4) $\forall t = 1, \ldots, K$, $\forall x, y \in M_t$, $u_t(x) > u_t(y) \Rightarrow p(x) > p(y)$, where the $M_t \subseteq H$ and partition H.

The result of this paper is:

THEOREM 1 *An economy $\mathcal{E}$ has a quasi-equilibrium distribution.*

This theorem is proved in Section 5. The next section is a digression on the cooperative game associated with an economy.

4 Balancedness of $\mathcal{E}$

This section considers the relationship between an economy, $\mathcal{E}$, of the kind described in this paper and the result in Weber (1981). Weber proves that the weak core of a certain class of games with a continuum of agents is nonempty. It will be shown that the cooperative game associated with $\mathcal{E}$ does not satisfy Weber's balancedness condition, which is stronger than the usual definition of balanced for finite player games. However, the core is nonempty in such games. The following are Weber's definitions of the characteristic function of a game and balancedness that are needed to discuss this issue.

DEFINITION 4 *The* characteristic function *of a game with a measure space, $(M, \mathcal{M}, \mu)$, of players is a set function, V from $\mathcal{M}$ to subsets of L_∞, such that $\forall S \in \mathcal{M}$, $V(S)$ is a closed, comprehensive subset of*

$$L_\infty^S \equiv \{f \in L_\infty | f(x) = 0 \text{ almost everywhere in } M \setminus S\}.$$

DEFINITION 5 *A characteristic function, V, is* balanced *if for every finite collection of measurable sets, $(S_1, \ldots, S_n)$, with positive measure and every vector of nonnegative numbers, $(\alpha_1, \ldots, \alpha_n)$ such that $\sum_{i=1}^n \alpha_i 1_{S_i} \leq 1_M$,*[3]

$$\sum_{i=1}^n \alpha_i V(S_i) \subseteq V(M).$$

Note that if M is a finite set Weber's definition of balanced is a stronger condition than the usual definition. The usual definition of balanced requires that the sets $V(S)$ and $V(M)$ satisfy $\cap_{S \in \mathcal{B}} V(S) \subseteq V(M)$, for only all balanced families, $\mathcal{B}$, of coalitions. However, Weber's definition requires more. For example, in a game with 3 agents, Weber's balancedness requires $V(\{1,2\})/2 + V(\{2,3\})/2 \subseteq V(M)$. Since $\{\{1,2\},\{2,3\}\}$ is not a balanced family, the usual definition of balanced does not require any relationship between $V(\{1,2\}), V(\{2,3\})$, and $V(M)$.

This difference will be exploited to give an example of a economy that is not balanced by Weber's definition. Let $H = [0,1]$ with two types of agents, where $E_1 = (3/8, 5/8)$ and $E_2 = H \setminus E_1$. Their utility functions are given by

$$u_1(x) = \mid x - \frac{1}{2} \mid$$

and

$$u_2(x) = \begin{cases} \frac{1}{2} - \mid x - \frac{1}{2} \mid & \text{if } x \in E_1 \\ \frac{11}{16} - \frac{5}{2} \mid x - \frac{1}{2} \mid & \text{if } x \in [\frac{1}{4}, \frac{3}{8}] \cup [\frac{5}{8}, \frac{3}{4}] \\ \frac{1}{8} - \frac{1}{4} \mid x - \frac{1}{2} \mid & \text{otherwise.} \end{cases}$$

The characteristic function of the game associated with this economy is defined by

$$V(S) = \left\{ u \in L_\infty^S \;\middle|\; \begin{array}{l} \exists m : S \to S \text{ that is 1-1, onto and measure preserving} \\ \text{such that for } t = 1, 2,\ u_t(a) \leq u_t(m(a)) \\ \text{for almost every } a \in S \cap E_t. \end{array} \right\}$$

[3] 1_S is the indicator function of $S \in \mathcal{M}$.

Now it is shown that this V is not balanced. Let $S_1 = [0, 5/8]$ and $S_2 = [3/8, 1]$. If V were balanced then $V(S_1)/2 + V(S_2)/2 \subseteq V(H)$. The functions, f_1 and f_2, are in $V(S_1)$ and $V(S_2)$, respectively, where

$$f_1(x) = \begin{cases} x - \frac{1}{8} & \text{if } x \in E_1 \\ \frac{1}{2} - \mid x - \frac{1}{8} \mid & \text{if } x \in (0, \frac{1}{4}) \\ u_2(x) & \text{if } x \in (\frac{1}{4}, \frac{3}{8}] \\ 0 & \text{otherwise} \end{cases}$$

and

$$f_2(x) = \begin{cases} x - \frac{1}{8} & \text{if } x \in E_1 \\ \frac{1}{2} - \mid x - \frac{7}{8} \mid & \text{if } x \in (\frac{3}{4}, 1) \\ u_2(x) & \text{if } x \in [\frac{5}{8}, \frac{3}{4}) \\ 0 & \text{otherwise.} \end{cases}$$

The function f_1 corresponds to agents in E_1 trading houses with type 2 agents in (0, 1/4), and f_2 corresponds to agents in E_1 trading houses with agents in (3/4, 1).

Define $f(x) \equiv f_1(x)/2 + f_2(x)/2$. Balancedness requires f to be in $V(H)$. f has the property that $f(x) \geq 3/16$ on $(0, 1/4) \cup (3/4, 1)$. So, in order for $f \in V(H)$, there must be some way to place type 2 agents so that a set of measure 1/2 will get a utility level of at least 3/16. However, $u_2(x) \geq 3/16$ only on the set [0.3, 0.7], which has measure less than 1/2. So $f \in V(H)$ and this V is not balanced.

However, this economy does have an equilibrium. The equilibrium price function is

$$p(x) = \begin{cases} 1 - x & \text{if } x \in [0, \frac{1}{8}) \\ 1 - \mid x - \frac{1}{2} \mid & \text{if } x \in E_1 \\ x & \text{if } x \in (\frac{7}{8}, 1] \\ u_2(x) & \text{otherwise.} \end{cases}$$

The movement function of this equilibrium is

$$m(x) = \begin{cases} \frac{1}{2} - x & \text{if } x \in [0, \frac{1}{8}) \cup (\frac{3}{8}, \frac{1}{2}) \\ \frac{3}{2} - x & \text{if } x \in (\frac{7}{8}, 1] \cup [\frac{1}{2}, \frac{5}{8}) \\ x & \text{otherwise} \end{cases}$$

which corresponds to agents in [0, 1/8) trading houses with agents in (3/8, 1/2], agents in (7/8, 1] and [1/2, 5/8) trading houses, and all other agents cannot afford to move to a better house.

5 Proof of the Existence of Equilibria

In this section the existence of a quasi-equilibrium distribution is proved. The proof will use nonstandard analysis. The main result that will be used is Lemma 1, which is proved in Bernstein and Wattenberg (1969).

LEMMA 1 *Let μ be Lebesgue measure on* [0, 1]. *Then there exists an internal *finite set, F, such that* $[0,1] \subseteq F \subseteq {}^*[0,1]$ *and* $\mu(S) = {}^\circ[\#({}^*S \cap F)/\#F]$, *where* ${}^\circ A$ *represents the standard part of A and $\#A$ is the (possibly nonstandard) cardinality of A.*

This result allows one to think of Lebesgue measure as being essentially a counting measure on a finite set. This lemma and the transfer principle, which loosely speaking states that the *version of any sentence is true in a nonstandard model if and only if the sentence is true in the standard model.[4] All of the nonstandard analysis that will be used is described in Bernstein and Wattenberg. For more complete descriptions of nonstandard analysis see Robinson (1966) or Davis (1977).

The structure of the proof of the theorem is straightforward. First, useful properties of an equilibrium distribution of an economy with finite H are described. This is done in Lemma 2 using the existence result in Shapley and Scarf (1974). Then the transfer principle is applied to these properties to get nonstandard sentences that are true in the nonstandard model whose existence is given by Lemma 1. Finally, it is shown that a quasi-equilibrium distribution can be defined by taking the standard part of certain nonstandard objects.

LEMMA 2 *Let $\mathcal{E}$ be an economy with H a finite set. Then there exist $N \leq \#H$ sets, $S_1, \ldots, S_N$; a map $m : H \to H$ that is 1-1 and onto; and a function $p : H \to H$ such that, for all n, $p(h) = p_n$ for all $h \in S_n$ satisfying*

A) $\forall n, t,\ \#[S_n \cap E_t] = 0$ *or* 1 ;

B) $\forall n, t,\ S_n \cap m(E_t) \neq \emptyset \Rightarrow S_n \cap m(E_t) \subseteq argmax\{u_t(h) | h \in H \setminus \cup_{i<n} S_i\}$;

C) $p_{i-1} - p_i \equiv max\ \{\bar{u}_t^i - u_t(y) | y \in m(E_t) \cap S_i$ *and* t *such that* $m(E_t) \cap S_i \neq \emptyset\}$, *where* $p_0 \geq max\{B_t\}$ *and*

$$\bar{u}_t^i \equiv min\{u_t(h) | h \in \cup_{j<i}[m(E_t) \cap S_j]\} \text{ or } B_t \text{ if this set is } \emptyset;$$

D) $\forall t, \forall a \in H \cap E_t,\ m(a) \in argmax\{u_t(h) | p(h) \leq p(a)\}$; *and*

E) $\sum_{i=2}^{N}(p_{i-1} - p_i) \leq \sum_{t=1}^{K} B_t$.

PROOF: As in Shapley and Scarf (1974) the sets $S_1, \ldots, S_N$ are defined so that S_i is a top trading cycle of $H \setminus \cup_{j<i} S_j$. The map m is determined by these sets. So, for $a \in S_i, m(a)$ is an element of S_i that agent a likes at least as much as any other element of $H \setminus \cup_{j<i} S_j$. By construction of a top trading cycle m can be defined so that it is 1-1 and onto. Properties A and B are clearly implied by the definition of a top trading cycle.

Note that D says that p, as defined by C, represents equilibrium prices and m where the agents want to move for $\mathcal{E}$. Shapley and Scarf have shown that any prices, $p_1 > \cdots > p_N$, where all houses in S_i are assigned the price p_i are equilibrium prices. Therefore, C and D will be satisfied if C defines prices such that $p_1 > \cdots > p_N$.

[4]There are restrictions on transferring sentences like: "$\forall$ set S, property P is true", which transfers to "$\forall$ internal set $^*S$, property $^*P$ is true." However, the transfer principle is true without restriction for first-order sentences; for example, sentences where all quantifiers refer only to points. These are the only kind of sentences to which the transfer principle will be applied in the proof. So it will not be necessary to worry about internal sets.

However this is not necessarily true. It is however from true that $p_{i-1} \geq p_i$ for all $N \geq i > 2$. This follows from the fact that $\bar{u}_t^1 \geq u_t(h)$ for all $h \in m(E_t) \cap S_i$. This is true since, by the definition of a top trading cycle, $u_t(h) \geq u_t(h')$ for all $h \in S_i \cap m(E_t), h' \in S_i \cap m(E_t)$, and $i < j$.

It is now shown that D holds. Suppose the contrary. So, suppose $a \in E_t$ such that there exists a h such that $p(h) \leq p(a)$ and $u_t(h) > u_t(m(a))$. Let $a, m(a) \in S_j$ and $h \in S_i$. By definition of S_j, $i < j$. This implies that $p(h) \geq p(m(a)) = p(a)$ and therefore $p(h) = p(a)$. Note that $p_i - p_j \geq u_t(h_i) - u_t(h_j)$ where $h_i \in S_i$ and $h_j \in S_j$. So $p_i - p_j > u_t(h) - u_t(a) > 0$ which contradicts $p(a) = p(h)$. Therefore D holds where prices are defined by C.

All that remains is to verify that property E holds. Let t_i be the type of agent such that $p_{i-1} - p_i = \bar{u}_{t_i}^i - u_{t_i}(h)$ for some $h \in m(E_{t_i}) \cap S_i$. By definition of $\bar{u}_t^i$, for all types $\bar{t}$,

$$\sum_{i \ni t_i = \bar{t}} (p_{i-1} - p_i) \leq max\{u_{\bar{t}}(h)|h \in H\} - min\{u_{\bar{t}}(h)|h \in H\} \leq B_t.$$

So

$$\sum_{i=2}^{N} (p_{i-1} - p_i) = \sum_{\bar{t}=1}^{K} \sum_{i \ni t_i = \bar{t}} (p_{i-1} - p_i) \leq \sum_{t=1}^{K} B_t.$$

Q.E.D.

PROOF OF THEOREM 1: Let $^*\mathcal{E} = \langle (F, 2^F, \#), (^*E_1, \ldots, {}^*E_K), (^*u_1, \ldots, {}^*u_K) \rangle$, where F and $\#$ are as given in Lemma 1. Applying the transfer principle to Lemma 2 and $^*\mathcal{E}$ yields a nonstandard natural number $N[\leq \#F]$ of subsets of F, $S_1, \ldots, S_N$; a map $m : F \to F$ that is 1-1 and onto; and a function $p : F \to {}^*\Re$ such that, for all $n, p(h) = p_n$ for all $h \in S_n$ satisfying:[5]

* A) $\forall n, t, \#[S_n \cap {}^*E_t \cap F] = 0$ or 1;

* B) $\forall n, t$,

$$S_n \cap m(^*E_t \cap F) \neq \emptyset \Rightarrow S_n \cap m(^*E_t \cap F) \subseteq argmax\{^*u_t(h)|h \in \cup_{i<n} S_i\};$$

* C) $p_0 \geq max\{B_t\}$ and $p_{i-1} - p_i \equiv$

$$max\{\bar{u}_t^i - {}^*u_t(h)|h \in m(^*E_t \cap F) \cap S_i \text{ and } t \text{ such that } m(^*E_t \cap F) \cap S_i \neq \emptyset\},$$

where $^*\bar{u}_t^i \equiv min\{^*u_t(h)|h \in \cup_{j<i}[m(^*E_t \cap F) \cap S_j]\}$ or B_t if this set is empty;

* D) for all t and $a \in F \cap {}^*E_t, m(a) \in argmax\{^*u_t(h)|p(h) \leq p(a)\}$; and

* E) $\sum_{i=2}^{N}(p_{i-1} - p_i) \leq \sum_{t=1}^{K} B_t$.

For $t = 1, \ldots, K$, define $\nu_t(A) \equiv {}^\circ[\#(^*A \cap m(^*E_t \cap F) \cap F)/\#F]$ where A $\in \mathcal{H}$. It will be shown that $\langle (\nu_t), t = 1, \ldots, K; {}^\circ p \rangle$ is a quasi-equilibrium distribution for $\mathcal{E}$.

Consider E_t for some types t. Since m is 1-1,

$$\#(^*E_t \cap F) = \#(m(^*E_t \cap F)).$$

Therefore,

$$\mu(E_t) = {}^\circ[\frac{\#(^*E_t \cap F)}{\#F}]$$

[5]Note that in these properties the indices i, j, n are nonstandard integers between 1 and N. The index t stills runs between 1 and K.

$$\begin{aligned} &= {}^\circ[\frac{\#(m({}^*E_t \cap F) \cap F)}{\#F}] \\ &= {}^\circ[\frac{\#({}^*H \cap m({}^*E_t \cap F)}{\#F}] \\ &= \nu_t(H). \end{aligned}$$

This is the first condition required of a quasi-equilibrium distribution.

Let $A \in \mathcal{H}$. Since the ${}^*E_t \cap F$ are pairwise disjoint and partition F, so do the sets $m({}^*E_t \cap F)$. Therefore, ${}^*S = \cup_{t=1}^K (m({}^*E_t \cap F) \cap {}^*S)$ and

$$\frac{\#({}^*S \cap F)}{\#F} = \sum_{t=1}^{K} \frac{\#(m({}^*E_t \cap F) \cap {}^*S \cap F)}{\#F}.$$

Taking the standard part of this equality gives $\mu(S) = \sum_{t=1}^K \nu_t(S)$ which is the second condition.

Let $S \subseteq E_t$ be a measurable set. Define

$$M \equiv \{h \in H | a \in S, {}^\circ p(h) \leq {}^\circ p(a) \text{ and } \forall y, {}^\circ p(y) < {}^\circ p(a) \Rightarrow u_t(h) \geq u_t(y)\}.$$

It must be shown that $\nu_t(M) \geq \mu(S)$. Note that

$${}^*M = \left\{ h \in {}^*H \;\middle|\; \begin{array}{l} a \in {}^*S,\ {}^*({}^\circ p(h)) \leq {}^*({}^\circ p(a)) \text{ and} \\ \forall y,\ {}^*({}^\circ p(y)) < {}^*({}^\circ p(a)) \Rightarrow {}^*u_t(h) \geq {}^*u_t(y) \end{array} \right\}$$

Also define $M' \equiv \{x \in {}^*H | x \in argmax\{{}^*u_t(x) | p(x) \leq p(a)\}, a \in {}^*S\}$. By *D, $m({}^*S) \subseteq M'$, and since m is 1-1, $\#(M') \geq \#({}^*S)$.

Next it is shown that $M' \subseteq {}^*M$. Let $x \in M'$. So there exists an $a \in {}^*S$ such that $p(x) \leq p(a)$ and ${}^*u_t(x) \geq {}^*u_t(y)$ for all y such that ${}^*({}^\circ p(y)) < {}^*({}^\circ p(a))$. So ${}^\circ p(y) < {}^\circ p(a)$ and $p(y) \leq p(a)$.[6] Therefore ${}^*u_t(x) \geq {}^*u_t(y)$ since $x \in M'$. So $x \in {}^*M$. Therefore

$$\begin{aligned} \nu_t(M) &\equiv {}^\circ(\#[{}^*M \cap m({}^*E_t \cap F) \cap F]/\#F) \\ &\geq {}^\circ(\#[M' \cap m({}^*E_t \cap F) \cap F]/\#F) \\ &\geq {}^\circ(\#[M' \cap m({}^*S \cap F) \cap F]/\#F) \\ &= {}^\circ(\#[m({}^*S \cap F) \cap F]/\#F) \\ &= {}^\circ(\#[{}^*S \cap F]/\#F) \\ &\equiv \mu(S). \end{aligned}$$

This is the third condition required of a quasi-equilibrium distribution.

Finally, it is shown that this quasi-equilibrium is nontrivial. Let $M_t \equiv m({}^*E_t \cap F) \cap H$ for $t = 1, \ldots, K$. Note that these M_t need not be internal subsets of F. Also these sets need not be measurable. It is shown that these sets satisfy the final

[6]Note that if the first inequality were $\leq$ then it would be possible that $p(y) > p(a)$. So it would be possible for a house that an agent prefers to be in his standard budget set with prices ${}^\circ p$ but not in his nonstandard budget set with prices p. This is the technical reason why the proof yields a quasi-equilibrium instead of an equilibrium.

condition of a quasi-equilibrium distribution. Since the $m({}^*E_t \cap F)$ partition F, the M_t partition $H \subseteq F$.

Let $x, y \in M_t$ such that $u_t(x) > u_t(y)$. It must be shown that ${}^\circ p(x) > {}^\circ p(y)$. Let $x \in S_i \subseteq {}^*H$ and $y \in S_j \subseteq {}^*H$. By definition of the trading cycle sets and since $x, y \in m({}^*E_t \cap F), i < j$. Otherwise ${}^*u_t(x) \leq {}^*u_t(y)$. Therefore $p(x) > p(y)$. It must be shown that $p(x) - p(y)$ is not infinitesimal.

Note

$$p(x) - p(y) = \sum_{k=i}^{j-1} (p_k - p_{k+1})$$

where $p_i = p(h)$ for $h \in S_i$. Let h_k be the element of $m({}^*E_t \cap F) \cap S_k$ if this set is nonempty. If it is empty let $h_k = h_{k'}$ where $k' < k$ is the largest index such that $m({}^*E_t \cap F) \cap S_{k'} \neq \emptyset$. Then

$$\begin{aligned} p(x) - p(y) &\geq \sum_{k=i}^{j-1} ({}^*u_t(h_k) - {}^*u_t(h_{k+1})) \\ &= {}^*u_t(h_i) - {}^*u_t(h_j) \\ &= {}^*u_t(x) - {}^*u_t(y) \\ &> r \end{aligned}$$

where r is a (standard) real such that $u_t(x) - u_t(y) > r > 0$. Therefore ${}^\circ p(x) - {}^\circ p(y) > 0$ which verifies that $\langle \nu_t, {}^\circ p \rangle$ is a quasi-equilibrium distribution. Q.E.D.

References

BERNSTEIN, A. AND F. WATTENBERG (1969): "Nonstandard Measure Theory," in *Applications of Model Theory to Algebra, Analysis, and Probability.* Ed. W. Luxemburg, New York: Holt, Rinehart, and Winston.

DAVIS, M. (1977): *Applied Nonstandard Analysis.* New York: John Wiley and Sons.

HART, S., W. HILDENBRAND, AND E. KOHLBERG (1974): "On Equilibrium Allocations as Distributions on the Commodity Space," *Journal of Mathematical Economics,* 1, 159-167.

JONES, L. (1983): "Existence of Equilibria with Infinitely Many Consumers and Infinitely Many Commodities," *Journal of Mathematical Economics,* 12, 119-138.

MAS-COLELL, A. (1975): "A Model of Equilibrium with Differentiated Commodities," *Journal of Mathematical Economics,* 2, 263-295.

OSTROY, J. (1984): "On the Existence of Walrasian Equilibrium in Large-Square Economies," *Journal of Mathematical Economics,* 13, 143-163.

ROBINSON, A. (1966): *Non-standard Analysis.* Amsterdam: North-Holland.

SHAPLEY, L. AND H. SCARF (1974): "On Cores and Indivisibility," *Journal of Mathematical Economics,* 1, 23-37.

WEBER, S. (1981): "Some Results on the Weak Core of a Non-side-payment Game with Infinitely Many Players," *Journal of Mathematical Economics,* 8, 101-111.

Oligopoly with Price Inertia and Bounded Rationality

JAMES W. FRIEDMAN
University of North Carolina, Chapel Hill

1 Introduction

This paper is an exploratory piece aimed toward developing useful approaches to bounded rationality and also toward a more realistic modeling of consumer demand in oligopoly. Regarding the bounded rationality side of the model, anyone familiar with economics knows that the bulk of the theory supposes well informed economic agents who have well defined preferences and who make decisions that are optimal for them in an environment in which neither resources nor time are needed to carry out calculations. Additionally, much, though not all, theory abstracts from uncertainty of every sort. This body of theory is impressive, beautiful, and full of insight into human economic behavior. It provides valuable early steps on a very long path. At the same time, it does great and obvious violence to reality.

In the nineteen fifties and sixties there was a great burst of fine work in capital theory, (see Sen (1970) and McKenzie (1986) for references) giving us important, rigorous results on economic behavior in an intertemporal setting. The inspiration and, to some extent, technique, of that work spread to other areas encouraging the development of intertemporal models of consumer behavior, of firms, as well as of competitive, monopolistic and oligopolistic markets. In the corner of the discipline that I know best, oligopoly theory, that work had two effects. One was to show which results from the static theory go through and which do not when you introduce firms that look ahead and behave rationally in light of their knowledge that they have a long future life. The other effect was to expose the extreme unreality of the assumptions that agents know their cost and demand functions at any future date and that they can do any optimizing calculations required to maximize an infinite discounted profit stream.

Ignorance about the future and expensive calculations can each be dealt with in various ways. Looking first at ignorance about the future, a common approach is to assume the future holds a list of known possibilities, that the agent has a prior probability distribution over these possibilities, and that, as information is acquired over time, the prior distribution is revised again and again to reflect the new data. Typically Bayesian updating is used to carry out the preceding program. This approach is within the classic optimizing tradition, which is both a strength and a weakness. The strength is that the optimizing tradition is widely accepted and aesthetically appealing. The weakness is that Bayesian revision suffers even more from excessive information and calculation demands. Thus, on the one had, the agent must have a specific list of possible demand and cost functions as well as a distribution over these possibilities. It is easy to envision circumstances in which an economic agent does not have such a distribution and does not even know the list of possibilities. On the other hand, the process of Bayesian updating requires an amount of computation that dwarfs the amount required under certainty.

Another facet of the optimizing theory is that it is usually geared to showing existence, and sometimes characteristics, of equilibrium. Meanwhile equilibrium is not always unique. The ingenious Kreps and Wilson (1982) sequential equilibrium is notoriously nonunique. In particular, at an equilibrium in which some strategies of some players receive zero weight in the player's mixed strategy, there will be a variety of beliefs about behavior on unreached parts of the game that are consistent and that give rise to different equilibrium strategies. The well publicized *folk theorem for repeated games* is another example of multiplicity of equilibria. (See, for example, Friedman (1971) or Fudenberg and Maskin (1986).) These equilibria tell us much that is insightful, but they do not allow us to see precisely what players will do.

Bounded rationality can cut through both the unreasonably extreme knowledge assumptions and the large calculation demands by postulating that agents make decisions using limited knowledge and that they use decision procedures that fall short of full-blown optimization. Bounded rationality will not, in general, solve the problem of multiplicity of equilibria. It is true that the equilibrium paths in the family of models investigated below are unique; however, there are some arbitrary elements in the decision process that could be redesigned possibly giving rise to different unique equilibrium paths. This is not necessarily a bad thing. If the model and decision process are reasonable, it may prove possible to empirically estimate the parameters of the decision process for specific markets.

Turning now to the modeling of consumer demand in oligopoly, consumers are represented in oligopoly models either explicitly or implicitly. If the latter, they are represented by market demand functions; if the former, they are endowed with preferences and their individual demand functions are then derived. Most of the literature goes directly to demand functions, although it is conventional to regard the explicit modeling of consumers as a superior approach. In the present paper, the consumers will not be explicitly modeled and this requires some justification. The modeling of consumers explicitly has typically required assuming both a representative consumer and a very special utility function. Such assumptions are so restrictive that it is doubtful whether it is worthwhile to model the consumers directly. Consumers are surely not identical and results based on this restrictive assumption are likely to be highly misleading. Furthermore, the combination of identical consumers and tractable utility functions greatly restricts the scope of analysis. It is by no means clear that the class to which one is thus restricted is interesting and that it yields results which would survive any generalization of the model. These considerations lead me to believe that it remains worthwhile to continue the parallel track of modeling demand directly. Perhaps each approach will prove useful and, in time, it may be possible to unite the results of both lines of work within a single framework.[1]

[1]Gabszewicz and Thisse (1986) exposits much work done in the spatial framework where indi-

The demand structure used below divides consumers among firms and then models the amount bought in a period per consumer as a function of that firm's price. The distribution of consumers among firms is a state variable whose transition rule is critical to the model. The most important feature of the transition rule is that when a firm changes its price, it causes a number of consumers to search, whether the price change is upward or downward. The basic idea here is that a price change of any size engages the consumers' attention making them more prone to check out alternatives. This interpretation of the form of demand relies on a bounded rationality argument, because the search/not-search decision of the consumer is not portrayed as the result of an optimality calculation.

In the remainder of the paper, Section 2 is devoted to a further discussion of the general issues raised in the present section. Non-optimizing approaches in economics are highly suspect because they are unusual; whereas, the optimization paradigm is deeply entrenched. Therefore, fuller discussion of the shortcomings of full-blown optimization and of the need for other approaches is worthwhile. Section 3 contains an oligopoly model that will be described and then used to show how it can generate various outcomes. Finally, Section 4 contains concluding remarks.

2 Comments on Bounded Rationality and Conventional Optimization

This section is organized into several subsections dealing with complaints against the traditional methods and with alternative approaches to decisionmaking. In section 2.1 the disadvantages of the Bayesian approach and doubts about the soundness of perfect foresight assumptions are elaborated. Section 2.2 further discusses limits on the ability of economic agents to perform costless and extensive calculations and Section 2.3 deals with rules of thumb versus partial optimizing as particular means of implementing bounded rationality.

2.1 Bayesian revision and foresight

In a Bayesian analysis it is typical to regard the underlying stochastic phenomena of the model as being governed by some particular distribution. This distribution is not necessarily known to the agent within the model, but these agents do have distributions over matters relevant to them, they have techniques for recalculating such distributions as they receive new information, and a researcher can, given knowledge of how the system really works and how the agents will make decisions, figure out the probability distribution over the various possible states the model can attain at arbitrary times in the future. The seminal game theoretic work in this

vidual consumers are represented in the model and firms must decide which variant of a good to produce (i.e., where to locate). It has been typical in the literature dealing with product choice by firms that consumers are directly represented, with the market demand functions derived from their preferences. For the product choice question this is probably the most fruitful way to proceed; the work of Gabszewicz, Thisse, Shaked, Sutton, Economides, and others bears this out (see the references in Gabszewicz and Thisse (1986)). It is possible that the fruits of this line of work will both grow greatly and spread to other parts of the oligopoly literature.

vein is Harsanyi (1967-68). In this world an agent will never observe an event that she regarded as impossible and will never observe an event that does not appear on her list of conceivable events.

In contrast with this picture, I believe that people observe events from time to time that they regarded as impossible, and that they observe some events whose possible occurrence never crossed their minds. Here are two examples. As I write now it is mid-summer of 1990. A year ago the events presently taking place in the Soviet Union and Eastern Europe would have been regarded as unthinkable by many people and, by most who would acknowledge the possibility, would be regarded as possible in only the very distant future. Even if there are a few experts in the world who were so well informed and so prescient as to see the possibility, I strongly suspect there are many others who never believed they could occur around this time. The second example is technological. As I write I use the now conventional "typewriting" technology; namely, a small computer. Fifteen years ago there were probably a few visionaries who thought computers would become both so small and so inexpensive that ordinary folks could own a powerful computer small enough to fit into a briefcase. Apart from such visionaries, probably no one had an inkling that such a thing was possible. Furthermore, I wonder if it even crossed the minds of the visionaries that a major use of these computers would be as highly automated typewriters.

The point of the preceding examples is that people may frequently face decisions in circumstances where they cannot be nearly so precise about uncertainty as Bayesian analysis requires. How do you come up with a suitable probability distribution over a set of alternatives when you do not even know what elements should be in the set? How do you assign probabilities to unusual non-repetitive events? I know the theoretical answers à la Savage (1954); however, I doubt the descriptive accuracy and relevance of these answers. That is, some of the Savage axioms may be violated and the best mode in which to carry out analysis may not be the Bayesian.

I am not trying to say Bayesian analysis should be forgotten, but am arguing for the development of alternatives even though such alternatives maybe messy. All of our usual optimizing analysis is intellectually neat and tidy; that which benefits an economic agent (i.e., what are her preferences) is clear to her and that which is a benefit maximizing decision is also clear. This is intellectually satisfying and has served economics and economists well. But we should explore other avenues too. Other avenues, because they are new and not yet worked out, will necessarily be less tidy and will seem less appealing.

2.2 Optimality calculations, even under complete information

Sometimes we postulate elaborate models in which the amount of calculation that must be done for a full optimization is very great. In addition, we may assume that agents can gather information instantly and costlessly. Bounded rationality is a way to allow agents to operate on less than the totality of potentially available information or to use shortcut calculations even if all information is present. Buy why do this? Gathering information is costly. Who has not set out to buy something such as a consumer durable, searched a few sellers, found some price dispersion, and then bought from one of these sellers despite being confident that a lower price could be found from yet some other seller? The justification for stopping such a search is, of course, the *guess* that any further price reduction will not pay for the time and inconvenience of locating it. This justification is not the result of any calculation on data; it merely expresses an intuition that is *not* grounded in careful analysis. Many people might find that, on average, additional search would be beneficial (given their own preferences). But they not only do not try it, they do not even keep sufficiently good records to quite know what they do. Indeed, keeping such records would not be worthwhile unless those records were analyzed; however, carrying out such analysis is costly.

Similar remarks apply to calculations made with available data. People will sometimes replace a consumer durable, making the argument that the item has become so costly to maintain that replacement is superior to the maintenance of the old unit; however, I strongly suspect that these decisions are often made with little any analysis of any data. In summary, collecting and analyzing information uses resources and delays final decisions, both of which are costly. Figuring out how far to carry these activities also takes time and is costly. Figuring out how far to carry the evaluation of how far to search and analyze takes time and is costly. The process is an infinite regress that, carried to its logical extreme, might totally immobilize a person who takes it seriously. This Gordian knot can be cut with bounded rationality.

2.3 Rules of thumb and partial optimizing

It is one thing to make various complaints about knowledge assumptions and the difficulties of costly calculation and quite another to propose appealing alternatives. If there is a unified, general, best methodology to apply, it will take years for it to become apparent. In the meantime my own view of the best way to proceed is by dealing with specific economic problems using approaches that seem reasonable for them. As time goes on, a body of such efforts will accumulate and it may be possible to see some coherence in that body.

There are two general approaches to bounded rationality that are easily identified: rules of thumb and partial optimizing. Rules of thumb are, on the surface, totally unconnected with optimizing. Examples are (1) setting one's price at some fixed multiple of marginal cost, (2) ordering more of an input when the current stock equals the needs of some arbitrary number of days, (3) regulating one's production to keep inventories of finished goods at some arbitrary number of days' sales, (4) visiting three stores before making a purchase, (5) visiting stores until the lowest price has been quoted a second time, etc. By partial optimizing I mean optimizing within a framework that is less than the fullest one available. For example, a firm might set its price to maximize today's profit or to maximize a profit stream for a limited time instead of attempting to maximize from the present to infinity. Another example is that of choosing price on the assumption that other firms' prices will remain constant instead of analyzing the model for a jointly determined equilibrium and choosing one's own price in that equilibrium. Also, searching an arbitrary number of sellers, then buying from the lowest price quoted is also an example of partial optimization.

One cannot come to bounded rationality without recalling the early advocacy of Herbert Simon (1957), the pioneering work of Alchian (1950) and Winter (1964), as well as the study of rules of thumb in business decisions in Hall and Hitch (1939). More recently the interaction of game theory and biology has inspired renewed interest in biological analogies and rule of thumb behavior (see, for example, Friedman and Rosenthal (1986)). Limited optimization is also well represented in recent work based on *finite automata* as in Kalai and Stanford (1988) and Abreu and Rubinstein (1988).[2]

A partial optimization approach is taken in Section 3 below in which the firms will make decisions under the assumption that other firms are making no changes and in which their explicit objectives are short run. The procedure can be given heuristic justifications. With respect to assuming other firms will not change prices, it will be true in practice that in most periods no firms change their prices and, typically, firms will change their prices in different periods. This provides some justification for the way the firms take one another's prices for granted when calculating the current optimal price. With respect to the short runover which firms optimize, I have in mind market conditions that can change randomly and quite unpredictably. This kind of change is not built into the examples that I calculate, however. Even in the presence of firms that exhibit behavior patterns that can, over time, be observed and used to predict price changes, it is possible that making such predictions is too expensive to be useful.

The reader will, of course, judge for himself or herself whether the decision process seems at all reasonable. It should be judged within the context of oligopoly models, as other economic situations may call for other formulations. My own inclination in modeling bounded rationality is to try first to use some form of partial optimizing, because it seems to me very believable. The basic process of decision I have in mind is that the decision maker takes his very difficult, complicated decision problem and simplifies it into something quite tractable. Then he optimizes within this simplified context.

Granting that full optimization is unreasonable and that bounded rationality with partial optimization is appealing, how do we decide how to model the decision process? What bounded rationality shortcuts are made and what is the limited domain over which the agents are assumed to optimize? These questions cannot be answered in the abstract. It is preferable to model a specific economic problem (e.g., an oligopoly) and answer the modeling questions in that special setting in ways that are heuristically acceptable. Perhaps general principles will become more apparent after a number of such investigations have been made.

[2]Lest it be thought that one must be better off by knowing more and optimizing more completely, see Gilboa and Samet (1989) where two players in a game differ in just this way. The complete optimizer is at a disadvantage compared with the boundedly rational player.

3 The Model

The model has n firms that live forever. The number of consumers is fixed and, at any given period, they are distributed among the n firms so that in a single time period a consumer buys from only one firm. Whether a consumer searches at time t depends on whether the firm he bought from at time $t-1$ has changed its price. Few consumers search if their firm does not change its price; however, even a tiny price change will trigger a large increase in the number searching. The number of units sold by a firm at time t depends only upon its own price and the number of consumers attached to the firm at the time. The only cost a firm faces is a constant marginal cost of production. The decision making process of the firm depends only on phenomena of the current time period and assumes that rival firms will not change their prices. The firm makes the following calculations: (a) What will be its profit in the current period if it does not change its price? (b) What is the maximum profit the firm can have in the current period, given that it changes its price? Each firm compares the profits under (a) and (b) and then follows the more profitable alternative. The ensuing paragraphs spell out the model and the decision process in more detail.

3.1 The demand structure and single period profits

The demand side of the model reflects demand inertia and is constructed using a variant of the notion of market share. Demand inertia is the phenomenon that consumers are somewhat slow to change the firm from which they purchase. The basic form of demand is that, at any given time, the fixed total of m consumers are parceled out among the n firms with m_{it} consumers buying from firm i at time t. Thus $m = \sum_{i=1}^{n} m_{it}$. The m_{it} consumers who buy from firm i at time t are assumed to be a representative sample of the m consumers, so that the per capita demand function facing a firm may depend upon i and t, but may not depend upon m_{it}. The per capita demand function facing any firm i at time t depends only on that firm's price. Thus the per capita demand function for firm i could be, for example, $a_{i0} - a_{i1}p_{it}$ making the total unit sales of firm i, $q_{it} = m_{it}(a_{i0} - a_{i1}p_{it})$. As the firms produce differentiated products, their demand functions may have different parameters (a_{i0}, a_{i1}). At any specific period a consumer buys from just one firm, so that the m_{it}/m give market shares of a sort; namely, the fraction of consumers that buy from firm i at time t. Clearly m_{it}/m is not the fraction of total industry units sold by firm i nor is it the fraction of total industry revenue going to firm i.

Consumers exhibit inertia in the sense that they tend to stay with the same firm from period to period, but they engage in some search depending on the price policy of the firm they currently buy from. If the price of firm i at time t, p_{it} is unchanged from the preceding period then a fraction a of the $m_{i,t-1}$ consumers return to firm i at time t and $1-a$ search. If, however, $p_{it} \neq p_{i,t-1}$ then a smaller fraction of consumers return to firm i. The returning fraction, denoted θ_{it}, is decreasing in $|p_{it} - p_{i,t-1}|$ and is bounded above by $\alpha < a$. A price change of a given amount is assumed to have the same effect on θ_{it} whether it is an increase or decrease. The postulated underlying behavior of the consumers is that, given no change, some fraction $(1-a)$ of them search. The slightest price change induces a larger fraction $(1-\alpha)$ to search, and, as the price change increases, the searching fraction also increases. The searching consumers from all firms form a pool that is distributed back to the n firms according to the previous period's distribution of consumers. Specifically

$$\theta_{it}^0 = \alpha - b\left[\frac{p_{it}-p_{i,t-1}}{p_{i,t-1}+c}\right]^2 - d\frac{|\, p_{it}-p_{i,t-1}\,|}{p_{i,t-1}+c}\frac{m-m_{i,t-1}}{m} \quad for \quad p_{it} \neq p_{i,t-1} \qquad (1)$$

$$= a \qquad for \quad p_{it} = p_{i,t-1} \qquad (2)$$

with

$$\theta_{it} = max\{0, \theta_{it}^0\} \qquad (3)$$

and

$$m_{it} = m_{i,t-1}\theta_{it} + \frac{m_{i,t-1}^{\delta}}{\sum_{j=1}^{n} m_{j,t-1}^{\delta}} \sum_{j=1}^{n} m_{j,t-1}(1-\theta_{jt}) \qquad (4)$$

The restrictions on parameters in eqs. (1) to (4) are $b, c, d > 0, \delta \in (0,1]$, and $0 < \alpha < a < 1$. In eq. (4) the number of returning consumers who do not search is the left hand term, $m_{i,t-1}\theta_{it}$. The right hand term in eq. (4) is the number of searching consumers that go to firm i. Thus the total number of searching consumers is $\sum_{j=1}^{n} m_{j,t-1}(1-\theta_{jt})$ and the fraction of these going to firm i is $m_{i,t-1}^{\delta}/\sum_{j=1}^{n} m_{j,t-1}^{\delta}$. If $\delta = 1$, this fraction equals $m_{i,t-1}/m$; however, if $\delta \in (0,1)$, then the fraction exceeds $m_{i,t-1}/m$ whenever $m_{i,t-1}/m < 1/n$. That is, when $\delta < 1$ the *small* firms pick up a larger than proportionate share of the searching consumers while the opposite holds for *large* firms.

In a model with price inertia and consumer search occurring as described above it is difficult to see how the model works unless prices are actually changing from time to time. Incentive for such change is built into the model by incorporating a steady rate of inflation. Thus demand is given by

$$q_{it} = max\{0, m_{it}(a_{i0} - a_{i1}\beta^t p_{it})\} \qquad (5)$$

where $a_{i0}, a_{i1} > 0$ and $\beta \in (0,1)$. The rate of inflation is $1/\beta - 1$ and the form of demand in eq. (5) implies that the demand per consumer does not change in real terms over time. Similarly, each firm has a marginal cost that is constant in real terms. Letting $\gamma_i > 0$ be the marginal cost parameter of firm i, marginal cost at time t is γ_i/β^t and period t profit is

$$\pi_{it} = (p_{it} - \frac{\gamma_i}{\beta^t})q_{it} \qquad (6)$$

3.2 The firms' decision process

Equations (1) to (6) thus specify single period profit functions in which marginal cost is constant and demand exhibits consumer inertia with price changes stimulating search. Having $\alpha < a$ endows the model with a fixed cost for price change through a net loss of consumers of approximately $m_{it}(a-\alpha)$. The true loss is slightly less because some of these searching consumers will return to firm i. The search behavior of the consumers is not based on any underlying optimization by them; instead it reflects a hunch about what consumers do – at least in some markets. The relevant markets would be products that are relatively cheap per unit and are bought fairly frequently such as food items, restaurant meals, dry cleaning, household supplies, etc. Products that do not fit include major consumer durables. A specific durable is bought sufficiently seldom that search is needed for many reasons of which price is just one; typically before searching for a durable the consumer does not even know the range of variety available in the item. In contrast, for frequently purchased items habit can easily take over. There are many such items, frequent search for each would consume excessive amounts of time, and the customary price is easily noticed.

The firms' behavior is characterized by a limited sort of profit maximization. In period t, firm i chooses p_{it} so as to maximize eq. (6) on the presumption that all other prices will be unchanged. If the maximum profit achieved by changing price is equal to the profit the firm receives without changing, then the firm will keep the old price. Bounded rationality enters here in two ways. First, the firm takes no account whatever of the possibility that its rivals will change their prices. For many sets of parameter values this is reasonable in that no prices change in most periods and, in periods when prices do change, typically only one changes. Second, the future is ignored and no long term plan is made. On one hand, the firms never seem to learn that there is a steady inflation rate. On the other, their current price change ignores the effect that its size or timing might have on the size and timing of its own future price changes. Contrary to typical infinite horizon models, the firm does not develop a plan for price changes over time that maximizes its discounted profits. Given the regularity of the inflation in the model and the stationarity of real demand per capita, ignoring the future in this way will seem unreasonable. Against this I would argue that the firms' simple decision procedure makes more sense in a world in which demand per capita is subject to random fluctuations produced by distributions unknown to the firms, distributions that may themselves be shifting unpredictably over time, and where the inflation rate may also vary unpredictably over time. It is for such a world that the decision process is intended. The steady inflation rate is used here because it permits simple calculations and allows a chance to determine steady state characteristics of the model as a function of parameter values – at least for any specific parameter values that are used for computations.

If all firms except firm i keep their prices unchanged, then eq. (4) becomes

$$m_{it} = m_{i,t-1}\theta_{it} + \frac{m_{i,t-1}^{\delta}}{\sum_{j=1}^{n} m_{j,t-1}^{\delta}}[m(1-a) + m_{i,t-1}(a - \theta_{it})] \tag{7}$$

3.3 Some analytical results

In this section some results are established that ensure a degree of regularity to the numerical illustrations given in Section 3.4. The key result is Lemma 2, ensuring that the behavior of the firms implies a unique path for the market over time starting from an arbitrary distribution of consumers. Lemma 1 is needed in establishing this result.

An important characteristic of the model is that π_{it} is quasiconcave in p_{it} on the intervals $[\gamma_i/\beta^t, p_{i,t-1})$ and $(p_{i,t-1}, a_{i0}/a_{i1}\beta^t]$. Prices below γ_i/β^t and above $a_{i0}/a_{i1}\beta^t$ are not relevant; the former, being below marginal cost, can never be profit maximizers and the latter correspond to zero demand and, likewise, cannot be profit maximizers.

Lemma 1 *π_{it} is strictly quasiconcave in p_{it} on $[\gamma_i/\beta^t, p_{i,t-1})$ and $(p_{i,t-1}, a_{i0}/a_{i1}\beta^t]$.*

Proof: This is implied by the quasiconcavity of π_{it} on $[\gamma_i/\beta^t, a_{i0}/a_{i1}\beta^t]$ when $a = \alpha$. Suppose, then, that $a = \alpha$. Then

$$\frac{\partial \pi_{it}}{\partial p_{it}} = m_{it}(a_{i0} - 2\beta^t a_{i1} p_{it} + \gamma_i a_{i1}) + (p_{it} - \frac{\gamma_i}{\beta^t})(a_{i0} - a_{i1}\beta^t p_{it})\frac{\partial m_{it}}{\partial p_{it}} \tag{8}$$

and

$$\frac{\partial^2 \pi_{it}}{\partial p_{it}^2} = -2\beta^t a_{i1} m_{it} + 2(a_{i0} - 2\beta^t a_{i1} p_{it} + \gamma_i a_{i1})\frac{\partial m_{it}}{\partial p_{it}} + (p_{it} - \frac{\gamma_i}{\beta^t})(a_{i0} - a_{i1}\beta^t p_{it})\frac{\partial^2 m_{it}}{\partial p_{it}^2} \tag{9}$$

where

$$\frac{\partial m_{it}}{\partial p_{it}} = -m_{i,t-1}\left[1 - \frac{m_{i,t-1}^{\delta}}{\sum_{j=1}^{n} m_{j,t-1}^{\delta}}\right]\left[\frac{2b(p_{it} - p_{i,t-1})}{(p_{i,t-1}+c)^2} + \frac{d(m - m_{i,t-1})(p_{it} - p_{i,t-1})}{m(p_{i,t-1}+c) \mid p_{it} - p_{i,t-1} \mid}\right] \tag{10}$$

and

$$\frac{\partial^2 m_{it}}{\partial p_{it}^2} = -m_{i,t-1}[1 - \frac{m_{i,t-1}^{\delta}}{\sum_{j=1}^{n} m_{j,t-1}^{\delta}}]\frac{2b}{(p_{i,t-1}+c)^2} \tag{11}$$

The interval $[\gamma_i/\beta^t, a_{i0}/a_{i1}\beta^t]$ can be partitioned into three subintervals. These are $[\gamma_i/\beta^t, I_M]$, (I_M, I_X), and $[I_X, a_{i0}/a_{i1}\beta^t]$ where I_M is the smaller of $p_{i,t-1}$ and $(a_{i0} + \gamma_i a_{i1})/2\beta^t a_{i1}$ and I_X is the larger of the two. Eq. (8) is clearly positive on $[\gamma_i/\beta^t, I_M]$ and negative on $[I_X, a_{i0}/a_{i1}\beta^t]$. It remains to show that eq. (8) is falling on the middle interval, (I_M, I_X). This latter is ensured by eq. (9) being negative. That eq. (9) is negative on this middle interval is because $\partial m_{it}/\partial p_{it}$ and $(a_{i0} - 2\beta^t a_{i1} p_{it} + \gamma_i a_{i1})$ are necessarily of opposite sign on this interval. □

The significance of Lemma 1 is that, given $(m_{i,t-1}, p_{i,t-1})$, there is a unique price, p_{it}, that the firm will choose under the decision procedure that is postulated. This, in turn, means that a given vector (m_{t-1}, p_{t-1}) will transform uniquely into (m_t, p_t). Consequently, starting from some initial condition, (m_o, p_0), the postulated decision process implies a unique path for the market.

Lemma 2 *Let $m_0 = (m_{10}, \ldots, m_{n0})$ be an initial distribution of consumers and let $p_0 = (p_{10}, \ldots, p_{n0})$ be an initial vector of prices. Given the postulated decision procedure, a unique time path (m_t, p_t) is induced.*

Proof: Clearly if an arbitrary (m_{t-1}, p_{t-1}) leads to a unique (m_t, p_t) the lemma is proved by induction. Consider first the determination of p_{it} given (m_{t-1}, p_{t-1}). The firm will find its new price in the following way. First, maximize π_{it} with respect to

p_{it} with $a = \alpha$. The price thus found, p_{it}^0, (a) exists, (b) is unique, and (c) lies in the compact interval $[\gamma_i/\beta^t, a_{i0}/a_{i1}\beta^t]$ on which π_{it} is continuous. To see that (a) to (c) are true, note that $p_{it}^0 < \gamma_i/\beta^t$ implies price below marginal cost, which cannot be as profitable as $p_{it}^0 = \gamma_i/\beta^t$. At the other extreme, $p_{it}^0 > a_{i0}/a_{i1}\beta^t$ is exactly as profitable as $p_{it}^0 = a_{i0}/a_{i1}\beta^t$ because sales will be zero as long as $p_{it}^0 \geq a_{i0}/a_{i1}\beta^t$. Consequently no price outside the interval $[\gamma_i/\beta^t, a_{i0}/a_{i1}\beta^t]$ can be more profitable than some price in the interval, so that the optimum must lie in the interval. That an optimum exists follows from the existence of a maximum of a continuous function on a compact set and uniqueness follows from Lemma 1 asserting the strict quasiconcavity of π_{it} on the interval $[\gamma_i/\beta^t, a_{i0}/a_{i1}\beta^t]$. If $p_{it}^0 = p_{i,t-1}$ then p_{it}^0 is the optimum we seek (recall that a $a \geq \alpha$). If $p_{it}^0 \neq p_{i,t-1}$, then $p_{it} = p_{i,t-1}$ unless the profit at p_{it}^0 is higher. Thus there is a unique p_{it} and the same holds for all firms, yielding a unique p_t. From eq. (4) p_t and m_{t-1} uniquely determine m_t. □

As a step toward determining whether long run equilibrium market shares are unique in the model, consider steady state equilibrium in a model where there is no inflation ($\beta = 1$) and no lump-sum penalty for changing price ($a = \alpha$). Equilibrium prices are given by $\partial\pi_i/\partial p_i = 0$ which, in a steady state equilibrium, requires $p_i = (a_{i0} + \gamma_i a_{i1})/2a_{i1}$. Equilibrium market shares must satisfy eq. (4) with $m_{it} = m_{i,t-1}$ and $\theta_{it} = a$. This reduces to $m_i/m = m_i^\delta / \sum_{j=1}^n m_j^\delta$, which, in turn, is equivalent to $m_i \sum_{j=1}^n m_j^\delta = m_i^\delta \sum_{j=1}^n m_j$. Clearly this relationship will hold for all i when $m_i = m/n$. Suppose the m_i are not all equal and, without loss of generality, suppose m_1 is the smallest. Then we have the requirement that

$$m_1^{1+\delta} + m_1 m_2^\delta + \ldots + m_1 m_n^\delta = m_1^{1+\delta} + m_1^\delta m_2 + \ldots + m_1^\delta m_n \qquad (12)$$

Comparing corresponding terms on the right and left sides of the equality in eq. (12), the first terms are equal. For any later term we have $m_1 m_i^\delta < m_1^\delta m_i$ whenever $m_1 < m_i$. To see this note that $m_1 m_i^\delta < m_1^\delta m_i$ is equivalent to $m_1^{1-\delta} < m_i^{1-\delta}$. This latter inequality holds whenever $\delta \in (0,1)$ and $0 < m_1 < m_i$. Given that m_1 is the smallest of the m_i, and all are not equal, the left hand side of eq.(12) must be strictly smaller than the right. Thus the only equilibrium distribution of consumers is $m_i = m/n$.

The introduction of $a > \alpha$ into the model, along with inflation, permits along run distribution of consumers that is unequal. The reason is that the existence of the inflation element means firms will wish to change prices from time to time. If $a = \alpha$ they would adjust in each period and adjust by the same proportion; however, having $a > \alpha$ means that they adjust only occasionally and the number of periods between adjustments is not identical across firms, permitting differential effects on the consumer distribution.

3.4 Some numerical illustrations

Tables 1 to 3 exhibit results of running the model with various parameter values. Most parameter values were constant for all runs reported within a single table; these values are listed at the bottom of the table. Parameters that change from one run to another within the same table are a, α, and δ. Their values are given

TABLE 1

firm	price	output	buyers	profit	change	a	α	δ
1	668.321	3,810.781	106.88	963,587.71	.0204	.8	.72	.95
2	128.933	1,787.306	86.37	44,662.23	.0416			
3	838.340	9,454.903	106.75	3,016,223.38	.0204			
1	368.274	3,670.902	109.52	538,514.47	.0204	.8	.72	.97
2	68.738	1,678.045	80.95	22,317.48	.0416			
3	460.342	9,177.253	109.52	1,682,857.37	.0204			
1	1,852.444	4,374.101	124.59	3,108,215.56	.0212	.8	.72	.99
2	353.380	1,065.394	50.81	71,973.72	.0392			
3	2,315.555	10,935.248	124.59	9,713,168.76	.0212			
1	1,815.911	4,761.692	138.23	3,370,525.96	.0216	.8	.72	.995
2	342.072	499.382	23.54	32,113.01	.038			
3	2,269.889	11,904.196	138.23	10,532,859.61	.0216			
1	1,880.019	5,402.020	146.58	3,722,751.72	.0216	.8	.72	.997
2	366.921	146.252	6.83	9,718.86	.0376			
3	2,350.023	13,504.974	146.58	11,633,524.46	.0216			
1	1,957.454	4,773.667	147.41	3,816,501.39	.022	.8	.72	.999
2	356.707	110.882	5.18	7,062.23	.0368			
3	2,446.816	11,934.024	147.41	11,926,407.84	.022			

b	c	d	β	a_{10}	a_{11}	γ_1	a_{20}	a_{21}	γ_2	a_{30}	a_{31}	γ_3
1	.001	.5	.998	100	5	8	120	40	2	250	10	10

in the appropriately labeled columns. Each run lasted for 2,500 iterations which was much longer than needed for the model to settle into a pattern under which the customer distribution was essentially unchanging and the frequency of price changes was also stabilized. The column headed *change* is the observed frequency of price change. For example, in the first set of parameter values in Table 1, firms 1 and 3 show price change frequencies of .0204 indicating 20.4 price changes per firm per thousand periods. Clearly, in any period that one firm alone changed its price, its customer base would fall. Customer distributions could eventually remain roughly constant over time because each firm would change its price from time to time so that the losses of customers suffered by a firm when it changed its price would be restored when the other firms changed their prices.

In Table 1 the figures suggest that firm 2 is in a weak position. Across the runs in that table only δ changes. The smaller is δ the more a firm with a small fraction of the customer base (below $\frac{1}{3}$) gains a disproportionate share of searching consumers. With $a = .8$ for all firms, 20% of the consumers search in any period where no price change occurs and the relative advantage of the small consumer base increases as that base shrinks. Again, the smaller is δ (within the (0, 1] interval) the stronger is this effect. With $\delta = .95$ firm 2 has about 27% of the consumers in a three firm market with the other two firms having about 36.5% each. However, as δ rises the consumer base of firm 2 shrinks; with $\delta = .999$ firm 2 has only 1.7%.

In Table 2, firm 1 seems to have a potential dominance with firm 3 being particularly weak. Again, when a and α have the same values as in Table 1 and $\delta =$ .95, the firms share the consumers almost equally, as in Table 1. When $\delta = .999$, the respective shares of the consumer base are 85.9%, 13.9%, and 0.2%. With $\delta =$ .95 and α taking on various values, again, as α falls, firm 1 gains consumers, firm 3 loses them, and firm 2 remains in the middle.

Within Table 3 the parameter a_{31} is 15, intermediate between the values in the other two tables, and the long run share of consumers going to firm 3 is correspondingly higher than in Table 2 (where $a_{31} = 20$) and Table 1 (where $a_{31} = 10$). All in all, the lessons from the tables boil down to showing that the model will accommodate a wide range of equilibrium circumstances, suggesting the model may prove to be a helpful descriptive device.

4 Concluding Comments

Some complaints that can be made against the model presented above are (1) firms at totally shortsighted, (2) evidence is ignored on the behavior of rival firms that could be profitably utilized, and (3) the discussion of the model envisioned unpredictable randomness, but none was examined. Taking these in turn, it would be easy to have the firms optimize over some fixed number of periods, say T. Using a procedure that is otherwise like the postulated procedure, a firm would assume all other firms would keep their prices constant and would assume its own price would be unchanged for T periods. It would then determine the most profitable price to use over that T period horizon. A further degree of sophistication would have the firms determining the optimal value of T; however, that seems to me to move too far back toward the computational difficulties that the model seeks to avoid. Concerning the behavior of other firms, over time the firms acquire track records that a firm can use in making its plans. Suppose, for example, that a firm can see that a certain rival changes its price by k% on the average at intervals of approximately τ periods. It can build this price behavior into it optimal price decision when it uses a planning horizon of T periods. This complicates the decision process a bit, but appears to be easy to cope with. For example, it would probably not be very difficult to put this into the computer program that was used to generate the illustrative tables. Similarly, occasional random parameter shifts could be incorporated into the model. Suppose this were done by two separate random draws. The first decides whether any parameters change and the second takes place only if parameters are to change. Call the former random draw the determination of whether there is a *regime switch*. The probability of a regime switch should be very small so that a firm has no opportunity to obtain a good reading on the distribution of regime switches or on the nature of switches when they occur. If this were done, then any attempt to predict the behavior of another firm might naturally be based on past data *within the present regime only.*

TABLE 2

firm	price	output	buyers	profit	change	a	α	δ
1	2,008.300	3,951.599	121.93	3,237,040.38	.0168	.8	.672	.95
2	368.075	2,108.825	100.92	149,623.01	.0336			
3	1,650.686	2,143.165	77.15	353,763.65	.0556			
1	1,911.654	4,373.451	123.08	3,173,091.15	.0176	.8	.668	.95
2	352.419	2,655.944	106.57	148,438.01	.0356			
3	1,664.159	1,794.906	70.35	324,200.05	.0624			
1	2,012.266	3,683.599	113.65	3,023,043.00	.0192	.8	.704	.95
2	351.692	2,758.393	108.18	148,878.13	.0384			
3	1,644.404	2,271.887	78.16	353,974.71	.0664			
1	1,991.627	3,816.019	117.67	3,100,934.26	.0208	.8	.72	.95
2	366.244	2,083.552	101.16	148,555.00	.042			
3	1,647.841	2,141.200	81.17	372,717.55	.0712			
1	1,885.636	4,303.509	117.38	2,989,897.81	.0204	.8	.72	.93
2	364.686	2,215.424	100.68	148,359.68	.0416			
3	1,671.342	2,085.341	81.95	379,408.71	.0728			
1	1,916.129	3,916.855	109.90	2,840,700.97	.02	.8	.72	.85
2	369.835	2,026.581	98.27	145,745.67	.0416			
3	1,664.895	2,416.271	91.83	425,982.09	.0768			
1	1,944.305	6,560.803	190.55	4,974,303.42	.0248	.8	.72	.99
2	367.961	1,671.232	80.62	118,977.76	.0416			
3	1,623.174	894.976	28.83	125,766.07	.0668			
1	2,046.739	7,843.217	257.81	6,824,223.71	.0352	.8	.72	.999
2	349.459	1,040.602	41.69	57,539.66	.0388			
3	1,648.098	12.928	0.50	637.06	.0636			
1	2,001.666	3,566.558	108.85	2,891,722.92	.0444	.8	.784	.95
2	370.242	2,072.314	101.03	149,850.68	.0908			
3	1,665.215	2,367.697	90.13	418,175.56	.1664			

b	c	d	β	a_{10}	a_{11}	γ_1	a_{20}	a_{21}	γ_2	a_{30}	a_{31}	γ_3
1	.001	.5	.998	100	5	8	120	40	2	250	20	10

TABLE 3

firm	price	output	buyers	profit	change	a	α	δ
1	2,071.933	7,234.744	239.03	6,388,764.14	.0284	.7	.63	.999
2	351.424	283.211	11.16	15,378.42	.0404			
3	1,905.889	2,867.434	49.81	1,205,092.96	.0344			
1	1,919.467	3,965.135	111.61	2,888,954.67	.0204	.8	.72	.95
2	369.659	1,863.493	90.16	133,657.72	.0416			
3	1,936.387	5,390.922	98.23	2,413,994.71	.034			
1	1,888.939	5,260.797	149.16	3,796,531.81	.022	.8	.72	.99
2	361.610	1,300.173	62.31	90,347.61	.04			
3	1,877.190	5,048.085	88.53	2,110,595.16	.0332			
1	2,022.464	5,539.793	178.87	4,708,998.00	.024	.8	.72	.995
2	355.935	1,030.760	45.18	64,881.67	.0388			
3	1,896.426	4,239.421	75.95	1,829,223.13	.0328			
1	1,974.761	7,586.011	245.02	6,301,117.77	.028	.8	.72	.999
2	352.657	233.346	10.92	15,160.09	.0376			
3	1,873.892	2,355.421	44.06	1,043,002.81	.032			
1	1,839.603	4,680.621	125.36	3,114,006.37	.0196	.9	.81	.95
2	364.254	1,690.448	81.51	119,081.07	.0388			
3	1,923.418	4,976.110	93.14	2,267,708.42	.032			
1	2,017.088	8,100.052	253.31	6,730,889.06	.0272	.9	.81	.999
2	365.138	75.145	3.50	4,755.24	.0352			
3	1,886.604	2,554.127	43.19	1,031,752.27	.03			
1	1,926.911	4,769.779	139.33	3,600,965.30	.02	.95	.855	.95
2	352.430	1,737.315	73.09	103,266.47	.0368			
3	1,930.317	4,584.616	87.58	2,131,350.42	.0308			
1	2,030.822	5,506.336	177.05	4,687,674.28	.0216	.98	.882	.95
2	363.733	947.592	44.53	65,363.53	.0352			
3	1,861.369	4,748.417	78.42	1,840,474.74	.0296			
1	2,035.295	6,633.058	217.24	5,723,935.72	.0228	.99	.891	.95
2	360.883	538.884	25.11	36,587.03	.0344			
3	1,913.147	3,119.391	57.65	1,398,114.08	.0292			
1	2,075.405	7,248.697	239.31	6,408,989.48	.0252	.99	.891	.98
2	355.943	275.443	11.31	16,037.28	.0336			
3	1,850.147	3,138.986	49.38	1,134,897.40	.0284			

b	c	d	β	a_{10}	a_{11}	γ_1	a_{20}	a_{21}	γ_2	a_{30}	a_{31}	γ_3
1	.001	.5	.998	100	5	8	120	40	2	250	15	10

With the aim of getting nearer to descriptive accuracy while maintaining analytical tractability and some degree of optimizing behavior, this paper has presented a model of oligopoly with boundedly rational firms and consumers. Until unifying results become available, the most promising avenue for developing bounded rationality models lies in trying to design specific models for relatively narrow applications. The reason is that we do not have any clearly acceptable bounded rationality approaches; therefore, developing models that are heuristically attractive in the narrow setting for which they are designed seems the best way to start. When much work of this sort has been done, it is possible that general principles will emerge.

Appendix

The computer program used to generate the examples is below. It was written for Turbo Pascal 5.0.

```
program inertia6;
  uses Crt;
  type vecint = array[1..20] of integer;
  type vector = array[1..20] of real;
  var a,b,c,d,m,ms,be,bet,mc,tl,ths,fs,del,rel : real;
    i,idx,n,t,tm,tn,ctr : integer;
    fi,fp : text; a0,a1,ga,m0,m1,p0,p1,pi,q,th,fm : vector; mk,nch : vecint;

procedure inread (var a,b,c,d,be,m,mc,del,tl : real; var n,tm,tn : integer;
  var a0,a1,ga,m0,p0 : vector; var fi,fp : text);
  var i : integer; ma : real;
  begin
    assign (fi,'c: \ tp\ data\ para6.in');
    assign (fp,'c: \ tp\ data\ dat6.out');
    reset (fi);
    rewrite (fp);
    readln (fi,n,tm,a,b,c,d,be,tl,mc,del,tn);
    if (del <= 0) then del := 1;
    ma := a*mc;
    writeln (fp,'itrs = ',tm:3,' theta params:',a:6:4,b:7:2,c:6:3,d:6:3);
    writeln (fp,'beta = ',be:5:3,' tol = ',tl:7:5,' alpha = ', ma:6:4,' del = ',del:6:4);
    writeln (fp);
    m := 0;
    for i := 1 to n do
      begin
        readln (fi,a0[i],a1[i],ga[i],m0[i]);
        m := m + m0[i];
        writeln (fp, 'firm',i:3,' a0 = ',a0[i]:8:3,' a1 = ',a1[i]:8:3,
            ' gamma = ',ga[i]:8:3,' m0 = ',m0[i]:8:3);
        p0[i] := 0.5*(ga[i] + a0[i]/a1[i])
      end;
    writeln (fp);
```

```
    close (fi)
  end;

procedure price (var a,b,c,d,a0,a1,bet,ga,m,mc,mo,tl,po,p1,th,fs,fm : real);
  var d1,dm,mu,pd,pm,px,ff : real;
  begin
    if ((a0-2*a1*bet*po+a1*ga) = 0) then
      begin
        p1 := po;
        th := a
      end
    else
      begin
        dm := 1-mo/m;
        ff := 1-fm/fs;
        if ((a0-2*a1*bet*po+a1*ga) < 0) then
          begin
            pm := ga/bet;
            px := po
          end
        else
          begin
            pm := po;
            px := a0/(a1*bet)
          end;
        repeat
          if keypressed then
            begin
              close (fp);
              halt
            end;
          p1 := (px+pm)/2;
          pd := (p1-po)/(po+c);
          th := a*mc-b*sqr(pd)-d*abs(pd)*dm;
          mu := mo*th+fm*(m*(1-a)+mo*(a-th))/fs;
          d1 := mu*(a0-2*a1*bet*p1+a1*ga)-(p1-ga/bet)*(a0- a1*bet*p1)*
                  mo*ff*(2*b/(po+c)+d*dm/abs(p1-po))*(p1- po)/(po+c);
            if (d1 <= 0) then px := p1;
            if (d1 >= 0) then pm := p1
          until (((px-pm)/px) < tl)
      end;
      if ((mu*(p1-ga/bet)*(a0-a1*bet*p1)) < {A price change will be }
          (mo*(po-ga/bet)*(a0-a1*bet*po))) then {undertaken if it will }
      begin {lower profit given the }
        p1 := po; {change cost. The change }
        th := a {cost must be absorbed in }
```

```
      end {one period. }
  end;

procedure beep(var tn : integer);
  begin
    sound(tn);
    delay(80);
    nosound
  end;

  begin
    inread (a,b,c,d,be,m,mc,del,tl,n,tm,tn,a0,a1,ga,m0,p0,fi,fp);
    for i := 1 to n do nch[i] := 0;
    bet := 1;
    idx := 1;
    ctr := 0;
    writeln (fp,' t i price output # cst profit');
    for t := 1 to tm do
      begin
        if (t mod 10 = 0) then write (t:6);
        if (t mod 100 = 0) then
            begin
                writeln;
                beep(tn)
            end;
        if (t mod 1000 = 0) then
            begin
                delay(100);
                beep(tn);
            end;
        fs := 0;
        for i := 1 to n do
            begin
                fm[i] := exp(del*ln(m0[i]/m));
                fs := fs + fm[i]
            end;
        for i := 1 to n do
            price (a,b,c,d,a0[i],a1[i],bet,ga[i],m,mc,
                m0[i],tl,p0[i],p1[i],th[i],fs,fm[i]);
        ths := 0;
        for i := 1 to n do ths := ths + m0[i]*(1-th[i])/m;
        for i := 1 to n do m1[i] := m0[i]*th[i] + m*ths*fm[i]/fs;
        for i := 1 to n do if (m1[i] < 0) then m1[i] := 0;
        ms := 0;
        for i := 1 to n do ms := ms + m1[i];
        if ms = 0 then for i := 1 to n do m1[i] := m0[i]
```

```
            else for i := 1 to n do m1[i] := m*m1[i]/ms;
        for i := 1 to n do
            begin
                mk[i] := 0;
                q[i] := m1[i]*(a0[i]-a1[i]*bet*p1[i]);
                pi[i] := (p1[i]-ga[i]/bet)*q[i];
                if (p1[i] <> p0[i]) then
                    begin
                        mk[i] := 1;
                        nch[i] := nch[i]+1;
                        pi[i] := pi[i]-a0[i]*mc/(a1[i]*bet);
                        idx := idx+1
                    end;
                m0[i] := m1[i]
                p0[i] := p1[i]
            end;
        if (idx>0) then
            begin
                writeln (fp);
                ctr := ctr + 1;
                for i := 1 to n do
                    if (mk[i] = 0) then writeln (fp,t:4,i:3,'',p1[i]:11:3,
                        q[i]:12:3,m1[i]:7:2,pi[i]:16:2)
                        else writeln (fp,t:4,i:3,'*',p1[i]:11:3,
                        q[i]:12:3,m1[i]:7:2,pi[i]:16:2)
            end;
        idx := 0;
        bet := bet*be
    end;
  rel := tm/ctr;
  writeln (fp);
  writeln (fp,'number of changes was ',ctr:4);
  write (fp,'distribution ');
  for i := 1 to n do q[i] := nch[i]/tm;
  for i := 1 to n do write (fp,q[i]:10:6);
  writeln (fp,'relative frequency ',rel:7:2);
  repeat
    sound(tn);
  until(keypressed);
  nosound;
  close (fp)
end.
```

References

ABREU, DILIP AND ARIEL RUBINSTEIN (1988): "The Structure of Nash Equilibrium in Repeated Games with Finite Automata," *Econometrica,* 56, 1259-1282.

ALCHIAN, ARMEN A. (1950): "Uncertainty, Evolution and Economic Theory," *Journal of Political Economy,* 58, 211-222.

FRIEDMAN, JAMES W. (1971): "A Non-Cooperative Equilibrium for Supergames," *Review of Economic Studies,* 38, 1-12.

FRIEDMAN, JAMES W. AND ROBERT W. ROSENTHAL (1986): "A Positive Approach to Noncooperative Games," *Journal of Economic Behavior and Organization,* 7, 235-251.

FUDENBERG, DREW AND ERIC MASKIN (1986): "The Folk Theorem in Repeated Games with Discounting and with Incomplete Information," *Econometrica,* 54, 533-554.

GABSZEWICZ, JEAN JASKOLD AND JACQUES-FRANÇOIS THISSE (1986): *Location Theory.* In *Fundamentals of Pure and Applied Economics 5.* Eds. Jacques Lesourne and Hugo Sonnenschein. Chur: Harwood.

GILBOA, ITZHAK AND DOV SAMET (1989): "Bounded versus Unbounded Rationality: The Tyranny of the Weak," *Games and Economic Behavior,* 1, 213-221.

HALL, R.L. AND C.J. HITCH (1939): "Price Theory and Business Behavior," *Oxford Economic Papers,* 12-45.

HARSANYI, JOHN C. (1967-68): "Games with Incomplete Information Played by 'Bayesian' Players," *Management Science,* 14, 159-82, 14, 320-334, 14, 486-502.

KALAI, EHUD AND WILLIAM STANFORD (1988): "Finite Rationality and Interpersonal Complexity in Repeated Games," *Econometrica,* 56, 397-410.

KREPS, DAVID M. AND ROBERT WILSON (1982): "Sequential Equilibrium," *Econometrica,* 50, 863-894.

MCKENZIE, LIONEL W. (1986): "Optimal Economic Growth, Turnpike Theorems and Comparative Dynamics," in *Handbook of Mathematical Economics,* vol III, 1281-1355, ed. by Kenneth Arrow and Michael Intriligator, North-Holland: Amsterdam.

SAVAGE, LEONARD J. (1954): *The Foundations of Statistics.* Wiley: New York.

SEN, AMARTYA K., ED. (1970): *Growth Economics.* Penguin: Harmondsworth.

SIMON, HERBERT A. (1957): *Models of Man.* Wiley: New York.

WINTER, SIDNEY G. (1964): "Economic 'Natural Selection' and the Theory of the Firm," *Yale Economic Essays,* 4, 225-272.

International Trade and Endogenous Production Structures

RONALD W. JONES
University of Rochester
AND
SUGATA MARJIT
Jadavpur University

No single production structure has become dominant in models of the pure theory of international trade, even those characterized by perfect competition. Most models are represented by Ricardian, Heckscher-Ohlin, or Specific-Factors structures, or variants and combinations of these, with the selection often dictated by the problem being investigated. However, it is well known that if a country is freed from the bonds of autarky and allowed to engage in trade in goods or factors, a certain degree of specialization is encouraged so that the production structure with trade can differ significantly from that postulated in autarky. In that sense production structures are endogenously affected by trade.

Several examples in which trade alters production structure come readily to mind. Intermediate goods that are used specifically in each of two individual sectors may be exchanged for each other with trade; as Sanyal and Jones (1982) pointed out, such trade tends to convert a 3 × 2 specific-factors framework into a 2 × 2 Heckscher-Ohlin one.[1] Similarly, a two-country Heckscher-Ohlin trade model adopts many of the Ricardian characteristics should international movement of capital be allowed (see Jones and Ruffin (1975)). Perhaps the most frequently cited example is one involving time rather than trade, *viz* the interpretation of the Heckscher-Ohlin model as a long-run variant of the specific factors model, with time allowing the transformation (or replacement) of one type of sector-specific capital with another (see Neary (1978)). (Alternatively, the transformation of a specific-factors model into a Heckscher-Ohlin structure results if the "mobile" factor is itself produced by the specific factors.)[2]

All these examples involve trade or transformation at the input level. In this paper we analyze how trade in final commodities in a country with many productive

[1] To repeat Doug Purvis's remark about this model, "Heckscher-Ohlin does not explain trade, trade explains Heckscher-Ohlin."

[2] This is the "Produced Mobile Factor" structure discussed in Jones and Marjit (1991). Somewhat related is recent work by Ali Khan (1991), in which separate ethnic groups (specific factors) are joined by mobile capital, either to produce rural outputs in isolation or to join forces with each other in an urban environment to produce a separate urban product.

factors causes one of two production structures to emerge. On the one hand is the familiar $(n+1)$-factor, n-commodity version of the specific-factor model (Jones, 1975), and on the other is a generalization to many commodities of a model proposed by Gruen and Corden (1970), in which one industry is tied to a production "nugget" by the common use of a single factor (labor), whereas the "nugget" contains two industries in a standard 2 × 2 Heckscher-Ohlin structure. In what follows we focus on the manner in which external shocks to such an economy, in the form of changes in the terms of trade (or technical progress or endowment discoveries), get spread from industry to industry. A particular phenomenon of interest to trade theorists has been labelled the "Dutch Disease", whereby a shock favorable to one trading sector spells trouble for other sectors, usually through passing on cost increases to these sectors. Our multi-commodity framework facilitates such an investigation and reveals that such shocks may require some industries to be completely wiped out and encourage new industries to emerge — industries which have experienced no external change in market conditions. As well, we investigate how the existence or creation of industries which are shielded from the direct competition of trade can crowd out industries which otherwise could compete successfully in the world market, or how non-traded industries modify the pattern of the Dutch Disease phenomenon. Once non-traded goods are introduced, our structure can be used to examine the frequently-held view that a country's terms of trade and real exchange rate go hand in hand.

1 Production Structure in Autarky

The country's economic activity in autarky is broken down into N productive sectors. Each sector, i, is characterized by the existence of a number of industries which employ labor and a type of capital, K^i, fixed in total amount but used only by the industries in sector i. Labor is homogeneous, fixed in total amount, and available on the same terms to all sectors of the economy. Thus one factor (labor) trades in a national market while all types of capital are limited by sector. If local demand maintains production even at high prices in autarky, a competitive equilibrium in each sector is of the type illustrated by the set of unit-value isoquants in Figure 1. These unit-value isoquants are all tangent to a line whose slope indicates the ratio of wages to rentals on the type of capital specific to that sector. Thus each sector of the economy is characterized by the two-factor, many-commodity version of the Heckscher-Ohlin model in which the non- traded status of all commodities in autarky ensures that commodity prices adjust to reflect unit costs. Sector j is composed of n_j industries, and the total number of commodities produced, $\sum_{j=1}^{N} n_j$, substantially exceeds the number of productive factors, $(N+1)$.

2 Free Trade in All Commodities

If all commodities in all sectors are freely traded at a given set of world prices — the economy being deemed to be too small to affect these prices — a considerable degree of specialization takes place in each sector. The analysis of this phenomenon within each sector follows closely that given in Jones (1974), except that the supply of labor provided each sector is to be determined endogenously. Figure 2 illustrates a set of unit-value isoquants for a 4-industry sector (i) facing given world prices. Technology at home is not assumed to be reflected in world prices, and this helps explain the existence of commodities such as industry 4 in sector i. The country has inefficient technology in this industry, and cannot effectively compete at these prices regardless of the quantity of labor employed in this sector. A further reflection of the independence of home technology is the assumption that no more than two industries have unit-value isoquants tangent to a common line.

The unit-value isoquants depicted in Figure 2 reflect a combination of the country's technology and world prices. Further information about factor supplies is required to determine which commodity or pair of commodities the country produces in this sector. If a ray whose slope represents the capital/labor ratio available in sector i is drawn in Figure 2, the composition of output is determined. Thus for ray k^i the country would produce commodities 1 and 2, with the wage/rent ratio reflected in the common tangent line and industries 3 and 4 ruled out at these factor prices since unit costs would exceed given world prices. The convex hull of unit-value isoquants in Figure 2 represents a Hicksian composite traded-commodity isoquant for sector i, and which particular industries survive in a competitive equilibrium depends upon how much labor this sector can attract.

The demand for labor in sector i is a function of the wage rate, given specific factor K^i and prevailing world prices. Figure 3 illustrates this demand curve. High wage rates imply that only industry 1, the most capital-intensive industry in sector i, would survive. The wage rate and given price for x_1^i would determine the rental on K^i and techniques. As w falls, the first industry adopts more labor-intensive techniques (and thus increases its demand for labor) until the next industry in ranking according to capital-intensity has its costs lowered to the level of world price. The flat at this wage rate in Figure 3 shows that x_2^i output can expand, with x_1^i output contracting, without requiring any change in factor prices or techniques. However, such a compositional shift raises the demand for labor from this sector until specialization in the second industry is complete. Further lowering of the wage rate encourages more labor-intensive techniques. The demand for labor schedule from sector i in Figure 3 thus consists of downward-sloping portions along which only one commodity is produced and flat stretches along which sector i produces two commodities. Which pattern emerges depends on the equilibrium wage rate and this, in turn, reflects the overall supply of labor to the economy.

Figure 4 illustrates the demand for labor in the entire economy, and its shape and position depends on the technology and prices in all industries and the array of specific capital endowments, K^i. We assume the absence of "ties" — each horizontal step in Figure 4 corresponds to some sector exhibiting a single pair of industries which could be simultaneously operated at the appropriate wage (and world prices). The given supply of labor may intersect the demand curve along a downward-sloping portion, in which case each sector devotes all its specific capital to a single industry. Alternatively, the supply curve may intersect at a flat (as shown), in which case one sector of the economy has a Heckscher-Ohlin "nugget" comprising two commodities using a common pair of factors (labor and the type of capital specific to that sector), with all other sectors specialized.

Two alternative outcomes characterize the possible equilibrium. One of these corresponds to the $(N + 1) \times N$ specific-factor model. Free trade induces each sector to focus on a single producing industry, utilizing a type of capital used in no other activity (at the equilibrium wage) and mobile labor. In the other alternative there exists a single sector displaying a Heckscher-Ohlin 2×2 "nugget".[3] Our assumption that the country's technology is independent of world prices rules out as purely accidental the possibility of two or more sectors displaying such a nugget at the same wage rate or the existence of more than two commodities in any single nugget. Such a structure is reminiscent of the three-factor, three-commodity model analyzed by Gruen and Corden (1970):[4] An economy (say, Australia) produces two commodities in one sector (wool and grain, each using land and labor), and as well a single commodity (textiles) in an alternative sector, requiring capital and labor as inputs. Such a structure was imposed arbitrarily in their model. Here it emerges endogenously (extended to encompass many sectors of the "textile" variety but only a single 2×2 nugget) as a consequence of the forces of free trade.

3 Small Shocks in World Prices

The pattern of response in local income distribution and outputs to a change in world prices depends sensitively on which of these alternative production structures emerges with free trade. The response depends as well on the size of the shock. A "small" shock is one which, by definition, does not disturb the qualitative pattern of production in the economy.

Review, first, the familiar pattern of factor-price and output response in the absence of any sector displaying a "nugget" in free-trade equilibrium. A small increase in any commodity price has no effect on the distribution of income if this commodity is not locally produced. Indeed, it lowers all factors' real income by an amount proportional to that factor's consumption of the commodity. Should that commodity be produced, however, the community as a whole would gain if production is sufficiently large to support exports. As to local income distribution, the real return to the type of capital found in that sector unambiguously rises, the wage rate is driven up, but by less, relatively, than the price of the commodity, while the return to capital in all other sectors falls. The familiar result on output patterns also emerges: the industry whose price has risen expands with industries in all other sectors contracting.

In the alternative Gruen/Corden setting, in which some sector displays a 2×2 nugget, production patterns and income distribution depend upon whether the industry experiencing the price rise lies in the nugget or in some other sector, assuming the commodity is produced somewhere in the economy. If the commodity lies within the nugget, the response depends in typical Heckscher-Ohlin fashion upon the relative factor intensity ranking of industries found in the nugget. Suppose the favored

[3] For earlier uses of this concept see Marjit (1990).

[4] Deardorff (1984) discusses in detail Krueger's (1977) model, which is similar in structure to that of Gruen and Corden.

industry is labor-intensive. The wage rate unambiguously rises, the return to capital in that sector falls, and the wage increase spreads to all other sectors of the economy to force decreases in the returns to capital everywhere. Thus the income distribution response for this particular price rise is precisely that of the strong Stolper/Samuelson variety in this $(N+1) \times (N+1)$ model. As for outputs, within the favored sector the labor-intensive industry expands at the expense of the more capital-intensive industry. Such a change in outputs is supported from two sources. For any given allocation of labor among sectors there emerges the familiar movement along a transformation curve for the two industries in the nugget. In addition, the increase in the wage rate causes all other sectors of the economy to release labor to the favored sector, encouraging a further expansion of the labor-intensive commodity in the nugget and a contraction of the capital-intensive industry (a la Rybczynski). The pattern of output changes is similar to that of the specific-factors model described earlier.

A rise in the world price of the more capital-intensive of the two commodities produced in the nugget can be expected to alter these findings. Most directly, within the nugget it is the return to capital which is unambiguously raised and the wage rate which falls. This wage drop spreads throughout other sectors, in which commodity prices have not changed, to cause an increase in the rate of return to all other sector-specific capitals. (These returns may or may not rise by relatively more than the price of the capital-intensive good in the nugget). The pattern of income distribution is now that modeled by Inada (1971): One factor loses unambiguously, and all others gain (at least nominally). As for outputs, the fall in the wage rate causes the nugget to lose labor to all other sectors. Nonetheless, the favored capital-intensive sector in the nugget expands, both because of a move along a fixed transformation schedule in the nugget before the labor reallocation and because the nugget's loss of labor to the rest of the economy causes a further transfer of resources within the sector to this industry. Thus the price rise for the single (capital-intensive) industry in the nugget encourages an expansion of output in all industries in the economy save the labor-intensive industry in the nugget.

Consider, finally, a price rise in some industry produced in a sector not containing the nugget. Now the repercussions get contained. The 2×2 nugget faces fixed world prices for the commodities it produces, implying no change in the wage rate and thus no change in any return to capital except in the single favored sector. This we may label as the case of "Isolated Rents". The price rise, of course, attracts labor to the favored sector, but all this labor is supplied by the nugget, causing an expansion there of the capital-intensive commodity and a reduction of the labor-intensive commodity. The rise in price has allowed two industries to expand at the expense of the third, with all other sectors left undisturbed.

A rich variety of outcomes, both in income distribution and in outputs, thus emerges, depending upon the endogenously determined production structure. With all commodities traded, it becomes natural to ask about the necessity of a Dutch-Disease phenomenon, whereby a rise in the price of one traded commodity causes outputs in other active industries to contract. This is certainly the case for the pair of commodities found in the nugget should the price change take place there. If it does, however, industries in all other sectors will experience a Dutch-Disease contraction if and only if the favored nugget sector is labor-intensive. The point of contact these other sectors have with the nugget is through the labor market, so that the spread effect on their outputs depends entirely on the behavior of the wage rate. If a nugget exists but the price rise is for a produced industry in a different sector, all other non-nugget industries are insulated from this change, but the labor-intensive commodity in the nugget is adversely affected.

The patterns of output response to price changes in the case in which some sector (say the nth) contains a nugget so that the same number of productive activities $(n+1)$ survive as the number of factors, is displayed in the output substitution matrix, S :

$$
\begin{array}{cc}
 & \begin{array}{cc} (n-1) \text{ sectors} & \begin{array}{c} n\text{th} \\ \text{sector} \end{array} \end{array} \\
S = \begin{array}{c} (n-1) \\ \text{sectors} \\ \\ \\ n\text{th} \quad x_1^{(n)} \\ \text{sector} \quad x_2^{(n)} \end{array} &
\left[\begin{array}{ccccccc|cc}
+ & & & & & & & + & - \\
 & + & & & & & & + & - \\
 & & + & & & & & + & - \\
 & & & \ddots & & & & \vdots & \vdots \\
 & & & & \ddots & & & \vdots & \vdots \\
 & & & & & \ddots & & \vdots & \vdots \\
 & & & & & & + & + & - \\
\hline
+ & + & + & \cdots & \cdots & \cdots & + & + & - \\
- & - & - & \cdots & \cdots & \cdots & - & - & +
\end{array}\right]
\end{array}
$$

$x_2^{(n)}$ labor-intensive

$$\hat{x} = \mathrm{S}\hat{\mathrm{p}}$$

The positive sign of the diagonal terms of S reveals that the output in any industry responds positively to a price increase for that industry. Off-diagonal elements in the jth column disclose the fate of other industries in the economy when p_j rises. The nth sector contains the nugget, and the first industry in that sector, $x_1^{(n)}$, is assumed to be capital-intensive relative to the second.[5]

With reference to output-price matrix, S, the price change most closely associated with Dutch Disease phenomena would be an increase in the price of the labor-intensive industry in the nugget $(x_2^{(n)})$; own-output rises and labor is released from all other sectors of the economy. By contrast, a price rise for the capital-intensive industry in the nugget hurts the other (labor-intensive) industry in the nugget but, since the wage rate is depressed, all other industries in the economy are allowed to expand. The first $(n-1)$ columns of S depict the "isolated rent" phenomenon; the

[5]Consider the matrix, $[\alpha]$, which links the change in relative factor returns to changes in commodity prices, such that $\hat{w} = \alpha\hat{p}$, where $w_1, \ldots, w_{n-1}$ indicate returns to specific types of capital in sectors $1, \ldots, n-1$, $w_1^{(n)}$ is the return to capital in the nth sector and $w_2^{(n)}$ is the wage rate, w. $[\alpha]$ has the same sign pattern as $[S]$ except the last two rows (not counting the last two columns) contain all zeroes.

industry favored by the price rise expands, all other non-nugget industries experience no output change, but in the nugget the labor-intensive industry contracts, releasing labor both to the favored industry and to the capital-intensive industry in the nugget. Of the output response patterns thus illustrated by the S-matrix, the one most closely approximating the alternative $(N+1) \times N$ specific factors structure is the one in which the favored industry is the labor-intensive activity in the nugget; a single output rises at the expense of all other industries.

4 Finite Shocks and Transmission Mechanisms

The movement from autarky to free trade suggests the potential existence of many productive activities ruled out by one set of prices but capable of being competitively viable at other sets. Price shocks that are not "small" are capable of inducing a significant alteration in the pattern of production (and trade). Concerns over the Dutch Disease phenomenon highlight the importance of identifying the channels through which new-found successes in some industries brought about by external price shocks get transmitted to other industries. As we show, much depends upon whether these other industries lie in the same sector or elsewhere in the economy.

A useful starting point is the demand curve for labor from a particular sector, as illustrated in Figure 3.[6] Consider a commodity such as x_2^i, neither the most capital-intensive nor the most labor-intensive commodity in sector i. A finite rise in p_2^i in world markets causes a shift in sector i's demand schedule, reflected in the position of the dotted curves in Figure 5. Two characteristics of this shift are noteworthy. First, in the range of wage rates for which x_2^i was initially produced, the price rise encourages a greater demand for labor. Secondly, the range of wages which allow positive production of x_2^i is increased at both ends. As illustrated in Figure 5 such a price rise cuts into the range of wages for which only commodity one, more capital-intensive than two, or only commodity three (more labor-intensive) would be produced. A sufficient rise in commodity 2's price could wipe out the possibility of industry 3, say, being viable at any wage rate.[7]

Perhaps the most surprising feature illustrated in Figure 5 is the possibility that a price rise for industry 2 in sector i could reduce that sector's demand for labor. For example, initially production might have been located at point B, with the ith sector only producing commodity 3. The price rise for x_2^i could eventuate in a move to point C, with a switch from industry 3 to more capital-intensive industry 2, thereby reducing sector i's demand for labor and the wage rate.

Equilibrium in the economy's labor market can be analyzed by confronting sector i's demand curve for labor with that of the rest of the economy. One possibility is illustrated in Figure 6. Initial equilibrium is at A, with sector i displaying a productive nugget in which commodities 1 and 2 are produced and all other sectors are

[6]This kind of diagram has also been utilized by Deardorff (1984).

[7]Further detail should be noted: corner point A' showing incipient production of commodity 1 after the increase in commodity 2's price, lies northwest of corner point A associated with original prices. The rationale: If the sector initially produces only commodity 2, the relative vertical shift in the demand curve equals the percentage rise in p_2^i, whereas if both x_1^i and x_2^i are produced, the relative vertical shift exceeds the price rise, a reflection of the magnification effect.

completely specialized to their "best" traded good corresponding to the equilibrium wage at A. The increase in the world price of sector i's second commodity causes production of x_1^i to cease and production of x_2^i to expand, with labor drawn both from x_1^i and from the rest of the economy, driving up the wage rate. Adjustments in perhaps several other sectors entail switches to more capital intensive goods, with some sector displaying a nugget in which a pair of commodities is produced.

Other cases could be illustrated, but the pattern is clear: The possibility of a Dutch Disease response in another industry when the world price of industry 2 in sector i rises depends on whether this other industry shares the same kind of capital as x_2^i. Of course if commodity 2 is initially not produced in sector i, the price rise may be insufficient to warrant its production in the new equilibrium. But, suppose it is produced. Then any other industry previously producing in that sector is either wiped out or finds its output diminished. As Figure 5 illustrates, the wage rate may fall (in the move from B to C), but this is of no comfort to other industries in sector i, even those that are more labor-intensive, since such a fall must reflect the movement of labor out of such industries towards the more capital-intensive industry whose price has risen.

The fate of industries in the rest of the economy is not generally as severe. These industries are linked to the favored sector only through a single market — that for labor. An increase in the wage rate, as illustrated in Figure 6, causes Dutch Disease distress to industries that are initially active, but there may exist more capital-intensive industries in these sectors which benefit from the change. In effect, all these other sectors experience two factor price changes: the wage rate rises but the rental that must be paid to sector-specific capitals falls. On the other hand, an externally-induced price change which leads to a fall in the wage rate benefits some industries in the rest of the economy which are more labor-intensive than the ones whose activity has been eliminated by the price rise in sector i.

5 Non-traded Goods and Crowding-Out

In order to analyze the nature of the equilibrium production pattern when not all commodities are traded on world markets we examine the consequences of having some commodity in sector i change its status from being fully traded to having natural or artificial transport costs or barriers (such as prohibitive import quotas) imposed so that local consumption must be locally produced. Does positive production of such a commodity crowd out any other industry in this sector, precluding it from competing in world markets? The country must export something, but export activities in other sectors do exist with industries that provide export earnings.

The possibilities are analyzed in Figure 7, a diagram which, like previous Figure 6, confronts sector i's demand for labor with that in all other sectors combined. The demand curve for the rest of the economy has been purged of any flats in order to simplify the analysis. As well, we suppose that only a single traded commodity, T^i, exists in sector i; the issue is whether it will be produced at all. Finally, at this stage of the analysis we assume that the single non-traded commodity in sector i, N^i, is labor-intensive compared with T^i.

Given the world price of T^i, whether or not it will be produced depends on the market price of non-tradeables in sector i. Point A in Figure 7 is associated with a relatively high price of non-tradeables, one which allows only incipient production of T^i; call this price p'_N. If the price of non-tradeables were to fall somewhat from this level, sector i's demand curve for labor would shift inwards, so that a new equilibrium would exist at point C, with a lower wage rate. This price drop for non-tradeables has allowed production of T^i to co-exist with that of N^i, although sector i now attracts less labor overall. Further reductions in the price of non-tradeables in sector i cause output N^i to fall until point B is reached. At that low price (p''_N), output of non-tradeables vanishes, and sector i only produces T^i.

The range of prices for which sector i tolerates simultaneous production activity in tradeables and non-tradeables, the range p''_N to p'_N, is illustrated by the supply curve for non-tradeables, S_N, in Figure 8. Below p''_N output of non-tradeables is closed down, whereas above p'_N the favorable prices for non-tradeables has crowded out the possibility of traded goods production. Note that the S_N curve above p'_N becomes more inelastic, a reflection of the fact that there is no longer another industry in sector i (T^i) from which resources (labor and sector-specific K^i) can be drawn. Instead, increases in N^i can be fueled only by attracting labor from the rest of the economy. Figure 8 shows an initial equilibrium at point E, but a sufficient rise in demand for non-tradeables could wipe out the tradeable industry in this sector.

If the non-tradeable industry in sector i had been capital-intensive, some modification in this scenario would be required. Figure 7 would have to be re-drawn to show N^i produced at higher wages, and T^i at lower. In Figure 8, increases in the price of non-tradeables between p''_N and p'_N would be accompanied by a fall in the wage rate and a loss of labor to the rest of the economy, a loss which, a la Rybczynski, promotes production of capital-intensive non-tradeables.

If sector i's non-tradeable sector had initially been freely traded, much can be gleaned from the trading pattern in such a state, assuming local demand conditions and technology to be invariant to the changed nature of impediments to trade. Thus if production of N^i were not initially viable, as a traded good it must have been imported. Therefore changing its status to a non-traded good must result in a price increase to sustain production. The price could lie anywhere above p''_N, with a co-existing traded goods industry if demand is not too strong. If the industry that becomes non- traded were originally viable as a traded industry, it might nonetheless have been imported. In this case a price rise as a non-tradeable is to be expected. However, suppose it was originally produced and exported. Conversion to non-traded goods status must lower its price. If initially it had shared a nugget with another traded good, the price fall as it becomes non-traded must encourage the production of the other traded good in the nugget. Thus the change in market status of an industry from an exported tradeable to the non-tradeable category helps production of another tradeable in the nugget whereas, if the good had originally been imported, the other tradeable produced in that sector finds its production reduced or, if p_N rises above p'_N, the industry is wiped out.

6 Non-Traded Goods and the Dutch Disease

The doctrine of comparative advantage proclaims the importance of the relative ranking of industries; if one traded sector improves its status via a price rise or productivity improvement, other tradeables move down in the relative ranking. In its starkest form the Dutch Disease proclaims that an increase in the fortunes of one traded sector spells contraction or elimination for others.

If all goods are tradeables, in our model these stark predictions are not always fulfilled. The exceptions require the existence of a nugget. In such a case the increase in the price of any traded good outside the nugget has no effect on the wage rate. The latter is determined in the nugget in standard 2×2 fashion. Returns to capital in the favored sector rise and industries in other sectors outside the nugget are insulated from the price rise. The favored sector expands by attracting labor from the nugget. Thus, most industries are left undisturbed, the Dutch Disease hits the labor-intensive industry in the nugget, and its contraction fuels not only an expansion in the traded sector initially favored by a price rise but also an expansion in the other industry in the nugget. A price rise for one of the traded industries in the nugget does cause all other industries to contract if it is the labor-intensive industry, but if, instead, the capital intensive industry in the nugget experiences a favorable price rise in world markets, the wage rate falls, and this is of positive benefit to all traded industries outside the nugget. The labor-intensive nugget industry is the sole loser, and this case represents the most radical departure from the pattern predicted by the Dutch Disease.

The existence of non-tradeables complicates the response. As often remarked, a non-tradeable industry is in many ways shielded from the brisk competition of world markets. It may even gain from a situation in which an export industry is favored by a price rise. The resultant favorable real income effects may so cause the price of non-tradeables to rise that output of non-tradeables expands despite any cost increases triggered by the export price rise. Indeed, as pointed out by Corden and Neary (1982), the rate of return to capital employed by the non-traded sector may rise by an even greater extent than in the booming export sector.

Our focus in this section is not directly on the fate of the non-tradeable sector. Instead, we analyze how the existence of non-tradeables alters the channels described earlier whereby the Dutch Disease gets spread (or thwarted) from a favored traded industry to other traded sectors. A useful starting point is the scenario in which no nuggets exist and, in the absence of non-tradeables, no resource transfers of any kind would take place in the small, price-taking economy. This is the case in which the exogenous rise in a commodity's price is insufficient to cause it to be produced in this economy. But such a price increase does represent a deterioration of the terms of trade, and if non-tradeables are normal, demand for non-tradeables may shift inwards. There is a caveat, however, in the form of a cross-effect in consumer demand between the traded import experiencing the price rise and non-tradeables. If these are good substitutes, the net effect could be a rightward shift in the demand for non-tradeables. If income effects are more important, the price of non-tradeables is driven down, and all traded productive industries actually gain labor since the wage rate falls. In this sense the non-traded industry serves as a "reservoir" from which other industries can extract labor. Alternatively, if high substitutability in demand causes the price of non-tradeables to rise, other tradeables are hit by the subsequent wage increase; the non-traded industry acts more like a "sponge" soaking up labor from the other sectors.

Continuing with the scenario in which the world price of a traded good not produced in the home country rises, suppose the non-traded good shares a nugget with some traded good (whose price is unchanged). Assuming income effects are stronger than cross-substitution effects, the resulting fall in the demand for non-tradeables would reduce p_N, but the effect of such a change on all tradeables depends on factor intensities in the nugget. The companion traded industry in the nugget must in any case expand, but this entails a contraction in all other traded industries if and only if non-tradeables are capital-intensive. If a nugget exists with two traded industries (with the non-traded good found in a separate sector), the economy's wage rate is frozen at the level determined by world prices of the goods produced in the nugget. But assuming (again) that income effects dominate in reducing the price of non-tradeables (produced outside the nugget), such a price change now is cauterized in its effect on other sectors; the price fall gets absorbed completely by a magnified reduction in rents to the sector-specific type of capital used by the non-traded industry. The labor released by the non- traded sector gets absorbed by the nugget, causing the appropriate asymmetric output response for the two tradeables produced there.[8]

Of more relevance in appraising the Dutch Disease phenomenon is a rise in the world price of a commodity produced at home. If the commodity is nonetheless imported, the income effects are detrimental, although not to the extent of the earlier scenario where imports supply the entire local demand. With weaker income effects, the cross-effect in demand, presumably shifting demand onto the non-tradeable, has more chance of raising p_N. If the commodity is exported, perhaps the most interesting setting for the Dutch Disease phenomenon, the price of non-tradeables must rise. The effect this has on the wage rate must be combined with the effect on wages of the initial rise in the price of the favored tradeable before the impact on other traded goods can be appraised.

Suppose, therefore, that the price of an exportable rises, and that this commodity does not lie in a nugget. If there exists a nugget with a pair of tradeables elsewhere in the economy, the wage rate is frozen so that all tradeables outside the nugget other than the favored traded good are insulated. Assuming the non-tradeable lies outside the nugget, its price is bid up, and the newly produced rents are all captured by its sector-specific capital. Thus two types of rent rise, and the non-tradeable joins the favored sector in drawing labor away from the nugget, at the magnified expense of the labor-intensive industry in the nugget. If, instead, a nugget exists but consists of one tradeable and the non-tradeable, the wage rate is no longer frozen. Figures 9

[8]It is possible that the non-traded good shares a nugget with two tradeables. In that case a downward shift in the demand for non-tradeables does not affect its price, the wage rate, or the return to any type of capital. Output changes of tradeables in the nugget depend on the ranking of factor intensities there. For example, if the capital/labor ratio of non-tradeables lies between those of the two tradeables, both their outputs would expand if the demand for non-tradeables falls. No other outputs are disturbed. Details of such interactions when the nugget is the only sector are found in Jones (1974).

and 10 depict some of the possibilities that may transpire if the non-tradeable lies in the nugget.

The non-tradeable is the labor-intensive nugget industry in Figure 9. The upper diagram shows an initial equilibrium at A, disturbed by a rise in price of some produced export good lying outside the nugget. The bottom diagram illustrates the original equilibrium at point F where demand and supply for non-tradeables match. The improvement in the terms of trade, coupled with a normal cross-effect in demand away from the favored export commodity, has shifted the demand curve out to D'_N. There is, as well, an inward shift in the supply curve of non-tradeables that is also attributable to the rise in price of the favored export commodity. At given p_N this price rise does not affect wages, but it does siphon labor out of the nugget, and this loss must reduce the output of labor-intensive x_N at given price. The rightward shift in D_N and leftward shift in S_N must raise the price of non-tradeables; as shown in Figure 9 by point G, the output of non-tradeables may actually fall. In any case in the upper diagram the broken demand for labor curve for sector i shifts as drawn, with a wage increase from A to B a magnified reflection of the rise in the price of non-tradeables. Dutch Disease is rampant — all non-nugget export industries except the favored one have contracted, and the non-tradeable industry has also contracted despite a price (and demand) rise. The capital-intensive traded industry in the nugget could either contract or expand.

Figure 10 traces through the adjustment if the non-traded nugget industry is capital-intensive. The initial equilibrium, once again shown by points A and F in the two graphs, respectively, is disturbed by an outward shift in the demand for labor in the favored export sector (and thus for the entire$\sum_{s\neq i} L^s$ schedule). At initial price for non-tradeables this would shift the S'_N schedule to the right since the departure of labor from the nugget causes capital-intensive non-tradeables to expand.[9] Combined with the outward shift of demand as the terms of trade improve, the supply shift encourages a rise in non-tradeable output from F to G. However, the bottom graph in Figure 10 shows the possibility that the price of non-tradeables may actually fall. This price fall is reflected in the shift in the labor-demand schedule for nugget sector i in the top graph, with the wage increase in moving from A to B a consequence of the fall in capital- intensive non-tradeables price. Dutch Disease is once again rampant since the wage increase squeezes other tradeables — despite the fall in the price of non-tradeables in Figure 10 (or the contraction of the non-tradeable sector in Figure 9.)

As a final case suppose the favored export industry is found in a nugget with the non-tradeable. If the export industry is capital-intensive and if p_N were kept constant, our earlier analysis highlighted this as the case in which all other tradeables gain since the wage rate would have to fall — all at the expense of non-tradeables. But with demand for non-tradeables shifting out, the price of non-tradeables must rise.[10] The fate of other tradeable industries depends on whether the rise in the

[9] That part of the S_N schedule at higher p_N, where the traded industry in the nugget has been driven out, would shift leftwards with the loss of labor from sector i. Thus the S_N and S'_n curves intersect.

[10] It is unlikely that non-tradeables would rise in price by more than the rise in price for the export industry in the nugget. Without income effects a comparable rise in both nugget prices would raise the wage rate by the same amount, bringing in labor from other sectors and expanding

price of non-tradeables is sufficient to increase the wage rate.[11]

If the export industry is labor-intensive in the nugget and p_N were constant, the wage would by driven up by a magnified amount and all other industries would lose — the extreme form of Dutch Disease. With non-tradeables also produced in the nugget the price must rise — both because demand shifts out and because the inflow of labor to the nugget caused by the wage increase penalizes capital-intensive non-tradeables. Indeed, if p_N rises to keep pace with the world-inspired rise in the export price, the supply of non-tradeables would still fall short of the original amount. The reason: the wage rate would rise by the same relative amount as the price of exports (instead of by a magnified amount), so that the nugget has drawn labor from the rest of the economy. This eventuates in a lower production of capital-intensive non-tradeables than initially. Unless non-tradeables are extremely good substitutes with other tradeables in demand, the non- tradeable industry would find its price driven up even relative to the favored export sectors. The existence of a capital-intensive non-tradeable industry in the nugget has not prevented all non-favored tradeables from succumbing to the Dutch Disease.

7 Real Exchange Rates and the Terms of Trade

The real exchange rate has often been defined as the price ratio between non-tradeables and a market basket of tradeables. An appreciation of the real exchange rate is an increase in the ratio p_N/p_T, where p_T is the price index for the tradeables basket. It has frequently been asserted that an improvement in the terms of trade leads to (or is accompanied by) an appreciation of the real exchange rate. As others have recently argued [Edwards and van Wijnbergen (1987), Neary (1988) and (1990)], there is no necessity for this relationship to hold. Here we remark briefly on the manner in which complementarities in production, associated with the existence of a nugget in the production structure, bear upon the relationship between the terms of trade and the real exchange rate.

Demand as well as production structure are relevant for this issue. To simplify, suppose all goods are net substitutes in demand. That is, suppose that an increase in any commodity price at given levels of real income, which causes "own" demand to fall, causes a positive spill-over in demand for all other commodities. The consequence in a simple exchange model with one export good (X), one import good (M), and a non-traded commodity (N) whose price must adjust to clear markets is that ignoring income effects, if the terms of trade improve,[12] $\hat{p}_X > \hat{p}_N > \hat{p}_M$

Therefore p_T, the tradeables price index representing some composite of p_X and p_M, may or may not rise relative to p_N. Income effects, however, do lend a presumption and, it can be argued, are crucial. Assuming all goods are normal, an improvement in the terms of trade will shift the demand curve outwards and serve

especially the supply of labor-intensive non-tradeables. In addition, consumers would shift away from non-tradeables since all other prices (except for the favored exportable) have not risen in price. Income effects would have to be powerful to offset such a gap in excess supply.

[11]The wage rate remains unchanged if, in sector i, $\hat{p}_N$ equals $(\theta^i_{KN}/\theta^i_{KT})\hat{p}^i_T$, where the θ's represent distributive shares. Their ratio is a fraction in this case.

[12]See, for example, Jones (1976).

further to increase p_N. (By assumption p_X and p_M are determined in larger world markets). This makes it more likely that the real exchange rate appreciates.

Of concern here is the manner in which the production structure alters this conclusion. If trade induces an $(N+1) \times N$ commodity structure of the specific-factors kind, with one of the sectors producing the non-traded good, the production structure lends support to the agnosticism about the relationship between changes in the terms of trade and the real exchange rate voiced above for the exchange model (ignoring income effects) when goods are net substitutes in demand. The rationale for this view is that an increase in the price of any tradeable reduces all other outputs at initial prices, and thus tends to raise the price of any commodity which serves only a national market. That is, the change in the price of non-tradeables is once again trapped between the rise in an export item and the no-change exhibited by other traded-goods prices.

The existence of a nugget has potential to alter this conclusion. Refer again to the S-matrix of output responses (along any column) to a rise in a single price of the commodity on the diagonal. Complementarity in production is revealed by positive elements off the diagonal such as the first $(n-1)$ elements in the nth row or nth column. Suppose, first, that the nugget consists of two traded commodities and that the non-traded commodity is the sole industry in some other (non-nugget) sector. If the capital-intensive commodity in the nugget ($x_1^{(n)}$ in the S-matrix) is an export commodity and increases in price on world markets, the output of the non-tradeable (and all non-nugget industries) will rise as labor is drawn away from the labor-intensive industry in the nugget.[13] Although the favorable income effect once again encourages a price rise for non-tradeables, the increased production tends to reduce p_N. If the latter effect dominates, an improvement in the terms of trade will have worsened the real exchange rate.

Alternatively, consider the scenario in which there is a nugget which contains the non-tradeable, and that it is capital intensive relative to the other industry in the nugget. If there is a rise in the world price of some export commodity not in the nugget, output of the non-tradeable would, at initial prices, also increase in complementary fashion. Once again these supply changes encourage a fall in the price of non-tradeables in the face of a terms-of-trade improvement.

Consideration of the specific-factors outcome or of all the other possibilities in the S-matrix reflecting a substitutive relationship between non- tradeables and exportables reveals the tenuous character of these exceptions to the positive relationship between the terms of trade and the real exchange rate. Of more importance, in our view, is that the production links among sectors exhibited in the S-matrix are invariant to whether the industry represents an export activity or import-competing activity. If the latter, in the cases of complementarity discussed above it is a deterioration (instead of improvement) in the terms of trade which is accompanied by a fall in the real exchange rate. Income effects, however, consistently work towards supporting a positive connection between terms of trade improvements and real exchange rate appreciation.

---

[13]This case is cited by Neary (1990) for the three-commodity Gruen- Corden model.

8 Concluding Remarks

Production structures in the theory of international trade are often imposed by assumption. However, the opening up of commodity markets to trade frees up the necessity of as diverse a production base as a nation would wish in autarky. Both the number of productive activities and the selection of those which survive in a competitive world are endogenous outcomes of conditions in world markets. We started with a rich array of sectors in autarky, with N different sectors each utilizing a separate type of capital but accommodating a variety of industries, and all activities employing as well a homogeneous type of labor whose return is thus uniform throughout the economy. That is, each sector represented a many-commodity, two-factor version of Heckscher- Ohlin structure. Free trade in all commodities resulted in a shutting down of most industries in each sector. The resulting structure exhibited either the survival of only a single "best" industry in each sector — an $(N+1) \times N$ version of the specific-factors model — or such a solution for all sectors except one, in which labor and the type of capital specific to that sector are actively employed by a pair of industries — a 2×2 Heckscher-Ohlin "nugget". The latter possibility, in full an $(N+1) \times (N+1)$ productive structure, represents the appropriate extension to many sectors of the simple three-commodity model put forth over twenty years ago by Fred Gruen and Max Corden.

These two alternative structures were compared, first, as to the manner in which a small price change in one affected outputs in all the others (and the distribution of income). Secondly, we considered finite shocks to the economy. If the wage rate falls, some industries which would have expanded if these shocks had been small instead are wiped out and replaced by a more labor-intensive industry in that sector. If the wage rate rises, an initially active industry in a sector may be replaced by a more capital-intensive industry using the same type of capital. Such finite wage changes may "pass through" one or more levels which would support simultaneous production of two industries in a nugget sector.

Non-traded productive activities can be embodied in this framework. We analyzed in detail the circumstances under which a nugget might exist in which a traded industry and a non-traded industry share a common type of capital.

Although this may occur, such a traded industry would be crowded out if the non-traded price rises sufficiently. The case of a single non-traded industry was the only scenario investigated, but it should be stressed that although only one nugget can in general exist if all goods are traded, any number of nuggets may operate simultaneously as long as at most only a single nugget contains more than one traded commodity. If demand conditions warrant, non-traded commodities may be produced at prices dictated by factor prices which are linked to world market prices for traded goods.

The phenomenon labelled the "Dutch Disease" refers to the loss of resources available to some traded industries when world prices rise for others. As with many general phenomena there are exceptions, and these are reflections of the possibility complementarity in the production structure. Of special interest was the role of non-tradeables in providing a "reservoir" of resources available to traded industries in some circumstances, or acting like a "sponge" to absorb resources and exacerbate the Dutch Disease difficulties faced by fixed-price traded industries in other circumstances.

Income effects tend to support the proposition that an improvement in the terms of trade is accompanied by an appreciation of the real exchange rate. On the side of production links, our structure is capable of exhibiting complementarity between a traded commodity and a non-traded activity if one of them is in a nugget in the Gruen-Corden outcome. The difficulty in tying this phenomenon into a systematic negative relationship between the terms of trade and the real exchange rate is that it requires the produced traded industry to be an export activity instead of an import-competing activity. It can be argued that in the present model there does exist a presumption that any traded industry engages in exports since only the "best" traded good in each sector is produced, with the rest being imported. However, complementarity seems no more likely than substitutability.

The pair of endogenous production outcomes analyzed here — the specific-factors model and the generalized Gruen-Corden structure containing a Heckscher-Ohlin 2×2 nugget — exhibit a rich variety of links among factor prices and industry outputs. More general settings can be envisioned. These involve the existence of industries utilizing a great number of inputs, some possessing a national market, others more restricted in their domain. However, trade theory often prefers to deal with more simple structures in which some hope of obtaining understandable comparative static results exist. The structures dealt with in our model are more robust in terms of dimension than the more standard models while, at the same time, allowing the force of trade and competition to determine which variant of more simple versions prevails in equilibrium.

Figures

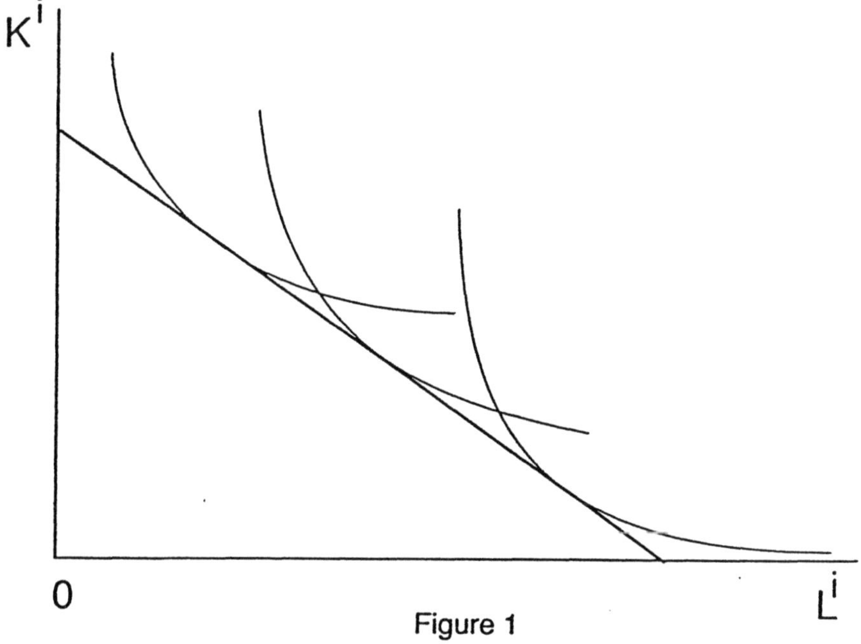

Figure 1

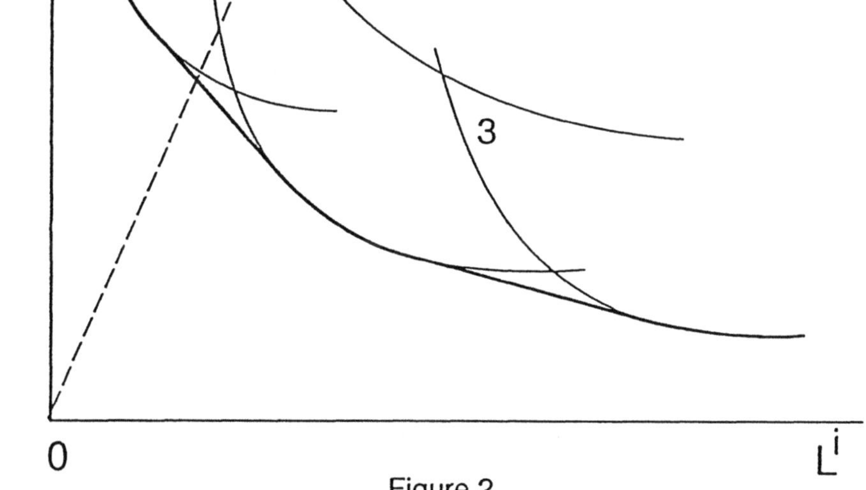

Figure 2

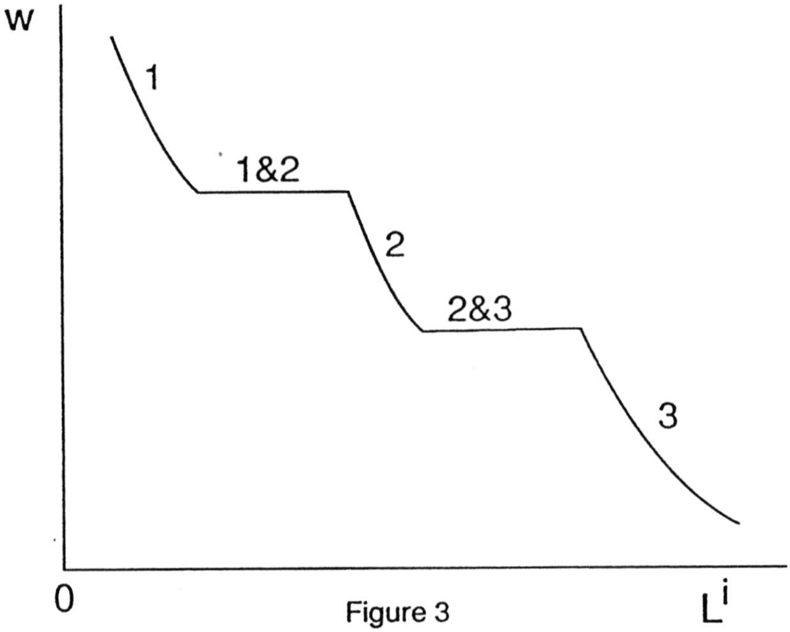

Figure 3

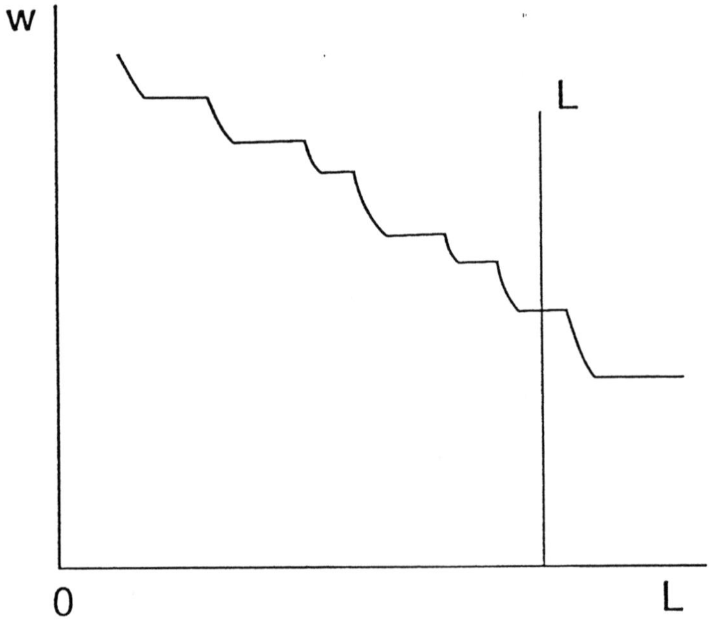

Figure 4

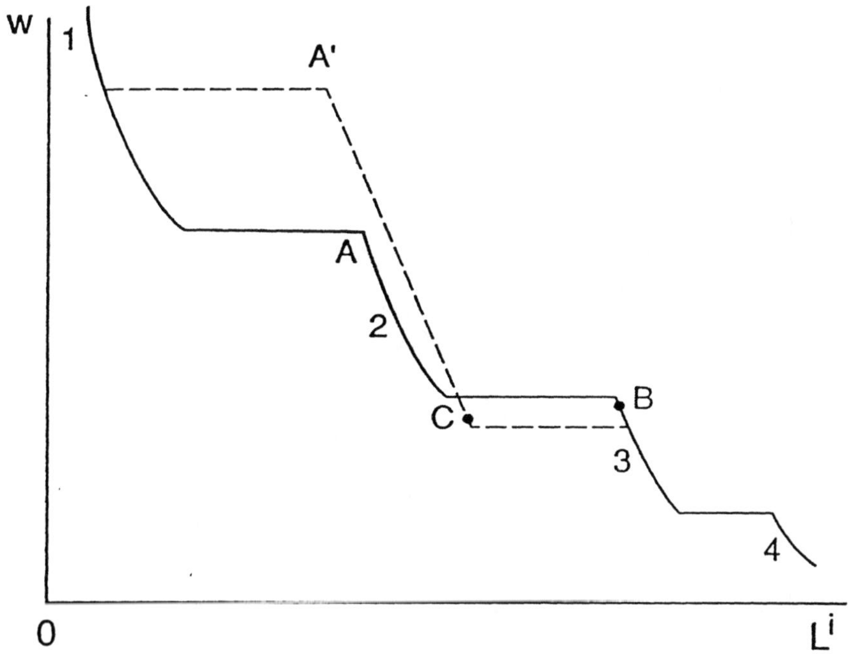

Figure 5

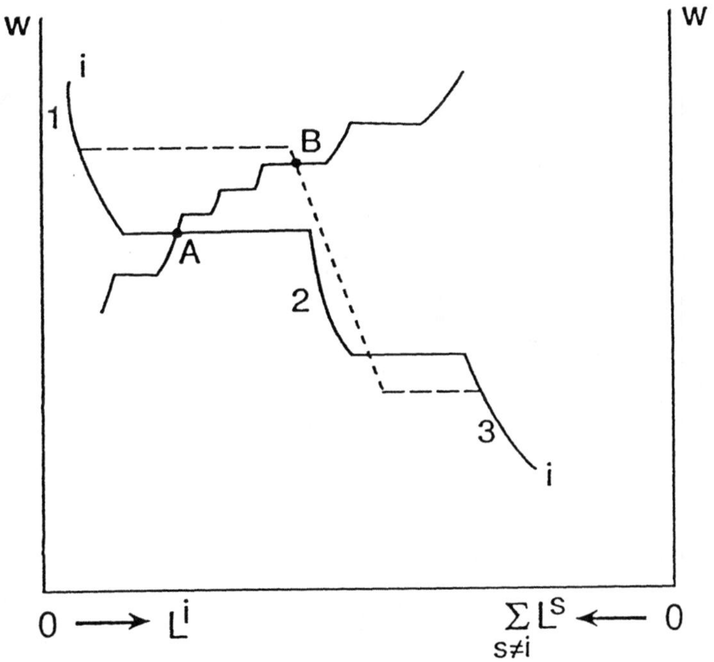

Figure 6

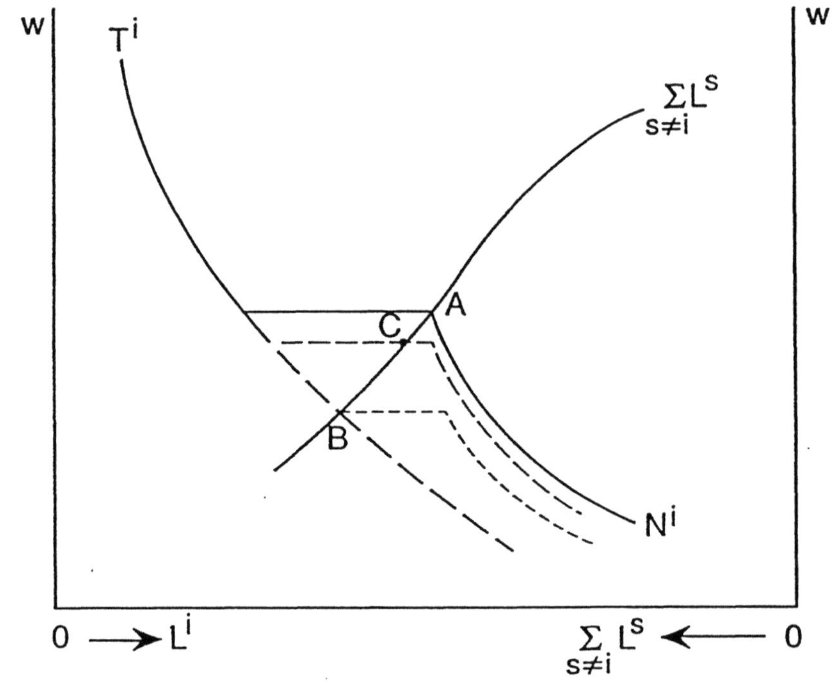

Figure 7

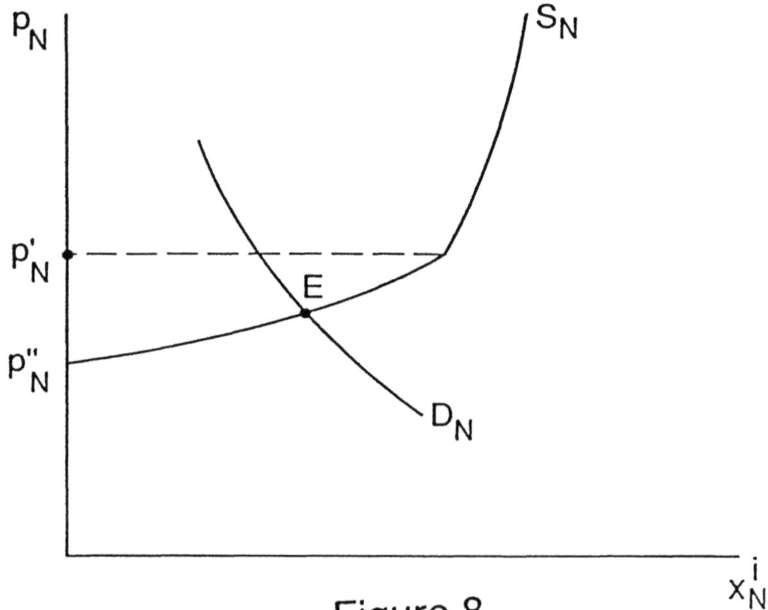

Figure 8

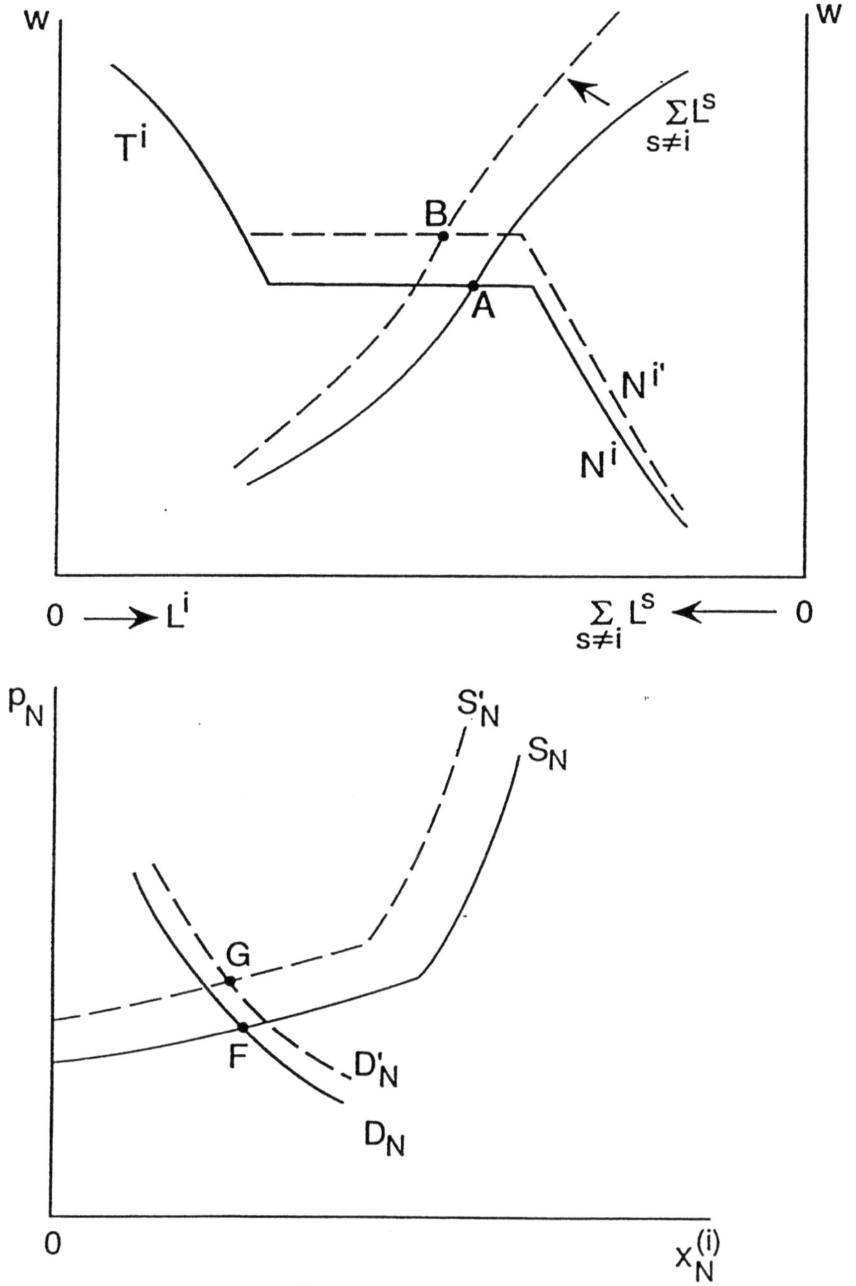

Figure 9

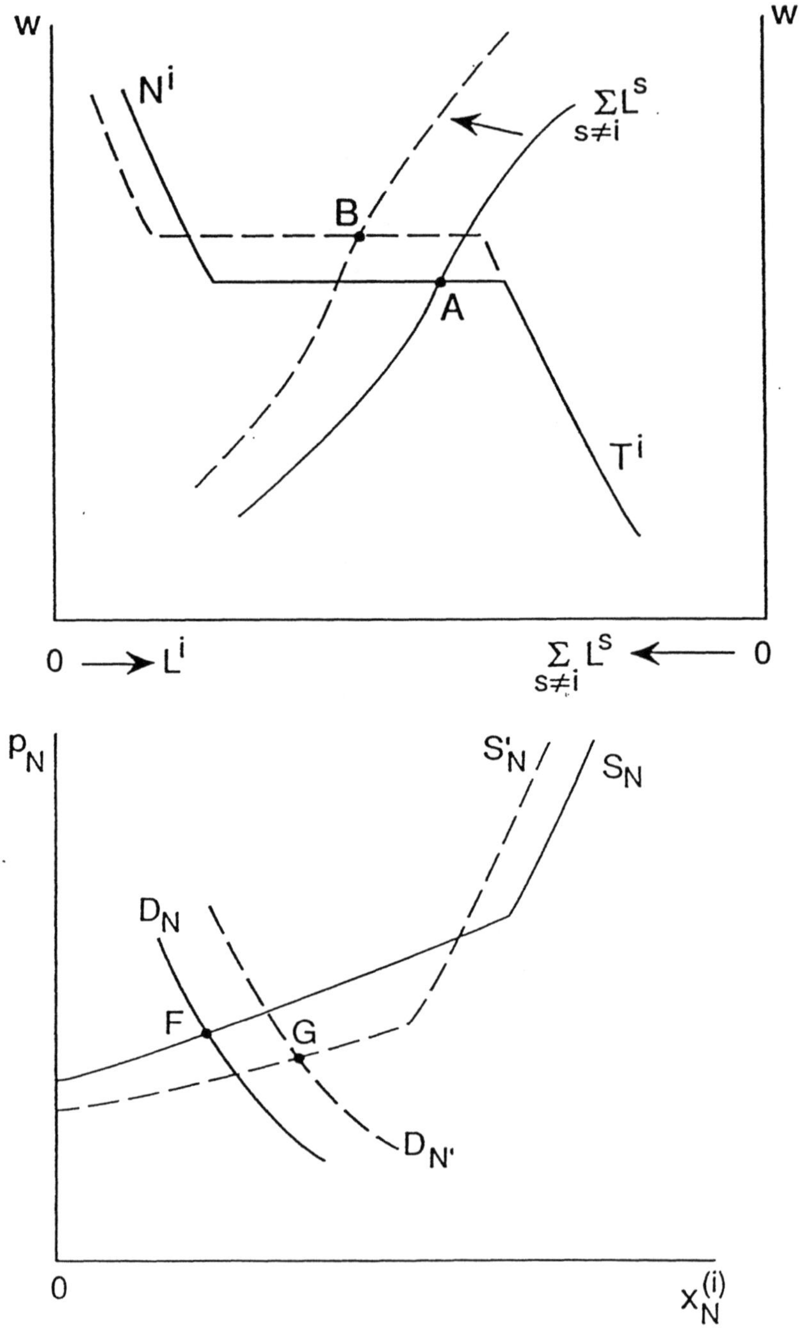

Figure 10

References

CORDEN, W.M. AND J.P. NEARY (1982): "Booming Sector and Deindustrialisation in a Small Open Economy," *Economic Journal,* 92, 825-48.

DEARDORFF, A. (1984) "An Exposition and Exploration of Krueger's Trade Model," *Canadian Journal of Economics,* November, 731-46.

EDWARDS, S. AND S. VAN WIJNBERGEN (1987): "Tariffs, The Real Exchange Rate and the Terms of Trade: On Two Popular Propositions in International Economics," *Oxford Economic Papers,* 39, 458-64.

GRUEN, F. AND W.M. CORDEN (1970): "A Tariff that Worsens the Terms of Trade," in I. McDougall and R. Snape (eds), *Studies in International Economics,* North-Holland, Amsterdam.

INADA, K. (1971): "The Production Coefficient Matrix and the Stolper- Samuelson Condition," *Econometrica,* 39, 219-40.

JONES, R.W. (1974): "The Small Country in a Many-Commodity World," *Australian Economic Papers,* (December), 225-36, reprinted as Ch. 2 in R.W. Jones: *International Trade: Essays in Theory* (North-Holland, 1979).

JONES, R.W. (1975): "Income Distribution and Effective Protection in a Multi-Commodity Trade Model," *Journal of Economic Theory,* (August), 1- 15.

JONES, R.W. (1976): "The Terms of Trade and Transfers: The Relevance of the Literature," Ch. 4 in Leipziger, D. (ed), *The International Monetary System and the Developing Nations* (A.I.D., Washington, D.C.), reprinted as Ch. 11 in Jones, R. W., *International Trade: Essays in Theory* (North-Holland, 1979).

JONES, R.W. AND S. MARJIT (1991): "The Stolper-Samuelson Theorem, the Leamer Triangle and the Produced Mobile Factor Structure," in Takayama, A., M. Ohyama, and H. Ohta (eds.), *Trade, Policy, and International Adjustments* (Academic Press).

JONES, R.W. AND R.J. RUFFIN (1975): "Trade Patterns with Capital Mobility," in M. Parkin and A. Nobay (eds), *Current Economic Problems* (Cambridge) 307-32, with abridged version as Ch. 13 in Jones, R. W., *International Trade: Essays in Theory* (North-Holland, 1979).

KHAN, M.A. (1991): "Ethnic Groups and the Heckscher-Ohlin-Samuelson Trade Model," *Economic Theory,* forthcoming.

KRUEGER, A. (1977): "Growth, Distortions, and Patterns of Trade Among Many Countries," *Princeton Studies in International Finance,* No. 40.

MARJIT, S. (1990): "A Simple Production Model in Trade and its Applications," *Economic Letters,* 257-260.

NEARY, J.P. (1978): "Short-run Capital Specificity and the Pure Theory of International Trade," *Economic Journal,* 88, 488-510.

NEARY, J.P. (1988): "Determinants of the Equilibrium Real Exchange Rate," *American Economic Review,* 78, 210-15.

NEARY, J.P. (1990): "Comments on 'Exchange Rate Policies in Developing Countries,' " unpublished.

SANYAL, K. AND R.W. JONES (1982): "The Theory of Trade in Middle Products," *American Economic Review,* 72, 16-31.

Regular Exchange Economies with Negative Prices

DONALD KEENAN *
The University of Georgia

1 Introduction

The standard model of regular exchange economies assumes monotone preferences ("more is always better"), which then assures that only positive prices need to be considered. Trout Rader (1972) has introduced a general equilibrium model where negative prices are allowed, and has provided a proof of existence of equilibrium.[1] In the current paper we consider a version of Rader's model simplified to exchange economies, and explore the results possible when regularity conditions are introduced. While static results on the number of equilibria are considered, emphasis is also given to a dynamic interpretation of the model. It is found that most static results from the standard model transfer appropriately to the current model. This process of transfer may also be reversed, however. The simplicity of the current model permits new results to be derived with minimal complications. The derivations then suggest whether the results may be extended back to the standard model. An example of this process is given in the context of comparative statics.

2 The Economic Model

2.1 First Formulation of the Model

Since we are interested in positive properties of the overall economy, we may work entirely with aggregate excess demand. What we require is that a single-valued demand exist for all non-zero price systems, that demand vary smoothly over prices, that demand depend only on relative prices, and that Walras' Law hold strictly. Normalizing prices p so that $p \epsilon S^n = \{p \epsilon R^{n+1}: \| p \| = 1\}$, we then have an excess demand $Z(p)$ where

(1) $$Z : S^n \to R^{n+1} \qquad Z \epsilon C^r(S^n, R^{n+1}),\ r \geq 1$$

(2) $$Z(p) = Z(-p)$$

*The author is deeply indebted to Trout Rader for his guidance in this work and in much else.
[1]See Hart & Kuhn (1983) for a further development of this model.

$$p \cdot Z(p) = 0. \tag{3}$$

While this is sufficient for our purposes, we remark briefly on the microfoundations permitting such aggregate economic behavior.

2.2 Microfoundations

The standard model of regular exchange economies works with positive prices, free disposal, monotone preferences, and a weak budget constraint. The framework best lending itself to the current model works with both positive and negative prices, no free disposal, satiated preferences, and a strict budget constraint.[2]

Presumably, the reason why a weak budget constraint is permitted in the standard model is that free disposal and positive prices allow one to obtain consumption bundles of lesser value from one of greater value, through disposal. With some prices being negative, however, were free disposal possible, then one could just as well afford bundles of value greater than the endowment as afford ones of smaller value.

Clearly, if negative prices are to be permitted, free disposal must be dropped. We would consider the disposal of goods to be a consumption activity that should be reflected in preferences over consumption bundles and not in the budget constraint. We would also regard such disposal as involving real costs, like any other physical activity.

Without free disposal, the budget constraint must be satisfied as a strict equality. Perfectly competitive consumers believe that they can trade any amounts on the market they wish, but only at the terms of trade set there.[3] Value is therefore always conserved by the trades being planned.

While it is not strictly required, the framework for the current model works most reasonably with preferences that exhibit global satiation.[4] We regard it as inevitable that too much of any kind of good would be undesirable.[5] Satiation naturally leads to compact and convex upper-contour sets, such as might be given by a smooth, concave utility function taking its maximum at an interior point of global satiation. There is then no difficulty generating smooth demand behavior from such an environment.[6]

[2]See Rader [(1972), p. 95] for a definition and discussion of competitive equilibrium with strict budget constraints required. The analysis in the current paper concerns only positive properties of the overall economy. Rader (1972), however, provides a discussion of the classical welfare and core theorems for competitive equilibria when strict budget constraints are introduced.

[3]If one does not trade through impersonal markets, then one presumably engages in personal trade. In this case conservation of quantity continues to give the strict Walras' Law, which is all that we actually require for our aggregate analysis.

[4]One can also obtain bounded demand from boundedness of the consumption set. Of course, this effectively requires satiation, though not necessarily in the interior of the consumption set.

[5]While one may seldom encounter the problem of satiation in practice, this is presumably due to most goods being scarce at the margin. Demand is concerned with what you would want to consume at various prices; the limits of what are actually possible can be captured by the feasibility condition for an equilibrium.

[6]While Mas-Colell (1977) rightly points out that satiation can prevent smoothness of demand, this only occurs when a weak budget constraint is permitted, i.e. when there is free disposal. With free disposal, demand would come to a sudden halt as the budget line passed through the bliss

2.3 Reformulation of the Model

While we have expressed aggregate demand in terms of an even vectorfield on the unit sphere (equations (1)-(3)), in a number of regards it is more economically natural to work in terms of the projective space P^n. This is the manifold obtained by identifying antipodal points on the unit sphere. It may also be considered the manifold consisting of equivalence classes of points along punctured lines through the origin of R^{n+1}. Thus, the very structure of projective space P^n incorporates the requirement that only relative prices count.

In terms of the unit sphere of normalized prices, S^n, equilibria always occur in pairs of antipodal prices. These price pairs, however, represent the same real price system and allocation, so that it is natural to identify these prices with one another, as is done when working on the projective price space P^n.

It turns out, though, that the even vectorfields on S^n do not correspond to vectorfields on P^n; that is they are not sections of the projection of the tangent bundle $\tilde{\pi} : TP^n \to P^n$. They are, however, the sections of the projection $\pi : \gamma_1^n(P^n) \to P^n$, where $\gamma_1^n(P^n)$ is the universal bundle over P^n. Much use of this fact is made in our analysis, particularly in obtaining static results.[7] The C^r-uniform topology on this Banach space of sections (Abraham and Robbin (1967)) provides the framework for our genericity results. We denote this space of sections by $\Gamma^r(\gamma_1^n(P^n))$.

3 Static Results

Since their proofs are so elementary, we first review the existence argument when regarding demand as being on the unit sphere S^n, and then, provide another argument making use of the projective space P^n.

Theorem 1 *(Existence): Given the economic model (1)-(3), equilibria always exist.*

Proof: Suppose to the contrary that $Z(p) \neq 0$ for all $p \epsilon S^n$. Then define

$$g : S^n \to S^n \qquad g(p) = \frac{Z(p)}{\|Z(p)\|}.$$

Since Z is even, so is g. It is a standard result that any even spherical map has even degree. It is also well known (Spanier (1966)) that, for spherical maps, the Lefschetz number is related to degree by

$$Lef(g) = 1 + (-1)^n deg\ g.$$

point, whereas without free disposal demand would continue to smoothly follow the budget line throughout.

[7] The universal bundle $\gamma_1^n(P^n)$ is a vector bundle defined as follows. (Milnor & Statsheef (1974)). The base space is P^n, whereas the fiber space consists of all pairs $([\pm p], v) \epsilon P^n \oplus R^{n+1}$ where $v \cdot p = 0$, the term $[\pm p]$ being the equivalence class of antipodal points on the unit sphere. The projection map $\pi : \gamma_1^n(P^n) \to P^n$ is the natural one, i.e. $\pi([\pm p], v) = [\pm p]$, whereas the vector space structure on the fiber over $[\pm p]$ is

$$\alpha([\pm p], u) + \beta([\pm p], v) = ([\pm p], \alpha u + \beta v).$$

It is well known that $\gamma_1^n(P^n)$ has a differentiable structure.

Thus, in the case of even degree, it is assured that $Lef(g) \neq 0$, and so a fixed point exists. That is, there is a p such that

$$Z(p) = \lambda p \qquad \lambda > 0,$$

which implies $p \cdot Z(p) = \lambda p \cdot p > 0$, in contradiction to Walras' Law.[8] QED

Theorem 1′ *(Existence): Each* $\xi \epsilon \Gamma^0(\gamma_1^n(P^n))$ *has a zero.*

Proof: It is a property of the Stiefel-Whitney classes $W_i[\lambda]$ of a vector bundle λ, (Milnor & Statsheef (1974)), that if λ has a nowhere zero section, then $W_n[\lambda] = 0$. As shown in Milnor and Statsheef (1974) [ex. 3, p. 43], all the Stiefel-Whitney classes for $\gamma_1^n(P^n)$ are nonzero, giving the desired result. QED

Theorem 2 *(Generic Finiteness): For an open, dense set of economies, there are but a finite number of equilibria. In our notation, for an open dense set in* $\Gamma^r(\gamma_1^n(P^n))$, *each section has a finite number of zeros.*

Proof: Consider the image E_0 of the zero section in $\Gamma^r(\gamma_1^n(P^n))$. E_0 is then a closed subset of the vector bundle $\gamma_1^n(P^n)$. Being a diffeomorphic copy of P^n, E_0 is of dimension n, whereas $\gamma_1^n(P^n)$ is of dimension $2n$. Now consider the C^r representation $\rho : \Gamma^r(\gamma_1^n(P^n)) \to C^r(P^n, \gamma_1^n(P^n))$, which is the identity projection. By application of the transversal density and openness of transversality theorems (Abraham and Robbin (1967)), one sees for an open, dense set of sections ξ in $\Gamma^r(\gamma_1^n(P^n))$, that $\xi^{-1}(E_0)$ is a manifold of dimension zero. Since P^n is compact, $\xi^{-1}(E_0)$ is in fact finite, but this set is nothing other than the zeros of ξ. QED

The only delicate point in the argument is in establishing that ev: $\Gamma^r(\gamma_1^n(P^n)) \times P^n \to \gamma_1^n(P^n)$ is transverse to E_0, as required by the transversal density theorem, but it is known by th. 12.4 of Abraham and Robbin (1967) that ev is in fact a submersion.

The result corresponds, of course, to that of Debreu (1970) obtained in the standard framework. The result shows that, in the typical case, equilibria are locally unique.

We speak of an economy as regular if its equilibria are nondegenerate. This requires that the Jacobian of excess demand at any such equilibrium have a non-vanishing determinant when considered in the vectorfield's local representation. A degenerate equilibrium and the associated economy are said to be critical.

Corollary 1 : *In the open, dense set of regular economies, the number of equilibria is locally constant. Over components of the set of regular economies, the equilibria vary smoothly.*

Proof: Since the proof is standard, we omit it. See the transversal isotopy theorem in Abraham and Robbin (1967). QED

The results on the local uniqueness and the smooth parameterization of equilibria among regular economies greatly simplify comparative statics among regular economies. We return to a discussion of comparative statics shortly.

---

[8]The proof of theorem 1 is a minor variation of that in Hart & Kuhn (1973). Rader (1972) provides a more general argument, applicable to upper semicontinuous correspondences, by making use of the Eilenberg-Montgomery fixed point theorem.

Theorem 3 *(Generic Oddness): For an open, dense set of economies, there are an odd number of equilibria. That is, for an open, dense set in $\Gamma^r(\gamma_1^n(P^n))$, there are an odd number of zeros for any such section.*

Proof: It is simple to exhibit an even vectorfield on S^n with a single antipodal pair of equilibria. For instance, Milnor and Statsteef (1974) [p. 142] construct the section f for $\gamma_1^n(P^n)$ given by the formula $[u_0, -u] \to (u \cdot u_0)u$ for some chosen u_0. The pair $[u_0, -u_0]$ is the single zero of this section.

Consider the zero section's image E_0. Then for the section f we selected above, $f^{-1}(E_0)$ is a unique element, so that f has 1 as its mod 2 intersection number (Milnor (1965)). Now, all sections of a vector bundle are homotopic, since pointwise their range is a vector space. (To see this, select as the homotopy $F(t,x) = tg(x) + (1-t)h(x)$ for any two sections g and h). It is well known that homotopic maps transverse to a manifold keep the same intersection number for their inverse image. For any section g of $\gamma_1^n(P^n)$, the mod 2 intersection number of $g^{-1}(E_0)$ must therefore be 1, and so the number of zeros must be odd.[9] QED

We have spoken of the above generic results as being static, since they serve only to count the number of equilibria. The results correspond exactly to those available in the standard model, where Mas-Colell (1977) has shown them to be the only such generic results possible. In addition, however, Dierker (1972) has observed that the Poincaré-Hopf index theorem applied to the standard model gives the result that a regular economy with only locally stable equilibria has in fact a unique equilibrium. Now, a locally stable price equilibrium of an even vectorfield on S^n has its antipodal set of prices being completely unstable (see section 5); thus, no result quite like that of Dierker is possible in the present context. Clearly, however, the analogous claim would be that an economy with all equilibrium allocations supported by a stable price system must have but one equilibrium allocation. It turns out that, while this result if true in even dimensions, it is false in odd ones. A failure in S^1 is easily obtained by drawing a vectorfield with three pairs of antipodal zeros, corresponding to three different equilibrium allocations, and arranging them so that stable prices alternate with unstable ones.

While it may be considered disturbing that a result should hold in dimensions of one parity and not another, this cannot be considered as a criticism of just the current model. The same sort of phenomena exist in the standard model. For instance, Scarf's celebrated counterexample to global stability of equilibrium involves a unique, completely unstable equilibrium. While this is possible with an even number of dimensions (e.g., two dimensions in Scarf's example), a consideration of the Poincaré-Hopf index theorem for the standard model shows that this situation is not possible in odd dimensions.

It is possible to interpret the difficulty under discussion as a manifestation of the intrinsically static character of equilibrium theory. All static results transfer nicely between the standard model and the current one, but the introduction of

[9]We remark that a straightforward counting argument to get this result from the Poincaré-Hopf index theorem, such as works in the standard model, will only work here in even dimensions and not in odd dimensions. It is possible, however, to obtain the oddness result in all dimensions by use of a more detailed version of the Poincaré-Hopf theorem (Pugh (1968)) applied to the unit half-sphere with boundary.

even the local notion of stability causes results to fail across dimensions and across models. While the view that equilibrium theory is entirely static is a tenable one, we do not ourselves share it. It should be pointed out that indices of equilibria used in the Poincaré-Hopf index theorem could be considered as just devices for counting equilibria, without imparting any dynamic interpretation to them, and still the difficulties under discussion would continue to exist. We will shortly engage in an explicitly dynamic interpretation of the current model.

4 Global Comparative Statics

Bifurcation theory constitutes the coordinate-free study of qualitative economics.[10] Given a parameterized family of economies, $Z_\lambda(p) \equiv Z(p, \lambda)$, one studies how the equilibrium set $Z_\lambda^{-1}(E_0)$ changes structure with λ. The corollary to theorem 2 shows that to locate such changes one may restrict attention to instances where this family of vectorfields encounters the set of critical economies.

The complexity of typical bifurcations of the equilibrium set depends on the dimension of the parameter space. It seems natural, at least as a first step, to restrict the parameterization to being one-dimensional. The interpretation then is that this represents the change in aggregate demand over time.[11] It may be that many aspects of preferences and endowments are changing, but if this is happening over time, the path of aggregate economies must still be one-dimensional.

With a one-parameter family of vectorfields, the typical change in the number of zeros occurs as a saddle-node bifurcation (Guckenheimer & Holmes (1983)). A saddle-node bifurcation formally corresponds to a real eigenvalue of a zero's Jacobian crossing the imaginary axis in the vectorfield's local representation, so that the zero is momentarily critical.[12] In such instances, two zeros merge as the critical one and then disappear, or running this picture backwards, a pair of zeros are born and then separate.

If one is maintaining a static point of view, then the main issue of global qualitative economies concerns what happens to the size of the equilibrium set. Note that since each saddle-node bifurcation changes the number of equilibrium allocations by two, parity in the number of equilibria is conserved, as required by the result on the oddness of equilibria. We now present a result showing that saddle-node bifurcations do indeed describe typical changes in our model's equilibrium set and that, in general, these bifurcations occur in isolation from one another over time. Typically, then, the set of equilibrium allocations changes by exactly two in number.

[10] See Mas-Colell (1985) for an integrated exposition of global comparative statics. Also, see Balasko (1988).

[11] By changes in demand over time, we do not mean price adjustment, which are assumed to occur instantaneously or in idealized time, but rather changes in the structure of aggregate demand due to eventual modifications of preferences or endowments. The distinction being made is the one between "fast" dynamics and "slow" dynamics.

[12] The other elementary case is where a pair of complex eigenvalues crosses the imaginary axis, giving rise to a Hopf bifurcation (Guckenheimer & Holmes (1983).) In this case, a cycle is thrown off the equilibrium, or in reverse time, a shrinking cycle coalesces with the equilibrium. This is only of interest in dynamic analysis, however, since the number of equilibria does not actually change with a Hopf bifurcation.

Theorem 4 : *There is an open, dense set A of $\Phi^r = C^r(\Lambda, \Gamma^r(\gamma_1^n(P^n)))$, for Λ a closed interval, such that $\xi \epsilon A$ has only a finite number of equilibria for each $\lambda \epsilon \Lambda$, and if a change in the size of the equilibrium set occurs, then the number of equilibria changes by exactly two. Such bifurcations occur on only a finite number of occasions.*

Proof: The proof consists basically of the observation that the result of Sotomayor (1973) for arbitrary vectorfields goes over to the case of even vectorfields, once the space of sections of TS^n is replaced by those of $\gamma_1^n(P^n)$.

The parameterized center manifold theorem (Arnold (1983)) provides a complete local description of families of vectorfields. The Jacobian of a vectorfields' equilibrium (zero) will have n^+, n^-, and n^0 eigenvalues with positive, negative, and vanishing real part, respectively, in any local representation. Since we are only giving a local description, one may consider the equilibrium to be $p_0 = 0 \epsilon R^n$ for $\lambda_0 = 0 \epsilon R$. The parameterized center manifold theorem then tells us that near (p_0, λ_0) the family of vectorfields is topologically equivalent to

$$dx/dt = f(x, \lambda) \quad x \epsilon R^{n^0}$$

$$dy/dt = \; -y \quad y \epsilon R^{n^-}$$

$$dz/dt = \; z \quad z \epsilon R^{n^+}.$$

Now, a vectorfield's critical equilibrium is said to be simple if the Jacobian is of rank one, so that the Jacobian has 0 as simple eigenvalue. In this case, R^{n^0} is one-dimensional and one has the dynamics on R^{n^0} being of the form

$$dx/dt = \pm x^2 + \lambda \qquad x_0 = 0, \lambda_0 = 0.$$

A saddle-node is merely a simple zero satisfying the further regularity condition that $D_p^2 Z(p, \lambda)(v, v)$ is transverse to $R^{n^-} \oplus R^{n^+}, v \epsilon R^{n^0}$. From the characterization of a simple zero in the parameterized center manifold theorem, one then obtains Sotomayor's result, in the case of even vectorfields:

Proposition G. *Let $Z \epsilon \Gamma^r(\gamma_1^n(P^n))$ have a saddle-node zero p, when regarded as an even vectorfield. Then there are neighborhoods $N(Z)$ of Z, $N(p)$ of p, and a submanifold S_1 in $N(Z)$, such that S_1 divides $N(Z)$ into two connected component S_1^- and S_1^+, and*

(1) $Y \epsilon N(Z)$ has a zero $p(Y)$ in $N(p)$ which is a saddle node if and only if $Y \epsilon S_1$

(2) $Y \epsilon N(Z)$ has two nondegenerate zeros p_1, p_2 in $N(p)$ if and only if $Y \epsilon S_1^-$

(3) $Y \epsilon N(Z)$ has no zero in $N(p)$ if and only if $Y \epsilon S_1^+$.

The sought for result will then follow once the following genericity argument of Sotomayor is established for the case of even vectorfields:

Proposition H. *Let Λ be a closed interval. Denote by A the subset of Φ^r such that*

(1) $\xi(\lambda)$ has only regular and saddle-node zeros

(2) $\hat{\xi}$ is transverse to E_0, where $\hat{\xi} : P^n \times \Lambda \to \gamma_1^n(P^n)$ and $\hat{\xi}(p, \lambda) \equiv \xi(\lambda)(p)$

(3) for every $\lambda \epsilon \Lambda$, $\xi(\lambda)$ has at most one saddle-node.

Then A is open and dense in Φ^r.

Openness in Proposition H follows immediately from the general result for arbitrary vectorfields, restricted to the set of even vectorfields. For the density portion, we follow the steps of Sotomayor's argument.

One may obtain an ξ of sufficient smoothness by approximation, since the class of C^k maps is always dense in the C^j class, $k \geq j$. Applying the transversality theorem (Abraham & Robbin (1967)), one obtains for any ξ an approximation ξ_1 with $\hat{\xi}_1$ transverse to E_0, considering the universal bundle as being over $P^n \times \Lambda$. Letting $\theta(\xi) = \{(p, \lambda) : \hat{\xi}(p, \lambda) = 0\}$ then $\theta(\xi)$ is a submanifold of codimension n in $P^n \times \Lambda$, that is a curve. Since the projection π of such a curve into Λ is an open map, one can approximate $\theta(S_1)$ by a curve θ_1 such that its projection is a Morse function.

The remainder of the proof proceeds by local approximations around critical zeros, so that one can return to the expression of sections as even vectorfields on the sphere and duplicate any perturbation in a neighborhood of a critical zero in the corresponding neighborhood of the antipodal zero.

By Sotomayor (1973), one can construct an ξ_2 approximating ξ_1 such that $\theta(\xi_2) = \theta_1$ and $\xi_2 = \xi_1$ outside a neighborhood of the set of critical points of π. The regular points of p_i correspond to regular zeros of the vectorfield. As a Morse function, $\pi(\xi)$ has finite many critical points and at most one for any λ. We denote these $(p_1, \lambda_1), (p_2, \lambda_2) \ldots (p_k, \lambda_k)$. By a perturbation in a neighborhood of each (p_i, λ_i) on the linear and quadratic terms of $\xi(\lambda_i)$ at p_i, we obtain saddlenodes for $\xi_3(\lambda_i)$, where ξ_3 satisfies the conditions of Proposition H.

Combining Propositions G and H, we then obtain the desired result. For any λ there are but a finite number of equilibria, since all but at most one are regular. By the stability of vectorfields in a neighborhood of regular zeros, bifurcations of the equilibrium set occur for only the saddle-nodes. Proposition H and its proof shows that there can only be a finite number of such saddle-node occurrences, and but one for any λ. Thus, by Proposition G, the number of price equilibria changes by exactly two antipodal pairs when the section to the universal bundle is regarded as an even vectorfield. Actually, the proof has thus far proceeded as if Λ is a compact manifold; but as Sotomayor notes, the result extends to Λ a compact manifold with boundary, which is just a closed interval when $dim\ \Lambda = 1$. QED

Results of the above type were first obtained by Balasko (1978, 1988) for a standard model with two consumers and two goods. The derivation in the current model is simplified by the fact that here, unlike the standard model, the price domain S^n is compact. Nonetheless, the result is a straightforward one and so it is not surprising that with a little effort the result in the current model can be extended back to the standard model in any number of dimensions (see Keenan (1984)). This bifurcation result is a generalization to paths of economies ($dim\ \Lambda = 1$) of the generic results on the number of equilibria obtained for single economies ($dim\ \Lambda = 0$).

5 Dynamic Analysis

5.1 Tatonnement

The standard model describes an economy as a vectorfield that, in rough terms, points inwards along the boundary of S^{n+}. This then leads naturally to consideration of the tatonnement process:

$$\dot{p} = Z(p).$$

The inward pointing condition assures that trajectories continue to exist on S^{n+} in forward time. This means that the standard model is consistent as a dynamic process.

In the current model, we have an even vectorfield on the entire unit sphere S^n, and so, again, the interpretation as a tatonnement process is a natural one. Compactness of this unit sphere then immediately assures the continuation of trajectories in forward (and backward) time.

We pursue a dynamic analysis of the current model. We will be interested, in particular, in a further examination of Dierker's (1972) result on the instability of multiple equilibrium allocations.

We first describe the property that characterizes even vectorfields on the unit sphere, when regarded as dynamic processes. Let $\phi_t(p)$ be the trajectory over time of the tatonnement process passing through $p \epsilon S^n$ at time zero.

Lemma 1 : *The dynamics of tatonnement for the current model are such that* $-\phi_t(p) = \phi_{-t}(-p)$.

Proof: One defines a dynamic system on S^n to be reversible (Abraham & Marsden (1978)) if there exists an involution $\mu : S^n \to S^n$ such that $\mu o \phi_{-t}(p) = \phi_t(\mu(p))$ (An involution is a mapping μ where $\mu o \mu = i$, with i being the identity mapping). It is immediately apparent that even vectorfields are reversible, taking μ to be the antipodal Z_2 action on S^n. The statement of the lemma then immediately follows from $T\mu o Z = -Z o \mu$. QED

The above property has a number of immediate implications. It requires that if $(-1)^k$ is the index of the equilibrium prices p^*, then $(-1)^{n-k}$ is the index of the antipodal prices $-p^*$.[13] The stability behavior of antipodal equilibria will be exactly opposite to one another, with the stable manifold of p^* corresponding to the unstable manifold of $-p^*$.

The current model has had built into it the property that only relative prices count, so that the all negative equilibrium prices of $-p^*$ would be just as valid as the all positive equilibrium prices p^*. Nonetheless, the dynamic action of the tatonnement process does not preserve relative prices, in the sense that the relative prices obtained over time beginning from the nonequilibrium prices p will not be the same as those obtained over the same time beginning from prices $-p$. This

[13] A hyperbolic equilibrium is one whose Jacobian has no eigenvalue with zero real part. The index of a hyperbolic equilibrium is $(-1)^k$, where k is the number of eigenvalues having negative real part.

bias works in a fashion that accords with one's intuition of which of two antipodal equilibria is the more natural. For instance, in the case of, say, two goods, where preferences are locally monotone at the unique equilibrium allocation, with the law of demand holding there, then it will be the all positive price combination (p_1^*, p_2^*) that will be stable. On the other hand, the combination $(-p_1^*, -p_2^*)$ will be unstable and hence presumably unobserved. If, instead, good 1 is desirable but good 2 is undesirable at the margin for the unique equilibrium allocation, then, given the law of demand there, it will be a price combination with p_1^* positive and p_2^* negative that will be stable, whereas the antipodal price combination will be unstable. Thus, tatonnement creates a presumption, not otherwise present, as to why desirable goods bear positive prices and undesirable ones negative prices, as opposed to the exact opposite situation.

5.2 Dynamic Analysis of Multiple Stable Equilibria

Economists often hold the opinion that, though economic models may have multiple equilibria, one will always reach one or another equilibrium over time. This property of system stability corresponds to gradient-like dynamical systems (Nitecki (1971)). For such systems, there is a series of so-called Morse inequalities relating the indices of dynamic equilibria to the shape of the underlying manifold. Since the shape of the unit sphere is well understood, this yields considerable information in our current model.

It will be recalled that, using the Poincaré-Hopf index theorem, Dierker (1972) was able to prove the result that, in the standard model, all equilibrium allocations being supported by stable prices requires that there be but one equilibrium allocation. It is easily seen that, in the current model, the Poincaré-Hopf index theorem continues to give the corresponding result in even dimensions, but not in odd ones. As observed in Section III, it is simple to construct counterexamples to the result in the case of two goods (one dimension). It is also possible to construct counterexamples in higher odd dimensions, but the possibilities are not as straightforward as in one dimension. We have, instead, the following result.

Theorem 5 : *For gradient-like dynamics of an economy with three or more goods, there is a unique equilibrium allocation if (and only if) all equilibrium allocations support a stable price.*

Proof: The Morse inequalities require that

$$m_0 \geq \beta_0$$

$$m_r - m_{r-1} + \cdots \pm m_0 \geq \beta_r - \beta_{r-1} + \cdots \pm \beta_0$$

and for $r = n$

$$m_0 - m_1 + \cdots \pm m_n = \beta_0 - \beta_1 + \cdots \pm \beta_n = \chi(S^n).$$

The last is the familiar Poincaré-Hopf index theorem. The coefficients m_i give the number of zeros of index i. The coefficients β_i are known as the Betti numbers, and for the unit sphere, it is found that

$$\beta_i = 1 \qquad i = 0, n$$
$$0 \qquad \text{otherwise.}$$

The Poincaré-Hopf index theorem implies in even dimensions only that if there are j pairs of stable/unstable antipodal pairs, then there must be $j-1$ additional pairs having odd indices. When the flow is gradient-like, this result continues to hold in odd dimensions, due to the Morse inequalities. Indeed, if there are j stable equilibria, then there must be at least $j-1$ unstable equilibria whose stable manifolds are of dimension $n-1$, and hence whose indices are odd.[14] QED

An implication of this result is that, except in the case of but two goods, economies whose multiple equilibrium allocations all support stable prices must have elements other than equilibria in the nonwandering set of their dynamics.[15] Therefore, the failure of Dierker's result in the current model only arises in the presence of more complex dynamic phenomena than just equilibria. Thus, even if one is only interested in results counting the number of equilibria, one will still need to be concerned with dynamic phenomena outside the neighborhood of equilibria. It is also easily seen that the dynamic phenomena that arise in the failure of Dierker's result cannot all themselves be attractors (or their repelling partners). Indeed, we have the following result:

Theorem 6 : *With three or more commodities, for an open, dense set of economies in our current model, those whose multiple equilibrium allocations all support stable prices have symmetric components of their nonwandering set that are neither equilibria nor attracting.*

Proof: By theorem 2, an open, dense set of economies have a finite number of equilibria, all regular. It is a standard argument to make C^r perturbations of these equilibria to obtain hyperbolic ones. The property of equilibria being hyperbolic is therefore dense; it is also clearly an open property.

Now, the stable manifold of a stable hyperbolic equilibrium is an open set, while that of a completely unstable hyperbolic equilibrium is just that equilibrium. The stable manifolds of multiple stable/unstable pairs cannot therefore decompose S^n as required, when n is two or greater.

Deleting the stable manifolds of attractors, we have a closed, invariant set whose every trajectory must have an ω-limit set. These limit points clearly cannot be repellers, so there must exist other elements of the nonwandering set. QED

Thus, even if one takes the position that only attractors are of economic concern, since only they will be observed, one still needs to account for the presence of dynamic phenomena, other than equilibria, whose stable sets are of lower dimension. Without them, Dierker's result goes through in the current model; with them, it need not. One may argue as a sort of global correspondence principle that a complete treatment of only the equilibrium set nonetheless requires consideration of the economy's global dynamic structure.

[14] There are similar inequalities for the so-called Morse- Smale flows (Nitecki (1971)), as well as for the Smale flows (Zeeman (1975)). This last class has the genericity property that it is C^0-dense among all vectorfields.

[15] See Abraham & Marsden (1978) for a definition of a dynamic's nonwandering set. This set contains the limiting motion of the dynamic flow.

5.3 Cycles and other Complex Dynamic Behavior

Closed orbits, like equilibria, appear in antipodal pairs. This follows quickly once it is realized that the alternative, a single, symmetric closed orbit, would be just the same as an even vectorfield on S^1 without equilibria, which we already know cannot happen. The stability behavior of each closed orbit in a pair is exactly opposite to its partner, just as with antipodal equilibria. It is interesting whether other elements of the nonwandering set, more complex than isolated equilibria or closed orbits, must also exist as antipodal pairs. If so, there is a sense in which the current dynamics is but a pure duplication of typical dynamic behavior. If on the other hand, connected components of the nonwandering set can be symmetric, so that they constitute their own antipodal partner, then the evenness property is creating novel dynamic phenomena.

One way to obtain such a symmetric component is through an Ω-explosion (Nitecki (1970)). Here a nonwandering set containing, say, two antipodal closed orbits suddenly expands, so that the closed orbits are then contained in a single enlarged component of the nonwandering set. For instance, let the dimension of S^n be odd, $n > 2$, and have the stable and unstable manifolds of each closed orbit be of the same dimension. Arrange that an arm of the stable manifold $W^s(\gamma)$ of one closed orbit γ coincides with part of the unstable manifold $W^u(-\gamma)$ of the antipodal closed orbit $-\gamma$. Then do the same for the stable manifold of the closed orbit $-\gamma$. This creates a so called heteroclinic cycle of trajectories between the two closed orbits. The coincidence of stable and unstable manifolds of these two orbits is atypical, and so a slight even perturbation will make the manifolds transverse to one another.

The orbits that then remain in, say, $W^s(\gamma) \bigcap W^u(-\gamma)$ are called transverse heteroclinic orbits and will themselves be in the nonwandering set. They will in fact be in the closure of the set of closed orbits, indicating that an infinite number of closed orbits have appeared in the neighborhoods of these stable and unstable manifolds. Transverse heteroclinic orbits going from say γ to $-\gamma$ will return via the unstable manifold of $-\gamma$ back to γ, becoming so-called homoclinic orbits in $W^s(\gamma) \bigcap W^u(\gamma)$. The resulting chaotic outcome is referred to as a homoclinic tangle (For further discussion, see Abraham & Marsden (1978), or Guckenheimer & Holmes (1983)). Thus, the dynamics allows two opposite regimes of price behavior to mix together in such a fashion that they become inseparable and indistinguishable. While this may be regarded as disturbing, it should be noted that such behavior can only occur for nonattracting sets. That is, attractors cannot be symmetric, since the set of antipodal trajectories necessarily forms an isolated repeller. Thus, if one ascribes to the notion that only attractors are of abiding interest, since only they are likely to be observed, then the problem that symmetric components of the nonwandering set mix up opposite modes of behavior becomes a secondary issue.

6 Conclusion

We have introduced regularity conditions to a model first developed by Trout Rader. This model differs from the standard one for regular economies in that negative prices are allowed, to account for goods that are not always desirable. It was found that the usual static results on existence, finiteness, and oddness of equilibrium allocations continue to go through from the standard to the current model. However, Dierker's result that multiple equilibrium allocations must involve allocations unsupportable by stable prices fails to hold in our model in the case of odd dimensions. A more careful analysis of the dynamic structure of the economy revealed, though, that such a failure could only occur in the presence of dynamic phenomena more complicated than just equilibria. This calls attention to a dynamic analysis of general equilibrium theory, for which the current model proves well suited. The model also turns out to be convenient for doing global comparative statics. A result was obtained showing that typical changes in the equilibrium set involve the number of allocations changing by a single pair. With similar techniques, this result may then be extended back to the standard model.

References

ABRAHAM, R. AND J. E. MARSDEN (1978): *Foundation of Mechanics.* Second Edition, Benjamin: New York.

ABRAHAM, R. AND J. W. ROBBIN (1967): *Transversal Mappings and Flows.* Benjamin: New York.

ARNOLD, V. I. (1983): *Geometrical Methods in the Theory of Ordinary Differential Equations.* Springer-Verlag: New York.

BALASKO, Y. (1978): "Economic equilibrium and catastrophe theory: An introduction," *Econometrica,* 46, 557–69.

BALASKO, Y. (1988): *Foundations of the Theory of General Equilibrium.* Academic: New York.

DEBREU, G. (1970): "Economies with a finite set of equilibria," *Econometrica,* 38, 387–92.

DIERKER, E. (1972): *Topological Methods in Walrasian Economics.* Lecture Notes in Economics and Mathematical Systems 92, Springer: Berlin.

GUCKENHEIMER, J. AND P HOLMES (1983): *Nonlinear Oscillations, Dynamical Systems and Bifurcations on Vector Fields.* Springer-Verlag: New York.

HART, O. AND H. KUHN (1973): "A proof of existence of equilibrium without the free disposal assumption," *Journal of Mathematical Economics,* 2, 335–44.

KEENAN, D. (1984): "Comparative statics in general equilibrium theory," Working Paper, University of Georgia.

MAS-COLELL, A. (1977): "On the equilibrium price set of a pure exchange economy," *Journal of Mathematical Economics,* 4, 117–26.

MAS-COLELL, A. (1985): *The Theory of General Economic Equilibrium: A Differentiable Approach.* Cambridge University Press: Cambridge.

MILNOR, J. W. (1965): *Topology from the Differential Viewpoint.* University Press of Virginia: Charlottesville.

MILNOR, J. W. AND J. STATSHEEF (1974): *Characteristic Classes.* Princeton University Press: Princeton, N. J.

NITECKI, Z. (1971): *Differential Dynamics.* MIT Press: Cambridge, MA.

PUGH, C. (1968): "A generalized Poincaré index formula," *Topology,* 7, 217–26.

RADER, J. T. (1972): *Theory of General Economic Equilibrium.* Academic Press: New York.

SOTOMAYOR, J. (1973): "Generic bifurcations of dynamical systems," in *Dynamic Systems.* Ed. M. M. Peixoto, Academic Press: New York.

SPANIER, E. H. (1966): *Algebraic Topology.* McGraw-Hill: New York.

ZEEMAN, E. C. (1975): "C^0 density of stable diffeomorphisms and flows," in *Proceedings of Colloquium on Smooth Dynamical Systems.* Ed. D. R. J. Chillingworth, Southampton University: 1972.

The Economics of the Atlantic Slave Trade *

M. Ali Khan
The Johns Hopkins University

1 Introduction

Trout J. Rader III is an economist with an impressive range. He is unique among mathematical economists in terms of his interests in the Protestant ethic[1] and in the economics of feudalism and slavery,[2] and unique among development economists in terms of his reliance on rigorous economic theory and in the importance he gives to purely technical issues such as, for example, the differentiability of solutions to general optimization problems and to the properties of preference relations.[3] As such, his work can be looked on and admired from many angles. In this essay, I follow Trout Rader the development economist, and taking Chapter 2 of his book on *The Economics of Feudalism* as an example and guide, propose a model of the Atlantic slave trade. The methodology behind my work can be stated best in Rader's own words.

> The main focus ... is upon the feudal economy [but] a secondary aim is to show how social, economic, and political forces interact. For this purpose, one can construct ... a reasonable but quite general picture of the world and then impose certain empirical constraints on the general system. This is the approach of the economic theorist or more precisely

*Preliminary versions of this paper were presented at the *Fall 1990 Mid-West International Economics Meetings*; at the *Second Chittagong Conference on Mathematical Economics and its Relevance for Development*; at the *Trade and Development Workshops* at Rochester and Yale; and at the *Economic Theory Workshops* at Georgetown and Notre Dame. I am grateful to all the participants for their encouragement and interest but I must single out Steve Blough and Jota Ishikawa for pointing out an incompleteness of the analysis in the first draft; to Sidney Mintz for directing me to the work of R. Sheridan; to Stan Engerman for his detailed comments and for references, especially to the Eltis-Jennings paper; to John Chipman, Tatsuo Hatta, Ron Jones, Amartya Sen and T. N. Srinivasan for their questions, some of which still remain in this version; and to Jeff Fischer, Lou Maccini, John Pomery and Hugh Rose for discussion and help at various points.

[1]See Rader (1982). The following quotation from page 22 of this work is both amusing and indicative of his sweep: "Such results as above could be avoided by the Protestant ethic whereby sustainable consumption paths were preferred. In this way, our analysis supports the mother's view in *Look Homeward Angel*."

[2]See, for example, Rader (1971a).

[3]See, for example, Rader (1963), (1973a) and (1973b).

> of the mathematical economist. "Explanation" is interpreted as the deductive system associated with inductive constraints upon a more or less *a priori* theoretical framework.[4]

The last sentence bears particular emphasis. It departs from a preoccupation with "prediction" and accents instead "understanding." Furthermore, the qualification *more or less* applied to the term *a priori* tends to bring out, for me at any rate, that

> the maxims of scientific methodology cannot be presented simply as abstract principles, in the realm ... of scientific jurisprudence: in addition, we must assemble a body of "case law" to flesh them out and give them content.[5]

As such, I would like to view the model presented here, as well as those of Bergstrom (1971), Darity (1982) and Findlay (1989), as an ongoing passage from the abstract to the concrete but with a privileged position for neither. The model, in giving a particular specificity to the reality of the Atlantic slave trade, brings out the importance of certain parameters hitherto neglected. Equally importantly, it furnishes a vantage point from which to view other purely theoretical constructions both in international trade and in development economics.[6] Moreover, it will hopefully allow, once its implications are fully understood and digested, a better handle on reality, and hence facilitate the construction of other better models for the Atlantic slave trade itself. Accordingly, the work here is not, and obviously cannot be, presented as an end in itself, and is done with some sensitivity to Curtin's complaint that

> development economists in particular have been led by their concern with the future to ignore the present and imagine the past.[7]

Of course, I have to squarely face that this is primarily a study in pure theory, and to the extent that

> ... historians are still concerned [in disassociating] themselves from Toynbeesque metahistory, [and eager] to avoid the trapdoors associated with holistic terms and to steer clear of charges of determinism [and of] large units, ... generalities, or [associations] with a single cause or model, whether linear, circular or any other shape,[8]

they will find little here that is not superficial. However, this is obviously not the place to attempt a justification of my point of view.[9]

Moving from method to substance, Rader's 1971 words introduce my model as aptly as they did his own.

---

[4] Rader (1971; p. 1).

[5] Toulmin (1977; p. 154)

[6] See Section 4 below.

[7] Curtin (1975; p. 197). However, see White (1978) and Woodward (1989; Part IV).

[8] Hopkins (1978; p. 5).

[9] And presumably Rader's. But see Heckscher (1926), Conrad-Meyer (1964; Part 1) and Temin (1971); also Khan (1989b) and the concluding remarks in Section 9 below.

> The model is one of general market equilibrium. Ideally, a theory based upon coalition structure would be best. However, the present state of game theory is such as to present a bewildering variety of possible solutions without any information about any one. The mechanistic market system of economics is more explored and better understood.[10]

Two other introductory points, both of which relate to Rader's work. As we shall see below, my model gives especial prominence to production and questions of consumer demand, as opposed to producers' derived demands, do not play any active role. There is some irony in this in that Rader's Yale Ph.D dissertation[11] was devoted to establishing how the Walrasian general equilibrium model with production can be conceived of and analyzed, without any loss of generality, as one pertaining *solely* to exchange. My second observation relates to the fact that the issue of whether slave labor is a substitute or a complement for machinery plays a crucial role in the sequel.[12] This is of some interest in view of Rader's investigation and emphasis on the importance of these properties in the context of the Walrasian model.[13]

The outline of this paper is as follows. In Section 2, I present the model and the equilibrium concept. Section 3 presents the historical references and material which served as my background reading for the formulation of the model. Section 4 relates the model to previous theoretical work on the Atlantic slave trade as well as to some work in trade and development. Section 5 begins the analysis by deriving the necessary conditions for optimality of the four representative agents of the model. Section 6 and 7 report preliminary analysis of the model and Section 8 presents the general equilibrium effects of British suppression of the slave trade. My focus on British suppression policies is in keeping with Rader's interest in showing "how social, economic, and political forces interact." Finally, Section 9 concludes the paper with two observations.

2 The Model and the Notion of Equilibrium

The setting involves three different economies: the British economy in which there is production of manufactures in general, and armaments in particular, with machinery and labor as inputs, and with part of this machinery being invested in the Caribbean; the Caribbean economy in which there is production of sugar with British machinery, African slaves and land as inputs; and the African economy in which there is production of slaves with British armaments as an input. The model comprises of four agents: the representative Caribbean plantation owner, the representative transporter of slaves from Africa to the Caribbean, the representative African supplier and the representative British manufacturer. I consider each agent in turn.

---

[10]See the Preface to Rader (1971).
[11]See Rader (1964).
[12]See the Standing Hypothesis in Section 6 below.
[13]See Rader (1968a) and Rader (1972).

2.1 The Planter's Problem

In addition to the technology for the production of sugar, there are three basic relationships involved here. The first relates to the productivity of slave labor, the second to its longevity and the third to the rate of depreciation of the stock of slaves. I take each in turn.

Following its recent popularity in the literature of development economics, I shall assume that the productivity of slave labor λ depends on the food that is given to him[14] and that this relationship is given by[15]

$$\lambda = \lambda(w),\ \lambda'(w) > 0,\ \lambda''(w)\begin{cases} > 0 & \text{if } w \leq \bar{w} \\ < 0 & \text{if } w \geq \bar{w} \end{cases} \tag{1}$$

A typical example of such a function is presented in Figure 1a. I refer the reader particularly to Bliss-Stern (1978) for justification as to its particular shape.

I shall also assume that the longevity of slave labor, Γ, depends on the food that is given to him, primarily in terms of increasing his resistance to disease, and thus postulate

$$\Gamma = \Gamma(w),\ \Gamma'(w) > 0,\ \Gamma'' < 0. \tag{2}$$

Finally, in this connection, I shall assume that the rate of depreciation ϕ in the stock of slaves depends on an exogenously given variable μ signifying all the variables that are not captured; on food and on longevity. I can thus write[16]

$$\phi = \phi(\mu, w, \Gamma(w)),\ \phi^i(\mu, w, \Gamma(w)) < 0,\ \ i = 1, 2, 3. \tag{3}$$

I shall assume that sugar X_r is produced by machinery K_r, slave labor S and land T according to the relationship

$$X_r = F_r(K_r, \lambda(w)S, T), \tag{4}$$

where F_r is twice continuously differentiable, and exhibits both constant returns to scale and diminishing marginal productivity to each factor.

I shall assume that the Caribbean economy is too small to influence the international price of sugar which is exogenously given by p_r. Let the rental to capital be given by ρ and that to land by τ. Let the international interest rate be exogenously given by i. Finally, let the buying price of a slave be p_s. Then the profit made by an individual planter is given by

$$\int_0^\infty (p_r F_r(K_r, \lambda(w)S, T) - \rho K_r - wS - \tau T - p_s I)e^{-it} dt, \tag{5}$$

where

$$\dot{S} = I - \phi(\mu, w, \Gamma(w))S, \tag{6}$$

[14]The pioneering work seems to be that of Leibenstein (1957). For more detailed analyses of the implications of this hypothesis, the reader should see Myrdal (1968; p. 1603), Mirrlees (1975), Stiglitz (1976) and Bliss-Stern (1978). The relationship between slave productivity and caloric intake was, of course, recognized much earlier; see David-Temin (1974), Sutch (1975) and their references.

[15]Throughout the sequel, primes denote differentials for a function of a single variable.

[16]Throughout the sequel, for a function of many variables, a numbered superscript will denote the partial derivative with respect to that variable.

and I is the investment in slaves and the initial stock of slaves is given. The planter assumes that all the relevant prices remain constant over the foreseeable future and are known with certainty.[17] The planter has to decide how many slaves to buy each year, how much capital and land to rent and how much to expend in sustaining each slave. Once these decisions are made, he has then automatically determined how much sugar he is to put on the world market. Thus the planter's unknowns are K_r, I, $S(t)$, T and w, and his parameters are p_r, p_s, ρ, τ and i. I shall assume that the planter maximizes the present discounted value of his surplus, and this gives me a standard version of neoclassical theory of investment[18] and from a technical point of view, a simple problem in the calculus of variations.[19]

One final observation which is somewhat anticipatory in nature. The equilibrium which I am in the process of formulating and for which the planter's problem is one particular constituent, pertains only to the stationary state. The procedure is to formulate the planter's problem as a dynamic one and then to impose the assumption of stationarity on the solution. An alternative procedure would have been to work under the behavioral assumption whereby the representative planter focusses only on steady states. In this case, the problem formulated as (5) and (6) would lead me to assume that $\dot{S} = 0$, and to integrate out the objective function. I would then obtain from (5)

$$(1/i)(p_r F_r(K_r, \lambda(w)S, T) - \rho K_r - wS - \tau T - p_s \phi(\mu, w, \Gamma(w))S. \tag{7}$$

On maximizing this with respect to the variables K_r, S, T and w, the only change would be that i would play no role in the necessary conditions.[20] Indeed, students of capital theory will recognize this as precisely the difference between the *golden rule* and the *modified golden rule* in the theory of optimal planning.[21]

2.2 The British Manufacturer

I shall assume that firearms[22] X_g are produced by machinery K_g and labor L_g according to the relationship

$$X_g = F_g(K_g, L_g), \tag{8}$$

[17] We now have a better developed theory of investment which takes into account uncertainty. It is not clear to me that application of this theory at this stage would not really be giving the subject more precision than it deserves.

[18] See, for example, Lucas (1967). Of course, in our set-up it is reasonable to assume that there are no costs of adjustment to capital stock. However, what makes the problem technically more complicated is the non-convexity introduced by the function $\lambda(\cdot)$. I do not do anything in the sequel to cope with this technical difficulty.

[19] With constant returns to scale in the production of sugar, the scale of the inputs is indeterminate and the problem is simpler still. I am indebted to Hugh Rose for this point.

[20] Equations (27) to (30) below.

[21] For details, see, for example, Koopmans (1967) and his references.

[22] The subscript g in X_g stands for guns. Readers uncomfortable with the interpretation in terms of firearms can alternatively think of X_g as a composite commodity denoting manufactures. However, it needs to be emphasized that, from an analytical point of view, I am explicitly assuming that X_g is a necessary input in the capture of slaves. I return to the question of firearms in Section 3 below.

where F_g is twice continuously differentiable, and exhibits both constant returns to scale and diminishing marginal productivity to each factor.

I shall also assume that the British economy is too small to influence the price p_g of firearms and the representative British manufacturer chooses (K_g, L_g) to maximize profits given by

$$p_g F_g(K_g, L_g) - \rho K_g - w_g L_g, \tag{9}$$

where w_g represents the British wage rate.

2.3 The Transporter's Problem

The transporter takes labor from Africa L and with the help of maritime inputs M delivers slave labor to the Caribbean according to the technology[23]

$$X_s = F_s(M, L), \tag{10}$$

where F_s is twice continuously differentiable, and exhibits both constant returns to scale and diminishing marginal productivity to each factor. The transporter rents the ships at an exogenously given rental price p_m, buys slaves at the price p_ℓ and sells them at the price p_s.

At this stage, I have two alternative possibilities as regards the behavioral assumption underlying the transporter's actions. The first is to assume that he is a monopsonist who sets p_s. Under this hypothesis, he maximizes

$$p_s F_s(M, L) - p_m M - p_\ell L, \tag{11}$$

while explicitly taking into account the fact that p_s depends on the stock of slave labor S. Somewhat more formally, the transporter knows the representative planter's derived demand and chooses L and M so as to solve

$$p_s F_s^1(L, M) + F_s(L, M)\frac{\partial p_s}{\partial L} = p_\ell \tag{12}$$

$$p_s F_s^2(L, M) + F_s(L, M)\frac{\partial p_s}{\partial M} = p_m \tag{13}$$

What complicates the problem is that the relationship between S and p_s obtained from Subsection 2.1 already involves the partial derivatives of F_r in the form of marginal productivities, and hence when one turns to comparative statics, one is dealing with third derivatives and swimming in algebra.[24]

Fortunately, as discussed in Section 3 below, the monopolies granted to transporters in the form of Royal Charters were always undercut, and hence a competitive hypothesis is not only technically easier to work with, but also more in consonant with the facts. Accordingly, I shall work with it.

---

[23] Note that X_s is not assumed to equal L and as such, F_s captures the death rate on the Atlantic voyage.

[24] This is both standard and well-known; see Ferguson (1968).

2.4 The African Supplier

The supply of slave labor is directly dependent on the discord in the African continent and hence on the amount of firearms consumed. I shall assume that slave labor $L \equiv X_s$ is produced by British manufactures G according to the relationship

$$L = F_\ell(G, Z), \tag{14}$$

where Z is a composite input or a proxy for the surplus, and where as before, F_r is twice continuously differentiable and strictly concave in terms of G.

I shall also assume that African supply is regulated so as to maximize the surplus from the selling of slaves. In other words, G is chosen so as to maximize

$$p_\ell F_\ell(G) - p_g G, \tag{15}$$

with p_g and p_ℓ being taken as exogenously to the supplier. As we shall see below in Section 3, this latter assumption does not do full justice to the facts.

2.5 Equilibrium

Putting all these aspects together yields the equilibrium concept studied in this paper.

Definition 1 *An equilibrium is a strictly positive quadruple constituted by a sextuple of outputs $(X_g^*, X_s^*, X_r^*, X_\ell^*, G^*, L^*)$, by a quintuple of inputs $(K_r^*, K_g^*, L_g^*, T^*, M^*)$, by the quintuple of factor prices $(w_g^*, \tau^*, \rho^*, p_g^*, p_\ell^*)$ and by the quadruple of variables pertaining to slavery $(p_\ell^*, S^*, I^*, w^*)$ such that:*

(i) (K_g^*, L_g^*) *maximizes* $p_g^* F_g(L_g, K_g) - w_g^* L_g - \rho^* K_g$,

(ii) (L^*, M^*) *maximizes* $p_s^* F_s(L, M) - p_\ell^* L - p_m M$,

(iii) G^* *maximizes* $p_\ell^* F_\ell(G, Z) - p_g G$,

(iv) $(K_r^*, w^*, T^*, S(t), I^*)$ *maximizes* $\int_0^\infty (p_r F_r(K_r, \lambda(w)S, T)) - \rho^* K_r - wS(t) - \tau^* T - p_s^* I)e^{-it}dt$, *subject to* $\dot{S} = I - \phi(w)S$ *and* $S(0) = S^* = (1/\phi(w^*))I^*$,

(v) $X_r^* = F_r(K_r^*, \lambda(w^*)S^*, T^*)$,

(vi) $X_s^* = I^* = F_s(L^*, M^*)$,

(vii) $X_g^* = G^* = F_g(K_g^*, L_g^*)$,

(viii) $X_\ell^* = L^* = F_\ell(G^*, Z)$,

(ix) $T^* = \mathcal{T}$ *and* $L_g^* = \mathcal{L}$,

(x) $K_r^* + K_g^* = \mathcal{K}$.

The equilibrium brings out the fact that the unknowns of the model are the output levels of armaments, slaves, sugar and African labor; the price of armaments; the allocation of machinery between Britain and the Caribbean and the input levels of British labor, Caribbean land and shipping services; the return to this labor and land as well as to machinery and African labor; and finally, the price and stock of slaves, the changes in this stock and the slave consumption levels. More specifically, the first four conditions bring out the behavioral hypothesis that the four representative agents of the model are all maximizers and that they are all "small" in the conventional sense of taking the relevant prices as given parameters. Condition (v) is a definitional identity and the next five conditions can be simply summarized in the statement that demand equals supply in each relevant market. Note that out of the four outputs, three are also inputs. This is in keeping with my emphasis on outputs of one sector constituting imported inputs in another.

From a technical point of view, the model has twenty unknown variables and six parameters given by $(\mathcal{L}, \mathcal{T}, \mathcal{K}, p_r, p_m, i)$. The necessary conditions for maximization furnish ten equations obtained from the maximization problems laid out in conditions (i) to (iv) of Definition 1. On adding the ten equations constituting conditions (v) to (x), I obtain twenty equations to determine twenty unknowns. However, it is by now well understood that counting equations and unknowns hardly suffices to establish that an equilibrium exists, and that a first step in the analysis of any model is to establish the viability of the equilibrium notion. In other words, I must guarantee that the equilibrium defined above not only exists, but is locally unique and continuously differentiable in terms of its parameters. Such an analysis is outside the scope of this paper.[25]

3 Discussion of the Model

In this section I present an attempt at a justification, or alternatively a critique, of the model presented in Section 2 in light of the basic facts of the Atlantic slave trade.[26]

A preliminary point can be quickly disposed. This concerns a recent controversy as regards the triangularity of the trade.[27] The issue primarily seems to be whether ships from the Caribbean returned to Britain laden or not[28] and the argument has been reduced to evidence of the duration of stay of these ships in Caribbean ports.[29] This controversy has little relevance for my work which is primarily focussed on the commerce in slaves, sugar and firearms. The existence of such commerce is beyond dispute. Moreover, since I assume that the price of sugar p_r to be exogenously given, it matters little from an analytical point of view whether the sugar was primarily going to Britain or to other European ports.

The interpretation of X_r as sugar and the producing region as the Caribbean

[25]On these issues, see, for example, Debreu (1976) and Mas-Colell's (1987) recent book.

[26]Also see Section V of Findlay's (1989) Frank Graham Lecture.

[27]The proponents seem to be Ostrander, Sheridan and Rice. See Minchinton (1979) for a point of view opposite to theirs as well as for detailed references.

[28]The technical term seems to be to "sail back in ballast."

[29]See Tables 13.1 to 13.8 in Minchinton (1979).

is of greater import and not really a simple choice of label. I am not assuming that the output of the plantation is an intermediate input in the production of British manufactures, and in so doing, I explicitly rule out the interpretation of X_r as any commodity that can be used as an input in British manufacturing. As such, X_r cannot be interpreted as raw cotton, or any composite commodity including cotton, serving as an input in the production of textiles. If any flexibility of commodity composition is allowed, it would have to be limited to consumption goods such as tobacco and tea.[30]

However, one has to be slightly careful here. Sidney Mintz has recently emphasized the importance of sugar and tea as an input into the productivity of factory labor in Britain and my work already emphasizes this point of view in the inclusion of the $\lambda(\cdot)$ function in the modelling of the plantation. Mintz' insightful overview bears repetition.

> It was once thought that plantations producing goods could benefit the homeland economy in two ways: through direct capital transfers to homeland banks for reinvestment; and as markets for such metropolitan products as machinery, cloth, instruments of torture and other industrial commodities. ...there is yet a third potential contribution: the provision of low-cost food substitutes, such as tobacco, tea and sugar, for the metropolitan laboring classes. By positively affecting the worker's energy output and productivity, such substitutes figured importantly in balancing the accounts of capitalism.[31]

I ignore this feedback here.[32]

I now move on to the consideration of the four representative agents of my model, beginning with the representative planter. The first question that needs some justification is the treatment of a plantation in the relatively sophisticated terms that I have given it. For this, I simply refer the reader to look at the work of Curtin (1990), Mintz (1959 and 1974; Chapter 4) and Wolf-Mintz (1957), and invite him to make his own judgement. If, in the light of this evidence as well as the considerations discussed below, this entails the view that the treatment is not sophisticated enough, I would rather leave generalizations to future work, once we have better judgement on the contribution of this exercise to our understanding of the Atlantic slave trade.

The exogeneity to the planter's decision of the price of sugar, p_r, has already been mentioned; the same is true of the rental rate, ρ, on machinery being imported from Europe, the rental to land, τ, as well as the rate of interest, i. Of course, one alternative is to argue that both machinery and land were bought rather than rented[33] but under the assumption of perfect markets for these commodities and under the other assumptions of the model, it is a matter of indifference as to whether

[30] On these issues, see Chapter 1 in Tomich (1990) and, in particular, his Table 1.1 on international sugar production during the period 1791-1842.

[31] Mintz (1985; p.148). Also see Sheridan (1974) and the reference by Engerman (1975; footnote 7) to the Lewis Henry Morgan Lectures delivered by Sidney Mintz at the University of Rochester.

[32] The work of Bliss-Stern, Mirrlees, Stiglitz, in particular, can be seen as an investigation of the importance of this feedback for development economics.

[33] But see Mintz (1959; p. 45) in the case of land.

I consider a stream or its capitalized value. A more serious objection relates to the relationship[34] between ρ and i as well as to the influence of the planters' lobby on lowering rates of interest. In this context, the following quotation is illuminating.

> Out of a total capital investment of £70,000,000 in the West India colonies in 1790, George Hibbert estimated the debt at not 'less than twenty millions'. .. a reviewer ...asserted in 1804, '.. the West Indies have now chiefly become the property of the commercial body of the city of London'.[35]
>
> Debtors and creditors crossed swords on the rate of interest as they did on so many issues. Planter governments reduced the legal maximum rate of interest from time to time. Creditors retaliated by forcing debtors to pay extra fees and disguised forms of interest on frozen trade credit and loans. An act of the Antigua legislature in 1738 raised the price of gold and reduced the rate of interest from ten to six per cent. This measure met with vigorous opposition from local merchants and factors.[36]

It needs to be emphasized that even though p_s, ρ and τ are considered exogenous to the planter's decision, unlike p_r, they are endogenous to the model and their values determined in equilibrium.

Finally, the assumptions of constant returns to scale in the production of sugar needs to be mentioned. This is motivated purely from a technical point of view; economic theory has only recently begun investigating the consequences of relaxing the *convexity* assumption on technology.[37]

Next, I turn to the economics of the supply of slaves. One cannot do better than begin with Engerman's summary statement.

> As shown dramatically in Curtin's forthcoming study of Senegambian trade,[38] the image of a static African society, or more accurately societies, out-bargained and out-maneuvered by European traders is not accurate, and is clearly in the process of revision.[39]

In terms of broad conception, I have modelled the economics of African supply in competitive terms. The extent to which this is justified can be gauged from the following quotations.

> The operations of the slave trade can be divided into three functionally and institutionally distinct segments. As a first step, the slave had to be captured in Africa – a process equivalent to the production of some other commodity that later becomes an article of commerce. Evidence indicates that the captors received only a small part of the price that

[34] More precisely, the absence of such a relationship in this work. As discussed below, in contrast, Findlay (1989) works with the assumption that $\rho = i$.

[35] See Sheridan (1958; p. 258).

[36] See Sheridan (1958; p. 250).

[37] See Khan (1989b, especially Section 2) and his references.

[38] See Curtin (1975).

[39] See Engerman in Engerman-Genovese (1975; p. 496).

> would ultimately be paid for the slave once he arrived in the New World. A larger part of the final selling price went to those who performed the second function – the shipment of slaves to a coastal point and accumulation of enough slaves to create an attractive market for slave ships. The third and final segment of the slave trade was shipment by sea to the Americas. European shipowners who managed this part of the trade normally received at least half of the sale price, which meant that theirs was the largest of the three shares... but the risks were also great, and the trade was intensely competitive.[40]

The same classification is repeated elsewhere.

> In the slave trade three distinct but connected activities were subject to technical change: the gathering of slaves in Africa: slave merchandizing in Africa, including transport to the coast and sale to the Europeans; and the transport of slaves to the Americas.[41]

In the model presented in Section 2, slave gathering and slave delivery has been subsumed under one technology which uses armaments, X_g, and a composite factor, Z, and takes the selling pricc, p_ℓ, as well as the price of armaments, p_g, as exogenously given. This, of course, limits me to one particular conceptual level of explanation, especially in light of the following.

> [As regards] the general structure of slave delivery mechanisms in West Africa, [a] major finding has been ... the existence of restrictive trade associations.
>
> ... the restrictive arrangements themselves underwent frequent alteration. In spite of a changing nature, some type of cartel or state trading was very likely to be encountered at any time in almost every region in which slave marketing was undertaken.
>
> "Membership" in such systems, however defined, was likely to encompass significant economic advantages. An individual traders' operations would thereafter be supported by an organic and often powerful commercial structure. He would usually find easier access to credit, important for successful trading when working capital is short. If he were not always licensed to or by state officials, he would at least be represented by the authorities of the trade association. Without their support, his "capital equipment," particularly firearms and other weapons... might be difficult or impossible to acquire.[42]

As far as the selling of slave labor to the Caribbean is concerned, my model assumes that British labor is internationally immobile and that as much slave labor can be had from Africa as cost conditions permit. Curtin has given a justification of

[40] Curtin (1971a; p. 315-316).

[41] Gemery-Hogendorn (1978; p. 246).

[42] Lovejoy-Hogendorn (1975; pp.232-235). In this context, the reader should also see Curtin (1975; Sections 4 and 5 of Chapter 7).

this in epidemiological terms[43] but this too has an economic basis once one weights the price of the two kinds of labor by the probability of survival.

> Whether [the planters] purchased the indenture of a European bondsman, bought the labor of a European criminal condemned to transportation or bought a slave from Africa, they were laying out capital in return for a claim to later labor. If the prices of African born slaves had not been competitive with those of labor from other sources – native born or European – the slave trade could never have come into existence, no matter what the epidemiological consequences of movement across the Atlantic. The cost conditions of the slave trade itself were therefore equally basic to the South Atlantic system.[44]

On the question of armaments as a relevant input, I can refer the reader to the excellent studies of Inikori,[45] and Gemery-Hogendorn.[46] The following quotation is illuminating.

> On the coasts, near the end of the seventeenth century, the gun/slave exchange ratio was eight trade muskets for one slave. In the interior slave prices were much lower, perhaps only one-fifth of coastal prices. It is therefore reasonable to conclude that expense alone can explain the relative scarcity of muskets in interior regions – especially when the scarcity was induced artificially by coastal states which controlled the trade routes to the interior.[47]

It is clear that armaments were not the only European, or even British, import into Africa,[48] and thus my exclusive emphasis on this can be seen, in part, as a reaction to its total omission in earlier studies.

> It is possible that firearms did not merely make a gun-slave cycle, where an African state used the arms to capture more slaves, to buy more arms, and so on. The availability of firearms may also have forced African sates to take up slave raiding in self-protection since guns could only be bought with slaves. But the importance of the gun-slave cycle is still a matter of controversy among historians.[49]

Whether X_g is regarded as manufactures or armaments is simply a matter of interpretation; what is important is that I am assuming it to be an input into slave-gathering. A different question however arises,

---

[43]See Curtin (1971a; pp. 313-314) and Curtin (1971b; paragraphs 2 and 3 on page 84).

[44]Curtin (1976; p. 315).

[45]See especially Tables 1, 3 and 4 in Inikori (1977). Also Curtin (1971b; p. 88).

[46]See especially the section titled *Technical Change in Slave Gathering* and the references in Gemery-Hogendorn (1978).

[47]Gemery-Hogendorn (1978; p. 246).

[48]See Curtin (1990; Figures 10.1 and 10.2 and Table 4). Also Table 2 in Eltis-Jennings (1988) and Chapter 5 in Curtin (1975).

[49]Curtin (1976; p. 318).

> ... given high import cost, as to why were firearms never manufactured in Africa on anything but a tiny scale? Despite their high costs, imported muskets were a better bargain than the local product. This most important form of technical change, with its enormous impact on slave gathering in Africa, was therefore an almost wholly external borrowing of technology.[50]

Next I turn to the economics of the transporter. The three principal agents seem to be, in chronological order and from a British perspective, *The Royal Adventurers into Africa,*[51] *The Royal African Company,*[52] and *The South Sea Company.*[53] The circumstances leading to the formation of *The South Sea Company* are interesting.

> As part of the price for ending the war, the English wrung an *asiento*[54] from the reluctant Spanish. The *asiento* gave the English sole rights to supply the Spanish colonies with slaves for the next thirty years, amounting to 4,800 piezas de Indias[55] annually, an overall total of 144,000 piezas. A duty of $33\frac{1}{3}$ would be paid the Spanish crown on each of the first 4,000 piezas; the remaining 800 would be admitted duty free. In the event that thc company dclivered more than 4,800 piezas in a year, it would pay a duty of $16\frac{2}{3}$ pesos on each excess pieza.[56]

In the context of *The Royal African Company,*

> The charter granted the company a monopoly to trade, for a period of 1,000 years, between Cape Blanco in the north and the Cape of Good Hope in the south. It was empowered specifically to deal in slaves, gold, and silver and to establish forts and factories at appropriate places on the African coast. As a monopoly company, it could seize the ships and effects of interlopers, and a court was created to adjudicate such cases. These interlopers received a ready acceptance from the planters, who justified their behavior by blaming the company for undersupplying them with African workers.[57]

It is precisely the last sentence of the above quotation that serves as a basis for modelling the transporter in competitive terms. In his chapter on the illegal slave trade, Palmer[58] documents how competition forced the Company to reduce

[50] Gemery-Hogendorn (1978; p. 251).

[51] This was chartered in 1660 and signed a contract to deliver 3500 slaves annually to the Spanish colonies; see Palmer (1981; p. 4).

[52] This was chartered in 1672 at the time of the demise of *The Royal Adventurers into Africa,* and survived until 1752.

[53] This company was chartered in 1711 and "granted a monopoly to trade with South America "for ever" on September 7, 1713;" see Palmer (1981; p. 10).

[54] For details on the meaning of this term, see Curtin (1969; pp. 21-25).

[55] A *pieza* was the standard slave unit.

[56] See Palmer (1981; p.9).

[57] See Palmer (1981; p.5).

[58] Chapter 5 in Palmer (1981).

prices on several occasions. The *Ten Percent Act,* passed in 1698, the prohibitions on the Captains of the ships not to engage in private dealings, the way these and other infractions of the law were dealt with, and the institution of the *Indulto,* all give insight into how the economics of the transport were evolving in the direction that economic theory suggests.

Finally, I refer the reader to the Appendices of Palmer (1981) for balance sheets relating to voyages from Africa to the Caribbean.

The British manufacturer, and more generally, the British economy is the crudest building block of the model. The extent of this can be appreciated to some extent by my discussion in the next section of some other models in the literature.

4 Relationship to Other Work

In this section I relate my model to some work in economic theory and in trade and development. I begin with Conrad-Meyer (1958). Their primary concern is with the profitability of slavery in the antebellum South and as such empirical. Nevertheless, their theoretical conception is one of a "neoclassical two-region, two-commodity trade system" with a slave as a produced intermediate capital input explicitly recognized. However, they do not propose, and analyze, a theoretical model of the kind presented here.

Next, I turn to Bergstrom (1971). Bergstrom constructs a general equilibrium model of the Arrow-Debreu-McKenzie[59] variety with a finite number of commodities and a finite number of consumers and producers. In Bergstrom's model, a subset of the consumers are designated as slaves by which is meant that they do not own shares in the profits of the firms and that the other consumers have shares in the value of their aggregate expenditures.

Bergstrom formulates two notions of equilibria: a *slave equilibrium* and a *slave exploitation equilibrium.* Under the first equilibrium notion, the slaves also maximize their preferences but over a restricted consumption set, one which does not guarantee *survival* in the sense of McKenzie.[60] Under the second equilibrium notion, the slaves are given consumption bundles which minimize their expenditure over a restricted consumption set. Under either notion, and under the notational convention that positive elements of a consumption plan denote commodities acquired and negative elements commodities furnished by the consumer, the price of a slave is the value of his expenditure in equilibrium. Bergstrom presents sufficient conditions for the existence of his equilibria and also presents versions of the two fundamental theorems of welfare economics. In particular, he formulates two notions of Pareto optimality: the conventional one and another phrased only in terms of the consumers who are not slaves.

This is, of course, not the place for a detailed investigation of Bergstrom's work but it is clear that such an examination would have to reckon with the insightful remarks of David-Temin (1974) on the applicability of neoclassical welfare economics

[59]The *locus classicus* is, of course, Debreu (1959). The interested reader is also referred to Khan (1989a) and his references.

[60]For details, see Khan (1989a) and his references to McKenzie's work.

to economies with slaves.[61]

Prior to the consideration of work that is of a style more in line with the one pursued here, I recall two canonical models in the theory of trade and development. The first is the so-called Ricardo-Viner model, henceforth RV model.[62] This is a production model with two outputs and three inputs, only one of which is intersectorally mobile, and with prices of the two outputs and the endowments of the three inputs as given parameters. The model is well-suited to answering standard questions in trade and development without a commitment to the decomposability property[63] of the Heckscher-Ohlin-Samuelson model, henceforth HOS model.[64]

The other model, due to Kemp-Ohyama, is of more recent vintage[65] and I shall refer to it as the KO model. The KO model is also a production model with two outputs and two non-produced inputs, only one of which is intersectorally mobile, but a model in which one of the outputs is also used as an input in the production of the other. Furthermore, in contrast to the RV and the HOS models, the price of the produced input is endogenously determined. The KO model is well-suited to highlighting trade between a capital-poor, resource-rich country with another sharing opposite characteristics. As such, it departs in an essential way from the assumption of symmetry between trading partners.

Both models have seen extensions and varied application in recent years. However, the relevant observation in our context is that Darity's (1982) work on the Atlantic slave trade can be seen as a synthesis of these two canonical models.[66] I turn to this.

In the notation of Section 2, the production structure of Darity's model is given by

$$X_g = F_g(K_g, L_g, X_r), \tag{16}$$

$$X_r = F_r(K_r, S), \tag{17}$$

$$X_a = F_a(Z, L_a), \tag{18}$$

$$K_g + K_r = \mathcal{K}, \tag{19}$$

$$L_a + S = \mathcal{L}, \tag{20}$$

where X_a is "food" produced in Africa with African labor L_a and there is perfect competition in all factor markets. Note that the subsystem consisting of African food and Caribbean sugar constitutes the RV model where K_r and Z are the sector-specific fixed factors and African labor is the intersectorally mobile factor. On the

[61]It seems to be fitting to remark here that Bergstrom was Rader's colleague when his work on slavery was done.

[62]See Jones (1971), Samuelson (1971) and Caves-Jones (1981; Chapter 4), for example, for a textbook treatment.

[63]This also goes under the guise of the factor price equalization theorem, as in Rader (1978). It is simply the result that the factor-prices are independent of factor endowments, a result as non-neoclassical in spirit as you can get.

[64]See, for example, Caves-Jones (1981; Chapter 5). Chipman, in his entry in *The New Palgrave* prefers the label Harberler-Lerner-Samuelson model.

[65]See Kemp-Ohyama (1978) and Findlay (1979, 1984).

[66]Darity is well aware of the relationship of his work to the RV model but does not mention the KO model.

other hand, the subsystem consisting of British manufactures and Caribbean sugar constitutes the KO model.

The fundamental difference between Darity's model and the one presented in this paper seems to be the treatment of African migration to the Caribbean. In particular, the equilibrating condition for this migration is the equalization of African and Caribbean wages and a disregard of a slave as a produced capital input.[67] On the other hand, Darity does not assume that any price is exogenously given, and in particular, determines the value of p_r in equilibrium.[68]

In terms of results, Darity's primary emphasis is to test the central propositions of the Caribbean School,[69] which in terms of my notation, amounts to an investigation of the effect of changes in $\mathcal{K}$ on African and British incomes. However, what is most interesting about Darity's work is that it can be seen as a precursor of recent extensions of the KO model. Thus Darity's production structure, and more generally the model,[70] is *identical* to Khan (1984), and a direct generalization of the work of Jones-Dei (1983) who do not assume that the output of the Caribbean sector is an input in British manufacturing, i.e., they omit the variable X_r from (16). The primary emphasis of the work of both Khan and Jones-Dei, in keeping with Kemp-Ohyama-Findlay, is on commercial policy.

Once I connect Darity's work to the research on international trade with asymmetric production structures, I can turn the matter around, and attempt to view the latter in terms of the modelling perspective of the Atlantic triangular trade. In the context of Darity's system (16) to (20), the work of Chaudhuri-Khan (1984), Young (1986) and Chaudhuri-Khan-Tang (1987) can then be seen as attempts to disaggregate the Caribbean sector and allow the production of X_g there, with or without the mobility of machinery. Chaudhuri-Khan (1986) stay within the same set-up but suppress the African food sector. All of this work follows Arthur Lewis and assumes labor is surplus at an exogenously given wage. In my context here, this assumption can simply be seen as an perfectly elastic supply of slave labor at either an exogenously given sustenance cost or one rationalized in terms of the $\lambda(\cdot)$ function. At any rate, from a substantive point of view, it is interesting to see work on the slave trade being tied into that on North-South trade. The problem, however, with all of this literature as contributing to our understanding of the slave trade is its fundamental disregard of a slave as a capital input.[71]

The first theoretical work to face up to this fact is, to my knowledge, that of Ron Findlay. In Findlay (1975) he presents a rigorous formulation of the idea but his primary emphasis is on issues relating to manumission. We have to wait for his

[67] Darity introduces some externality variables in his cost functions but disregards them in his simulations.

[68] In my view, this has led, in the words of Findlay (1989; p.6), to "some unwieldiness in the resulting formulas and solutions and difficulty in grasping the reasons for some of the results of numerical simulations."

[69] These are identified as the writings of Eric Williams, Walter Rodney and C. L. R. James. The extent to which Arthur Lewis can be seen as belonging to this School is to me a fascinating question with which I shall not burden the reader.

[70] Darity's specification of consumer demand is more detailed. I leave it for future work to see whether this constitutes an essential difference.

[71] This seems to me the basic message of Gemery-Hogendorn (1974) and, of course, as noted above, of Conrad-Meyer (1958). The idea was clearly in the air for many years before.

Frank Graham Lecture for an integration into a general equilibrium setting.[72] The simpler version of Findlay's model, in terms of the notation of my work, can be presented as

$$X_g = Min[F_g(K_g, L_g), X_r/\alpha], \quad \alpha > 0, \tag{21}$$

$$X_r = F_r(S), \tag{22}$$

$$I(p_s) = \phi S, \quad I'(\cdot) > 0, \quad \phi > 0, \tag{23}$$

$$(i + \phi)p_s = p_r F_r'(S), \tag{24}$$

$$(1 - \alpha p_r)F_g^1 = i, \tag{25}$$

where $I(\cdot)$ is an exogenously given supply function of slaves. Note the resemblance of (23) and (24) to the relevant part of condition (iv) of Definition 1 and to the equilibrium condition spelt out in (29) below.

The locations Findlay has in mind are Africa, Europe and America and the commodities he mentions are manufactures, raw materials and slaves.[73] Thus, he focusses more sharply on the British manufacturer rather than on questions of African supply and transport.[74] Unlike the model of this paper, he has X_r entering as an input into X_g and p_r is an unknown. Moreover, as remarked earlier, Findlay assumes, in my terminology, that, ρ and i are identical. The relationship of these slavery models to intertemporal models of international trade,[75] and more generally to Wicksellian capital theory must await another occasion.

Findlay conducts four comparative static investigations. An increase in L_g and changes in technical progress in F_g and F_r and in the supply function $I(\cdot)$. Moreover, in his second model, he disaggregates British manufacturing by adding another sector, that producing a non-tradeable using land and labor.

A final observation for this subsection. The KO model emphasizes intersectoral mobility of a non-produced input and the use of one output as an input in the production of the other. Even though the second aspect may appear to be absent in my model, a simple rewriting of

$$I = X_s = F_s(L, M) = F_s(F_\ell(G, Z), M) = F_s(F_\ell(F_g(K_g, L_g), Z)), M) \tag{26}$$

shows it to be also a driving force of the model presented here. The RV model, on the other hand, is evident in the side of the triangle connecting Britain to the Caribbean.

5 Necessary Conditions for Optimization

Before I can attempt a comparative static analysis of the equilibrium, I have to supplement Definition 1 of the equilibrium by the necessary conditions for optimality of each of the four representative agents of the model. I turn to this.

---

[72]See Findlay (1989).

[73]See Figure 1 in Findlay (1989) for a schematic overview.

[74]However, he leaves "for a future occasion the pursuit of this fascinating link between the formation of predatory states through the import of firearms."

[75]See, for example, Samuelson (1975) and Findlay (1978).

5.1 Necessary Conditions for Optimization: The Planter's Case

The Euler-Lagrange conditions for the optimization problem laid out in (5) and (6) can be written as follows.[76]

$$p_r F_r^1(K_r, \lambda(w)S, T) = \rho, \tag{27}$$

$$p_r F_r^3(K_r, \lambda(w)S, T) = \tau, \tag{28}$$

$$p_r F_r^2(K_r, \lambda(w)S, T)\lambda(w) = w + p_s(i + \phi(\mu, w, \Gamma(w))), \tag{29}$$

$$p_r F_r^2(K_r, \lambda(w)S, T)\lambda'(w) = \left(1 + p_s[\phi^2 + \phi^3\Gamma'(w)]\right), \tag{30}$$

The first two equations are routine: the plantation rents machines and land so as to equate the marginal revenue product of each factor to its marginal cost. (29) departs from this only to the extent that the marginal revenue product has to be reckoned in terms of efficiency units,[77] and emphasizes that the marginal cost of an additional slave must equal the cost of his subsistence w, plus the foregone interest payment on the money spent to acquire him, plus the cost of his depreciation. Finally, (30) requires that the equilibrium wage must be such that, at the margin, the benefits from increasing the wage equal the cost, correctly measured.[78]

Given the importance of these variables for what follows, some additional notation is warranted. Let the marginal cost of maintaining a slave be denoted by $c(w; p_s, i)$ where

$$c(w; p_s, i) = w + p_s(i + \phi(\mu, w, \Gamma(w))), \tag{31}$$

$$\gamma_w = \frac{w}{w + p_s(i + \phi)}, \quad \gamma_i = \frac{ip_s}{w + p_s(i + \phi)}, \quad \gamma_d = \frac{p_s\phi}{w + p_s(i + \phi)}. \tag{32}$$

I shall also need to consider the elasticity of marginal cost with respect to w and shall denote this by ϵ_{mc}, where

$$\epsilon_{mc} = \frac{w}{c}\frac{\partial c(w; p_s, i)}{\partial w} = \frac{w}{c}\left(1 + p_s[\phi^2 + \phi^3\Gamma'(w)]\right). \tag{33}$$

I can now compose (29) and (30) to obtain

$$\lambda'(w) = \epsilon_{mc}\frac{\lambda(w)}{w}. \tag{34}$$

This is a particularly interesting equation in light of previous work. Go back to (5) and (6) and suppose a regime of wage labor, with S now representing the number of

[76] See, for example, Gelfand-Fomin (1963). Also compare with the relevant equations in Lucas (1967). Note that one also needs to include the transversality condition $lim_{t\to\infty} e^{-it}S(t) = 0$. Since I assume that the initial stock of slaves is the steady state stock, I am justified in assuming that this condition is automatically fulfilled.

[77] Which is to say that $p_r F_r^2$ has to be multiplied by $\lambda(\cdot)$.

[78] Note that under constant returns to scale in the production of sugar, only the ratios $K_r/\lambda(w)S$, $T/\lambda(w)S$ can be determined; and hence (29) should be seen as a market equilibrium condition determining τ and with the supply of land T determining the scale.

laborers hired by the plantation owner. On equating I to zero in (5) and on ignoring (6), I obtain from the necessary conditions for optimality yield that

$$\lambda'(w) = \frac{\lambda(w)}{w}. \tag{35}$$

The value of w satisfying this equation is termed the *efficiency wage* in the development literature[79] and denoted by w_e in Figure 1b. The point to be noted in my context is that a negative value of ϵ_{mc} precludes the existence of a solution to (34). Thus let me assume that

$$\epsilon_{mc} > 0 \Longleftrightarrow \left(1 + p_s[\phi^2 + \phi^3\Gamma'(w)]\right) > 0. \tag{36}$$

However, in this case,

$$\epsilon_{mc} - 1 = \frac{w\,(1 + p_s[\phi^2 + \phi^3\Gamma'(w)])}{w + p_s(i + \phi(\mu, w, \Gamma(w)))} - 1 = -\frac{p_s(i + (\phi - w[\phi^2 + \phi^3\Gamma'(w)])}{w + p_s(i + \phi(\mu, w, \Gamma(w)))} < 0. \tag{37}$$

I can now state

Proposition 1 *Under the assumption that the elasticity of marginal cost ϵ_{mc} is positive, a planter furnishes sustenance to his slaves in an amount higher than the efficiency wage; this differential depends on the rate of interest, on the price of the slave, on the rate of depreciation of the slave stock and on the rate of change of this rate of depreciation with respect to w.*

If the rate of depreciation is a constant, which is to say that it depends only on μ, then $\epsilon_{mc} = w/c$, and (34) can be rewritten as

$$\lambda'(w) = \left(\frac{w}{c(w; p_s, i)}\right)\left(\frac{\lambda(w)}{w}\right). \tag{38}$$

If i and ϕ are zero,[80] then $w = c(w; p_s, i)$ and the planter would furnish his slaves the efficiency wage.

It should be emphasized, particularly because of some past confusion on this topic, that Proposition 1 in no way implies that "free labor would therefore volunteer for slavery!" For a comparison between the two regimes, a general equilibrium solution would have to take other factors, particularly the amount of land, explicitly into account.

5.2 Slave Price and Slave Sustenance

Next, still remaining with the planter's partial equilibrium problem, I consider the effect on w of a change in p_s, all other parameters remaining constant. Observe that once p_s is given, w can be determined from (34) and that this equation can be rewritten in the form

$$\frac{\lambda'(w)}{\lambda(w)} = \frac{1 + p_s[\phi^2 + \phi^3\Gamma'(w)]}{w + p_s(i + \phi(\mu, w, \Gamma(w)))}. \tag{39}$$

[79]See, in particular, Mirrlees (1975), Stiglitz (1976) and Bliss-Stern (1978).

[80]ϕ equal to zero implies that the stock of slaves is self-sustaining.

On totally differentiating (19) and on using Jones' hat calculus,[81] I obtain

$$\xi\widehat{w} = (\epsilon_{\lambda'} - \epsilon_{\lambda} + \epsilon_{mc} - \epsilon_{\Delta mc})\widehat{w} = \zeta\widehat{p}_s - \gamma_i\widehat{i}, \tag{40}$$

where ϵ_{mc} and $\epsilon_{\lambda'}$ are the elasticities of $\lambda(w)$ and $(\lambda'(w))$ respectively; $\epsilon_{\Delta mc}$ the elasticity of the marginal change in marginal cost with respect to the wage, i.e.,

$$\epsilon_{\Delta mc} = \frac{w}{c^1(w;p_s,i)}\frac{\partial^2 c(w;p_s,i)}{\partial^2 w} = \frac{p_s w(\phi^{22} + 2\Gamma'(w)\phi^{23} + \Gamma''(w)\phi^3 + \phi^{33}(\Gamma'(w))^2)}{1 + p_s[\phi^2 + \phi^3\Gamma'(w)]}; \tag{41}$$

$$\begin{aligned}\zeta &= p_s[\phi^2 + \phi^3\Gamma'(w)]/c^1(w;p_s,i) - p_s(i+\phi)/c(w;p_s,i),\\ &= \frac{p_s}{c(w;p_s,i)}\left(\frac{w}{\epsilon_{mc}}[\phi^2 + \phi^3\Gamma'(w)] - (i + \phi(\mu, w, \Gamma(w))\right) < 0.\end{aligned} \tag{42}$$

I can now present

Proposition 2 *Under the assumption that the elasticity of marginal cost ϵ_{mc} is positive, an increase in the price of a slave increases the sustenance that a planter furnishes to him if and only if*

$$\xi = (\epsilon_{\lambda'} - \epsilon_{\lambda} + \epsilon_{mc} - \epsilon_{\Delta mc}) < 0.$$

If the depreciation rate is independent of w, then $\xi < 0$.

5.3 Necessary Conditions for Optimization for the Other Agents

I begin with the necessary conditions for the British manufacturer obtained from (9) and condition (ix) of Definition 1.

$$p_g F_g^1(K_g, \mathcal{L}) = \rho \text{ and } p_g F_g^2(K_g, \mathcal{L}) = w_g. \tag{43}$$

The necessary condition for the African supplier, obtained from (15), is simply

$$p_\ell F_\ell^1(X_g, Z) = p_g. \tag{44}$$

All that remains is the transporter. As brought out in my discussion above, I assume, under the competitive hypothesis, that $\partial p_s/\partial L$ and $\partial p_s/\partial M$ in (12) and (13) are both equal to zero.

6 The Mechanics of the Model

Definition 1 of the equilibrium is well-suited towards giving an overview of the model, but it is somewhat pedantic when one moves on to the analysis of the equilibrium. In particular, even when supplemented by the necessary conditions of the previous

[81] As students of international trade are particularly aware, this simply means that the analysis is conducted in terms of proportional changes, i.e, in terms of $\hat{x} \equiv dx/x$ rather than in terms of dx. See, for example, Caves-Jones (1981).

section, it does not clearly bring out the important observation that the twenty equation, twenty unknowns system decomposes into three subsystems linked by p_s and p_g, the endogenous prices of a slave and of armaments. In this section, I draw out the implications of this observation and lay out the basic logic underlying the comparative static results. However, before I get to the algebra, it is worth stating that the first subsystem assumes the constancy of both p_s and p_g, the second only that of p_g, and the third determines p_g.

6.1 Subsystem I

Ignore, for the moment, the complete specification of the equilibrium, and observe that once p_s and p_g are given, w, K_r, K_g and S can all be determined. The relationship between w and p_s has already been discussed in Proposition 2. Since the stock of machinery is divided between Britain and the Caribbean (condition (x) of Definition 1), since the stocks of British labor and Caribbean land are given (conditions (ix) of Definition 1), and since perfect markets prevail, I obtain from (43) and (27) that,

$$p_g F_g^1(K_g, \mathcal{L}) = p_g F_g^1(\mathcal{K} - K_r, \mathcal{L}) = \rho = p_r F_r^1(K_r, \lambda(w)S, \mathcal{T}). \tag{45}$$

This, coupled with (29), gives us two equations in the remaining two unknowns, K_r and S. On including (40), I obtain our first subsystem of three equations in three unknowns. Total differentiation leads me to

$$\begin{bmatrix} \eta_r^1 + (\kappa_r/\kappa_g)\eta_g^1 & \sigma_r^{12} & \sigma_r^{12}\epsilon_\lambda \\ \sigma_r^{21} & \eta_r^2 & \epsilon_\lambda(1+\eta_r^2) - \epsilon_{mc} \\ 0 & 0 & \xi \end{bmatrix} \begin{bmatrix} \widehat{K}_r \\ \widehat{S} \\ \widehat{w} \end{bmatrix} = \begin{bmatrix} \widehat{p}_g - \widehat{p}_r + (\eta_g^1/\kappa_g)\widehat{\mathcal{K}} + \sigma_g^{12}\widehat{\mathcal{L}} - \sigma_r^{13}\widehat{\mathcal{T}} \\ (\gamma_i + \gamma_d)\widehat{p}_s + \gamma_i\widehat{i} - \widehat{p}_r \\ \zeta\widehat{p}_s - \gamma_i\widehat{i} \end{bmatrix} \tag{46}$$

where η_k^m is the elasticity of demand for factor m in sector k; σ_k^{mn} is the elasticity of demand for factor m in terms of the price of factor n in sector k; and all other variables have been defined before.

The first point to be noticed is that the determinant D of the 3×3 matrix in (46) is given by

$$D = \xi[\eta_r^2(\eta_r^1 + (\kappa_r/\kappa_g)\eta_g^1) - (\sigma_r^{12}\sigma_r^{21})]. \tag{47}$$

Since F_r and F_g are assumed to be concave, I obtain

Lemma 1 *$D < 0$ if and only if $\xi < 0$.*

Next, I turn to the effect of a change in p_s on the level of the slave stock S.

$$\frac{\widehat{S}}{\widehat{p}_s} = (1/D) \begin{bmatrix} \eta_r^1 + (\kappa_r/\kappa_g)\eta_g^1 & 0 & \sigma_r^{12}\epsilon_\lambda \\ \sigma_r^{21} & (\gamma_i + \gamma_d) & \epsilon_\lambda(1+\eta_r^2) - \epsilon_{mc} \\ 0 & \zeta & \xi \end{bmatrix} \tag{48}$$

$$\begin{aligned} &= (1/D)[\sigma_r^{12}\sigma_r^{21}\zeta\epsilon_\lambda + (\eta_r^1 + (\kappa_r/\kappa_g)\eta_g^1)\{\xi(\gamma_i+\gamma_d) - \zeta(\epsilon_\lambda(1+\eta_r^2) - \epsilon_{mc})\}] \\ &= (1/D)[\zeta\epsilon_\lambda\{\sigma_r^{12}\sigma_r^{21} - \eta_r^2(\eta_r^1 + (\kappa_r/\kappa_g)\eta_g^1)\} \\ &+ (\eta_r^1 + (\kappa_r/\kappa_g)\eta_g^1)\{\xi(\gamma_i+\gamma_d) - \zeta(\epsilon_\lambda - \epsilon_{mc})\}] \end{aligned} \tag{49}$$

Lemma 2 *If $\xi < 0$ and $\epsilon_{mc} > \epsilon_\lambda$, then $\widehat{S}/\widehat{p}_s < 0$.*

Finally, I turn to the effect of changes in p_s on the effect of the amount of machinery invested in the Caribbean.

$$\frac{\widehat{K}_r}{\widehat{p}_s} = (1/D)\begin{bmatrix} 0 & \sigma_r^{12} & \sigma_r^{12}\epsilon_\lambda \\ \gamma_i + \gamma_d & \eta_r^2 & \epsilon_\lambda(1+\eta_r^2) - \epsilon_{mc} \\ \zeta & 0 & \xi \end{bmatrix} \tag{50}$$

$$= -(1/D)\sigma_r^{12}[\xi(\gamma_i + \gamma_d) - \zeta(\epsilon_\lambda - \epsilon_{mc})] \tag{51}$$

Lemma 3 *Under the hypotheses of Lemma 2, $\widehat{K}_r/\widehat{p}_s > 0$ if and only if $\sigma_r^{12} < 0$.*

I shall conclude this subsection by emphasizing that p_s is an endogenous variable in the model and hence (48) and (50) very much represent an intermediate partial equilibrium stage in the analysis even when p_g is taken to be a constant.

6.2 Subsystem II

Given my competitive assumption, I can rewrite the necessary conditions for the transporters problem more compactly in terms of the unit cost function. This gives me my second subsystem

$$p_s = C_s(p_\ell, p_m), \tag{52}$$

$$p_g = p_\ell F_\ell^1(F_g(K_g, \mathcal{L}), Z). \tag{53}$$

On total differentiation, I obtain

$$\begin{bmatrix} 1 & -\theta_{sL} \\ \eta_\ell^1\theta_{gK}(\widehat{K}_g/\widehat{p}_s) & 1 \end{bmatrix}\begin{bmatrix} \widehat{p}_s \\ \widehat{p}_\ell \end{bmatrix} = \begin{bmatrix} \theta_{sm}\widehat{p}_m \\ \widehat{p}_g - \eta_\ell^1\theta_{gL}\widehat{\mathcal{L}} - \eta_\ell^1\theta_{gK}(\widehat{K}_g/\widehat{\tau})\widehat{\tau} \end{bmatrix}, \tag{54}$$

where θ_{ij} is the share of factor j in the value of output i, τ stands for any of the indices $p_g, p_r, \mathcal{K}, \mathcal{L}, \mathcal{T}$ and i, and where the determinant of the 2×2 matrix above is denoted by

$$\Lambda \equiv 1 + \theta_{sL}\theta_{gK}\eta_g^1\frac{\widehat{K}_g}{\widehat{p}_s} = 1 - \theta_{sL}\theta_{gK}\eta_g^1\frac{\kappa_r}{\kappa_g}\frac{\widehat{K}_r}{\widehat{p}_s}. \tag{55}$$

Lemma 4 *If $\widehat{K}_r/\widehat{p}_s > 0$, $\Lambda > 0$. Thus, under the hypotheses of Lemma 2, $\Lambda > 0$ if $\sigma_r^{12} < 0$.*

6.3 Subsystem III

I now get to the final stage of the analysis in which the endogenous price of armaments p_g is determined. Note that I have not used so far the equality of G and X_g given by condition (vii) of Definition 1. On using this, I can rewrite (53) as

$$p_g = p_\ell F_\ell^1(G, Z) \equiv \psi(p_g), \tag{56}$$

which relies on the fact that G and p_ℓ have been determined as functions of p_g from the first two subsystems.

7 Partial Equilibrium Results

In this section, I shall focus on the case[82] where there is complete rigidity in the price of armaments p_g. I can thus completely neglect Subsystem III.

I shall now assume the following

Standing Hypothesis: $\xi < 0$, $\sigma_r^{12} < 0$ and $\epsilon_{mc} > \epsilon_\lambda$.

Recall from Proposition 2 the implication of the first part of our standing hypothesis for the response of the slave sustenance levels to changes in the slave prices. The second part of the hypothesis requires that the marginal product of slave labor to decrease with an increase in machinery.

7.1 An Increase in the Price of Maritime Inputs

My first set of comparative static investigations center on the effect of changes in p_m. From (54), I obtain

$$\frac{\widehat{p}_s}{\widehat{p}_m} = \frac{\theta_{sm}}{\Lambda} \tag{57}$$

Once I have (57), I can turn to the effect on supply, i.e., the effect of an increase in p_m on X_r, X_g, X_ℓ and on $X_s = \phi S$.

I begin with the effect on the output of guns, X_g.

$$\widehat{X}_g = \theta_{gK}\widehat{K}_g + \theta_{gL}\widehat{L}_g = \theta_{gK}\widehat{K}_g + \theta_{gL}\widehat{\mathcal{L}}. \tag{58}$$

Since L_g is not being changed, I can write

$$\begin{aligned}\frac{\widehat{X}_g}{\widehat{p}_m} &= \theta_{gK}\frac{\widehat{K}_g}{\widehat{p}_m} = \theta_{gK}\frac{\widehat{K}_g}{\widehat{p}_s}\frac{\widehat{p}_s}{\widehat{p}_m}, \\ &= \theta_{gK}\frac{\kappa_r}{\kappa_g}\frac{\theta_{sm}}{\Lambda D}\sigma_r^{12}[\xi(\gamma_i + \gamma_d) - \zeta(\epsilon_\lambda - \epsilon_{mc})].\end{aligned} \tag{59}$$

The effect on the supply of African labor is given by

$$\frac{\widehat{X}_\ell}{\widehat{p}_m} = \frac{\widehat{L}}{\widehat{p}_m} = \theta_{\ell g}\frac{\widehat{X}_g}{\widehat{p}_m}. \tag{60}$$

Once I have the effect on the equilibrium stock of slaves,

$$\frac{\widehat{S}}{\widehat{p}_m} = \frac{\widehat{S}}{\widehat{p}_s}\frac{\widehat{p}_s}{\widehat{p}_m}, \tag{61}$$

I can present

[82] If the reader balks on thinking of these as results, nothing is changed if they are thought of as intermediate steps in the analysis.

Proposition 3 *Under the Standing Hypothesis, an increase in maritime costs leads to an increase in the price of slaves as well as in the sustenance levels of the slaves. Furthermore, it leads to a decrease in the supply of armaments, the supply of African labor and in the stock of slaves. The effect on the supply of sugar is ambiguous with the decrease in the stock of slaves being counteracted both by an increase in slave productivity and by an increase in the amount of machinery invested in the Caribbean.*

The validity of the last part of the proposition can be seen easily once we recall that w does not depend on p_m. This yields

$$\frac{\widehat{w}}{\widehat{p}_m} = \frac{\widehat{w}}{\widehat{p}_s}\frac{\widehat{p}_s}{\widehat{p}_m} = \frac{\zeta}{\xi}\frac{\theta_{sm}}{\Lambda}. \tag{62}$$

I can now turn to the effects on the supply of sugar.

$$\frac{\widehat{X}_r}{\widehat{p}_m} = \theta_{rK}\frac{\widehat{K}_r}{\widehat{p}_m} + \theta_{\lambda S}\left(\frac{\widehat{S}}{\widehat{p}_s}\frac{\widehat{p}_s}{\widehat{p}_m} + \epsilon_\lambda\frac{\widehat{w}}{\widehat{p}_s}\frac{\widehat{p}_s}{\widehat{p}_m}\right). \tag{63}$$

Next, I consider the effect on factor returns ρ, τ and p_ℓ. From (27), (28) and (54), I obtain

$$\frac{\hat{\rho}}{\widehat{p}_m} = \eta_g^1\frac{\widehat{K}_g}{\widehat{p}_m}, \tag{64}$$

$$\frac{\hat{\tau}}{\widehat{p}_m} = \sigma_r^{31}\frac{\widehat{K}_r}{\widehat{p}_m} + \sigma_r^{32}\left(\epsilon_\lambda\frac{\widehat{w}}{\widehat{p}_m} + \frac{\widehat{S}}{\widehat{p}_m}\right), \tag{65}$$

$$\frac{\widehat{p}_\ell}{\widehat{p}_m} = (1/\Lambda)\begin{bmatrix} 1 & \theta_{sm} \\ \eta_\ell^1\theta_{gK}(\widehat{K}_g/\widehat{p}_s) & 0 \end{bmatrix} = -(1/\Lambda)\eta_\ell^1\theta_{sm}\theta_{gK}\frac{\widehat{K}_g}{\widehat{p}_s}. \tag{66}$$

Proposition 4 *Under the Standing Hypothesis, an increase in maritime costs leads to an increase in the return to machinery and to a decrease in the price of African labor. The effect on the rental to Caribbean land is ambiguous with the change in the stock of slaves being counteracted both by an increase in slave productivity and by an increase in the amount of machinery invested in the Caribbean.*

All that remains is to highlight the effect on $y \equiv (p_s/p_\ell)$.

$$\widehat{y} = \theta_{sm}\widehat{p}_m - (1-\theta_{s\ell})\widehat{p}_\ell \Longleftrightarrow \widehat{y}/\widehat{p}_m = \theta_{sm} - (1-\theta_{s\ell})(\widehat{p}_\ell/\widehat{p}_m). \tag{67}$$

Proposition 5 *Under the Standing Hypothesis, an increase in maritime costs leads to an increase in the differential between the price of slaves and the price of African labor.*

7.2 An Increase in the Price of Armaments

Next, I turn to my second set of comparative static investigations. The basic technical complication here is due to the fact that a change in the price of armaments, p_g, on a particular unknown has two effects: a direct effect operating through (46) and subsystem I, and an indirect effect through the change in p_s, and hence from

(54) and subsystem II. This direct effect did not operate in the comparative static exercises presented in Section 7.1.

I first obtain from (46),

$$\left(\frac{\widehat{K}_g}{\widehat{p}_g}\right)_{p_s \text{ constant}} = \frac{\xi\eta_r^2}{D} = \frac{\eta_r^2}{\eta_r^2(\eta_r^1 + (\kappa_r/\kappa_g)\eta_g^1) - (\sigma_r^{12}\sigma_r^{21})}. \tag{68}$$

I now note that

$$\frac{\widehat{p}_s}{\widehat{p}_g} = (1/\Lambda)\begin{bmatrix} 0 & -\theta_{sL} \\ \nu & 1 \end{bmatrix} = \frac{\nu\theta_{sL}}{\Lambda}, \tag{69}$$

$$\nu \equiv 1 - \frac{\eta_r^2\eta_\ell^1\theta_{gK}}{\eta_r^2(\eta_r^1 + (\kappa_r/\kappa_g)\eta_g^1) - (\sigma_r^{12}\sigma_r^{21})}. \tag{70}$$

and begin with the effect on the output of guns, X_g. Since $\widehat{X}_g = \theta_{gK}\widehat{K}_g + \theta_{gL}\widehat{\mathcal{L}}$, I can write

$$\frac{\widehat{X}_g}{\widehat{p}_g} = \theta_{gK}\frac{\widehat{K}_g}{\widehat{p}_g} = \theta_{gK}\left[\frac{\widehat{K}_g}{\widehat{p}_s}\frac{\widehat{p}_s}{\widehat{p}_g} + \left(\frac{\widehat{K}_g}{\widehat{p}_g}\right)_{p_s \text{ constant}}\right]. \tag{71}$$

The effect on the supply of African labor is straightforward and given by

$$\frac{\widehat{X}_\ell}{\widehat{p}_g} = \frac{\widehat{L}}{\widehat{p}_g} = \theta_{\ell g}\frac{\widehat{X}_g}{\widehat{p}_g}, \tag{72}$$

whereas the effect on the equilibrium stock of slaves is

$$\frac{\widehat{S}}{\widehat{p}_g} = \left(\frac{\widehat{S}}{\widehat{p}_g}\right)_{p_s \text{ constant}} + \frac{\widehat{S}}{\widehat{p}_s}\frac{\widehat{p}_s}{\widehat{p}_g} = -\frac{\xi\sigma_r^{21}}{D} + \frac{\nu\theta_{sL}}{\Lambda}\frac{\widehat{S}}{\widehat{p}_s}. \tag{73}$$

Finally, recall that w does not depend on p_g directly but only indirectly through p_s. I thus obtain

$$\frac{\widehat{w}}{\widehat{p}_g} = \frac{\widehat{w}}{\widehat{p}_s}\frac{\widehat{p}_s}{\widehat{p}_g} = \frac{\zeta}{\xi}\frac{\theta_{sL}}{\Lambda}. \tag{74}$$

Once I have the effect on the supply of sugar,

$$\frac{\widehat{X}_r}{\widehat{p}_g} = \theta_{rK}\frac{\widehat{K}_r}{\widehat{p}_g} + \theta_{\lambda S}\left(\frac{\widehat{S}}{\widehat{p}_g} + \epsilon_\lambda\frac{\widehat{w}}{\widehat{p}_g}\right), \tag{75}$$

I can present

Proposition 6 *Under the Standing Hypothesis, an increase in the price of armaments leads to an increase in the price of slaves as well as in the sustenance levels of the slaves if and only if $\nu > 0$. In this case, it leads to a decrease in the supply of armaments and in the supply of African labor. The effect on the stock of slaves and on the supply of sugar is ambiguous, with the ambiguity in the former contributing to that in the latter.*

All that remains is to consider the effect on factor returns ρ, τ and p_ℓ. From (27), (28) and (54), I obtain

$$\frac{\hat{\rho}}{\widehat{p}_g} = \eta_g^1 \frac{\widehat{K}_g}{\widehat{p}_g} \tag{76}$$

$$\frac{\hat{\tau}}{\widehat{p}_g} = \sigma_r^{31} \frac{\widehat{K}_r}{\widehat{p}_g} + \sigma_r^{32} \left(\epsilon_\lambda \frac{\widehat{w}}{\widehat{p}_g} + \frac{\widehat{S}}{\widehat{p}_g} \right) \tag{77}$$

$$\frac{\widehat{p}_\ell}{\widehat{p}_g} = (1/\Lambda) \begin{bmatrix} 1 & 0 \\ \eta_\ell^1 \theta_{gK}(\widehat{K}_g/\widehat{p}_s) & (1 - \eta_\ell^1 \theta_{gK}(\widehat{K}_g/\widehat{p}_g)) \end{bmatrix} = -(1/\Lambda)(1 - \eta_\ell^1 \theta_{gK}(\widehat{K}_g/\widehat{p}_g)) \tag{78}$$

Proposition 7 *Under the Standing Hypothesis, an increase in the price of armaments leads to an increase in the price of African labor if and only if $\nu > 0$. In this case, it leads to an increase in the return to machinery. The effect on the rental to Caribbean land is ambiguous with the effect of the change in the slave sustenance level counteracted by the ambiguity of the change in the slave stock.*

8 British Suppression Policies

The only set of complete general comparative static investigations I present relates to the period around 1808 when slavery was declared illegal by Britain. The definitive empirical results on the subject seem to be those of LeVeen.

> Our analysis presents evidence which demonstrates that the navy's influence forced the prices of newly imported slaves to Brazil and Cuba to rise as much as twice what they would have been without such interference. .. not only did the navy prevent some slave cargoes from reaching their destination, but also, through the combined effects of higher operating costs and greater risk of loss, the navy deterred some potential traders from entering the trade and caused some buyers to seek substitutes for slave labor, or to produce less sugar and coffee.[83]

I formulate[84] this question as the effect of an increase in the price of maritime inputs, namely p_m. Note that, unlike Section 7.1, I no longer assume the constancy of the price of armaments.

Consider (56) and in particular, the right hand side $\psi(\cdot)$ as a function of p_g. On differentiating this with respect to p_g, and on appealing to Propositions 6 and 7, we obtain

Lemma 5 *If $\nu > 0$, $\psi(\cdot)$ as a function of p_g is upward sloping.*

Given Lemma 5, we can represent (56) as in Figure 2. Now the remaining part of the analysis is clear. As p_m increases, it has a direct effect as studied in Propositions 3, 4 and 5, but it also has an indirect effect through changes in p_g and the consequent effects charted out in Propositions 6 and 7. I can now present the final result of the paper.

[83]See LeVeen (1975; pp. 52-54).

[84]Also see Findlay (1989) who views these policies as an export tax and a consequent shift in the supply function $I(\cdot)$.

Proposition 8 *Under the Standing Hypothesis and the conditions that*

$$\nu > 0 \text{ and } p_\ell F_\ell'' \frac{\partial G}{\partial p_m} > -F_\ell' \frac{\partial p_\ell}{\partial p_m},$$

British suppression policies lead to an increase in the price of armaments, an increase in the price of slaves as well as in the sustenance levels of the slaves.

In terms of basic intuition, an increase in the cost of maritime inputs restricts the supply of slaves thereby making them more expensive, and leading the plantation owners both to treat them better as well as to substitute for them by machinery from England. Given the constancy of British labor supply, this leads to a decrease in the output of guns and hence an increase in their price, p_g. How all of these forces work out depends on factor shares and the elasticities of substitutions involved and this is precisely captured in the assumptions of Proposition 8.

9 Concluding Remarks

I conclude the paper with two observations. First, the extent to which the model presented in this paper contributes to our understanding of the economics of the Atlantic slave trade depends on the variety of questions that it can be used to pose and answer, and in terms of its

> capacity [to be] deformed and transformed.[85]

This constitutes plans for my future work. Second, while pointing to my attempt at historical "justification" of the model in Section 3, I would like to remind the reader of Heisenberg's warning that

> one should be particularly circumspect in using phrases such as "in reality," which satisfy the imagination but are cognitively "empty" and operationally inconsequential.[86]

[85]Weber (1987; p. xi).
[86]Weber (1987; p. xii).

Figures

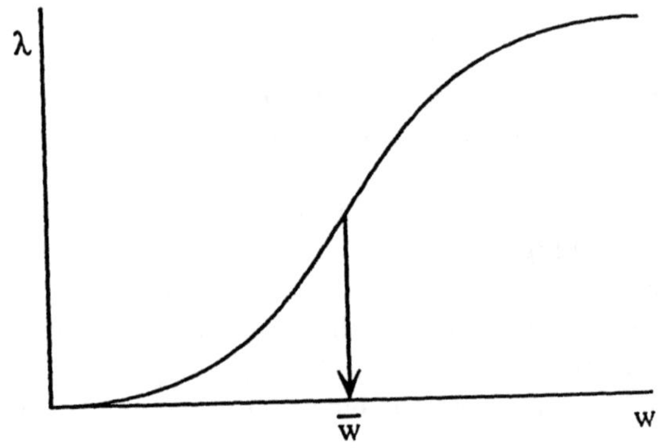

Figure 1.a

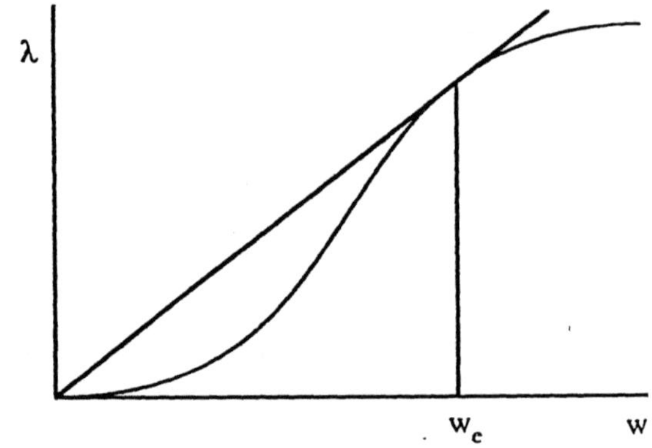

Figure 1.b

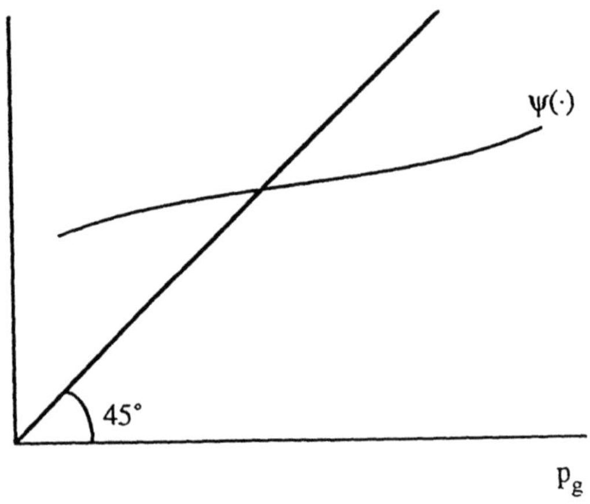

Figure 2

References

BERGSTROM, T. C. (1971): "On the existence and optimality of competitive equilibrium for a slave economy," *Review of Economic Studies* 38, 23-36.

BERGSTROM): "T. C., R. PARKS AND T. RADER (1976): "Preferences which have open graphs," *Journal of Mathematical Economics* 3, 265-268.

BLISS, C. J. AND N. H. STERN (1978): "Productivity, wages and nutrition," Parts 1 and 2, *Journal of Development Economics* 5, 331-398.

CAVES, R. E. AND R. W. JONES (1981): *World Trade and Payments,* Little Brown and Company, New York.

CHAUDHURI, T. DATTA AND M. ALI KHAN (1984): "Sector-specific capital, interconnectedness in production, and welfare," *Canadian Journal of Economics* 17, 489-507.

CHAUDHURI, T. DATTA AND M. ALI KHAN (1986): "Commercial policy in an asymmetric world economy," *Zeitschrift für Nationalökonomie* 46, 143-161.

CHAUDHURI, T. DATTA, M. ALI KHAN AND M. TANG (1987): "Technical progress and structural change," *Journal of Institutional and Theoretical Economics* 143, 310-323.

CONRAD, A. H. AND J. R. MEYER (1958): "The economics of slavery in the antebellum South," *Journal of Political Economy* 66, 95-130.

CONRAD, A. H. AND J. R. MEYER (1964): *The Economics of Slavery.* Aldine Publishing Co., Chicago.

CURTIN, P. D. (1969): *The Atlantic Slave Trade.* The University of Wisconsin Press, Wisconsin.

CURTIN, P. D. (1971a): " The Atlantic slave trade 1600-1800," in J. F. A. Ajayi and M. Crowder (eds.) *History of West Africa,* Volume 1. Columbia University Press, New York

CURTIN, P. D. (1971b): " The slave trade and the Atlantic basin: intercontinental perspectives," in N. I. Huggins, M. Kilson and D. M. Fox (eds.): *Key Issues in the Afro-American Experience.* Harcourt Brace Jovanovich, New York.

CURTIN, P. D. (1975): *Economic Change in Precolonial Africa.* The University of Wisconsin Press, Wisconsin.

CURTIN, P. D. (1990): *The Rise and Fall of the Plantation Complex.* Cambridge University Press, New York.

DAVID, P. A. AND P. TEMIN (1974): "Slavery: the progressive institution," *Journal of Economic History* 34, 739-783.

DARITY, W. A. (1982): "A general equilibrium model of the 18th century Atlantic slave trade," *Research In Economic History* 7, 287-326.

DEBREU, G. (1976): "Regular differentiable economies," *American Economic Review* 66, 280-287.

DEBREU, G. (1959): *Theory of Value.* John Wiley and Sons, New Haven.

ELTIS, D. AND L. C. JENNINGS (1988): "Trade between Western Africa and the Atlantic world in the pre-colonial era," *American History Review* 93, 936-959.

ENGERMAN, S. L. AND E. D. GENOVESE (EDS.) (1975): *Race and Slavery in the Western Hemisphere.* Princeton University Press, Princeton.

FERGUSON, C. E. (1968): "Inferior factors and the theories of production and input demand," *Economica* 138, 140-150.

FINDLAY, R. (1975): "Slavery, incentives and manumission," *Journal of Political Economy* 83, 923-933.

FINDLAY, R. (1978): "An "Austrian" model of international trade and interest rate equalization," *Journal of Political Economy* 86, 989-1007.

FINDLAY, R. (1979): "Economic development and the theory of international trade," *American Economic Review* 69, 186-190.

FINDLAY, R. (1984): "Growth and development in trade models," in P. B. Kenen and R. W. Jones (eds.) *Handbook of International Economics,* Volume 1. North Holland, Amsterdam.

FINDLAY, R. (1989): "The "triangular trade" and the Atlantic economy of the eighteenth century," Frank Graham Lecture, Discussion Paper No. 424, Columbia University.

GELFAND, I. M. AND S. V. FOMIN (1963): *Calculus of Variations.* Prentice-Hall, Englewood Cliffs.

GEMERY, H. A. AND J. S. HOGENDORN (1974): "The Atlantic slave trade: a tentative economic model," *Journal of African History* 15, 223-246.

GEMERY, H. A. AND J. S. HOGENDORN (1978): "Technological change, slavery and the slave trade," in C. Dewey and A. G. Hopkins (eds.), *The Imperial Impact: Studies in the Economic History of Africa and India.* The Athlone Press, London.

HECKSCHER, E. (1926): "A plea for theory in economic history," in F. C. Lane and J. C. Riemersma (eds.), *Enterprise and Secular Change.* Richard Irwin, Illinois (1953).

HOPKINS, A. G. (1978): "Imperial connections," in C. Dewey and A. G. Hopkins (eds.), *The Imperial Impact: Studies in the Economic History of Africa and India.* The Athlone Press, London.

INIKORI, J. E. (1977): "The import of firearms into West Africa 1750-1807: a quantitative analysis", *Journal of African History* 18, 339-368.

JONES, R. W. (1971): "A three factor model in theory, trade and history," in J. N. Bhagwati et al., *Trade, Balance of Payments and Growth.* North Holland, Amsterdam.

JONES, R. W. AND F. DEI (1983): "International trade and foreign investment: a simple model in theory," *Economic Enquiry* 21, 449-464.

KEMP, M. C. AND M. OHYAMA (1978): "On the sharing of trade gains by resource-poor and resource-rich countries," *Journal of International Economics* 10, 245-256.

KHAN, M. ALI (1984): "International trade and foreign investment: a model with asymmetric production," *Pakistan Development Review* 23, 510-530.

KHAN, M. ALI (1989a): "Lionel McKenzie on the existence of competitive equilibrium," Johns Hopkins Working Paper . Forthcoming in *General Equilibrium and Growth: The Legacy of Lionel McKenzie.* Academic Press, New York.

KHAN, M. ALI (1989b): "In praise of development economics," *Pakistan Development Review* 28, 337-378.

KOOPMANS, T.C. (1967): "Objectives, constraints and outcomes in optimal growth models," *Econometrica* 35, 1-15.

LEIBENSTEIN, H. (1957): *Economic Backwardness and Economic Growth.* John Wiley, New York.

LEVEEN, E. P. (1975): "A quantitative analysis of British suppression policies on the volume of the nineteenth century Atlantic slave trade," in S. L. Engerman and E. D. Genovese (eds.), 1975, *Race and Slavery in the Western Hemisphere.* Princeton University Press, Princeton.

LOVEJOY, P. E. AND J. S. HOGENDORN (1979): "Slave marketing in West Africa," in H. A. Gemery and J. S. Hogendorn (eds.) *The Uncommon Market: Essays in the Economic History of the Slave Trade.* Academic Press, New York.

LUCAS, R. J. (1967): "Optimal investment policy and the flexible accelerator," *International Economic Review* 8, 78-85.

MAS-COLELL, A. (1985): *The Theory of General Economic Equilibrium: A Differential Approach.* Cambridge University Press, New York.

MINCHINTON, W. E. (1979): "The triangular trade revisited," in H. A. Gemery and J. S. Hogendorn (eds.) *The Uncommon Market: Essays in the Economic History of the Slave Trade.* Academic Press, New York.

MINTZ, S. W. (1959): "Plantation systems of the new world," *Social Science Monograph* No. VII, Pan American Union, Washington D.C.

MINTZ, S. W. (1974): *Caribbean Transformations.* Columbia University Press, New York.

MINTZ, S. W. (1985): *Sweetness and Power.* Penguin Books, New York.

MIRRLEES, J. A. (1975): "A pure theory of underdeveloped economies," in L. G. Reynolds (ed.) *Agriculture in Development Theory.* Yale University Press, New Haven.

MYRDAL, G. (1968): *Asian Drama,* Volume III. Allen Lane, Middlesex.

PALMER, C. A. (1981): *Human Cargoes.* University of Illinois Press, Urbana.

RADER, T. (1963): "Existence of a utility function to represent preferences," *Review of Economic Studies* 30, 299-232.

RADER, T. (1964): "Edgeworth exchange and general economic equilibrium," *Yale Economic Essays* 4, 133-180.

RADER, T. (1968a): "Normally factor inputs are never gross substitutes," *Journal of Political Economy* 76, 38-43.

RADER, T. (1968b): "International trade and development in a small country," in J. Quirk and R. M. Saposnik (eds.) *Papers in Quantitative Economics,* Volume 1. The University Press of Kansas, Lawrence.

RADER, T. (1971a): *The Economics of Feudalism.* Gordon and Breach Science Publishers, New York.

RADER, T. (1971b): "International trade and development in a small country, II," in A. M. Zarley (ed.) *Papers in Quantitative Economics,* Volume 2. The University Press of Kansas, Lawrence.

RADER, T. (1972): "General equilibrium theory with complementary factors," *Journal of Economic Theory* 4, 372-380.

RADER, T. (1973a): "Nice demand functions," *Econometrica* 30, 913-926.

RADER, T. (1973b): "Absolutely constrained maximizers," *Journal of Optimization Theory and Applications* 12, 107-128.

RADER, T. (1978): "On factor price equalization," *Journal of Mathematical Economics* 5, 71-82.
RADER, T. (1982): "Growth in a many (non-Protestant ethic) consumer, many good economy leads to immiserization of all but one consumer,"" Washington University, mimeo.
SAMUELSON, P. A. (1971): "Ohlin was right," *Swedish Journal of Economics* 73, 365-384.
SAMUELSON, P. A. (1975): "Trade pattern reversals in time-phased Ricardian systems and intertemporal efficiency," *Journal of International Economics* 5, 309-363.
SHERIDAN, R. B. (1958): "The commercial and financial organization of the British slave trade," 1750-1807, *Economic History Review* 11, 249-263.
SHERIDAN, R. B. (1974): *Sugar and Slavery: An Economic History of the British West Indies 1623-1775.* Johns Hopkins University Press, Baltimore.
STIGLITZ, J. E. (1976): "The efficiency wage hypothesis, surplus labor and the distribution of income in LDCs," *Oxford Economic Papers* 28,
SUTCH, R. (1975): "The treatment received by American slaves: a critical review of the evidence" presented in *Time on the Cross. Explorations in Economic History* 12, 335-439.
TEMIN, P. (1971): "General equilibrium models in economic history," *Journal of Economic History* 31, 58-75.
TOMICH, D. W. (1990): *Slavery in the Circuit of Sugar.* Johns Hopkins University Press, Baltimore.
TOULMIN, S. (1977): "From form to function: philosophy and history of science in the 1950s and now," *Daedalus* 143-162.
WEBER, S. (1985): *Institution and Interpretation.* University of Minnesota Press, Minneapolis.
WHITE, H. (1978): *Tropics of Discourse: Essays in Cultural Criticism.* Johns Hopkins University Press, Baltimore.
WOLF, E. R. AND S. W. MINTZ (1957): "Haciendas and plantations in Middle America and the Antilles," *Institute of Social and Economic Research,* 6. 380-412.
WOODWARD, C. VANN (1989): *The Future of the Past.* Oxford University Press, Oxford.
YOUNG, L. (1986): "A note on 'sector-specific capital, interconnectedness in production, and welfare' ", *Canadian Journal of Economics* 19, 678-684.

On Aggregate Demand in a Measure Space of Agents*

ANDREU MAS-COLELL

Harvard University

Preface (1991): This paper first appeared in May 1973 as Working Paper IP-183 of the Center for Research in Management Science of the University of California - Berkeley. In spite of the high regard that this author had for it, it remained unpublished. It is on a topic very close to Trout Rader's interest and it belongs to a line of the literature which grew considerably after 1973 (see W. Trockel: *Market Demand: An Analysis of Large Economies with Non-convex Preferences*, 1989 *Lecture Notes in Economics and Mathematical Systems* 223, Springer-Verlag). It is dedicated to Trout Rader with much sympathy.

We are concerned in this paper with an instance in equilibrium theory of the general phenomenon of smoothing by aggregation.

It is known that without a convexity assumption on preferences the demand correspondence of a consumer will not, in general, be convex valued. However, if the economy is large, actually if there is a continuum of agents, one gets an aggregate demand correspondence which is convex valued (see R. Aumann (1964)). This is a consequence of Liapunov's theorem, and the fact that the correspondences being integrated (i.e., aggregated) are demand ones is immaterial; by integrating a correspondence with respect to an atomless measure one always obtains a convex set. Recently, G. Debreu (1972, p. 614) has suggested that, precisely because of the economic structure of the problem, one may expect, under reasonable regularity conditions, the aggregate demand to be a function. This is, indeed, very plausible; of course, not every economy (not even atomless) will have this property; the contention is, rather, that classes of economies having it are significant ones and can be distinguished in a natural manner.

We want to report here a result which gives support to this intuition. It is not a difficult one; its key features are the reduction of the problem to one dealing with finite-dimensional objects and the exploitation of smoothness hypothesis on preferences. Representing an economy by a measure over a space of agents' characteristics (see W. Hildenbrand (1970)) the result says, very roughly, that if the

***Research for this paper has been supported by the National Science Foundation under Grants GS-35890X and GS-3274. Without implicating him I want to express acknowledgement to Professor G. Debreu for valuable conversation on the topic discussed here.**

measure is supported by and evenly spread over the set of agents which preferences are representable by polynomial utility functions, then the economy generates a continuous demand function. Obviously, this does not go very far but at least it gives some flavor of the sort of the theorems one would like to have; we shall defer more detailed comments to the remarks after the precise statement (1) and to the final section (3).

As it is clear from the above paragraphs we are emphasizing an interpretation in terms of large economies. We want to remark, however, that the results given (especially the theorem in 2) could be interpreted as well in an uncertainty of preferences framework.[1]

1 Statement of the Proposition

For the following concepts and description of an economy see W. Hildenbrand (1970). The commodity space, as well as the price domain, will be $P = \{x \in \mathbb{R}^\ell : x \gg 0\}$.[2] The set of continuous, monotone preference relations on P is denoted by $\mathcal{R}$;[3] it is endowed with the topology of closed convergence of sets;[4] the space of preferences-endowments pairs is $\mathcal{E} = \mathcal{R} \times P$ (with the product topology). The demand correspondence[5] $h : \mathcal{E} \times P \to P$ is defined by $h(R, \omega, p) = \{x \in P : (x, y) \in R$ for every $y \in P$ such that $py \leq p\omega\}$. An economy will be described by a probability measure ν on $(\mathcal{E}, \mathcal{B}(\mathcal{E}))$[6] satisfying $\int_{\mathcal{E}} \omega(\cdot) d\nu < \infty$. Let $\mathcal{V}$ be the set of such measures endowed with the weak convergence topology. For every $\nu \in \mathcal{V}$ the aggregate demand correspondence h^ν: $P \to \mathbb{R}^\ell$ is given by $h^\nu(p) = \int_{\mathcal{E}} h(\cdot, p) d\nu$. It is well defined.

The set of polynomial functions f: $\mathbb{R}^\ell \to \mathbb{R}$ shall be denoted by $\mathcal{P}$ and endowed with the topology of uniform convergence on compact sets; $\mathcal{P}^* = \{f \in \mathcal{P}: Df(x) \gg 0$ for every $x \in \overline{P}\}$. Let $\Phi : \mathcal{P}^* \to \mathcal{R}$ assign to every $f \in \mathcal{P}^*$ the preference relation which it represents. One has (see 1.18, 1.19 in Mas-Colell (1972)):

(1) Φ *is continuous.*

Let $\mathcal{P}_n$ (resp. $\mathcal{P}_n^*$) be the subspace of $\mathcal{P}$ (resp. $\mathcal{P}^*$) formed by the polynomials of degree less than or equal to $n > 0$. Obviously, by adapting some uniform notational convention, every $f \in \mathcal{P}$ can be identified with its (ordered) set of coefficients and so, if s_n designates the cardinality of the set of coefficients of a n-th degree polynomial, then, for every n, a continuous mapping $\pi_n : \mathbb{R}^{s_n} \to \mathcal{P}_n$ can be defined by assigning to every $a \in \mathcal{R}^{s_n}$ the n-th degree polynomial whose coefficients equal a. Let $\pi_n' : \mathbb{R}^{s_n} \times P \to \mathcal{P}_n \times P$, $\Phi' : \mathcal{P}_n^* \times P \to \mathcal{E}$ be given by, respectively, $\pi_n'(a, \omega) = (\pi_n(a), \omega), \Phi'(f, \omega) = (\Phi(f), \omega)$.

[1] This observation is motivated by remarks of Professor R. Radner.

[2] As usual, $x > 0$ means $x \neq 0$ and $x \geq 0$; $x \gg 0$ means $x^i > 0$ for every i.

[3] A preference relation R on P is a subset of $P \times P$ which is complete, reflexive, and transitive; R is monotone if $x - y \in P$, $x, y \in P$ implies $(y, x) \notin R$; R is continuous if it is closed (rel. to $P \times P$).

[4] The fact that we are taking the consumption set to be open is immaterial for the definition of this topology.

[5] We shall allow correspondences to be empty valued.

[6] If X is a topological space we denote by $\mathcal{B}(X)$ the Borel σ-field generated by the open subsets of X.

For every positive integer r let μ_r be a probability measure on $\mathbb{R}^r$ which is absolutely continuous with respect to Lebesgue measure and reciprocally.[7] Our results do not depend on the particular ones chosen. Define then a measure m on $(\mathcal{E}, \mathcal{B}(\mathcal{E}))$ by $m = \sum_{n=1}^{\infty} \frac{1}{2^n} m_n$, $m_n = \mu_{s_n+\ell}(\Phi' \circ \pi_n')^{-1}$. By the continuity of the functions involved all this is well defined.

PROPOSITION. *If $\nu \in \mathcal{V}$ is absolutely continuous with respect to m then, for every $p \in P$, $\#h^\nu(p) \leq 1$ (i.e., h^ν is a function in the domain $\{p \in P : h^\nu(p) \neq \phi\}$).*

Remarks.

1. It is easily checked that $m(\mathcal{E}) > 0$, hence the Proposition is nonvacuous.
2. *Mutatis mutandis*, the statement and proof of the Proposition can be adapted to cover the situation (appropriate to an uncertainty interpretation where preferences, but not income, are random) in which every agent has the same ω and the demand correspondence is defined for every p and ω.
3. Informally, the hypothesis of the Proposition can be divided into two parts; the first, which is very strong and difficult to interpret, says that the economy (i.e., ν) is fully concentrated on the set of agents whose preferences are representable by polynomial utility functions; the second, which is very natural, says that it is not the case that positive weight is given to a family of agents for which, for every n, the Lebesgue measure of the set of pairs of "endowments-coefficients of polynomial utility functions of the n-th degree" corresponding to agents in this family is zero.

2 Proof of the Proposition

We shall prove first a purely formal result and show then how it implies the Proposition.

For every $(p, w) \in P \times (0, \infty)$ define $\gamma(p, w) = \{x \in \overline{P}: px \leq w\}$. Let $f: \overline{P} \to \mathbb{R}$ be a C^2 strictly increasing[8] function. Define $g: \overline{P} \times \mathbb{R}^\ell \to \mathbb{R}$ by $g(x, a) = f(x) + ax$ and, for every $a \in \mathbb{R}^\ell$, $g_a: \overline{P} \to R$ by $g_a(x) = g(x, a)$. For every $p \in P$ form the open subset of $\mathbb{R}^{2\ell}$, $A(p) = \{(a, \omega) \in \mathbb{R}^\ell \times P: Dg_a(x) \gg 0$ for every $x \in \gamma(p, p\omega)\}$. For every $(p, a, \omega) \in P \times A(p)$, let $h'(p, a, \omega) = \{x \in P$: x is a maximum of g_a on $\gamma(p, p\omega)\}$.

THEOREM. *For every $p \in P$ the set $C(p) = \{(a, \omega) \in A(p): \#h'(p, a, \omega) > 1\}$ has (2ℓ–dimensional) Lebesgue measure zero.*

Proof of the Theorem. Take a $p \in P$. From now on this p will be kept fixed. Define a correspondence $\hat{h}: A(p) \to P$ by $\hat{h}(a, \omega) = \{x \in P$: x is a critical point of $g_a \mid Bdry\ \gamma(p, p\omega)\}$.[9]

[7] That is to say, $\mu_r(A) = 0$ if and only if the Lebesgue measure of A is zero.

[8] In other words, $Df(x) \gg 0$ for every $x \in \overline{P}$.

[9] This is an "extended demand correspondence" in the same sense of the "extended equilibrium" of S. Smale (1972).

If F: $X \to Y$ is a correspondence, $G(F)(= \{(x,y) \in X \times Y, y \in F(x)\})$ denotes its graph. A C^1 function F: $S \to \mathbb{R}^r, S \subset \mathbb{R}^t, r \geq t$, is regular if, for every $x \in S$, $DF(x)$ has full rank.

(2) *There is a set* $J \subset A(p)$ *such that*

(i) J *has Lebesgue measure zero;*

(ii) *If* $(a,\omega) \in A(p) \sim J$ *and* $x \in \hat{h}(a,\omega)$, *then there are open neighborhoods of* (a,ω) *and* x, $B_1(a,\omega,x)$, $B_2(a,\omega,x)$, *respectively, and a* C^1 *function* $v_{a,\omega,x}$: $B_1(a,\omega,x) \to B_2(a,\omega,x)$ *such that* $G(v_{a,\omega,x}) = G(\hat{h}) \cap B_1(a,\omega,x) \times B_2(a,\omega,x)$.

Proof: Define the C^1 function Ψ: $A(p) \times P \times (0,\infty) \to \mathbb{R}^{\ell+1}$ by $\Psi(a,\omega,x,\lambda) = (Dg_a(x) - \lambda p, px - p\omega)$; for every $(a,\omega) \in A(p)$ let $\Psi_{a,\omega}$: $P \times (0,\infty) \to \mathbb{R}^{\ell+1}$ be given by $\Psi_{a,\omega}(x,\lambda) = \Psi(a,\omega,x,\lambda)$. Then $(a,\omega,x) \in G(\hat{h})$ if any only if, for some $\lambda > 0$, $(x,\lambda) \in \Psi^{-1}_{a,\omega}(0)$.

The map Ψ is regular since for every $(a,\omega,x,\lambda) \in A(p) \times P \times (0,\infty) \subset \mathbb{R}^{2\ell}$ the following submatrix of the Jacobian matrix of Ψ has full rank:

$$[D_{x^1}\Psi, D_{a^1}\Psi, \ldots, D_{a^n}\Psi] = \begin{bmatrix} D^2_{x^1x^1}g & 1 & 0 & \ldots & 0 \\ & 0 & 1 & \ldots & 0 \\ \vdots & \vdots & & \ddots & \\ D^2_{x^1x^\ell}g & 0 & 0 & \ldots & 1 \\ p^1 & 0 & 0 & \ldots & 0 \end{bmatrix}$$

Therefore $\Psi^{-1}(0)$ is a C^1 2ℓ-manifold and by Sard's Theorem (see S. Sternberg (1964, p. 47)) there is a set $J \subset A(p)$ of null measure such that if $(a,\omega) \notin J$ then zero is a regular value of $\Psi_{a,\omega}$; by the Implicit Function Theorem this yields the second conclusion of the lemma and finishes its proof.

Let $E = G(h' \mid A(p) \sim J)$. Then, by (2), $\{G(v_{a,\omega,x})$: $(a,\omega,x) \in E\}$ is an open covering of E (in the relative topology). Take a countable subcovering $\{G(v_{a_n,\omega_n,x_n})\}_{n=1}^{\infty}$ and call $v_n = v_{a_n,\omega_n,x_n}$, $U_n = B_1(a_n,\omega_n,x_n)$. Denoting the natural numbers by Z, let, for every $i \in Z$, $T_i = \{j \in Z$: $U_i \cap U_j \neq \phi$ and $v_i \mid U_i \cap U_j \neq v_j \mid U_i \cap U_j\}$. For every $i,j \in Z$ such that $j \in T_i$, define a C^1 function φ_{ij}: $U_i \cap U_j \to \mathbb{R}$ by $\varphi_{ij}(a,\omega) = g(v_i(a,\omega),a) - g(v_j(a,\omega),a)$.

(3) *For every* $i,j \in Z$ *such that* $j \in T_i$, $\varphi_{ij}^{-1}(0)$ *has Lebesgue measure zero.*

Proof: It is sufficient to show that φ_{ij} is a regular map, then $\varphi_{ij}^{-1}(0)$ will be a C^1 manifold of dimension $< 2\ell$ and, therefore, a null set. Let $(a,\omega) \in U_i \cap U_j$, $x_i = v_i(a,\omega)$, $x_j = v_j(a,\omega)$. Since $j \in T_i$, it follows, by construction and (2(*ii*)), that $x_i \neq x_j$. Let $x_i^1 \neq x_j^1$. For $k = i,j$ we have $D_{a^1}g(v_k(a,\omega),a) = D_x g(v_k(a,\omega),a) \circ D_{a^1}v_k(a,\omega) + x_k^1$, but since $pD_{a^1}v_k(a,\omega) = 0$ (because $pv_k(\cdot,\omega) = p\omega$) and $D_x g(v_k(a),a) = \lambda p$ for some $\lambda \in \mathbb{R}$, the first term of the sum vanishes so that $D_{a^1} g(v_k(a,\omega), a) = x_k^1$ $(k = i, j)$ and, therefore, $D_{a^1}\phi_{ij}(a,\omega) \neq 0$. This ends the proof of (3).

The proof of the theorem is now completed: let $(a,\omega) \in A(p) \sim J$ and $x', x'' \in h'(p,a,\omega), x' \neq x''$; of course, $g_{a,\omega}(x') = g_{a,\omega}(x'')$. For some $i, j \in Z$, $(a,\omega,x') \in G(v_i)$, $(a,\omega,x'') \in G(v_j)$ which implies that $j \in T_i$ and $(a,\omega) \in \phi_{ij}^{-1}(0)$. Therefore $C(p) \subset J \cup \bigcup_{i,j \in Z, j \in T_i} \phi_{ij}^{-1}(0)$, the last set being null by (2) and (3).

The Proposition follows immediately from the Theorem: take a $p \in P$ and let $\mathcal{E}' = \{(R,\omega) \in \mathcal{E} : \#h(R,\omega,p) > 1\}$; it is not hard to see that $\mathcal{E}'$ is an $\mathcal{F}_\sigma$ set, hence measurable. Therefore, by Fubini's Theorem and the Theorem above, $\mu_{s_n+\ell}(\phi' \circ \pi_n')^{-1}(\mathcal{E}') = 0$ for every n. Thus, $m(\mathcal{E}') = 0$ and so $\nu(\mathcal{E}') = 0$. **Q.E.D.**

3 Final Comments and Extensions

The result in this paper can be straightforwardly extended in a variety of directions, but the two lines of further research which we regard as more interesting do not seem quite so simple. They are suggested by the following two comments on the limitations of the Proposition.

(i) The hypotheses of the Proposition are far from guaranteeing that the aggregate demand function (if it exists) be differentiable or even Lipschitzian. Clearly, this limits the appeal of the result, since with the much weaker assumption of atomlessness of the economy one already has that the aggregate demand correspondence is convex-valued.

(ii) No characterization independent of the choice of utility function is available for the class of preferences representable by polynomial utility. This is troublesome because it makes the results difficult to interpret. The class of preferences representable by analytic utility functions can be easily and naturally described without reference to utility. One could perhaps surmise that some analog of the Proposition (i.e., some consequence of the Theorem in Part 2) holds for economies fully concentrated in the set of agents with preferences in this class.

We finish by mentioning, in an informal manner, an application of the Theorem in Part 2 to approximation problems. Consider the following elementary proposition: "...every finite (pure exchange) economy whose agents have convex preferences can be approximated by economies yielding continuous excess demand functions." Theorem 2 in (Mas-Colell, 1972) (see, also, G. Debreu (1972, p. 613)) implies that the Proposition can be improved by substituting C^1 for continuous. By applying the Theorem in 2 one obtains a different extension, namely, if approximation is understood in the sense of weak convergence for measures (and the word "finite" is dropped) then the above statement remains true without the convexity of preferences assumption. A somewhat more significant question remains open: can every pure exchange economy (nonconvex preferences allowed) be approximated (in the sense of weak convergence for measures) by economies yielding C^1 excess demand functions?

References

AUMANN, R. (1964): "Markets with a Continuum of Traders," *Econometrica,* 32, 39-50

DEBREU, G. (1972): "Smooth Preferences," *Econometrica,* 40, 603-615

HILDENBRAND, W. (1970): "On Economies with Many Agents," *Journal of Economic Theory,* 2, 161-188

MAS-COLELL, A. (1972): "Continuous and Smooth Consumers: Approximation Theorems," WP 171, Center for Research in Management Sciences, University of California, Berkeley[10].

SMALE, S. (1972): "Global Analysis and Economics, II: Extension of a Theorem of Debreu," mimeo, University of California-Berkeley[11].

STERNBERG, S., (1964): *Lectures on Differential Geometry.* New Jersey: Prentice-Hall and New Jersey: Princeton University Press, 1966.

[10] Published in the *Journal of Economic Theory* (1974), 305-336.

[11] Published in the *Journal of Mathematical Economics* (1974), 1-14

Existence of Competitive Equilibrium in a Growing Economy

LIONEL W. MCKENZIE*
University of Rochester

It may be reasonable to suppose that an infinity of goods for delivery on one date belong to a compact space which can be adequately approximated by a finite subset of goods. However if we wish to deal with an economy which has an indefinite or infinite horizon this approximation is not available. Goods for delivery at different dates must be regarded as different goods. It was a major contribution of *Value and Capital* (Hicks (1939)) to provide a full scale analysis of an economy in which this fact is properly recognized. Then if the horizon is infinite the number of goods must be infinite even when deliveries are scheduled at discrete intervals. The infinity of goods must be dealt with together since the market is analyzed as though all trades occur simultaneously. This is a limiting form of the futures economy of Hicks. When uncertainty is introduced in the manner of Debreu (1959) by also distinguishing goods by the states of the world in which they are delivered, the sets of possible future states in each period must be foreseen. It may be possible to do with only a finite number of states of the world in each period, but to give an infinite horizon a finite approximation is difficult unless an arbitrary truncation of time is used with goods in the terminal period valued in an arbitrary way.

We will prove a theorem which generalizes a theorem of Peleg and Yaari (1970) for an exchange economy to the case of a growing economy with production. The expansion of the economy may be regarded as the consequence of an expansion of population where there are no natural resources which cannot be augmented through investment. The method of proof used by Peleg and Yaari is based on a theorem of Scarf on the nonemptiness of the core. Scarf assumes that the traders have utility functions over their possible consumption sets $C^h(p)$. Peleg and Yaari assume that utility functions exist which are strictly quasiconcave. Our assumptions will imply that these functions exist.

The commodity space s^n is the Cartesian product $\Pi_{t=0}^{\infty}\mathbf{R}^n(t)$, endowed with the product topology where $\mathbf{R}^n(t)$ has the norm topology. If $z \in s^n$ then $z = \Pi_{t=1}^{\infty} z_t$, and $z_t \in \mathbf{R}^n(t)$ represents quantities of goods in period t. There is a finite number of traders, 1 to H. The set of possible net trades for the hth trader in period t is C_t^h. The set of net trades for the hth trader over the infinite horizon is $C^h \subset s^n$ where $C^h = \Pi_{t=1}^{\infty} C_t^h$. If $w_t \in C_t^h$ then $w_{it} < 0$ implies that the quantity w_{it} of the ith good is provided by the hth consumer and $w_{it} > 0$ implies that the quantity w_{it} of the ith good is received by the hth consumer. For C_0^h the hth consumer will be able to

*I would like to thank John Boyd for his assistance.

provide any initial stocks of goods which he may possess including produced goods. However for C_t^h with $t > 0$ the hth consumer can provide only labor services and other unproduced goods. Since the economy will be expanding the consumer may be thought of as representing an expanding family extending through the indefinite future.

A binary relation Q is said to be *irreflexive* if zQz does not hold for any z. The relation Q is said to be *antisymmetric* if zQw implies not wQz. Q is *transitive* if xQz and zQw implies zQw. There is an irreflexive, antisymmetric, and transitive relation P^h of strict preference defined on C^h and a correspondence, also denoted by P^h, defined on C^h by $P^h(z) = \{w|w \in C^h \text{ and } wP^h z\}$.

The production set is $Y = \sum_{t=1}^{\infty} \bar{Y}_t$ where $\bar{Y}_t \subset 0 \times \cdots \times 0 \times \mathbf{R}_-^n(t-1) \times \mathbf{R}_+^n(t) \times 0 \times \cdots$. $\bar{Y}_t$ represents the possibilities of producing goods belonging to the tth period from goods belonging to the $(t-1)$th period. Inputs are negative numbers and outputs are positive numbers. Let Y_t be the projection of $\bar{Y}_t$ into the coordinate subspace $\mathbf{R}^n(t-1) \times \mathbf{R}^n(t)$. Then $(u_{t-1}, v_t) \in \bar{Y}_t$ implies $u_{t-1} \leq 0$ and $v_t \geq 0$. The inputs and outputs of the production sector include the capital stocks, which do not appear in the consumers' net trading sets C_t^h except for C_0^h. In an economy with certainty the ownership of capital stocks is inessential. Only the value of investment is significant for the consumer and the sequence of investment values over time is implicit in the pattern of consumption of the consumer.

The economy $E(\bar{\rho})$ is given by the list $(Y, C^1, \cdots, C^H, P^1, \cdots, P^H, \bar{\rho})$ where $\bar{\rho}$ is the maximum of factors ρ of proportional growth for the economy along paths in which all goods appear in positive amounts. Recall that a *lower section* of the correspondence $f : X \to \{\text{subsets of } X\}$, at a point $y \in X$, is the set $\{z|y \in f(z)\}$. The *graph* of f is the set $\{(y,z)|z \in f(y)\}$. We define $C = \sum_{h=1}^{H} C^h$. Define the *preference relation* R^h by $x^h R^h y^h$ if and only if not $y^h P^h x^h$. The economy is *strongly irreducible* if, whenever I_1, I_2 is a nontrivial partition of $\{1, \ldots, H\}$ and $x_{I_1} + x_{I_2} \in Y$, there are $z_{I_1} + z_{I_2} \in Y$ with $z^h P^h x^h$ for $h \in I_1$, and, for $h \in I_2$, $z^h \in C^h$.

Let $l_\infty^n = \{z \in s^n|$ there is ζ and $|z_t| < \zeta$ for all $t\}$. We give l_∞^n the norm topology where $|z|_\infty = \sup_{t \geq 0} |z_t|$. Let $e_t \in \mathbf{R}^n(t)$ have each component equal to 1.

The assumptions are

1. Y_t is a closed convex cone with vertex at the origin.
2. $Y_t \cap (\{0\} \times \mathbf{R}_n^+) = (\{0\}, \{0\})$. Also $\bar{\rho} > 1$.
3. C^h is convex, closed, and bounded below. There is an interval $[\bar{z}, \bar{w}] \subset l_\infty^n$ where $\bar{z}_t = \bar{\rho}\bar{z}_{t-1}$ and $\bar{w}_t = \bar{\rho}\bar{w}_{t-1}$ for all $t > 0$ and $C^h = (C^h \cap [\bar{z}, \bar{w}]) + s_+^n$.
4. For all h the correspondence P^h is convex and open valued relative to C^h with open lower sections. $R^h(x)$ is the closure of $P^h(x)$ for all $x \in C^h$.
5. The economy $E(\bar{\rho})$ is strongly irreducible. Also $x \in C^h$ with $z \geq x$, and $z_t > x_t$ for some t, implies $z \in P^h(x)$.
6. There is $\bar{x}^h \in C^h - Y$ with $\bar{x}^h \leq 0$ for all h. Moreover, $\sum_{h=1}^{H} \bar{x}^h = \bar{x} < 0$ and the $\bar{x}^h$ may be chosen so that $\bar{x}_t = \bar{\rho}\bar{x}_{t-1}$ for all $t > 0$. For any h and any x^h let $z^h \in R^h(x^h) - Y$. Then for any $\delta > 0$ there is a τ_0 and an $\alpha > 0$ such that $(z_0^h + \delta e_0, z_1^h, \cdots, z_\tau^h, \alpha\bar{x}_{\tau+1}^h, \cdots) \in R^h(x^h) - Y$ for all $\tau > \tau_0$.

The purpose of the second part of Assumption 3 is to insure that given a nonnegative price vector there is a cheapest bundle of consumption goods, which allows the consumer to subsist, and which is finite in each period while expanding by a factor equal to ρ from one period to the next. Assumption 4 implies that a continuous utility function exists. The second part of Assumption 5 says that an increase in the quantity of all goods for some period leads to a preferred stream. The first part of Assumption 6 provides for an expanding path of production and consumption for the economy as a whole in which all goods exceed subsistence requirements in every period. This may be thought of as a kind of Slater Condition (See Uzawa (1958), p. 34). The existence of a path of steady expansion excludes natural resources which are not augmentable through production. Thus this economy is a type of von Neumann economy in which consumption is allowed for. Paths of proportional expansion in economies of this type have been studied by Morishima (1964) and numerous others.

In an exchange economy a lower bound $-b^h$ for C^h has often been taken to be the negative of a vector of endowments held by the hth trader which lies in C^h. In a production economy where productive services are traded the requirement that $-b^h$ lie in C^h would be very restrictive. Even in a trading economy it is not satisfactory since it implies that the subsistence level for consumers allows no substitution between goods. In this model the last part of Assumption 3 makes $-b^h \in C^h$ unnecessary.

We mean by an *allocation* of net trades a list $x = (x^1, ..., x^H)$ such that $x^h \in C^h$ for all h. A *feasible allocation* must also satisfy the condition $\sum_{h=1}^H x^h \in Y$. Then the set of feasible allocations for the economy is $F = \{(x^1, \cdots, x^H) | x^h \in C^h$, all h, and $\sum_{h=1}^H x^h \in Y\}$. The set of *feasible net trades* for the hth consumer is the projection of F into the hth consumer's net trading set.

Lemma 1. *F and F^h are nonempty, compact, and convex.*

Proof. By Assumption 6 there is $\bar{x} = w - y$ where $w \in C$ and $y \in Y$. Then $w - \bar{x} = y$ and $w - \bar{x} \in C$ by monotonicity since $\bar{x} < 0$. Thus F is nonempty. F is convex by the convexity of Y and of C^h for each h. F is closed since Y is closed and C^h is closed for each h. To prove compactness it is sufficient to prove that the projection of F into each term F_t of the product is compact. Since F_t is closed we must show that F_t is bounded. Consider $x_t^s = u_t^s + v_t^s$ for $x_t^s \in F_t$, $s = 1, 2, \cdots$. Suppose $|x_t^s| \to \infty$ as $s \to \infty$. Since $x_t^s \in C$ and C is bounded below while $0 \geq u_t^s$, $|x_t^s| \to \infty$ if and only if $|v_t^s| \to \infty$. Then $(u_{t-1}^s, v_t^s)/|v_t^s| \to (\bar{u}_{t-1}, \bar{v}_t) \neq 0$. If u_{t-1}^s is bounded, $\bar{u}_{t-1} = 0$. This contradicts Assumption 2. Thus it must be that u_{t-1}^s is unbounded, but then x_{t-1}^s bounded below implies that $|v_{t-1}^s| \to \infty$, so by the same argument u_s^{t-2} is unbounded. By backwards induction it follows that $u_0^s \leq 0$ is unbounded. However $u_0^s = x_0^s$ which is bounded below by Assumption 3. Since this is a contradiction we conclude that y_t^s is bounded for all t. Thus F_t is bounded for all t and F is compact by Tychonoff's theorem (Berge (1963), p.79). Since the projection into the hth subspace is a linear mapping the compactness and convexity of F^h follows immediately from these properties for F. Also $x \in F$ implies $x^h \in F$ so that if F is nonempty then F^h is nonempty. ∎

The assumptions allow us to prove that a continuous utility exists which represents the preference order P^h. First we will show that Assumption 4 implies that R^h is transitive.

Lemma 2. *R^h is transitive.*

Proof. Assume that xR^hz and zR^hy. Since $R^h(z)$ is the closure of $P^h(z)$, in every neighborhood U of x there is a point $x' \in P^h(z)$. Also for any z' sufficiently close to z we have $x' \in P^h(z')$ since lower sections are open. As before for any neighborhood V of z there is a point $z'' \in P^h(y)$. By choosing V small enough we may take $z' = z''$ to get $x'P^hz''P^hy$ so that $x'P^hy$ by transitivity of strict preference. Since x' may be chosen in an arbitrary neighborhood U of x it follows that $x \in$ *closure* $P^h(y)$ or $x \in R^h(y)$. In other words R^h is transitive. ∎

In order to apply the theorem of Scarf on the nonemptiness of the core we need to show that the preference order R^h may be represented by a utility function, that is, a numerical function on the commodity bundles in C^h.

Lemma 3. *There is a continuous function $u^h : F^h \to \mathbf{R}$ such that $x^hR^hz^h$ if and only if $u^h(x^h) \geq u^h(x^h)$.*

Proof. Since F^h is compact and s^n with the product topology is metrizable and complete, it follows that F^h is separable (Berge (1963), p. 94). Therefore the theorem of Debreu (1954) may be applied to obtain a continuous numerical representation of R^h. ∎

Let u^h be the continuous utility function representing R^h on F^h. Let $U(\tilde{x})$ be the vector of utilities $(u^h(x^h))$ and $\tilde{F} = U(F)$. The set $\tilde{F}$ is the utility possibility set of the economy. Note $\tilde{F}$ is compact, hence bounded. For any coalition S define

$$V(S) = \{z \in \mathbf{R}^H | z_h \leq u^h(x^h) \text{ for all } h \in S, \text{ with } x^h \in C^h \text{ and } \sum_{h \in S} x^h \in Y\}.$$

$V(S)$ is the set of utility vectors whose projection on the utility subspace of the coalition S lies in or below the utility possibility set of S. A set W is *comprehensive* if $z \in W$ and $y \leq z$ implies $y \in W$. Note that $V(S)$ is closed, nonempty, comprehensive, and bounded above in $\mathbf{R}^S$. Moreover, if $x \in V(S)$ and $x_h = y_h$ for all $h \in S$, then $y \in V(S)$.

Let $\mathcal{B}$ be a nonempty family of subsets of $I = \{1, \cdots, H\}$. Define $\mathcal{B}_h = \{S \in \mathcal{B} | h \in S\}$. A family $\mathcal{B}$ is balanced if there exist nonnegative weights w_S with $\sum_{S \in \mathcal{B}_h} w_S^h = 1$ for all $h \in I$. A *V-allocation* is an element of $V(\{1, \cdots, H\})$. A coalition S can *improve* on a V-allocation x if there is a $y \in V(S)$ with $y_h > x_h$ for all $h \in S$. The V-core is the set of V-allocations that cannot be improved upon by any coalition. The following theorem is from Scarf (1967).

Theorem (Scarf). *Suppose $\cap_{S \in \mathcal{B}} V(S) \subset V(\{1, \cdots, H\})$ whenever $\mathcal{B}$ is a balanced family. Then the V-core is nonempty.*

Lemma 4. *Under Assumptions 1-5 the economy has a nonempty core.*

Proof. Let $\mathcal{B}$ be a balanced family of sets with balancing weights w_S and let $(z_1, \cdots, z_H) \in \cap_{S \in \mathcal{B}} V(S)$. For each coalition S there are $x_S^h \in C^h$ for $h \in S$ with $\sum_{h \in S} x_S^h = y^S \in Y$ and $u^h(x_S^h) \geq z_h$ for all $h \in S$. Now consider $x^h = \sum_{S \in \mathcal{B}_h} w_S x_S^h$. Note that $u^h(x^h) \geq z_h$ by convexity of preferences. Also

$$\sum_{h=1}^H x^h = \sum_{h=1}^H \sum_{S \in \mathcal{B}_h} w_S x_S^h = \sum_{S \in \mathcal{B}} w_S (\sum_{h \in S} x_S^h) = \sum_{S \in \mathcal{B}} w_S y^S \in Y.$$

Thus $(z_1, \cdots, z_H)$ is feasible for the entire economy due to the feasibility of $(x^1, \cdots, x^H)$. Therefore $(z_1, \cdots, z_H) \in V(\{1, \cdots, H\})$. Scarf's theorem now shows that the V-core is nonempty.

Now let $\tilde{z} = (z^1, \cdots, z^H)$ be in the V-core and take $\tilde{x} \in F$ with $U(\tilde{x}) \geq \tilde{z}$. It is clear that $\tilde{x}$ must be a core allocation. Therefore the core of the economy is not empty. ∎

We consider the set $C^h - Y$ of possible trades with production for the hth consumer. Let $\bar{x} = \sum_{h=1}^{H} \bar{x}^h$. Take units of measurement for goods so that $|\bar{x}| = 1$. The *set of admissible price vectors* will be $S = \{p \in s_+^n | p\bar{x} < \infty\}$ where $p\bar{x} = \sum_{t=1}^{\infty} p_t \bar{x}_t$. Unlike the admissible price vectors used in most models of the competitive economy the price vectors in S are not all contained in the dual space of the commodity space. The dual space $(s^n)^*$ contains only those $p \in S$ which have a finite number of nonzero components. For $p \in P$ the *budget set* of the hth trader is $B^h(p) = \{x | x \in C^h$ and $px \leq 0\}$. A *competitive equilibrium* for the economy $E(\bar{\rho}) = \{Y, C^1, \cdots, C^h, P^1, \cdots, P^h, \bar{\rho}\}$ is a list $(p, y, x^1, \cdots, x^H)$ such that p is admissible and the following conditions are met.

I. $px^h \leq 0$ and $z \in P^h(x^h)$ implies $pz > 0$.

II. $y \in Y$ and $y_t = u_t + v_t$ for $t \geq 1$, where $p_{t-1}u_{t-1} + p_t v_t = 0$ for $t \geq 1$. Also $z \in Y$, with $z_t = u'_t + v'_t$, implies $p_{t-1}u'_{t-1} + p_t v'_t \leq 0$ for all $t \geq 1$. $y_0 = u_0 \leq 0$.

III. $\sum_{h \in I} x^h = y$.

The first condition is the usual demand condition. The second condition is the profit condition. The third condition is the balance condition. Our objective is to prove

Theorem 1. *The economy $E(\bar{\rho})$ has a competitive equilibrium under Assumptions 1-6.*

The proof of Theorem 1 will begin with a series of lemmas. Consider the replication of the economy $E(\bar{\rho})$. In the economy E_r where $E(\bar{\rho})$ has been replicated r times there are r copies of each trader who appears in $E(\bar{\rho})$. Each copy has the same trading set and preference correspondence as the original trader. We will use the idea of the equal treatment core. The equal treatment core is equal to the set of allocations in the core of the replicated economy E_r such that each trader in E_r who is a replica of a given trader in $E(\bar{\rho})$ undertakes the same net trade. Then an allocation in the equal treatment core K_r of E_r may be represented by $\{x^h\}_r$ where $\{x^h\}_1$ is the allocation of net trades to the original traders and r is the number of replications. Let K_1 be the core of the economy $E_1 = E(\bar{\rho})$. We must first show that the equal treatment core is not empty for any r.

Lemma 5. *Under Assumption 4 if zP^hx and wR^hx then yP^hx for $y = \alpha w + (1-\alpha)z$ for any α with $0 < \alpha < 1$.*

Proof. Since $P^h(x)$ is open relative to C^h by Assumption 4, zP^hx implies that $z \in$ *interior* $P^h(x)$ relative to C^h. If $w \in P^h(x)$, $y \in P^h(x)$ by convexity. If $w \notin P^h(x)$ then $w \in$ *boundary* $P^h(x)$ by Assumption 4. Thus all intermediate points y on the line segment from w to z are interior to $P^h(x)$ or yP^hx. ∎

We may now prove

Lemma 6. *If $\{x^{hk}\}_r$, $h = 1, ..., H$, and $k = 1, ..., r$, is an allocation in the core of E_r then, for h given, $x^{hk}I^hx^{hk'}$ holds for all k and k'.*

Proof. Let the allocation $\{x^{hk}\}_r$ where $h = 1, ..., H$ and $k = 1, ..., r$ lie in the core for the economy E_r. I claim that $x^{hk} I^h x^{hj}$ for all h, k, j. Suppose not. From convexity of $P^h(x)$ it follows that $R^h(x)$ is convex as the closure of $P^h(x)$. Consider a replicate with index $hj(h)$, for each original consumer with index h, where $hj(h)$ satisfies $x^{hk} R^h x^{hj(h)}$ for all $k = 1, \cdots, r$. That is, $hj(h)$ has a net trade which no better, and perhaps poorer, than the net trade of any other replicate of h. Consider the coalition $B = \{1j(1), ..., Hj(H)\}$ and the allocation to the member of B with index $hj(h)$ of $(1/r)\sum_{k=1}^{r} x^{hk} = x^h$. For each h it follows that $x^h R^h x^{hj(h)}$ by convexity of $R^h(x)$ and, if $x^{ik} P^i x^{ij(i)}$ for some i, k, then $x^i P^i x^{ij(i)}$ holds by Lemma 5.

Now $\sum_{h=1}^{H} x^h = (1/r)\sum_{k=1}^{r}\sum_{h=1}^{H} x^{hk}$ which lies in Y since $\{x^{hk}\}$ is feasible and Y is a cone. Thus $\{x^h\}_B$ is a feasible allocation for B. By strong irreducibility and convexity it is possible to spread the gain received by $ij(i)$ from the new allocation to all $hj(h)$. Let $\{I_1, I_2\}$ be the partition of B where $I_1 = \{hj(h)|h \neq i\}$ and $I_2 = \{ij(i)\}$. B has the same list of preferences and initial stocks as the original economy $E_1 = E(\bar{\rho})$. Therefore by strong irreducibility for $E(\bar{\rho})$ there is a feasible allocation $\{z^h\}$ over B with $z^h = z^{hj(h)}$ and $z^h P^h x^h$ for $h \in I_1$. Take the convex combination $\{\lambda x^h + (1 - \lambda) z^h\}$ for $0 \leq \lambda \leq 1$. This a feasible allocation which is preferred by all $h \in I_1$ to $\{x^h\}$ and, since $x^i P^i x^{ij(i)}$, also preferred by i for λ sufficiently close to 1. Thus B is an improving coalition and $\{x^{hk}\}_r$ is not an allocation in the core of E_r contrary to the assumption. Therefore $x^{hk} I^h x^{hk'}$ must hold for all k, k'. ∎

Lemma 7. *K_r is nonempty if the core of E_r is nonempty.*

Proof. According to Lemma 6 for any allocation in the core the allocations received by the copies of a given h in the original economy are indifferent. Then by the convex valuedness of the relation R^h the equal treatment allocation in which each copy of h receives x^h, as defined in the proof of Lemma 6, satisfies $x^h R^h x^{hk}$ for all h, k. Thus if there is no improving coalition for the allocation $\{x^{hk}\}_r$ there is also no improving coalition for the allocation $\{z^{hk}\}_r$ in which $z^{hk} = x^h$ for all h, k. Therefore $\{z^{hk}\}_r$ is in the core of E_r. ∎

Lemma 8. *$K_r \neq \phi$ for any $r \geq 1$.*

Proof. Since E_r satisfies the assumptions if $E(\bar{\rho})$ does Lemma 4 implies that the core of E_r is not empty for all r. Then Lemma 7 implies that K_r is not empty either. ∎

It is not enough that the equal treatment core be nonempty. We must also prove that it is closed.

Lemma 9. *The equal treatment core K_r is closed for all r.*

Proof. Suppose that the allocations $\{x^{h^s}\}_r$, $s = 1, 2, ...$, lie in K_r and converge to $\{x^h\}_r$. Suppose that $\{x^h\}_r$ is not in K_r. Let w^{hi} be a net trade for the ith copy of the hth original trader. Then there is an improving coalition B such that $w^{hi} \in P(x^h)$ for $hi \in B$ and $\sum_{hi \in B} w^{hi} \in Y$. By the fact that $P(x^h)$ has open lower sections $w^{hi} \in P(x^{h^s})$ will hold when s is large. This implies that B is improving for $\{x^{h^s}\}_r$ for large s and thus $\{x^{h^s}\}_r$ is not in K_r contrary to the assumption. Therefore $\{x^h\}_r \in K_r$ must hold and K_r is closed. ∎

Let $K = \cap_{r=1}^{\infty} K_r$. That is, $\{x^h\} \in K$ if $\{x^h\}_r \in K_r$ for all r.

Lemma 10. *K is not empty.*

Proof. If B is an improving coalition for an allocation $\{x^h\}_r$ in E_r it is also an improving coalition for the allocation $\{x^h\}_{r+1}$ in E_{r+1}. Thus $K_{r+1} \subset K_r$ and the K_r, $r = 1, 2, ...$, form a nested sequence of sets which are nonempty by Lemma 8, closed by Lemma 9, and bounded by Lemma 1. Thus K_r is compact and any infinite set in K_r has a point of accumulation. However any subsequence of $\{x^h\}_r$ for $r > r'$ lies in $K_{r'}$. Thus K_r contains any accumulation point of $\{x^h\}_r$ for all r. This implies that there is an accumulation point $\{x_h\} \in K$. ▮

To prove Theorem 1 we will show that $(x^1, ..., x^H) \in K$ implies that there is p and y such that $(p, y, x^1, \cdots, x^H)$ is a competitive equilibrium for $E(\bar{\rho})$. Let $G =$ *convex hull* $(\cup_{h=1}^{H} R^h(x^h))$.

Lemma 11. *G is closed in s^n.*

Proof. I first show that G is closed. C^h is bounded below for all h from its definition and therefore G is bounded below. Suppose $z^s \rightarrow z$, $s = 1, 2, ...$, where $z^s \in G$ for all s. We must show that $z \in G$. Let I be the set of all traders. Let $z^s = \sum_{h \in I} w^{hs} = \sum_{h \in I} \alpha_{hs} z^{hs}$ where $\sum_{h \in I} \alpha_{hs} = 1$, $\alpha_{hs} \geq 0$, and $z^{hs} \in C^h$. Suppose there is w^{hs} which is unbounded as $s \rightarrow \infty$. Since z^{hs} is bounded below by Assumption 3 and $0 \leq \alpha_{hs} \leq 1$ this implies that z^s is unbounded above in contradiction to $z^s \rightarrow z$. Therefore w^{hs} is bounded and there is a subsequence w^{hs} (retain notation) such that w^{hs} converges to a point w^h.

Let $J = \{h | \alpha_h > 0\}$. For $h \in J$ we have $w^{hs}/\alpha_{hs} = z^{hs} \rightarrow w^h/\alpha_h$. Since C^h is closed $w^h/\alpha_h \in C^h$. For $h \notin J$ we have $\alpha_{hs}\bar{z} \leq w^{hs}$ where $\bar{z}$ is the lower bound on C^h from Assumption 3. Taking the limit shows $0 \leq w^h$. Now consider $w^h/\alpha_h + \sum_{i \notin J} w^i$ which is in $R(x^h)$ by periodwise monotonicity. Moreover $\sum_{h \in J} \alpha_h (w^h/\alpha_h + \sum_{i \notin J} w^i) = \sum_{h=1}^{H} w^h = z$. Therefore $z \in G$. ▮

We will need the following theorem adapted from Choquet (1962).

Theorem (Choquet). *Let Z be a convex set in s^n closed in the product topology. If Z contains no straight lines, then for any two subsets X and Y of Z closed in the product topology the sum $X + Y$ is closed.*

Lemma 12. *$G - Y$ is closed in s^n.*

Proof. From Assumption 3 we have $G - Y \subset \bar{z} + s^n_+ - Y$. Both $G - \bar{z}$and $-Y$ are closed and contained in $s^n_+ - Y$. Also $s^n_+ - Y$ contains no straight lines since $-Y$ contains no nonzero vectors in s^n_- by Assumption 2. Thus we need only show that $s^n_+ - Y$ is closed and apply Choquet's theorem.

Let $z^n \rightarrow z$ with $z^n \in Y - s^n_+$. Then there are $y^n \in Y$ with $z^n \leq y^n$. Since z^n converges the $y^n_0 \leq 0$ are bounded below. But $y^n_0 \leq 0$ so the y^n_0 are bounded. By the proof of Lemma 1, this implies y^n_t is bounded for each t. Then a Cantor diagonal process gives a convergent subsequence of y^n with limit $y \in Y$. Since $z^n \leq y^n$, $z \leq y$ and $z \in Y - s^n_+$. Thus $Y - s^n_+$ is closed. ▮

Lemma 13. *$K \neq \phi$ implies that there is no $z \in G$ and $y \in Y$ such that $z - y \leq 0$ and $z_t - y_t < 0$ for some t.*

Proof. It was proved by Debreu and Scarf (1963) that $0 \notin G - Y$ in the finite dimensional case. The argument is not changed in the infinite dimensional case.

Thus it cannot hold that there are

$$w^h \in P^h(x^h) \text{ such that } \sum_{h \in I} \alpha_h w^h \in Y \text{ and } \alpha^h \geq 0, \sum \alpha^h = 1. \quad (1)$$

Let $z \in G$, $y \in Y$, with $z \leq y$ and $z_t < y_t$ for some t. We have $z = \sum_{h \in I} \alpha_h z^h$ for some $z^h \in G^h$, $\alpha_h \geq 0$, $\sum_{h \in I} \alpha_h = 1$. Therefore $\sum_h \alpha_h (z^h + (y - z)) = y \in Y$. But $z^h \in R^h(x^h)$ by definition of G, and $z^h + (y-z) \in P(x^h)$ by periodwise monotonicity. Letting $w^h = z^h + (y - z)$ gives an instance of (1), since $\sum_{h=1}^{H} w^h = y \in Y$. Thus no such z can exist. ∎

Lemma 14. *For any $\epsilon > 0$ there is $p \in (s^n)^*$ such that $pz > -\epsilon|p_0|$ for all $z \in G - Y$. Also $p \geq 0$, $|p_0| > 0$, and $p_{t-1}u_{t-1} + p_t v_t \leq 0$ for all $(u_{t-1} + v_t) \in Y_t$ for all $t \geq 1$.*

Proof. For $\epsilon > 0$ let $a(\epsilon) = (-\epsilon e_0, 0, 0, ...)$ where $e_0 = (1, \cdots, 1)$. By Lemma 13, $a(\epsilon) \notin G - Y$. By Lemma 12, $G - Y$ is closed. Also the set $\{a(\epsilon)\}$ is compact. By a separation theorem (Berge (1963), p. 251) there is a continuous linear functional $f \in (s^n)^*$ with $f \neq 0$ such that $f(z) > f(a(\epsilon)) + \delta$ for any $z \in G - Y$ and some $\delta > 0$. However any such f may be represented by a vector $p \in s^n$ with $p \neq 0$ but $p_t = 0$ for all but finitely many t, where

$$f(z) = pz = \sum_{t=0}^{\infty} p_t z_t \geq -\epsilon|p_0| + \delta,$$

for any $z \in G - Y$ and some $\delta > 0$. Periodwise monotonicity implies that $p \geq 0$. Thus we have for some $p \geq 0$, $p \neq 0$,

$$pz > -\epsilon|p_0| \text{ for all } z \in G - Y. \quad (2)$$

On the other hand $x^h \in R^h(x^h)$ for all h and $\sum_{h=1}^{H} x^h = y$ for some $y \in Y$ implies that $0 \in G - Y$. Since $Y = Y + Y$ and $0 \in G - Y$ it follows that $-Y \subset G - Y$. Therefore (2) implies $pz < \epsilon|p_0|$ for all $z \in Y$ and $|p_0| \neq 0$. Since $\alpha z \in Y$ for any $\alpha > 0$ it follows that $pz \leq 0$ for all $z \in Y$. However $(0, \cdots, 0, u_{t-1}, v_t, 0, \cdots) \in Y$ for all $t \geq 1$ and $(u_{t-1}, v_t) \in Y_t$. Therefore $p_{t-1}u_{t-1} + p_t v_t \leq 0$ for all $(u_{t-1}, v_t) \in Y_t$. ∎

Define d^h by $d_0^h = x_0^h + e_0$, $d_t^h = x_t^h$ for $t = 1, \cdots, \tau$, and $d_t^h = \alpha \bar{x}_t^h$ for $t > \tau$. By Assumption 6 and monotonicity we may choose τ and α so that $d^h \in R^h(x^h) - Y$ for all h. Thus $d^h \in G - Y$ and we have $pd^h > -\epsilon|p_0|$ by Lemma 14. Let $d_0^{h\prime} = d_0^h + 2e_0$ and $d_t^{h\prime} = d_t^h$ for $t > 0$. It follows from periodwise monotonicity that $d^{h\prime}$ is also in $R^h(x^h) - Y$. Define $\bar{c}^h$ by $\bar{c}^h = d^{h\prime} - \alpha \bar{x}^h$. Then $\bar{c}^h = 0$ for $t > \tau$. Since $\alpha p \bar{x}^h \leq 0$ we have $p\bar{c}^h > |p_0|$ whenever $\epsilon < 1$ from the definition of $d^{h\prime}$. Let $\bar{c} = 1/H \sum_{h=1}^{H} \bar{c}^h$.

For $\epsilon < 1$ we define the price set

$$S(\epsilon) = \{p \in s_+^n | pw \geq -\epsilon \text{ for all } w \in G - Y \text{ and } p\bar{c} = 1\}.$$

In the definition of $S(\epsilon)$ we allow the possibility that $pw = \sum_{t=0}^{\infty} p_t w_t = \infty$.

Lemma 15. *$S(\epsilon)$ is not empty for $1 > \epsilon > 0$.*

Proof. By Lemma 14 there is $p \geq 0$ such that $pz \geq -\epsilon|p_0|$ for all $z \in G - Y$. Thus $(1/|p_0|)pz \geq -\epsilon$. Let αp satisfy $\alpha p\bar{c} = 1$. α is well defined and positive since $p\bar{c} > |p_0|$. We must show that $\alpha pz \geq -\epsilon$ holds for all $z \in G - Y$. Since $z < 0$

is possible and $\alpha > 0$ holds we require $\alpha < 1/|p_0|$. The normalization rule implies $\alpha = 1/p\bar{c}$. Thus we require $p\bar{c} \geq |p_0|$. But we have seen that this holds from the definition of $\bar{c}$. Then $\alpha p \in S(\epsilon)$ and $S(\epsilon)$ is not empty for any ϵ with $1 > \epsilon > 0$. ∎

Let $l_1^n = \{z \in s^n | \sum_{t=0}^{\infty} |z_t| < \infty\}$. We give l_1^n its norm topology where $|z|_1 = \sum_{t=0}^{\infty} |z_t|$.

Proposition 1. *Let $z^s \in l_1^n$, $s = 1, 2, \cdots$, where $\sum_{t=0}^{\infty} |z_t^s| < \zeta < \infty$ for all s. If $\sum_{t=\tau}^{\infty} |z_t^s| \to 0$ as $\tau \to \infty$ uniformly for all s then the z^s have a point of accumulation in the norm topology of l_1^n.*

Proof. Since each component of z^s is bounded it is clear that z exists which is a pointwise limit of a subsequence $z^{s'}$. Therefore for any $\epsilon > 0$ and any $\tau > 0$ there is σ with $\sum_{t=1}^{\tau} |z_t^{s'} - z| < \epsilon/2$ for all $s' > \sigma$. Choose τ so that $\sum_{\tau+1}^{\infty} |z_t^s| < \epsilon/2$ for all z^s. Then $\sum_{t=1}^{\infty} |z_t^{s'} - z| < \epsilon$ for all $s' > \sigma$. By a Cantor diagonal process we may choose a subsequence of z^swhich converges to z. ∎

Lemma 16. *For $\epsilon < 1$, $S(\epsilon)$ is compact if it is closed.*

Proof. Let p be an arbitrary element of $S(\epsilon)$. Consider the point w of $G - Y$ where $w = \bar{c} + \alpha\bar{x}/H$. By definition of $S(\epsilon)$ we have $pw = p(\bar{c} + \alpha\bar{x}/H) \geq -\epsilon$ or

$$-p\bar{x} \leq H(1+\epsilon)/\alpha. \tag{3}$$

Note that $p \geq 0$ and $\bar{x} < 0$. It is implied by (3) and Assumption 6 that $-p\bar{x} = -\sum_{t=0}^{\infty} p_t \bar{x}_t = -\bar{x}_0 \sum_{t=0}^{\infty} \bar{\rho}^t p_t$. Thus $\bar{\rho}^t p \in l_1^n$ and *a fortiori* $p \in l_1^n$. Also (3) implies that p is uniformly bounded for $p \in S(\epsilon)$. Moreover $-\bar{x}_0 \sum_{t=\tau}^{\infty} p_t \leq \bar{\rho}^{-\tau} H(1+\epsilon)$. In other words $-\bar{x}_0 \sum_{t=\tau}^{\infty} p_t \to 0$ as $\tau \to \infty$ uniformly over $S(\epsilon)$. Since $-\bar{x}_0 > 0$ and $p_t \geq 0$, all t, this implies $|\sum_{t=\tau} p_t| \to 0$ uniformly.

Consider p^s, $s = 1, 2, \cdots$, with $p^s \in S(\epsilon)$. Proposition 1 implies that p^s has a point of accumulation. Since l_1^n is a metric space this implies that $S(\epsilon)$ is compact (Berge (1963), pp. 89). ∎

According to Assumption 3, $\bar{z} \in l_\infty^n$ is a lower bound for all the C^h where $\bar{z}_t = \rho^t \bar{z}_0$. Then $\sum_{t=0}^{\infty} p_t w_t$ is well defined as a finite number *or* $+\infty$ for all $w \in C^h$ for all h. Then for any $p \in S(\epsilon)$, pz achieves a finite minimum at a point $z^h(p) \in [\bar{z}, \bar{w}]$. We will prove that $S(\epsilon)$ is closed with an argument that uses $z^h(p)$ in place *of* $-b$, the negative of endowment. Peleg and Yaari used $-b$ for their exchange economy in which the positive orthant is the consumption set. This is a crucial step in the generalization of their theorem.

Lemma 17. *The set $S(\epsilon)$ is closed for $0 < \epsilon < 1$.*

Let $p^s \to \bar{p}$ in the norm topology of l_1^n where $p^s \in S(\epsilon)$. It must be shown that $\bar{p} \in S(\epsilon)$. There is no difficulty with the normalization condition since $\bar{c}$ has only a finite number of nonzero components. However to establish that $\bar{p}z \geq -\epsilon$ holds for an arbitrary $z \in G - Y$ is more difficult. Any such z satisfies $z = w - y$ where $w \in G$ and $y \in Y$. Then it suffices to prove that $\bar{p}w \geq -\epsilon$ and $\bar{p}y \leq 0$. Consider any $w^h \in P^h(x^h)$. Note that pz is well defined for $z \in C^h$ since C^h is bounded below and $p \in l_1^n$. However pz may *be* $+\infty$. Define c^h by $c^h(w^h) = w^h - z^h(\bar{p})$. It follows that $\bar{p}c^h(w^h) \geq 0$. If $w \in G$ then $w = \sum_{h=1}^{H} \alpha_h w^h$ with $\alpha_h \geq 0$ and $\sum_{h=1}^{H} \alpha_h = 1$.

We have $pw \geq -\epsilon$ for $p \in S(\epsilon)$ if and only if

$$p\sum_{h=1}^{H} \alpha_h c^h(w^h) \geq -p\sum_{h=1}^{H} \alpha_h z^h(p) - \epsilon. \tag{4}$$

Define $w(\tau)$ by $w_0(\tau) = w_0 + \delta e_0$, $w_t(\tau) = w_t$ for $t = 1, \cdots, \tau$, and $w_t(\tau) = z_t^h(\bar{p})$ for $t > \tau$. By periodwise monotonicity, Assumption 6, and the fact that $P^h(w^h)$ is open a function $\tau(\delta)$ may be defined that is monotone decreasing and satisfies $w^h(\tau(\delta)) \in P^h(w^h)$ for all h and for all $\delta > 0$. Let $c^h(\tau) = c^h(w(\tau))$. Then $p^s \in S(\epsilon)$ and $w \in G$ imply

$$\delta|p_0^s| + \sum_{h=1}^{H} \alpha_h p^s c^h(\tau(\delta)) \geq -\sum_{h=1}^{H} \alpha_h p^s z^h(p^s) - \epsilon, \tag{5}$$

for $s = 1, 2, \cdots$, and all $\delta > 0$. We must prove that the function $pz^h(p)$ is continuous.

Write $m(p) = pz^h(p)$. The concavity of $m(p)$ implies that it is continuous in the interior of its domain, that is, for $p > 0$. However a general proof may be given which includes the boundary points, except for $p = 0$, and depends on the special properties of $m(p)$.

Proposition 2. *$m(p)$ is continuous for $p \geq 0$, $p \neq 0$.*

Proof. Suppose $m(p)$ is not continuous in l_1^n at some $p \geq 0$, $p \neq 0$. Note that $m(p)$ is finite, since $m(p) = pw$ for some $w \in [\bar{z}, \bar{w}]$ which is contained in l_∞^n by Assumption 3,and $p \in l_1$. Then there is $\epsilon > 0$ and a sequence $p^s \geq 0$, $s = 1, 2, \cdots$, such that $p^s \to p$ in l_1^n and $|m(p^s) - m(p)| \geq \epsilon$ for all s. Thus there is a subsequence $p^s \to p$ (retain notation) and either

(a) $m(p^s) \geq m(p) + \epsilon$, or

(b)$m(p^s) \leq m(p) - \epsilon$.

In case (a) let $w \in (C^h \cap [\bar{z}, \bar{w}])$ be a point where

$$pw \leq m(p) + \epsilon/2. \tag{6}$$

Since $w \in l_\infty^n$, pw is well defined. According to (a) there is a subsequence p^s such that $p^s \to p$ and $p^s w \geq m(p) + \epsilon$. But by (6) for large s we have $p^s w < m(p) + \epsilon$. Therefore case (a) cannot arise.

In case (b) let $w^s \in (C^h \cap [\bar{z}, \bar{w}])$ be a point where

$$p^s w^s \leq m(p^s) + \epsilon/4. \tag{7}$$

According to (b) there is a subsequence w^s such that $p^s w^s \leq m(p) - \epsilon$ for $s = 1, 2, \cdots$ and $p^s \to p$. Let $J = \{i | p_i > 0\}$ and $J' = \{i | p_i = 0\}$. For all i, w_i^s is bounded below. This implies

$$\sum_{i \in J'} p_i^s w_i^s \geq -\epsilon/4 \tag{8}$$

for large s. It follows from the definition of $S(\epsilon)$ that $J \neq \phi$. Note that w_i^s is bounded above for $i \in J$ since $p^s w^s \leq m(p) - \epsilon < p\bar{w}$. Therefore

$$\sum_{i \in J} (p_i - p_i^s) w_i^s \to 0. \tag{9}$$

For s large enough we have

$$m(p) \leq pw^s = \sum_{i\in J} p_i w_i^s \leq \sum_{i\in J} p_i^s w_i^s + \epsilon/4$$
$$= p^s w^s - \sum_{i\in J'} p_i^s w_i^s + \epsilon/4 \leq p^s w^s + \epsilon/2 \leq m(p^s) + 3\epsilon/4. \tag{10}$$

The second inequality is implied by (9) since w_i^s is bounded. The third inequality is implied by (8). The fourth inequality is implied by (7). However (10) contradicts (b). Thus case (b) cannot arise either. ∎

Using Proposition 2 and taking the limit of (5) for given δ as $s \to \infty$ we obtain

$$\delta|\bar{p}_0| + \sum_{h=1}^{H} \alpha_h \bar{p} c^h(\tau(\delta)) \geq -\sum_{h=1}^{H} \alpha_h \bar{p} z^h(\bar{p}) - \epsilon. \tag{11}$$

Now let δ approach 0. The first term vanishes in the limit. Note that $p^s z^h(p^s)$ is well defined since $z^h(\tau(\delta))$ lies in the interval $[\bar{z}^h, \bar{w}^h]$ as a consequence of Assumption 3. Moreover $\bar{p}_t c_t^h(w) \geq 0$ since $\bar{p}_t w_t^h \geq \bar{p}_t z_t^h(\bar{p})$ by the definition of $\bar{z}_t^h(\bar{p})$. Thus $\sum_{h=1}^{H} \alpha_h \bar{p} c^h(\tau(\delta))$ converges to a finite limit *or* $+\infty$ as $\tau(\delta)$ increases. In the limit as $\delta \to 0$ we have

$$\sum_{h=1}^{H} \alpha_h \bar{p} c^h(w) + \sum_{h=1}^{H} \alpha_h \bar{p} z^h(\bar{p}) = \bar{p}w \geq -\epsilon, \tag{12}$$

where $\bar{p}w$ is a finite number *or* $+\infty$. This implies that $\bar{p}$ satisfies the definition of $S(\epsilon)$ for $w \in G$.

We must also show that $\bar{p}$ satisfies the definition of $S(\epsilon)$ for $y \in Y$. We may write $y = \sum_{t=0}^{\infty} y_t$ where $y_t = (0, \cdots, 0, u_{t-1}, v_t, 0, \cdots) \in \bar{Y}_t$ and $u_{t-1} \leq 0$, $v_t \geq 0$. Then $(u_{t-1}, v_t) \in Y_t$ and by Lemma 12 we have $\bar{p}_{t-1}^s u_{t-1} + \bar{p}_t v_t^s \leq 0$ for all s and t. This implies $\bar{p}_{t-1} u_{t-1} + \bar{p}_t v_t \leq 0$ for all t. Since $\sum_{t=0}^{\tau}(\bar{p}_{t-1} u_{t-1} + \bar{p}_t v_t)$ is a sequence indexed by τ which is monotone decreasing it converges to a finite value $\bar{p}y \leq 0$ *or* $-\infty$. This completes the proof that $S(\epsilon)$ is closed. ∎

Since $S(\epsilon)$ is not empty by Lemma 15 and compact and therefore closed by Lemma 16, $S(\epsilon) \subset S(\epsilon')$, for $\epsilon < \epsilon'$, implies by the argument of Lemma 10 that $S^* = \cap_{\epsilon>0} S(\epsilon) \neq \phi$. Let p^* lie in S^*. I claim that $(p^*, y, x^1, ..., x^H)$ where $y = \sum_{h=1}^{H} x^h$ is a competitive equilibrium for $E(\bar{\rho})$. Since $p^* \in S(\epsilon)$ implies $p^* z \geq -\epsilon$ for $z \in G - Y$ and $0 < \epsilon < 1$, we have

$$p^* z \geq 0 \tag{13}$$

for $z \in G - Y$. On the other hand $x = (x^1, ..., x^H) \in G$ implies that $x^h \in G$, so $p^* x^h \geq 0$ for all h. Also $(x^1, ..., x^H)$ feasible implies $\sum_{h=1}^{\infty} x^h \in Y$. Therefore $p^* \cdot \sum_{h=1} x^h \leq 0$ by Lemma 14. This implies

$$p^* x^h = 0 \tag{14}$$

must hold for all h. Then $p^* y = 0$ also holds. Equation (14) establishes the first part of Condition I and the first part of Condition II for competitive equilibrium.

To complete the proof that condition I holds we must show that $w^h \in P^h(x^h)$ implies $w^h \notin B^h(p^*) = \{z^h | p^* z^h \leq 0\}$. A final lemma is

Lemma 18. *If there is $w^h \in C^h$ such that $pw^h < 0$ and $pz^h \geq 0$ for all $z^h \in P^h(x^h)$ then $pz^h > 0$ for all $z^h \in P^h(x^h)$.*

Proof. Suppose $z^h \in P^h(x^h)$ and $pz^h = 0$. Since $P^h(x^h)$ is open in C^h in the product topology by Assumption 4 there is a point $y^h \in \alpha w^h + (1-\alpha)z^h$ such that $y^h \in P^h(x^h)$ and $py^h < 0$. This contradicts the hypothesis. Therefore no such z^h can exist. ∎

From Lemma 18 we see that Condition I will be completed if it can be proved that every consumer has a net trade w^h such that $p^*w^h < 0$. Suppose no consumer has such a net trade. Then it must be that $p^*\bar{x} = 0$ where $\bar{x} = \sum_{h=1}^H \bar{x}^h$. However $\bar{x} \in C$ and $\bar{x} < 0$ implies that $p^*\bar{x}^h < 0$ for some h.

Let I_1 be the set of indices h such that there is $w^h \in C^h$ with $p^*w^h < 0$. Let I_2 be the complementary subset of indices. We have just shown that I_1 is not empty. Suppose that $I_2 \neq \phi$. By Assumption 5 there is a feasible allocation $\{z^h\}$ with $z^h P^h x^h$ for all $h \in I_1$ and $z^h \in C^h$ for all $h \in I_2$ where $y' = z_{I_1} + z_{I_2} \in Y$. By Lemma 18 we have $p^*z_{I_1}^h > 0$. However $p^*z_{I_2}^h \geq 0$ by assumption. Thus $p^*(z_{I_1} + z_{I_2}) = p^*y' > 0$. But feasibility implies $y' \in Y$ which implies $p^*z \leq 0$ for all $z \in Y$. Thus I_2 must be empty. Then by Lemma 18, $w^h \in P^h(x^h)$ implies $p^*w^h > 0$ for all h. This establishes the second part of Condition I for competitive equilibrium. Condition II is implied by $p^*y = 0$ and Lemma 14, and condition III follows from the definition of a feasible trade. Therefore $(p^*, y, x^1, ..., x^h)$, where $y = \sum_{h=1}^H x^h$, is a competitive equilibrium of $E(\bar{\rho})$. This concludes the proof of Theorem 1. ∎

Using stronger topological arguments based on the duality (ba, l_∞) it is possible to extend Theorem 1 to the case of $E(\bar{\rho})$ with $\bar{\rho} = 1$. See Boyd and McKenzie (forthcoming). Apparently that extension cannot be made on Assumptions 1-6 with the more elementary methods used here.

References

Berge, Claude (1963): *Topological Spaces.* Edinburgh: Oliver and Boyd.

Boyd, John H. III, and Lionel W. McKenzie (1991): "The Existence of Competitive Equilibrium over an Infinite Horizon with Production and General Consumption Sets," Working Paper No. 254 (revised), University of Rochester.

Choquet, G. (1962): *Ensembles et cones convexes faiblement complets.* Paris: C. *R.* Acad. Sci.

Debreu, Gerard (1954): "Representation of a Preference Ordering by a Numerical Function," in *Decision Processes.* Ed. R. M. Thrall, C.H. Coombs, and *R.* L. Davis. Wiley: New York.

Debreu, Gerard, and Scarf Herbert (1963): "A Limit Theorem on the Core of an Economy," *International Economic Review,* 4, 235–46.

Hicks, John R. (1939): *Value and Capital.* Oxford: Oxford University Press.

Morishima, Michio (1952): "On the Laws of Change of the Price-System in an Economy which Contains Complementary Commodities," *Osaka Economic Papers,* 1, 101–13.

Peleg, Bezalel, and Menahem E. Yaari (1970): "Markets with Countably Many Commodities," *International Economic Review,* 11, 369-377.

Uzawa, Hirofumi (1958): "The Kuhn-Tucker Theorem in Concave Programming," in *Studies in Linear and Non-Linear Programming.* Ed. K. Arrow, *L.* Hurwicz, and H. Uzawa. Stanford, California: Stanford University Press.

Promoting Capital Improvements by Public Utilities: A Supergame Approach*

DAVID SALANT AND GLENN WOROCH

GTE Laboratories Incorporated

1 Introduction

A public utility undertakes capital improvements only if it expects to earn revenues that cover necessary investments and provide a competitive return. Typically, outlays occur within a short span of time while the returns are spread over a much longer period. This applies to expenditures for cost-reducing investments, capacity expansion, or product enhancements. It is especially true of utilities that adopt new technologies such as the latest advances in telecommunications networks.

Between the time costs are incurred and returns begin to flow, a regulator could reverse the profitability of the investment by driving down output prices or by opening the market to competition. Such actions will cause the firm to revise its expectations and, in turn, to scale back on its plans to expand and improve its operations. This could work to the regulator's disadvantage especially if deteriorating facilities require repeated investments to maintain productive capacity and service quality.

The regulatory agency must offer credible assurances of adequate future rewards to induce the firm to continually invest. Otherwise, the risk of opportunistic behavior could jeopardize projects that are both socially beneficial and privately profitable.

Formal contracts between regulators and their client firms could offer a remedy, but often institutional constraints preclude such contracts. Furthermore, the great uncertainty typical when evaluating benefits and costs for large-scale, long-term investments makes the cost of contract negotiation prohibitive.

In an ongoing relationship, however, contracts may be unnecessary. They become superfluous when long-term considerations outweigh the benefits of opportunistic behavior. In this paper we analyze control of natural monopoly as a

* This paper has benefitted from suggestions made by Bob Rosenthal, Ingo Vogelsang, and Tom Lyon, and comments received in seminars delivered at The Telecommunications Policy Research Conference, The Midwest Mathematical Economics Conference and Virginia Polytechnic Institute. The views expressed in this paper should not be attributed to GTE nor any of its subsidiaries. Remaining errors are, of course, the responsibility of the authors.

repeated interaction between a profit-maximizing firm and a welfare-maximizing regulatory agency. We present conditions where long-run considerations on both sides prevail over the short-run gains of opportunism.

Beginning with an initial stock of capital and a given technology, the utility invests in a capital improvement. Physical immobility and industry specificity make the entire outlay irreversible. In addition, capital depreciates as plant and equipment undergo wear and tear and old technologies become obsolete.

We first characterize the "planning solution" which maximizes welfare subject to the constraint that the discounted value of the firm's future income never falls below some specified value. Under a wide class of circumstances the solution is characterized by the path of capital stock, price and output levels, each converging to some limiting value. In every period, it satisfies a modified Ramsey-Boiteux pricing rule. Rader (1970) characterized the efficient allocation under increasing returns to scale, and derived a static Ramsey-Boiteux pricing rule for the types of scale economies consider here.

The planning solution provides a reference point against which we compare non-cooperative equilibria of the firm-regulator game. The bulk of this paper shows how closely this solution can be approximated at a non-cooperative equilibrium. "Trigger strategies" are employed to achieve near-optimal outcomes. When capital depreciates or investment costs are convex increasing, the firm must continue investing to stay close to the planning solution. And rates which continue to allow the firm to recover part of its capital costs are needed to induce such investment. Should either side deviate too far from the planning solution, trigger strategies call for investment to cease and prices to fall to operating costs.

In general, the greater the punishment for defection, the more each player wants to cooperate. The more the regulator can reduce firm profits, the less likely the firm is to retard investment and the faster capital depreciates, the less likely is the regulator to try to reduce rates. Indeed, the lower the discount rate and the more severe the costs of a breakdown of cooperation, the larger is the equilibrium set and the more closely it can approximate the planning solution.

The analysis suggests several unorthodox prescriptions for regulatory policy. Gradual increases in the capital stock that accompany an uninterrupted, but protracted investment program can be a necessary part of any nearly optimal equilibrium policy.

We also note that lumpiness in the investment technology can preclude realization of all but very inefficient outcomes under price ceiling regulation. Under such circumstances, rate-of-return regulation may be preferable to price regulation. There has long been a suspicion that regulatory institutions fail to erect incentives for efficient investment. Averch and Johnson (1962) found that a regulated firm overinvests when it is allowed to earn a supercompetitive return on capital. Just the opposite tendencies may occur under strict cost-based pricing. The desire to equate prices to current costs generates inadequate revenues to cover the large up-front costs for many projects. Woroch (1987) demonstrates that underinvestment results when regulators pursue this goal.

Weak investment incentives is a particularly serious problem for outlays on drastic product or process innovations. By delaying the price adjustment following an innovation, Bailey (1974) struck a balance between the exercise of market power and strong incentives offered by supernormal profits.

Whether in fact the regulator will permit such profits after the firm has made an investment in the new technology is another story. When the investment is irreversible there may be little desire for the regulator to follow through on its promises. Klein, Crawford and Alchian (1978) and Williamson (1975) emphasize the role of capital sunkness in raising the temptation to behave opportunistically. Goldberg (1976) finds that public utility regulation illustrates the possibilities for bilateral opportunism and herein finds a purpose in traditional administrative regulation.

Salant and Woroch (1992) re-examine these conclusions when the firm and the regulator are long lived. That paper applies the logic of the Folk Theorem to the time-dependent supergame formed from the pricing and investment decisions of the two players. We find that payoffs close to the planning solution can be supported as equilibria through the use of trigger strategies.

This result rests on an extension of the Folk Theorem of repeated games (see Friedman (1990)). The classical Folk Theorem does not apply directly to the supergame when capital is durable. In that case the set of attainable outcomes in a period depends on the previous investment decisions of the firm. Our examples suggest limits to the applicability of the trigger-strategies underpinning the Folk Theorem. In a different setting, Benhabib and Radner (1988) characterize a time-dependent supergame equilibrium. Gilbert and Newbery (1989) examine trigger equilibria in a repeated stochastic game without time dependence.

2 The Model

Both the firm and the regulatory authority have an infinite horizon. Their production, consumption and investment decisions occur at discrete intervals of time. Except for the capital accumulation process, demand and cost conditions are static.

2.1 *Demand*

Demand in each period t depends on both price, p_t, and possibly product quality, z_t. Direct demand is written

$$q_t = Q(p_t, z_t) \tag{1}$$

and inverse demand is

$$p_t = P(q_t, z_t)$$

In this context, the variable z measures investment that can affect consumer perception of product quality. Various interpretations are discussed below.

As usual, we assume that $\partial Q/\partial p \leq 0$. We also assume that $\partial Q/\partial z \geq 0$. When z represents a factor of production (e.g., ordinary plant and equipment), it has no effect on service, so that $\partial Q/\partial z$ is zero.

2.2 *Consumer Surplus*

Consumer surplus is obtained by integrating willingness to pay over all output levels to get

$$S(p,q,z) = \int_0^{Min[q,Q(p,z)]} P(x,z)dx - pq. \tag{2}$$

When $p = P(q,z)$, (2) equals Marshallian surplus, $S(q,z) \equiv S(P(q,z),q,z)$. In that case, notice that $S_q(q,z) = p\varepsilon > 0$ where $\varepsilon \equiv \partial lnQ(p,z)/\partial lnp$ is the price elasticity of demand for a fixed product quality. In what follows $S(q,z)$ is assumed to be (weakly) concave in (q,z).

2.3 *Costs*

Costs are divided into operating and capital components. Total operating cost in period t is

$$v_t = V(q_t, z_t) \tag{3}$$

Marginal costs V_q are non-negative, while V_z can be either positive or negative. Capital costs are a function of gross investment, $I_t \equiv z_t - sz_{t-1}$, where $s \equiv 1 - \delta$ and δ is the depreciation rate making s the "survival" rate of capital. Let k_t be expenditures on capital in period t,

$$k_t = K(I_t) \tag{4}$$

For most of what follows we assume that $K' \geq 0$ and $K'' \geq 0$. The irreversibility of investment is captured by the inequality $z_t \geq sz_{t-1}$.

2.4 *Revenues*

With price set by the regulator, and quantity and quality determined by the firm, revenues in period t can be written as

$$r_t = R(p_t, q_t, z_t) = p_t Min\{q_t, Q(p_t, z_t)\} \tag{5}$$

When the firm operates along its demand curve, we have $r_t = R(q_t, z_t) = q_t P(q_t, z_t)$.

2.5 *Profits*

The firm earns an operating profit in period t equal to the difference between revenues and operating cost $r_t - v_t$. Capital expenses must then be deducted to yield net profit

$$\pi_t(p_t, q_t, z_t, z_{t-1}) = R(p_t, q_t, z_t) - V(q_t, z_t) - K(z_t - sz_{t-1}) \tag{6}$$

2.6 *Objective Functions*

Both the firm and the regulator use the same factor $\rho\epsilon[0,1]$ to discount future payoffs. The regulator maximizes the discounted sum of consumer surpluses

$$\mathcal{S} = \sum_{t=1}^{\infty} \rho^t S(p_t, q_t, z_t) \tag{7}$$

The firm maximizes the discounted sum of profits

$$\Pi = \sum_{t=1}^{\infty} \pi_t(p_t, q_t, z_t, z_{t-1})\rho^t \tag{8}$$

Observe that the regulator places no explicit weight on the firm's profit. However, feasibility dictates that discounted profits never falls below the firm's opportunity costs. When a regulator's plan offers less than its opportunity costs, the firm will never voluntarily enter into the relationship. So, unless the firm can be forced to operate, no optimum nor equilibrium plan can imply a profit level below the opportunity cost.

3 Three Types of Investment

The way in which capital enters our setup allows for a wide variety of interpretations. Three types of investment are highlighted: (I) cost-reducing investment, (II) capacity expansion, and (III) product enhancement. Each case imposes its own special restrictions on demand and cost conditions, and has a different interpretation of depreciation.

(I) Cost-Reducing Investment

When capital is a normal factor of production, investment permits more output to be produced from fixed amounts of all other inputs. As a result, variable cost decreases with the stock of capital, i.e., $V_z < 0$. This corresponds to the usual interpretation of capital as plant and equipment. Alternatively, capital could amount to cumulative knowledge derived from a research and development program or from learning by doing. Whether the capital is physical or not, the passage of time diminishes its contribution to production at a geometric rate.

Either way, demand is independent of capital, i.e., Q_z (and P_z) $= 0$. We also assume that $V_{qq} = 0, V_{qz} \leq 0$, and $V_{zz} > 0$. These last two assumptions mean that investment reduces marginal cost at a decreasing rate. These properties effectively put an upper bound on capital.

(II) Capacity Expansion

A special case of case (I) is where investment determines the level of productive capacity. Demand is once again unaffected by investment. This case can be expressed as

$$V(q,z) = \begin{cases} vq & \text{if } q \leq z, \\ \infty & \text{otherwise} \end{cases}$$

where unit variable cost is constant up to capacity. In this case depreciation amounts to a reduction in the maximum output flow due to physical wear and tear on the facilities.

(III) Product Enhancements

Additional investment can improve products in consumers eyes in either of two ways. Increases in "vertical quality" raise the flow of services provided by a unit of the good for all consumers. This could come from adding nodes and links to a communications network or widening the traffic lanes of a highway.

When the product varies in terms of "horizontal quality," some consumers are made better off when the product is more closely adapted to their tastes. Other consumers disagree. For instance, communications systems can be optimized for voice traffic or for data transmission.

For investments which improve product quality, we assume $\partial Q/\partial z > 0$ (equivalently, $\partial P/\partial z > 0$) and $\partial V/\partial z > 0$. Additionally, we assume that $S(q,z)$ is concave in $(q,z), P_{qz} \geq 0$, $P_{zz} < 0$ and $V(q,z)$ has the multiplicative form $V(q,z) = q\nu(z)$ with $\nu'(z) > 0$ and $\nu''(z) < 0$.

Investments in product improvements depreciate over time just like physical capital. This occurs when competitors introduce new brands or make style changes that carve into demand for the incumbent's product. The substitution could occur smoothly as customers slowly migrate to the new offering, provided it is not a drastic innovation.

4 The Planning Solution

Here we characterize the second-best plan which maximizes discounted consumer surplus S subject to the constraint that the firm earns a given level of profit Π_0. Π_0 measures the firm's opportunity cost of participating in this market. The planning solution is a sequence of prices, quantities, and capital stocks $\{p_t^*, q_t^*, z_t^*\}$ which solves the planning problem

$$\max \quad S \quad \text{subject to} \quad \Pi \geq \Pi_0, p_t \leq P(q_t, z_t), z_t \geq sz_{t-1} \qquad \text{(PP)}$$

for each $t = 1, 2, \ldots, \infty$. The solution reduces to finding a singularity of the following Lagrangean

$$\mathcal{L} = \sum_{t=1}^{\infty} \rho^t \Big\{ S\big[P(q_t, z_t), q_t, z_t\big] + \lambda \pi_t(p_t, q_t, z_t, z_{t-1}) \Big\} \tag{9}$$

The solution to (9) and the corresponding price path depend on the initial capital z_0 as well as the discount factor ρ, the depreciation rate δ, and the opportunity cost Π_0. Let $\{p_t^*(\rho,\delta,\Pi_0,z_0), q_t^*(\rho,\delta,\Pi_0,z_0), z_t^*(\rho,\delta,\Pi_0,z_0)\}$ be the solution where $p_t^* = P(q_t^*, z_t^*)$.

When (PP) has an interior optimum, necessary conditions for a solution include (see Luenberger (1969), p. 249):

$$\rho^t \Big[S_q(q_t, z_t) + \lambda \big[p_t + q_t P_q(q_t, z_t) - V_q(q_t, z_t)\big] \Big] = 0$$

and

$$\rho^t\Big\{S_z(q_t,z_t)+\lambda\big[q_tP_z(q_t,z_t)-V_z(q_t,z_t)-K'(z_t-sz_{t-1})+s\rho K'(z_{t+1}-sz_t)\big]\Big\}=0$$

The first condition reduces to a period-by-period Ramsey pricing rule. The Lerner index of monopoly markup is inversely proportional to the price elasticity

$$\big[p_t - V_q(q_t,z_t)\big]/p_t = \eta/\varepsilon_t \tag{10}$$

where $\varepsilon_t = -p_t/[q_tP_q(q_t,z_t)]$ is the price elasticity of demand at date t and given z_t, and $\eta \in [0,1]$ is the so-called "Ramsey number." For case (II) where z represents capacity, (10) and the first-order condition for capacity can be combined to yield

$$\frac{p_t - MC_t}{p_t} = \frac{\eta}{\varepsilon_t} \tag{11}$$

where

$$MC_t = V_q(q_t,z_t) + K'(z_t - sz_{t-1})$$

is a *dynamic* marginal cost.

We more fully characterize the planning solution in Section 6 below, but examine a few examples before doing so.

5 Some Examples

In this Section we characterize the planning solution for a few examples. We also introduce a regulatory game. In one example we show how the planning solution can be approximated with an equilibrium pair of "trigger strategies." In a second example we show that a unique equilibrium exists where the firm never invests and the regulator never allows recovery of capital costs. Throughout this Section the firm's opportunity cost Π_0 is zero.

5.1 *Capacity with Linear Accumulation Costs*[1]

Here we consider a variant of case (II) in which capital represents capacity. This means z does not directly enter demand so that $P(q,z) = P(q)$, and so

$$S(q,z) = \int_0^{q(z)} P(x)dx - q(z)P\big(q(z)\big)$$

where $q(z) = Min(q,z)$. Also, variable costs take the form

$$V(q,z) = \begin{cases} vq & \text{if } q \le z, \\ \infty & \text{otherwise.} \end{cases}$$

Additionally, capital costs are linear in investment: $K(I_t) = kI_t$.

[1] Taken from Salant and Woroch (1992).

The Planning Solution

Whenever $z_0 \leq \bar{z}^*(\delta) \equiv Max\{z|\ P(z)z - vz - K(\delta z) \geq 0\}$, the optimal planning solution has $z_t^* = \bar{z}^*(\rho, \delta, z_0), q_t = z_t$ and $p_t = \bar{p}^*(\rho, \delta, z_0)$ for each t, where $\bar{z}^*$ and $\bar{p}^*$ satisfy

$$\bar{p}^*(\rho, \delta, z_0) = v + k\big[\delta + (\frac{1-\rho}{\rho})[\bar{z}^*(\rho, \delta, z_0) - z_0]\big].$$

Thus, at an optimum, the firm immediately brings its capacity up to some steady-state value and maintains that level indefinitely. Prices are constant and just sufficient for the firm to recover its operating and capital costs.

The Supergame

In a long-term regulatory relationship, the firm typically chooses price, investment and output levels within the constraints imposed by the regulatory agency. Here we assume that the regulator can set a ceiling price, $\hat{p}_t$, in each period t but has no direct control over investment or output. The firm chooses its output and investment in each period subject to the constraints that (i) $z_t \geq sz_{t-1}$, i.e., the firm cannot divest at a rate faster than the depreciation rate, (ii) $q_t \leq Q(p_t, z_t)$, i.e, the firm cannot sell more than the quantity demanded, and (iii) $p_t \leq \hat{p}_t$, i.e., price does not exceed the ceiling.

Thus a strategy for the regulator is a sequence of rules, $\hat{p}_t(h_t)$, determining a price ceiling at each date t as a function of the history up to that date,

$$h_t = (z_0, \hat{p}_1, z_1, \hat{p}_2, z_2, \ldots, \hat{p}_{t-1}, z_{t-1}).$$

For the firm, a strategy is a sequence of decision rules, $z_t(h_t)$, giving its capacity at any date t as a function of the history, h_t.

A subgame perfect equilibrium is a pair of sequences of decision rules such that at any date t and for any history, h_t, the continuation of play dictated by the rules are such that neither the firm nor the regulator can change its rule for any later date and expect to earn a larger payoff.

Notice that price and quantity are not part of the firm's strategy. At each date t, the firm chooses p_t and q_t after $\hat{p}_t$ and z_t are determined. The prices the firm chooses at a subgame perfect equilibrium will maximize its current profits. This follows because payoffs at any later date in no way depend on the firm's current price and output decisions. Thus, the subgame perfect equilibrium values for price and quantity are completely determined by the ceiling price and capacity at that date.

Equilibria

This game has multiple equilibria. We characterize two extreme types. One is the grim equilibrium in which the firm never invests and the regulator disallows any operating profits: $z_t = sz_{t-1}$ and $\hat{p}_t = v$ for each period t and for all histories h_t. These minmax strategies have each player hold down payoff to the other to the maximum that they can achieve.

Second, we consider a strategy in which players adhere to stationary actions unless one or the other deviates. A deviation "triggers" a reversion to the minmax strategies. For $\delta < 1$, let the strategies be:

$$(12) \qquad \hat{p}_t(h_t) = \begin{cases} \bar{p} & \text{if } \hat{p}_t = \bar{p} \text{ and } z_\tau = \bar{z} \text{ for all } \tau \in \{1,\ldots,t-1\}, \\ v & \text{otherwise.} \end{cases}$$

and

$$(13) \qquad z_t(h_t) = \begin{cases} \bar{z} & \text{if } \hat{p}_t = \bar{p} \text{ and } z_\tau = \bar{z} \text{ for all } \tau \in \{1,\ldots,t-1\}, \\ s z_{t-1} & \text{otherwise.} \end{cases}$$

Salant and Woroch (1992) show that, for some $\bar{z}$, with $z_0 < \bar{z} < \bar{z}^*(\delta)$, and for ρ sufficiently close to one, this pair of strategies is a subgame perfect equilibrium. It is also shown that any $\bar{z}$ such that $[P(\bar{z}) - v]\bar{z} - K(\delta\bar{z}) \geq \frac{s(1-\rho)}{\rho - s(1-\rho)}$ can emerge at an equilibrium.

The reasoning behind the result follows by a simple check of the incentives for both players to deviate from the stationary path. By defecting from $\bar{z}$, the firm saves the replacement investment of $k\delta\bar{z}$ in that period. In exchange, it must forsake a profit flow equal to $[\bar{p} - v - k\delta\bar{z}] > 0$ in all subsequent periods. The present value of continued cooperation will exceed the one-time gain of defection for ρ sufficiently close to one.

The regulator can likewise generate a higher short-run surplus for consumers by cutting price down to v. However, defection from $\bar{p}$ results in declining capacity over time as capital depreciates. Consumer surplus will decline accordingly. For ρ close enough to one, the regulator will prefer the long-run benefits of continued cooperation to the short-run gains of a defection.

5.2 *Perfectly Durable Capacity and Fixed Demand*

We now simplify the above example slightly. Let demand be perfectly inelastic up to some reservation price

$$Q(p) = \begin{cases} \bar{q} & \text{if } 0 \leq p \leq \bar{p}, \\ 0 & \text{otherwise.} \end{cases}$$

Also ignore any variable costs, i.e., $V(q,z) = 0$ for all q and z, and assume that capital does not depreciate, i.e., $\delta = 0$. Finally, let $K(z - \tilde{z}) = \alpha(z - \tilde{z})$ where $\alpha < 1$.

In this example the planning solution calls for $z_t = \bar{q}$ and $p_t = \alpha(1-\rho)(\bar{q}-z_0)/\rho\bar{q}$ for all t. This is not an equilibrium since after the firm sinks its investment, the regulator has no incentive to allow a positive price. However, the trigger strategies from the last example can be modified to support other equilibria. They have the property that, when discounting is sufficiently slow, capacity comes arbitrarily close to $\bar{q}$ after any finite number of periods.

Such equilibria require the triggers be based on capacity increments $I_t = (z_t - z_{t-1}) = \beta^t I_0$, and prices such that $p_t z_t = I_t$ for each t. Whenever $\beta > (1-\rho)/\rho$, such a price and investment path can be supported as an equilibrium using trigger strategies described above.

The firm's per-period profit decreases over time as does price along the equilibrium path. Discounted future profits from cooperation always outweigh the one-time increase in profit the firm can earn by terminating investment. Similarly, the amount of additional capacity that the regulator can expect the firm to add falls over time, but so also does the price ceiling it imposes on the firm. The regulator's benefit from cooperation declines, but continues to exceed the benefit of dropping price to zero. As price goes to zero, the additional surplus the regulator can provide consumers through price reductions also vanishes, and this term is always less than the present discounted value of the anticipated additional capacity accumulation.

5.3 *Cost-Reducing Investment*

Now we consider a special version of case (I) in which capital represents the cumulative stock of cost-reducing investment. In particular, we suppose $V(q, z) = q/z$ and that $K(I) = I^2/2$. Further, since z does not enter demand, $P(q, z) = P(q)$ for all z. After briefly describing the optimal plan, we return to this case in Section 6 to establish that the optimal plan can be approximated at an equilibrium by means of trigger strategies.

Investment has a declining marginal value. The planning solution will select a sequence $\{(q_t, z_t)\}$ which solves: $\max \sum_{t=1}^{\infty} \rho^t S(q_t)$ subject to $\sum_{t=1}^{\infty} \rho^t \{q_t P(q_t) - q_t/z_t - (z_t - z_{t-1})^2/2\} \geq 0$. This sequence has the property that q_t and z_t are both monotone increasing and converge to $\bar{q}$ and $\bar{z}$, respectively. Price, $p_t = P(q_t)$, will gradually fall toward a limit value $\bar{p}$.

5.4 *Lumpy Investment*

Here we modify case (II) by supposing that capacity increments up to some fixed level $\bar{I} > 0$ incur a fixed cost $f > 0$

$$K(z_t - z_{t-1}) = \begin{cases} 0 & \text{if } z_t - z_{t-1} = 0, \\ f & \text{if } 0 < z_t - z_{t-1} \leq \bar{I}, \\ \infty & \text{if } z_t - z_{t-1} > \bar{I}. \end{cases}$$

Note that this construction technology implies that the firm will wish to add capacity $\bar{I}$ units at a time, since faster accumulation is prohibitively expensive and a slower rate is uneconomical. The planning solution calls for the firm to invest until demand saturation $\bar{q}$ is reached after which the firm ceases all investment. Prices should be constant over time and just sufficient for the firm to recover its investment outlays.

However, this outcome can never be approximated at an equilibrium. In this example, for any initial capacity, equilibrium is unique: the firm never invests and the regulator never allows any return. Because of the fixed investment cost and no depreciation, there is at most a finite number of periods in which investment occurs. After the last period investment occurs, the regulator has no incentive for further cooperation. Essentially, the game reduces to a finite-horizon game. As with all finitely repeated perfect information games having a unique equilibrium in the stage game, cooperation breaks down.

6 The Game

Typically a regulator lacks the ability to implement the planning solution. A privately-owned enterprise will invariably want to maintain a higher price and lower output than levels dictated by efficiency. A regulator can much more easily constrain a firm than directly control it, which he does through the limitation on price. In addition, regulators often impose quality standards and obligation to serve constraints as well. The regulated firm can choose investment levels and may have some flexibility in its choice of quantity and quality.

A principal goal of this paper is to determine how close the planning solution can be approximated at an equilibrium when the regulator has less than complete control over the firm's operations. We assume that at the beginning of each period, the regulator chooses a price ceiling at the same time the firm decides on its level of capital. This simultaneity represents an information lag of a discrete time model: neither player can react simultaneously to unexpected deviations by the other. They both need time to detect and respond to policy changes. The information and response lag determines the length of the period which, in turn, affects the discount rate. The shorter the lag, the closer the discount rate is to zero.

More importantly, the information-response lag allows either party to "cheat" by deviating from any anticipated price ceiling or capital level. The longer the lag, the more transitory profit the firm can earn by curtailing investment before the regulator can retaliate with a drop in the ceiling. Similarly, with a longer lag, the regulator can boost surplus for a longer period of time before the firm can react and cut its investment.

Given a price ceiling and capital stock, the firm is free to choose any price-quantity pair such that (i) price does not exceed the ceiling, (ii) quantity does not exceed demand at the ceiling, and (iii) quantity does not exceed capacity. We assume that the firm will pick that price-quantity pair that maximizes, over all pairs that meet the constraints, its revenues minus costs for the period.

The strategic variables are the price ceiling and capital investment, respectively. (Incorporating a separate stage for the firm to pick price and quantity does not change the equilibrium set, as subgame perfection dictates that in each period the actual price and quantity maximize the firm's profits for the period.) A strategy for the regulator is a sequence of rules, $\{\hat{p}_t(h_t) : t = 1, 2, \ldots, \infty\}$, where for each t, $\hat{p}_t(h_t)$ determines a price ceiling for period t as a function of the history, $h_t = (z_0, \hat{p}_1, z_1, \ldots, \hat{p}_{t-1}, z_{t-1})$, up to date t. For the firm a strategy is a sequence of decision rules $\{z_t(h_t) : t = 1, 2, \ldots, \infty\}$, where for each t, $z_t(h_t)$ determines a capital level for period t, $z_t \geq sz_{t-1}$, as a function of the history through that period.

A subgame perfect equilibrium is a pair of strategies $(\{\hat{p}_t(h_t)\}, \{z_t(h_t)\})$ such that given any date t and history h_t, neither the firm nor the regulator can earn a higher profit or surplus, discounted back to that date, by changing their strategy.

Strategies that select an action at every date independent of earlier moves are called open-loop strategies. Salant and Woroch (1992) show that a unique equilibrium in open-loop strategies exists where in each period no investment is undertaken and price equals unit operating cost. These strategies are equilibrium minmax (and maxmin) strategies in all continuation games. From any date t on, the firm can guarantee zero profits, and the regulator can always hold it down to zero profits. The worst outcome that can befall the regulator from any date t on occurs when the firm stops investing.

In the next Section we see that there are often many equilibria in the regulatory game. For the class of models we consider we show that the optimal planning solution can be approximated arbitrarily closely at an equilibrium when discounting is sufficiently slow.

7 Optima and Equilibria

7.1 *Optima*

Here we characterize the optimal planning solution. Recall there are three classes of investment being considered: (I) cost-reducing investment, (II) capacity expansion, and (III) product enhancement.

In each case the surplus $S(q,z)$ is concave, investment cost $K(I)$ is convex increasing, variable cost $V(q,k)$ is linear in output up to capacity, and revenue $R(q,z)$ is concave. This implies that the planning solution will have output, price and capital paths that approach finite limits as time goes to infinity.

Consider a close relative to the planning problem (PP)

$$\max\left\{\sum_{1}^{\infty}\rho^t S(q_t,z_t)\right\} \tag{14}$$

subject to:

$$\sum_{t=\tau}^{\infty}\rho^t\{q_tP(q_t,z_t)-V(q_t,z_t)-K(z_t-sz_{t-1})\}\geq\rho^{\tau}\Pi_0, \tag{15}$$

for each $\tau=1,2,\ldots$ and $p_t=P(q_t,z_t)$.

The solution depends on (ρ,δ,z_0,Π_0). Denote it by

$$\{p_t^{**}(\rho,\delta,z_0,\Pi_0),q_t^{**}(\rho,\delta,z_0,\Pi_0),z_t^{**}(\rho,\delta,z_0,\Pi_0)\}$$

where $t=1,2,\ldots,\infty$. Let $\mathbf{P}^{**}(\rho,\delta,z_0,\Pi_0)$ be shorthand for the entire sequence $p_t^{**}(\rho,\delta,z_0,\Pi_0)$ for $t=1,2,\ldots,\infty$. Likewise for $\mathbf{Q}^{**}(\rho,\delta,z_0,\Pi_0)$ and $\mathbf{Z}^{**}(\rho,\delta,z_0,\Pi_0)$.

The inequality (15) constrains discounted profits from any date τ on to never fall below Π_0 in current terms. It is more severe than that imposed by the planning solution (PP) which merely requires that (15) be satisfied for $\tau=1$.

LEMMA 1: *(i) For $\rho<1, p_t^{**}(\rho,\delta,z_0,\Pi_0)\to\bar{p}^*(\rho,\delta,z_0,\Pi_0)<\infty, q_t^{**}(\rho,\delta,z_0,\Pi_0)\to\bar{q}^*(\rho,\delta,z_0,\Pi_0)<\infty$ and $z_t^{**}(\rho,\delta,z_0,\Pi_0)\to\bar{z}^*(\rho,\delta,z_0,\Pi_0)$ as $t\to\infty$ for some $\bar{p}^*(\rho,\delta,z_0,\Pi_0)$, $\bar{q}^*(\rho,\delta,z_0,\Pi_0)$, and $\bar{z}^*(\rho,\delta,z_0,\Pi_0)$. (ii) $\bar{p}^*(\rho,\delta,z_0,\Pi_0)\to\bar{p}^*(\delta),\bar{q}^*(\rho,\delta,z_0,\Pi_0)\to\bar{q}^*(\delta)$ and $\bar{z}^*(\rho,\delta,z_0,\Pi_0)\to\bar{z}^*(\delta)$ as $\rho\to 1$, where $[\bar{q}^*(\delta),\bar{z}^*(\delta)]=\operatorname{argmax}\{S(q,z)\mid qP(q,z)-V(q,z)-K(\delta z)\geq 0\}$ and $\bar{p}^*(\delta)=P(\bar{q}^*(\delta),\bar{z}^*(\delta))$.*

PROOF: See Appendix.

Part (i) of the above lemma says that the solution (14) subject to (15) approaches a finite limit. Part (ii) says that as the discount factor approaches one, this limit converges to the surplus-maximal price-quantity-capital triple which can be sustained and still allow the firm to break even. Note that for $\Pi_0 = 0$, Lemma 1 provides a characterization of the optimal planning solution for that special case.

7.2 *Equilibria*

Here we characterize one extreme of the equilibrium set. In particular, we show that equilibrium can result in *normalized* payoffs arbitrarily close to that of the planning solution as the discount factor approaches one. We normalize payoffs because otherwise they diverge to infinity when $\rho = 1$. Normalized consumer surplus for the regulator is

$$NS(\mathbf{Q}, \mathbf{Z}, \rho) = \frac{1}{1-\rho}\left[\sum_{t=1}^{\infty} \rho^t S(q_t, z_t)\right].$$

and normalized profit for the firm is

$$N\Pi(\mathbf{Q}, \mathbf{Z}, \rho) = \frac{1}{1-\rho}\left[\sum_{t=1}^{\infty} \rho^t \big(q_t P(q_t, z_t) - V(q_t, z_t) - K(z_t - s z_{t-1})\big)\right].$$

Recall that $\bar{z}^*(\delta)$ is the surplus-maximal capital stock that can be sustained and still allow the firm to break even. The following pair of trigger strategies:

$$\hat{s}_t^*(h_t) = \begin{cases} p_t^{**}(\rho_0, \delta, z_0, \Pi_0) & \text{if } h_t = h_t^* \\ V_q(q, s q_{t-1}) & \text{otherwise} \end{cases} \tag{16}$$

and

$$z_t^*(h_t) = \begin{cases} z_t^{**}(\rho_0, \delta, z_0, \Pi_0) & \text{if } h_t = h_t^* \\ s z_{t-1} & \text{otherwise.} \end{cases} \tag{17}$$

are used to in the following proposition to show that the plan that solves (14) and (15), and which also provides greater profits than the planning solution, is an equilibrium outcome.

PROPOSITION 1: *Given $z_0 \leq \bar{z}^*(\delta), 0 < \rho_0 < 1, \Pi_0 > 0$, and $\epsilon > 0$, there exists $\rho(\epsilon) < 1$ such that for all ρ with $\rho(\epsilon) < \rho < 1$, the pair of strategies (16) and (17) is a subgame perfect equilibrium.*

PROOF: See Appendix.

Lemma 1 and Proposition 1 together are used to establish that the outcome of the strategies (16) and (17) can, in terms of normalized payoffs, come arbitrarily close to the planning solution.

PROPOSITION 2: *Given $\epsilon > 0$, there exists $\rho(\epsilon) < 1$ such that the normalized payoffs to the regulator from the equilibrium outcome* $\Big(\mathbf{Q}^{**}(\rho, \delta, z_0, \Pi_0),$ $\mathbf{Z}^{**}(\rho, \delta, z_0, \Pi_0)\Big)$ *determined by (16) and (17) above, satisfies*

$$\left|NS\Big(\mathbf{Q}^{**}(\rho, \delta, z_0, \Pi_0), \mathbf{Z}^{**}(\rho, \delta, z_0, \Pi_0)\Big) - S\Big(\bar{q}^*(\delta), \bar{z}^*(\delta)\Big)\right| < \epsilon$$

whenever $1 \geq \rho > \rho(\epsilon)$.

PROOF: See Appendix.

When $z_0 < \bar{z}^*(\delta)$, the normalized total profits at any equilibrium in which investment occurs must be bounded away from zero. This is because the firm can always earn a one-time positive profit by foregoing investment in a period in which it is supposed to invest and then ceasing all investment thereafter. However, as $\rho \rightarrow 1$, the firm's per-period profit along an equilibrium path converging to some $\bar{z}$ can be made to approach zero.

Similarly, the equilibrium per-period surplus will always fall short of $S(\bar{q}^*(\delta), \bar{z}^*(\delta))$ whenever $z_0 < \bar{z}^*(\delta)$. This follows because the cost of building up the capital stock to $\bar{z}^*(\delta)$ can never be completely recovered, although its discounted average value can be made arbitrarily small as the discount factor approaches one.

Implicit in (16) and (17) are perhaps unrealistically grim punishments. Usually regulations prevent firms from abandoning plants. And laws against "takings" make it costly for a regulator to confiscate the firm's plant or deny it any opportunity for a profit. However, it can easily be shown that only minor modifications in the proofs of Propositions 1 and 2 are needed to allow for less severe punishments.

8 Conclusions

Our analysis offers several significant lessons regarding regulation of investment in infrastructure. It indicates that levels of investment and prices which approximate the planning solution can emerge at stable equilibria when long-term considerations outweigh short-term benefits of opportunism. To support such cooperation, it must be the case that (i) discounting is slow enough to induce both sides to continue cooperating, (ii) the firm and regulator each can react in a way that will punish the other side for deviating from the cooperative plan, and (iii) these threats of punishments are credible. When both believe that a deviation will results in abandonment of the cooperative plan, the firm will want to continue investing and the regulator will want to reward the investment with a reasonable return.

Our examples reveal that it is particularly difficult to support lumpy and durable investment typical of so many public utility projects. There is a desire to build up capital stocks rapidly when capital is durable. In this way the firm is able to capture the productive services over a longer horizon. Never-the-less, if the construction technology allows it, successful completion of the project in a strategic relationship may require the firm to accumulate capital gradually.

By slowly approaching a target level of capacity, both sides have a continued stake in the relationship: incremental additions to capacity promise the regulator additional consumer surplus, and future rates above operating costs allow the firm additional profit. The prospect for more future surplus and profit may not be large, and will generally diminish over time, but each side retains the expectation of future payoff exceeding the payoff from terminating their relationship.

Some other conclusions emerge from our analysis. We see that the larger the costs of a breakdown in cooperation, the better are the outcomes that can emerge at equilibrium. Further, slower discounting implies that any target level of capital can be approached more rapidly, and higher target levels can be reached, at equilibrium.

On a final note, we wish to stress that although outcomes that approximate optima can be equilibria, their realization requires extensive communication and coordination. Without coordination, the firm and the regulator will miss out on opportunities to achieve Pareto improving equilibria in the underlying non-cooperative game.

9 Appendix

PROOF OF LEMMA 1:

(i) By assumption $S(q,z)$ is concave, $K(I)$ are convex increasing, and in each of cases (I)-(III) it can be seen that (1) if $z_0 > \bar{z}^*(\delta)$, z_t^{**} is monotone decreasing in t, (2) for $z_0 < \bar{z}^*(\delta)$, z_t^{**} is monotone increasing in t, and (3) q_t^{**} is monotone increasing (respectively decreasing) whenever z_t^{**} is increasing (respectively decreasing). Further q_t^{**} and z_t^{**} are bounded by assumption. So $\{q_t^{**}, z_t^{**}\}$ has a limit point, $[\bar{q}^*(\rho,\delta,\Pi_0,z_0), \bar{z}^*(\rho,\delta,\Pi_0,z_0)]$. Let $\bar{p}^*(\rho,\delta,\Pi_0,z_0)$ be the corresponding inverse demand price. Then by continuity of demand, $\bar{p}^*(\rho,\delta,\Pi_0,z_0)$ must be a limit point of $\{p_t^{**}\}$.

(ii) As $\rho \to 1$, it must be the case that $\{\bar{q}^*(\rho,\delta,\Pi_0,z_0), \bar{z}^*(\rho,\delta,\Pi_0,z_0)\} \to \{\bar{q}^*(\delta), \bar{z}^*(\delta)\}$, and if not, it must be the case that $\{\bar{q}^*(\rho,\delta,\Pi_0,z_0), \bar{z}^*(\rho,\delta,\Pi_0,z_0)\} \to (q',z') \neq \{\bar{q}^*(\delta), \bar{z}^*(\delta)\}$. In each case (I)-(III), welfare in each period is higher the larger is capital, and as $(\bar{z}^*(\delta), \bar{q}^*(\delta))$ maximize S(q,z) subject to $qP(q,z) - V(q,z) - K(sz) \geq 0$, and the solution for (14) subject to (15) requires higher output in each period the larger is capital in that period, it also must be the case that both $z' < \bar{z}^*(\delta)$ and $q' < \bar{q}^*(\delta)$.

But for ρ sufficiently close to one, a path can be constructed that satisfies (15) and provides the regulator with greater surplus than any path converging to (q',z') with $q' < \bar{q}^*(\delta)$ and $z' < \bar{z}^*(\delta)$. Consider

$$(18) \qquad (q_r, z_r) = Argmax_{q,z}\{S(q,z) \mid qP(q,z) - V(q,z) - K(sz) \geq r\Pi_0\}$$

where $r = \frac{1-\rho}{\rho}$. Notice that as $r \to 0$, $\rho \to 1$, and $(q_r, z_r) \to (\bar{q}^*(\delta), \bar{z}^*(\delta))$. Let $(\mathbf{Q}(r), \mathbf{Z}(r))$ be the "fastest" path to (q_r, z_r), that is, the one with the fewest number of periods to satisfy (18). As $r \to 0$, $\rho \to 1$, and $NS(\mathbf{Q}(r), \mathbf{Z}(r)) \to$

$S[\bar{q}^*(\delta), \bar{z}^*(\delta)] > S(q', z')$. Thus, $\left(q^*(\rho, \delta, \Pi_0, \hat{z}_0), (z^*(\rho, \delta, \Pi_0, \hat{z}_0)\right) \rightarrow \left(\bar{q}^*(\delta), \bar{z}^*(\delta)\right)$ as $\rho \rightarrow 1$. ∎

PROOF OF PROPOSITION 1:

Cooperation for the firm, i.e., adherence to (17), implies payoffs of at least $\Pi_0(\frac{1-\rho_0}{\rho_0})(\frac{\rho}{1-\rho})$ in any continuation game. Defection at t yields a payoff of no more than $p_t^{**}Q(p_t^{**}, sz_{t-1}^{**}) - V(q_t^{**}, sz_{t-1}^{**})$. For ρ sufficiently close to 1, the former must exceed the latter.

Similarly for the regulator, continued adherence to (16) implies payoffs close to

$$\left(\frac{1-\rho}{\rho}\right) S(\bar{q}^*(\delta), \bar{z}^*(\delta))$$

(discounted to date t) for ρ sufficiently close too one. Deviation at date t leads to payoffs, discounted to that date, not exceeding

$$\sum_{\tau=t}^{\infty} \rho^{\tau-t+1} S(s^{\tau-t+1} z_t)$$

where $S(z) = Max\{S(q, z) \mid q = Q(p, z)$ for some q such that $qP(q, z) \geq V(q, z)\}$. If $s < 1$, the former expression must exceed the latter for ρ sufficiently near 1. ∎

PROOF OF PROPOSITION 2:

For $\frac{1-\rho}{\rho}\Pi_0 < \Pi^M \equiv \max\{qP(q, z) - V(q, z) - K(\delta z) : q \geq 0, z \geq 0\}$, Lemma 1 establishes that the plan that maximizes (14) subject to (18) satisfies:

$$[q_t^{**}(\rho, \delta, \Pi_0, z_0), z_t^{**}(\rho, \delta, \Pi_0, z_0)] \rightarrow [\bar{q}^*(\delta), \bar{z}^*(\delta)]$$

as $\rho \rightarrow 1$. Thus, the strategies (16) and (17) imply that, along the equilibrium path, $S[q_t^{**}(\rho, \delta, \Pi_0, z_0), z_t^{**}(\rho, \delta, \Pi_0, z_0)] \rightarrow S(\bar{q}^*(\delta), \bar{z}^*(\delta))$ as $\rho \rightarrow 1$ for any z_0 with $0 \leq z_0 \leq \bar{z}^*(\delta)$. So for ρ_0 in Proposition 1 for which surplus converges fast enough to $S(\bar{q}^*(\delta), \bar{z}^*(\delta))$, the strategy pair (16) and (17) will have the desired properties for ρ sufficiently close to 1. ∎

References

AVERCH, H. AND L. JOHNSON (1962): "Behavior of the firm under regulatory constraint," *American Economic Review,* 52, 1052-69.

BAILEY, E. (1974): "Innovation and regulation," *Journal of Public Economics,* 3, 285-95.

BARON, D. AND R. MYERSON (1982): "Regulating a monopolist with unknown cost," *Econometrica,* 50, 911-30.

BENHABIB, J., AND R. RADNER (1988): "Joint exploitation of a productive asset: a game-theoretic approach," New York University Research Report 88-17.

BROCK, W. AND W.D. DECHERT (1985): "Dynamic Ramsey pricing," *International Economic Review,* 26, 569-91.

FRIEDMAN, J. (1990): "A modification of the Folk Theorem to apply to time-dependent supergames," *Oxford Economic Papers*, 317-35.

GILBERT, R. AND D. NEWBERY (1989): "Dynamic efficiency of regulatory constitutions," University of California-Berkeley.

GOLDBERG, V. (1976): "Regulation and administered contracts," *Bell Journal of Economics,* 7, 426-48.

KYDLAND, F. AND E. PRESCOTT (1977): "Rules rather than discretion: the inconsistency of optimal plans," *Journal of Political Economy,* 85, 473-91.

KLEIN, B., R. CRAWFORD, AND A. ALCHIAN (1978): "Vertical integration, appropriable rents, and the competitive contracting process," *Journal of Law and Economics,* 21, 279-326.

LAFFONT, J.-J. AND J. TIROLE (1986): "Using cost observations to regulate firms," *Journal of Political Economy,* 94, 614-641.

LINHART, P., R. RADNER AND F. SINDEN (1983): "A sequential Principal-Agent approach to regulation," in *Proceedings of the 10th Telecommunications Conference*, ed. by H. Gandy, P. Espinosa and J. Ordover. Norwood, NJ: ABLEX Publishing Co..

LUENBERGER, D. (1969): *Optimization by Vector Space Methods.* John Wiley: New York.

RADER, T. (1970): "Resource allocation with increasing returns to scale," *American Economic Review,* 55, no. 5, 814-25.

SALANT, D. AND G. WOROCH (1992): "Trigger price regulation," *Rand Journal of Economics*, forthcoming.

VOGELSANG, I. (1988): "Price cap regulation of telecommunications services: a long-run approach," Rand Note N-2704-MF.

WILLIAMSON, O. (1975): *Markets and Hierarchies.* Free Press: New York.

WOROCH, G. (1987): "Credible price control," GTE Laboratories Economics Discussion Paper.

Kernels of Replicated Market Games

LLOYD S. SHAPLEY*
UCLA

1 Introduction

Our subject is replicated TU economies and the kernels of the cooperative games that they generate. The kernel is a multi-bilateral bargaining equilibrium; it contains the nucleolus and is contained in most bargaining sets. Two players are considered to be in equilibrium if at the given outcome they split their combined payoff equally between what they could claim on the basis of marginal worth to coalitions containing one but not the other. To qualify for the kernel, an outcome must have *all* pairs of players in equilibrium simultaneously. It is somewhat remarkable that the kernel is never empty.

The kernel has a special relationship to the core. Any core point is at the center of a (possibly degenerate) "asterisk" of line segments in the core, radiating in all directions of possible two-player transfers. A core point is a member of the kernel if and only if it *bisects* all the line segments that make up its "asterisk." Despite the fact that the core provides at most $n-1$ dimensions in which to satisfy up to $\binom{n}{2}$ conditions, there is always at least one point that does this, assuming of course that the core is not empty.[1] Indeed, the nucleolus has this property. Unlike the nucleolus, however, kernel points can also appear outside the core, even when the core is not empty.

Although the kernel often turns out to contain just one point, it is generally a formidable task to verify that there are no other points.[2] It is therefore pleasant to be able to report here on a class of games that have played a historical role in economic theory—the replicated market games—in which the kernels are easy to work with and yet exhibit very interesting behavior.

*This paper grew out of joint work with Martin Shubik, begun in the 1970's and supported then by both the National Science Foundation and the Office of Naval Research, but not heretofore published. It was presented at an International Conference on Game Theory at SUNY Stony Brook in July 1990.

[1]This bisection property also holds for any nonempty *strong* ε*-core*; see Maschler, Peleg and Shapley (1979).

[2]Even in the case of *convex* games, where most cooperative solutions shed their complexities under the benign influence of an all-powerful core, the kernel remains a "hard nut" to crack. Though it's easily shown that the kernel of a convex game is in the core, the additional fact that it is a single point requires a most elaborate argument (Maschler, Peleg, Shapley (1972)).

Just as the nucleolus was first presented as a way of explaining the nonemptiness of the kernel, the kernel began as a way of proving the nonemptiness of a certain bargaining set.[3] Our example in §6 of a nonconvergent kernel in a replication sequence of TU markets therefore serves as a counterexample to the convergence of certain bargaining sets as well. The counterexample will be seen to depend on the piecewise-linearity of the underlying utility functions and may be compared with the more positive results that have been obtained for smooth utility functions.[4]

Recognizing that many readers will be unfamiliar with the kernel concept, we have taken this opportunity to review many of its basic properties along the way.

2 Definitions and Notation

We shall follow, with a few exceptions, the terminology and notation of Maschler, Peleg and Shapley (1979).

Let N be a finite set of size $n = |N|$, and let $\mathcal{N}$ stand for its power set 2^N. It will be convenient to define[5]

$$\mathcal{N}_i \;=:\; \{S \in \mathcal{N} : i \in S\}, \qquad \text{all } i \in N, \text{ and}$$

$$\mathcal{N}_{i\backslash j} =: \; \{S \in \mathcal{N} : i \in S,\, j \notin S\}, \qquad \text{all } i, j \in N,\ i \neq j.$$

By a *game*[6] Γ we shall mean an ordered pair (N, v), where v is a function from $\mathcal{N}$ to the real numbers $\mathbf{R}$ such that $v(\oslash) = 0$. We call v (or Γ) *monotonic* if

$$S \supseteq T \implies v(S) \geq v(T), \qquad \text{all } S, T \in \mathcal{N},$$

and *0-monotonic* if v_0 is monotonic, where v_0 is the "0-normalization" of v :

$$v_0(S) \;=:\; v(S) - \textstyle\sum_{i \in S} v(\{i\}), \qquad \text{all } S \in \mathcal{N}.$$

We note that in the standard interpretation of the characteristic function v is automatically superadditive, and hence 0-monotonic. As customary in this context, $\mathbf{R}^N$ will denote the n-dimensional product space $\mathbf{R}^n$ with coordinates indexed by $i \in N$. If $x \in \mathbf{R}^N$, then "x" will be used both for the real vector $(x_i : i \in N)$ and the additive set function $x(S) =: \sum_{i \in S} x_i$.

Given $\Gamma = (N, v)$, certain basic subsets of $\mathbf{R}^N$ are

$${}_{\mathbf{p}}\mathbf{X}(\Gamma) \;=:\; \{x \in \mathbf{R}^N : x(N) = v(N)\}, \qquad \text{(the \textit{pre-imputations} of } \Gamma)$$

$$\mathbf{X}(\Gamma) \;=:\; \{x \in {}_{\mathbf{p}}\mathbf{X}(\Gamma) : x_i \geq v(\{i\}),\ \text{all } i \in N\}, \qquad \text{(the \textit{imputations} of } \Gamma)$$

$$\mathbf{C}(\Gamma) \;=:\; \{x \in \mathbf{X}(\Gamma) : x(S) \geq v(S),\ \text{all } S \in \mathcal{N}\}. \qquad \text{(the \textit{core} of } \Gamma)$$

---

[3] See Schmeidler (1969) for the nucleolus; Maschler (1966), Maschler and Peleg (1966), and Davis and Maschler (1965) for the kernel.

[4] Shapley and Shubik, in Shubik (1984; App. B); see also Mas-Colell (1989).

[5] The symbol "=:" indicates a definition.

[6] More fully, a "cooperative TU game in characteristic-function form."

(The argument "Γ" will be omitted when there is no danger of confusion.)

We now introduce the sequence of concepts leading to the "multi-bilateral" equilibrium. First the *excess* of S at x:

$$e(S,x) =: v(S) - x(S), \qquad \text{all } S \in \mathcal{N},\ x \in {}_{\mathbf{p}}\mathbf{X}; \tag{2.1}$$

then the *surplus of i against j* at x:

$$\sigma_{ij}(x) =: \max_{S \in \mathcal{N}_{i \setminus j}} e(S,x), \qquad \text{all } i,j \in N,\ i \neq j; \tag{2.2}$$

then the *pre-kernel*:

$${}_{\mathbf{p}}\mathbf{K}(\Gamma) =: \{\, x \in {}_{\mathbf{p}}\mathbf{X} : \sigma_{ij}(x) = \sigma_{ji}(x),\ \text{all } i,j \in N,\ i \neq j \,\}; \tag{2.3}$$

and finally, the *kernel* itself:

$$\begin{aligned} \mathbf{K}(\Gamma) \ =: \ \{\, x \in \mathbf{X} : \ & \text{for each } i,j \in N,\ i \neq j, \ \ldots \\ & \underline{\text{either}}\ \ \sigma_{ij}(x) = \sigma_{ji}(x), \\ & \underline{\text{or}}\ \ \sigma_{ij}(x) < \sigma_{ji}(x) \text{ and } x_i = v(\{i\}), \\ & \underline{\text{or}}\ \ \sigma_{ij}(x) > \sigma_{ji}(x) \text{ and } x_j = v(\{j\}) \,\}. \end{aligned} \tag{2.4}$$

The last definition—though historically correct—is needlessly complicated in the standard interpretation, in view of Proposition 2 below. Indeed, (2.3) is increasingly being used now as the definition of $\mathbf{K}$, since for non 0-monotonic games the consideration of "individual rationality" that motivates (2.4) has no particular appeal.

The following results are basic to the theory of the kernel:[7]

Proposition 1. If $\mathbf{X} \neq \emptyset$ then $\mathbf{K} \neq \emptyset$ and $\mathbf{K} \subseteq \mathbf{X}$.

Proposition 2. If Γ is 0-monotonic, then $\mathbf{K}(\Gamma) = {}_{\mathbf{p}}\mathbf{K}(\Gamma)$.

Proposition 3. If $\mathbf{C} \neq \emptyset$ then $\mathbf{C} \cap \mathbf{K} \neq \emptyset$.

The next proposition sets forth the "bisection" property, which is helpful in both visualizing and calculating the kernel. Let $x \in \mathbf{C}$, and for any $i \neq j$ let $\mathbf{L}_{ij}(x)$ be the line that passes through x in the "i-j direction," i.e., the line in ${}_{\mathbf{p}}\mathbf{X}$ along which only x_i and x_j are allowed to vary.

Proposition 4. If $x \in \mathbf{C}$, then $x \in \mathbf{K}$ if and only if x bisects the segment $\mathbf{C} \cap \mathbf{L}_{ij}(x)$ for each $i \neq j$. (If $\mathbf{C} \cap \mathbf{L}_{ij}(x)$ is a single point, then x is that point.)

Figure 1 shows a kernel point bisecting the "asterisk" of line segments that pass through it in the six possible directions. No other core point in Figure 1 enjoys this

[7] See e.g. Maschler, Peleg and Shapley (1979).

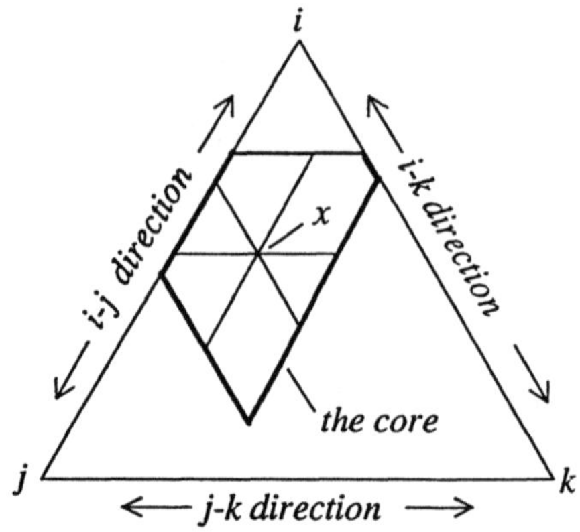

Figure 1. Illustrating the bisection property.

property, and indeed, as in all 3-person games, the kernel is a singleton. For larger n, however, there can be many core points with the bisection property. Indeed, we shall soon be dealing with a class of games in which *all* points in the core are multi-bilateral bisectors, and there may be kernel points outside the core as well.

For those who may be puzzled by the bisection property's success in imposing up to $(n^2-n)/2$ constraints on the kernel when the core itself is at most $(n-1)$-dimensional, the following remarks may provide some clues: (1) the constraints are actually not linear but piecewise linear; (2) the boundary faces of the core are severely restricted in the directions of their normals, since the coefficients of the defining inequalities are all 0 or 1 (note the parallel faces in Figure 1); (3) if $n \geq 4$ and the dimension of the core is less than $n-2$, it is quite possible for the core to be skewed in such a way that none of the transfer lines L_{ij} intersect it in more than a point. Then all the asterisks are trivial, and we have $\mathbf{K} \supseteq \mathbf{C}$. We shall soon see that this is a common occurrence in replicated market games.[8]

3 Symmetries, Types and Profiles

By a *symmetry* of a game, we shall mean any permutation of the players that leaves the characteristic function unchanged. Thus, if $\Gamma = (N, v)$ and $\pi : N \leftrightarrow N$ is a permutation of the players, then the symmetries of Γ comprise the set

$$\Pi \;=\; \Pi(\Gamma) \;=:\; \{\pi : \pi v = v\},$$

where πv is defined by $(\pi v)(S) =: v(\pi S) =: v(\{\pi(i) : i \in S\})$. Π is obviously a group under composition: $(\pi \cdot \rho)v =: \pi(\rho v)$.

While two players i, j will be called *symmetric* if $\pi(i) = j$ for some $\pi \in \Pi$, the stronger relationship of "perfect substitutes" is also important; it requires that the simple transposition of i and j—i.e., leaving the other players fixed—is itself an

[8]See Proposition 7.

element of Π. Both symmetry and substitutability are equivalence relations[9] and therefore induce partitions of N; we shall call them *symmetry classes* and *substitution classes* respectively, the latter being in general a refinement of the former.

For an example, let $N = \{1,2,3,4\}$ and let $v(S)$ be 1 if S is $\{1,2\}$, $\{2,3\}$, $\{3,4\}$ or $\{1,4\}$, 2 if $|S| = 3$ or 4, and 0 otherwise. Then $\Pi(v)$ is the familiar group of the square (with 1 and 3 sitting at opposite corners). All six pairs of players are symmetric, but players 1 and 2, for example, are not substitutes. The unique symmetry class is N, while the substitution classes are $\{1,3\}$ and $\{2,4\}$.

Given Γ, we may distinguish two special classes of pre-imputations:

$$_{\mathbf{P}}\mathbf{X}_{\mathrm{sym}} =: \{x \in {}_{\mathbf{P}}\mathbf{X} : x_i = x_j \text{ whenever } i \text{ and } j \text{ are symmetric in } \Gamma\},$$

$$_{\mathbf{P}}\mathbf{X}_{\mathrm{subs}} =: \{x \in {}_{\mathbf{P}}\mathbf{X} : x_i = x_j \text{ whenever } i \text{ and } j \text{ are substitutes in } \Gamma\}.$$

We observe that always $_{\mathbf{P}}\mathbf{X}_{\mathrm{sym}} \subseteq {}_{\mathbf{P}}\mathbf{X}_{\mathrm{subs}}$. (In the example above, $(1,0,1,0)$ is in $_{\mathbf{P}}\mathbf{X}_{\mathrm{subs}}$ but not $_{\mathbf{P}}\mathbf{X}_{\mathrm{sym}}$.) Of course if Γ has no symmetries except the identity permutation, then $_{\mathbf{P}}\mathbf{X}_{\mathrm{sym}} = {}_{\mathbf{P}}\mathbf{X}_{\mathrm{subs}} = {}_{\mathbf{P}}\mathbf{X}$. We shall write $\mathbf{X}_{\mathrm{sym}}$ for $\mathbf{X} \cap {}_{\mathbf{P}}\mathbf{X}_{\mathrm{sym}}$ and $\mathbf{X}_{\mathrm{subs}}$ for $\mathbf{X} \cap {}_{\mathbf{P}}\mathbf{X}_{\mathrm{subs}}$.

The following is an easily proved but important property of the kernel:

Proposition 5. $\mathbf{K}(\Gamma) \subseteq \mathbf{X}_{\mathrm{subs}}(\Gamma)$.

In other words, every kernel point gives "equal treatment" to all members of each substitution class. This is not true in general for core points, nor is it generally true that kernel points give equal treatment to players who are symmetric but not substitutes.[10]

We shall be dealing in the sequel with games whose players can be classified into *types*, a type being any nonempty subset of a substitution class. We define a *regular type-partition of order k* to be any refinement of the substitution partition with the property that all types have size k. Thus, even though a game may have many substitution classes of different sizes, it may not have any regular type-partitions beyond the trivial $k = 1$. In fact, it is easily seen that the order of any regular type-partition must be a common divisor of all the substitution-class sizes.

It would appear, then, that games with nontrivial regular type-partitions are rare in practice. Nevertheless they are of much interest in economics because of their connection with the procedure of "replication," which traditionally has served as an important point of entry into the study of large economies. The present note continues that tradition.

[9]To verify the transitivity of substitution, let $(ijk...m)$ denote the *cyclic permutation* in which i takes j's seat, j takes k's seat ..., and m takes i's seat. Then $(ij)=(ji)$ is just the transposition of i and j. We must show that if (ij) and (jk) are in Π then so is (ik). But $(ij)\cdot(jk)$ (read "(jk), then (ij)") is (ikj), which is a symmetry but not a transposition. Another application of (jk) does the trick, however, since $(jk)\cdot(ikj) = (ik)$.

[10]But see Proposition 6 below. Of course, both the kernel and the core—*as sets*—enjoy the full symmetry of the game. It follows that in the case of a one-point kernel or a one-point core, all members of each *symmetry* class get equal treatment.

Let $\{N_t : t = 1, \ldots, m\}$ be a partition of N into m types of size k. To each $S \in \mathcal{N}$ we associate an integer-valued m-vector $\mathbf{s} = (\mathbf{s}_1, \ldots, \mathbf{s}_m)$, called the *profile* of S, where $\mathbf{s}_t = |S \cap N_t|$. Because the members of a type are substitutes, the characteristic function on coalitions can be replaced by a simpler, "characterizing" function on profiles, defined by the identity

$$(3.1) \qquad v(S) = \phi(\mathbf{s}).$$

The precise domain of ϕ is the cubic lattice of integer points $\mathbf{s} \in \mathbf{R}_+^m$ with $\mathbf{0} \leq \mathbf{s} \leq \mathbf{k}$, where $\mathbf{0}$ denotes $(0, 0, \ldots 0)$ and $\mathbf{k}$ denotes $(k, k, \ldots k)$.

4 TU Markets and Market Games

Following Shapley and Shubik (1969, 1975), a *TU market* $\mathrm{M} = (T, G, a, u)$ is composed of (1) a finite set T of *traders*, (2) a finite set G of *commodities* with the associated *consumption set* $\mathbf{R}_+^G$, (3) a family $a = \{a^t\}_{t \in T} \subset \mathbf{R}_+^G$ of *initial bundles*, and (4) a family $u = \{u^t\}_{t \in T}$ of *utility functions*, $u^t : \mathbf{R}_+^G \to \mathbf{R}(t)$, assumed to be continuous, concave, and nondecreasing. (Here the $\mathbf{R}(t)$ are copies of $\mathbf{R}$ representing the individual *utility scales* of the respective traders t.)

The "TU" designation means that utility is treated as an additional, money-like good, valuable in itself and freely transferable, but serving also as a common unit of measurement for the $\mathbf{R}(t)$. To obtain the final utility levels or "payoffs" of the traders we take their utilities of consumption $u^t(z^t)$, where $z^t \in \mathbf{R}_+^G$ is t's final bundle, and add their net balances of transfered utility.[11]

The market $\mathrm{M} = (T, G, a, u)$ generates a cooperative TU game $\Gamma = (T, v)$ in a very natural way. First, define an *S-allocation* to be any $x^S = \{x^i \in \mathbf{R}_+^G : i \in S\}$, and call it *feasible* if

$$(4.1) \qquad \sum_{i \in S} x^i = \sum_{i \in S} a^i.$$

Then, for each nonempty $S \subseteq T$ define[12]

$$(4.2) \qquad v(S) =: \max \left\{ \sum_{i \in S} u^i(x^i) : x^S \text{ is a feasible } S\text{-allocation} \right\}.$$

Finally, set $v(\oslash) = 0$. It is easy to see that v is automatically superadditive.

By a *TU market game* we shall mean any $\Gamma = (T, v)$ that can be derived from a TU market $\mathrm{M} = (T, G, a, u)$ in this way. These games have been widely studied, a central result being that the TU market games are precisely those that are "totally balanced," a property which, among other things, assures a non-empty core.[13]

[11] An early statement of the role of transferable utility in economic theory, applicable to the present context, will be found in Shapley and Shubik (1966; pp. 807-808).

[12] Note that transfered utility does not enter into the definition. No help for S can be expected from outside, and utility transfers among members of S do not affect the total.

[13] Shapley and Shubik (1969, 1975); see also Shapley (1967), Scarf (1967), Billera (1970), Billera and Bixby (1973) (who apply Rader's (1972) "Principle of Equivalence" between production economies and pure exchange economies), Mas-Colell (1975), Hart (1982), Qin (1991).

A *replicated* TU market has a special structure. We may imagine constructing one by starting with any TU market M, making k exact copies, arranging them side by side on a map, then finally erasing all boundaries and barriers to create a "common market," denoted by ^{k}M. If we start with $|T| = n$ traders in M then we end up with $|{}^kT| = kn$ traders in ^{k}M; moreover ${}^kT$ will admit a regular type-partition $\{T_1, \ldots, T_n\}$ of order k. Of course, this type-partition applies equally to the *market* ^{k}M and the associated TU market *game*, which we denote by ${}^k\Gamma$.[14]

It is not difficult to see that ${}^k\Gamma = ({}^kT, {}^kv)$ is positively homogeneous in the following, discrete sense: let $S \in {}^kT$, and let ${}^hS$ be any coalition in ${}^kT$ having exactly h times as many traders of each type as S; then ${}^kv({}^hS) = h\,{}^kv(S)$.

This suggests that in dealing with games of the form ${}^k\Gamma$ we should speak of *profiles* rather than coalitions, and introduce an alternative characterizing function ϕ, as in (3.1), defined on the lattice of integer n-vectors between $\mathbf{0}$ and $\mathbf{k}$, inclusive. The homogeneity property then has a more familiar appearance:

$$(4.3) \qquad \phi(h\mathbf{s}) = h\phi(\mathbf{s}),$$

for all positive integers h such that $\mathbf{0} \leq h\mathbf{s} \leq \mathbf{k}$.

Referring to (4.2), we see that ϕ is given by

$$(4.4) \qquad \phi(\mathbf{s}) = \max_{x} \sum_{t \in T} \mathbf{s}_t u^t(x^t),$$

where x runs over n-dimensional space of the feasible *type-symmetric* allocations—i.e., sets of bundles $\{x^t\}_{t\in T}$ such that $\sum_{t\in T} s_t x^t = \sum_{t\in T} s_t a^t$, since the concavity of the u^t ensures that the maximum over all allocations will be achieved at an equal-treatment allocation. To see this, observe that if two members of S are of the same type but receive different bundles, then the total utility to S will not be decreased if they both are given the average of the two bundles.

We see also that the natural superadditivity of ${}^kv$ implies that ϕ is (discretely) *concave*, in the sense that if $p\mathbf{r} + (1-p)\mathbf{s}$ is an integer vector for any $\mathbf{r} \leq \mathbf{k}$, $\mathbf{s} \leq \mathbf{k}$ and $0 \leq p \leq 1$, then $\phi(p\mathbf{r} + (1-p)\mathbf{s}) \geq p\phi(\mathbf{r}) + (1-p)\phi(\mathbf{s})$.

We now state the well-known "equal treatment" property of core points in k-replicated economies, $k \geq 2$. With its aid we shall establish an important fact about the kernel in the TU case.

> **Proposition 6.** Let $x \in \mathbf{C}({}^k\Gamma)$, $k \geq 2$. Then if i and j are members of the same type, we have $x_i = x_j$.

The proof consists in forming an n-player coalition S with profile $\mathbf{s} = (1, \ldots, 1)$ by selecting a worst-treated player of each type. Then in the absence of equal treatment, S can improve.

> **Proposition 7.** If $k \geq 2$, then $\mathbf{K}({}^k\Gamma) \supseteq \mathbf{C}({}^k\Gamma)$.

[14] We do not define the replication of games *per se*. Indeed, two TU markets that generate the same game can easily have k-replications that generate different games.

Proof. In defining the asterisk at any $x \in \mathbf{C}({}^k\Gamma)$, only two players can depart from their x coordinates at the same time—one up and one down. Thus, the equal treatment that exists at x by Proposition 6 is necessarily spoiled by any movement away from x on a transfer line $L_{ij}(x)$. So all core points have trivial asterisks, and the result follows at once by Proposition 4.

It will be convenient now to extend the domain of the "characterizing" function ϕ to a continuous, nondecreasing, concave, positively homogeneous function $\bar{\phi}$ on the full positive orthant $\mathbf{R}^n_+$. We begin by releasing the h of (4.3) from its integer constraint, thereby extending ϕ to all the rays in $\mathbf{R}^n_+$ that hit lattice points in the k-cube. If k is allowed to increase indefinitely these "rational rays" become dense in $\mathbf{R}^n_+$, and an appeal to continuity completes the extension.

Proposition 8. Given a TU market $\mathrm{M} = (T, G, a, u)$ together with its k-replications, $k=2,3,\ldots,$ there is a unique continuous function $\bar{\phi} : \mathbf{R}^n_+ \to \mathbf{R}$ such that the characteristic function ${}^kv$ of ${}^k\Gamma(\mathrm{M})$ is given by

$$ {}^kv(S) = \bar{\phi}(\mathbf{s}), \qquad \text{all } S \in {}^kT; $$

moreover, $\bar{\phi}$ is positively homogeneous, nondecreasing, and concave.

The converse is also of interest:

Proposition 9. Every continuous, concave, nondecreasing, positively homogeneous function $\bar{\phi} : \mathbf{R}^n_+ \to \mathbf{R}$ is represented by some TU market $\mathrm{M}(T, G, a, u)$ together with its k-replications.

Proof. An easy way to set up an $\mathrm{M}(T, G, a, u)$ with the desired properties is to take $|T| = |G| = n$ and match trader types to commodities.[15] Initially endow each member of type t with one unit of good t, and nothing else, so that a^i for i in type t is just the t-th unit vector of $\mathbf{R}^G_+$. The utility functions u^t are then defined to be equal to each other and to the given function $\bar{\phi}$:

$$ (4.5) \qquad u^t(x_1, \ldots x_n) \equiv u^o(x_1, \ldots x_n) = \bar{\phi}(x_1, \ldots x_n), \qquad \text{all } t \in T. $$

Under this set-up, the total bundle available to a coalition to distribute is exactly its profile. Concavity of u^o implies that total utility is maximized for any S is attained by an equal split, each player turning in his endowment for the bundle $\mathbf{s}/|S|$. This of course yields $v(S)$ or ${}^kv(S)$ equal to $\phi(\mathbf{s})$, as in (4.4).

Of course with the positive homogeneity of (4.5), the maximum is attained by by other, nonsymmetric distributions—for example, by giving the whole of $\mathbf{s}$ to one player. But homogeneity of u^o is not at all essential to the construction. It suffices that u^o be concave, continuous and nondecreasing, and agree with $\bar{\phi}+u^o(0)$ on the simplex formed by the convex hull of the unit vectors of $\mathbf{R}^G_+$. These remarks are easily verified.

[15] Cf. the *direct market of a game*, utilized by Shapley and Shubik (1969, 1975).

5 The Kernel for Two Types.

We now restrict ourselves to the case $n = 2$ and consider the sequence of $2k$-person games ${}^k\Gamma$ that derive from a fixed continuous, concave, positively homogeneous function $\bar{\phi}$ on $\mathbf{R}^2_+$, restricted for each ${}^k\Gamma$ to the profiles $\mathbf{s}$ in the $k{\times}k$-square $\mathbf{0} \leq \mathbf{s} \leq \mathbf{k}$.

Consider an equal-treatment imputation of ${}^k\Gamma$:

(5.1) $$(a, \ldots, a, b, \ldots, b) \quad \text{or, for short,} \quad (a; b).$$

where $a \geq \phi(1, 0)$, $b \geq \phi(0, 1)$ and $a + b = \phi(1, 1)$. The excess at $(a; b)$ of any coalition $S \subseteq {}^kT$ with profile $\mathbf{s}$ is given by[16]

(5.2) $$e(S, (a; b)) = \varepsilon(\mathbf{s}, (a, b)) =: \phi(\mathbf{s}_1 + \mathbf{s}_2) - (a\mathbf{s}_1 + b\mathbf{s}_2)$$

(cf. (2.1)), and the surplus of any $i \in T_1$ against any $j \in T_2$ is given by

(5.3) $$\sigma_{12}((a, b)) =: \max_{\mathbf{s} \in \mathrm{D}_{12}} \{\varepsilon(\mathbf{s}, (a, b))\}$$

where

(5.4) $$\mathrm{D}_{12} =: \{\mathbf{s} : 1 \leq \mathbf{s}_1 \leq k \text{ and } 0 \leq \mathbf{s}_2 \leq k - 1\}$$

(cf. (2.2)), with corresponding expressions defining $\sigma_{21}((a, b))$ and D_{21}. Of course, if the two players are of the same type their surpluses against each other are automatically equal, since the maximization problems they face are the same.

So in order for $(a; b)$ to be in the kernel, it is necessary and sufficient that

(5.5) $$\sigma_{12}((a, b)) = \sigma_{21}((a, b)),$$

by (5.3), (2.3) and Proposition 2. Our problem therefore reduces to maximizing ε over the two finite domains D_{12} and D_{21} and comparing the results (Figure 2).

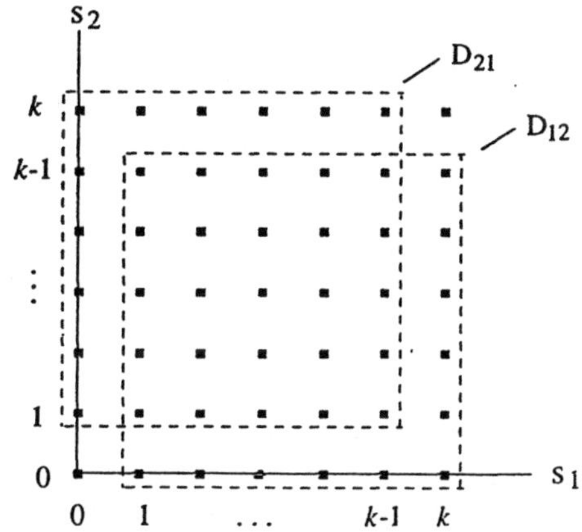

Figure 2. Illustrating the squares D_{12} and D_{21}.

[16]Note that "$(a; b)$" denotes a point in $\mathbf{R}^{2k}$, "(a, b)" a point in $\mathbf{R}^2$.

If we extend ϕ and ε to functions $\hat{\phi}$, $\hat{\varepsilon}$ on the full $k\times k$-square by replacing $\mathbf{s}_1$ and $\mathbf{s}_2$ by real variables s_1 and s_2 in $[0,k]$, we see that $\hat{\varepsilon}$ is just another continuous, concave, positively homogeneous function for each (a,b), resembling ϕ but with the added property that it is 0 along the diagonal $s_1 = s_2$.

Figure 3 below shows the positive and negative regions of a typical $\hat{\varepsilon}$ for $k=6$. Because of the concavity there can be at most one "+" sector; moreover, there can be no "0" sector of positive area if a "+" sector exists. If there is no "+" sector, the maximum of $\varepsilon(\mathbf{s},(a,b))$ is 0 in both D_{12} and D_{21} and so $(a;b)$ is in the core *and* the kernel.[17]

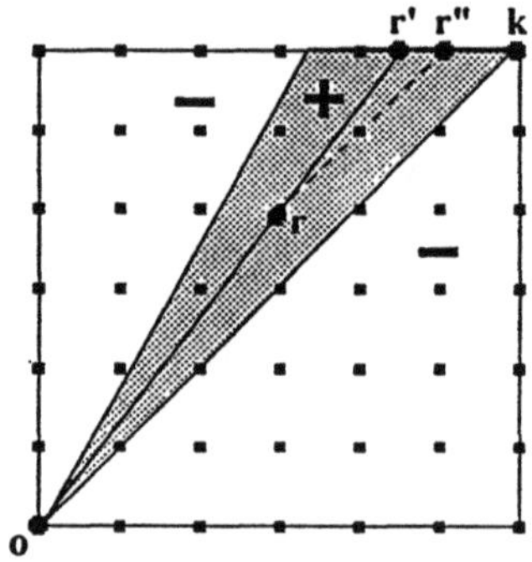

Figure 3. An excess function in the $k\times k$-square.

Attempting to construct kernel points $(a;b)$ outside the core, we choose (a,b) so that the "+" sector of $\hat{\varepsilon}(\mathbf{s},(a,b))$ contains at least one lattice point, like $\langle k-1,k\rangle$ in Figure 3, say. Then $\max\varepsilon(\mathbf{s})$[18] is positive in $\mathrm{D}_{21}\backslash\mathrm{D}_{12}$ but negative in $\mathrm{D}_{12}\backslash\mathrm{D}_{21}$. So the only way that (5.5) can hold is if $\max\varepsilon(\mathbf{s})$ over $\mathbf{s}\in\mathrm{D}_{12}\cup\mathrm{D}_{21}$ is attained at some $\mathbf{r}\in\mathrm{D}_{12}\cap\mathrm{D}_{21}$.

Let $\mu>0$ be that maximum, and let it be attained at a lattice point $\mathbf{r}$ with $r_1<r_2\le k-1$, like $\langle 3,4\rangle$ in Figure 3. Extend the ray $\mathbf{0r}$ to the boundary of the square at $\mathbf{r}'=\langle r_1k/r_2,k\rangle$. By homogeneity, $\hat{\varepsilon}(\mathbf{r}')=k\mu/r_2>\mu$. So r_1k/r_2 cannot be an integer. Indeed, there must be no lattice points on the segment $\mathbf{rr}'$ other than $\mathbf{r}$ itself. But note that since $\mathbf{r}_1<\mathbf{r}_2$, there is at least one boundary lattice point strictly between $\mathbf{r}'$ and the corner $\mathbf{k}=\langle k,k\rangle$, namely $\mathbf{r}''=:\langle k-(r_2-r_1),k\rangle$. So concavity of $\hat{\varepsilon}$ entails that

$$\hat{\varepsilon}(\mathbf{r}'') \ \ge\ \frac{k-\mathbf{r}_1''}{k-\mathbf{r}_1'}\,\hat{\varepsilon}(\mathbf{r}')+\frac{\mathbf{r}_1''-\mathbf{r}_1'}{k-\mathbf{r}_1'}\,\hat{\varepsilon}(\mathbf{k}').$$

Observing that the triangles $\mathbf{rr}'\mathbf{r}''$ and $\mathbf{0r}'\mathbf{k}$ are similar, we have at once

$$\text{(5.6)}\qquad \hat{\varepsilon}(\mathbf{r}'') \ \ge\ \frac{\mathbf{r}_2}{k}\frac{k\mu}{\mathbf{r}}+\frac{k-\mathbf{r}_2}{k}0 \ =\ \mu.$$

[17]Indeed, $(a;b)$ is a CE payoff of the underlying market. A sharper condition for core membership is that the "+" sector contain no lattice points. Thus, as k increases we get a glimpse of how and why the core is generally larger than the CE set but closes in on it as $k\to\infty$. (The "shrinkage" takes place in $\mathbf{R}^2$, however, not $\mathbf{R}^{2k}$.)

[18]We shall suppress the argument (a,b) until it is needed again.

Since μ is the maximum on lattice points, equality holds in (5.6), and it follows that the triangle $\mathbf{Okr'}$ represents a "flat" sector of $\hat{\varepsilon}$ (i.e., linear, not level). Hence $\hat{\varepsilon}$ is identically μ along the line $\mathbf{rr''}$ which runs parallel to the diagonal.

In short, a lattice point in $D_{12} \cap D_{21}$ that is maximal in $D_{12} \cup D_{21}$ *can* be constructed, but only just barely, by making a considerable portion of $\hat{\varepsilon}$ linear.

What more is demanded of $\hat{\varepsilon}$ (and hence $\bar{\phi}$) to ensure that $(a; b)$ has the kernel property? Not much. To the right of the "flat" sector, concavity keeps $\hat{\varepsilon}$ safely negative. To the left, however, $\hat{\varepsilon}$ must drop off rather quickly, so as not to exceed μ at any lattice point. But apart from this condition, which is easily fulfilled, there is nothing more to assume. Indeed, other than the need for a flat region adjacent to the diagonal $\mathbf{Ok}$, the existence of kernel points outside the core is a robust phenomenon. Let us make two further observations:

(1) The kernel is readily seen to be convex. If the $(a; b)$ of Figure 3 is thought of as a plane in $\mathbf{R}^3$ that contains the line $\mathbf{Ok}$ in $\mathbf{R}^2$, then consider decreasing a and increasing b by the same amount.[19] This will tilt it to the right, and so by (5.2) cause the graph of $\hat{\varepsilon}$ to tilt to the left, turning on the $\mathbf{Ok}$ hinge, until the "flat" becomes level and the "+" sector disappears. This means that $(a; b)$ has entered the core. But throughout the tilting process the point $\mathbf{r}$ continues to maximize $\varepsilon(\mathbf{s})$ on both D_{12} and D_{21}, even as $\mu \to 0$. So the kernel extends all the way from the original $(a; b)$ to the core.

(2) Due to the absence of requirements on $\hat{\varepsilon}$ on the negative side of $\mathbf{Ok}$, there is nothing to prevent a similar construction in that region as well, resulting in another segment of the kernel protruding from the core in the opposite direction. If the two "flats" are given the same slope then the core will be a single point in the interior of $\mathbf{K}$. But if they are given different slopes there will be a "crease" along $\mathbf{Ok}$, and the core will be a closed line segment interior to $\mathbf{K}$, representing the family of planes that support $\phi(\mathbf{s})$ along the crease.

We expect that the situation described for $n = 2$ carries over in most respects to larger n. The core, at least, is always convex and generically $(n-1)$-dimensional, and it appears that the kernel too will be convex.

6 A Nonconvergent Example

We now apply the analysis of §5 to a special case. The characterizing function, $\bar{\phi} : \mathbf{R}^2_+ \to \mathbf{R}$ is deceptively simple:

$$\bar{\phi}(s) = \min\{s_1, \alpha s_2\}, \tag{6.1}$$

where α is a parameter > 1; $\bar{\phi}$ is of course also the utility function for all traders in the two-commodity "direct market" that represents ϕ.[20] This piecewise linear function has two flat sectors joined along a ray R whose slope is $1/\alpha$, as depicted

[19] Recall that $a + b$ is a constant.

[20] See the proof of Proposition 9.

in Figure 4(a) for $\alpha = 2$. (The small numbers are the values of $\bar{\phi}$ on the L-shaped contours.) By (5.2), we have

$$\begin{aligned}\bar{\varepsilon}(s, (a,b)) &= \min\{s_1 - as_1 - bs_2,\ \ \alpha s_2 - as_1 - bs_2\} \\ &= bs_1 - bs_2 + \min\{0,\ -s_1 + \alpha s_2\},\end{aligned}$$

(eliminating a by the identity $a + b = \bar{\varepsilon}(1,1) = 1$). Figure 4(b) indicates the signed sectors of $\bar{\varepsilon}$ for $(a,b) = (.2, .8)$ with $\alpha = 2$; the shading is parallel to the contours.

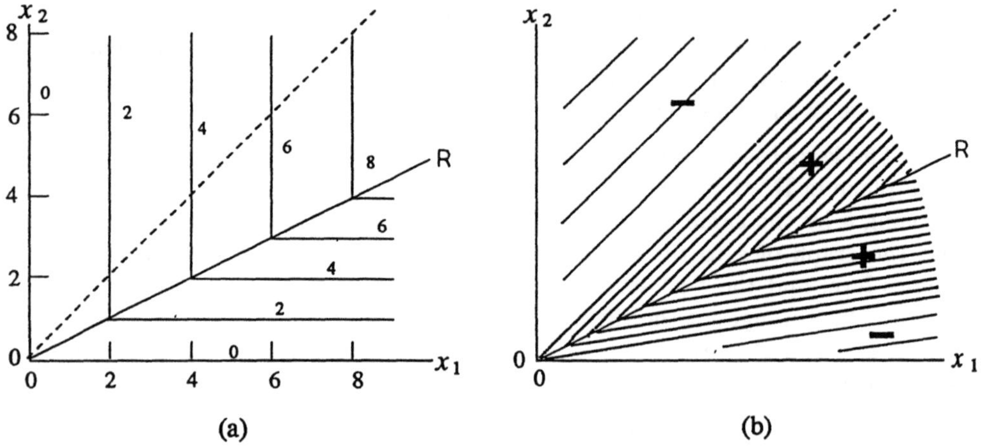

Figure 4. The extended functions $\bar{\phi}$ and $\bar{\varepsilon}$.

We note that the type-symmetric imputations form a line segment in $\mathbf{R}^{2n}$:

$$\mathbf{X}_{\text{sym}} = [(1;0),(0;1)] = \{(a;b) : 0 \le a = 1 - b \le 1\},$$

while the core $\mathbf{C}$ consists of the single point (1; 0), which is situated at one end of $\mathbf{X}_{\text{sym}}$. As we saw in §5, $\mathbf{K}$ is a closed line segment (or point) containing $\mathbf{C}$ and contained in $\mathbf{X}_{\text{sym}}$.[21]

We now fix $\alpha = 2$ and determine $\mathbf{K}$ for all values of k. Figure 5 (next page) graphically tabulates the $\varepsilon(\mathbf{s})$ values at lattice points in the critical region around $(k, k/2)$. The parity of k now becomes critical.

If k happens to be even, then $\varepsilon(\mathbf{s})$ takes its maximum in D_{12} at $\langle k, k/2\rangle$ and—if $b > 0$—nowhere else in D_{12}. This means that we can never equate the two surpluses: $\sigma_{12} = \sigma_{21}$ unless $(a;b)$ is the core point (1; 0). So, by Proposition 7, $\mathbf{K} = \mathbf{C}$.

If k is odd, however, the situation is quite different. From Figure 5(b) we see that $\varepsilon(\mathbf{s})$ is maximized at both $\langle k, (k+1)/2\rangle$ and $\langle k-1, (k-1)/2\rangle$. So $\sigma_{12} = \sigma_{21}$ throughout the entire range, and we have $\mathbf{K} = \mathbf{X}_{\text{sym}}$.

[21]Note that in the present example, the type partition *is* the symmetry partition.

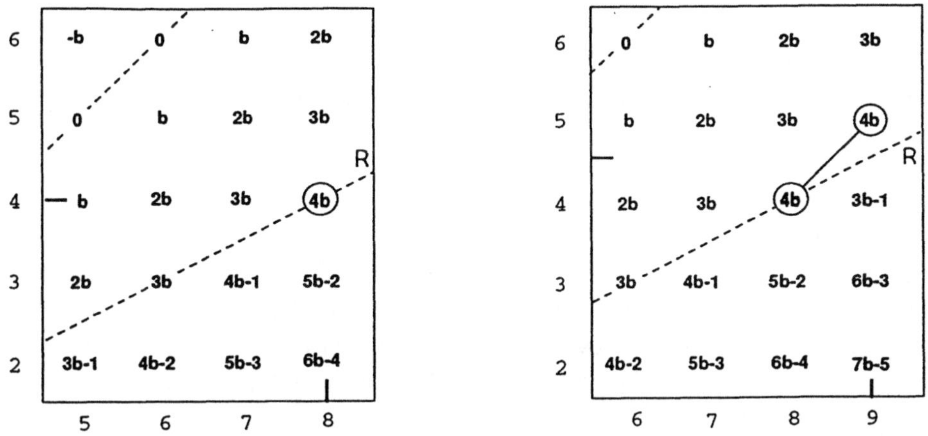

(a) $k=8$, unique maximum. (b) $k=9$, two maxima.

Figure 5. Excesses in the neighborhood of $\langle k, k/2\rangle$.

To summarize: The kernel flips in and out of the core according to whether the replication number is even or odd. Viewed in the "type" space (i.e., $\mathbf{R}^2$), the oscillation is exact:

$$[(1,0),(0,1)] \text{ for } k=1,3,5,\ldots, \qquad \{(1,0)\} \text{ for } k=2,4,6,\ldots.$$

Viewed in the payoff space, or rather, the increasing sequence of payoff spaces of dimension $kn-1$, the even-odd oscillation is at least as bad. Indeed, depending on the metric or sequence of metrics employed, the diameter of the "odd" kernels may even grow without bound—e.g., like $\sqrt{k}$ if the Euclidean norm is used. Certainly in this case the kernel cannot be said to "shrink" to the core.[22]

It is worth remarking that $\alpha = 2$ is not a special case. In fact, any real number $\alpha > 1$ will yield double maxima as in Figure 5(b) for infinitely many k. If α is rational, the ray R will pass through a lattice point at regular intervals, and a periodic pattern of $\mathbf{C}$ kernels and $\mathbf{X}_{\text{sym}}$ kernels will result. If α is irrational, the ray will not hit any lattice points and the oscillation will be irregular. Nevertheless, infinitely many kernels of each kind will occur.

References

BILLERA, L. J. (1970): "Some Theorems on the Core of an n-Person Game Without Side Payments," *SIAM Journal of Applied Mathematics*, 18, 567–579.

BILLERA, L .J. AND BIXBY R. E. (1974): "Market Representations of n-Person Games," *Bulletin of the American Mathematical Society*, 80, 522–526.

DAVIS, M. AND M. MASCHLER (1965): "The Kernel of a Cooperative Game," *Naval Research Logistics Quarterly*, 12, 223–259.

[22]Similar metric considerations arise in connection with the "shrinking" of both the classical core (see e.g. Shapley (1975)) and the bargaining set $\mathbf{B}$ treated by Shapley and Shubik (see Shubik (1984)).

HART, S. (1982): "The Number of Commodities Required to Represent a Market Game," *Journal of Economic Theory*, 27, 163–170.

MASCHLER, M. (1966): "The Inequalities that Determine the Bargaining Set $\mathcal{M}_1^{(i)}$," *Israel Journal of Mathematics*, 4, 127–134.

MASCHLER, M. AND B. PELEG (1966): "A Characterization, Existence Proof and Dimension Bounds for the Kernel of a Game," *Pacific Journal of Mathematics*, 18, 289–328.

MASCHLER, M., B. PELEG, AND L. S. SHAPLEY (1972): "The Kernel and Bargaining Set for Convex Games," *International Journal of Game Theory*, 1, 73–93.

MASCHLER, M., B. PELEG, AND L. S. SHAPLEY (1979): "Geometric Properties of the Kernel, Nucleolus, and Related Solution Concepts," *Mathematics of Operations Research*, 4, 303–338.

MAS-COLELL, A. (1975): "A Further Result on the Representation of Games by Markets," *Journal of Economic Theory*, 10, 117–122.

MAS-COLELL, A. (1989): "An Equivalence Theorem for a Bargaining Set," *Journal of Mathematical Economics*, 18, 129–139.

QIN, C. Z. (1991): "On a Conjecture of Shapley and Shubik" (to appear).

RADER, T. (1972): *Theory of Microeconomics*, Academic Press, New York, NY; see esp. 258–261.

SCARF, H. E. (1967): "The Core of an n-Person Game," *Econometrica*, 35, 50–69.

SCHMEIDLER, D. (1969): "The Nucleolus of a Characteristic Function Game," *SIAM Journal of Applied Mathematics*, 17, 1163–1170.

SHAPLEY, L. S. (1967): "On Balanced Sets and Cores," *Naval Research Logistics Quarterly*, 14, 453–460.

SHAPLEY, L. S. (1975): "An Example of a Slow-Converging Core," *International Economic Review*, 16, 345–351.

SHAPLEY, L. S. AND M. SHUBIK (1966): "Quasi-cores in a Monetary Economy with Non-convex Preferences," *Econometrica*, 34, 805–827.

SHAPLEY, L. S. AND M. SHUBIK (1969): "On Market Games," *Journal of Economic Theory*, 1, 9–25.

SHAPLEY, L. S. AND M. SHUBIK (1975): "Competitive Outcomes in the Cores of Market Games," *International Journal of Game Theory*, 4, 229–237.

SHUBIK, M. (1984): *A Game-Theoretic Approach to Political Economy*, MIT Press, Cambridge, MA; see esp. App. B.

Nice Demand in Rough Neighborhoods: Continuity in Non-Convex, Dispersed Economies

STEPHEN SHEPPARD
Oberlin College

1 Introduction

The technology available to households for transforming and producing goods to be consumed, and even for engaging in commercial transactions, will naturally be a significant factor in determining the structure of demand. Two general approaches have been used in modeling the role of these technologies. One is to incorporate the technology directly into the household preferences. The second is to incorporate the technology into the structure of the budget correspondence. The first approach is exemplified in Rader (1964), and (1978). The second has been used in Kurz (1974).

When we consider actual transactions technologies or processes of household production, we often encounter non-convexities. Virtually every transportation process, for example, seems to involve either some sort of fixed cost or economies of scale. Bargaining and trading also would seem to involve costs which must be paid even for the smallest of transactions. In such situations, what can we expect for the structure of household demand?

Clearly, we cannot expect individual demand to be 'nice' in the sense analyzed by Rader (1973), (1979). Indeed in such a situation the induced preferences may not even be representable, let alone representable by analytic utility. We are unlikely to find nice demand in this kind of neighborhood.

Even aggregate demand may be unpleasant in such situations, although there are some reasons for hope. The notion of *dispersedness* has been shown to be of considerable power in obtaining continuity or differentiability of aggregate demand. Assuming that consumers are dispersed with respect to wealth or with respect to a parameterization of their preferences has been combined with transversality theorems to obtain continuous mean demand and generically differentiable mean demand. [For example, see Sondermann (1975), (1980) and Dierker, Dierker, and Trockel (1980a), (1980b).] Hildenbrand (1980), Allen (1982), and Trockel (1984) have obtained results without using the transversality theorems, but retaining various notions of dispersedness of consumer preferences. The main goal of this line of research has been to obtain nice aggregate demand, not to allow non-convex consumption sets or budgets. Nevertheless, it may be possible to use some sort of dispersedness of consumers to obtain aggregate demand which is reasonably nice.

Such dispersedness assumptions might be an acceptable structure to impose on models in exchange for the ability to model non-convexity in household production.

The analysis of Yamazaki (1978) introduced a notion of dispersedness of the endowment distribution, and established that for any price vector, almost every agent has a budget set which satisfies the 'Local Cheaper Point' condition. From this condition and continuity of preferences one then obtains upper hemi-continuity of demand. [This latter step is illustrated in Yamazaki (1978) and explored at length and generalized in Heller (1977).] Yamazaki's analysis does not make use of transversality, but instead establishes the desired result directly.

The purpose of this paper is to construct a framework which can be used in these intrinsically non-convex settings to obtain upper hemi-continuity of demand via dispersedness. The idea is to provide an approach which can be applied to a variety of situations, with different notions of dispersedness. (Although the dispersedness is always based on budget situations, not dispersedness of preferences.) From this we can obtain a form of Yamazaki's result. Other examples are provided to illustrate the types of problems to which this approach might be applied.

2 Local Cheaper Points and Transversality

Two considerations constrain the action $x \in \Re^n$ taken by an economic agent. First, it must be physically or biologically feasible. We represent this by requiring that $x \in C$. Here C is the 'consumption set'.

Second, an action must be economically feasible. This can be represented by the mapping

$$V : A \times \Re^{3n} \rightarrow \Re \ .$$

$V(a,p,e,x) \leq 0$ is then interpreted as meaning 'x is economically feasible for an agent facing prices p, having endowments e, and having other characteristics a'. The vector $a \in A$ of 'other characteristics' is for the moment left vague, but we want it to be capable of representing such things as the location of the consumer or household technology. We do require that A be finite-dimensional.

The budget set (or choice set) of the consumer is then given by:

$$B(a,p,e) = \{x \in C | V(a,p,e,x) \leq 0\} \ .$$

The budget set is said to satisfy the **local cheaper point condition (LCP)** if: $\forall \ x \in B(a,p,e)$ such that $V(a,p,e,x) = 0$, given any open $O \subset \Re^n$ such that $x \in O$, $\exists \ y \in O \cap C$ such that $V(a,p,e,y) < 0$.

As mentioned above, LCP combined with continuity of preferences is used to ensure that demand is upper hemi-continuous. Since continuity of preferences cannot be refuted with finite observations of behavior, it might be reasonably argued that satisfaction of LCP is the critical requirement for continuity of demand.

We now introduce three assumptions which are made throughout the discussion which follows:

A1. $C \subset \Re^n$ is a smooth manifold with boundary. The manifold C has dimension greater than or equal to one.

A2. The function V is smooth, and 0 is a regular value of V.

A3. The set of characteristics A is a smooth sub-manifold without boundary having dimension k, and $A \subset \Re^k$.

The boundary of C is denoted ∂C. By 'smooth' we mean having derivatives of all orders, i.e. C^∞. The notation adopted follows closely that used in Hirsch (1976) or Guillemin and Pollack (1974).

Let G be the inclusion map for the set $A \times \Re^n \times \Re^n \times C$, and let ∂G be the inclusion map for $A \times \Re^n \times \Re^n \times \partial C$. Then define the map $g^{a,p,e} : C \to A \times \Re^{3n}$ by $g^{a,p,e}(x) = (a, p, e, x)$. In a similar manner we can define $\partial g^{a,p,e}$.

Define the set F by $F = V^{-1}(0)$. Since V is a smooth map and 0 is a regular value of V, F is a smooth manifold having dimension $(k+3n-1)$. Also, $F \subseteq \Re^{k+3n}$. The set F plays an important role in the results that follow, and it has a clear, intuitive, interpretation. It represents the set of points (a, p, e, x) with the property that given prices p, the consumption x is just *barely affordable* to a consumer having endowment e and other characteristics a.

The following lemma establishes a link between the Local Cheaper Point condition and $g^{a,p,e}$ being transversal to F.

LEMMA 1: *If $g^{a,p,e} \pitchfork F$ and $\partial g^{a,p,e} \pitchfork F$, then $B(a,p,e)$ satisfies LCP.*

The proof for the lemma is presented in the final section of the paper. The intuitive idea behind the result can be easily visualized. Consider the two budget situations which are illustrated in Figure 1.

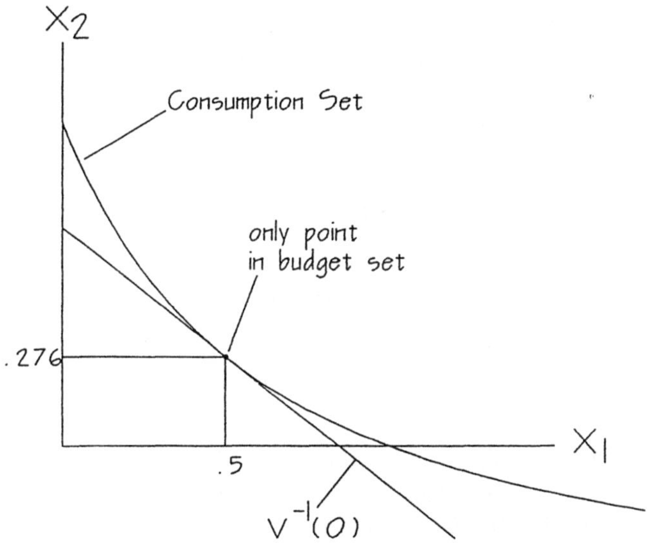

FIGURE 1.—LCP and Transversality.

In both diagrams the consumption set (or rather, the boundary ∂C) is drawn in and labeled. Also drawn and labeled is the manifold F. Imagine that points above and to the left of F have the property that for such points $V(a,p,e,x) > 0$. That is, such points are not affordable. Transversal intersection between the mapping $g^{a,p,e}$ and F requires that at points of intersection – such as point A in the left diagram, the tangent to the consumption set and the tangent to F should together span the entire space. Intuitively, this requires that the two manifolds cut across one another as shown. In such circumstances, we can move down to local cheaper points such as the one indicated in the diagram.

In the diagram on the right, however, problems arise. The set of affordable actions available to the consumer is the 'lens-shaped' area indicated plus the point C. It is this point C which violates transversal intersection. At a point such as B, the same general structure holds as is seen in the left diagram. Point B has local cheaper points. At point C, however, the 'budget line' F is tangent to the consumption set C. The tangent space of the two manifolds at point C is then the same one-dimensional subspace, which of course does not span $\Re^2$. Transversal intersection thus fails at point C. We can also see that point C fails to have local cheaper points. Attempts to move to some action which is less costly takes the consumer out of the set of actions which are biologically feasible. Lemma 1 generalizes and formally establishes these intuitive observations.

3 Dispersed Economies and LCP

Let $(S, \mathcal{B}(S), \mu)$ be a non-atomic measure space of traders or consumers. An **economy** is a measurable mapping which assigns preferences, endowments, and other characteristics to each agent. Thus $\xi : S \to A \times \Re^n \times \mathcal{P}$, where $\xi^1(s) = a(s)$ represents the 'other characteristics' of agent s, $\xi^2(s) = e(s)$ is the vector of endowments for s, and $\xi^3(s) = \succeq_s$ is the preference order of s. All agents have the same consumption set $\mathcal{C}$.

Let ν be a measure defined on $(A \times \Re^n, \mathcal{B}(A \times \Re^n))$ by:

$$\nu(M) = \mu\{s \in S | (\xi^1(s), \xi^2(s)) \in M\} .$$

Similarly, define the measure γ on $(A, \mathcal{B}(A))$ by:

$$\gamma(M) = \mu\{s \in S | \xi^1(s) \in M\} .$$

Finally, let λ_A be the restriction of k-dimensional lebesgue measure to A, λ_n be ordinary n-dimensional lebesgue measure on $\Re^n$, and let λ be the product measure $(\lambda_A \times \lambda_n)$ defined on $(A \times \Re^n, \mathcal{B}(A \times \Re^n))$.

The economy ξ is *dispersed with respect to endowments and other characteristics* if ν is absolutely continuous with respect to λ ($\nu \ll \lambda$). The economy is *dispersed with respect to characteristics* if $\gamma \ll \lambda_A$.

In the analysis below we will need some additional regularity properties for the function V. We introduce two assumptions which are designed to capture the requirement that in modeling the consumer the 'other characteristics' or the endowment vector, or both should be important in determining those actions which are economically feasible.

A4. For every $(a,p,e,x) \in \mathcal{A} \times \Re^{3n}$ with $p \neq 0$,

$$\exists\, i \text{ such that } \frac{\partial V(a,p,e,x)}{\partial a^i} \neq 0\,,$$

or

$$\exists\, j \text{ such that } \frac{\partial V(a,p,e,x)}{\partial e^j} \neq 0\,,$$

or both.

A5. For every $(a,p,e,x) \in \mathcal{A} \times \Re^{3n}$ with $p \neq 0$,

$$\exists\, i \text{ such that } \frac{\partial V(a,p,e,x)}{\partial a^i} \neq 0\,.$$

Obviously, A5 $\Rightarrow$ A4. Which of the two assumptions are being used will be clearly stated in each result below.

The interpretation of the two assumptions is clear. Assumption A5 states that for every type of consumer and every possible budget situation with prices not all equal to zero, there is some characteristic of the consumer which, if it changes, affects the affordability of the consumption bundle x. Assumption A4 states that either this is true or there is some element of the endowment vector e which, if it changes, affects the affordability of the consumption bundle x.

Next, consider the mapping $g^p : \mathcal{A} \times \Re^n \times C \to \mathcal{A} \times \Re^{3n}$, defined by $g^p(a,e,x) = (a,p,e,x)$. Let $\partial g^p = g^p|_{\mathcal{A}\times\Re^n\times\partial C}$, that is, the restriction of the mapping g^p to a domain which is the product of the space of agent characteristics, the n-dimensional reals, and the boundary of the consumption set. The next lemma establishes a relation between the manifold F and the mappings g^p and ∂g^p.

LEMMA 2: *For all $p \neq 0$, A1 – A4 implies $g^p \pitchfork F$ and $\partial g^p \pitchfork F$.*

The intuition behind lemma 2 is to make use of the differential structure guaranteed by A1 - A3, plus the regularity assumption A4 to establish transversality. The idea of the proof is straightforward: the manifold C does not vary as endowments or other characteristics change. Assumption A4 guarantees that the 'budget line', that is manifold F, does change as endowments or other characteristics (or both) change. This guaranteed change in one manifold along with a constancy in the other is sufficient to establish that the two manifolds are in 'general position', which is what is asserted by lemma 2.

We can now apply a standard transversality theorem to the results of Lemma 2.

LEMMA 3: *A1-A4 imply that for λ-almost every $(a,e) \in \mathcal{A} \times \Re^n$, we have $g^{a,p,e} \pitchfork F$ and $\partial g^{a,p,e} \pitchfork F$ for fixed but arbitrary $p \neq 0$.*

Proof: Since g^p may be viewed as the evaluation map for $g^{a,p,e}$, and since by Lemma 2 $g^p \pitchfork F$, the result follows from the parametric transversality theorem (see Guillemin and Pollack (1974, p. 68) or Hirsch (1976, p. 79)). ∎

Remark: The degree of smoothness we have imposed is actually stronger than is needed. It would suffice for all manifolds and for V to be C^r, where $r > 2k+5n-1$ (see Hirsch (1974)).

We can now state the main result of this paper, which links lemma 1 with lemma 3.

THEOREM 4: *If the economy ξ is dispersed with respect to endowments and other characteristics, and if A1 - A4 are satisfied, then for any $p \neq 0$, μ-almost every agent $s \in S$ has a budget set $B(a(s), p, e(s))$ which satisfies LCP.*

Proof: Let $p \neq 0$ be fixed. Let $L \subseteq \mathcal{A} \times \Re^n$ be defined by:

$$L = \{(a, e) \mid \text{ it is not the case that } (g^{a,p,e} \pitchfork F \text{ or } \partial g^{a,p,e} \pitchfork F) \ \} .$$

By lemma 1, then, we have:

$$L = \{(a, e) \mid B(a, p, e) \text{ fails LCP} \} .$$

By lemma 3, we have $\lambda(L) = 0$. By dispersedness, we have $\nu(L) = 0$, which establishes the theorem. ∎

The result established in Theorem 4 allows us to use dispersedness to obtain LCP and hence upper hemi-continuity of aggregate demand. There are, however, circumstances under which the dispersedness assumption might be felt to be inappropriately strong. For example, the dispersedness required in Theorem 4 implies that almost every agent has a non-zero endowment of every commodity.

By strengthening the assumed regularity of V, and restricting the endowment distribution to have countable support we can weaken the type of dispersedness required.

THEOREM 5: *If A1 – A3 and A5 are satisfied, if $\xi^2(S)$ is countable, and the economy ξ is dispersed with respect to characteristics, then for any $p \neq 0$, μ-almost every agent has a budget set $B(a(s), p, e(s))$ which satisfies LCP.*

Proof: Let $p \neq 0$ be fixed. Let $\hat{e} \in \xi^2(S)$ be fixed. Consider the mapping $g^{p,\hat{e}} : \mathcal{A} \times C \to \mathcal{A} \times \Re^{3n}$ defined by $g^{p,\hat{e}}(a, x) = (a, p, \hat{e}, x)$, and let $\partial g^{p,\hat{e}} = g^{p,\hat{e}}|_{\mathcal{A} \times C}$. An argument exactly parallel to that given in the proof of lemma 2, using the regularity assumption A5 yields the result $g^{p,\hat{e}} \pitchfork F$ and $\partial g^{p,\hat{e}} \pitchfork F$.

Then, as in the proof of lemma 3, we let $g^{p,\hat{e}}$ be the evaluation map for $g^{a,p,\hat{e}}$, and $\partial g^{p,\hat{e}}$ be the evaluation map for $\partial g^{a,p,\hat{e}}$. Then apply the parametric transversality theorem to obtain:

$$g^{a,p,\hat{e}} \pitchfork F \text{ and } \partial g^{a,p,\hat{e}} \pitchfork F \text{ for } \lambda\text{-almost every } a \in \mathcal{A} .$$

Then the analysis of lemma 1 plus dispersedness with respect to characteristics yields:

$$\mu\{s \in S \mid \xi^2(s) = \hat{e}, \text{ and } B(a(s), p, \hat{e}) \text{ fails LCP} \} = 0 .$$

This result can be obtained for every $e \in \xi^2(S)$. Since $\xi^2(S)$ is countable, we obtain:

$$\mu\left[\bigcup_{e \in \xi^2(S)} \{s \in S \mid \xi^2(s) = e, \text{ and } B(a(s), p, e) \text{ fails LCP} \}\right] = 0$$

$$\Rightarrow \quad \mu\left[\{s \in S \mid B(a(s),p,e(s)) \text{ fails LCP }\}\right] = 0 \,,$$

which establishes the desired result. ∎

There is an interesting gap between Theorems 4 and 5. In Theorem 4, there must be uncountably many distinct endowment vectors, and in Theorem 5 we require that there are only countably many distinct endowments – a sort of *anti-dispersedness* with respect to endowments. The function of this restriction is illustrated by the following example, in which there are uncountably many endowments, agents are dispersed with respect to characteristics but not dispersed in the sense required in Theorem 4.

Example: Let $S = (0,1)$, and $\mathcal{A} = (0,1)$. Let the commodity space be $\Re^2$, and let $\xi^1(s) = a(s) = s$ and $\xi^2(s) = (e_1, e_2) = (s, 1-s)$. Then let $\mathcal{C}$ be given by:

$$\mathcal{C} = \left\{ x \in \Re^2 \mid x_2 \geq \frac{1}{x_1 + .6180339} - .6180339 \right\} .$$

Finally, let V be given by:

$$V(a,p,e,x) = p \cdot x - p \cdot e + .3236066 - .2a \ .$$

One possible interpretation for the economy in this example might be a situation in which agents face transport costs in connection with obtaining or trading their initial endowments, and the transport costs include a fixed-cost component. The 'other characteristic' is then location, and the market is located at $a_m = 1$. At the price vector $p = (.8, 1)$, we have:

$$V^{-1}(0) = \{x \in \Re^2 \mid .8x_1 + x_2 = .6763934\} .$$

The budget set for every agent consists only of the point $(.5, .2763934)$, and LCP fails for every agent. The situation is illustrated in Figure 2.

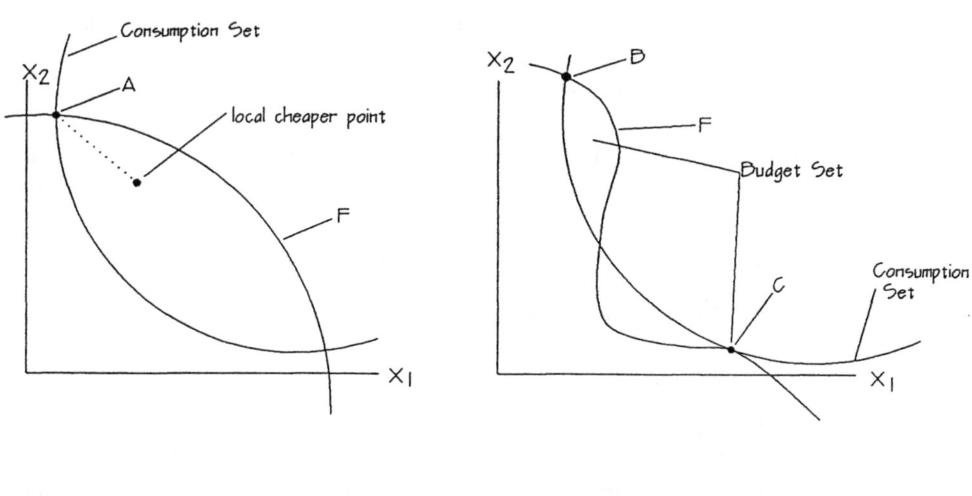

FIGURE 2.—Failure of LCP property.

Note that in this example assumptions A1 - A5 are all fulfilled. The agents in the model are dispersed with respect to characteristics. The one assumption stated in theorem 5 which fails to hold is that there are a continuum of different endowments. Note also that μ-almost every agent has an endowment which is in the interior of the consumption set, and the consumption set itself is convex. The non-convexity, in the form of fixed costs of transportation, destroys the LCP property and for some preference profiles the aggregate demand of this economy will not be upper hemi-continuous.

We close this section with a remark concerning the regularity assumptions A4 and A5. They are presented here in a form which can be concisely stated, but slightly weaker versions may be substituted by requiring them to be true only for those consumption vectors that 'matter', i.e. for $x \in \mathcal{C}$, but for most applications this is unlikely to represent a significant generalization.

4 Applications

We now consider some examples which serve to illustrate the possible applications of the theorems presented in the preceding section. As mentioned in the introduction, the role of LCP in obtaining upper hemi-continuity is shown in Yamazaki (1978) and Heller (1977), so that in the applications discussed we concentrate on establishing LCP. The first examples consider economies with transaction costs and economies in which some commodity is traded under non-linear pricing. We then show that a slightly less general version of Yamazaki's result can be derived based on the results obtained above.

4.1 *Economies with transaction costs*

Suppose an agent must pay transaction costs to collect and trade his endowment. These costs depend upon the agent's endowments e, consumption x, and other characteristics a. The characteristic might, for example, represent the agent's skill in bargaining. The costs are given as resource costs by the function $\mathcal{T} : \mathcal{A} \times \Re^{2n} \to \Re^n$, where $\mathcal{T}(a, e, x)$ is the vector of resources used by an agent with bargaining skill a, endowments e, and consumption x. We assume that $\mathcal{T}$ is a smooth function, but it may otherwise incorporate a variety of non-convexities in the relation between bargaining skill and transactions costs and hence affordable consumption plans.

We can suppose that bargaining skill is measured unidimensionally, and take $\mathcal{A} = (0, 1)$. Furthermore, we can assume that bargaining skill is always important, so that:

$$\forall\, (a, e, x) \in \mathcal{A} \times \Re^{2n} \,,\; \frac{\partial \mathcal{T}_i}{\partial a}(a, e, x) \neq 0 \,, i = 1 \ldots n \,.$$

In this economy, the feasibility of some consumption x, given (a, e), is determined by:

$$V(a, p, e, x) = p \cdot x + p \cdot \mathcal{T}(a, e, x) - p \cdot e \,.$$

Each agent has the consumption set C, which need not be convex but is a smooth manifold with boundary.

If, in addition to the structure imposed in this description, the mapping ξ which defines the economy is dispersed with respect to endowments and other characteristics, then Theorem 4 may be applied to obtain the result that at any non-zero price vector p, almost every agent has a budget set which satisfies LCP.

4.2 *Non-linear pricing*

Although the interpretation may seem somewhat strained since the economies discussed in this paper have all been exchange economies, the basic idea is relevant to the problem of establishing continuity properties of aggregate demand under non-linear pricing of some commodity. Consider a consumer sector in which all agents have zero endowment of some commodity, say x_j, and suppose that x_j is sold to these consumers using a (potentially) non-linear pricing function which depends on the amount consumed and the 'other characteristics' of the consumer, for example location or age.

Then assume that all these consumers have the same consumption set $\mathcal{C}$, which is a smooth manifold (again, not necessarily convex), and $\mathcal{A}$, the set of possible locations or ages, is a manifold without boundary. Let the cost of consuming amount x_j of good j be given by $f(a, x)$, which is assumed to be a smooth function, but need have no convexity properties. Then we have the function:

$$V(a, p, e, x) = p \cdot x + f(a, x) - p_j \cdot x_j - p \cdot e\,.$$

Assume that the price function f satisfies $\partial f/\partial a \neq 0$ for all $(a, x) \in \mathcal{A} \times \mathcal{C}$, and assume that there are only countably many distinct endowments. Then if the economy is dispersed with respect to locations and ages $\mathcal{A}$, we may apply theorem 5.

Clearly, more structure would be needed to turn this into an equilibrium model, but the basic idea for obtaining LCP for almost every agent is clear. One might also consider a similar application in which the function f is a tax function in an economy with public goods. The basic notion is that if the economy has some dispersedness, then price equilibrium may be a robust concept in spite of non-convexities in individual choice sets resulting from tax or pricing rules.

4.3 *Wealth dispersedness and LCP*

Finally, we show how a slightly less general version of Yamazaki's lemma (1978) can be obtained using the techniques presented above. The result in less general only in that our approach requires the consumption set to have manifold structure, which is not required in Yamazaki. The consumption set $\mathcal{C}$ may still be non-convex.

By considering the function

$$V(a, p, e, x) = p \cdot x - p \cdot e\,,$$

it is clear that if agents were dispersed with respect to endowments, then by theorem 4 almost every agent would have a budget set satisfying LCP. Yamazaki used a more general notion of dispersedness. The economy is assumed to be dispersed with respect to wealth at any price vector. That is, for any fixed $p \neq 0$, $\lambda(M) = 0 \Rightarrow \mu[\{s \in S \mid p \cdot e(s) = m \in M\}] = 0$. If the economy is dispersed in this sense, then Yamazaki shows that almost every agent has a budget set which satisfies LCP.

To apply the framework used in this paper, let ξ be the economy being considered. Let $\hat{p} \neq 0$ be fixed, and construct an associated economy $\xi_{\hat{p}}$ as follows:

$$\xi^1_{\hat{p}}(s) = \hat{a}(s) = \hat{p} \cdot e(s) \ ,$$

$$\xi^2_{\hat{p}}(s) = \hat{e}(s) = \{0\} \ ,$$

$$\xi^3_{\hat{p}}(s) = \succeq_s \ ,$$

where $e(s)$ and $\succeq_s$ are the endowments and preferences assigned to agent $s \in S$ under the economy ξ. The idea here is to construct an associated economy in which the 'other characteristic' $\hat{a}(s)$ of the agent is the wealth or value of the agent's endowment at the price $\hat{p}$. Then consider the function $V(a,p,e,x) = p \cdot x - a$. Clearly, for every (a,p,e,x), we have $\partial V(a,p,e,x)/\partial a \neq 0$. Also, if ξ is dispersed with respect to wealth (in the sense of Yamazaki) then $\xi_{\hat{p}}$ is dispersed with respect to characteristics.

Finally, taking $\mathcal{A} = (0, \infty)$, and assuming that $\mathcal{C}$ is a manifold with boundary, we can apply theorem 5 to obtain that for all $p \neq 0$, almost every consumer associated with the economy $\xi_{\hat{p}}$ has a budget set which satisfies LCP. This holds in particular for $p = \hat{p}$. But for $p = \hat{p}$, we have

$$B\left(\hat{a}(s), \hat{p}, \hat{e}(s)\right) = \{x \in \mathcal{C} \mid \hat{p} \cdot x - \hat{a}(s) \leq 0\} = \{x \in \mathcal{C} \mid \hat{p} \cdot x \leq \hat{p} \cdot \hat{e}(s)\} \ .$$

Hence, since $B\left(\hat{a}(s), \hat{p}, \hat{e}(s)\right)$ satisfies LCP for μ-almost every $s \in S$, we obtain the result that the budget set

$$B\left(a(s), \hat{p}, e(s)\right) = \{x \in \mathcal{C} \mid \hat{p} \cdot x \leq \hat{p} \cdot e(s)\}$$

satisfies LCP for almost every agent $s \in S$. This can be done for every $\hat{p} \neq 0$, and we thereby obtain the result.

5 Proofs for Lemmas 1 and 2

Finally, we restate and present formal proofs for Lemmas 1 and 2, which were presented above.

LEMMA 1: *If $g^{a,p,e} \pitchfork F$ and $\partial g^{a,p,e} \pitchfork F$, then $B(a,p,e)$ satisfies LCP.*

Proof: First, note that $dim(F) = k + 3n - 1$, and

$$T_{a,p,e,x}F = \{h \mid dV_{a,p,e,x}(h) = 0\} \ .$$

(To simplify notation somewhat, for the rest of the proof we drop the superscripts to the functions $g^{a,p,e}$ and $\partial g^{a,p,e}$, writing them as g and ∂g, respectively.)

Let $x \in \mathcal{C}$ be such that $g(x) \in F$. Then making use of the fact that g is transversal to F, we note that:

$$g \pitchfork F \ \Rightarrow \ T_x g(T_x \mathcal{C}) + T_{a,p,e,x}F = \Re^{k+3n} \ ,$$

and that

$$g \pitchfork F \ \Rightarrow \ T_x g(T_x \mathcal{C}) \not\subseteq T_{a,p,e,x}F \ .$$

Then, since $dim(C) \geq 1$, we have:

$$\exists\, z \text{ such that } (0,0,0,z) \in T_x g(T_x C)\ ,$$

where

$$dV_{a,p,e,x}(0,0,0,z) = \delta < 0\,, \text{ and } \|z\| = \|(0,0,0,z)\| = 1\,.$$

Let $z_n = \frac{z}{n}$, for $n = 1, 2, 3, \ldots$. Applying Taylor's formula to V, we obtain:

$$V\left((a,p,e,x) + (0,0,0,z_n)\right) = V(a,p,e,x) + dV_{a,p,e,x}(0,0,0,z_n) + \|z_n\| \cdot \varepsilon(z_n)\,.$$

Now, if $g(x) \in F$, then $V(a,p,e,x) = 0$, so we have:

$$\begin{aligned} V\left((a,p,e,x) + (0,0,0,z_n)\right) &= dV_{a,p,e,x}(0,0,0,z_n) + \|z_n\| \cdot \varepsilon(z_n) \\ &= \frac{1}{n} \cdot dV_{a,p,e,x}(0,0,0,z) + \frac{1}{n} \cdot \|z\| \cdot \varepsilon(z_n) \end{aligned}$$

$$\Rightarrow n \cdot V\left((a,p,e,x) + (0,0,0,z_n)\right) = \delta + \varepsilon(z_n)\,,$$
$$\text{where } \varepsilon(z_n) \to 0 \text{ as } n \to \infty\,.$$

Thus

$$\exists\, N \text{ such that } \forall n > N, V((a,p,e,x) + (0,0,0,z_n)) < \delta + \varepsilon_N < 0\,,$$

where $\varepsilon_N = \varepsilon(z_N)$.

By construction, $(0,0,0,z_n) \in T_x g(T_x C)$. Thus:

$$\exists\, v_n \to 0 \text{ such that } T_x g(v_n) = (0,0,0,z_n), \text{ and } v_n \in T_x C\,.$$

Let ψ be a local parameterization for C at x with $\psi(0) = x$.
Then $T_x g = D(g \circ \psi)_0$, so that:

$$(g \circ \psi)(v_n) = g \circ \psi(0) + D(g \circ \psi)_0(v_n) + \|v_n\| \cdot \varepsilon(v_n)\,.$$

For n sufficiently large, we have $\psi(v_n) \in C$. Let $y_n = \psi(v_n)$. Then:

$$\begin{aligned} &(a,p,e,y_n) = (a,p,e,x) + T_x g(v_n) + \|v_n\| \cdot \varepsilon(v_n)\,, \\ &\Rightarrow (a,p,e,x) + T_x g(v_n) = (a,p,e,y_n) - \|v_n\| \cdot \varepsilon(v_n) \\ &\Rightarrow (a,p,e,x) + (0,0,0,z_n) = (a,p,e,y_n) - \|v_n\| \cdot \varepsilon(v_n) \\ &\Rightarrow V\left((a,p,e,x+z_n)\right) = V\left((a,p,e,y_n) - \|v_n\| \cdot \varepsilon(v_n)\right) \\ &\Rightarrow \forall n > N,\ V\left((a,p,e,y_n) - \|v_n\| \cdot \varepsilon(v_n)\right) < \hat{\delta} < 0\,, \end{aligned}$$

where

$$\hat{\delta} = \delta + \varepsilon_N, \text{ and } \varepsilon(v_n) \to 0 \text{ as } v_n \to 0\,.$$

Then, continuity of V implies that $\forall \beta > 0$, $\exists \alpha > 0$ such that $\|r - s\| < \alpha \Rightarrow |V(r) - V(s)| < \beta$. Let $\beta = \frac{\hat{\delta}}{2}$, and let α be the associated constant. Since $v_n \to 0$, we note that:

$$\exists\, M \text{ such that } \forall n > M, \left\| \, \|v_n\| \cdot \varepsilon(v_n) \right\| < \alpha\,.$$

Thus for $n > \max\{M, N\}$, we have:

$$V\left((a,p,e,y_n) - \|v_n\| \cdot \varepsilon(v_n)\right) < \hat{\delta} < 0 ,$$

so that

$$\left| V\left((a,p,e,y_n)\right) - V\left((a,p,e,y_n) - \|v_n\| \cdot \varepsilon(v_n)\right) \right| < \frac{\hat{\delta}}{2}$$

implies

$$V(a,p,e,y_n) < 0 .$$

We then have a sequence $y_n \to x$, $y_n \in C$, and $V(a,p,e,y_n) < 0\ \forall n$. These y_n are the local cheaper points for x.

If we have $x \in C$ such that $\partial g(x) \in F$, then of course $x \in \partial C$. If $dim(C) > 2$, then $dim(\partial C) \geq 1$, and the argument presented above demonstrates the existence of local cheaper points for such x. If $dim(C) = 1$, then $dim(\partial C) = 0$, and if this is true, then:

$$\partial g \pitchfork F \;\Rightarrow\; \partial g(\partial C) \cap F = \emptyset, \text{ so } \;\; \partial g(x) \in F \quad \Rightarrow \quad x \notin \partial C .$$

Hence, we can write:

$$\forall x \in C \;\; \text{such that } V(a,p,e,x) = 0, \; \exists\, y_n \to x, \; y_n \in C, \text{ and } V(a,p,e,y_n) < 0 .$$

That is, $B(a,p,e)$ satisfies LCP. ∎

Remark: In the event that $dim(C) = 0$, then C consists of isolated points. In this case the usual definitions of transversal intersection cannot, strictly speaking, be applied. Using the most natural generalizations, however, we would have for any $x \in C$, the tangent to C at x is given by $T_x C = \{0\}$, and thus $T_x g(T_x C) = 0$. Thus we could only have $g \pitchfork F$ if $g(C) \cap F = \emptyset$, so that LCP would then be vacuously true. In this sense the assumption that $dim(C) \geq 1$ can be relaxed.

LEMMA 2: *For all $p \neq 0$, A1 – A4 implies $g^p \pitchfork F$ and $\partial g^p \pitchfork F$.*

Proof: Let (a,e,x) be such that $g^p(a,e,x) \in F$, where p is arbitrary but fixed. To establish transversal intersection between the mappings g^p and ∂g^p and the manifold F, we must show that at such a point (a,e,x), the tangent space of the mapping and the tangent space of the manifold together span the space which contains both. Thus given any $b \in \Re^{k+3n}$, we seek c, d such that:

i. $c + d = b$
ii. $c \in T_{a,p,e,x}F$
iii. $d \in T_{a,e,x}g^p(T_a\mathcal{A} \times \Re^n \times T_x C)$.

Let $b = (b_1, b_2, b_3, b_4)$ be given. Note that

$$T_{a,p,e,x}F = \{c \in \Re^{3n} \mid dV_{a,p,e,x}(c) = 0\} ,$$

and

$$T_{a,e,x}g^p(T_a\mathcal{A} \times \Re^n \times T_x C) = \Re^k \times \{0\} \times \Re^n \times T_x C .$$

Using notation similar to our representation of the vector b, we denote the vector c by (c_1, c_2, c_3, c_4) and d by (d_1, d_2, d_3, d_4), where for each of these vectors the first component is in $\Re^k$, and the remaining three are each contained in $\Re^n$. Choose any $d_4 \in T_x C$. Set

$$c_4 = b_4 - d_4 \text{ and } c_2 = b_2 .$$

We must then select c_1 and c_3 so that:

$$\sum_{i=1}^{k} \frac{\partial V}{\partial a_i} c_1^i + \sum_{i=1}^{n} \frac{\partial V}{\partial e_i} c_3^i + \sum_{i=1}^{n} \frac{\partial V}{\partial p_i} bi_2 + \sum_{i=1}^{n} \frac{\partial V}{\partial x_i} (b_4^i - d_4^i) = 0 ,$$

where all partial derivatives are evaluated at (a, p, e, x). This is equivalent to:

$$\sum_{i=1}^{k} \frac{\partial V}{\partial a_i} c_1^i + \sum_{i=1}^{n} \frac{\partial V}{\partial e_i} c_3^i = \sum_{i=1}^{n} \frac{\partial V}{\partial x_i} (d_4^i - b_4^i) - \sum_{i=1}^{n} \frac{\partial V}{\partial p_i} bi_2 .$$

Since V is smooth, the terms on the right are well-defined, and sum to some constant, say K. So we must solve:

$$\sum_{i=1}^{k} \frac{\partial V}{\partial a_i} c_1^i + \sum_{i=1}^{n} \frac{\partial V}{\partial e_i} c_3^i = K .$$

But A4 implies that there exists c_1 and c_3 to solve this equation.

We then have $c = (c_1, c_2, c_3, c_4)$. Letting $d_2 = 0$, $d1 = b_1 - c_1$, and $d_3 = b_3 - c_3$ yields the corresponding $d = (d_1, d_2, d_3, d_4)$. Thus $g^p \pitchfork F$.

An exactly parallel argument yields $\partial g^p \pitchfork F$. The only change in the argument is that when we select d_4, we take $d_4 \in T_x \partial C$. The resulting vector $d = (d_1, d_2, d_3, d_4)$ will be an element of the tangent space $T_{a,e,x} g^p (T_a \mathcal{A} \times \Re^n \times T_x \partial C)$. ∎

References

ALLEN, BETH (1982): "A Non-parametric Approach to Smoothing by Aggregation Over Preferences," *Journal of Mathematical Economics*, 10, 279–297.

DIERKER, E., DIERKER, H., AND TROCKEL, W. (1980): "Continuous Mean Demand Functions Derived from Non-Convex Preferences," *Journal of Mathematical Economics*, 7, 27-33.

DIERKER, E., DIERKER, H., AND TROCKEL, W. (1980): "Smoothing Demand by Aggregation With Respect to Wealth," *Journal of Mathematical Economics*, 7, 227–247.

GUILLEMIN, V. AND POLLACK, A. (1974): *Differential Topology*. Englewood Cliffs: Prentice-Hall.

HELLER, W. P. (1977): "Continuity in General Non-Convex Economies (With Applications to the Convex Case)," in *Equilibrium and Disequilibrium in Economic Theory*, ed. by G. Schwödiauer. Dordrecht, Holland: D. Reidel.

HILDENBRAND, W. (1980): "On the Uniqueness of Mean Demand for Dispersed Families of Preferences," *Econometrica,* 48, 1703–1710.

HIRSCH, M. (1976): *Differential Topology.* New York: Springer-Verlag.

KURZ, M. (1974): "Arrow-Debreu Equilibrium of an Exchange Economy with Transaction Cost," *International Economic Review,* 15, 699–717.

RADER, TROUT (1964): "Edgeworth Exchange and General Economic Equilibrium," *Yale Economic Essays,* 4, 133–180.

RADER, TROUT (1973): "Nice Demand Functions," *Econometrica,* 41, 913–935.

RADER, TROUT (1978): "Induced Preferences on Trades When Preferences May Be Intransitive and Incomplete," *Econometrica,* 46, 137–146.

RADER, TROUT (1979): "Nice Demand Functions – II," *Journal of Mathematical Economics,* 6, 253–262.

SONDERMANN, D. (1975): "Smoothing Demand by Aggregation," *Journal of Mathematical Economics,* 2, 201–224.

SONDERMANN, D. (1980): "Uniqueness of Mean Maximizers and Continuity of Aggregate Demand," *Journal of Mathematical Economics,* 7, 135–144.

TROCKEL, W. (1984): *Market Demand.* Berlin: Springer-Verlag.

YAMAZAKI, A. (1978): "An Equilibrium Existence Theorem Without Convexity Assumptions," *Econometrica,* 46, 541–555.

Printing: Druckhaus Beltz, Hemsbach
Binding: Buchbinderei Kränkl, Heppenheim

MIX
Papier aus verantwortungsvollen Quellen
Paper from responsible sources
FSC® C105338

If you have any concerns about our products,
you can contact us on
ProductSafety@springernature.com

In case Publisher is established outside the EU,
the EU authorized representative is:
Springer Nature Customer Service Center GmbH
Europaplatz 3, 69115 Heidelberg, Germany

Printed by Libri Plureos GmbH
in Hamburg, Germany